THEGREENGUIDE
Brittany

Presqu'île de Crozon © R. Mattes/MICHELIN

| **General Manager** | Cynthia Clayton Ochterbeck |

THE GREEN GUIDE **BRITTANY**

Editorial Manager	Jonathan Gilbert
Editor	Clive Hebard
Principal Writers	Paul Shawcross, Victoria Trott
Production Manager	Natasha G. George
Cartography	Stéphane Anton, Thierry Lemasson
Photo Editor	Yoshimi Kanazawa
Photo Researcher	Nicole D. Jordan
Proofreader	Hannah Witchell, Anne McDowall
Interior Design	Chris Bell
Cover Design	Chris Bell, Christelle Le Déan
Layout	Michelin Apa Publications Ltd., Nicole D. Jordan
Cover Layout	Michelin Apa Publications Ltd.

Contact Us	The Green Guide
	Michelin Maps and Guides
	One Parkway South
	Greenville, SC 29615, USA
	www.michelintravel.com
	Michelin Maps and Guides
	Hannay House
	39 Clarendon Road
	Watford, Herts WD17 1JA, UK
	✆01923 205240
	www.ViaMichelin.com
	travelpubsales@uk.michelin.com

Special Sales	For information regarding bulk sales, customized editions and premium sales, please contact our Customer Service Departments:
	USA 1-800-432-6277
	UK 01923 205240
	Canada 1-800-361-8236

HOW TO USE THIS GUIDE

PLANNING YOUR TRIP

The blue-tabbed PLANNING YOUR TRIP section gives you **ideas for your trip** and **practical information** to help you organize it. You'll find tours, practical information, a host of outdoor activities, a calendar of events, information on shopping, sightseeing, kids' activities and more.

INTRODUCTION

The orange-tabbed INTRODUCTION section explores Brittany's **Nature** and geology. The **History** section spans from the arrival of the Celts to the role of folklore in contemporary life. The **Art and Culture** section covers architecture, art and literature, while **Brittany Today** delves into the modern region.

DISCOVERING

The green-tabbed DISCOVERING section features Principal Sights by region, featuring the most interesting local **Sights**, **Walking Tours**, nearby **Excursions**, and detailed **Driving Tours**. Admission prices shown are normally for a single adult.

ADDRESSES

We've selected the best hotels, restaurants, cafes, shops, nightlife and entertainment to fit all budgets. See the Legend on the cover flap for an explanation of the price categories. See the back of the guide for an index of hotels and restaurants.

Sidebars

Throughout the guide you will find blue, orange and green-colored text boxes with lively anecdotes, detailed history and background information.

😊 A Bit of Advice 😊

Green advice boxes found in this guide contain practical tips and handy information relevant to the sight in the Discovering section.

STAR RATINGS★★★

Michelin has given star ratings for more than 100 years. If you're pressed for time, we recommend you visit the ★★★ or ★★ sights first:

★★★	**Highly recommended**
★★	**Recommended**
★	**Interesting**

MAPS

- 😊 Regional Driving Tours map, Places to Stay map and Sights map.
- 😊 Region maps.
- 😊 Maps for major cities and villages.
- 😊 Local tour maps.

All maps in this guide are oriented north, unless otherwise indicated by a directional arrow. The term "Local Map" refers to a map within the chapter or Tourism Region. A complete list of the maps found in the guide appears at the back of this book.

© Chris Warren/Pictures Colours Library

PLANNING YOUR TRIP

INTRODUCTION TO BRITTANY

S. Sauvignier/MICHELIN

CONTENTS

DISCOVERING BRITTANY

Welcome to Brittany

With the longest coastline of any of the French Regions, the Breton peninsula stretches from the River Loire in the south right around the aptly named Finistère in the west to the UNESCO World Heritage Site of Mont-St-Michel on the north coast. Populated by Celtic settlers, who arrived here from Cornwall in the 5C, Brittany retains many affinities with other Celtic lands fringing the Atlantic. Its identity, quite distinct from that of the rest of France, is expressed in language and traditions as well as in its landscape.

RENNES AND AROUND *(pp86–121)*

Rennes is the largest city in modern Brittany and is the regional capital, a title it took over from Nantes. Being ideally located at the confluence of the Ille and the Vilaine Rivers, there has been a settlement here since Celtic times. The region to the east of Rennes was known as the Brittany Marches, and the fortresses at Fougères, Vitré and Châteaubriant all bear witness to the need to protect the province from the French kings during the medieval period. To the west, and only a short drive from Rennes, lies the mysterious Forest of Paimpont, a place of myths and legends. Although it is much reduced from its original size, recent replanting has reversed this process.

CÔTE D'ÉMERAUDE *(pp122–170)*

The Côte d'Émeraude, or Emerald Coast, named for the beautiful colour of the sea off this coastline in the northeast of the region, stretches from the Bay of St-Michel in the east to the Bay of St-Brieuc in the west. It encompasses the fascinating walled city of St-Malo, out of which privateers used to operate, and quiet seaside towns with splendid beaches, including Dinard, which has managed to keep its old-world charm, and pleasant resorts such as St-Briac and St-Cast. Divided by the Rance river estuary, which reaches up to the remarkable old port of Dinan a short distance to the south, the Emerald Coast is one of Brittany's most varied destinations.

ST-BRIEUC AND TRÉGOR
(pp171–222)

Trégor and St-Brieuc are two of the nine historic regions of Brittany and today make up the western half of the Côtes d'Armor *département*. This section of the Guide includes the regional administrative capital of the Côtes-d'Armor, St-Brieuc, and several other quiet Breton towns, such as Lannion, Guincamp and the ports of Tréguier, which was the old capital, and Paimpol. In the heart of the Argoat (inland Brittany) to the south is the Lac de Guerlédan with its many recreational activities. The most spectacular part of this region is the beautiful Pink Granite Coast in the north with its unusual rock formations, many of which resemble a variety of animals, stretching from Perros-Guirec to Trébeurden.

Place du Champ-Jacquet, Rennes

A. de Valroger/MICHELIN

NORTH FINISTÈRE *(pp223–269)*

This small region makes up the northeast corner of Brittany from the Bay of Morlaix to the rural Presqu'île de Plougastel opposite the large naval port of Brest. In the north, the Abers or Breton fjords of the Côte des Légendes funnel deep into the heart of the countryside, while 20km/12.5m off to the west lies the rocky, windy Île de Ouessant with its colony of grey seals and its many lighthouses, which illuminate the approaches to the English Channel. Much nearer the mainland, the Île de Batz is separated from the port of Roscoff by a narrow channel. Here the climate is so mild that it is suited to market gardening.

SOUTH FINISTÈRE *(pp270–340)*

The southern part of the Finistère *département* is in many ways characterised by the Presqu'île de Crozon and the Pointe de Raz jutting out into the Atlantic Ocean in the west and separated by the deep Bay of Douarnenez. From the Pointe de Raz, with its macabre-sounding Bay of the Deceased overlooking the Île de Sein, the Cornouaille Coast sweeps round to the Odet River and the pleasant seaside resort of Bénodet, encompassing many fine beaches and fishing ports on the way. Further east the spectacular walled town of Concarneau and the charming old port of Pont-Aven at the head of the Aven River are both, deservedly, much-visited destinations.

MORBIHAN *(pp341–403)*

In Breton the name *mor bihan* means "little sea" and in fact the modern *département* of Morbihan does contain a beautiful inland sea dotted with islands called the Gulf of Morbihan. Spectacular though the

Phare de Créac'h, Île d'Ouessant

©Tips Images

Gulf is, there is much more to this tranquil area, which boasts a mild climate, mysterious dolmens and menhirs, the medieval city of Vannes and some fascinating ports, not to mention its many myths involving such legendary characters as Merlin and Lancelot that are still familiar to us today. The ancient standing stones around Carnac indicate the presence of settlers here in prehistoric times. A visit to these, especially at sunset or sunrise, will evoke a sense of awe in the visitor.

NANTES AND AROUND
(pp404–447)

Previously the capital of Brittany, Nantes is a very large city at the confluence of several rivers. Despite being no longer in the administrative region of Brittany, it is steeped in Breton history and there is much of interest here, including the Château of the Dukes of Brittany. Nearby is the Presqu'île de Guérende, the fine beach at Le Baule and the unusual medieval walled town of Guérende at the centre of the salt industry. Just to the north is the exceptional Regional Nature Park of Brière, providing opportunities for many outdoor pursuits, including bird-watching and rambling. A short drive south of Nantes is the renowned wine region of Muscadet.

Rue du Petit Fort, Dinan
© Chris Warren/Pictures Colours Library

Michelin Driving Tours

Refer to the Driving Tours Map on p13–15.

1 THE LOIRE ESTUARY

240km/149mi starting from Nantes
The Loire-Atlantique *département* benefits from healthy, economic activity: tourism centres around La Baule, which boasts one of Europe's finest beaches; shipbuilding in St-Nazaire where luxurious cruise liners are built; and the sea-salt industry around the medieval town of Guérande.

There are four other drives in the area:
(i) *Circular drive of 65km/40mi.* Starting at Clisson just south of Nantes this tour takes in some of the wine villages and châteaux of the Pays de Muscadet and passes through the Marais de Goulaine before reaching the château of the same name.
(ii) *Tour of 70km/44mi.* Takes in the popular resorts of the Jade Coast, starting at Pornic and visiting Pointe de St-Gildas before going on to St-Brévin-les-Pis opposite St-Nazaire and returning via Paimboeuf where there is a fine view of the Loire estuary.
(iii) *Circular drive of 130km/81mi.* This longer tour explores the Pays de Retz and is partly coastal and partly rural. The drive offers the opportunity to visit the fascinating Carolingian church of St-Philbert-de-Grand-Lieu, the Lac de Grand Lieu and the important wildlife centre of Planète sauvage as well as the capital of the Retz country, Machecoul.
(iv) *Drive of 62km/39mi.* This tour on the north side of the estuary departing from Guérande allows a visit to the Château de Careil with its fine renaissance facade before proceding along the Côte Sauvage to Saillé and the Maison des Paludiers to learn all about salt production. Return to Guérande via the Pointe du Castelli and the fishing village of Piriac-sur-Mer.

2 BRITTANY'S BORDER COUNTRY

220km/137mi starting from Rennes
Old stones, old houses, old castles and legends of this region that for many centuries have preserved the secrets of the Kingdom of France. These may belong to the past, but are by no means forgotten. Strolling along the lively streets of Rennes today, one has the impression that this modern capital has passed its forward-looking dynamism on to the towns, villages and historic sites of the area.

There are four other drives either from Rennes or nearby towns:
(i) *Round trip of 36km/22.5mi.* From Rennes drive to the country town of Bruz with its tiny square on the

Locmariaquer

©Sylvaine Poitau/Apa Publications

north side of the modern church. An ornithological park may be visited before moving onto Le Boël to enjoy a short walk by the river and then return to Rennes.

(ii) *Round trip of 80km/50mi.* From the superbly preserved old-world town of Vitré, a 80km/50mi drive takes in the Château des Rochers-Sévigné, one of the finest megalithic monuments in the region at La Roche-aux-Fées, and the historic church at Retiers.

(iii) *48km/30mi.* From Redon this drive takes you to the delightful Jardin Anglais du Manoir de la Chaussée and then on to St-Just (look out for megaliths) before visiting the exceptional Manoir de l'Autombile à Lohéac, which contains more than 160 cars of all types.

(iv) *43km/27mi.* The itinerary through the forest of Paimpont takes about one day. Starting from St-Léry with its lovely 14C church, drive to the Château de Comper where many great families have lived. Don't miss the Centre Arthurien and the tomb of Merlin before visiting the pleasant market town of Paimpont. Pass by, stopping if time allows, the pretty hamlet of Les Forges de Paimpont and Beignon before reaching the Château de Trecesson and finally Tréhorentec from where you can enter the Val sans retour (the Valley of no return)!

3 MERLIN'S REALM

250km/155mi starting from Josselin
Experience the magic of Merlin the Magician along this drive. First, the venerable and stately Château de Josselin overlooking the River Oust; next, a feast of international contemporary art at the heart of the formal grounds of the 18C Kerguéhennec castle; and then a succession of old, carefully restored towns livened up by summer events. All this could be Merlin's doing! For the magician and his sweetheart fairy are not far away; their memory pervades the vast Paimpont Forest, known as Brocéliande in Arthurian legend.

Alignements de menhirs à Carnac

4 MEGALITHS AND PREHISTORY

190km/118mi starting from Vannes
Natural beauty and splendid vestiges of earlier civilisations are the main attractions of this drive. The megalith civilisation, known for its standing stones, flourished among magnificent scenery around the Golfe du Morbihan. Towns like Vannes, Auray, Port-Louis and Hennebont are definitely worth the trip. There are several drives starting from either Vannes or other towns in the Morbihan:

(i) *Round trip of 55km/34mi.* From Vannes head for the imposing ruins of the Forrtresse de Largoët standing in the middle of a park before going on to the Landes de Lanvaux, passing the restored Château de Trédlon. At Callac a footpath lead to a fine view of the Landes before you return to Vannes.

(ii) *Tour of 49km/31mi.* From Vannes head for the Pointe d'Arradon for a good view of the Golfe du Morbihan before moving onto Larmor-Baden in order to visit the Gavrinis Tumulous, the most interesting megalithic site in Brittany, situated on an island in the Gulf. After this don't miss the lovely port of Le Bono before moving onto Auray and perhaps to Locmariaquer.

(iii) *23km/14.4mi round trip.* This short drive from Auray around the Pays de

Alréan goes first to the Chartreuse d'Auray and the Champs des Martyrs, where the Chouans were shot during the Royalist Insurrection of 1793–1804. Move on to St-Degan passing the site of the Battle of Auray (1364) to Ste-Anne d'Auray, Brittany's premier place of pilgrimage, before returning to Auray via Pluneret and the pretty cottages and chapel at Ste-Avoye. (iv) *18km/11.25mi round trip.* This drive on the Presqu'île de Quiberon should take about two hours but during July and August the Peninsula becomes very congested. Good views are available from the Pointe de Percho; there are 22 menhirs to be seen at St-Pierre-Quiberon.

Phare d'Eckmühl, La Cornouaille
S. Sauvignier/MICHELIN

5 THE HEART OF BRITTANY

225km/140mi starting from Pontivy
Bretons have maintained strong religious inclinations throughout the region's history. Rostrenen, Le Faouët and Kernascléden boast some of the most beautiful religious monuments in inland Brittany (Argoat) where mystery is never very far away, as illustrated by the legends of Guerlédan lake, Toul Goulic Gorge and Castennec. The heart of Brittany is granite; the stone bares its many subtle colours to the light, both in its natural state and in man-made creations.

6 PONT-AVEN, LAND OF PAINTERS

180km/112mi starting from Pont-Aven
Pont-Aven and the surrounding countryside enjoy a special light that attracted world-famous painters such as Paul Gauguin and Émile Bernard. However, you don't have to be a painter to appreciate Pont-Aven and bask in the unique Breton light.

7 PAYS BIGOUDEN AND CORNOUAILLE

*170km/106mi starting from Quimper*As its name suggests, Finistère feels like land's end. This feeling becomes overwhelming as one drives west from Quimper or Locronan towards

the ocean's edge, where the rocks, the waves, the sky and the sea all seem to mingle. Admire the vastness of the Pointe du Raz, the noble robustness of Notre-Dame-de-Tronoën and the Penmarsh reefs, all bathed in maritime air. There are several other drives from either Quimper or nearby towns, two of which are described below:
(i) *27km/17mi round trip.* This short drive from Quimper follows the banks of the Odet and allows a visit to the 16C church Ergué-Gabéric before going on to the Chapelle de Kerévot with its interesting calvary and 15C alterpiece. Leaving Kerdévot head for the Site du Stangala which offer good views of the Odet, the hamlet of Tréouzon and the Locronan mountain to the the northwest.
(ii) *128km/80mi.* This itinerary from Quimper to Plozévet on the Bay of Audierne takes about one day. From Quimper head to Plogonnec and Locronan before reaching Keriaz where there is a good view of Douarnenez. From this important fishing port, head west to the medieval Chapelle de Nôtre-Dame de Kérinac and the nearby church of Nôtre-Dame de Confort. On the coast the Réserve du Cap Sizun is a must for bird-watchers, especially from March to early July, where you can see the

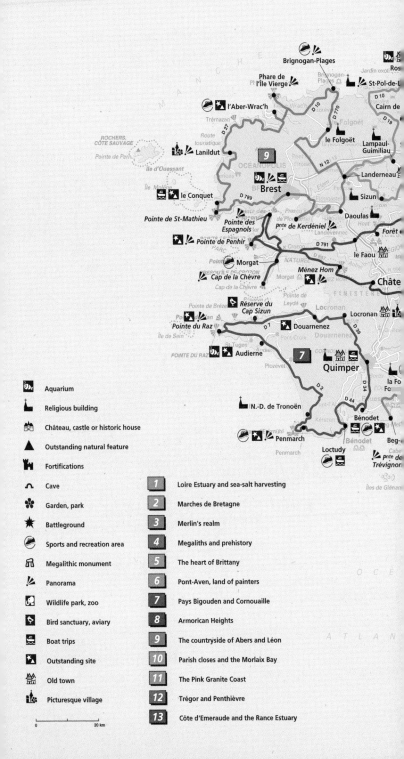

Brignogan-Plages

Phare de
l'Île Vierge

l'Aber-Wrac'h

Trémazan

Route
touristique

ROCHERS,
CÔTE SAUVAGE

Pointe de Penh.

Lanildut

Île d'Ouessant

Île Molène

le Conquet

Brignogan-
Plages

St-Pol-de-L

Jardin exoti

Ros

Cairn de

le Folgoët

Lampaul-
Guimiliau

Landerneau

OCÉANOPOLIS

Brest

9

Sizun

Pointe de St-Mathieu

D 789

Daoulas

Pointe des
Espagnols

pnte de Kerdéniel

Forêt

Pointe de Penhir

D 791

le Faou

Châte

Morgat

Pointe

Ménez Hom

Cap de la Chèvre

Cap de la Chèvre

Pointe de
Leyde

Pointe de Brézé

Réserve du
Cap Sizun

Locronan

Locronan

Pointe du Raz

Île de Sein

D 7

Douarnenez

D 39

POINTE DU RAZ

Audierne

Plozévet

7

Quimper

la Fo
Fo

N.-D. de Tronoën

D 2

D 44

Bénodet

Beg-

Penmarch

Bénodet

Loctudy

pnte de
Trévignon

Penmarch

Îles de Glénan

OCÉ

ATLAN

🐟	Aquarium
⛪	Religious building
🏰	Château, castle or historic house
🔺	Outstanding natural feature
🏰	Fortifications
∩	Cave
❀	Garden, park
✳	Battleground
⊘	Sports and recreation area
⌂	Megalithic monument
⚐	Panorama
🐾	Wildlife park, zoo
🐦	Bird sanctuary, aviary
🚤	Boat trips
★	Outstanding site
🏛	Old town
🏘	Picturesque village

0   20 km

1	Loire Estuary and sea-salt harvesting
2	Marches de Bretagne
3	Merlin's realm
4	Megaliths and prehistory
5	The heart of Brittany
6	Pont-Aven, land of painters
7	Pays Bigouden and Cornouaille
8	Armorican Heights
9	The countryside of Abers and Léon
10	Parish closes and the Morlaix Bay
11	The Pink Granite Coast
12	Trégor and Penthièvre
13	Côte d'Emeraude and the Rance Estuary

Driving tours

For descriptions of these tours, turn
to the Planning Your Trip section following.

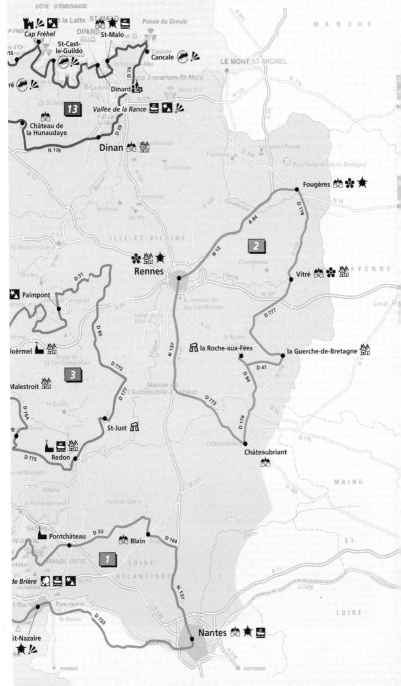

birds nesting. Heading west past the Pointe du Van you will come to the Bay of the Dead leading to the rocky promontory of the Pointe du Raz and its panoramic views of the Île de Sein. Follow the D784 back along the Peninsula visiting Audierne and the Aquashow (allow two hrs). There are several fishing vilages and interesting churches on the way back to Plozévet.

8 ARMORICAN HEIGHTS

250km/155mi starting from Châteaulin
Visitors who like vast panoramas will enjoy the Breton "mountains", or rather these hills culminating at 1,280ft/384m. From Roc Trévézel to the Pointe de Penhir, from the Ménez-Hom to the Pointe des Espagnols, the road rises only slightly, but the vastness and the colours of the landscapes are unique. Leave your car in the parking areas dotted across the heath and listen to the wind playing in syncopation with the raging sea.

9 THE COUNTRYSIDE OF ABERS AND LÉON

250km/155mi starting from Brest
This drive is a must for nature lovers: cliffs, sand dunes, estuaries, peat bogs and rivers form the landscape of this still-unspoilt part of North Finistère. There is an infinite variety of colours, from the dark grey slates and Kersanton granite of the Brest area to the golden sands and lichens of Brignogan and Lanildut. Despite the impact of humans on the local environment, it many places the wild beauty of this region survives. It is a sanctuary for thousands of migrating birds each autumn. There are several other drives in North Finistère, two of which are described below:
(i) *Half-day round trip of 56km/35mi.* Leave Brest by crossing the Élorn Estuary via the Pont Albert-Louppe, with its sculptures by Quillac, and the Pont d'Iroise then bear right towards Plougastel-Daoulas and the Peninsula.
(ii) *Two-hour rund trip of 56km/35mi.* Leave Brest heading west to Ste-Anne du Portzic for a coastal walk with fine views. Drive further west to pass through Plougonvelin towards the Pointe de St-Mathieu. Note Vauban's Fort de Bertheaume guarding the entrance to the Brest Channel and visit the Abbey Church at the old village of St-Matthieu before climbing the lighthouse, from which there is superb view.

10 PARISH CLOSES AND THE MORLAIX BAY

325km/202mi starting from Morlaix
Corbelled houses in Morlaix, churches in St-Pol-de-Léon and Roscoff, parish closes in Lampaul-Guimiliau and St-Thégonnec, the bridge in Landerneau, religious treasure in St-Jean-du-Doigt and passage graves in Barnenez are all found along this

View of the city from the Fort National, St-Malo

R. Mattes/MICHELIN

route. You will also discover Morlaix Bay and the rocky Locquirec Peninsula, whose natural beauty and attractive beaches will appeal to visitors fond of bathing.

1 1 THE PINK GRANITE COAST

180km/112mi starting from Lannion
In a beautiful mineral transformation, granite worn smooth by erosion takes on pink or reddish-beige hues depending on the place and intensity of the sun's rays. This phenomenon is perhaps best enjoyed at the region's resorts (St-Michel-en-Grève, Port-Blanc, Perros-Guirec and Trégastel). The inland areas offer different but equally enchanting features, such as the Château de Tonquédec and the Menez-Bré summit.

1 2 TRÉGOR AND PENTHIÈVRE COUNTRY

160km/100mi starting from St-Brieuc
With the advent of rail travel in the 19C, the bay of St-Brieuc became the birthplace of seaside tourism. However, the Côtes-du-Nord *département* was later neglected by holiday-makers, perhaps because of the uninspiring name. This was changed in 1990 to Côtes-d'Armor, a name that does more justice to this part of the Breton coast facing the lovely island of Bréhat with its remarkably mild climate.
There are several other drives in the Trégor/St-Brieuc area, two of which are described below:
(i) *Two-hour round-trip of 25km/15.5mi.* Head north out of St-Brieuc to the Pointe du Roselier for a fine view. Follow the road back to the pretty beach of Martin-Plage and go on to Plage des Rosaries for another fine view of St-Breiuc Bay before returning to St-Brieuc.
(ii) *47km/29.5mi round trip.* Leaving Paimpol head for the Pointe de Guilben for a good view of the coast. Return to the Abbaye de Beauport, which used to be very important in this area – there is a great deal of interesting architecture still to be seen. Follow the route past Ste-Barbe and Port Lazo to the Pointe de Bilfot, which has a fine view across the Anse de Paimpol to the the Île de Bréhat as does the view from the Pointe de Minard, which gives a wider perspective including the Bay St-Brieuc. Further along you will come to the small port and resort of Bréhec en Plouha, said to be the place where St-Brieuc and the first celtic emigrants landed from Britain during the 5C.

1 3 CÔTE D'EMERAUDE AND THE RANCE ESTUARY

270km/168mi starting from Dinan
Whatever the weather, the sea remains a beautiful emerald colour. The very name of some of the sights along this itinerary appeals to the imagination: the Rance estuary, Cancale, St-Malo, Cap Fréhel, Les Sables-d'Or … but there are also less renowned yet equally enchanting places such as Dinan, St-Cast, Le Val-André, Montcontour and the Château de la Hunaudaye with its cloak-and-dagger atmosphere. There are several other drives in the Côte d'Emeraude, one of which is described below:
28km/17.5mi half day. From Dinard go straight to the tidal power station, *Usine Marémotrice de la Rance,* (open Apr–Sept), which is very interesting and well worth seeing if time allows. Enjoy the view of Dinard and St-Malo from the platform across the top of the dam. Continue to the small village of Le Richardais, where there is a fine church and good views of the Rance Estuary, and then carry on to the Jardins de Montmarin, where the gardens descend on terraces to the river. At Le Landrais further on there are naval dockyards and a 2km/1.25mi walk along the Hures Promenade starting at the car park and skirting the Rance. Drive on to the old village of Taden, where there is a porch and a keep flanked by a 14C turret, and follow the road along the banks of the river into to the fascinating old port of Dinan.

When and Where to Go

WHEN TO GO

Brittany and Cornwall have much in common both culturally and meteorologically. The Breton peninsula, rather like the Cornish Peninsula on the other side of the Channel, has a reputation for rainy weather and heavy fog, which rolls in from the Atlantic Ocean, but it is rarely very cold for much the same reason. The climate is mild, thanks to the surrounding ocean waters and the tides, which keep the clouds moving and allow the sun to shine through regularly. The flora is a unique blend of Mediterranean and northern species. In summer, the weather is generally pleasant and usually not too hot. The Morbihan and Île-et-Villaine tend to be the warmest and driest areas of the region.

WEATHER FORECAST

For any outdoor activity, on sea or land, it is useful to have reliable weather forecasts. The French weather reporting service, Météo-France, can be consulted by telephone: ✆08 92 68 02 followed by the number of the *département* in question. For example, to obtain the forecast for the Morbihan you would dial ✆08 92 68 02 56. (0.34€ per min) For holiday weather conditions, for example at sea, on the beach, in towns dial 3250 (0.34€ per min) or go to www.meteo france.com.

WHERE TO GO
HISTORICAL ROUTES

Created in 1975 by the Demeure Historique and Caisse Nationale des Monuments Historiques et des Sites (CNMHS), these 80 historical routes cover the whole of France. Well signposted, they explore architectural, archaeological, botanical or geological heritage within a historical context: the Dukes of Brittany, the Painters of Cornouaille.

Five historical routes run through Brittany: Châteaubriand; the regions of Léon and Tréguier the Painters of Cornouaille; the Dukes of Brittany; and the Breton Marches. Further information from CNMHS at *Hôtel de Sully, 62 rue Ste-Antoine, 75004 Paris.* ✆01 44 61 20 00.

ARTISTIC AND HISTORICAL CENTRES

Breton towns designated by the CNMHS as *Villes d'Art et d'Histoire* 🏛 (Towns of Art and History) have been regrouped as a special unit in Brittany since 1984. Similarly, smaller towns of particular local character – *Petites Cités de Caractère* – have been administered as a regional association since 1977. These towns regularly hold medieval pageants, *son et lumière* (sound and light) shows, and traditional and modern festivals in their historic town centres.

Tours accompanied by CNMHS-approved guides are also available. Visitors can obtain relevant literature from tourist offices, rest places alongside main roads and motorways, or from the local town hall *(mairie)*. Ten Breton towns have been designated as *Villes d'Art et d'Histoire*:

- **Auray** ✆02 97 24 09 75
  contact@ville-auray.fr
  www.auray-tourisme.com
- **Concarneau** ✆02 98 97 01 44
  contact@tourismeconcarneau.fr
  www.tourismeconcarneau.fr
- **Dinan** ✆02 96 87 69 76
  infos@dinan-tourisme.com
  www.dinan-tourisme.com
- **Fougères** ✆02 99 94 12 20
  ot.fougeres@wanadoo.fr
  www.ot-fougeres.fr
- **Nantes** ✆08 92 46 40 44
  office@nantes-tourisme.com
  www.nantes-tourisme.com
- **Quimper** ✆02 98 53 04 05
  contact@quimper-tourisme.com
  www.quimper-tourisme.com
- **Rennes** ✆02 99 67 11 11
  infos@tourisme-rennes.com
  www.tourisme-rennes.com

- **St-Malo** ✆ 08 25 13 52 00
  info@saint-malo-tourisme.com
  www.saint-malo-tourisme.com
- **Vannes** ✆ 08 25 13 56 10
  info@tourisme-vannes.com
  www.tourisme-vannes.com
- **Vitré** ✆ 02 99 75 04 46
  info@ot-vitre.fr
  www.ot-vitre.fr

There are 20 *Petites Cités de Caractère*: Bécherel, Châteaugiron, Châtelaudren, Combourg, Le Faou, Guerlesquin, Josselin, Jugon-les-Lacs, Léhon, Lizio, Locronan, Malestroit, Moncontour, Pont-Croix, Pontrieux, Quintin, La Roche-Bernard, Rochefort-en-Terre, Roscoff and Tréguier.
For details, contact the *Associations régionales des Villes d'Art et d'Histoire et des Petites Cités de Caractère de Bretagne,* 1 rue Raoul Ponchon, 35069 Rennes Cedex, ✆ 02 99 28 44 30 or see www.brittanytourism.com.

LIGHTHOUSES AND BEACONS
The Breton coast has the highest concentration of lighthouses and beacons on the French coast. A route running along the north Finistère coast leads past some of the most important lighthouses in Europe. For details, contact *Les Pays de Brest, BP 24, 29266 Brest Cedex,* ✆ 02 98 44 24 96, www.bretagne.com.

SITES REMARQUABLES DU GOÛT
French authorities have created a quality label for places where the unique quality of local produce deserves special mention.
In Brittany, these places include: Cancale, the salt marshes of Guérande, La Guilvinec, the salt marshes and the farming plain of Noirmoutier, and Riec-sur-Belon.

SIGHTSEEING
FROM ABOVE
Up, up and away – enjoy the Breton countryside at dawn in a **hot-air balloon**. In the Côtes d'Armor contact the Association Aérostatique Nord

Museum Passes
If you are intending to stay in Rennes or Nantes for a few days then consider purchasing a Museum Pass.

Nantes Pass: Free entry to 30 attractions, free public transport and discounts. 24hr (16.20€), 48 hr (25.20€) and 72 hr (32.40€) passes are available.

Rennes Metropole City Pass: Free admission to museums, discounted bus and metro fares and reductions for leisure activities (ⓒ see p95). Two-day pass from 13€.

Bretagne (*www.montgolfiere-bretagne. com,* ✆ 02 96 79 80 69), in Ille-et-Vilaine, contact Ballons d'Emeraude (*www.ballons-emeradue.com,* ✆ 06 12 25 44 83) and in Morbihan contact Montgolfière Morbihan (*www.mont golfieremorbihan.com,* ✆ 02 97 62 76 00). Just imagine **paragliding** over the Breton coast. Contact the École Celtic Vol Libre in Finistère (*www.vol-libre-menez-hom.com,* ✆ 02 98 81 50 27) and your dream could become a reality. See www.brittanytourism.com for other schools.

FROM THE WATER
As well as a rugged windswept coastline, Brittany also has its fair share of canals, such as the Nantes-Brest, the Blavet between Pontivy and Hennebont, Ille-et-Rance from Dinan to Rennes and the Vilaine in Rennes. Croisières Chateaubriand (*www. chateaubriand.com,* ✆ 02 99 46 44 40) runs boat trips of varying duration in Dinard and St-Malo, Vedettes Odets (*www.vedettes-odet.com,* ✆ 02 98 57 00 58) offers trips in the Finistère region including around the Îles Glénans and Vedettes Jaunes runs trips down the River Vilaine from Arzal (*www. vedettesjaunes.com,* ✆ 02 97 45 02 81). Ask in local tourist offices for details of other trips.

What to See and Do

OUTDOOR FUN
CANOEING AND KAYAKING (RIVER AND SEA)

A canoe is propelled by a single-bladed paddle, whereas a kayak is propelled by a double-bladed paddle: Sea kayaks are increasingly popular and are available for sale or for hire in the main seaside resorts. Sea-kayaking offers a wonderful opportunity to discover the magnificent Breton coastline. There are many opportunities to take part in kayaking or canoeing in several locations around the coast of the Breton Peninsula and also on the Lac de Guerléden in the Côtes-d'Armor *département*.

Sea kayaking
©G. Targat/MICHELIN

SAILING AND WINDSURFING

The rugged Breton coastline shelters numerous bays, which make an ideal setting for sailing enthusiasts to practise their sport. Many of the Breton yacht clubs have a sailing school attached to them, for example the centre at Glénan (*℘01 53 92 86 00. www.glenans.asso.fr*). Sailing is possible from Carnac, Quiberon and La Trinité, all in the southern Morbihan, and also on the Rance Estuary between St Malo and Dinan. Windsurfing is also possible from these locations and from many beaches, although it is subject to certain rules; contact the yacht clubs for details. Windsurfers can be hired at all the major beaches, as can boats – with or without a crew – in season. For further information, contact the **Fédération Française de Voile** (*17, rue Henri Bocquillon 75015 Paris, ℘01 40 60 37 00, www.ffvoile.net*), or **France Stations Nautiques** (*17, rue Henri Bocquillon 75 015 Paris, ℘01 44 05 96 55, www.france-nautisme.com*). Regattas are organised throughout the season in all the major resorts.

DIVING

This activity is becoming very popular in Brittany. The clear waters of the inlets along Brittany's south coast (Port-Manech, Port-Goulphar to Belle-Île) are rich in fish and marine plantlife, providing interest for underwater anglers and admirers of underwater landscapes alike. The *Îles de Glénan* diving centre attracts deep-sea divers, who can practise in the swimming pool during the winter. Further information can be obtained from the **Comité Interrégional Bretagne-Pays de Loire de la Fédération Française d'Études et de Sports Sous-Marins** (*39 rue de la Villeneuve, 56100 Lorient, ℘02 97 37 51 51*).

FISHING
Freshwater Fishing

Obey national and local laws. You may have to become a member (for the year in progress) of an affiliated angling association in the *département* of your choice, pay the annual angling tax or buy a day card. If you wish to fish on private land you must obtain permission from the landowner. Fishing permits for public waters can be obtained from local newsagents (*tabac*) or bars and a fishing licence covers local areas and costs about 7€ per day. Special two-week holiday fishing permits are also available.

Deep-Sea Fishing

From Mont-St-Michel Bay to the River Loire estuary, Breton coastal waters offer infinite possibilities to amateur deep-sea fishermen. Contact the local marine authorities, Service des

Affaires Maritimes (*www.chasse-sous-marine.com*) to find out about regulations governing fishing from boats or under water. Fishing from the shore is not subject to any formal regulations, apart from the use of nets, which requires permission from the marine authorities. Different areas may, however, have particular coastal rules; it is advisable to find out what these are from the appropriate local authority. Deep sea fishing for sea bass or pollock is possible from Dinard in the Île-et-Vilaine or off the coast of Brest or the coast of Cornouaille in Finistère.

RAMBLING

Several long-distance footpaths (**Sentiers de Grande Randonnée – GR**) cover the region described in this guide. Walking holidays and rambles are organised by a number of organisations. See www.headwater. com, www.inntravel.co.uk and www. ramblersholidays.co.uk for ideas. Otherwise, contact the local tourist office nearest to where you're staying. Argoat is criss-crossed by the GR footpaths 34, 37, 38, 341 and 380, which offer a range of pleasant rambles to walkers of all abilities. The GR 34, often called the *Sentier des Douaniers* is the most well known of the Breton long-distance footpaths following as it does almost the entire coastline of the region from Vitré in the Ile-et-Vilaine to Quimperlé in Finistère. The GR 37 and 39 cross the Peninsula – the former goes east to west from Vitré to Douarnenez and the latter north to south from Mont-St-Michel to Guérende. Please note that the GRs often include quite difficult sections and therefore it is advisable to purchase the appropriate Topo-Guide beforehand. The Topo-Guides are published by the **Fédération Française de la Randonnée Pédestre** (*www.ffrandonnee.fr* ✆ 01 44 89 93 93) and give detailed maps of the paths and offer valuable information to ramblers. You can find these and other guides and maps to local short-distance footpaths in local tourist information centres and sports shops.

CYCLING

Brittany, like much of France, is ideal for cycling, both in terms of provision for the activity and the generally sympathetic attitude of other road users towards cyclists. The countryside, especially around the coastal areas, tends to be relatively flat, and even the hillier parts are not too strenuous. For families and less experienced riders, cycling the Nantes–Brest Canal in easy stages using the well-maintained towpaths would be ideal and there are organised itineraries of varying lengths. With careful planning, round trips for more experienced cyclists, such as from Roscoff to Carhaix-Plouguer and on to Concarneau returning to Roscoff via Pleyben (333km/208mi), could be done over several days. More serious riders might like to tackle sections used by the professionals of the Tour de France, which regularly passes through the region, such as Brest to Plumelec; Auray to St-Brieuc or St-Malo to Nantes. For information contact the **Fédération Française de Cyclotourisme,** (*12 rue Louis Bertrand, 94207 Ivry-sur-Seine Cedex,* ✆*01 56 20 88 88, www.ffct.org*), which will give you the details of its local representatives. Tourist Information Centres have lists of places to hire bicycles, which include some main railway stations.

GOLF

Brittany boasts a large number of golf courses, often located in very picturesque settings. The *Comité Régional du Tourisme de Bretagne* publishes a brochure listing some 30 golf clubs throughout the region's four *départements*. The best golfing in Brittany can be found around St-Malo (Ile-et-Vilaine), Val André (Côtes-d'Armor), Bénodet (Finistère) and Auray (Morbihan).

WRESTLING

Have you heard of *gouren*? This traditional Breton wrestling competition, of Celtic origin, has its own federation. Its values are fair play and loyalty. The sport, practised within a club, offers exciting competitive matches (indoors in winter, but also outdoors in summer, during traditional festivals). **Information**: Comité National de Gouren (*ZA St Ernel, 29800 Landerneau, ℘02 98 85 40 48, www.gouren.com*).

VOIE VERTE

Whether you are keen on roller-skating, cycling or walking, the **Voie Verte** from Mauron to Questembert, in the Morbihan area, is the perfect playing field. The old railway line has been renovated for the enjoyment of families and people with disabilities. This 53km/33mi itinerary, west of Paimpont Forest, passes near Loyat, Malestroit, Molac, Montertelot, Ploërmel, Le Roc-St-André and St-Marcel. You can join it in several places. Information at the Tourist offices of Tréhorenteuc (*℘02 97 93 05 12*), Ploërmel (*℘02 97 74 02 70*), Malestroit (*℘02 97 75 14 57*) and Questembert (*℘02 97 26 56 00*).

BOATING

The Channel and Atlantic coasts lend themselves particularly well to exploration by boat, be it under sail or motor-power. The main marinas are indicated on the *Places to Stay* map; criteria dictating their selection include number of berths available and range of facilites offered (fuel, fresh water and electricity on the quayside, toilets and washing facilities, elevators or cranes for loading, repair workshops, security guards).Boating opportunities can be found around much of the coast although many sailors favour the west coast of Finistère. Camaret-sut-Mer is an ideal centre from which to explore the Rade de Brest or the Bay of Douarnenez, and the islands of Ouessant, Sein, Glenan and Molene can all be reached easily.

SPAS

A seaside setting (with the healthy sea air and seaweed) is well known as an excellent natural restorative for those suffering from fatigue or stress. *Thalassotherapy* (medical sea treatment, from the Greek *thalassa* (meaning sea) involves various techniques maximise the beneficial effects of a seaside climate: *algotherapie* (seaweed and sea mud baths), *hydrotherapie* (spray-jets, sea-water showers or baths), *kinesitherapie* (massages, gymnastics), saunas, and sea-water spray treatments. The average length of a treatment at one of these thalassotherapy centres is around 7–10 days.
Brittany's major sea-water therapy centres are at La Baule, Belle-Île-en-Mer, Carnac, Le Crouesty, Dinard, Perros-Guirec, Quiberon, Roscoff and St-Malo. For **information** and bookings, contact Brittany Tourism (1 rue Raoul Ponchon 35069, Rennes Cedex, ℘01 53 63 11 69, www. brittany-best-breaks.com).

HORSE RIDING

The possibilities for riding holidays in Brittany are numerous and open to riders of all abilities. Contact: Comité Régional pour le Tourisme Equestre en Bretagne (CRTEB), 5 bis rue Waldeck Rousseau BP 307 56103 Lorient Cedex, ℘02 97 84 44 03, www.equibreizh.com.
Clearly signed with orange markers, the **Equibreizh Trail** is a series of bridle paths that covers about 2000km/1250mi of the Breton countryside. Accommodation for horse and rider is available at regular intervals (25–30km/15–20m). A detailed guide is essential before setting out and there is a "Equibreizh Topoguide" available giving details of routes and accommodation.

ACTIVITIES FOR KIDS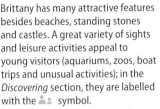

Brittany has many attractive features besides beaches, standing stones and castles. A great variety of sights and leisure activities appeal to young visitors (aquariums, zoos, boat trips and unusual activities); in the *Discovering* section, they are labelled with the symbol.
Many of the larger, more popular campsites have organised activities for children aged from 3–16 years.

VILLES D'ART ET D'HISTOIRE
Towns designated by the Ministry of Culture as *Villes d'Art et d'Histoire* organise discovery tours and cultural-heritage workshops for children. Fun books and specially designed tools are provided and the activities on offer are supervised by various professionals such as architects, stone masons, story-tellers and actors. This scheme, called *L'été des 6–12 ans* (summer activities for 6–12-year-olds) operates during school holidays.

BEACHES
Beaches are, of course, one of the main reasons to come to Brittany for a family holiday: **Bénodet** is considered the best family resort in the region, Beg Meil has its excellent Plage des Dunes and Plage de Kerambigorn, La Baule has 4km/2.5mi of uninterrupted sand, and Carnac's beaches are south-facing and sheltered. Active sea lovers can **learn to surf** at St-Malo Surf School (*www.surfschool.org, ℘02 99 40 07 47*), which gives lessons to 3–13-year-olds as well as adults.

LAND ACTIVITIES
Landlubbers will find plenty of amusement at the Labyrinthe du Corsaire (*www.labyrintheducorsaire. com, ℘02 99 81 17 23*), the Pirate's Maze, in both St-Malo and Lorient. Cobac Park (www.cobac-parc. com) near St-Malo offers boating, swimming, water slides, children's island, bouncy castles, horses and a picnic area. Le Vapeur du Trieux (*www.vapeurdutrieux.com, ℘08 92 39 14 27*) in Paimpol is a **steam train** that runs alongside the River Trieux, delighting both young and old. **Car enthusiasts** should head to Le Manoir de l'Automobile (*www.manoir-automobile.fr, ℘02 99 34 02 32*) near Rennes, which has more than 400 cars on display and a mini-racetrack where adults can enquire about taking a spin.

ANIMAL PARKS
Animal lovers are spoilt for choice with several **animal parks** and aquariums to choose from, such as La Bourbansais (*www.labourbansais. com, ℘02 99 69 40 07*) near Dinan, the Parc de Branféré (*℘02 97 42 94 66*) near Vannes and Océanopolis (*www. oceanopolis.com, ℘02 98 34 40 40*) near Brest, which has 40 aquariums full of fish from around the world. Kids have the opportunity to feed and touch some of the inhabitants and they'll also love the sea lions. In a similar vein, the Océarium at Le Croisic, (www.ocearium.fr), offers the visitor the chance to see a colony of penguins before encountering various forms of marine life.

FISHING
To find out about Brittany's **fishing heritage**, families should make a date to visit Haliotika (*www.leguilvinec. com, ℘02 98 58 28 38*) near Quimper, to learn about the fishing industry and attend a fish auction, witnessing the day's catch.

ADVENTURE
Adventurous sorts can swing or abseil through the trees at Parc des Grands Chênes as well as do some serious orienteering, go walking on the GR39 long-distance path (Trans Brittany Trail) or the gentler Sentier Botanique (botanical footpath) (*www. parcdesgrandschenes.fr, ℘06 88 72 73 40*) near Mont St-Michel and Tépacap (*www.tepacap.fr, ℘02 40 58 30 30*) near St-Nazaire, where you can also swim, play tennis and go mountain-biking.

SHOPPING
SOUVENIRS

Oysters from Cancale, *charcuterie* such as *rillettes* or *boudin noir* (black pudding), globe artichokes, chestnuts, cider, Muscadet and Gros Plant wine, Breton mead (*hydromel*), Breton butter biscuits, and local crafts such as carved wood, lace and Quimper pottery.

Travellers from the USA should note that they are not allowed to take food and plant products home, so this rules out unpasteurised French cheeses and fruit.

North American citizens are allowed to take home, tax-free, up to US$800 worth of goods, Canadians up to CND$700, Australians up to AUS$900 and New Zealanders up to NZ$700.

MAIN MARKETS

Market day is an important event in the lives of local communities, and also provides visitors with an opportunity to meet people, exchange news and views, and find out about the region and local produce from those who live and work there. Le *marché* is a way of life in France, a tradition which has been lost in many other parts of the world. One of the pleasures of visiting French towns on market day is to share in that experience.

Sunday

Brest (St-Louis), Cameret-sur-Mer, Cancale, Carnac, Étables-sur-Mer, La Forêt-Fouesnant, Plouigneau, St-Gildas-de-Rhuys.

Brest Market in the Halles St-Louis (covered market) opens daily but Sundays are the most spectacular, with stalls spreading out along the Rue de Siam where on average about 100 stalls sell everything from local produce like cheese from the Monts d'Arrée, bread, preserves and seafood to clothing and novelties. The market at Carnac (Morbihan) in the Place du Marché is also has around 100 stalls.

Monday

Auray, Bénodet, Châtelaudren, Combourg, Concarneau, Dinard, Douarnenez, Guerlesquin, Pontivy Pontrieux, Redon, Vitré.

While most markets take place in the morning only, twoof the above last all day: Redon (Ile-et-Vilaine) which has a good mix of stalls; and Pontivy in the Morbihan which is smaller with but is nevertheless a worth a visit. Vitré (Ile-et-Vilaine) has a medium-sized morning market (45 stalls) in the Place du Marchix while Combourg (Ile-et-Vilaine) has an excellent market in the town centre with a large number of stalls selling everything from local produce to clothing and accessories.

Colourful tins of biscuits

©Sylvaine Poitau/Apa Publications

Tuesday

Brest, Le Croisic (Jul–Aug), Guilvinec Landerneau, La Roche-Bernard, Locmariaquer, Loctudy, Pont-Aven, Quintin, St-Pol-de-Léon, La Trinité-sur-Mer.

La Roche-Bernard in the Morbihan has an excellent market in the morning with 120 stalls selling a variety of produce. Guilvinec in Finistère is smaller but provides a good choice, while the excellent medium-sized market in the Place de l'Évéché at St-Pol-de-Léon lasts all day. Loctudy has organic veg.

Wednesday

Carnac, Châteaubriant, Châteauneuf-du-Faou, Guérande, Lorient, Morlaix, Nantes, Quiberon (seasonal) Quimper, St-Brieuc, Roscoff, Tréguier, Vannes.

Carnac in the Morbihan has a good morning market (about 100) stalls in the Place du Marché, while nearby Quiberon has a small summer market in the Port. Quimper (Finistère) has an excellent small market with a wide variety of goods that lasts all day.

Thursday

Châteaugiron, Dinard, Le Croisic, Dinan, Hennebont, Lamballe, Lannion, Malestroit, Pont-l'Abbé, Pont-Croix, La Roche-Bernard, Sarzeau.

Several excellent markets with more than 200 stalls and everything from local produce to clothing, tools and novelties take place on Thursday. Lannion (Côtes-d'Armor) lasts all day while Dinan (Côtes-d'Armor), Hennebont and Sarzeau (both Morbihan) take place in the morning.

Friday

Arradon, Concarneau, Fouesnant, Guingamp, Jugon-les-Lacs, Landerneau, Paimpol, Perros-Guerec, Quimper, Quimperlé, St-Malo, La Trinité- sur -Mer.

Quimperlé in Finistère has a good medium-sized market lasting all day in the Place St-Michel. Perros-Guirec

Alternative Markets

For markets on slightly more unusual themes, try: the Book Market at Bécherel *(first Sun of every month)*; the Flea Market *(Marché aux Puces)* at Dinan *(every Wed Jul and Aug otherwise the first Wed of the month)*; and one of the largest cattle markets in Europe, the Aumaillerie Market at Fougères *(from 5am Fri, but arrive around 7am)*.

(Côtes-d'Armor), which is morning only, has excellent selection of locally produced goods, clothes and books spreading right through the town. St-Malo has a varied morning market at St-Servan.

Saturday

Bécherel, Le Bono, Le Croisic, Dol-de-Bretagne, Fougères, Guérande, Guingamp, Josselin, Landerneau, Locmariaquer, Lorient, Morlaix, Nantes, Plancoët, Pontivy, Port-Louis, Quiberon, Quimper, Redon, Rennes, St-Brieuc, Vannes, Vitré.

Rennes has one of the best markets in Brittany. It takes place in the Place des Lices, with more than 300 stalls selling the finest farm produce from all over Brittany, plus high-quality seafood. Vannes has a first-class market in its Place des Lices, with about 150 stalls selling a huge variety of products.

FRESH FISH AUCTIONS

The fresh fish auctions, which take place on the return of the fishing fleets, are lively and colourful affairs. They are generally held every day of the week 30mins after the boats come in, and last for about two hours. The major ones are to be found at Audierne, Concarneau, Douarnenez, Erquy, Le Guilvinec, Loctudy and Lorient. All of these markets are open to the public but you have to be there at about 6am. Lesconil and Roscoff have good auctions as does Ploubazlanec/ Loguivy-de-la-Mer near Paimpol (Nov–Apr) on Mondays and Wednesdays.

BOOKS AND FILMS
BOOKS
History
Discovering the History of Brittany by Wendy Mewes (Red Dog Books, 2007)
> Former teacher and now Finistère resident Wendy charts the history of Brittany in a lively fashion from its origins to the present day in this informative book.

Memoirs of a Breton Peasant by Jean-Marie Deguignet (Seven Stories Press, 2004). The views of a literate "peasant" on religion, science and life – recently published after being found in his granddaughter's cupboard.

Food
Trop mad, trop bonne la cuisine bretonne by Nathalie Beauvais (2006)
> Voted the world's best regional cookbook for 2007, this mouth-watering *oeuvre* is published by Nathalie herself. She also finds time to cook in her restaurant, Le Jardin Gourmand de Lorient.

General Interest
The Most Beautiful Villages of Brittany by James Bentley and Hugh Palmer (Thames & Hudson, 1999).
> A look at the unique aspects and architecure of 31 Breton villages and islands accompanied by stunning and evocative photography.

Fiction
The Five of Cups by Wendy Mewes (Red Dog Books, 2007)
> A newly single woman embarks on a journey of self-discovery in the region of the *Monts d'Arrée.*

FILMS
L'Homme du Large/Man of the Sea (1920) by Marcel l'Herbier.
> A wayward son is cast out to sea in a boat by his despairing father. Based on a book by Honoré de Balzac, this film, believed to be set around Carnac, marked Charles Boyer's debut. An insight into early 20C Breton life and culture.

Chère Inconnue/I Sent a Letter to My Love (1980) by Moshé Mizrahi
> Starring the Finistère coast and Simone Signoret, this is the story of a middle-aged woman who places an ad in a lonely hearts column only to discover that her correspondent is her disabled brother for whom she is carer.

Conte d'Été/A Summer's Tale (1996) by Eric Rhomer
> A young man, Gaspard, spends the summer in Dinard waiting for his girlfriend to arrive. In the meantime, he meets Margot and Solene. Which one will he choose?

Marthe (1997) by Jean-Loup Hubert
> Set in 1915, this is a love story between a schoolteacher and an injured soldier, torn between his feelings and his sense of duty, who is recuperating in the Loire-Atlantique region.

Au Coeur du Mensonge/The Colour of Lies (1999) by Claude Chabrol
> A young girl is raped and murdered in a small, middle-class Breton community. Whodunnit? Perhaps the hard-up artist/art teacher? Stars Sandrine Bonnaire and Valeria Bruni Tedeschi (actress sister of France's First Lady).

Les Femmes ou les Enfants d'Abord/ Women or Children First (2002) by Manuel Poirier
> Set in Auray, Morbihan, the film focuses on a Spaniard, Tom, whose married life is turned upside down when his ex-lover turns up with some news: he's got a daughter.

L'Ennemi Naturel (Natural Enemy) (2004) by Pierre-Erwan Guillaume
> A young policeman has an existential (and sexuality) crisis while investigating a teen's death in a small Breton village. Not for the faint of heart!

Calendar of Events

PARDONS

A *pardon* is a type of pilgrimage unique to the western parts of Brittany that takes place on the feast days of particular Breton saints.

PALM SUNDAY

Callac — Stations of the Cross
☎02 96 45 50 19
Quintin — Pardon of Nôtre-Dame-de-Délivrance, ☎02 96 74 92 17

MAY

St-Herbot — Pardon of St-Herbot
Third Sunday in May
Tréguier — Pardon of St-Yves, 3rd Sunday in May, ☎02 96 92 95 11
Bubry — Pardon of St-Yves,
☎02 97 51 74 83

WHIT SATURDAY AND SUNDAY

Moncontour — Pardon of St-Mathurin, ☎02 96 73 49 57
Île St-Gildas — Blessing of the horses
Notre-Dame-du-Crann — Pardon,
☎02 98 93 94 27 (Chapel)

SUNDAY AFTER WHIT SUNDAY

Rumengol Le Faou —
Pardon of the Trinity

SAT EVE AND SUNDAY BEFORE THE FEAST OF ST-JOHN THE BAPTIST (MID-JUNE)

St-Tugen — Pardon,
☎02 98 74 80 28

LAST SUNDAY IN JUNE

St-Jean-du-Doigt — Pardon of St-John the Baptist,
☎02 98 79 92 92
Plouguerneau — Pardon of St-Peter and St-Paul, ☎02 98 04 70 93
Le Faouët (Morbihan) —
Summer Pardon of St-Barbara,
☎02 97 23 15 27

FIRST SUNDAY IN JULY (AND PRECEDING FRIDAY AND SATURDAY)

Guingamp — Pardon of Notre-Dame-de-Bon-Secours (Procession on Sat night), ☎02 96 43 73 89
Montautour — Pardon Notre-Dame du Roc

SECOND SUNDAY IN JULY

Locronan — *Petite Troménie* (the *Grande Troménie* takes place every 6 years; next one will be Jul 2015),
☎02 98 91 70 14

THIRD SUNDAY IN JULY

Carantec — Pardon St-Carantec,
☎02 98 67 00 43

La grande troménie at Locronan

R. Mattès/MICHELIN

**25 AND 26 JULY
(FEAST OF ST-ANNE)**

Ste-Anne-d'Auray — Grand Pardon
of St-Anne, ☎02 97 57 68 80

**26 JULY (FEAST OF ST-ANNE)
AND FOLLOWING SUNDAY**

Fouesnant — Grand and Petit
Pardons of St-Anne,
☎02 98 56 00 91

THIRD SUNDAY IN JULY

Le Vieux Marché — Islamic-Christian
pilgrimage to the Chapelle des
Sept-Saints, ☎02 96 38 91 73

FOURTH SUNDAY IN JULY

Le Relecq — Pardon of St-Anne –
Breton mass; festival of Celtic
Music

Bubry — Pardon of Ste-Hélène,
☎02 97 51 70 38

FIRST SUNDAY IN AUGUST

Persquen — Pardon of Notre-Dame-
de-Pénéty, ☎02 97 39 35 30

**15 AUGUST (FEAST OF THE
ASSUMPTION) AND EVE OF 14TH**

Perros-Guirec — Pardon of Nôtre-
Dame-de-Clarté,
☎02 96 23 21 64

Quelven — Pardon of Notre-Dame
☎02 97 25 04 10

Loudeac —Pardon de Querrien,
☎02 96 28 01 32

Rumengol — Pardon of Notre-
Dame-de-Rumengol

Porcaro — Pardon of *"La Madone des
Motards"* (Our Lady of Bikers),
☎02 97 22 10 70, http://madone
desmotards.ifrance.com

Bécherel — *Troménie de Haute-
Bretagne*, ☎02 99 66 75 23

Pont-Croix — Pardon of Notre-
Dame-de-Roscudon,
(www.pont-croix.info)

SUNDAY AFTER 15 AUGUST

Rochefort-en-Terre — Pardon of
Nôtre-Dame-de-la-Tronchaye,
☎02 97 43 33 57

Carantec — Pardon of Notre-Dame-
de-Callot, ☎02 98 67 07 88

Ploërdut — Pardon of Notre-Dame-
de-Crénenan, ☎02 97 39 44 43

Le Faouët — Pardon of St-Fiacre, 3rd
weekend, ☎02 97 23 23 23

La Baule —La Baule Pardon, 3rd
weekend, ☎02 40 24 56 29.

**LAST SUNDAY IN AUGUST (AND EVE,
AND FOLLOWING TUESDAY)**

Plonévez-Porzay— Ste-Anne-
la-Palud Grand Pardon,
☎02 98 26 53 57

FIRST SUNDAY IN SEPTEMBER

Camaret — Pardon of Notre-Dame-
de-Rocamadour (blessing of
the sea), ☎02 98 27 90 48

Le Folgoët — Grand Pardon of
Notre-Dame, 8 Sept,
☎02 98 83 00 61

Lamballe — Pardon of Notre-Dame-
de-la-Grande-Puissance,
☎02 96 31 92 06

Pouldreuzic — Pardon of Notre-
Dame-de-Penhors,
☎02 98 51 55 91

SECOND SUNDAY IN SEPTEMBER

Carnac — Pardon of St-Cornély,
☎02 97 52 08 08

7/8 SEPTEMBER

Josselin — Pardon of Notre-Dame-
du-Roncier, ☎02 97 22 20 18.
www.notre-dame-du-roncier.fr

THIRD SUNDAY IN SEPTEMBER

Hennebont — Pardon of Notre-
Dame-du-Vœu, ☎02 97 36 24 52

Notre-Dame-de-Tronoën —
Pardon, ☎02 98 82 03 16

Pontivy — Pardon of Notre-Dame-
de-la-Joie, 12 Sept or Sun
following, ☎02 97 25 04 10

LAST SUNDAY IN SEPTEMBER

Plouguerneau — Pardon of
St-Michel, ☎02 98 44 24 96

SUNDAY NEAREST 29 SEPTEMBER

Mont-St-Michel — Feast of the
Archangel St-Michael,
☎02 33 60 14 30

Gourin — Bellringers' Pardon,
☎02 97 23 41 83

2ND WEEKEND IN OCTOBER
Vannes — Pardon de la Chapelle
de Hamon
Fougères — Pardon de Notre-Dame
des Marais, ☎02 99 94 12 20

FIRST SUNDAY IN DECEMBER
Le Faouët — Winter Pardon of
St-Barbara ☎02 97 23 23 23

OTHER MAJOR FESTIVALS
Brittany is usually associated with the
Pardon but there are, however, many
other festivals in the region, ranging
from classical music to jazz and rock
to festivals celebrating celtic culture,
many of which are listed below:

LAST WEEKEND OF JANUARY/FIRST WEEKEND FEBRUARY
Nantes — *La Folle Journée* (classical
music festival), ☎08 92 70 52 05
www.follejournee.fr

APRIL
La Trinité-sur-Mer — Spi Ouest-
France sailing event, early Apr,
www.spi-ouestfrance.com
Nantes — Carnival, ☎02 40 35 75 42
Concarneau— Book festival,
☎02 98 97 52 52
Châteauneuf-du-Faou — *Printemps
de Châteauneuf-du-Faou* music
and dance festival, early Apr,
☎02 98 21 97 57, www.printemps-
de-chateauneuf.org
Dinard — International Fashion
Festival, ☎02 99 46 94 12
www.festival-dinard.com
Loguivy de la Mer — *Fête de la
Coquille St-Jacques* (scallop
festival), www.cotesdarmor.com

MAY–JUNE
Morbihan — *La Semaine du Golfe*
(week-long vintage boat festival),
☎02 97 62 20 09
www.semainedugolfe.asso.fr
St-Brieuc — Festival Art Rock,
www.artrock.org

Binic — *Fête de la Morue* (Cod Festival
– sea shanties, tall ships, cooking),
☎02 96 73 39 90.
www.ville-binic.fr
Guérande —La Fête Médievale,
☎02 40 15 60 40.
www.villie-guerande.fr

JULY
Vitré — *Festival du Bocage*
(rural festival), first 2 weeks of Jul,
☎02 99 75 02 25
www.paysdevitre.org
Rennes — *Les tombées de la nuit*
(Breton art festival), early Jul,
☎02 99 32 56 56
www.lestombeesdelanuit.com
Carhaix-Plouger — *Vieilles Charrues*
(music festival) third week of Jul,
☎08 20 89 00 66,
www.vieillescharrues.asso.fr
Dinan — Celtic Harp Festival, 2nd/3rd
week of Jul, ☎02 96 87 36 69.
www.harpe-celtique.com
Morlaix — *Festival des Arts de la Rue*
(street festival), ☎02 98 46 19 46,
www.artsdanslarue.com
Polignac — Festival of Classical Music
and Jazz, ☎02 97 65 06 13,
www.festivalpolignac.com
Quimper — Cornouaille Festival,
endJul, ☎02 98 55 53 53.
www.festival-cornouaille.com
Vannes — Jazz Festival, last week of
Jul, ☎02 97 01 62 44
www.mairie-vannes.fr
Hennebont — Fêtes Médiévales
(medieval festival),
☎02 97 36 24 52.
www.hennebont.net
Gourin — Fête de la Crêpe
(pancake festival)
http://fetedelacrepe.free.fr

FIRST FORTNIGHT OF AUGUST (INCLUDING 15 AUGUST)
Paimpol — Festival of Sea Shanties,
every two years (2011, 2013, 2015)
first fortnight of Aug, ☎02 96 20
83 16. www.paimpol-goelo.com
Erquy — Festival of the Sea, (first
Sun), ☎02 96 72 30 12
www.erquy-tourisme.com

Inter-Celtic Festival

This vast annual gathering of Celts from all the celtic regions of Europe, including those who now live further afield, attracts about 650,000 spectators and 4,500 artists each year with the aim of celebrating this rich cultural heritage. Fiddles, bagpipes and ceilidhs plus traditional food and drink.

Office du Tourisme de Pays de Lorient, 2 rue Paul-Bert 56100. ℘*02 97 21 24 29. www.lorient-tourisme.fr.*

Pont-Aven — *Fête des Fleurs d'Ajonc* (Gorse Flower Festival) 31 Jul–1 Aug, ℘02 98 06 04 70, www.pontaven.com

Lorient — Interceltic Festival, ℘02 97 21 24 29, www.festival-interceltique.com

Moncontour —Medieval Festival, every 2 years (2011, 2013, 2015), ℘02 96 73 49 57 www.moncontour-medievale.com

St-Malo — *La Route du Rock,* ℘02 99 54 01 11 www.laroutedurock.com

Crozon — Festival du Bout du Monde (music), ℘02 98 27 00 32, www.festivalduboutdu monde.com

Guingamp — Festivals of Breton Dance St-Loup, ℘02 96 43 73 89, www.dansebretonne.com

Plomodiern — Ménez-Hom Folk Festival, ℘02 98 8127 37, www.tourisme-porzay.com

Guérande — Celtic Festival, ℘02 40 24 96 71, www.ot-guerande.fr

Vannes — Grand Festival of Arvor, ℘02 97 47 24 34 or 02 97 01 60 00, www.fetes-arvor.org

MID TO LATE AUGUST

Roscoff — Fête de l'Oignon Rosé (Pink Onion Festival) ℘02 98 61 12 13, www.roscoff-tourisme.com

Concarneau — Festival of the Blue Nets, ℘02 98 97 09 09, www.concarneautourisme.fr

SEPTEMBER

Fougères — *Le Rando'patrimoine* (outdoor heritage days), ℘02 96 73 49 57, www.bretagnes-fougeres.com

Rennes — Gallo (local dialect) Festival, ℘02 99 38 97 65

Vannes —*Les Celti'Vannes* (Celtic culture festival), ℘0825 13 56 10, www.tourisme-vannes.com

OCTOBER

Finistère — Atlantique Jazz Festival ℘02 29 00 40 01, www.atlantiquejazzfestival.com

Dinard — British Film Festival, ℘02 99 88 19 04, www.festivaldufilm-dinard.com

St-Malo — *Quai des Bulles* (Comic-Strip Festival), ℘08 25 13 52 00, www.quaidesbulles.com

Redon — *La Teilloue* chestnut festival, ℘02 99 71 06 04, www.tourisme-pays-redon.com/ fete/bogue_d_or.htm

Lanvellec — Baroque Music Festival, 9–24 Oct, ℘02 96 35 14 14, www.festival-lanvellec.fr

Nantes — Celtomania Festival, all Oct, ℘02 40 54 20 18, www.celtomania.fr

NOVEMBER

Nantes —3 Continents Film Festival, last week Nov, ℘02 40 69 74 14 www.3continents.com

Quévert — Fête de la Pomme (Apple Festival), www.fruitsdebretagne.net

DECEMBER

Rennes — Transmusicales, first week Dec, ℘02 99 31 12 10, www.lestrans.com

Know Before You Go

USEFUL WEBSITES

www.ambafrance.org.uk
The French Embassy's website provides basic information (geography, demographics, history), a news digest and business-related information. It offers special pages for children, and pages devoted to culture, language study and travel. You can reach other selected French sites (regions, cities, ministries) with a hypertext link.

www.franceguide.com
The French Government Tourist Office – *Maison de la France* – site is packed with practical information and tips for travelling to France. Choose your country of origin and then click on the French region you're interested in. Alternatively, go directly to www.brittanytourism.com.

www.visiteurope.com
The European Travel Commission provides useful information on travelling to and around 34 European countries, and includes links to some commercial booking services (i.e. vehicle hire), rail schedules, weather reports and more.

www.FranceKeys.com
This site has plenty of practical information for visiting France. It covers all the regions, with links to tourist offices and related sites. Very useful for planning the details of your tour in France.

www.francetourism.com
The official website of the French Tourist Office offers a hotel reservation service, information on flights etc, the regions and cultural sites.

www.france-for-visitors.com
Easily accessible information on France, all its regions and cities plus downloadable maps and useful suggestions about what to see.

TOURIST OFFICES ABROAD

For information, brochures, maps and assistance in planning a trip to France, travellers should apply to the official French Tourist Office in their own country:

AUSTRALIA – NEW ZEALAND

- **Sydney**
  Level 13, 25 Bligh Street, NSW 2000 Sydney
  ✆(0)2 92 31 52 44
  Fax: (0)2 9221 8682

CANADA

- **Montreal**
  1800 Ave. McGill College, Suite 1010, Montreal Que H3A 3J6
  ✆(514) 288 20 26
  Fax: (514) 845 48 68.

EIRE

- **Dublin**
  10 Suffolk St, 2
  ✆01560 235 235

UNITED KINGDOM

- **London**
  178 Piccadilly, London W1J 9AL
  ✆09068 244 123 (60p/min at all times), Fax: 0207 493 6594

UNITED STATES

- **East Coast – New York**
  825 Third Ave, 29th Floor, NY 10022
  ✆(514) 288 1904
  Fax: (212) 838 7855

- **Midwest – Chicago**
  205 North Michigan Avenue, Suite 3770, Chicago, IL 60601
  ✆(514) 288 1904

- **West Coast – Los Angeles**
  9454 Wilshire Boulevard, Suite 210, Beverly Hills, CA 90212.
  ✆(514) 288 1904
  Fax: (310) 276 2835

TOURIST OFFICES IN FRANCE

Visitors may also contact local tourist offices for more precise information and to receive brochures and maps. The addresses, telephone numbers and websites of local tourist offices are listed after the symbol 🏛 at the beginning of most of the Principal Sights described in this book. Below are addresses for the regional tourist offices and the departmental tourist offices for Brittany.

COMITÉ RÉGIONAL DE TOURISME

♦ **Bretagne**
1 rue Raoul-Ponchon,
35000 Rennes Cedex.
☎02 99 28 44 30
Fax: 02 99 28 44 40
www.tourismebretagne.com

COMITÉ DÉPARTEMENTAL DE TOURISME

♦ **Ille-et-Villaine**
4 rue Jean-Jaurès, BP 6046,
35060 Rennes Cedex 3.
☎02 99 78 47 47
Fax: 02 99 78 33 24
www.bretagne35.com

♦ **Loire-Atlantique**
11, rue du Chàteau de l´Eraudière,
CS40698 44306 Nantes Cedex 3
☎02 51 72 95 38
Fax: 02 40 20 44 54
www.loire-atlantique-tourisme.com

♦ **Côtes-d'Armor:**
7 rue St-Benoît, BP 4620, 22406
St-Brieuc Cedex 2.
☎02 96 62 72 01
Fax: 02 96 33 59 10
www.cotesdarmor.com

♦ **Finistère:**
4 rue du 19 mars 1962,
29018 Quimper Cedex.
☎02 98 76 24 77
Fax: 02 98 52 19 19
www.finisteretourisme.com

♦ **Morbihan:**
PIBS, Allée Nicolas-Leblanc,
BP 408, 56010 Vannes Cedex
☎0 825 13 56 56
Fax: 02 97 42 71 02
www.morbihan.com

INTERNATIONAL VISITORS
EMBASSIES AND CONSULATES IN FRANCE

Australia Embassy
4, rue Jean-Rey, 75015 Paris
☎01 40 59 33 00; Fax: 01 40 59 33 10
www.france.embassy.gov.au

Canada Embassy
35, avenue Montaigne, 75008 Paris
☎01 44 43 29 90; Fax: 01 44 43 29 99.
ww.france.gc.ca

Eire Embassy
4 rue Rude/12 ave Foch, 75116 Paris
☎01 44 17 67 00; Fax: 01 44 17 67 50
www.embassyofireland.com

New Zealand Embassy
7 rue Léonard-de-Vinci, 75116 Paris
☎01 45 01 43 43; Fax: 01 45 01 43 44
www.nzembassy.com/france.

UK Embassy
35, rue du Faubourg-St-Honoré,
75363 Paris
☎01 44 51 31 00; Fax: 01 44 51 31 88
http://ukinfrance.fco.gov.uk/fr

UK Consulate
18 bis rue d'Anjou, 75008 Paris
☎01 44 51 31 00; Fax: 01 44 51 31 27

USA Embassy
2, avenue Gabriel, 75382 Paris
☎01 43 12 22 22; Fax: 01 42 66 97 83
http://france.usembassy.gov

USA Consulate
2, rue St-Florentin, 75382 Paris
☎01 43 12 22 22

ENTRY REQUIREMENTS
PASSPORT

Nationals of countries within the European Union entering France need only a national identity card (or for UK citizens, a passport). Nationals of other countries must be in possession of a valid national **passport**.

VISA

No **entry visa** is required for Canadian, US, Australian or New Zealand citizens for a stay of less than three months – except for students planning to study in France. Citizens of non-EU countries should check with their French Consulate.

US citizens should obtain the booklet *Safe Trip Abroad*, which provides useful information on visa requirements, customs regulations, medical care, etc. for international travellers. Published by the Government Printing Office, it can be ordered by phone (☎(202) 512 1800 DC Metro area; Toll free 866 512 1800) or consulted online at www.access.gpo.gov.

CUSTOMS REGULATIONS

Call the Customs Office (UK) for a leaflet on customs regulations and the full range of "duty free" allowances on ☎0845 010 9000 (☎+44 208 929 0152 outside UK) or see www. hmrc.gov.uk. The US Customs Service offers a downloadable publication *Know Before You Go* for US citizens, obtainable from www.customs. ustreas.gov. There are no customs formalities for holidaymakers bringing their caravans or pleasure boats into France for a stay of less than six

DUTY-FREE ALLOWANCES

Spirits (whisky, gin, vodka, etc.)	10l/2.6gal
Fortified wines (vermouth, port, etc.)	20l/5.3gal
Wine (not more than 60 sparkling)	90l/23.7gal
Beer	110l/29gal
Cigarettes	3,200
Cigarillos	400
Cigars	200
Smoking tobacco	1kg/2.2lb

months but registration documents should be carried. Americans can bring home, tax-free, up to US$800 worth of goods; Canadians up to CND$750 ; Australians up to AUS$900 and New Zealanders up to NZ$700. Persons living in a Member State of the European Union are not restricted in regard to purchasing goods for private use, but the recommended allowances for alcoholic beverages and tobacco are as given in the Duty-Free Allowance table.

HEALTH

First aid, medical advice and chemists' night service are provided by chemists/drugstores (*pharmacie*), identified by the green cross sign. Since the recipient of medical treatment in French hospitals or clinics must pay the bill, it is advisable to take out comprehensive insurance cover. Nationals of non-EU countries should check with their insurance companies about policy limitations. Reimbursement can then be negotiated with the insurance company according to the policy held. All prescription drugs should be clearly labelled; it is recommended that you carry a copy of the prescription.

British and Irish citizens need to carry their European Health Insurance Card (EHIC) as proof of entitlement to free or reduced-cost medical treatment in EU countries. You can get one at www.ehic.org.uk, call ☎0845 606 2030 or get a form from the post office. You pay upfront but can reclaim most of the money (see website for details). **Americans** concerned about travel and health can contact the International Association for Medical Assistance to Travellers, which can also provide details of English-speaking doctors in different parts of France: ☎(716) 754 4883, www.iamat.org.

ACCESSIBILITY

The sights described in this guide that are easily accessible to people of reduced mobility are indicated in the

Admission times and charges section by the symbol &.
Many of France's historic buildings, have limited or no wheelchair access. Older hotels tend to lack lifts. Useful information on transport, holidaymaking and sports associations for the disabled is available from the *Comité National Français de Liaison pour la Réadaptation des Handicapés (CNRH)*. Call their international information number ℘01 53 80 66 66 or visit www.accessproject-phsp.org. Holiday Care (*℘0845 124 9971, www.tourismforall.org.uk*) is a charity that publishes overseas information guides listing accommodation it believes to be accessible for disabled travellers. Useful information on transportation, holidaymaking and sports associations for disabled travellers is available from the French-language website www.handica.com.

In the UK, www.radar.org.uk is a good source of information and support, as is US website www.access-able.com. For information on museum access, contact *Les Musées de France* on ℘01 40 15 73 00. Michelin publishes **The Michelin Guide France** and the **Michelin Camping Caravaning France**, which indicate hotels and campsites with facilities suitable for people with physical disabilities.

Getting There and Getting Around

BY PLANE

FROM THE UK AND IRELAND

Aer Arann (www.aerarann.com) from various airports in Ireland to Lorient.
Aer Lingus (www.aerlingus.com) from Dublin to Rennes.
Aurigny (www.aurigny.com, ℘01481 822 886) from Guernsey to Dinard.
easyJet (www.easyjet.com, ℘0905 821 0905) to Rennes.
Flybe (www.flybe.com, ℘0871 700 0535) to Rennes and Brest.
Ryanair (www.ryanair.com, ℘0871 246 0000) to Brest, Dinard and Nantes.

FROM THE USA

All flights via Paris
Air Canada (www.aircanada.com, ℘1-888-247-2262, opt 3) from New York
Air France (www.airfrance.fr) from New York, Detroit, LA, Washington DC
Delta (www.delta.com. ℘800-241-4141) from Atlanta, Philadelphia, San Francisco

FROM PARIS

From Paris, use inland flights (Charles de Gaulle airport). **Air France** (www.airfrance.fr) is one such airline which flies from Paris to Brest, Lorient, Quimper and Rennes.

BY FERRY

There are numerous **cross-Channel services** from the United Kingdom and Ireland and also the Eurotunnel rail shuttle through the Channel Tunnel (www.eurotunnel.com, ℘08705 353535). To compare prices see www.ferrysavers.co.uk or contact:

- **Condor Ferries**
  ℘0845 609 1024
  www.condorferries.co.uk
- **P &O**
  ℘08716 645 645
  www.poferries.com
- **Brittany Ferries**
  ℘0870 907 6103
  www.brittanyferries.co.uk
  Irish Ferries
  ℘0818 300 400
  www.irishferries.com

BY TRAIN

Eurostar (www.eurostar.com, ℘08705 186 186) operates a 2hr 15min service via the Channel Tunnel from **London** (St Pancras) to **Paris** (Gare du Nord). From Paris-Gare

Montparnasse, the TGV Atlantique (high-speed rail service) serves Nantes, St-Nazaire and La Baule, Rennes, Lorient and Quimper, as well as Rennes, St-Brieuc and Brest. To book your return tickets from the UK to Brittany contact **Rail Europe** (www.raileurope.co.uk, ✆08448 484 064). **France Railpass**, **Global Pass**, **One Country Pass, Interail Flexi**, **Interail Continuous and France Youthpass** and are travel passes that may be purchased by residents of countries outside the European Union (see www.eurorailways.com). In the USA, contact your travel agent or **Rail Europe** (✆1-888-382-RAIL or ✆1-888-382-7245, www.raileurope. com). Information on schedules can also be obtained from **SNCF** at www.sncf.fr.

Tickets in France must be validated (*composté*) by using the orange automatic date-stamping machines at the platform entrance (✆failure to do so may result in a fine).

The French railway company SNCF operates a telephone information, reservation and pre-pay service in English from 7am to 10pm (French time). In France, call ✆08 92 35 35 35. For details of local train services and buses in Brittany see www.ter-sncf. com/bretagne.

BY COACH/BUS

Eurolines runs regular coach services from London to various towns and cities in Brittany. For further information, see www.eurolines.co.uk or call ✆08717 818181 in the UK. For local travel, bus times can be obtained from train stations, bus stations (*gare routière*) or tourist offices.

BY CAR
ROUTES

The area covered in this guide is easily reached by main motorways and national routes. **Michelin map 726** indicates the main itineraries as well as alternative routes for avoiding heavy traffic during busy holiday periods, and gives estimated travel times. **Michelin map 723** is a detailed atlas of French motorways, indicating tolls, rest areas and services along the route; it includes a table for calculating distances and times. **Michelin Local maps 308, 309** and **316** cover the areas included in this guide. There is a listing of Michelin maps and plans at the back of the guide. The latest Michelin route-planning service is available on the internet at **www. ViaMichelin.com**. Travellers can calculate a precise route using such options as shortest route, quickest route or Michelin-recommended route and gain access to tourist information (hotels, restaurants, attractions). The service is available on a pay-per-route basis or by subscription.

DRIVING LICENCE

Travellers from other European Union countries and North America can drive in France with a valid national or home-state driving licence. An international driving licence is useful because the information on it appears in nine languages (bear in mind that traffic officers are empowered to fine motorists). A permit is available (US$10) from the National Auto Club, Touring Department (*1151 E. Hillsdale Blvd. Foster City, CA 94404, ✆1 800 622 2136, www.nationalautoclub.com*) or contact your local branch of the American Automobile Association. In the UK an International Driving Licence can be obtained from the Post Office or one of the motoring organisations.

Registration papers

It is imperative that you carry your vehichle's registration papers (logbook) and display a nationality plate or sticker.

INSURANCE

Certain motoring organisations (AAA, AA, RAC and The Caravan Club) offer accident insurance and breakdown service schemes for members. Check with your current insurance company with regards to coverage while abroad. If you plan to hire a car using your credit card, check with the company, which may provide liability insurance automatically (and thus save you having to pay the cost for optimum coverage).

HIGHWAY CODE

The minimum driving age in France is 18. Traffic drives on the **right**. All passengers must wear **seat belts**. Children under the age of 10 must travel in the back seat of the vehicle. **Headlights** must be switched on in poor visibility and at night; **dipped headlights** should be used at all times outside built up areas. Use **side-lights** only when the vehicle is stationary. In the case of a **breakdown**, at least one red warning triangle or hazard warning lights are obligatory and reflective safety jackets are recommended. In the absence of stop signs at intersections, cars must **yield to the right**. Traffic on main roads outside built-up areas (priority indicated by a yellow diamond sign) and on **roundabouts** has right of way. Vehicles must stop when the lights turn red at road junctions and may filter to the right only when indicated by an amber arrow.

The regulations on **drinking and driving** (limited to 0.5g/l or 0.017oz/gal) and **speeding** are strictly enforced – usually by an on-the-spot fine and/or confiscation of the vehicle.

SPEED LIMITS

- toll motorways (autoroutes) 130kph/80mph (110kph/68mph when raining);
- dual carriageways and motorways without tolls 110kph/68mph (100kph/62mph when raining);
- other roads 90kph/56mph (80kph/50mph when raining) and in towns 50kph/31mph;
- outside lane on motorways during daylight, on level ground and with good visibility – minimum speed limit of 80kph/50mph.

PARKING REGULATIONS

In town there are zones where parking is either restricted or subject to a fee; tickets should be obtained from the ticket machines (horodateurs – small change necessary) and displayed inside the windscreen on the driver's side; failure to display may result in a fine, or towing and impoundment. In some towns you may find blue parking zones (zone bleue) marked by a blue line on the pavement or road and a blue signpost with a P and a small square underneath. In this case you have to display a cardboard disc with various times indicated on it. This will enable you to stay for 1hr 30min (2hr 30min over lunchtime) free. Discs are available in supermarkets or petrol stations (ask for a disque de stationnement).

TOLLS

In France, most motorway sections are subject to a toll (péage). You can pay in cash or with a credit card (Visa, MasterCard).

CAR RENTAL

There are car rental agencies at airports, railway stations and in all large towns throughout France. European cars have manual

RENTAL CARS – CENTRAL RESERVATION IN FRANCE	
Avis	☏ 08 20 05 05 05 www.avis.fr
Europcar	☏ 08 25 35 83 58 www.europcar.fr
Budget France	☏ 08 25 00 35 64 www.budget.fr
Hertz France	☏ 08 25 86 18 61 www.hertz.fr
SIXT-Eurorent	☏ 08 20 00 74 98 www.sixt.fr
National-CITER	☏ 08 25 16 12 20 www.citer.fr
Ada	☏ 08 25 16 91 69 www.ada.fr

transmission; automatic cars are available in larger cities only if an advance reservation is made. Drivers must be over 21; between ages 21 and 25, drivers are required to pay an extra daily fee; some companies allow drivers under 23 only if the reservation has been made through a travel agent. It is relatively expensive to hire a car in France; US citizens in particular will notice the difference and should make arrangements before leaving, take advantage of fly-drive offers, or seek advice from a travel agent.

MOTORHOMES
Worldwide Motorhome Rentals offers fully equipped camper vans for rent. You can view them on the company's web page: www. mhrww.com or call ℘888-519-8969 in the USA (toll free) or ℘530-389-8316 outside the USA. Also try www.aviscaraway.com and www. motorhome-hire-france.com.

PETROL/GASOLINE
French service stations dispense: *sans plomb 98* (super unleaded 98), *sans plomb 95* (super unleaded 95), *diesel/gazole* (diesel) and *GPL* (LPG). Petrol is considerably more expensive in France than in the USA. Prices are listed on signboards on the motorways although it is usually cheaper to fill up after leaving the motorway. Check the hypermarkets on the outskirts of town for lower prices.

Where to Stay and Eat

WHERE TO STAY
Hotels and Restaurants are described in the Address Books within the *Discovering Brittany* section. Please 👜 *see the Places to Stay map* for a selection of recommended places for overnight stops. The Map Legend that appears on the inside cover flap of the guide explains the symbols and abbreviations used.

ECONOMY CHAIN HOTELS
If you need a place to stop en route, the following can be useful, as they are inexpensive (under 50€ for a double room) and generally located near the main road. While breakfast is available, there may not be a restaurant; rooms are small, with a television and bathroom. Central reservation details:

- **Akena**
  ℘01 69 84 85 17
  www.hotels-akena.com
- **B&B**
  ℘02 98 33 75 29
  www.hotel-bb.com

- **Etap Hôtel**
  ℘08 92 68 89 00
  www.etaphotel.com
- **Hotel Formule 1**
  ℘08 92 68 56 85
  www.hotelformule1.com
- **Villages Hôtel**
  ℘03 80 60 92 70
  www.villages-hotel.com

The hotels listed below are slightly more expensive (below 65€), and offer a few more amenities and services. Central reservation numbers:

- **Campanile, Kyriad**
  ℘08 25 00 30 03 (from abroad +33 1 64 62 46 46)
  www.louvrehotels.com
- **Ibis**
  ℘08 92 68 66 86
  www.ibishotel.com

RURAL ACCOMMODATION AND YOUTH HOSTELS
The **Maison des Gîtes de France** is an information service on self-catering accommodation in the regions of France. *Gîtes* usually take the form of a cottage or apartment decorated in the local style where visitors can make themselves at home.

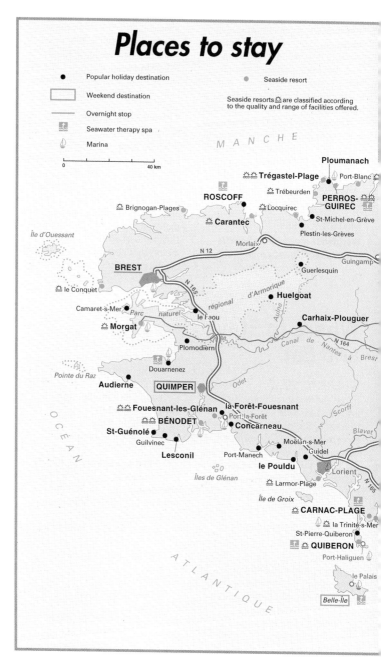

Places to stay

- Popular holiday destination
- ▭ Weekend destination
- — Overnight stop
- Seawater therapy spa
- ⚓ Marina
- Seaside resort

Seaside resorts ⚐ are classified according to the quality and range of facilities offered.

0 ——— 40 km

MANCHE

Ploumanach
⚐⚐ Trégastel-Plage ⚓ Port-Blanc
⚐ Trébeurden
ROSCOFF ⚐ Locquirec PERROS-GUIREC ⚐⚐
⚐ Brignogan-Plages ⚐ St-Michel-en-Grève
⚐ Carantec Plestin-les-Grèves
Île d'Ouessant Morlaix
N 12 Guingamp
BREST Guerlesquin
⚐ le Conquet régional d'Armorique Huelgoat
Camaret-s-Mer Parc naturel Carhaix-Plouguer
⚐ Morgat le Faou Aulne Canal de Nantes à Brest N 164
Plomodiern
Pointe du Raz Douarnenez Odet
Audierne QUIMPER Scorff
⚐⚐ Fouesnant-les-Glénan la Forêt-Fouesnant
⚐⚐ BÉNODET Port-la-Forêt Blavet
St-Guénolé Concarneau
Guilvinec Moëlan-s-Mer
Lesconil Port-Manech Guidel
Îles de Glénan le Pouldu Lorient
⚐ Larmor-Plage N 165
Île de Groix
⚐ CARNAC-PLAGE
⚐ ⚐ la Trinité-s-Mer
St-Pierre-Quiberon
⚐ QUIBERON
Port-Haliguen
le Palais
Belle-Île

ATLANTIQUE
OCÉAN

For a list of Gîtes in France and how to book, contact the Gîtes de France office in Paris: ✆01 49 70 75 75 or search online at www.gites-de-france.com (select English by clicking the flag on the home page). Try contacting the local tourist offices as they also publish lists of available properties. Gîtes de France publishes a booklet on bed and breakfast accommodation

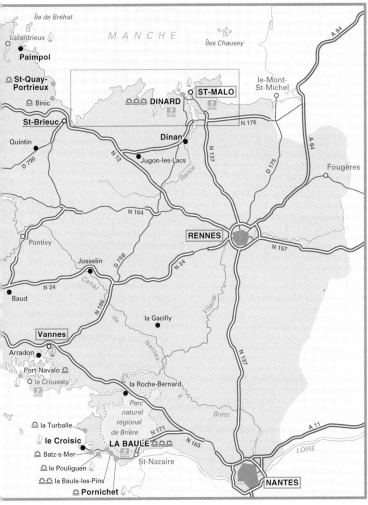

(chambres d'hôtes) entitled *Chambres et tables d'hôtes*. These include a room and breakfast at a reasonable price. Also visit www.bed-breakfast-france. com which has a good selection of accommodation throughout the region.

The **Fédération Française des Stations Vertes de Vacances** (BP 71698, 21016 Dijon Cedex, ℘03 80 54

Michelin Red Guide

For an even greater selection, use the *Michelin Guide France* with its well-known star-rating system and hundreds of establishments throughout France. The *Michelin Charming Places to Stay* guide contains a selection of 1,000 hotels and guesthouses at reasonable prices. Be sure to book ahead, especially during the high season, as Brittany is a very popular holiday destination.

For further information, **Loisirs Accueil** (280 boulevard St-Germain, 75007 Paris, ℘01 44 11 10 44, www.resinfrance.com) is a booking service that has offices in most French *départements*.

A guide to good-value, family-run hotels, **Logis et Auberges de France** (www.logis-de-france.fr), is available from the French Tourist Office, as are lists of other kinds of accommodation such as hotel-châteaux, bed and breakfasts. **Relais et Châteaux** (www.relaischateaux.com) provides information on booking in luxury hotels with character: ℘0 823 32 32 32 (France); ℘0 800 2000 00 22 (UK); ℘1 800 735 2478 (US).

10 50, www.stationsvertes.com) lists accommodation, leisure facilities and natural attractions in rural locations on the website.

There are two main youth hostel (*auberge de jeunesse*) associations in France:

- **Ligue Française pour les Auberges de Jeunesse**,
  67, rue Vergniaud Bat.K
  75013 Paris
  ℘01 44 16 78 78,
  www.auberges-de-jeunesse.com
- **Fédération Unie des Auberges de Jeunesse**,
  27 rue Pajol, 75018 Paris
  ℘01 44 89 87 27
  www.fuaj.org.

To obtain an **International Youth Hostel Federation card** (there is no age requirement and a "senior card" is available, too) contact the IYHF in your own country for information and membership applications.

- **USA** ℘1-301-495-1240 or www.hiusa.org
- **England and Wales** ℘01707 324 170 or www.yha.org.uk
- **Scotland** ℘01786 891 400 or www.syha.org.uk
- **Canada** ℘1-613-237-7884;
- **Australia** ℘61-2 9283-7195 or www.yha.com.au.

There is an online booking service (www.iyhf.org), which you may use to reserve a room as far as six months in advance.

CAMPING

There are numerous officially graded sites with varying standards of facilities throughout Brittany; the **Michelin Guide Camping and Caravanning France** lists a selection of the best campsites.

An International Camping Carnet for caravans is useful but not compulsory; it can be obtained from the motoring organisations or from the following:

- **Camping and Caravanning Club**
  ℘0845 130 7632,
  www.campingandcaravanning club.co.uk
- **The Caravan Club**
  ℘01342 326 944,
  www.caravanclub.co.uk

There are many excellent campsites in Brittany, most of which are scattered round the coast or slightly inland. "La Baie" at La Trinité-sur-Mer has direct access to the beach while "Ty Nadan" at Arzano is 18km/11.25m inland and generally very quiet.

WHERE TO EAT
FINDING A PLACE TO EAT

A selection of places to eat in the different locations covered in this guide can be found in the Address Books appearing in the *Discovering Brittany* section. The key on the cover flap explains the symbols and abbreviations used in this section. Use the red-cover **Michelin Guide France**, with its well-known star-rating system and hundreds of establishments all over France, for an even greater choice. If you would like to experience a meal in a highly rated restaurant from The Michelin Guide, be sure to book ahead. In the countryside, restaurants usually serve lunch between noon and 2pm and dinner between 7.30 and 10pm. It is not always easy to find something in-between those two meal times as the "non-stop" restaurant is still a rarity in the provinces. However, a hungry traveller can usually get a sandwich in a café, and ordinary hot dishes may be available in a *brasserie*. In French restaurants and cafés, a service charge is included. Tipping is not necessary, but French people often leave the small change from their bill on their table or about 5 percent for the waiter in a nice restaurant.

Restaurants

Restaurants are found in all towns and cities and usually only open at traditional meal times, that is, between noon and 2pm for lunch and 7pm–10pm for dinner. Food ranges from regional cooking to *nouvelle* and *haute cuisine* – expect to pay anything from 12€ upwards for a main course, depending on the type of food on offer. Many restaurants offer good value-for-money set menus at lunch times. You'll find restaurants specialising in fish *(poisson)*, but vegetarians will be disappointed to know that there are few places that cater exclusively for their needs. See www.frenchentree.com/fe-vegetarians for details of vegetarian establishments in France.

Brittany's wide range of fresh seafood

S. Sauvignier/MICHELIN

Café-Restaurants

These establishments are where to have a coffee or breakfast in the morning. You will often find men standing at the counter drinking a *pastis* (aniseed-flavour alcoholic drink). At lunchtime, the tables are set with cutlery and paper cloths and you'll find good-value, simple food. Of course quality will vary, so it's good to go somewhere that seems popular.

Brasseries

Brasseries are found in most cities and towns and often serve food 24/7. The white-aproned waiters buzz between the tables, taking orders for coffee, drinks or food – steak and chips, duck, chicken – from locals and tourists alike. If you're around in the early hours, you'll often find them welcoming post-club nightbirds.

Restaurants Rapides

The ubiquitous fast-food outlets McDonalds® and Burger King® (France even has it's own chain – Quick) can be found in the centre of most French cities these days as well as pizza places, kebab shops and take-away crêpes. Ideal for those on a budget or short of time.

Relais Routiers

These places, mainly frequented by lorry drivers, can be found on A roads. But food is cheap and they can be a good option if you're en route somewhere and don't want to waste time going into town. Do your research at www.relais-routiers.com.

Auberges

As well as serving food, auberges also traditionally offered accommodation to travellers. They are usually found in the countryside and can be an attractive option to both eat and stay.

They normally serve regional produce. See www.brittanytourism.com for more details.

Crêperies

There are thousands of *crêperies* across Brittany serving the region's traditional dish. A *crêpe* is made with sweet batter and a *galette* is made with salty batter – both are usually available with a choice of fillings. Accompany with a glass of cider. There's even an organisation to ensure quality!

Useful Words and Phrases

Commonly Used Words

	Translation
Hello	Bonjour
Goodbye	Au revoir
How?	Comment?
Excuse me	Excusez-moi
Thank you	Merci
Yes/no	Oui/non
Sorry	Pardon
Why?	Pourquoi?
When?	Quand?
Please	S'il vous plaît

Time

	Translation
Today	Aujourd'hui
Tomorrow	Demain
Yesterday	Hier
This week	Cette semaine
Next week	La semaine prochaine
Monday	Lundi
Tuesday	Mardi
Wednesday	Mercredi
Thursday	Jeudi
Friday	Vendredi
Saturday	Samedi
Sunday	Dimanche

Numbers

	Translation
One	Un
Two	Deux
Three	Trois
Four	Quatre
Five	Cinq
Six	Six
Seven	Sept
Eight	Huit
Nine	Neuf
Ten	Dix

Useful Phrases

Do you speak English?
Parlez-vous anglais?
I don't understand
Je ne comprends pas
Talk slowly, please
Parlez lentement, s'il vous plaît
Where is …?
Où est …?

When does the … leave?
À quelle heure part …?
When does the … arrive?
À quelle heure arrive …?
When does the museum open?
À quelle heure ouvre le musée?
When is breakfast served?
À quelle heure sert-on le petit déjeuner?
What does it cost?
Ça coûte combien?
Where can I buy an English newspaper?
Où puis-je acheter un journal anglais?
Where is the nearest petrol/gas station?
Où se trouve la station d'essence la plus proche?
Where are the toilets?
Où se trouve les toilettes?
Do you accept credit cards?
Acceptez-vous les cartes de crédit?

What time is it?
Quelle heure est-il?
Do you have a table for two please?
Est-ce que vous avez une table pour deux personnes, s'il vous plaît?

Breton To English

	Translation
Aber	Estuary
Armor	Coast
Bihan	Small
Breizh	Brittany
Demat	Hello
Kenavo	Goodbye
Ker	Village
Mad	Good
Mor	Sea

Basic Information

BUSINESS HOURS

Department stores and chain stores are usually open Mon–Sat 9am–6.30pm or 7.30pm. ☺*Smaller, more specialised shops may close during the lunch hour, usually from noon or 12.30pm to 2 or 2.30pm.*

Food stores (grocers, wine merchants and bakeries) are usually open Mon–Sat from 7am to 6.30pm or 7.30pm (some open Sun mornings). ☺*Many close noon–2pm and on Mon.*

Hypermarkets: Mon–Sat 9am–9pm or 10pm.

Banks are usually open Mon–Fri 9am–noon and 2pm–4pm. ☺*Many close Mon or Sat (except market days); some open for limited transactions on Sat. Banks close early the day before a bank holiday.*

Post offices: Mon–Fri 8am–7pm, Sat 8am–noon. ☺*Smaller branches often close noon–2pm and close of business is 4pm.*

Signpost of a crêperie

Crêperie

G. Targat/MICHELIN

COMMUNICATIONS
PUBLIC TELEPHONES

Most public phones in France use prepaid phone cards (*télécartes*), rather than coins. Some telephone booths accept credit cards (Visa, MasterCard/Eurocard). *Télécartes* (50 or 120 units) can be bought in post offices, branches of France Télécom, *bureaux de tabac* (cafés selling cigarettes) and newsagents and can be used to make calls in France and abroad. Some tabacs sell a telephone scratch card which gives better value for money.

TO USE YOUR PERSONAL CALLING CARD

AT&T	☎ 0-800 99 00 11
Sprint	☎ 0-800 99 00 87
MCI	☎ 0-800 99 00 19
Canada Direct	☎ 0-800 99 00 16

Calls can be received at phone boxes where the blue bell sign is shown; the phone will not ring, so keep your eye on the little message screen. Some phones even have internet access these days.

NATIONAL CALLS

French telephone numbers have 10 digits. Numbers begin with:
+ 01 in Paris and the Paris region
+ 02 in northwest France
+ 03 in northeast France
+ 04 in southeast France and Corsica
+ 05 in southwest France

INTERNATIONAL CALLS

To call France from abroad, dial the country code (33) + 9-digit number (omit the initial 0). When calling abroad from France dial 00, then dial the country code followed by the area code and number of your correspondent.
+ **International dialling codes**
  ☎00 + code
+ **International Information**
  ☎USA/Canada: 00 33 12 11
+ **International operator**
  ☎00 33 12 + country code
+ **Local directory assistance**
  ☎12

INTERNATIONAL DIALLING CODES
(00 + code)

Australia	☎61	New Zealand	☎64
Canada	☎1	United Kingdom	☎44
Eire	☎353	United States	☎1

MINITEL

France Télécom operates a system offering directory enquiries (free of charge up to 3min), travel and entertainment reservations, and other services (cost per minute varies). These small computer-like terminals can be found in some post offices, hotels and France Télécom agencies, as well as in many French homes. 3614 PAGES E is the code for directory assistance in English (turn on the unit, dial 3614, hit the connexion button when you get the tone, type in PAGES E and follow the instructions on the screen).

MOBILE PHONES

France has an efficient mobile phone service with several networks to choose from, including SFR, Orange™ and Bouygues Telecom. Check with your network provider that your phone is set up for international roaming before you go – your phone will automatically switch to the local network when you get to France. Bear in mind that calls are more expensive than those made within the UK or USA and you also pay to receive a call. If you're going to be making and receiving a lot of calls, it might be worth getting a global SIM card *(www.0044.co.uk* or *www.gosim.com)*, which will give you a local number and lower call rates. If you're going to be making a lot of calls in France you should consider buying a pay-as-you-go *(sans abonnement)* phone from a high-street shop or supermarket. Alternatively you could rent a phone from World Cellular Rentals *(www.worldcr.com)*.

ELECTRICITY

The electric current is 220V/50Hz. Circular two-pin plugs are the rule – an electrical adaptor may be necessary. Appliances (hairdryers, shavers, etc.) from North America will not work without one. Adapters are on sale in electrical stores and also at international airports.

EMERGENCIES

EMERGENCY NUMBERS

Police: ☏17

SAMU (Paramedics): ☏15

Fire (Pompiers): ☏18

INTERNET

You'll find internet access in most towns and cities in hotels (for residents), cyber-cafés, public libraries and tourist offices. Websites such as www.cybercafe.com, www.cybercafe.fr and www.cybercaptive.com are good sources of information for where to find such places in France and elsewhere.

Many hotels and public places have wireless internet access (Wi-Fi) if you have your laptop with you – see www.journaldunet.com/wifi for details.

MAIL/POST

Main post offices usually open Monday–Friday 9am–noon and 2pm–7pm, Saturday 9am–noon. Prices of postage for a 20g/0.7oz letter (July 2010):

- **France:** 0.58€
- **UK:** 0.75€
- **North America:** 0.87€
- **Australia & NZ:** 0.87€

Stamps (timbres) are also available from newsagents and bureaux de tabac. Stamp collectors should ask for timbres de collection in any post office.

MEDIA
NEWSPAPERS

You can get English newspapers at news stands in most large towns and cities, usually on the same day they are published.

American tourists will find copies of the International Herald Tribune or USA Today.

French News, France's English-language monthly newspaper, has a regional insert for Brittany and there's a community magazine called Central Brittany Journal.

LOCAL RADIO STATIONS

There are no English-language radio stations specific to the Brittany area, but you can listen to your favourite stations on the internet or tune in to the BBC World Service. See www.bbc.co.uk/worldservice for details of frequencies.

MONEY
CURRENCY

There are no restrictions on the amount of currency visitors can take into France. However, the amount of cash you may take out of France is subject to a limit, so visitors carrying a lot of cash should complete a currency declaration form on arrival because there are restrictions on currency export: if you are leaving the country with more than 7,600€ you must declare the amount to customs.

BANKS

Banks are open from 9am to noon and 2pm to 4pm and branches are closed on Monday or Saturday. Banks close early on the day before Bank Holiday. A passport is necessary as identification when cashing travellers cheques in banks. Commission charges vary and hotels usually charge more than banks for cashing cheques. One of the most economical ways to use your money in France is by using ATMs (cash machines) to get cash directly from your bank account or to use your credit card to get cash advances (but be aware that your bank may charge you for this service).

☺Be sure to remember your PIN number, you will need it to use cash dispensers and to pay with your card in most shops, restaurants, etc. Code pads are numeric; use a telephone pad to translate a letter code into numbers. PIN numbers have four digits in France; enquire with the issuing company or bank if the code you usually use is longer.

CREDIT CARDS

Visa is the most widely accepted credit card followed by MasterCard; other cards, credit and debit (Maestro, Plus, Cirrus, etc.) are also accepted in some cash machines. American Express is more often accepted in premium establishments. Research credit cards on the market that don't charge for transactions made abroad (apart from withdrawing money from ATMs) at www.moneysupermarket. com. Most places post signs indicating the cards they accept; if you don't see such a sign, ask before buying. Cards are widely accepted in shops, supermarkets, hotels and restaurants, at tollbooths and in petrol stations. If your card is lost or stolen, call one of the 24-hour hotlines in France (above):

American Express ✆ 01 47 77 72 00

Visa ✆ 08 00 90 11 79

Mastercard ✆ 08 00 90 13 87

Diners Club ✆ 08 10 31 41 59

PUBLIC HOLIDAYS

1 January	New Year's Day (Jour de l'An)
late March to late April	Easter Day and Easter Monday (Pâques)
1 May	May Day (Fête du Travail)
8 May	VE Day (Fête de la Libération)
Thurs 40 days after Easter	Ascension Day (Ascension)
7th Sun–Mon after Easter	Whit Sunday and Monday (Pentecôte)
14 July	Bastille Day (Fête nationale)
15 August	Assumption (Assomption)
1 November	All Saint's Day (Toussaint)
11 November	Armistice Day (Fête de la Victoire)
25 December	Christmas Day (Noël)

Such loss or theft must also be reported to the local police who will issue a certificate to show to the credit card company.

PUBLIC HOLIDAYS

Museums and other monuments may be closed or may vary their hours of admission on the public holidays listed in the table (opposite). National museums and art galleries are closed on Tuesdays; municipal museums are generally closed on Mondays. In addition to the usual school holidays at Christmas and in the spring and summer, there are long mid-term breaks (ten days to a fortnight) in February and early November.

REDUCED RATES

Some towns and cities sell passes, available from local tourist offices, which allow entry to several museums and monuments. For example, in **Rennes**, the two-day City Pass (available from the tourist office) costs 13€ and gives free access to museums as well as discounts in shops and on public transport (⚲ see RENNES). Significant discounts are available for senior citizens, students, youth under 25, teachers and groups for public transportation, museums and monuments and for some leisure activities such as movies (at certain times of day). Bring student or senior cards, as well as some extra passport-sized photos for discount travel cards. The **International Student travel Confederation** (www.istc.org), global administrator of the International Student and Teacher Identity Cards, is an association of student travel organisations around the world. ISTC members collectively negotiate benefits with airlines, governments, and providers of other goods and services for the student and teacher community, both in their own country and around the world. The non-profit association sells international ID cards for students, youth under age 25 and teachers (who may get discounts on museum entrances, for example).

Place de Merciers, Dinan

Y. Tierny/MICHELIN

SMOKING

Smoking is now banned in shopping malls, schools, offices and other public places including restaurants, bars and cafés, if not on the terrace.

TIME

France is 1hr ahead of Greenwich Mean Time (GMT). France goes on daylight-saving time from the last Sunday in March to the last Sunday in October. The 24-hour clock is widely applied in France.

WHEN IT IS NOON IN FRANCE**, IT IS**

3am	in Los Angeles
6am	in New York
11am	in Dublin
11am	in London
7pm	in Perth (6pm in summer)
9pm	in Sydney (8pm in summer)
11pm	in Auckland (10pm in summer)

TIPPING

Since a service charge is automatically included in the prices of meals and accommodation in France, it is not necessary to tip in restaurants and hotels. However if the service in a restaurant is especially good or if you have enjoyed a fine meal, an extra tip (this is the *pourboire*, rather than the *service*) is a much-appreciated gesture.

This is generally small change or about 5%. Taxi drivers and hairdressers are usually tipped 10–15%.

Restaurants usually charge for meals in two ways: a *menu* that is a fixed-price menu with 2 or 3 courses, sometimes a small pitcher of wine, all for a stated price, or *à la carte*, the more expensive way, with each course ordered separately.

Cafés have very different prices, depending on location. Drinks are cheaper if you stand at the counter (*comptoir*) than if you sit down (*salle*) and are sometimes even more expensive if you sit outdoors (*terrasse*).

Terrace outside a café on La Place du Commerce, Nantes

H. Le Gac/MICHELIN

47

Pleyben Calvary
S. Sauvignier/MICHELIN

Brittany Today

21ST CENTURY BRITTANY
LIFESTYLE

The lifestyle of the average Breton is nowadays much the same as that of any other French person. Local traditions remain very important, however, and it is true that the proximity of the sea still influences lives here, although less so than in former times. Life begins earlier in the day than in the UK and the two hour lunch break is still common. People retire earlier in the evening and most small towns and villages become quiet after 9 or 10 pm.

Life by the Sea

Many Bretons live near to the sea and not unnaturally have a great affection for it, whether they work in the fishing industry or simply live near the coast and perhaps take part in a little weekend sailing from time to time. In the past many more earned their living from the sea and today fishing remains a major activity, and important fishing ports right around the coast, including Roscoff, Douarnenez, Le Guilvinec and Concarneau all specialise in deep-sea fishing while at Cancale, round the Bay of St-Brieuc and the Golfe du Morbihan shellfish are harvested. The proximity of the sea has also meant that the Bretons have been able to exploit their many coastal towns by developing them into attractive seaside resorts such as Dinard, Carentec, Perros-Guirec and Bénodet, which all successfully attract those looking for a traditional seaside holiday.

A Blend of Old and New Towns

Brittany has a unique blend of old and new towns and it is difficult to find any basis of comparison between the old towns, with their historical associations, and their modern counterparts. Many towns, includin Dinan, Locronan, Vitré, Rennes, Vitré, Vannes and the marvellously reconstructed St-Malo, have retained their cultural heritage by carefully preserving or restoring their old town centres and their ramparts, which are enormously important in attracting tourism. It is impossible, however, not to be struck by the planning and grouping of buildings in modern such towns as Brest and Lorient. The wide streets with modern shops and huge, airy squares are elegant and have obviously been built to achieve harmony and unity. Visitors may well be surprised by certain buildings, but they will find something to admire in the upward sweep of a tall bell-tower, the simple lines of a concrete façade, the successful decorative effect of stone and cement combined.

SPORT
Water Sports

For many people Brittany is synonymous with water sports. The very nature of its wild coastline, with numerous bays, peninsulas and breakers crashing in from the Atlantic Ocean, draws water sport enthusiasts, both professional and amateur, from all over the world. The Bay of Audierne in southwest Finistère is one such place and the Pointe de la Torche, jutting out into its extreme southern end, is home to the French (and on occasion, World) Surf Championships. The beaches at Carnac in southern Morbihan host both national and international championships of the Windsurfing Tour, and Trébeurden on the Pink Granite Coast is where you will find the Trégor Kite Party and the Kite Surfing Championships of France in October each year.

Rugby

Rugby is a very popular sport in France but has never really become established in Brittany, unlike other Celtic nations, and no major club sides operate in the region. However, there are many small clubs, especially in Finistère, where most towns have their own sides. Many Breton fans of the sport tend to support Scotland, Ireland and Wales as fellow Celts, particularly in their matches against the French national side.

LANGUAGE
Brezhoneg

Breton, or "Brezhoneg" is a Celtic language with many similarities to Welsh, Cornish, Scottish Gaelic, Irish Gaelic and

Manx Gaelic. It is believed that the the Celts originated in Central Europe and gradually extended their territory until they were pushed by the Romans and other invaders to the western fringes. From a linguistic point of view, Bretons are more closely related to the Irish and the Welsh than to the French. From the 4C–7C, Armorica (present-day Brittany) was a refuge for Britons fleeing England after the Anglo-Saxon invasion. From that time on, the Breton language rivalled French, a derivative of Low Latin. The annexation of the province to France in the 15C and the French Revolution enhanced the trend in favour of French.

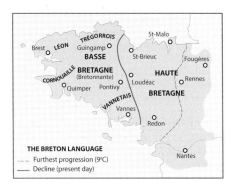

THE BRETON LANGUAGE
--- Furthest progression (9°C)
— Decline (present day)

The map *(opposite)* shows **Upper Brittany** (Haute-Bretagne), or the "Gallo" country, and **Lower Brittany** (Basse-Bretagne), or the Breton-speaking country. French is spoken in the first; French and Breton in the second. Lower Brittany has four regions, each of which has its customs and brings shades of diversity to the Breton language – the district of Tréguier or Trégorrois, the district of Léon, the district of Cornouaille and the district of Vannes or Vannetais.

Modern Breton *(brezhoneg)*, derived from Brythonic, belongs to the Celtic languages and manifests itself in four main dialects: *cornouaillais* (south Finistère), *léonard* (north Finistère), *trégorrois* (Tréguier and the bay of St-Brieuc) and *vannetais* (Vannes and the Golfe du Morbihan). *Vannetais* distinguishes itself from the other three, which are closely related, for example by replacing 'z' with 'h'; thus *Breiz* (Brittany) becomes *Breih*. In an attempt to overcome such differences, the use of 'zh' has been introduced for the relevant words, thus *Breizh*.

MEDIA

The main regional newspaper in Brittany is *Le Télégramme*, published in Morlaix Finistère, in French and not Breton as might be expected. It sells in excess of 200,000 copies daily and is available to read on the Internet. *Ouest France*, the daily newspaper available throughout western France, also has a Breton regional edition and is available via the internet too. With respect to TV, there are two regional channels, tvbreizh, which broadcasts totally in French, although it used to have some Breton programming, and TV Rennes 35, which broadcasts programmes of interest to Rennes and its region. France 3 TV also has regional programmes.

ECONOMY
AGRICULTURE

With 51,200 farmers, half the number of 15 years ago but farming on a larger scale, and 100,000 workers (of which a third are aged under 40), agriculture remains the most important economic activity in Brittany. This mainly involves the rearing of cows, pigs and poultry, as well as mixed farming. The region produces 20 per cent of France's milk, 33 per cent of veal, 50 per cent of pork, 38 per cent of poultry and 48 per cent of the country's eggs. Two-thirds of cereal-grown (corn, wheat and barley) is used for animal-feed. Most of France's vegetables (green beans, artichokes, and potatoes) are grown here.

Brittany is responsible for 51 percent of France's fish production and large and small fishing concerns work side by side. Around 7,700 people are employed in the industry, which includes those who work in preparing the caught fish.

The agri-food industry has grown considerably over the last 25 years and more than 5,000 jobs have been created in this industry in the last ten years. It specialises in the transformation of animal proteins (meat, fish, milk), vegetable production and animal food and is responsible for almost half of France's meat and fish exports.

OTHER INDUSTRIES

Brittany, whose other main industries are car manufacturing (Citroën has a large presence in the region), ship-building and telecommunications, is one of the few regions in France to have seen steady growth in industrial employment since 1980. The tertiary sector is also buoyant, notably in the area of banking.

With more than 2,700km/1,700mi of coastline, 3,700km/1,864mi of footpaths, eight "towns of art and history", ten *villes historiques* and almost 1,000 monuments, Brittany is France's fourth most-visited region, especially for holidays by the seaside. It has always been very popular with the British due to its proximity to the UK, but the Dutch, the Germans the Italians and even the French themselves also come here in large numbers. Tourism is extremely important to the economy of the region, (almost 50,000 workers are employed at peak season) along with fishing and agriculture. The service sector is expanding rapidly, as more jobs are created in hotels and restaurants.

In 2006, the GDP was 78.3€ billion (4.4 percent of the national GDP), making Brittany the seventh wealthiest region in France.

GOVERNMENT

Brittany has been a territory of France since 1532, and in 1982 the region became an administrative *Région* of the French Republic, with some devolved powers. There are four administrative divisions: Ile-et-Vilaine, Côtes-d'Armor, Morbihan and Finistère. The capital of the region is Rennes.

The *Région* consists of two Assemblies: the publicly elected *Conseil régional* is responsible for regional politics and the *Conseil économique et sociale régional*

(CESR) advises on regional matters. The president of the *Conseil régional* prepares and carries out decisions voted for by the elected members, the *administration régionale* puts them into practice. The *Conseil régional* consists of 83 elected members from the four administrative divisions who are elected for a period of six years. They debate regional politics and meet once every trimester.

The *administration régionale* has nine directorates, overseen by a *directeur général*, who carry out the decisions made by the elected members related to the following areas: educational establishments, higher education and apprenticeships, land and transport management, economic research and development, environment and tourism, culture, and the promotion and evaluation of local politics. There are also directorates of finance, technology and human resources.

The CESR, made up of 113 representatives from the business world and the social and cultural sectors, meets four times a year to give its opinions on the dossiers put forward by the *Conseil*.

FOOD AND DRINK

Breton cooking is characterised by the high quality and freshness of the ingredients used, many of which will have been plucked from land or sea and brought almost directly to table after the briefest of interventions in the kitchen. You can find details of local produce, plus recipes, on the tourist board's website, www.tastybrittany.com.

Galette de sarrasin with ham and egg

S. Sauvignier/MICHELIN

SEAFOOD, CRUSTACEANS AND FISH

Shellfish, crustaceans and fish are all excellent. Particularly outstanding are the spiny lobsters, grilled or stuffed clams, scallops, shrimp, crisp batter-covered fried fish morsels and crab pasties *Belon* oysters, Armorican oysters from Concarneau, La Forêt and Île-Tudy, and Cancale oysters are all well known in France, but are not at their best until the end of the tourist season.

Lobster is served grilled or with cream and especially in a *coulis*, the rich hot sauce that makes the dish called *Armoricaine* or *à l'Américaine* (the latter name is due to a mistake made in a Paris restaurant).

Try also *cotriade* (a Breton fish soup like *bouillabaisse*), conger-eel stew, the Aulne or Élorn salmon, trout from the Monts d'Arrée and the Montagnes Noires, or pike and shad served with "white butter" in the district near the Loire. This is a sauce made from slightly salted butter, vinegar and shallots, and its preparation requires real skill.

Finally, there are *civelles* (elvers), which are a speciality of Nantes.

Langoustines - speciality of Loctudy

S. Sauvignier/MICHELIN

MEAT, VEGETABLES AND FRUIT

The salt-pasture sheep *(prés-salés)* of the coast are famous. Breton leg of mutton (with white beans) is part of the great French gastronomic heritage. Grey partridges and heath-hares are tasty, as are the chickens from Rennes and Nantais ducks.

Pork butchers' meat is highly flavoured and includes Morlaix ham, bacon, black pudding, smoked sausage from Guéméné-sur-Scorff and chitterlings from Quimperlé.

Potatoes, artichokes, cauliflowers and green peas are the glory of the Golden Belt, the fertile northern coastal plain.

Kouign amann

This buttery Breton delight is made from 500g/1lb 2oz flour, 250g/9oz butter, 200g/7oz sugar, 10g/1tsp baking powder, pinch of salt and an egg yolk. Work the flour, baking powder and salt into a dough with a little water and leave to rise for 30min. Form the dough into a large flat pancake about 30cm/12in in diameter, spread half the butter on this, taking care not to go right up to the edge, and sprinkle on about a third of the sugar. Fold the pancake into four, pressing the outer edges firmly together, and leave for 10min.

S. Sauvignier/MICHELIN

Repeat this sequence four times, allowing the dough to rest for 10min each time. Flatten out to form a pancake of 25–30cm/10–12in in diameter and about 1–2cm/0.4–0.8in thick. Paint with the egg yolk and sprinkle with the rest of the sugar. Bake on a buttered tray in a hot oven (220ºC/425ºF/gas 7) for 30min. If the butter oozes out, use it to baste the *kouign amann* until it has finished cooking.

There are also strawberries and melons from Plougastel and cherries from Fouesnant.

CRÊPES, CAKES AND SWEETMEATS

Most towns have *crêperies* (pancake restaurants) where very flat pancakes called crêpes, made of either wheat or buckwheat, are often served with cider. In some of the smaller, picturesque *crêperies*, often decorated with Breton furnishings, you may see them being made. Crêpes are served plain or with jam, cheese, eggs, ham, etc. The buckwheat pancake *(crêpe de sarrasin,* also called *galette)* is salted and often served as a starter, while the wheat pancake *(crêpe de froment)* is sweet and served at dessert.

Also worth tasting are the Quimper wafer biscuits *(crêpes-dentelles),* Pont-Aven butter biscuits/cookies *(galettes),* Nantes biscuits, Quintin oatmeal porridge and the *far breton* and *kouign amann* cakes. Among the sweets are the pralines from Rennes and *berlingots* (sweet drops) from Nantes.

CIDER AND WINE

The local drink is cider *(cidre),* and of special note are the ciders from Fouesnant, Beg-Meil, and Pleudihen-sur-Rance.

The only Breton wine is **Muscadet**, which in 1936 was granted the *appellation d'origine contrôlée* (A.O.C.).

The grape used in Muscadet, the *Melon de Bretagne,* has been cultivated since the early 17C, and gives a dry and fruity white wine that complements fish and seafood particularly well. Muscadet is produced in three distinct geographical areas, each with its own *appellation: Muscadet*, produced in the Grand-Lieu region; *Muscadet de Sèvre et Maine,* produced south of Nantes; and *Muscadet des Coteaux de la Loire,* produced in the Ancenis region.

Other Breton drinks worth tasting are mead, also called *hydromel* or *chouchen,* strawberry liqueur *(liqueur de fraises),* a fortified cider apéritif *(pommeau)* and even a Breton whisky.

BRETON CULTURE
CELTIC AND BRETON MUSIC

After World War II, Celtic music found a new audience with the creation of the *Bogaged ar Sonérion,* a marching band *(bagad)* playing traditional bagpipes of different sizes and shapes and percussion instruments, in the style of Scottish pipe bands.

In the 1970s Alain Stival, a musical instrument craftsman and major fan of the traditional *festoùnoz* (the Breton word for an evening of music and entertainment), popularised the Celtic harp and became a leading force in the new wave of Breton music.

More recently, the artist Dan Ar Braz has contributed to revitalising traditional tunes. Today, Celtic music in Brittany is a lively mixture of the traditional and the modern; many groups perform around France and their recordings are widely distributed. Festivals abound, including the **Transmusicales** and **Tombées de la Nuit** in Rennes, the **Festival de Cornouaille** in Quimper, the **Festival Interceltique** in Lorient (marching bands from around the Celtic world attend to compete). Perhaps the most famous foot-stomping get-together is the **Festival des Vieilles Charrues** in Carhaix-Plouguer. The small town in central Brittany is suddenly home to a crowd of happy campers who dance the nights away in a carefree and anything-goes ambience.

In some places these manor farms add a great deal of character to the Breton countryside. This is the case in Léon, where they are numerous, and where Kergonadéac'h, Kerouzéré, Kergroadès and Traonjoly together form a background setting to Kerjean, pride of the province. Certain other châteaux, such as Rocher-Portail, were built later, and lack all appearance of being fortresses, but impress by their simplicity of outline and the grouping of the buildings; at such places as Lanrigan and La Bourbansais, on the other hand, it is the detail that charms the visitor.

Landal is one of those that gain enormously from its surroundings; others take great pride in a well laid-out garden or a fine park – these include Bonne-Fontaine, Caradeuc and Rosanbo.

TRADITIONS AND FOLKLORE
BRITTANY AND ITS SYMBOLS

Like other French regions, Brittany (population 3,146,654 million 2008 est.) has preserved its identity through the centuries by maintaining traditions. Costumes, religious observances, language and the arts all contribute to that identity. There is a special lifestyle in Brittany, a way of looking at the world: standing on a high cliff, leaning hard into the wind to keep your footing, listening to waves crashing below – this is the stance of the Breton people in the face of the modern world that values conformity and uniformity above all else.

More changes occured in the region in the first half of the 20C than had taken place in the two preceding centuries combined. Yet in the 1980s, a movement grew for the valorisation of the old ways, despite the diminishing population of the smaller villages and the inevitable changes brought about by modern trade and services, industrial development and tourism.

One symbol the visitor is not likely to miss is the **Breton flag**, *Gwenn ha du* (white and black). Morvan Marchal designed it in 1925. The five black stripes represent the five original bishoprics of Upper Brittany (Rennes, Nantes, Dol, St-

Malo, and St-Brieuc); the white bands represent those of Lower Brittany (Léon, Cornouaille, Vannes, and Tréguier). The **ermine** was the symbol of the Duchy of Brittany. In the 13C, ermine fur was worn by all of the Dukes of Brittany as a symbol of authority. Another symbol is the **Triskell**, an ornament in the form of a revolving cross with three arms or vortexes symbolising earth, fire and water. It is a Celtic symbol and has been found on old Celtic coins in the British Isles and Ireland, Denmark and even in South and North America.

COSTUMES AND HEADDRESSES
Costumes

Brittany possesses costumes of surprising richness and variety. The fine clothes passed down from one generation to another were to be seen at every family

Folk dance

The "Tro Breiz"

Until the 16C, tradition demanded that every Breton make a pilgrimage at least once in his or her lifetime to the seven cathedrals of Brittany. The **"Tro Breiz"**, or "Tour of Brittany", as it was known, drew people in their thousands from the 12C to the 16C, with its popularity reaching a peak in the 14C; estimates suggest that crowds numbering up to 30,000 to 40,000 pilgrims were taking

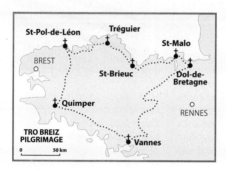

to the roads! The tour covered nearly 700km/435mi, and it enabled the faithful to pay homage to the holy relics of the founding saints of Brittany: St Brieuc and St Malo at the towns of those names, St Samson at Dol-de-Bretagne, St Patern at Vannes, St Corentine at Quimper, St Paul the Aurelian at St-Pol-de-Léon and St Tugdual at Tréguier. Whoever failed to carry out this duty was supposed to have to undertake the pilgrimage after death, advancing by one coffin-length every seven years.

festivity. It was customary for a girl at her marriage to acquire a costly and magnificent outfit that would last many years. Nowadays the traditional costumes are brought out only on great occasions such as *pardons*, and sometimes High Mass on feast days. In spite of attempts to modernise the dress, and the efforts of regional societies over the last few years – and they have had some success – to make the young appreciate the old finery, the tourist who travels through Brittany quickly is not likely to see many of the elaborate traditional dresses made familiar by picture postcards and books on the subject.

The most striking and attractive feature of the women's traditional costumes is their aprons, which reveal the wealth of the family by the abundance of their decoration. The aprons, of every shape and size, are made of satin or velvet and are brocaded, embroidered or edged with lace: at Quimper they have no bib, at Pont-Aven they have a small one, while at Lorient the bib reaches to the shoulders. Ceremonial dresses are usually black and are often ornamented with bands of velvet. The finest examples are those of Quimper, which are adorned with multi-coloured embroidery. The men's traditional costume includes a felt hat with ribbons and an embroidered waistcoat.

Headdresses

The most original feature of the Breton costume is the **coiffe** or headdress, once worn mainly in Finistère and Morbihan. One of the most attractive is the headdress of **Pont-Aven,** which has, as an accessory, a great starched lace collar. The **Bigouden** head-dress from the **Pont-l'Abbé** area is one of the most curious; it used to be quite small but since 1930 has become very tall. In **Quimper** the head-dress is much smaller and is worn on the crown of the head; in **Plougastel**, where tradition is still strong, it has a medieval appearance, with ribbons tied on the side. In **Tréguier**, the plainest of materials is allied with the most original of shapes. The **Douarnenez** headdress is small and fits tightly round the bun on the back of the head; that of **Auray** shades the forehead; and that of **Huelgoat** is almost like a lace hairnet.

In order to get a complete picture of the richness and variety of Breton costume, the tourist should visit the museums of Quimper, Guérande, Rennes, Nantes, Dinan and Pont-l'Abbé, which all have fine collections of traditional dress.

THE PARDONS

Above all, the Breton *pardons* are a manifestation of popular religious fervour. They take place in churches and chapels which may have witnessed the tradition for a thousand years, where the faithful come to seek forgiveness, fulfil a vow or beg for grace.

The great *pardons* are most impressive, while the smaller events, though less spectacular, are often more fervent. It is well worth arranging a trip so as to be present at one of them (👍 *see Calendar of Events)*. They can be a rare occasion to see traditional Breton costume, perhaps slightly modernised.

The Saints of Brittany

Brittany, with its magicians, spirits, fairies and demons – both male and female – has also claimed more haloes than any other part of France. Its saints number in hundreds and are represented by painted wooden statues adorning chapels and churches. Truth to tell, those who were canonised by the Vatican authorities (St Yves for example) can be counted on one's fingers.

The most 'official' among them were simply recognised by the bishops; the people themselves adopted others. Their fame goes no further than the borders of the province, or even the limits of the villages where they are venerated. (For the purposes of this guide, the names of saints revered in a particular region have been left in their local form.)

Healing and Protective Saints

The Bretons have always been on trusting, friendly and familiar terms with their saints. Some are invoked on all occasions; innumerable others are invoked against specified ailments: rheumatism,

baldness, etc. For centuries they took the place of doctors. Horned animals also have their appointed saints (St Herbot and St Cornély) – as do motorcyclists.

Monsieur St-Yves

The most popular saint in Brittany, St-Yves rights all wrongs and is the patron saint of the poor. Son of a gentleman, Yves Hélori was born in Minihy-Tréguier in 1253. Magistrate and barrister, he acquired a reputation for dispensing justice quickly and fairly, achieving reconciliation, and pleading with precision. One day, a local notable came before the magistrate with a complaint concerning a beggar who came to stand by his kitchen window every day to enjoy the smell of the rich man's meal.

Yves jingled some coins and sent the man on his way saying "the sound of the money pays for the smell of the food." This defender of the poor died in 1303 and was canonised in 1347.

Ste-Anne

Ste-Anne became a popular figure around the time when the crusaders were returning home. With the encouragement of Duchess Anne of Brittany, she became the patron saint of the region. One of the most famous *pardons* is devoted to Ste-Anne-d'Auray and another celebrates Ste-Anne-la-Palud. There is a saying among the faithful in Brittany:"Dead or alive, every Breton will see Ste-Anne". Statues often represent her in a green cloak, the colour symbolising hope, either alone or teaching her daughter Mary.

Notre-Dame des Motards

The little village of Porcaro (just 550 inhabitants) in the Morbihan region is known as the French capital of motorcyclists. Each year on 14 and 15 August, thousands of bikers from across France come to pay their respects to "Our Lady of the Bikers'" a statue of the Virgin Mary that the founder of the pilgrimage had brought from the shrine of Fatima. The event celebrated its 30th anniversary in 2008.

History

TIME LINE

Events in italics indicate milestones in world history.

ANCIENT ARMOR

6C BC — The Celts arrive in the peninsula and name it Armor (country of the sea). A little-known people who set up many megaliths were there before them.

56BC — Caesar destroys the fleet of the Veneti, the most powerful tribe in Armor (&see GOLFE DU MORBIHAN), and conquers the whole country. For four centuries Roman civilisation does its work. Then the Barbarian invasions wreck Armor, which returns almost to savagery.

ARMOR BECOMES BRITTANY

460 — Arrival of the Celts from Britain, driven out by the Angles and Saxons. Immigration continues for two centuries. These colonists revive and convert Armor and give it a new name, Little Britain, later shortened to Brittany. The Breton people make saints of their religious leaders, who become the patrons of many towns in the peninsula. The political state, made up of innumerable parishes, remains anarchic.

799 — Charlemagne subjugates all of Brittany.

THE DUCHY OF BRITTANY

826 — Louis the Pious makes Nominoé, a noble of Vannes, Duke of Brittany.

845 — Nominoë throws off Frankish suzerainty by defeating Charles the Bald, near Redon. He brings all of Brittany under his authority and founds an independent ducal dynasty which lasts for more than a century.

851 — Erispoë, son of Nominoé, takes the title King of Brittany. He is later assassinated by his cousin Salomon, who reigns from 857.

874 — Salomon (the Great, or St Salomon) assassinated. During his reign, the Kingdom of Brittany reached its zenith, embracing Anjou and Cotentin.

919 — Great invasion of Norsemen. Violent robbery and pillage.

939 — King Alain Barbe-Torte drives out the last Norsemen.

952 — Death of Alain, the last King of Brittany. In the fortresses built all over the country to resist the Norsemen, the nobles defy the successors of Barbe-Torte. There follows a period of disorder and poverty that lasts until nearly the end of the 14C.

1066 — *William the Conqueror lands in England.*

1215 — *The Magna Carta.*

1337 — Start of the Hundred Years' War (ending in 1453). This well-documented conflict between France and England lasted for 116 years, interspersed with several periods of peace. The Plantagenet Kings of England, with French ancestry, also lay claim to the French throne. After much early success, the English are finally overcome by the French, who are boosted by the passion of Joan of Arc.

1341 — The Breton War of Succession begins on the death of Duke Jean III. His niece, Jeanne de Penthièvre, wife of Charles of Blois, supported by the French, fights her brother Jean of Montfort, ally of the English, for the duchy. Vannes changes hands several times.

1351 — Battle of the Thirty. In a fight for succession to the Duchy of Brittany, both Jean de Beaumanoir of France and Robert Bramborough of England enlist the services of 30 champions, knights and squires, who enter into a bloody fight resulting in many deaths. The episode is regarded as one of great chivalry and was remembered in song and art.

1364 — Charles of Blois, though aided by Du Guesclin, is defeated and killed at Auray. Brittany emerges ruined from this war.

THE MONTFORTS

1364–1468 — The dukes of the House of Montfort restore the country. This is the most brilliant period of its history. The arts reach their highest development. The dukes are the real sovereigns and pay homage only in theory to the king of France. Constable de Richemont (*see VANNES*), the companion-in-arms of Joan of Arc, succeeds his brother in 1457 as Duke of Brittany.

1488 — Duke François II, who has entered into the federal coalition against the Regent of France, Anne of Beaujeu, is defeated at St-Aubin-du-Cormier and dies. His daughter, Anne of Brittany, succeeds him.

Anne of Brittany, Duchess of Brittany and Queen of France

REUNION OF BRITTANY WITH FRANCE

1491 — Anne of Brittany marries Charles VIII (*see VANNES*) but remains Duchess and sovereign of Brittany.

1492 — *Columbus discovers America on 12 October.*

1498 — Charles VIII dies. Anne returns to her duchy.

1499 — Anne again becomes Queen of France by marrying Louis XII, who has hastily repudiated his first wife. The duchy remains distinct from the Crown (*see VANNES*).

1514 — Anne of Brittany dies. Her daughter, Claude of France, inherits the duchy. She marries François of Angoulême, the future François I.

1532 — Claude cedes her duchy to the Crown. François I has this permanent reunion of Brittany with France ratified by the Parliament at Vannes.

FRENCH BRITTANY

1534 — Jacques Cartier discovers the St Lawrence estuary (*see ST-MALO*) and is the man who named Canada.

1588 — Brittany rebels against its governor, the Duke of Mercœur, who wants to profit from the troubles

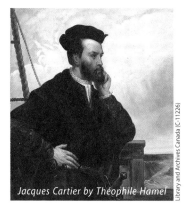

Jacques Cartier by Théophile Hamel

Library and Archives Canada (C-11226)

of the League to seize the province. Bandits like the famous La Fontenelle ravage the country (℃ *see DOUARNENEZ)*.

1598 — By the Edict of Nantes, Henri IV puts an end to religious strife (℃ *see NANTES)*.

1675 — The "Stamped Paper" Revolt develops into a peasants' uprising. The Bretons are not happy with the royal taxation (to raise money for war with Holland) on tobacco, pewter and all legal documents. Starting with riots in Nantes, Rennes and Guingamp, the unrest quickly spreads. The aristocracy wins, with violent and brutal consequences for the rioters.

1711 — Duguay-Trouin, the St-Malo-born *corsair* (legal pirate), takes Rio de Janeiro during an 11-day battle with 17 ships and 6,000 men.

1764 — The Rennes Parliament and its Public Prosecutor, La Chalotais, oppose Governor Aiguillon. The authority of the Crown is much weakened. The Revolution is near.

1765 — Arrival on Belle-Île of many Acadian families of French origin from Nova Scotia.

1773 — Birth of Surcouf, the Breton *corsair*, in St-Malo. Known as the King of Pirates, he takes 47 ships during his career.

1776 — *American Declaration of Independence.*

1789 — The Bretons welcome the Revolution with enthusiasm.

1793 — Jean-Baptiste Carrier, a violent French Revolutionary, is responsible for the brutal drowning of more than 2000 people, including clergy, in the Loire near Nantes.

1793–1804 — The laws against the priests and the mass levies give rise to the *Chouannerie* (revolt of Breton Royalists).

1795 — A landing by Royalist exiles is defeated at Quiberon.

1804 — Cadoudal, who tried to revive the *Chouannerie*, is executed.

1805 — Creation of the first Celtic Academy.

1826 — René Laënnec, the great physician, dies. Born in Quimper, he invents the stethoscope and gives the name to "cirrhosis".

1832 — Another attempted revolt, organised by the Duchess of Berry, fails. This is the last uprising.

1861 — *Start of the American Civil War.*

1870 — Trade Unions spring up in the main towns and cities following industrialisation. Strikes increase.

1871 — More than 500,000 Bretons emigrate over a period of 30 years due to over-population and the decline of traditional industries.

1909 — Strikes and riots among the Concarneau cannery workers.

1914–18 — Brittany pays a heavy toll in loss of life during World War I. More than 150,000 Bretons between the ages of 18 and 35 lose their lives.

BRITTANY TODAY

1927–8 —The Morbihan aviator Le Brix, accompanied by Costes, is the first to fly round the world. They cover 58,000km/36,000 miles in 338 hours.

1932 — A monument representing the Treaty of Everlasting Union between Brittany and France in Rennes is blown up by clandestine nationalist group *Gwenn ha du* ("white and black" – the colour of the Breton flag).

1940 — The islanders of Sein are the first to rally to General de Gaulle's call.

1942 — An Anglo-Canadian commando raids the St-Nazaire submarine base.

1944–5 — The end of the German Occupation leaves in its wake a trail of destruction, especially at Brest, Lorient and St-Nazaire.

1951 — Formation of the organisation *Comité d'Études et de Liaison des Intérêts Bretons* (CELIB), to safeguard Breton interests, is an initial step towards the rejuvenation of the local economy.

1956 — Detachment of Nantes, which becomes part of the Loire region.

1962 — First transatlantic transmission by satellite of a television programme by the station at Pleumeur-Bodou.

1966 — The opening of the Rance tidal power scheme and the Monts d'Arrée nuclear station near Brennilis.

1967 — The *Torrey Canyon* disaster off the English coast causes oil slicks to contaminate the beaches of Brittany.

1969 — Creation of the *Parc Naturel Régional d'Armorique*.

1970 — Creation of the *Parc Naturel Régional de Brière*.

1975 — First search for oil in the Iroise Sea off Finistère.

1978 — Establishment of a charter and council to safeguard the Breton cultural heritage. *Amoco Cadiz* oil spill on Brittany beaches. This was the fifth-largest oil-spill in world history and affected 76 beaches along 322km/206mi of coastline.

1982 — Political devolution: Brittany obtains limited autonomy over regional economy, infrastructure, environment, education and culture.

1985 — Introduction of bilingual road signs in French and Breton.

1994 — The Law Courts at Rennes, home to the Breton Parliament, are burned to the ground by rioting French farmers. The opening of the *Pont de l'Iroise* spanning the Eloen.

1996 — Inauguration of the La Roche-Bernard bridge.

2000 — The *Erica* founders in a storm. Once again,"black tides" damage the shore and wildlife. St-Nazaire receives a commission to build the *Queen Mary 2*, the world's largest ocean liner. Brest 2000 International Maritime Festival

2002 — Rennes becomes the smallest city in the world to have a subway system

2003 — Launch of the *Queen Mary 2* at St-Nazaire.

2006 — Tall Ships at St-Malo.

2007 — Nicolas Sarkozy elected President of France.

2008 — Brest 2008 International Maritime Festival

2010 — Tempest Xynthia hits western France in Feb. Several Breton towns flooded. Interceltic Festival at Lorient celebrates its 40th year.

Art and Culture

ARCHITECTURE
PREHISTORIC MONUMENTS

The megaliths or "great stones" – More than 3,000 'great stones' are still to be found in the Carnac district alone. These monuments were set up between 5000 and 2000 BC by the little-known race that preceded the Gauls.

The **menhir**, or single stone, was set up at a spring, near a tomb and more often on a slope. The exact use of a menhir is still in debate, but it did have some kind of symbolic meaning. In Brittany there are about 20 menhirs over 7m/23ft high; the biggest is at Locmariaquer (see LOCMARIAQUER).

The **alignments** or lines of menhirs are probably the remains of religious monuments associated with the worship of the sun or moon. Most are formed by only a few menhirs set in line (many of the menhirs now isolated are the remains of more complicated groups). There are, however, especially in the Carnac area, fields of menhirs arranged in parallel lines running from east to west and ending in a semicircle or **cromlech**. In the Lagatjar area the lines intersect. The lines of the menhirs also appear to be astronomically set, with an error of a few degrees, either by the cardinal points of the compass, or in line with sunrise and sunset at the solstices, from which it has been concluded that sun worship had something to do with the purpose of the monuments.

As for the **dolmens** (the best-known is the Table des marchands at Locmariaquer), these are considered to have been burial chambers. Some are preceded by an ante-chamber or corridor. Originally all were buried under mounds of earth or dry stones called **tumuli**, but most of them have been uncovered and now stand in the open air. The round tumuli found in the interior are of more recent date than the tumuli with closed chambers, like the one of St-Michel at Carnac, and the former were probably built up to 1000 BC. **Cairns** are tumuli composed entirely of stones, such as the ones at Barnenez, which dates back to over 5000 BC, and at Gavrinis, which is not so old. Some tumuli without burial chambers probably served as boundary markers.

In northern Brittany, **gallery graves** or **covered alleyways** are formed of a double row of upright stones with flat slabs laid on top of them, sometimes engraved.

Although tumuli have never been fully excavated, some have been found to contain beautiful artefacts: polished axes made of rare stone (jadeite), or jewellery and marvellous necklaces made of callaïs (a green stone). The museums of Carnac and Vannes contain particularly good collections of these early works of art (see CARNAC and VANNES).

Mystical tradition – For many centuries the menhirs were connected with the mystic life of the people. The Romans adapted some to their rites, carving pictures of their gods upon them. When the Christian religion became established, it acknowledged many raised stones that people still venerated by crowning them with a cross or cutting symbols on them.

CHURCHES AND CHAPELS

Nine cathedrals or former cathedrals, about 20 large churches and thousands of country churches and chapels make up an array of religious buildings altogether worthy of mystical Brittany.

The edifices were built by labourers following artists' designs that attempted to imbue the structures with obvious signes of their religious faith. This faith was manifested in a richness that was sometimes excessive – exaggeratedly decorated altarpieces – and a realism that was at times almost a caricature, as, for instance, the carvings on certain capitals and many purlins. Only affected in part by outside influences, the artists always preserved their individuality and remained faithful to their own traditions.

Cathedrals – These are inspired by the great buildings in Normandy and Île-de-France, although they do not rival their prototypes either in size or ornamentation. The small towns that built

St-BRIEUC – Ground plan of the Cathédrale St-Étienne (13C and 14C)

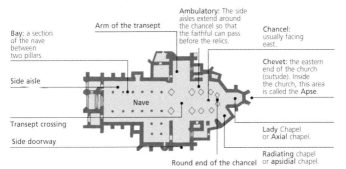

Bay: a section of the nave between two pillars.

Arm of the transept

Ambulatory: The side aisles extend around the chancel so that the faithful can pass before the relics.

Chancel: usually facing east.

Side aisle

Chevet: the eastern end of the church (outside). Inside the church, this area is called the Apse.

Nave

Transept crossing

Side doorway

Lady Chapel or Axial chapel.

Round end of the chancel

Radiating chapel or apsidial chapel.

ST-POL-DE-LÉON – Cross-section of the first two bays on the northern side of the cathedral nave (13C and 14C)

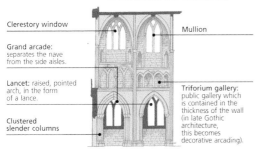

Clerestory window

Mullion

Grand arcade: separates the nave from the side aisles.

Lancet: raised, pointed arch, in the form of a lance.

Triforium gallery: public gallery which is contained in the thickness of the wall (in late Gothic architecture, this becomes decorative arcading).

Clustered slender columns

DINAN – Porch with three arches on the Basilique St-Sauveur (12C)

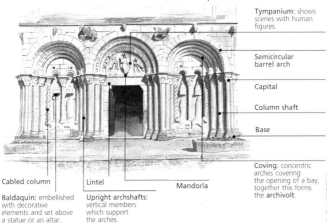

Tympanium: shows scenes with human figures.

Semicircular barrel arch

Capital

Column shaft

Base

Coving: concentric arches covering the opening of a bay; together this forms the archivolt.

Cabled column

Lintel

Mandorla

Baldaquin: embellished with decorative elements and set above a statue or an altar.

Upright archshafts: vertical members which support the arches.

R. Corbel/MICHELIN

QUIMPER – Cathédrale St-Corentin (13C to 19C)

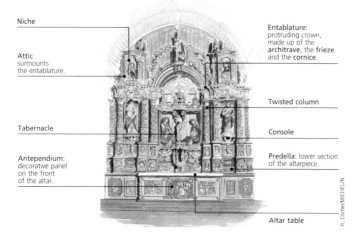

Finial

Spire

Waterspout:
protruding from the
building, drains off rain
water.

Pinnacle

English-style
clerestory window

Pinnacle: an
upright member
ending in a small
spire which gives
weight to a buttress
or angle pier.

Twin bays

Flying buttress

Flamboyant window:
stone tracery divides
the opening of the bay.

Buttress: supports
the wall from
the outside, protrudes
from the wall
to which it is bonded.

Gable: a decorative
element used above
certain doorways.

Main doorway

COMMANA – Église St-Derrien – St-Anne Altarpiece

Placed behind and above the altar, this altarpiece is a jewel of Baroque art in Brittany.

Niche

Entablature:
protruding crown,
made up of the
architrave, the frieze
and the cornice.

Attic:
surmounts
the entablature.

Twisted column

Tabernacle

Console

Antependium:
decorative panel
on the front
of the altar.

Predella: lower section
of the altarpiece.

Altar table

R. Corbel/MICHELIN

PLOUGASTEL-DAOULAS – Calvary (17C)

The words of the Evangelists are here written in stone; scenes from the life of Christ are sculpted on these imposing monuments, typical of religious expression in the region.

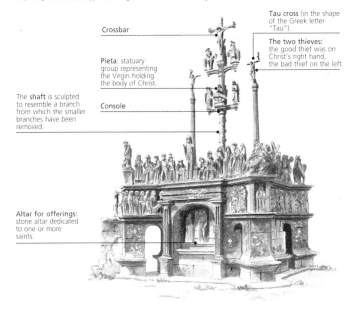

Crossbar

Tau cross (in the shape of the Greek letter "Tau").

The two thieves: the good thief was on Christ's right hand, the bad thief on the left.

Pieta: statuary group representing the Virgin holding the body of Christ.

The shaft is sculpted to resemble a branch from which the smaller branches have been removed.

Console

Altar for offerings: stone altar dedicated to one or more saints.

ST-THÉGONNEC – Triumphal gateway to the Parish Close (17C)

The "Gateway of the Dead", an ornately worked entranceway, marks the separation between the sacred and the profane; it was used for religious processions and funeral corteges.

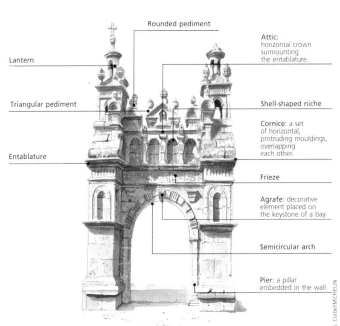

Rounded pediment

Attic: horizontal crown surmounting the entablature.

Lantern

Triangular pediment

Shell-shaped niche

Cornice: a set of horizontal, protruding mouldings, overlapping each other.

Entablature

Frieze

Agrafe: decorative element placed on the keystone of a bay.

Semicircular arch

Pier: a pillar embedded in the wall.

R. Corbel/MICHELIN

FORT LA LATTE – Fortified castle (14C)

More than 60m/200ft above the sea, this 14C fort was modified in the 17C and restored in the 20C, but remains medieval in appearance.

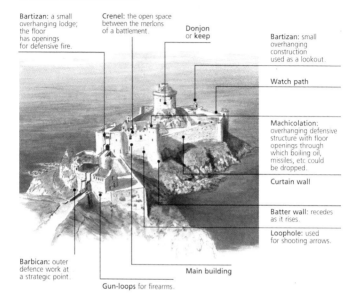

Bartizan: a small overhanging lodge; the floor has openings for defensive fire.

Crenel: the open space between the merlons of a battlement.

Donjon or keep

Bartizan: small overhanging construction used as a lookout.

Watch path

Machicolation: overhanging defensive structure with floor openings through which boiling oil, missiles, etc could be dropped.

Curtain wall

Batter wall: recedes as it rises.

Loophole: used for shooting arrows.

Barbican: outer defence work at a strategic point.

Main building

Gun-loops for firearms.

BELLE-ÎLE-EN-MER – Vauban Citadel (17C)

Built in the 16C, the citadel was entirely redesigned by Vauban in the 17C. It is in exceptionally good condition, and a remarkable illustration of military architecture.

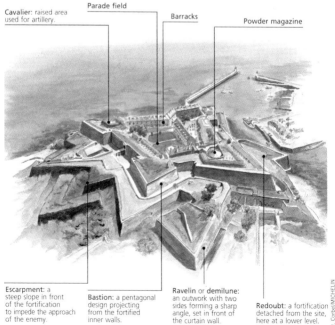

Cavalier: raised area used for artillery.

Parade field

Barracks

Powder magazine

Escarpment: a steep slope in front of the fortification to impede the approach of the enemy.

Bastion: a pentagonal design projecting from the fortified inner walls.

Ravelin or **demilune:** an outwork with two sides forming a sharp angle, set in front of the curtain wall.

Redoubt: a fortification detached from the site, here at a lower level.

R. Corbel/MICHELIN

JOSSELIN – Interior façade of the château (1490–1510)

Erected at the beginning of the 16C, this magnificent façade facing the courtyard illustrates the exuberance, the imagination and the abundance of sculpted dormer windows typical of the Renaissance.

Pinnacle: an upright member, which is a small, ornate spire rising from a square or polygonal base.

Finial

Dormer window: two storeys, extending out from the façade.

Gable

Polygonal roof

Flying shore

Mullion window with two crosspieces.

Mullion window (the window above it has two crosspieces).

Ogee arch

Mullion window: the mullion is the vertical bar; the horizontal crossbar is the transom.

Ashlar

R. Corbel/MICHELIN

67

RENNES – Hôtel de ville (1730–1742)

Built by the architect Jacques Gabriel; the belfry is set off by the concave form of the building, a typically Baroque touch of the spectacular.

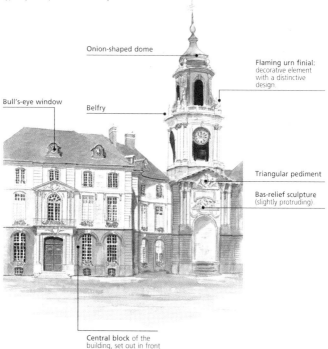

Onion-shaped dome

Flaming urn finial: decorative element with a distinctive design.

Bull's-eye window

Belfry

Triangular pediment

Bas-relief sculpture (slightly protruding).

Central block of the building, set out in front of the other parts.

JOSSELIN – Maison "Lovys Piechel" (1624)

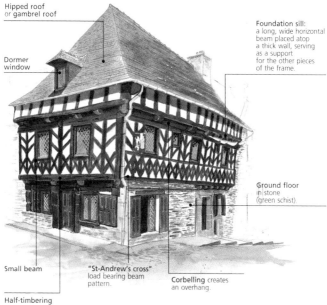

Hipped roof or gambrel roof

Foundation sill: a long, wide horizontal beam placed atop a thick wall, serving as a support for the other pieces of the frame.

Dormer window

Ground floor in stone (green schist).

Small beam

"St-Andrew's cross" load bearing beam pattern.

Corbelling creates an overhang.

Half-timbering

them had limited means. Moreover, their erection was influenced by the use of granite, a hard stone that is difficult to work. The builders had to be content with rather low vaulting and simplified decoration.

Financial difficulties dragged out the work for three to five centuries. As a result, every phase of Gothic architecture is found in the buildings, from the bare and simple arch of early times to the wild exuberance of the Flamboyant style; finishing touches were often added during the Renaissance.

The most interesting cathedrals are those of St-Pol-de-Léon, Tréguier, Quimper, Nantes and Dol-de-Bretagne.

The corresponding Gothic period in England lasted until the end of the 13C and included, in whole or in part, the cathedrals of Wells (1174), Lincoln (chancel and transept, 1186), Salisbury (1220–58), Westminster Abbey (c. 1250) and Durham (1242).

Country churches and chapels – In the Romanesque period (11C and 12C) Brittany was miserably poor. Buildings were few and small. Most of them were destroyed or transformed in the following centuries.

It was during the Gothic and the Renaissance periods, under the dukes and after the union with France, that the countryside saw the growth of churches and chapels.

Buildings constructed before the 16C are usually rectangular, though one also frequently sees the disconcerting T-plan, in which the nave, usually without side aisles, ends in a chancel flanked by often disproportionately large chapels. The chevet is flat; there are no side windows – light comes through openings pierced right at the east end of the church.

Stone vaulting is rare and is nearly always replaced by wooden panelling, often painted, whose crocodile-headed tie-beams (cross-beams dividing the roof timbers), wooden cornices at the base of the vaulting and hammerbeams are frequently carved and painted.

When there is no transept, a great stone arch separates the chancel from the nave.

Ste-Anne

Many of the statues ornamenting the churches of Brittany provide priceless information on the history of costume because they are faithful portraits of real people and the clothing that they wore. A common grouping is the Trinity of St Anne, the Virgin and Child, also seen frequently in Central European churches, but much more rarely in the rest of France.

From the 16C onwards there was a complete transformation in architectural design; it became necessary to include a transept, which, inevitably, gave rise to the Latin Cross outline. The central arch disappeared; the east end became three-sided; the nave was lit by windows in the aisles.

Belfries – The Bretons take great pride in their belfries. The towers did not serve only to hold bells, they were also symbolic of both religious and civic life. In older times the people prized them greatly, and it was a terrible punishment for them when an angry king demolished them.

The belfries are usually square in outline and their position on the building varies considerably. Small churches and chapels were often given the lighter and less-costly gable tower in preference to a belfry. The tower was placed either on the west front gable or on the roof itself, at the intersection of the chancel and the nave. It is reached by outside steps or by stairs in the turrets that flank it and are linked to it by a gallery. Sometimes these little belfries become so reduced as to be only walls in gable form, pierced by arcades. This form of architecture, while fairly widespread in southwest France, is somewhat rare in Brittany.

Porches – Breton churches have a large porch on the south side. For a long period the porch was used as a meeting place for parish notables, who sat on stone benches along the walls.

A double row of Apostles often decorates the porch. They can be recognised

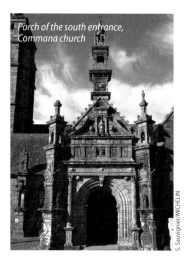

Porch of the south entrance, Commana church

S. Sauvignier/MICHELIN

by their attributes: St-Peter holds the key of Heaven; St-Paul, a book or a sword; St-John, a chalice; St-Thomas, a set square; St-James the Elder, a pilgrim's staff. Others carry the instruments of their martyrdom: St-Matthew, a hatchet; St-Simon, a saw; St-Andrew, a cross; St-Bartholomew, a knife.

RELIGIOUS FURNISHINGS

Sculpture – From the 15C to the 18C an army of Breton sculptors working in stone and more particularly in wood supplied the churches with countless examples of religous furnishings: pulpits, organ casings, baptisteries and fonts, choir screens, rood screens, rood beams, altarpieces, triptychs, confessionals, niches with panels, holy sepulchres and statues.

These works are, as a general rule, more highly developed than the figures carved on the Calvaries, since it is much easier to work in oak, chestnut or alabaster than in granite.

Visits to the churches and chapels of Guimiliau, Lampaul-Guimiliau, St-Thégonnec, St-Fiacre near Le Faouët and Tréguier Cathedral (stalls) will give a good general idea of Breton religious furnishings.

The many **rood screens** (*jubés*) to be found in the churches of Brittany are often of unparalleled richness. Some are cut in granite, as in the church at Le Folgoët, but most are carved in wood, which which makes them unique to Brittany. Their decoration is very varied and is different on both sides.

The rood screen serves two purposes: it separates the chancel from the part of the church reserved for worshippers and completes the side enclosures of the chancel; the upper gallery may also be used for preaching and reading prayers (the name derives from the first word of a prayer sung from the gallery). The screen is usually surmounted by a large crucifix flanked by statues of the Virgin and St John the Divine facing the congregation.

The **rood beam**, or *tref*, which supported the main arch of the church, was the origin of the rood screen. To prevent

A Myriad of Fountains

Fountains associated with the mystical or the miraculous are very common in Lower Brittany. Many are believed to produce healing waters. Almost every station of a *pardon* has a fountain for the faithful to drink from. The waters are placed under the protection of a saint or of the Virgin Mary, whose statues are found in little sanctuaries both humble and grand. In some places, such as the popular Ste-Anne-d'Auray, the fountain has been made into a grand display, with cascades and basins.

S. Sauvignier/MICHELIN

Depiction on the wooden frame in Chapelle de Trémalo, Pont-Aven

the beam from bowing it had to be supported by posts which were eventually replaced by a screen carved to a lesser degree. Rood beams are seen mostly in the small chapels and churches, where they serve as a symbolic boundary for the chancel; they are usually decorated with scenes from the Passion and always carry a group of Jesus Christ, the Virgin and St-John. Renaissance works are numerous and very elaborate. **Fonts** and **pulpits** are developed into richly decorated monuments.

Altarpieces, or retables, show an interesting development that can be traced through many stages in Breton churches. Originally the altar was simply a table; as the result of decoration it gradually lost its simplicity and reached a surprising size. In the 12C and 14C altars were furnished with a low step and altarpiece, the same length as the altar. Sculptors took possession of the feature and added groups of figures in scenes drawn from the Passion. From the 15C onwards, the altarpiece became a pretext for twisted columns, pediments, niches containing statues and sculpted panels, which reached their highest expression in the 17C.

Ultimately, the main subject was lost in decoration consisting of angels, garlands, etc. and the altarpiece occupied the whole of the chapel reserved for the altar. Sometimes it even fused to the retables of side altars and decorated the whole wall of the apse, as is the case at Ste-Marie-de-Ménez-Hom.

Of lesser importance, but equally numerous, are the niches that, when the two panels are open, reveal a **Tree of Jesse**. Jesse, who was a member of the tribe of Judah, had a son, King David, from whom the Virgin Mary was descended. Jesse is usually depicted lying on his side; from his heart and his body spring the roots of the tree whose branches bear the figures, in chronological order, of the kings and prophets who were Christ's forebears. In the centre the Virgin is portrayed representing the branch that bears the flower: Jesus Christ.

Stained-glass window, Château Combourg

Musée départemental breton, Quimper

Among the many statues ornamenting the churches, such as the Trinity of St Anne and the Virgin and Child, portraits of real people and items of great importance in the study of the history of costume in Brittany are often to be found. Such representation, seen frequently in Central Europe, is rare in France.

Stained-glass windows – Whereas the altarpieces, friezes and statues were often coloured, paintings and frescoes, as such, were rare; almost the only exception are those at Kernascléden. In contrast, there were a great many stained-glass windows, often Italian or Flemish inspired, but always made in Brittany. Some are especially fine, such as the cathedral at Dol, which has a beautiful 13C window.

The workshops at Rennes, Tréguier and Quimper produced stained glass between the 14C and 16C that should be seen: the most remarkable windows from these workshops are in the churches of Notre-Dame-du-Crann, La Roche and St-Fiacre near Le Faouët.

In the 20C the restoration and building of numerous churches and chapels offered the possibility of decorating these edifices with colourful, non-figurative stained-glass windows. The cathedral at St-Malo is a good example.

Gold and silver church plate – In spite of considerable losses, Brittany still possesses many wonderful pieces of gold and silver church plate. This was made by local craftsmen, most of them from Morlaix. Though fine chalices and shrines may be hidden away for security, magnificent reliquaries (shrines), chalices, richly decorated patens and superb processional crosses may be seen at Carantec, St-Jean-du-Doigt, St-Gildas-de-Rhuys, Paimpont and Locarn.

Parish closes

The parish close *(enclos paroissial)* is the most typical monumental grouping in Breton communities, and visitors should not leave Brittany without having seen a few examples.

The centre of the close was the cemetery, which was very small with gravestones of uniform size, something now tending to disappear. Around the cemetery, which is often reached through a **triumphal arch**, are grouped the **church** with its small square *(placître)*, the **calvary** and the **charnel house**, or ossuary. Thus the spiritual life of the parish is closely linked with the community of the dead. Death, *Ankou*, was a familiar idea to the Bretons who often depicted it in paintings. The extraordinary rivalry between neighbouring villages explains the richness of the closes which were built in Lower Brittany at the time of the Renaissance and in the 17C.

Competition between Guimiliau and St-Thégonnec went on for two centuries: a calvary answered a triumphal arch, a charnel house a porch, a tower replied to a belfry, a pulpit to a font, an organ loft to a set of confessionals, an Entombment to chancel woodwork. The two finest closes in Brittany sprang from this rivalry.

Triumphal arch – The entrance to a cemetery is often ornamented with a monumental gateway. This is treated as a triumphal arch to symbolise the accession of the Just to immortality.

Some arches built during the Renaissance, like those of Sizun and Berven, are surprisingly reminiscent of the triumphal arches of antiquity.

Charnel house or ossuary – In the tiny Breton cemeteries of olden days, bodies had to be exhumed to make room for new dead. The bones were piled in small shelters with ventilation openings, built against the church or cemetery wall. The skulls were placed there separately in special "skull caskets". Then these charnel houses became separate buildings, larger and more carefully built and finally reliquaries, which could be used as funerary chapels.

Calvary – This is the name of the hill, also known as Golgotha, where Christ was crucified; its name was inspired by its skull-like shape (skull is *calvaria* in Latin). Breton calvaries representing scenes from the Passion and Crucifixion are not to be confused with the wayside crosses often erected at crossroads or near churches to mark the site of a pilgrimage procession.

Parish close of Guimiliau

A.J. Cassaigne/Michelin

The unique Breton monuments illustrate episodes of the Passion, represented around Christ on the Cross. Many of them were built to ward off a plague epidemic as in 1598, or to give thanks after it ended. The priest preached from the dais, pointing out with a wand the scenes, which he described to his congregation.

The distant forerunners of the calvaries were the Christianised menhirs, which were still fairly common, and their immediate predecessors were the crosses, plain or ornate. Crosses along roads in this countryside are countless, certainly numbering tens of thousands at one time. In the 16C a bishop of Léon boasted that he alone had had 5,000 put up. The oldest remaining calvary is that of Tronoën, which dates from the end of the 15C. They were being erected as late as the end of the 17C. The most famous are those of Guimiliau, which has 200 figures, Plougastel-Daoulas with 180 and Pleyben.

The sculpture is rough and naïve – the work of a village stonemason – but it shows a great deal of observation and is often strikingly lifelike and expressive. Many figures, notably soldiers, wear the costumes of the 16C and 17C.

CASTLES AND FORTRESSES

Breton granite can be visually daunting to first-time visitors. Clean-cut and hard, it does not age or weather and it would, therefore, not be possible to give a date to the grey buildings that blend perfectly into the landscape were it not for the architectural design and methods employed in construction. With the exception of the fortresses, most of which stood guard on the eastern border in fear of the kings of France or along the coast to ward off raids of English invaders, there are few great castles in Brittany. This conveys the Breton character that turned all its artistic endeavour to the service of religion.

Nevertheless, it is easy to imagine Brittany in the Middle Ages. Few regions, in fact, had such fortresses and though many were destroyed or have fallen into ruin, a number are still standing. Before

Château de Fougères

Y. Tierny/MICHELIN

these walls, one can imagone the problems of war in the Middle Ages. Although some fortresses fell at once to a surprise attack, it was not unusual for a siege to go on for several months. The attacker then sapped the ramparts, brought up machines that could hurl stones weighing more than 100kg/220lb, and tried to smash the gates with battering rams before launching the final assault. In the mid-15C, artillery brought about new methods of attack and changes in military architecture.

At St-Malo and at Guérande, the stone walls that encircled these towns can be seen in their entirety. Remains of ramparts of varying extent can be seen in many other places; Vannes, Concarneau and Port-Louis have ramparts that are almost complete. There are many fortresses; those of Fougères and Vitré are among the finest in France. Dinan and Combourg have fortified castles still standing; Suscinio and Tonquédec have impressive ruins; and though of lesser importance, the towers of La Hunaudaye, Elven, Oudon and Châteaugiron still stand proudly upright. Fort la Latte, as upright as a sentinel, boasts a magnificent site.

Buildings, half fortress and half palace, like Kerjean, Josselin and the Château des Ducs de Bretagne at Nantes, are interesting to see, but there are few of them. The fact is that the Breton nobility, except for the duke and a few great families, were poor. They included many country gentlemen who lived in

Source of Inspiration

Between 1886 and 1896, more than 20 painters, including Charles Laval, Paul Sérusier, Charles Filiger and Maurice Denis, grouped around Pont-Aven resident Paul Gauguin seeking to invent new forms of artistic expression. The meeting between **Paul Gauguin** and **Émile Bernard** in 1888 was the beginning of the Synthetist group. Rejecting the Impressionist and Pointillist movements, their work was characterised by painting from memory, two-dimensional patterns, bright vivid colours and spiritual subjects.

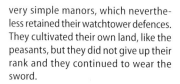

by a large group of friends, debunked their literal vision of pictorial art. The new movement, soon christened the Pont-Aven School, at first carried the name "synthetism".

Colours were bold and applied as solid tints, outlines and shapes were simplified and faces were often devoid of features: the Pont-Aven style established itself as a new artistic view of nature. Émile Bernard and Paul Gauguin, its founders, were soon joined by the young Sérusier, Maurice Denis, Armand Seguin and by foreign painters, informed by Paris critics greeting the birth of the movement.

Their peace disturbed by crowds of onlookers, the group settled in Le Pouldu. As for Gauguin, he left for the Pacific to seach for other sources of inspiration and explore other pictorial avenues. He made his last visit to Brittany in 1894, leaving Pont-Aven a reputation that endures today.

very simple manors, which nevertheless retained their watchtower defences. They cultivated their own land, like the peasants, but they did not give up their rank and they continued to wear the sword.

ART

Artists have found in Brittany an endless source of inspiration since the 19C. Painters and engravers have travelled the coast from the bay of Mont St-Michel to the Gulf of Morbihan in quest of the secrets of light and colour, while potters and sculptors have chosen instead ethnic and cultural themes.

PONT-AVEN SCHOOL

A painter friend described the market town of Pont-Aven to Paul Gauguin as a cheap little place in which to live and work. In 1886, Gauguin, then 38 years old, decided to leave his petty-bourgeois life for the bohemian lot of a painter. Built on the edge of the river Aven, the little town is famous for its windmills and the port activity generated by the flour mills. The surrounding area, with its wealth of churches and its fields scattered with yellow haystacks and megaliths, was already attracting a procession of French Academy painters, who were drawn by the exoticism of the region. Gauguin, soon followed

CONTEMPORARY ART IN BRITTANY

Since 1981, the Frac Bretagne (Fonds régional d'art contemporain – regional collection of contemporary art), located at Châteaugiron, has amassed nearly 2,000 works, which are regularly exhibited in Brittany's four départements. In addition to a resource centre and an educational service designed to familiarize young children with art, it also regularly publishes monographs of regional artists and collective catalogues. The region also has three approved contemporary art centres: La Criée in Rennes, Le Quartier in Quimper and La Passerelle in Brest.

Note that all Breton cities have contemporary art centres. The Musée des Beaux-Arts in Rennes regularly exhibits the work of local visual artists, while La Passerelle, in Brest, is an arts centre that focusses on dance, music and poetry. Not wanting to be restricted within the confines of its historical school, Pont-Aven opened its Centre international d'art contemporain in 2004. Its aim is to promote innovation by means of grants and masterclasses – in the field of visual

Faïence de Quimper

©S. Sauvignier/MICHELIN

arts, of course, but also in music, dance and poetry. Works are exhibited or performed throughout the year. If you like sculpture, don't miss a visit to the gardens of the Domaine de Kerguéhennec (👁 see p399), where sculptures are exhibited all year.

Also worth seeing is the studio of sculptor Pierre Manoli, which is located on the left bank of the Rance at La Richardais (👁 see p160).

Some deconsecrated places of worship today house temporary exhibitions of contemporary works. These include various chapels in the Blavet valley and the commune of Pontivy within the context of an annual event called "L'art dans les chapelles" ("Art in Chapels'") (👁 see p403).

The sea, too, plays its part in the revival of regional art with a new use for driftwood. In demand by coastal Bretons for centuries for use in furniture making, pieces of wood washed up by the tide are now gleaned and reworked by local artists.

DECORATIVE ARTS

Furniture

Over the centuries, Breton cabinetmakers have made *lits clos* (see below), sideboards, dressers, armoires and clock housings following identical patterns. Individual pieces differ from each other only in the minutest details of their ornamentation. This repetition has enabled these craftsmen to become highly skilled.

The *lit clos*, an essential piece of Breton furniture, provided protection from the cold while enabling one to isolate oneself in the large communal room. The bed is generally enclosed by two sliding doors (or by one large door in Le Léon or thick curtains in the regions of Audierne and Morbihan). It also includes a blanket chest where the bed linen is stored. *Lits clos* are covered with rich ornamentation: spindles, garlands, religious motifs, such as the monogram of Christ or the royalist heart, geometric figures, juxtaposed or interwoven, known as *au compas* decorations. These motifs are also found on armoires, which are often crested with a flat overhanging cornice, or sometimes by a double-bowed cornice, as in those made around Rennes. The chest also played an important role: it held linen or grain for domestic use.

Faïence pottery

Although faïence is more properly a decorative art, faience accessories were a regular element of home furnishings. Quimper faience, the most famous, has been enriched over the centuries by the contributions of numerous artisans, which have at various times revived this craft, developing its style and demonstrating its creativity. Skills handed down to these *peinteurs quimpérois* over generations have made this town home to a craft whose originality lies in its diversity of styles.

It was around 1840 that the first faience with a Breton theme was produced (notably the *petit Breton*, a caricatural figure that would replace traditional decorative themes), and that it began to be manufactured. The collection of *scènes bretonnes*, inspired by stories and engravings, and later of *légendes bretonnes*, made by A. Beau, were hugely successful.

Silverware

The Breton silversmith trade was at its most prosperous during the 14C and 15C. At that time, commissions were mostly religious, and magnifcent pieces, notably reliquaries, were produced. Many of them were melted down to finance wars. But despite its losses, Brittany secretly harbours many very beautiful pieces by local artists, particularly around Morlaix and Vannes, where they have been jealously guarded from the covetous. Notwithstanding, such work can be seen at Carantec, St-Jean-du-Doigt, St-Gildas-de-Rhuys, Paimpont, and Locarn, among other places.

Embroidery

Embroidery first appeared in Britanny after the French Revolution. Before that time, the materials used (silk thread, beads, velvet etc.) were so expensive that only the very rich could afford them. In the 19C, regional costumes underwent an extraordinary development: there were no less than 1,200 different ones in Brittany! Each region had its own embroidered ornamentation, used on both costumes and headdresses, which could be identified by its stitches and motifs (floral in the area around Aven, orange and yellow in the Bigouden region, etc.) The craft, along with the embroiderers' guilds, virtually disappeared during the years between the two world wars, but continues today as a cottage industry and has even undergone a revival of interest, linked to the blossoming of celtic culture.

LEGENDS AND LITERATURE
A LAND OF LEGENDS

Ancient beliefs, rituals and stories have, over the centuries, woven a tapestry of folklore and mysterious legends. Many of the stories told as fables are deep-rooted myths that have endured and continue to influence contemporary writers, just as they held the imagination of those who listened to them in the dark nights of the Middle Ages.

The Round Table

After the death of Christ, Joseph of Arimathea, one of his disciples, left Palestine carrying away a few drops of the divine blood in the cup from which the Redeemer drank during the Last Supper. He landed in Britain according to some legends, in Brittany according to others, where he lived for some time in the Forest of Brocéliande (now the Forêt de Paimpont) before vanishing without trace.

In the 6C King Arthur and 50 knights set out to find this precious cup. For them it was the Holy Grail, which only a warrior whose heart was pure could win. Percival (Wagner's *Parsifal*, 1882) was such a man. In the Middle Ages the search for the Grail gave rise to the endless stories of adventure that formed the Cycle of the Round Table. The most famous versions of the tale in English are Sir Thomas Malory's *Le Morte d'Arthur* (1471) and Alfred Lord Tennyson's *Idylls of the King* (1859).

Merlin and Viviane

One of King Arthur's companions, Merlin the Sorcerer (or Merlin the Magician), came to the Forest of Brocéliande to live in seclusion. But he met the fairy Viviane, and love inflamed them both. To ensure she kept Merlin, Viviane enclosed him in a magic circle. It would have been easy for him to escape, but he joyfully accepted this romantic captivity forever.

Tristan and Isolde

Tristan, Prince of Lyonesse, was sent to Ireland by his Uncle Mark, King of Cornouaille, to bring back the beautiful

Isolde, whom Mark wanted to marry. On board their ship, Tristan and Isolde accidentally drank a philtre that was intended to bind Isolde to her husband in eternal love. Passion stronger than duty sprang up in both their hearts. There are several versions of the end: sometimes Tristan is slain by Mark, furious at his betrayal; sometimes he marries and dies in his castle in Brittany. But Isolde always follows him to the grave. Richard Wagner's opera has made the love story famous.

The town of Is

At the time of good **King Gradlon**, about the 6C, Is was the capital of Cornouaille; finds in Trépassés and Douarnenez Bays and off the Presqu'île de Penmark are said to have come from Is. The town was protected from the sea by a dyke, opened by locks to which the King always carried the golden key.

The King had a beautiful but dissolute daughter, **Dahut**, also known as Ahès, who was seduced by the Devil in the form of an attractive young man. To test her love he asked her to open the sea gate. Dahut stole the key while the King was asleep, and soon the sea was rushing into the town.

King Gradlon fled on horseback, with his daughter on the crupper. But the waves pursued him and were about to swallow him up. At this moment a celestial voice ordered him, if he wished to be saved, to throw the demon who was riding behind him into the sea. With an aching heart the King obeyed, and the sea withdrew at once, but Is was destroyed.

For his new capital Gradlon chose Quimper; this is why his statue stands between the two towers of the cathedral. He ended his days in the "odour of sanctity", guided and sustained by St-Corentine. As for Dahut, she turned into a mermaid, who is known as **Marie-Morgane** and whose beauty still lures sailors to the bottom of the sea. This state of affairs will persist until Good Friday, when Mass is celebrated in one of the churches of the drowned city. Then Is will cease to be accursed, and Marie-Morgane will no longer be a siren.

A LAND OF LITERATURE
THE MIDDLE AGES AND THE RENAISSANCE

Learning was centred in the monasteries; the language used was Latin; the subjects studied were concerned, for the most part, with the history of the Church and of Brittany, moral philosophy and the lives of the saints. *La Vie de Saint Guénolé* (A Life of St Guénolé) was written by Gurdisten (Wurdisten), Abbot of Landévennec, in the 9C, and *La Vie de Saint-Pol-de-Léon* (A Life of St Pol de Léon) by Wrmonoc, a monk from the same abbey.

Authors are rarely known by name, but there are some exceptions from the 12C: the philosopher **Pierre Abélard**, one of the most brilliant figures of the Middle Ages, who was born at Le Pallet near Nantes and became Abbot of St-Gildas-de-Rhuys; **Étienne de Fougères**, who was named Bishop of Rennes in 1168, wrote *Livre des manières* (Book of Manners, 1174–78), which gave him free rein to lecture his contemporaries on moral issues; **Guillaume Le Breton**, a poet and historian at the court of Philippe-Auguste, whose reign he patriotically eulogised.

Students from Brittany first went to Paris University, and then to Nantes when that establishment was founded in the 15C. Schools were established to supplement the teaching provided by the churches and monasteries in out-of-the-way parishes. However, it was not until the 15C and 16C that one began hearing of names such as those of the historians Pierre Le Baud, Alain Bouchard and Bertrand d'Argentré; of the poet Meschinot from Nantes, who wrote a series of ballads entitled *Les Lunettes des princes* (The Princes' Spectacles), which became well known in his own time; of Noël du Fail, Councillor of the Rennes Parliament, who depicted the world around him so well; and of the Dominican Albert Legrand, who wrote *Vie des saints de la Bretagne armoricaine* (Life of the Saints of Armorican Brittany).

17C AND 18C

The best-known figures of the 17C and 18C are **Mme de Sévigné** – Breton by marriage – who wrote vivid descriptions of Rennes, Vitré, Vannes and Port-Louis; **Lesage**, the witty author of *Gil Blas*; and Duclos, moralist and historian, who was Mayor of Dinan. There was also **Élie Fréron**, who became known only through his disputes with Voltaire and who was the director of a literary journal published in Paris and, finally, the Benedictines Dom Lobineau and Dom Morice, historians of Brittany.

THE ROMANTICS AND CONTEMPORARY WRITERS

Three figures dominated literature in the 19C in Brittany: **François-René de Chateaubriand**, who had an immense influence on French literature. In his *Mémoires d'Outre-Tombe* (*Memoirs From Beyond the Grave*), he recounts his childhood at St-Malo and his youth at Combourg Castle; **Lamennais**, fervent apologist of theocracy, became a convinced democrat, reflected in his philosophical works the evolution of his thought.

Chateaubriand by Girodet de Roucy Trioson, 1811, Château de Versailles

Musée d'Histoire de la Ville, Saint-Malo/Bridgeman Art Library

Ernest Renan, philologist, historian and philosopher, wrote many books in an easy and brilliant prose, and in one, *Souvenirs d'enfance et de jeunesse* (Recollections of Childhood and Youth), described his native Brittany.

Henri Queffélec (1910–92) lauded Brittany in *Un Recteur de l'île de Sein*, *Un homme d'Ouessant*, *Au bout du monde*, *Franche et secrète Bretagne* and *Promenades en Bretagne*.

Nature

The relief of Brittany is the result of an evolutionary process that has taken place over millions of years. Crafted by the forces of the sea, the rugged coastline symbolises the mystical beauty of the region, while the dynamic between land and sea has come to define its people and their culture.

THE SEA
THE ARMOR

The name Armor (or, more rarely, Arvor) means "country near the sea". It was given to the coastal region by the Gauls; the interior was Argoat.

The Breton Coast

The coast of Brittany is extraordinarily indented, which makes it 2720km/

1700mi long; it would be only half that without its saw-teeth appearance. The jagged nature of this coastline, with its islands, islets and reefs is due only in part to the action of the sea and is one of the characteristics of Brittany.

The most typical seascapes are to be found at the western tip of the peninsula. Sombre cliffs, rugged capes 50–70m/164–230ft high, islands, rocks and reefs give the coastline a grimness that is reflected in sinister local names: the Channel of Fear *(Fromveur)*, the Bay of the Dead *(Baie des Trépassés)*, the Hell of Plogoff *(Enfer de Plogoff)*.

There are many other impressive features, too: piles of enormous blocks of pink granite sometimes as high as 20m/65ft, as at Ploumanach and Trégastel; the red-sandstone promontory of Cap Fréhel standing 57m/187ft above

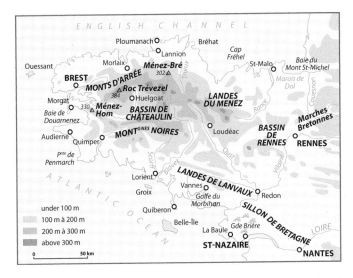

the sea; the brightly coloured caves of Morgat. Unforgettable are the Brest roadstead, the Bay of Douarnenez, the Golfe du Morbihan and its islands. The successive estuaries between the Rance and the Loire offer magnificent views at high tide as one crosses the impressive bridges that span them (Pont Albert-Louppe and Pont de Térénez).

Some low-lying sections of the coast contrast with the more usual rocks.

In the north, Mont-St-Michel Bay is bordered by a plain reclaimed from the sea; in the south, the inhospitable Bay of Audierne, the coast between Port-Louis and the base of the Presqu'île de Quiberon, and the beach at La Baule give a foretaste of the great expanses of sand that predominate south of the Loire.

Wherever the coast is directly open to the sea winds, it is completely barren. This is so on the points and on the summits of the cliffs; the salt with which the winds are impregnated destroys the vegetation. But in sheltered spots there are magnificent, profusely flowering shrubs. Arum lilies, camellias, hydrangeas and rhododendrons, that would be the pride of many a skilled gardener, grace the smallest gardens.

The climate is so mild that plants that grow in hot countries flourish in the open, e.g. mimosa, agave, pomegranate, palm, eucalyptus, myrtle, oleander and fig trees.

Tides and Waves

Visitors should first learn the rhythm of the tides, a division of time as regular as that of the sun. Twice every 24 hours the sea advances on the coast – this is the rising tide. It reaches high water mark, where it stays for a while, and then drops back – this is the falling or ebb tide – until it reaches low water mark. It remains at this low level for a while, and then the cycle begins again.

The timetables for the tides are displayed in hotels, on quays and in local papers. Look at them before planning a trip, as they may affect the timing of your programme.

It is at high tide that the coast of Brittany is at its most beautiful. The waves advance on the coast, break on the rocky outspurs and surge in parallel crests into the bays; a shining liquid carpet fills the estuaries. This is the time when a journey along a coastal road or a walk to the harbour is the most rewarding. At low tide, the uncovered rocks, stained with algae and seaweed, are often dirty and can be disappointing. At the mouths of the great coastal rivers there is only a poor thread of water winding between mudflats. The greater the tide and the gentler the slope, the greater the expanse of shore that is uncovered; in Mont-St-Michel Bay the sea retreats 15–20km/9.3–12.4mi. On the other hand, low tide is the joy of anyone fishing for crab, shrimp, clams or mussels. On the north coast, the tide sweeps in, in exceptional cases, to a height of 13.5m /44ft in the bay of St-Malo and 15m/49.2ft in Mont-St-Michel Bay.

When the wind blows, the battering-ram effect of the sea is tremendous – sometimes the shocks given to the rocks off Penmarch are felt as far off as Quimper, 30km/18.6mi away. Attacking the softest parts of the cliffs, the sea makes fissures and brings down slabs of rock. In this way, caves (&see MORGAT), tunnels and arches are formed. Peninsulas joined to the mainland by strips of softer material are turned gradually into islands.

The waves do not only destroy, they also have a constructive effect. The sand they carry, added to the alluvial deposits brought down by the rivers, forms beaches, gradually silts up the bays (Mont-St-Michel Bay is a striking example), and connects islands with the mainland; this is the case at Quiberon and it will also be the same, in due course, at Bréhat.

SAILING

Brittany, the most maritime region of France, is home to many devoted sailors. Breton people, if one is to believe a well-known proverb, "are born with the waters of the sea flowing round their eyes and the ocean has flowed in their veins from birth". Here, sailing is more than a sport: it's second nature, as inevitable as sunshine and rain. For some, it is part of daily life or earning a living, for others it is an abiding passion.

Regatta, a sport for everybody – In times past, sailing used to be a sport for the élite, but now it is a popular sport, as is windsurfing, which took off in the 1980s. The nautical industry abandoned craftwork to turn towards the mass production of boats made of synthetic materials. The change in production methods made recreational boats more affordable. There are now some 700 sailing schools operating within the French Federation of Sailing and another 1,000 centres located all around France. Sealovers enjoy going on regattas along the Breton coast, examining the sky, anticipating the thermal breeze, pondering over the depressions, in order to swell the spinnakers and the Genoa jibs better and to cleave through the waves of the big blue ocean.

Things have changed a lot since the first regattas, which were merely gatherings of fishing dinghies that took place around 1850. All kinds of single-hull and multi-hull ships are moored at the marinas' landing stages. If boats could dream, perhaps as they rock gently in their berths, they would imagine participating in a regatta, even a modest one, or perhaps the Spi Ouest-France, which is organised every year at La Trinité-sur-Mer. Famous competitive sailors attend this event and mingle with the crowd of enthusiastic wannabes and fans.

Great sailors – Not all the great French sailors are Breton, of course, but Brittany represents the sea to such an extent that most of the them have a strong attachment to the region. Many are well known to "old salts" from the seas of the world: Bernard Moitessier, Jacques-Yves Le Toumelin and Éric Tabarly (tragically lost at sea off Southwest Wales in June 1998). Tabarly had a reputation for fair play and love of the sea that inspired many landlubbers to consider the ocean as something more than a vast, liquid steppe without life. Among the sailors who trained by his side and are now following in his wake are Olivier de Kersauzon, Jean Le Cam, Marc Pajot, Yves Parlier, Philippe Poupon and Alain Thébault.

Sailing has grown in popularity as the number of competitive events has increased. High-performance craft are sponsored by a variety of companies eager for the visibility that media coverage of races provides. Shipyards in Lorient, Vannes and Nantes turn out racing craft made of highly resistant materials, such as spectra, kevlar or titanium, to be captained by the likes of Florence Arthaud, Isabelle Autissier, Laurent

Bourgnon, Franck Cammas, Alain Gautier, Loïck Peyron or Paul Vatine. Long-distance races can be especially dangerous: besides Tabarly, sailors who lost their lives whilst pursing their passion include Alain Colas in 1978, Loïc Caradec in 1986 and Gerry Roufs in 1997.

Great races – Solo and team races take place most of the year, in one corner of the world or another. The world of sailing is enlivened by solo or team races and crossing records almost all the year round. Websites allow aficionadi to follow the big events minute-by-minute without having to put on their rough weather gear!

Some prestigious races start or finish in Brittany. The most famous is probably the Route du Rhum race, for single-hulls and multi-hulls, which takes sailors from Pointe du Grouin to Pointe-à-Pitre in Guadeloupe. It takes place every four years (the next being in 2014). Other big events are La Baule–Dakar, (famous for the difficult crossing of the Bay of Biscay in autumn); Québec–St-Malo (featuring whales and icebergs); the transatlantic race Lorient–Bermuda–Lorient. The Figaro race in July occasionally starts from a Breton harbour; the Round Europe race calls at main ports from the north to the south of Europe, and many other races and regattas are organised in Brittany.

LIGHTHOUSES

Since man first took to the seas, means have existed to warn sailors about the dangers of approaching the shore. The first lighthouses were built in the 17C, but it wasn't until the 19C that they became the norm. The oldest Breton lighthouse is at Stiff on Ouessant, where construction began in 1685.

How do you build a lighthouse when there are dangerous rocks, currents and storms? The one at Armen took 14 years, because in 1870 the workers were able to work for a total of only eight hours during the whole year, and in 1873 for just six hours! The rock it is built on is just 1.5m/1.5ft at low tide.

These days, means are being developed to illuminate lighthouses with renewable energy from sun and wind. Originally, coal fires were used, then oil lamps in front of a reflector, until Augustin Fresnel invented a system of lens formations which is still in use today. This economised on fuel and increased luminosity. Today, most lighthouses are automated, which means that no direct human intervention is needed. The keeper monitors the automated systems, maintains the lighthouse and provides radio links and weather reports.

Eighty lighthouses are still working along the Breton coast and some can still be visited. These include St-Matthieu, Trézien, the Île Vierge, the Stiff and Créac'h. The latter boasts one of the most powerful lights in the world, reaching 120km/75.5mi in clear weather. The old engine room houses a museum of lighthouses and buoys.

FISHING

Coastal Fishing

Sole, turbot, skate, bass, sea bream, crustaceans, scallops... take your pick! On the Atlantic coast, the season for sardine fishing lasts from June to September, when the finest specimens are caught and canned for France's premier brands – Gonidec, La Belle Illoise, Quibéronnaise and Rodel.

Deep-Sea Fishing

Open-sea fishing takes place as far off as the coasts of Iceland, and represents the main activity of big Breton ports. For tuna fishing, both dragnets and live bait are used in the Bay of Biscay; *seines* (large fishing nets) are used along the African coasts. White tuna is fished from June to October; the season starts somewhere between Portugal and the Azores. Tropical or albacore tuna is the quarry of a fleet of some 30 boats with refrigerated holds, equipped at Concarneau and operating from the ports of West Africa during the season.

"La Grande Pêche"

This is the name given to cod fishing in the shoals of Newfoundland, Labrador and Greenland. It made Paimpol and St-Malo famous in the past, but nowadays

Digging for dinner

S. Sauvignier/MICHELIN

it is only a modest activity practised by factory ships equipped with machines for processing and freezing fish at sea.

Shellfish
Most shellfish is harvested along the rocky coasts using lobster pots and traps, but long-distance fishing is also common. Lobster boats, equipped with tanks as well as refrigeration or freezing facilities used to leave from Camaret-Audierne for the coast of Mauritania for several months at a time.

Along the coast, in deep waters and far from home, the fishermen of Brittany have succeeded in adapting to modern techniques, despite the implementation of restrictive quotas, due mainly to the internationalisation of the fishing indus-

try. Lorient and Concarneau make Brittany the leading French region for the fishing industry.

OTHER SEAFOOD

Canning Industry
At the instigation of Louis XIV's minister of Finances, Fouquet, the method of preserving fish in barrels gradually replaced the customary drying and salting of fish. Sardines used to be preserved in oil, until Nicolas Appert invented the canning process in 1810. In Brittany, the industry faces competition from developing countries, but there are still factories operating on the Presqu'ile de Quiberon and in the harbours of Douarnenez and Concarneau.

Oceanography and Aquaculture
Researchers at Ifremer (French Research Institute for the Exploitation of the Sea) work to find solutions to avoid depleting the resources of the sea. Aquaculture offers promise for the future. Fish farms in Finistère are already successfully breeding salmon and turbot.

Conchyliculture
Oyster and mussel breeding has become commercially important, which has long been the great production region for flat oysters (belons) and has also developed its Portuguese oyster beds (sold as creuses de Bretagne or fines de Bretagne). Brittany's annual oyster production amounts to 30,000 tonnes of creuses and 2,000 tonnes of plates, which is a quarter of France's national production. Mussel breeding on poles known as bouchots is carried out along the coast from Mont-St-Michel Bay to St-Brieuc Bay and in the Vilaine estuary.

Algae and Algae-Processing
Harvested and used as fertiliser for many years, then as raw materials for the chemical industry, the various types of algae are as likely nowadays to be found on restaurant tables as in sea-water spas. Wrack cultivating and harvesting, using specially equipped boats, is now subject to regulations. This activity is mainly based in the Abers area.

Bucket and Spade

The French call it pêche à pied, or fishing on foot. Take care to go crabbing and shrimping in authorised areas and in season (signs are posted on beaches). There are specified sizes for each species and you are expected to gather reasonable quantities – that is, not more than you can eat! Females bearing eggs should be released and any rocks you move or turn over set back in place. Keep your catch fresh by covering it with algae (cut it, don't pull it up). Respecting these simple rules will help preserve an ecosystem that is more fragile than you might suspect.

Naval Dockyards

With the creation of the Atlantic Dockyards at St-Nazaire, after years of crisis, the ship-building industry is once again competitive on an international scale. Capable of dealing with ships of up to 500,000 tonnes, they have, above all, turned to the production of container ships, oil rigs and cruise ships, including the largest-ever ocean liner, the *Queen Mary 2*.

THE ARGOAT
THE PLATEAUX

The Argoat is the inland plateau covering most of the region. Although you must not expect to find great expanses extending to far horizons, the traveller crosses a series of rises that may confuse the directionally challenged! Between the uplands flow deeply sunken rivers with brown, rushing waters. The land resembles a chequerboard, with banks and dry-stone walls forming the boundaries of fields and pastures. Pollarded oaks grow on most of the banks, and it is these that make the countryside, seen from a distance, seem heavily wooded.

THE MOUNTAINS

Mountains! The word rather overpowers the Breton hills, but this is what the coast-dwellers call the central part of Brittany. The barrenness of the heights, the saw-toothed crests contrasting with the undulating plains that they overshadow, and the strong wind give an impression of high altitude. In clear weather a vast expanse can be seen from the Roc Trévezel (384m/1259ft), the Ménez-Hom (330m/1083ft) and the Ménez-Bré (302m/991ft).

FORESTS AND MOORS

Brittany once had immense forests of oak and beech. Successive generations since the Romans have wielded the axe in these woods, and there are now only scattered strips of woodland: the forests of Paimpont, Loudéac, Huelgoat and Quénécan, for example. These woodlands are very hilly and intersected by gorges, ravines and tumbled rocks. A perfect example of this type of country is to be seen at Huelgoat. Unfortunately, most of the woodlands appear neglected, and brushwood predominates. Fine forests are rare and these Breton woodlands owe their picturesque quality more to their relief than to their trees.

Fallow moors, where the great forests once stood, now form empty stretches that are relieved from gloom when the gorse wears its golden cloak and the heather spreads a purple carpet on the hills. Elsewhere, moors have become tilled fields. Such are the Landes de Lanvaux, where the visitor finds reclaimed land, rich in promise for the future.

AGRICULTURE

For a long time the Argoat was essentially an agricultural and stock-rearing region, but more recently industrial development has been encouraged by local authorities.

Nearly a third of the land under cultivation is given over to cereal production, inclusing fodder crops (mainly corn).

There are still many apple orchards in Ille-et-Vilaine and in the south of the Finistère, but a certain decline is noticeable in Morbihan. The apples are used to make cider and apple juice.

The Argoat has a reputation for its dairy cattle, which produce a variety of dairy products enjoyed throughout France. Pig rearing has been industrialised and represents half of France's production. Brittany supplies national markets and the many firms that produce fresh, canned or salted pork products.

CANALS

Brittany has more than 600km/373mi of rivers and canals. Running north–south are the Rance, the Île-et-Rance canal and the Vilaine, flowing through Dinan, Rennes and Redon.

The Nantes–Brest canal runs east–west for 360km/224mi. It was originally built so that Napoleon's fleet could avoid the English off the coast. At the end of the 19C it became a key coal, slate and fertilizer route. Today, the canal is an ideal way to explore inland Brittany by barge, bike or on foot.

View of Le Palais with Citadelle Vauban, Belle-Île
©Bathilde Chaboche/Office de Tourisme de Belle Île en Mer

In the Breton language, Rennes is known as *Roazhon*, which is the name for the old province that roughly corresponds to the modern Ille-et-Vilaine *département* in which the sights and attractions of this part of the guide are included. Rennes, the largest city in the modern Brittany region and also its capital, has much to interest the visitor, particularly its architectural heritage. Between Rennes and the border with Mayenne in the Pays de Loire region lie the Breton Marches, whose castles in medieval times protected the province from invasion. To the west of Rennes can be found the Forêt de Paimpont (Paimpont Forest) which is thought to be the site of several ancient Breton myths and legends.

Highlights

1 Strolling the **old town** of Rennes (p92)

2 Visiting the **Palais du Parlement de Bretagne**, the first stone building in a town of wood (p94)

3 Taking a racing car for a spin at the **Manoir de l'Automobile** (p113)

4 On the trail of legends in the **Forêt de Paimpont** (p115)

5 Climbing the towers of the **Château de Combourg** (p120)

Regional Crossroads

The Ille-et-Vilaine *département* is often known, along with the Loire Atlantique and the eastern parts of Morbihan and Côtes-d'Armor, as Upper Brittany because here the people tended to use the Gallo language, which was very close to French; whereas in Lower Brittany (the western parts of Morbihan and Côtes-d'Armor as well as Finistère), Breton was traditionally spoken. This is the easternmost part of the region and for this reason it shares with the Loire Atlantique the distinction of being a little more "French" than the rest of Brittany. The economy is based on agriculture (it is the leading producer of dairy products in France), fisheries, food production, car production (Peugeut-Citroën) and IT. Rennes has been the regional capital since 1941, when it took over from Nantes following the detachment of the Loire-Atlantique *département* from Brittany by the Vichy Government, and is a thriving city in the centre of the Ille-et-Vilaine *département* with plenty of interesting architecture, including the 17C Palais du Parliament. There has been a settlement since Celtic times at the confluence of the Ille and Vilaine rivers and today Rennes is a bustling university town with hi-tech factories.

Castles at Fougères, Vitré and Châteaubriant in the Breton Marches east of Rennes still serve as a reminder that the Dukes of Brittany had to defend the province from the French during the Middle Ages.

Not far to the west of Rennes is the primeval oak and beech Forest of Paimpont, where myths and legends thrive. This ancient woodland, that many Celts believe to be the Brocéliande of Arthurian legend, has associations with Merlin the magician and the fairy Viviane, said to be the Lady of the Lake who raised the fabled knight Lancelot of Round Table fame. Though the forest covers a much smaller area today than hitherto, it is a fascinating place to explore, with four beautiful lakes, ethereal clearings and ancient Neolithic monuments, now associated with the fables shared by Celtic people everywhere. More recent historical events, such as being a refuge for Christian clergy during the Viking raids, means that anyone who likes a good story will enjoy discovering the secrets of the forest for themselves.

In the south of the Ille-et-Vilaine stands Redon, at the junction of three *départements*, two regions, two rivers and the Nantes–Brest Canal. With its elegant old houses in the Grande Rue and the sandstone and granite tower of the former Abbey Church of St-Sauveur, it is well worth a visit.

Well to the north of the region is Combourg, perhaps one of the most picturesque towns in Brittany, complete with its imposing feudal castle.

Market produce

© F1 Online/Tips Images

Rennes Market

Rennes has the distinction of hosting what is claimed to be the second largest market in France. Located in the centre of Rennes old town, it is only a few minutes walk from the bus station and the metro (Ste-Anne and République stations). The origins of the present day market, which takes place every Saturday from 7.30am–1.30pm, lie in the 17C when traders gathered in the Place des Lices to sell their wares to the members of the public who gathered there for games such as jousting, and to attend executions which took place in the vicinity. Every week, some 300 traders set up their colourful stalls, some starting as early as 4am in order to get everything perfect for the citizens of the Breton capital and visitors to the city.

Rennes market

H. Le Gac/MICHELIN

The market is always crowded so it pays to arrive as early as possible in order to make the most of it. The stalls are grouped by specialistion as far as possible in order to encourage competition. You will find fresh produce from all over Brittany, especially the fish and seafood for which the region is renowned. As well as fruit, vegetables, poultry, meat and charcuterie, cheese, bread, honey and preserves, a varity of other products such as pot plants and cut flowers are for sale. Rennes market is about more than shopping, however, and there is much banter between the traders and their regulars customers. There are also musicians to enliven the proceedings. Towards lunchtime, many people repair to the numerous outdoor cafés to enjoy a dozen oysters and a chilled Muscadet. In winter, the *marché de Noël* (Christmas market) is held in the Place des Lices.

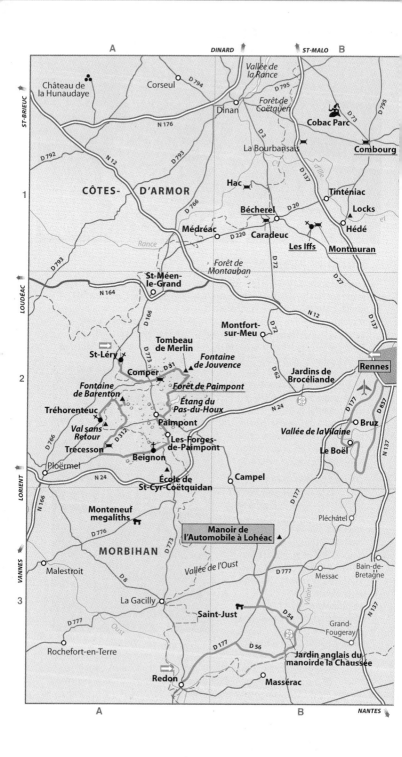

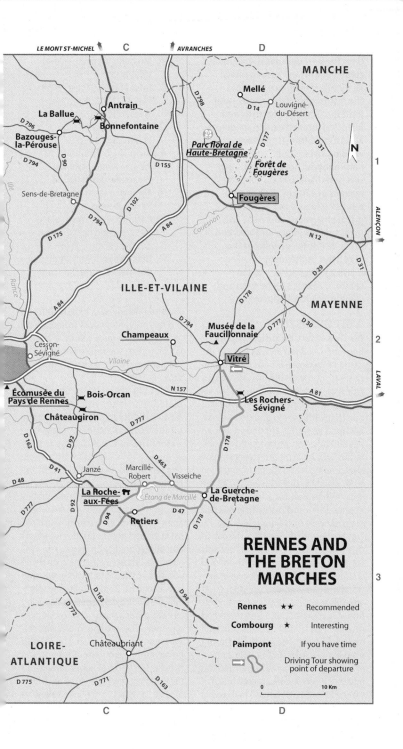

RENNES AND THE BRETON MARCHES

Rennes	★★	Recommended
Combourg	★	Interesting
Paimpont		If you have time
	⟹	Driving Tour showing point of departure

0   10 Km

Rennes★★

Over the past decades the regional capital of Brittany has regained its dignified elegance through the restoration of its architectural heritage. This city of artistic and historical interest exudes medieval atmosphere from its narrow, winding streets lined with charming half-timbered houses and carved sills that thankfully escaped the ravages of a fire in 1720. Stately public buildings and numerous private mansions adorn the two royal squares (place du Palais and place de l'Hôtel-de-Ville) at the very heart of the town. Rennes is also a university city at the centre of France's electronics and communications industries.

▶ **Population:** 209,613
◉ **Michelin Map:** L6 – Ille-et-Villaine (35).
▣ **Info:** 11 rue St-Yves, 35064 Rennes. ℘02 99 67 11 11. www.tourisme-rennes.com.
◉ **Location:** Capital city of Brittany.
▲▲ **Kids:** The Ecomuseum du Pays de Rennes and the Espace des Sciences.
◉ **Timing:** It takes a full day to visit Rennes.
▣ **Parking:** Car parks in place des Lices and near Champs Libres.
◉ **Don't Miss:** A walk through the streets of the Old Town.

A BIT OF HISTORY

Du Guesclin's beginnings (14C) – Bertrand Du Guesclin was born in the castle of La Motte-Broons (now disappeared), southwest of Dinan. He was the eldest of 10 children and by no means handsome. On the other hand, he was bursting with energy and good sense. Bertrand spent his childhood among peasant boys, whom he taught to fight. In this way he acquired strength, skill and cunning – and rough manners. In 1337, when Du Guesclin was 17, all the local nobles met for a tournament at Rennes. Du Guesclin arrived in peasant dress, mounted on a draught horse. He was kept out of the lists. His despair at this was such that one of his cousins from Rennes lent him his armour and charger. Without giving his name, Bertrand unseated several opponents. At last a lance thrust lifted his visor and his father recognised him. Delighted and proud, he exclaimed: "My fine son, I will no longer treat thee scurvily!" During his military career Du Guesclin, known as the Eagle of Brittany, supported the house of Valois and recaptured much of what was lost to the English in the early stages of the Hundred Years' War.

The duchess' marriage (1491) – In 1489, when François II died, his heiress, Anne of Brittany, was only 12, but this did not prevent wooers from coming forward. Her choice fell on Maximilian of Austria, the future Emperor. The religious marriage was performed by proxy in 1490.

Charles VIII, who had an unconsummated marriage with Margaret of Austria, daughter of Maximilian, asked for the Duchess' hand for himself; he was refused and laid siege to Rennes in August 1491. The starving people begged their sovereign to accept the marriage. She agreed and met Charles VIII. Anne was small and thin and slightly lame, but she had gaiety and charm; she knew Latin and Greek and took an interest in art and letters. Charles was short and ill-favoured, with large, pale eyes and thick lips always hanging open; he was slow-witted, but loved power and had a taste for pomp. Quite unexpectedly the two young people took a liking to each other, which grew into tender affection. Their engagement was celebrated at Rennes. There remained, however, the problem of freeing the fiancés. The Court of Rome agreed and the wedding took place in the royal Château de Langeais, in the Loire Valley, on 6 December 1491 (◉ see The Michelin Guide Châteaux of the Loire). The marriage united Brittany to France.

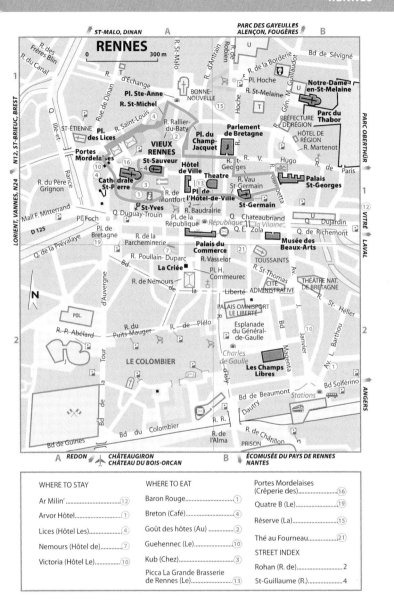

RENNES

The great fire of 1720 – At the beginning of the 18C the town still looked as it did in the Middle Ages, with narrow alleys and lath-and-plaster houses. There was no way of fighting fire, for there was no running water. In the evening of 22 December 1720, a drunken carpenter set fire to a heap of shavings with his lamp. The house burned like a torch and immediately others around it caught fire.

Ravaged areas were rebuilt to the plans of **Jacques Gabriel**, the descendant of a long line of architects and father of Gabriel who built the place de la Concorde in Paris. A large part of the town owes its rectangular street pattern and the uniform granite houses to this event. In order that they might be inhabited more quickly, new houses were divided into apartments that were sold separately, the beginning of co-ownership.

Old Houses

- ◆ **6 Rue St-Sauveur** was a 16C canon's residence.
- ◆ **3 Rue St-Guillaume**, a beautiful medieval house, known as Maison Du Guesclin, contains the restaurant Ti Koz.
- ◆ **Rue de la Psalette**. This street is lined with old houses.
- ◆ **22 Rue du Chapitre** is a Renaissance house; number 8 is the Hôtel de Brie (17C); number 6 the 18C Hôtel de Blossac with a fine granite staircase (on the left as you enter) with marble columns and a wrought-iron handrail.
- ◆ **6 and 8 Rue St-Yves** are 16C houses.
- ◆ **10 Rue des Dames** is the Hôtel Freslon de la Freslonnière.

The La Chalotais affair – In 1762, the Duke of Aiguillon, Governor of Brittany, clashed with Parliament over the Jesuits. The Jansenist lawyers (*robins*) opposed the Society of Jesus, whose colleges made it very powerful in Brittany – that of Rennes had 2,800 pupils. La Chalotais, the Public Prosecutor, induced Parliament to vote for the dissolution of the Order. His report had huge success: 12,000 copies were sold in a month. Voltaire wrote to the author: "This is the only work of philosophy that has ever come from the Bar."

The Duke of Aiguillon, who defended the Jesuits, asked Parliament to reverse its vote. It refused. Louis XV summoned the councillors to Versailles, scolded them and sent three into exile. On returning to Rennes, the members of Parliament resigned rather than submit. The King had La Chalotais arrested and sent him to Saintes; the other councillors were scattered over various provinces, but the Paris Parliament took the side of the Rennes Parliament and Louis XV hesitated to go further. The Duke of Aiguillon, lacking support, retired in 1768. The assemblies had defeated royal power and revolution was on the march.

WALKING TOUR
OLD TOWN ★★

This is the part of the old town that escaped the 1720 fire. It contains a maze of 15C and 16C houses with overhanging storeys and lordly mansions with sculpted façades. Begin at the Basilique St-Saveur.

Basilique St-Sauveur

Inside this 17C and 18C basilica are a fine gilded wooden **canopy** and an **organ loft** (17C). To the right is a chapel consecrated to Our Lady of Miracles who is belived to have saved Rennes from the English during the siege of 1357. Note the numerous ex-votos that have been donated in gratitude to Our Lady.

○ *Rue St-Guillaume leads to the cathedral.*

Cathédrale St-Pierre

Carrefour de la Cathédrale.
○ *Open 9am–noon, 3pm–6pm.*
₢ 02 99 78 48 80.

The third built on the site since the 6C, this cathedral was finished in 1844 after 57 years' work. The previous building collapsed in 1762 except for the two towers in the Classical style flanking the façade. The **interior**★ is very rich, its stucco facing covered with paintings and gilding. The cathedral contains a masterpiece: the gilded and carved wood **altarpiece** ★★ in the chapel before the south transept.

Both in size and in execution, this 16C Flemish work is one of the most important of its kind. The scenes represent the life of the Virgin.

○ *Follow rue du Griffon to rue St-Yves to visit the Tourist Office and a permanent exhibition on the cultural heritage of Rennes in the chapel of St-Yves. Rue des Dames leads to the Portes Mordelaises.*

Portes Mordelaises

The city's main entrance, these gates are all that remain of the 15C ramparts. The dukes of Brittany passed through it on their way to the cathedral for their

Place Ste-Anne

A. de Valroger/MICHELIN

coronation. In 1598 the silver-gilt keys of the city were presented there to Henri IV. At this kind of ceremony, a delegate from the Pyrenean province of Béarn made a statement which always went down well: "These are beautiful keys," he would say, "but I would rather have the keys to the hearts of your citizens." The drawbridge, modelled on that of Montmuran Castle, was reconstructed in 1997.

Walk away from the cathedral and join rue de Juilliet then turn right on to place des Lices.

Place des Lices

Jousts and tournaments were once held on this square. At 34 stands a 17C stone mansion, the Hôtel de Molant, with a mansard roof; inside, there is a sumptuous oak staircase with trompe-l'œil paintings (a skyscape) and woodwork decorating the ceiling of its stairwell.

Rue St-Michel leads off the square.

Rue St-Michel

This street is lined with half-timbered houses and still has the inns and taverns dating from the time when it was part of the city's suburbs.

Place Ste-Anne

The coloured half-timbered houses, Gothic and Renaissance in style, surround a 19C neo-Gothic church. The

house formerly occupied by Mayor Leperdit is at nunber 19. This square is next to rue d'Échange, which contains the Jacobin Convent where Anne of Brittany was betrothed to the King Charles Viii of France.

Rue du Pont-aux-Foulons

This is a shopping street leading off the square with 18C half-timbered houses.

Rue du Champ-Jacquet

This street leads to an oddly shaped triangular square of the same name. It is lined to the north with tall half-timbered 17C houses and is overlooked by the stone and wood façade of Hôtel de Tizé (number 5).
The itinerary continues along rue La Fayette and rue Nationale into the Classical part of the city with its majestic buildings, in particular the **Palais du Parlement de Bretagne**.

Turn left on to rue Nationale.

Palais du Parlement de Bretagne★★

Place du Parlement de Bretagne.
Guided tours only; reservations at the Tourist Office. Closed 1 May. 6.80€. 02 99 67 11 66.
www.parlement-bretagne.com
Brittany's Parliament, one of the 13 provincial parliaments that made up the Kingdom of France, initially had its seat in Rennes for part of the year and Nantes

Palais du Parlement de Bretagne

©José Mouret

for the other, before finally the decision was taken in 1561 to establish a single seat in Rennes. It was the Supreme Court of 2,300 Breton tribunals, as well as fulfilling a legislative and political function. The architecture and décor of the mansion, which was the first stone building in a town of wood, were to influence the whole of Haute-Bretagne. The design of local architect Germain Gaultier was reworked for the façade by the Court architect of Marie de' Medici, Salomon de Brosse. Building went on from 1618 to 1655 and its decoration was not completed until 1706. The jewel of the building is the Grand'Chambre with its gilt-wood ceiling decorated by Coypel and Errand.

The Palais du Parlement de Bretagne was badly damaged by fire in February 1994. While the firefighters struggled valiantly to save the building, tons of water were poured over and into it, resulting in damage that required more than 400,000 hours of work to repair. The restoration was completed in 1999, and the Court of Appeals of Rennes once again sits in this historic place. The ground floor gallery and the Court of Assizes on the floor above, as well as the French gardens in front, have been restored to their original appearance.

➲ *Walk away from the parliament building down rue Hoche and turn right.*

Rue St-Georges

This animated street, lined with cafés and restaurants, has many old houses: numbers 8, 10 and 12 form a remarkable group of 17C half-timbered houses. The 16C Hôtel de Moussaye at number 3 has a lovely Renaissance façade with sculptured pilasters.

Palais St-Georges

Preceded by a beautiful garden, this former Benedictine abbey (1670) now houses administrative services.

➲ *Take rue de Corbin leading away from Palais St-Georges.*

Église St-Germain

This Flamboyant church on rue de Coëtquen (15C–16C) with its 17C gable (on the south side) retains certain characteristics typical of a Breton cathedral: wood vaulting and its beams with sculpted ends. In the south transept the beautiful 16C **stained-glass window** recounts the life of the Virgin and the Passion. The nave contains modern stained-glass windows by Max Ingrand.

➲ *Continue along rue Coëtquen.*

Place de l'Hôtel-de-Ville

This regal square is the centre of the Classical district. On its west side stands the town hall and on the east side, the theatre, built in 1832. To the south, beyond rue d'Orléans, the view is blocked by the **Palais du Commerce** (Trade Hall), an imposing building decorated with monumental sculpture.

The **Hôtel de Ville** (◡ *open Mon–Sat, guided tours only;* ◉ *closed public holidays;* ♿*;* ⃠*02 99 67 11 08; www.tourisme. rennes.com*) was built to the plans of Jacques Gabriel in 1734–43, after the fire of 1720. A central tower, standing back from the façade, carries the great clock – *le gros*, as the townspeople call it – and is joined by two curved buildings to two large annexes. Inside are the former chapel and a lovely 17C Brussels tapestry. The right wing contains the Pantheon of Rennes, a hall dedicated to the memory of men who have died for

France. Provided no official reception is being held, the public is admitted to the left wing of the building and can see the monumental staircase, the 18C Brussels tapestries and the hall where wedding ceremonies are performed.

ADDITIONAL SIGHTS

Les Champs Libres★

10 cours Allié. ⊙Open Tue–Fri noon–7pm (Tue until 9pm), Sat–Sun 2pm–7pm. ⊛7€ (Passe Expos – access to all exhibitions, valid one day). & ℘02 23 40 66 00. www.leschampslibres.fr.
Opened in 2006, this cultural centre brings together three institutions: the Musée de Bretagne, the Espace des Sciences and the library. The ultra-modern building is the work of architect Christian de Portzamparc.

Musée de Bretagne – This museum recalls the history of Brittany. Through 2,300 exhibits (objects, models, carved figures) and audio-visual displays, different eras are evoked: prehistory, Gallo-Roman Armorica, medieval Brittany and the Ancien Régime. On the ground floor there is an exhibition of photographs of Brittany.

Espace des Sciences – This science space has several themes: the Salle de Terre (geography of the Armorica region); the Laboratoire de Merlin, where children can do their own scientific experiments and the Planétarium, where live programmes are shown.

Musée des Beaux-Arts★

20 Quai Émile Zola. ⊙Open Tue 10am–6pm, Wed–Sun 10am–noon, 2pm–6pm. ⟶Guided tours available (1hr). ⊙Closed Mon and public holidays. ⊛5.72€ (under 18 no charge). ℘02 23 62 17 45. www.mbar.org.
The permanent collection rooms at the Museum of Fine Arts have recently been restyled, extended and enriched with new works that have never been shown. It now contains fine examples of painting, sculpture, drawing, prints and objects from the 14C to the present. Among the 16C masters are Veronese *(Perseus Rescuing Andromeda)* and Maarten van Heemskerk *(St Luke Painting the Portrait of the Virgin)*. The 17C is well represented (Rubens, Jordaens, and Champaigne) and masterpieces include **The Newborn**★ by Georges de La Tour. The 18C is exemplified by the works of Chardin *(The Basket of Plums; Peaches and Grapes)* and Greuze *(Portrait of a Young Girl)*.

In the 19C are canvases by Jongkind, Corot, Boudin and Sisley. Works of the members of the Pont-Aven School are also on display: Bernard *(Yellow Tree)*, Gauguin *(Oranges)*, Sérusier *(Solitude, Paysage d'Argoat)* and Georges Lacombe (**Wave Effect**★).

The last gallery displays 20C works by Laurent, Picasso, Utrillo, Vlaminck, Tanguy and contemporary artists such as de

Staël, Poliakoff and Asse. Old drawings, porcelain and fine Egyptian, Greek and Etruscan archaeological artefacts are also on show.

A small room presents works by 19C and 20C Breton painters who painted local landscapes and activities, such as Blin, Lemordant and Cottet.

Jardin du Thabor★★

Entrances at 5 blvd. de la Duchesse Anne and Place Ste-Mélaine. Open daily 7.30am–8.30pm, winter 7.30am–6pm. *02 99 67 11 11*

In the 16C the Benedictine abbey of St-Mélaine stood on an elevated site, beyond the city walls. The monks called the place Thabor in memory of the biblical Mount Tabor. The former orchards were transformed in the 19C to their present appearance by Bülher and Martenot and completed by the placing of Lenoir's statues. There are different flowers (roses, dahlias, chrysan-themums, camellias, rhododendrons) and trees (oak, beech, sequoia, cedar), spread over more than 10ha/25 acres, composed of a French garden, botanical garden, rose garden, landscaped garden, a grotto, lake and an aviary. There is a water fountain and public toilets.

EXCURSIONS
Châteaugiron

16km/10mi SE along D 463.

This old town, which was famous for its hemp sailcloth used for rated ships in the 17C, has preserved picturesque half-timbered houses (mainly in rue de la Madeleine) and an impressive fortified **castle**. The moat, 13C keep, which in the 14C was capped by a pepper-pot roof, and 15C clock tower next to the chapel are all that remain of the often-besieged castle. The living quarters, rebuilt in the 18C, house administrative offices. From boulevard du Château there is a full view of the castle and its site.

Château du Bois-Orcan

3km/1.2mi N on the D 92.

Guided tours 1 Jul–4 Sept, Tue –Sun 10am–noon, 2.30pm–5.30pm. *02 99 37 74 74.*

This 15C stone manor house has a large collection of old furniture. The interior and gardens also display the work of 20C artist Étienne Martin.

Écomusée du Pays de Rennes★

8km/5mi S of rue Maréchal-Joffre.

Open Apr–Sept, Tue–Fri 9am–6pm, Sat 2pm–6pm, Sun 2pm–7pm; Oct–Mar, 9am–noon, 2pm–6pm, Sat 2pm–6pm, Sun 2pm–7pm. Closed 16–31 Jan and public holidays. 4.60€ (children 6–14, 2.30€). *02 99 51 38 15.*
www.ecomusee-rennes-metropole.fr.

Located between city and country, the **Ferme de la Bintinais** was for a long time one of the largest properties around Rennes. The museum illustrates by means of a collection of tools and farming equipment, reconstituted interiors, costumes and other items the evolution of rural life on a farm, near an urban area from the 16C. There is also a display on earlier construction methods. Take a walk across the 15ha/37-acre estate and discover some of the many sights: gardens, beehives, orchards, and cultivated plots of land that illustrate the evolution of local farming techniques.

The botanical park is complemented by the presence of livestock: 14 country breeds of endangered farm animals. All these animals are characteristic of Brittany and its surrounding region: horses (Breton draught post-horses), cows (Pie Noire, Froment du Léon, Nantaise and Armoricaine), pigs (Blanc de l'Ouest and Bayeux), goats, sheep (from Ushant, Landes de Bretagne and the Avranchin) and poultry (La Flèche hens, the Coucou de Rennes and the famous Gauloise Dorée).

This museum also organises demonstrations and other celebrations – lettuce competition, harnessing contest for Breton draught horses, feast of the swine– as well as many other festive events testifying to the vivacity of Rennes' long-standing traditions and customs.

Montfort-sur-Meu

17km/10.6mi W along D 125.
This charming small town, built of local red stone, is located at the confluence of the Meu and Garun rivers.

Écomusée du Pays de Montfort

The regional museum, the **Écomusée du Pays de Montfort** (◔*open Apr–Sept, Mon–Fri 8.30am–noon, 2pm–6pm, Sat 10am–noon, 2pm–6pm, Sun and public holidays 2pm–6pm; Oct–Mar, Tue–Fri 8.30am–noon, 2pm–6pm, Sun and public holidays 2pm–6pm;* ◕*closed Mon, Sat, Sun in winter, 1 Jan and 25 Dec;* ◌*4€;* ☎*02 99 09 31 81; http://ecomuseepaysmontfort.free.fr/*) is housed in the 14C **Tour de Papegaut** (Papegaut Tower), all that remains of the medieval construction. It is named after a game of skill. A spiral staircase takes you up to the temporary and permanent exhibits held on the different floors, which present Montfort and its region (landscapes, folklore: collection of dolls in traditional costumes and headdresses). There is a fine view from the top of the tower.

🚗 DRIVING TOUR

VILAINE VALLEY

Round trip of 36km/22.5mi – allow 1hr.

▷ *Leave Rennes on D 177 towards Redon. Cross the river at Pont-Réan. As you leave the town, turn left.*

Bruz

This country town is an example of successful urban planning in rural surroundings with its tiny square on the north side of the beautiful **church**★ (1950), which is built of pink veined schist. The interior blends well; daylight enters on all sides through square panes of glass decorated with a picture of three fishes within a circle.

The apse has stained-glass windows depicting the Seven Sacraments, while in the two arms of the transept, windows depict scenes from the Crucifixion and the Virgin Mary. The organ is flanked on either side by the long, narrow stained-glass windows of unequal height that can be seen in the façade. North of Bruz at 53 Blvd. Pasteur is the **Parc Ornithologique de Bretagne** (◔*open Jul–Aug, daily 10am–noon, 2pm–7pm, Apr–Jun and Sept, 2pm–7pm, rest of the year Sun and public holidays 2pm–6pm;* ◌*6.50€;* ♿ ☎*02 99 52 68 57; www.parc-ornithologique.com*). It contains an interesting collection of more than 1,000 birds from every continent.

▷ *Continue S along D 577. The road crosses the river at Pont-Réan.*

Le Boël

You can enjoy a pleasant walk by the river, which runs between rocky hills in a verdant setting. A small lock and a dam link the west bank of the river to the old mill situated on the opposite bank.

▷ *Return to Pont-Réan and after crossing the bridge over the Vilaine, go right.*

ADDRESSES

🛏️ STAY

🍴 **Hôtel Arvor** – *31 av. Louis-Barthou.* ☎*02 99 30 36 47. www.arvorhotel.com. 16 rooms.* ⊑ *7.50€. Restaurant*🍴. Located near the train station, this hotel-restaurant has simple, functional rooms and a friendly bar. Ideal location for exploring the city on foot.

🍴🍴 **Hôtel des Lices** – *7 pl. des Lices.* ☎*02 99 79 14 81. www.hotel-des-lices.com. 45 rooms.* ⊑*8€.* In the centre of Old Rennes, these comfortable rooms with soundproofing are decorated with vivid colours and equipped with contemporary furniture. Free Wi-Fi.

🍴🍴 **Hôtel de Nemours** – *5 rue de Nemours.* ☎*02 99 78 26 26. www.hotel nemours.com. 29 rooms.* ⊑ *8.50€.* Very well located in a busy street near the République metro, this hotel's rooms are soundproofed and reached by a small lift. Attractive breakfast room.

🍴🍴 **Le Victoria** – *35 av. Jean Janvier.* ☎*02 99 31 69 11. www.hotel-levictoria.com. 40 rooms.* ⊑*8€. Restaurant*🍴. This hotel near the station has been rejuvenated.

Its clean rooms make for a convenient stay. A brasserie atmosphere prevails in the restaurant and frescoes depict a trip made by Queen Victoria.

Ar Milin' – *24km/15mi E of Rennes by N 136 then N 157 at 30 r. de Paris, 35220 Châteaubourg. ℘02 99 00 30 91. www.armilin.com. Closed 20 Dec–5 Jan and Sun eve. Nov–Feb. 32 rooms. ⌷12 €. Restaurant closed Tue–Sat lunch and Mon Jul–Aug.* Ar Milin', "the windmill" in Breton, has been converted into an attractive hotel. Choose between the intimate style of the rooms with period furniture in the main building or the more contemporary park hotel. Panoramic views from the restaurant.

ⵠEAT

Le Baron Rouge – *15–17 rue du Chapitre. ℘02 99 79 08 09. Closed Sun.* Original cuisine and a wild atmosphere where Bacchus himself is celebrated makes for a rustic and surprisingly charming dining experience.

Chez Kub – *20 r. du Chapitre ℘02 99 31 19 31. www.chezkub.fr. Closed Sun lunch and Mon.* Grilled specialities prepared on a wood stove in convivial surroundings close to the chimney. In good weather the terrace opens out onto the medieval street.

Crêperie des Portes Mordelaises – *6 rue des Portes Mordelaises. ℘02 99 30 57 40.* Opposite one of the old town gates and the house of Anne of Brittany: you couldn't dream of a better location to taste crêpes and *galettes* made with organic flour. Family atmosphere with a terrace in summer and a choice of wines.

Au Goût des Hôtes – *8 pl. Rallier-du-Baty. ℘02 99 79 20 36 . Closed 2 Jan.* Away from the hubbub of the Quartier de la Soif, this restaurant boasts an inventive menu sustained by quality ingredients and an excellent wine cellar.

Thé au Fourneau – *6 rue du Capitaine Alfred Dreyfus. ℘02 99 78 25 36. Closed third week of Aug and Sun.* Under the low ceiling of this welcoming 17C tea house, you will taste wonderful homemade pies, prodigious salads and, of course, an excellent choice of teas.

Le Café Breton – *14 rue Nantaise. ℘02 99 30 74 95. Closed Mon evenings, Sun, 3 weeks in Aug.* The haphazard décor of this restaurant has created both a popular and an energetic dining atmosphere. Good choice of salads, salted pies, gratins and delicious pastries.

Le Guehennec – *33 r. Nantaise. ℘02 99 65 51 30. www.leguehennec.com . Closed 2 weeks in Aug, Sat lunch, Mon eve and Sun.* Light coloured panelling and dark brown contemporary furnishings contribute to a warm welcome in this small restaurant. The gourmet menu is inspired by market produce.

Le Picca La Grande Brasserie de Rennes – *pl. de la Mairie. Open daily 8am–midnight. ℘02 99 78 17 17. www.lepicca.com.* This Rennes institution founded in 1832 welcomes clients from midday to midnight in its attractive dining room. Pleasant terrace backs onto the theatre.

Le Quatre B – *4 pl. Bretagne. ℘02 99 30 42 01. www.quatreb.fr. Closed Mon & Sat lunch and Sun.* Refined dining room with red banquettes, modern chairs and large, floral-themed canvasses. Pleasant terrace. The modern style successfully extends to the cuisine.

La Réserve – *36 r. de la Visitation. ℘02 99 84 02 02. www.lareserve-rennes.com. Closed Sun & Mon.* Quality traditional cuisine. Don't miss the foie gras, the mango and pineapple chutney or the crème brûlée with vanilla and bourbon!

ⵠNIGHTLIFE

A number of listings magazines (*Le Rennais, Contact Hebdo Spectacles* and *Spectacles Info*) are available from the Tourist Office. You'll also find *La Griffe* in the town's bars. A haven for students, Rennes naturally comes to life at night. Most of the area's night life is concentrated in the Old Town, on St-Malo, St-Georges and St-Michel streets, also known as the "district of the thirst." More relaxing, especially on fine days, are the terraces and restaurants of *rue Vasselot* and *rue Ste-Madeleine.*

Le Dejazey – *54 rue de St-Malo.* ✆*02 99 38 70 72. Open Mon–Sat 6pm–3am.* Mecca for lovers of jazz, rhythm and blues and Latin music.

Théâtre National de Bretagne – *1 rue St Hélier.* ✆*02 99 31 12 31. www.t-n-b.fr. Open Tue–Fri 1–7pm, Sat 2pm–6.30pm. Closed 13 Jul–22 Aug.* As the place where cultures meet, the TNB has distinguished itself by the quality and diversity of its theatrical and musical productions.

Le Triangle – *bd. de Yougoslavie.* ✆*02 99 22 27 27. www.letriangle.org. Open Mon–Sat 2pm–7pm, Wed 9am–7pm, Sat 10am–5pm. Closed 17 Jul–17 Aug, 25 Dec–1 Jan, public holidays.* This cultural centre offers contemporary dance as well as poetry and music.

Opéra de Rennes – *pl. de la Mairie.* ✆*02 99 78 48 78. www.opera-rennes.fr. Open Tue–Sat noon–7pm. Closed 14 Jul–6 Sept.*

☆ACTIVITIES

Bike hire – *Vélo à la Carte – Parc de la Vilaine.* ✆*02 99 79 65 88. Open daily.* Since 1998, it has been possible to hire bikes at no cost in Rennes. With a deposit and proof of identity, you can use a bike for two hrs. Go to quai Duguay-Trouin.

Boat trips – *Urbavag – rue du Canal St-Martin.* ✆*02 99 33 16 88 or 06 82 37 67 72. www.urbavag.com.* An original way to visit Rennes: on board electric boats on the Ille-et-Rance canal.

Étang d'Apigné – ✆*02 99 31 68 95.* This former sandpit on the way to Vannes has become a favoured green space of the Rennais. The outdoor leisure centre has a supervised beach (lake).

Swimming – *Piscine St-Georges – 2 rue Gambetta.* ✆*02 23 62 15 40. Open Tue and Fri 12am–2pm; Wed 8am–11am and 3pm–10pm; Thur 12am–2pm and 6pm–9pm; Sat 9am–1pm and 3pm–7pm; Sun 8.30am–1pm. Closed Aug.* ⊚*2.45€.* Opened in 1926, this swimming pool, with its blue-and-white tiles, is a fine example of the Art Deco era: enjoy a swim in the 33m/108ft pool overlooked by the changing rooms, evoking the bygone days of cruise ships.

☆ FESTIVALS AND EVENTS

Les Tombées de la Nuit ✆*02 99 32 56 56. www.tdn.rennes.fr. First full week in July.* For 25 years, this festival has produced performances (theatre, concerts, opera) across many sites in the town centre.

Transmusicales de Rennes ✆*02 99 31 12 10.* Three days of music and partying in early December.

☆ SHOPPING

Market *Marché des Lices – Place des Lices Sat 7am–1pm.* Whatever the season, you will find here the best farm products from across Brittany; above all, an unequalled choice of fish and seafood.

Pâtisserie Thierry Bouvier *21 rue de la Motte Picquet.* ✆*02 99 67 23 60. Mon–Sat 7am–8pm.* Taste the Parlementin, a Rennaise speciality made with apple compote and cider, or the delicious macaroons, a speciality of this popular pastry chef. The same artisan offers a line of chocolates at 5 rue de la Parchminerie.

Chocolaterie Durand *5 quai Chateaubriand.* ✆*02 99 78 10 00. www.durandchocolatier.fr. Closed Sun.* Behind the beautiful façade of this 19C Rennaise institution lurk about 30 unexpected chocolate flavours: *fleur de sel*, basil, spices....

Boulangerie Hoche *17 rue Hoche.* ✆*02 99 63 61 01. www.boulangerie-hoche.com. Closed Sun, 3 wks in Aug.* One of the best bakeries in Rennes. More than 80 different breads made with organic flour; especially delicious are the Viennese varieties.

Cellier St-Germain *3 rue du Vau-St-Germain.* ✆*02 99 79 36 82. Closed Mon, 3 weeks in Aug.* A good wine shop where someone will help you find your way among more than 2,000 labels.

Fromagerie St-Hélier *19 rue St-Hélier.* ✆*02 99 30 63 76. Closed Sun–Mon, mid-Jul–mid-Aug.* Excellent Breton butters and refined AOC cheeses.

Fougères★★

This former stronghold is built in a picturesque setting on a promontory overlooking the winding valley of the Nançon. Below it, on a rocky height almost entirely encircled by the river, stands a magnificent feudal castle whose walls and 13 towers are among the largest in Europe. The town centre (place Aristide-Briand, place du Théâtre, rue Nationale and the neighbouring streets) make up a pedestrian precinct. The Classical buildings in this area are the works of Gabriel.

▶ **Population:** 20,941.
- **Michelin Map:** 4 - ille-et-Vilaine (35).
- **Info:** 2 rue Nationale, 35300 Fougères. ℘02 99 94 12 20. www.ot-fougeres.fr.
- **Location:** On the eastern edge of Brittany, 49km/30mi NE of Rennes.
- **Timing:** A leisurely day is enough time to explore the town.
- **Parking:** In the town centre, the blue zones are free for 1hr 30min. Avoid the centre on Saturday mornings (market day). Car parks on the periphery.
- **Don't Miss:** The view of the château from the public gardens.

A BIT OF HISTORY

A frontier post – Standing on the border of Brittany and France, Fougères acquired great military importance in the early Middle Ages, when its barons were very powerful. The most famous was Raoul II. He lived in the mid 12C under Conan IV, known as "the Little", Duke of Brittany. This weak duke submitted to Henry II Plantagenet, King of England and Duke of Normandy, but the proud Raoul revolted against the English yoke. He formed a league with some of the Breton nobles and rebelled against Henry II. In 1166 Henry II surrounded Fougères, which capitulated after a three-month siege. The castle was completely demolished, but Raoul immediately began to rebuild it, and part of his work still stands.

In the 13C the fief passed to some Poitou noblemen, the Lusignans. They claimed to be descendants of the fairy Mélusine and gave her name to the finest of the towers that they added to the walls.

Though formidable, Fougères fortress was often taken. Among those who fought their way into it were St Louis, Du Guesclin, Surienne, (a leader from Aragon in the service of the English who took the city at night without striking a blow), La Trémoille, the Duke of Mercœur and the men of the Vendée.

After the union of Brittany and France, there was a succession of governors at Fougères; ten of its towers bear their names. The castle was then mainly used as a prison. In the 18C it became private property. The town bought it in 1892.

THE CHÂTEAU★★

83 Place Pierre Simon. Open Feb–Mar and Oct–Dec, 10am–12.30pm, 2pm–5.30pm; May, Jun and Sept, 10am–12.30pm, 2pm–7pm; Jul–Aug, 10am–7pm. Closed Mon, 25 Dec and Jan. Guided tours (45min) 7.50€. ℘02 99 99 79 59.

Château de Fougères

R. Mattès/MICHELIN

The château is a fine example of military architecture of the Middle Ages. There is an interesting general view from the public garden.

The site is curious: a loop in the river, washing a rocky eminence, shaped like a very narrow peninsula, formed an excellent defensive position. Military architects took advantage of this site to build ramparts and towers and turn the peninsula into an island by a short diversion of the Nançon at the base of the loop. As the château was connected with the upper town by the city ramparts, the garrison could take part in its defence; they also had the advantage of being able to retire into the fortress and hold it as a frontier post for the Duchy of Brittany should the town fall. The fortress has suffered greatly over the centuries, but the wall, with its curtains closely following the lie of the land and its 13 towers, is complete.

Unfortunately, we can no longer see the high keep that commanded all the defences; it was razed in 1166 by King Henry II of England and there are now only traces which can be seen when visiting the château's interior. The main buildings that occupied part of the inner court were also demolished down to their foundations at the beginning of the 19C. History tells us that the defenders often succumbed and that attackers were able to seize these high walls, either by surprise attack or after long sieges. An outer tour of the château shows the attackers' point of view; an inner tour, that of the defenders.

☙ WALKING TOUR
FORTIFICATIONS★

Park your car in place Raoul-II, skirt the fortifications, then go left along rue Le Bouteiller.

As you circle the walls you will see the splendid towers in all their variety of appearance and structure. At the start is the 14C **Guibé Turret** in the middle of the north rampart: a corbelled sentry-post built onto the wall.

Going round the spur formed by the ramparts towards the west, notice how massively the defences are concentrated at this point. The whole forms a triangle with two towers at the base and a postern at the apex. The 15C postern today looks out onto empty space, but it was once connected with a double arcade that crossed the moat to communicate with an outwork. The 13C and 14C **Gobelin Tower**, to the left of the postern, and the 14C **Mélusine Tower**, to the right, are round and overlook the walls from a height. Stripped of their machicolations and with their upper parts probably rebuilt, they have lost much of their proud aspect. The Mélusine Tower is regarded as a masterpiece of military architecture of the period; it is over 13m/42.5ft in diameter, with walls 3.5m/11.5ft thick and rising 31m/102ft above the rock.

Further on are two squat, horseshoe-shaped towers, the **Surienne** and the **Raoul**, which mark the last stage in the building of the castle (15C). Built to serve as platforms for artillery, they contain several storeys of very strong and well-preserved gun platforms. To resist enemy artillery fire, their walls are 7m/22ft thick. At the end of the 15C, artillery had been in use for nearly a century-and-a-half, and siege warfare often took the form of an artillery duel at short range.

◔ Opposite the two towers stands the Église St-Sulpice. On the right is the Marchix District (◔ see The Medieval District, p104).

Still following the walls, you will see the 13C Cadran Tower, two centuries older than the others. It is small, square and badly damaged, not nearly as strong as its neighbours and recalling the time when firearms had not yet taken the place of bows and arrows.

Further on, **Our Lady's Gate** is the only one left of the four rampart gateways preceding the four gates in the walls that encircled the town. The left-hand tower, which is higher and is pierced with narrow loopholes, dates from the 14C; that on the right, with very ornamental machicolations, dates from the 15C.

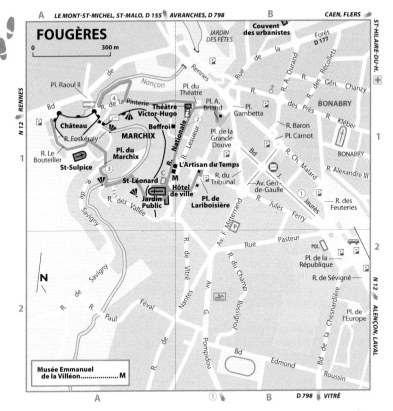

FOUGÈRES

0 ——— 300 m

Musée Emmanuel de la Villéon .... M

A LE MONT-ST-MICHEL, ST-MALO, D 155 — AVRANCHES, D 798 — *B* CAEN, FLERS

◐ *Go under the gate and follow rue de la Fourchette, then turn a sharp right onto rue de la Pinterie.*

Walk *(50m/55yds right)* through the gardens laid out along the reconstructed watch-path; there is a fine overall view of the Nançon Valley and the castle.

◐ *To leave the garden, go under the ruins of a beautiful chapel doorway and onto rue de la Pinterie on the left. This leads to the château entrance.*

Inside the château★★

The entrance, preceded by a moat filled from a diversion of the Nançon, is through the **square tower of La Haye-St-Hilaire.** To reach it, first go through a town gate and the wall before it. The castle has **three successive walls.** The *avancée* (advanced wall) was guarded by three 13C towers pierced with loopholes. When this line of resistance had

been crossed, attackers would enter a small courtyard on the island formed by a second diversion of the river, and would come under the converging fire of defenders posted on the four sides. Thus exposed, the attackers had to cross a second moat before reaching the main ring of fortifications, guarded by four towers dating from the 12C and 15C.

When both lines had been stormed, they would burst into the main inside courtyard where the **living quarters** and the **chapel** stood; but the defenders still had a chance to rally. A third position, the redoubt, girt with a wall and two towers, and the keep (demolished after the 12C), made a long resistance possible, and from these positions the garrison could still seek safety in flight through the postern.

Entering the main inside courtyard, go round the walls on the wall walk to appreciate the might of such a fortress and also to enjoy some good views of

Fougères. At the end of the highest wall of the castle is Mélusine Tower, which from the top (75 steps) commands a fine view of the castle and the town.

Further on are the remains of the keep and north wall, and beyond, the Guibé Turret and the Coigny Tower (13C and 14C), whose second and third storeys were turned into a chapel in the 17C. The summit was disfigured by the addition of a loggia during its first restoration in the 19C.

WALKING TOUR
UPPER TOWN

On leaving the chateau, take the promenade through the Val Nançon Gardens and you will come to a modern glass sculpture, *L'Œuvre à la Vie* by the artist Louis Marie-Catta, which was inaugurated in 2000 as a symbol of peace and representing all cultures.

Rejoin the rue de la Pinterie by the ruelle de Vaux and climb to the Place Aristide-Briand.

Place Aristide-Briand

Hôtel de la Belinaye, which presently houses the Magistrates' Court, was the birthplace of **Armand Taffin de la Rouërie** (a Breton hero). A statue was erected in 1993 to commemorate the bicentenary of his death.

Walk down rue Nationale.

Rue Nationale★

This is the town's most attractive street, with its 18C granite façades decorated with wrought-iron balconies. On the right as you walk down rue Nationale is an octagonal **Beffroi** (belfry), built in the 14C and 15C. It is decorated with gargoyles and topped by a slate-covered steeple.

L'Artisan du Temps – L'Atelier-Musée de l'Horlogerie

37 rue Nationale. Open 15 Jun–Aug, Tue–Sat 9am–noon, 2pm–7pm, Sun, Mon and public hols 2pm–6.30pm; Sept –14 Jun, Tue–Sat 9am–noon, 2pm–7pm. Closed Sun, Mon. Guided tours

(1hr 30min). 4.70€. 02 99 99 40 98. This small museum displays some 200 items presented by an enthusiastic clockmaker who keeps himself busy in his workshop.

Returning to rue Nationale, you'll see a square on the right.

Place de Lariboisière

This square is named after the **Comte de Lariboisière** (1759–1812), a native of Fougères and one of Napoleon's valiant officers, who died of exhaustion during the Russian campaign.

Musée Emmanuel de la Villéon

51 rue Nationale. Open mid-Jun–mid -Sept, 10.30am–12.30pm, 2pm–6pm. No charge. 02 99 99 19 98. The museum, located in a 16C house (restored), displays drawings and watercolours by **Emmanuel de la Villéon** (1858–1944), an Impressionist painter, born in Fougères who was inspired by the landscape and people of his native Brittany.

Église St-Léonard

The 15C–16C church at the bottom of rue Nationale has a richly decorated 16C north façade and a 17C tower. It is lit through modern stained-glass windows by Lorin; however, in the Chapel of the Cross, on the left as you go in, are two 12C scenes of St Benedict's life, and in the baptismal chapel pieces of 16C **stained-glass windows★**.

Adjacent is the 16C **Hôtel de Ville**, with a partly walled up Renaissance doorway (partly walled up).

Jardin Public★

This lovely garden, at the foot of the church of St-Léonard and the town hall, is laid out partly in terraces on the site of the former town walls and partly on the slopes down into the valley of the River Naçon. Follow the low wall that elongates the balustrade to the entrance for an extensive view of the woodlands typical of the Fougères region.

From the terrace closed off by the balustrade, there is an interesting general

view★ of the castle. *Steps lead from here to the castle and the river banks.*

Medieval District
Quartier du Marchix

This area around place du Marchix (the site of the former market at the heart of the old town), with its picturesque old houses, has always been of interest to painters. From rue Foskeraly, which skirts the Nançon, there are good views of the old ramparts now converted into a public garden. Take a walk along rue du Nançon with its 16C houses. There are other interesting houses at the corner of rue de la Providence and in rue de Lusignan.

On place du Marchix are two fine 16C houses, numbers 13 and 15. Take rue des Tanneurs to cross the bridge over the Nançon; looking back, you will see a picturesque group formed by the backs of the houses of place du Marchix.

Place de Marchix
G. Targat/MICHELIN

Église St-Sulpice★

12 ave. Général de Gaulle.
🕐 *Open daily. Free.*

A Gothic building in the Flamboyant style that, although erected between the 15C and the 18C, has great homogeneity. It has a slim 15C slate-covered steeple. The inside is enriched with 18C woodwork; but the 15C granite **altarpieces**★ in the chapels are the most noteworthy features.

The Lady Chapel (on the left) contains the altarpiece dedicated to Anne of Brittany, the church's donor. In the niche, underneath Brittany's coat of arms, is the miraculous 12C statue of the Nursing Virgin (Notre-Dame des Marais).

EXCURSIONS
Forêt Domaniale de Fougères

❯ *3km/1.8mi NE of the town centre. Leave Fougères on the D 177, the road to Flers.*

Those who like walking in a forest will spend hours strolling in the fine beech woods, along the forest roads. Notice the two dolmens in ruins and a line of megalithic stones called the Cordon des Druides (Druids' Cord)near the Carrefour de Chennedet (Chennedet crossroads).

At Landéan, on the edge of the forest, near the Carrefour de la Recouvrance (Recouvrance crossroads) are the 12C cellars (⊶ *closed*) once used as a secret hideout by the lords of Fougères.

Parc Floral de Haute-Bretagne★

❯ *Le Châtelier, 10km/6.2mi NW. Leave Fougères heading N on D 798 (towards St-James) until you reach D 19, then turn left and follow the signs.*
🕐*Mar–Jun and Sept–mid-Nov 10am–noon and 2pm–6pm, Sun and Public Hols 10.30am–6.30, Jul–Aug 10.30am–6.30pm.* 🕐*Closed mid-Nov–Feb.*
♿*9.80€.* ♿ 📞*02 99 95 48 32. www.parcfloralbretagne.com.*

The grounds of the Château de la Folletière have been laid out as a floral park. A discovery trail links the dozen gardens with evocative names (1001 nights garden, the city of Cnossus), offering a year-round festival of colour and fragrance.

ADDRESSES

STAY

FOUGÈRES

Balzac Hôtel – *15 rue Nationale.* $\mathscr{C}$*02 99 99 42 46. www.balzachotel.fr. 22 rooms.* Spa *6€.* Traditional hotel in an 18C house, with elegant rooms, a spa and a wellness centre. Cordial welcome.

SURROUNDING AREA

Chambres d'hôte La Haute Bourdière – *Landéan. 8km/5mi NE of Fougères by the D177.* $\mathscr{C}$*02 99 97 21 52. www.haute-bourdiere.com. 5 rooms. Restaurant.* Renovated farm with individually styled rooms, including a unit for up to six people. Be sure to reserve for dinner.

Chambre d'hôte Ferme de Mésauboin – *35133 Billé. 10km on the D 179 via Billé then the D 23.* $\mathscr{C}$*02 99 97 61 57. www.ferme-de-mesauboin.com. Closed two weeks in Mar and Oct. 5 rooms. included. Restaurant.* The calm and tranquility of this 17C farm should ensure a relaxing break in the country. Enjoy regional produce and comfortable beds in the B&B or one of the two gîtes.

EAT

FOUGÈRES

La Table de Cueillette – *1 rue Lesueur.* $\mathscr{C}$*02 99 99 60 38. Closed Wed and Sun Jul–Sept.* Welcoming tea shop to enjoy sweet or savoury tarts and excellent English teas.

Ti Vabro – *13 Place du Marchix.* $\mathscr{C}$*02 99 17 20 90. Closed Sun evening and Mon.* In a half-timbered house in the medieval district, this *crêperie* offers a menu of 15 ciders to enjoy with well- made crêpes.

Crepêrie Les Remparts – *102 rue de la Pinterie.* $\mathscr{C}$*02 99 94 53 53. Closed Feb school hols and Thu off season.* Two steps from the château, one of the oldest houses in town hides a traditional *crêperie*, with a terrace on fine days offering a beautiful view.

La Haute Sève – *37 blvd. Jean Jaurès.* $\mathscr{C}$*02 99 94 23 39. www.lehaute seve.fr. Closed 1–28 Jan, 9–19 Feb, 22 Jul– 22 Aug, Sun eve and Mon.* Behind the half-timber façade, you will find a welcoming art-clad dining room where inventive, market-fresh cuisine is served.

NIGHTLIFE

Le Coquelicot – *18 rue de Vitré.* $\mathscr{C}$*02 99 99 84 52. http://barlecoquelicot.free.fr. Closed Sun, Mon and mid-Jul–mid-Aug.* The liveliest night-spot in Fougères, this warm bar regularly schedules musical nights.

Café de Paris – *9 Place Aristide Briand.* $\mathscr{C}$*02 99 94 39 38.* Small pub in the town centre with musical nights in summer.

SHOPPING

Market – In the streets of the upper town on Saturday morning.

Lecourtiller – *21 Place Aristide Briand.* $\mathscr{C}$*02 99 99 38 70. Closed Mon and Sun afternoon. La Gâche,* a flat cake made with bread pastry, and the *Beffroi,* a meringue with hazelnut cream, are the specialities of this well-known pattisserie.

La Galette du Beffroi – *41 rue Nationale.* $\mathscr{C}$*02 99 99 31 23. Closed Sun and Mon.* Cakes, Breton far, cupcakes and apple cakes.

ACTIVITIES

Ferme de Chênedet – *7km/4.3mi N of Fougères, 35133 Landéan.* $\mathscr{C}$*02 99 97 35 46. www.chenedet-loisirs.com. Open 9am–6pm.* In the heart of the forest, this activity centre offers horse-riding, water-based activities and motorbike rental all year round. There's also accommodation available in four gîtes.

TOURS

Fougères is a designated "Ville d'art et d'histoire" and the Tourist Office provides guided tours (1hr 30mins) of the town from mid-Jun to mid-Sept at 3pm. You can also explore the town by following the "literary circuit" or take the little tourist train. Ask for details in the Tourist Office.

Vitré★★

This is the best-preserved "old world" town in Brittany; its fortified castle, its ramparts and its small streets have remained just as they were 400 or 500 years ago, giving the town a picturesque and evocative appeal that is long remembered. The old town is built on a spur, commanding the deep valley of the Vilaine on one side and a railway cutting on the other; the castle stands proudly on the extreme point. From the 15C to the 17C, Vitré was one of the more prosperous Breton cities; it made hemp, woollen cloth and cotton stockings that were sold not only in France, but also in England, Germany, Spain and even America and the Indies. Gathered together to form the powerful brotherhood known as "Marchands d'Outre-Mer", the Vitré tradesmen of this period commissioned the building of highly distinctive houses with half-timbering, many of which can still be seen today.

CHÂTEAU★★

Open Apr–Sept, daily 10.30am–12.30pm, 2pm–6.30 pm; Oct–Mar daily except Tue and Sun am, 10.30am–12.15pm, 2–5.30pm. Guided tours

- **Population:** 16,156.
- **Info:** place du Gen.-de-Gaulle, 35500 Vitré. ℘02 99 75 04 46. www.ot-vitre.fr.
- **Location:** Situated at the intersection of the D 857 and D 178.
- **Timing:** Allow a day and half to visit Vitré and the surrounding area.
- **Don't Miss:** A visit to the château and the medieval district below it.

available. Closed 1 Jan, Easter Sun, 1 Nov and 25 Dec. 4€ (combined ticket for 3 museums). ℘02 99 75 04 46. www.mairie-vitre.fr.

The château, dating from the 11C, was rebuilt from the 13C to the 15C. The entrance is guarded by a drawbridge and entrance fort (Châtelet) flanked by two big machicolated towers. At the south corner stands the main keep or Tour St-Laurent; at the northeast corner stands the Madeleine Tower, and at the northwest corner, the Montafilant Tower. These various works are linked by a wall, reinforced by other towers. As you enter the courtyard, you will see on the right a Romanesque porch (**1**)

Façade, Château de Vitré

G. Targat/MICHELIN

with archstones alternating in colour (red granite and black schist), the town hall (1913) abutting on the north front, and before you, the Oratoire Tower with an elegant Renaissance chapel (**2**).

From the platform of the Montafilant Tower *(82 steps)* there is a fine **view**★ of the town, the Tertres Noires and Moines Quarters, the River Vilaine and the old tannery.

The St-Laurent Tower houses the Musée St-Nicolas, which contains 15C and 16C sculpture from the houses of Vitré (a beautiful chimney has been remounted), the 15C tomb of Gui X (a local lord) as well as 16C Flemish and 17C Aubusson tapestries.

The Argenterie Tower presents exhibits of the region's natural history.

Via the curtain wall you arrive at the Oratoire Tower. In its chapel is a beautiful 16C **triptych**★ decorated with 32 Limoges enamels.

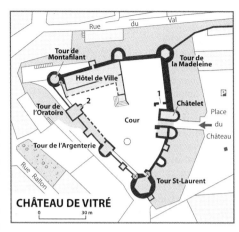

CHÂTEAU DE VITRÉ

🐾 WALKING TOUR
TOWN CENTRE★

🔖 *Starting from place du Château, take rue Notre-Dame and turn right.*

Rue de la Baudrairie★★

This, the most curious street in Vitré, gets its name from *baudroyeurs* (leather craftsmen).

Turn right on to Rue d'En Bas, a street that used to lead to the gate (partly destroyed in 1846) of the same name. It is lined with half-timbered houses; note number 10, the former **Hôtel du Bol d'Or** (1513).

🔖 *At the end of the street, turn left along Promenade St-Yves and continue to place du Général-de-Gaulle then turn left onto rue Garangeot.*

As you cross rue Sévigné, note number 9, a 17C mansion *(restoration work in progress)* known as "Tour de Sévigné", home to the famous writer.

🔖 *Turn right.*

Rue Poterie

Picturesque houses: some half-timbered, some with porches. Note in particular the **Maison de l'Île**, on the corner of *rue* Sévigné.

🔖 *From place du Marchix on the left, turn right onto rue Notre-Dame, which leads to place de la République.*

Ramparts★

From place de la République you will see one of the old rampart towers, the 15C Bridolle Tower (note the machicolations, openings through which rocks could be dropped on attackers). On the south side of the town the walls follow the line, at a little distance, of the present rue de la Borderie and place St-Yves and then join the castle. Only fragments remain, built into private properties. On the north and east sides the ramparts are still intact. Old houses line rue de Paris, which leads into place de la République.

🔖 *Go through the gate in promenade du Val to circle the ramparts. At the end of the alley, after passing a gate, take the ramp to the left, which passes under the St-Pierre postern; follow rue du Bas-Val uphill and turn right in the square, then left into rue Notre-Dame.*

Église Notre-Dame★

🕐Open 9am–7pm (if closed, call ☎02 99 74 52 30).

The church is 15C–16C. Outside, the most curious part is the south side, with its seven gables decorated with pinnacles and its pulpit from which preachers addressed the congregation assembled on the small square.

Inside, you will see many altarpieces and a fine Renaissance stained-glass window in the south aisle (third bay) depicting Christ's Entry into Jerusalem.

At number 27 rue Notre-Dame is the former Hôtel Hardy or de la Troussanais (16C) with its finely carved porches and dormer windows.

▷ *Return to place du Château.*

ADDITIONAL SIGHTS

Tertres Noirs★★

Access by rue de Brest and chemin des Tertres Noirs, to the right after the bridge over the Vilaine.

There is a fine **view**★★ of Vitré town centre and its castle from this shaded terrace.

Public garden★

Entrances on blvd. de Roches, blvd. de Châteaubriand and Champs de Foire.

A pleasant, well-kept, English-style garden.

Faubourg du Rachapt

During the Hundred Years' War, this suburb was occupied for several years by the English, while the town and the château resisted all their attacks. The people of Vitré paid the invaders to go away: hence the name of the suburb (*rachapt* means repurchase).

Lying at the foot of the castle, the area crosses the Vilaine Valley and rises on the north slope. Follow rue Pasteur, which affords picturesque views of the river and the **Pré des Lavandières**. Rue Pasteur leads to the **Musée St-Nicolas** (*enter by the little door on the left and skirt the chapel;* 🕐*open Apr–Sept, daily 10.30am–12.30pm, 2pm–6.30pm, Oct–Mar daily except Tue and Sun am,* 10.30am–12.15pm, 2–5.30pm; 🕐*closed 1 Jan, Easter Sun, 1 Nov and 25 Dec.;* ◉4€ *(combined ticket for 3 museums);* ☎02 99 75 04 46; www.mairie-vitre.fr.) The 15C chapel has retained original murals and now houses a museum of sacred art. The gilt-wood high altar is from the 18C.

EXCURSIONS

Champeaux★

▷ *Leave Vitré by the D857 towards Châteaubourg and Rennes. After 2km/ 1.25mi turn right onto the D29 for 9km/5.75mi.*

The **village square**★ forms a harmonious scene with its collegiate church, its small town hall with a large hipped roof, and the few houses (former canons' residences) around an old well.

Collégiale – This 14C and 15C collegiate church, with a single nave, has some fine Renaissance canopied **stalls**★ and an elegant door, of the same period, which opens onto the sacristy, the former chapter-house. To the left of the high altar and in a chapel to the left of the chancel are two stone and marble mausolea (1551–4) belonging to the d'Espinay family, who founded the church.The two handsome Renaissance **stained-glass windows**★, made in Rennes, are noteworthy: depicted in the apse is the Passion of Christ and in the sacristy the sacrifice of Abraham. In the nave, the south chapel contains a 17C altarpiece recounting scenes of the Passion and the north chapel is adorned with a 14C Virgin.

🧗 Parc du Boiscornillé

5km/3mi N of Champeaux by way of Val-d'Izé. 🕐*Open Jul–Sept, 10am–7pm.* ◉3€. ♿ ☎06 07 79 11 32.

The Bülher brothers, well-known landscape artists of the time, designed this park in 1872. Later, Edouard André used terraces to create different vantage points to view the grounds, as well as separate the meadows from the more formal, planted areas beloved by the aristocratic inhabitants. The result is a park with the formal lines of a French garden and a touch of fantasy typical of an English garden.

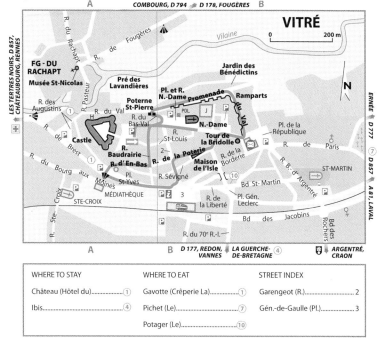

🚗 DRIVING TOUR

COUNTRY OF LEGENDS

Itinerary of 80km/50mi - half a day.
Leave Vitré by the D88 in the direction of
Argentré-du-Plessis. As you leave the
Argentré-du-Plessis wood, take l'allée
du château on the left.

Château des Rochers-Sévigné

Rte d'Argentré-du-Plessis. ℘ 02 99 75
04 46. ☜ Guided tours available.
Ⓧ Closed 1 Jan, Easter Sun, 1 Nov and
25 Dec. ☞ 4€ (combined ticket for 3
museums). ℘ 02 99 75 04 46.
www.mairie-vitre.fr.

The Rochers-Sévigné Château, which
was the home of the Marquise de
Sévigné (1626–96), is a place of literary
interest. Admirers of her famous letters
will enjoy visiting the castle, an unusual
octagonal chapel and the surrounding
grounds.

The château was built in the 15C and
remodelled in the 17C. It consists of
two wings set at right angles. In addition to the chapel built in 1671 for the

"exemplary" abbot of Coulanges (the
marquise's maternal uncle), two rooms
in the large north tower are open to
visitors. That on the ground floor was
the Cabinet Vert (Green Room). It still
contains some of Mme de Sévigné's
personal possessions, family pictures
and her portrait; there is a collection of
autographs and documents in a glass
case. The 16C chimney piece is adorned
with the Marquise's initials (Marie de
Rabutin-Chantal – MRC).

In the French-style **garden**, rearranged following 1689 designs by Le
Nôtre, is the semicircular wall that
Mme de Sévigné called "that little wall
that repeats words right into your ear"
because of its double echo (stones mark
the places where the two conversation-
alists should stand). Beyond the garden
lies the large, wooded **park**, which
is crossed by avenues, the names of
which recall the Marquise and her literary environment: the Mall, the Lone
Wolf, Infinity.

▶ *Take the D88 S, then at Cuillé turn*
right on the D32.

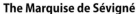

The Marquise de Sévigné

Château des Rochers-Sévigné

© Richard Semik/Dreamstime.com

The Marquise stayed frequently in Rochers, mainly for economic reasons: her husband and son had squandered most of her fortune. From 1678, she was there almost continually but she died at her daughter's house in Grignan (Drôme) in 1696. Her letters allow us to see how she lived at Rochers. Get up at 8am, mass at 9am, walk, lunch. Afternoon: sewing, walk, chatting, correspondence. Her son Charles sometimes used to read to her for five hours! Dinner at 8pm. The Marquise retired to her bedroom at 10pm, where she read or wrote until midnight.

La Guerche-de-Bretagne

North of the forest of the same name, La Guerche is crossed by the D178. Allow half a day, and try to coincide your visit with market day (Tues).

This small town (pop. 4,095), once a manorial estate with Du Guesclin as its overlord, still retains some old houses and an interesting church. An important fair and market has been held since 1211 around the town hall and the squares in the town centre.

Only the chancel, with its triple-sided apse, and the Romanesque tower, with its massive buttresses, remain from the original **church** building erected in 1206. The nave and south aisle were rebuilt in the 16C; the north aisle and the bell-tower, with openings at the top, date from the end of the 19C. Note the splendid 16C stalls with their amusing Gothic misericords – the carved decoration of the woodwork is clearly of the time of Henri II (1547–59) – and the remains of the 15C and 16C stained-glass windows in the south aisle.

▷ *Leave La Guerche by the D463 in the direction of Rennes, then at Vissieche take the D48 on the left to Marcillé-Robert. Proceed through the village then take the D107 on the left towards Retiers along the second branch of the lake. After 800m turn right in the direction of Thiel and 3km/2mi further on turn right again. 800m/0.5mi later you will come to la Roche-aux-Fées.*

Roche-aux-Fées★

This is one of the finest megalithic monuments in Brittany, dating from the Middle Neolithic period (fourth millennium BC) when it would have been surrounded by forest.

Built in purple schist, it consists of 42 stones, of which six weigh between 40t and 45t. There is a massive portico entrance with a perfectly horizontal lintel and a low-slung corridor leading to a large, very high compartmented room (14m/46ft long, 4m/13ft wide, 2m/6.5ft high). Scientists have established that these huge stones were moved over a distance of 4km/2.5mi. According to legend, this was done by fairies who simply put the stones in their aprons!

▷ *Return to Retiers via the D47.*

Retiers

The church In this charming village contains five paintings and three 17C and 18 restored wooden sculptures.

▷ *You can return to La Guerche via Arbrissel and Rannée along the D 47, then the D 178.*

ADDRESSES

STAY

VITRÉ AND SURROUNDINGS

Hôtel du Château – *5 rue Rallon. 02 99 74 58 59. 24 rooms. 8€. Closed Nov holidays.* In the heart of Old Town, this hotel offers cosy rooms; some even with castle-views. Breakfast is served on the patio in summer.

Ibis – *1 bd Chateaubriant. 02 99 75 51 70. www.ibishotel.com. 50 rooms. 7.50 €.* Located in the centre of Vitré, with the Jardin du Parc gardens nearby. Wi-Fi internet access and a terrace where you can enjoy breakfast.

EAT

VITRÉ

Le Potager – *5 Place du Gén. Leclerc. 02 99 74 68 88. www.restaurant-le potager.fr. Closed Mon, Sun eve and 2 weeks in Aug.* Everything from the vegetables to the decoration of the dining room deserves praise here for its colour. Fresh and inventive cuisine. Located near the station.

Le Pichet – *17 blvd. de Laval. 02 99 75 24 09. www.lepichet.fr. Closed 28 Jul –13 Aug, Wed and Thu eves, and Sun. Reservations necessary.* A pleasant terrace opens onto a garden during the summer, and a comfortable room with a fireplace offers warmth on colder days. Inspired by the market, the menu features produce of the sea most prominently.

Crêperie La Gavotte – *7 r. des Augustins (dir. Fougères). 02 99 74 47 74. Closed Mon.* Traditional galettes made with black flour can be washed down with regional ciders in this traditionally decorated restaurant situated at the foot of the Château.

LA GUERCHE-DE-BRETAGNE AND SURROUNDINGS

La Calèche – *16 av. du Gén. Leclerc. 02 99 96 21 63. www.lacaleche.com. 12 rooms. Restaurant . Closed first 3 weeks Aug, Fri and Sun eves and Mon.* This immense house offers functional and renovated rooms and a well-known restaurant.

NIGHTLIFE

The rue d'En-Bas is the street of bars and restaurants. Particularly lively at night are **Aston Bar** and the **Nain Jaune**.

Bar du Château des Rochers de Sévigné – *02 99 96 52 52. www.vitre-golf.com. Closed 25 Dec–3 Jan and Mon in winter.* You don't need to be a member of the golf club to enjoy a drink in the bar, formerly the old stables, of the château. Lovely view from the terrace.

ACTIVITIES

Walks – Guided walking tours around Vitré are available from the Tourist Office. A smooth 20km/12.4mi path along the old railway from Vitré to Moutiers is pleasant by foot or by bike.

Rent a bike – Cycles Dufeu – *6 rue de Paris. 02 99 75 01 41.*

Water sports – ANCPV – *Bassin de Haute Vilaine. 02 99 76 74 41. Open daily 9am–noon, 2pm–5pm. Closed winter.* This water sports centre offers courses and lessons in windsurfing and rowing. Possibility of hiring equipment.

Picnic – The Pré de Lavandières is an open space ideal for a picnic opposite the old wash-houses. The other possibility is the Jardin du Parc, an English-style public garden with a bandstand.

FESTIVALS

The concerts and shows of the **Festival du Bocage** bring Vitré and its surroundings to life from 30 Jun to 15 Jul. Jazz-lovers follow the tempo during **Jazz in Vitré**, the first week of Mar.

SHOPPING

Markets – Vitré, Mon morning place du Marchix. Small market Sat morning, rue de la Poterie. **La Guerche-de-Bretagne**, Tue morning (fowl and farm products).

Jarno – *50 rue Poterie. 02 99 75 06 23.* Good pastries and bread specialities.

Redon

Redon, the centre of an active region, is the meeting point of three *départements* (Ille-et-Vilaine, Loire-Atlantique and Morbihan) and two regions (Brittany and Pays de Loire). In Redon, the River Vilaine and the Nantes–Brest Canal converge at the pleasure boat harbour (tourism on inland waterways).

▶ **Population:** 9, 601.
◈ **Michelin Map:** Local map 309 J9 – Ille-et-Vilaine (35).
▪ **Info:** pl. de la République, 35600 Redon. ℘02 99 71 06 04. www.tourisme-pays-redon.com.
◔ **Timing:** Allow two hours to visit the town then take a walk along the river Vilaine or the Nantes-Brest canal.
◈ **Don't Miss:** The tower of St-Saveur church.

SIGHTS

Église St-Sauveur
◔*Open 9am–6pm.*
This former abbey church, founded in 832, was a great pilgrimage centre throughout the Middle Ages until the 17C. This accounts for the impressive size of the building. In 1622 Richelieu was the commendatory abbot. It was cut off from its 14C Gothic bell-towers (H) by a fire in 1780. A remarkable Romanesque sandstone and granite **tower**★ stands at the transept crossing. From the neighbouring **cloisters** (17C), occupied by the College of St Saviour, the superimposition of its arcades can be seen. From the esplanade planted with chestnut trees and overlooking rue Richelieu, one has a good view of the chevet and buttresses. The **interior** reveals a dimly lit low nave (11C) with wood vaulting separated from the side aisles by flat pillars. Note the carved pillars in the transept crossing; they support the octagonal stone vaulting.

The Old Town
The old town contains elegant 15C–18C town houses (◈*see tour marked on map opposite*). Leave from the Église St-Sauveur and walk along **Grande Rue,** noting numbers 22, 25, 38, 44, 52 and 54; look down rue d'Enfer and rue Jeanne-d'Arc. Cross the flower-decorated bridge that spans the Nantes–Brest Canal.
In **rue du Port** across from number 6, Hôtel Carmoy, are three corbelled houses. Go onto **rue du Jeu-de-Paume**, which has, at number 10, the old customs barracks, a four-storey building with a severe façade and a wall with a scene of swineherds and fishmongers dressed in costumes of the past. Return to rue du Port where old salt houses (number 40) can be seen; occupying number 3 **rue du Plessis** is the Hôtel Richelieu.
Quai Duguay-Trouin is lined with stately shipowners' homes of which numbers 15, 7, 6 and 5 are particularly worth looking at. Return to the church by way of **Quai St-Jacques**, where ramparts in ruins still stand.

EXCURSIONS

Massérac
▷ *15km/9.3mi E along D 775. Turn right towards Avessac.*
Lying at the confluence of the Vilaine and the Don rivers, this municipality is rich in wetlands (800ha/1,977 acres). The **Maison des Marais, de la Chasse et de la Pêche** (◔*open Jun–Sept, 2pm–6pm;* ⬭*1€* ♿*;* ℘*02 40 87 20 35*) offers insight into the lifestyle of waders, fish and other animals living in the ecosystem. Inside, the displays and films are informative, and guided walking tours (45min) can be arranged.

St-Gildas-des-Bois
▷ *19km/12mi south via the D164 then the D 77.*
Constructed in reddish brown sandstone, this ancient 12C and 13C Romanesque abbey, remodelled in the 19C, restored after the bombings of 1944 and fitted with modern windows by Maurice Rocher. See the beautiful 18C furniture, wrought-iron railings, remnants of the

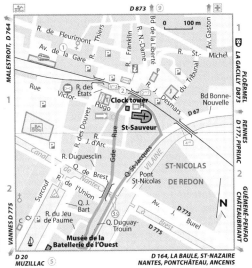

REDON

WHERE TO STAY

Queen Serenity Hotel..........①

WHERE TO EAT

Bogue (La).....................②

Gaudence (Le)..................⑤

Moulin de Via (Le)..............⑨

old choir wall, and the stalls and the interior porch in sculpted wood.

🚗 DRIVING TOUR

On the Road to Rennes

Itinerary of 48km/30mi, so allow half a day.

▷ *Leave Redon by the D177 in the direction of Rennes. At Renac, take the D55 in the direction of Langon. After Langon turn immediately left before the railway. The Manoir de la Chaussée is the first house on the left.*

Jardin anglais du manoir de la Chaussée

🕐*Daily 10am–6pm.* 🎫*5€.* 📞*02 99 08 64 41. www.chateau-france.co.uk.*
This garden offers a perfumed and colourful walk along pathways snaking through water courses and cascades, selections of small shrubs, a rose garden, box hedges and under trees.

▷ *From Port-de-Roche, take the D54 in the direction of St-Just.*

🚶 St-Just

19km/12mi NE.
▷ *Leave Redon on the D177 towards Rennes and turn left to St-Just.*

This small town lies at the centre of an area rich in **megaliths** (dating from c.3500 BC) and there are many interesting rambles starting from St-Just. A way-marked path lead to **Landes de Cojoux (**Cojoux Moor, megalith). From here there is a lovely view of the Étang de Val (rock-climbing).

▷ *Take the D177 in the direction of Rennes until Lohéac, then turn left onto the D772.*

Manoir de l'Automobile à Lohéac★★

Lohéac is near the D 177, which links Rennes (38km/23.6mi N) and Redon (31km/19.3mi S). Coming from Rennes take the D 772 towards Maure-de-Bretagne: the museum is on the D 50 towards Lieuron. 🕐*Open Jul–Aug 10am –7pm; Sept–Jun Tue–Sun 10am–1pm, 2pm–7pm.* 🎫*8.50€; children 7€.* ♿. 📞*02 99 34 02 32. www.manoir-automobile.fr.*

This **Motor Museum,** set up in La Courneuve manor house, contains a collection of more than 160 cars of all types, ages and nationalities, specializing particularly in private and sports cars.
The tour begins in the old manor house, taking in a collection of "golden oldies" from the turn of the century, before

moving on to an impressive line-up of Alpines (A210 Le Mans, Coach A106, Berlinette Tour de France A108, A110 GT4, A310 1600 VE).

Further on, there are examples of essentially the whole Lamborghini production (from the 350 GT to the Diablo). Dozens of Maseratis, Ferraris, Porsches and Rolls-Royces rub fenders with Dauphine Renaults, R8s or R12s, Citroëns, Peugeots (convertibles 301–403, from the 1960s and 70s) and Volkswagens.

The next stop on the tour is the **Chapelle des Moteurs** (Engine Chapel), an original display of several vintage engines in an old chapel.

Other features of the museum include the reconstructions of a forge, a garage and an old-fashioned filling station fully equipped with tools, materials and authentic equipment connected with vehicle repair and maintenance.

The spacious first floor houses an exhibition of lavish foreign cars known as the *belles étrangères*, and at the end of it is a wall of illuminated signs bearing the names of leading manufacturers associated with the motor industry.

The area devoted to miniature models relates the glorious history of the steam engine, illustrated by more than 3,000 exhibits.

Espace hippomobile is devoted to some 50 horse-drawn carriages of all types: travelling coaches, omnibus, etc. To finish your visit, take a seat in the projection room, and imagine yourself behind the wheel.

Adults can book a spin in a racing car with an experienced racing driver around the adjacent track. Follow it up with a crêpe and a cider in the bar before stopping off in the shop to buy some souvenirs.

To prolong this drive, see also the itinerary for the Vallée de la Vilaine, p97.

ADDRESSES

STAY

REDON

Queen Serenity Hotel – *16 av. de la Gare. ☎ 02 99 71 13 20. www.hotel redon.com. 20 rooms. ☐ 6.10 €.* Pleasant, comfortable rooms, some of which are individually decorated according to travel themes. The hotel is equipped with free internet access, bike hire, a bar and a room for breakfast. A conference room is available inside the hotel. Convenient central location opposite Redon railway station.

AROUND REDON

Château du Plessis Anger – *35550 Lieuron-Lohéac. ☎ 02 99 34 08 04. www.chateauduplessisanger.com.* Old hunting lodge in a park of 80ha/198acres convenient for the Lohéac motor museum. All rooms are tastefully decorated. In the wood can be found the remains of old moats and corner towers, a dovecote and a chapel. A superb pepperpot tower completes the ensemble.

EAT

Le Gaudence – *2 rue de Redon, 56350 Allaire. 9km/15.6mi W of Redon on the D 775 rte de Vannes. ☎ 02 99 71 93 64. www.hotel-legaudence.com. Closed Christmas holidays, Sun and Fri.* A useful address on the rte de Vannes. The outside is nothing to look at but the dining room has been recently redecorated and offers good regional cuisine.

La Bogue – *3 rue des États. ☎ 02 99 71 12 95. labogue@wanadoo.fr. Closed Sun eve and Mon.* Welcoming rustic dining room where you can taste the cuisine of the renowned Mr Chefdor. In autumn and winter, the famous *bogue* (Redon chestnut) finds its way into many dishes.

Le Moulin de Via – *3km/2mi rte de La Gacilly on the D 177 and D 873. ☎ 02 99 71 05 16. http://lemoulindevia.fr. Closed Tue eve, Mon eve and Sun.* Traditional cuisine in an old mill.

TOURS

The Tourist Office sells brochures of the footpaths in the Redon country (2–5€). Guided tours of the area in summer.

Forêt de Paimpont★

The Forest of Paimpont – the ancient Brocéliande where, according to the songs of the Middle Ages, the sorcerer Merlin and the fairy Viviane lived – is all that remains of a huge forest that for centuries covered a vast expanse of inner Brittany. Sustained logging has reduced the forest to its current 7,067ha/27.3sq mi, of which 500ha/1.93sq mi belong to the state. Recently, large areas have been replanted with conifers, which will increase the industry of the massif. A few charming corners remain, especially in the vicinity of the many streams and lakes.

EXCURSIONS

École de St-Cyr-Coëtquidan

16km/10mi E of Ploërmel on the D 724.
This military academy houses training schools for elite officers of the land forces: the *École Spéciale Militaire*, founded in 1802 by Napoleon Bonaparte, commonly known as St-Cyr or Coët in military circles; the *École Militaire Interarmes*, founded in 1961 by Général de Gaulle; the *École Militaire du Corps Technique et Administratif*, founded in 1977 by Giscard d'Estaing, and the *Bataillion des Élèves-Officiers en Réserve*.

Musée du Souvenir★

Open daily Feb–Dec (except Mon) 10am–noon, 2.30–6pm. Closed public holidays. 4€. *No charge 1st Sun of month.* 02 97 70 77 49.
This museum is famed for its memorial "La France" by Antoine Bourdelle in honour of 17,000 officers killed in action. It retraces the history of officer training from the *Ancien Régime* to today and contains documents, uniforms and military decorations of the elite.

St-Méen-le-Grand

20km/12.4mi N of Paimpont on the D 773 then the D 166 from Gaël.
In the 6C, St Méen (Mewan), a monk from Great Britain, founded an abbey on

Michelin Map: Local map 309 I6 Ille-et-Vilaine (35)

Info: Esplanade Brocéliande, 35380 Paimpont. 02 99 07 84 23.

Location: The forest is found between the N 24 and D 766, 30km W of Rennes.

Timing: Make time for lunch on the banks of Forges de Paimpont lake.

Don't Miss: Walks in the Val to immerse yourself in Breton legends.

this site, which was reconstructed several times from the 11C to the 18C. The abbey buildings now contain flats. The church retains a fine 12C square **tower**. Note the tombstone in the south aisle and, in the south transept, the statue and funerary monument of St Méen, all from the 15C. Some 13C and 14C frescoes recently discovered beneath the plasterwork, are currently undergoing restoration.

Musée Louison Bobet

5 rue de Gaël. *Open 2pm–5pm Closed Tue (Oct–Jun), 1 Jan, 1 Nov and 25 Dec.* 3€. 02 99 09 67 86.
A small museum is dedicated to the career of Louison Bobet, the legendary cycling champion and native of St-Méen, who won the **Tour de France** race several times in the early 1950s.

Site Mégalithique de Monteneuf

Centre Les Landes, rue des Menhirs. *Open daily Jul–Aug 10.30am–12.30pm, 2.30pm–6pm. Guided tours 2.30pm, 4pm and 5pm.* 3.50€. 02 97 22 04 74.
Located on the moor lying between Guer and Monteneuf, this megalithic site is seen as one of the most important in central Brittany; it is currently being excavated and restored. More than 20 huge blocks of purple schist

have been raised with the help of Engineers from the nearby military college of Coëtquidan.

 Two 7km/4.35mi-long pedestrian itineraries takes you past the Loge Morinais (schist gallery graves), the menhirs of Chomet, Coëplan and Pierres Droites (standing stones), the Pièce Couverte, the Rocher Maheux and the Bordoués (gallery graves). More than 420 officially listed menhirs, thought to have been knocked down towards the end of the first millenium on the orders of the Church, line the D 776.

DRIVING TOUR

CASTLES AND LEGENDS
43km/27mi.

This route leaves from St-Léry and follows a round trip through the forest of Paimpont, past the best-known sites.

In the wake of the great fire of September 1990, nature is gaining the upper hand, and, although some centuries-old trees have been lost forever, gorse, heather, broom and ferns are composing a new landscape, which clearly has its own charm.

St-Léry
On the south side of the 14C **church** is a Renaissance portico with two elegant basket-handle arched doors surmounted by delicately carved ogee mouldings. Sculpted figures frame the door on the right: the Virgin, the Angel Gabriel, St Michael slaying the dragon, and the damned. The leaves of the door are beautifully carved.

Inside, in the nave, is the 16C tomb of St Léry, and opposite it is a little bas-relief in sculpted wood depicting the life of the saint. The lovely Flamboyant chapel in the south side aisle is illuminated through a stained-glass window dating from 1493, which is dedicated to the Virgin Mary. Beneath the gallery, the clock can be seen through a glass door.

Near the church, note a 17C house decorated with three lovely dormer windows.

Château de Comper
Open Mar–Jun and Sept–mid Oct Thu–Mon 10am–5.30pm, Jul–Aug Thu–Tue 10am–7pm. 5.50€. Closed Jan–Mar, 1 Jan, 1 & 11 Nov, 25 Dec, Wed & Tue in low season. 02 97 22 79 96. www.centre-arthurien-broceliande.com.

The Montforts, Charettes, Rieux, Lavals, Colignys, La Trémoilles and Rosmadecs are the great families who have at some point been the owners of this site where the fairy Viviane is supposed to have been born. This is also where she is said to have brought up Lancelot, the gallant Knight of the Round Table. The castle was destroyed twice, in the 14C and in the 18C, and all that now remains of it are two sections of curtain wall, the postern and a huge tower; the body of the main building was restored in the 19C. The castle is the headquarters of the **Centre Arthurien**, which organises exhibitions and events every year on the Celtic world, Arthurian legend and the Middle Ages.

Merlin's supposed vault (**Tombeau de Merlin**) is indicated by two schist slabs and some holly.

An ordinary-looking fountain, the Fontaine de Jouvence, is said to have magic powers.

Étang du Pas-du-Houx
This lake is the largest in the forest (86ha/212 acres). Two châteaux were built on its shores in 1912: Brocéliande, in the Norman style, and Pas-du-Houx.

Paimpont
This market town, deep in the forest near a pool amid tall trees, dates back to the Revolution. It owes its origins to the founding of a monastery in the 7C, which was raised to the status of abbey in the late 12C and survived until the Revolution. The 17C north wing houses the town hall and the presbytery.

The 13C **abbey church** (open daily 9am–7pm) was decorated in the 17C with richly ornate **woodwork**. Busts, carved medallions and festoons of fruit and flowers have been executed with remarkable skill. Note in particular the 15C and 16C statues, including one of

St Judicaël, in stone and a St Méen. The **treasury** (🕐 *open Apr–Jun, Sat–Sun 2.30pm–6.30pm Jul–mid-Sept, 10am–12.30pm, 3pm–6.30pm;* & *02 99 07 81 37*), in the sacristy, displays a statue of St Anne carrying the Virgin and Child (15C), an interesting arm reliquary of St Judicaël (15C) and, most importantly, a magnificent ivory Christ (18C).

Les Forges de Paimpont
This pretty hamlet, next to a lake, owes its name to the forges that were here between the 16C and late 19C.
In nearby **Beignon**, a church contains some beautiful 16C stained-glass windows. In the chancel, behind the altar, there is a representation of the Crucifixion of St Peter, and, in the north transept, that of the Tree of Jesse.

Château de Trécesson
⊘ *Access is limited to the interior courtyard.*
This castle, surrounded by a moat, was built at the end of the 14C in reddish schist and still has its original medieval appearance. Accessible by foot only in a clearing signposted from the château is the **Fontaine de Barenton**. Endowed with supernatural powers (according to legend), this fountain could generate violent storms when water from the spring was poured onto the **Perron de Merlin** (Merlin's threshold), a nearby stone slab.

Tréhorenteuc
In the **church** (🕐 *open daily 9am–5pm; guided tours on request from the Tourist Office;* 💶 *2.50€;* *02 97 93 05 12*) and sacristy, mosaics and pictures illustrate the legend of the Val sans retour and the Barenton fountain.
In the chancel is a stained-glass window of the Holy Grail and a painting of the Knights of the Round Table.

Val sans retour
Known as the "Valley of No Return", this is one of the places most heavily steeped in legend in the Forêt de Paimpont. It can be found by taking the unsurfaced track, for pedestrians only, after the sec-

The Golden Tree by François Davin, Val sans retour.

M. Gurfinkel/MICHELIN

ond car park. This leads to the *Miroir des Fées et Rocher des Faux Amants* (Fairies' Mirror and False Lovers' Rock). Legend has it that Morgana the witch, jealous of a knight who had been unfaithful to her, cast a spell over the valley preventing anyone who had done wrong from leaving it. Only Lancelot, who remained faithful to Guinevere, was able to break the spell. At the Fairies' Mirror, note the splendid **Arbre d'Or** (Golden Tree), the work of François Davin, which marks the furthest spot reached by the fire of 1990. This "tree" (a chestnut tree covered in golden leaves), signifies the beauty of the forest and the respect it deserves.

Guided tours

From mid-Jun to mid-Sept, the Tourist Office at Tréhorenteuc (*pl. Abbé-Gillard,* *02 97 93 05 12, www.valsansretour.com*) organises day tours on foot and by car of the **Brocéliande Forest**. Cost: 15€ per person, no charge for children under 10.
Le *Centre de l'imaginaire Arthurien* at the Comper castle also offers guided tours focusing on **Arthurian legends** on Mon and Tue from mid-Jul to mid-Sept.

ADDRESSES

🛏STAY

☞☞**Chambre d'hôte La Corne de Cerf** – *2km/1.25mi S of Paimpont on the D 733 and D 71.* ✆*02 99 07 84 19. Closed Jan.* ⊅*3 rooms.* This elegant house offers bright and fresh rooms, giving onto a delightful English garden. Homemade jams and breads for breakfast.

☞☞**Au Relais du Porhoët** – *11 pl. de l'Église, 56490 Guilliers. 13km/8mi N of Ploërmel by the D 766 and D 13.* ✆*02 99 74 40 17. www.aurelaisduporhoet.com. Closed 4–18 Jan. 12 rooms. Rest. closed Sun eve and Mon exc eve Jul–Aug .* A charming inn offering a warm, family atmosphere. with pleasantly-furnished, functional rooms.

DISCOVER THE COUNTRYSIDE

The Brocéliande countryside is full of paths you can take on foot, by bike or on horseback. Several guides and maps are for sale at the Tourist Office of Paimpont or at the *Pays Touristique de Brocéliande, 1 rue des Korrigans 35380 Plélan-le-Grand.* ✆*02 99 06 86 07.*

🏃ACTIVITIES

Domaine de Tremelin – *3.5km/ 2.2mi S of Iffendic.* ✆ *02 99 09 73 79. www.domaine-de-tremelin.fr.* As well as water-based activities on the lake there are trampolines, quad bikes, mini golf…

Bécherel★

Perched on a hill (alt 176m/1557ft) overlooking the upper valley of the River Rance, Bécherel was once a seigneurial stronghold; only a few ruins and old granite houses still stand. In former times, flax was cultivated and the purest linen thread, the finest in Brittany, was produced here. Now the town is the leading book town in France (a town with a large number of second-hand or antiquarian book shops) and is known for its book market, held on the first Sunday of the month, which attracts 40,000 visitors annually. Bécherel is also among the 19 towns honoured for their typical Breton character. From Thabor Gardens the view extends as far as Dol, Dinan and Combourg.

▸ **Population:** 731.
 Michelin Map: Local map 309 K5 – Ille-et-Vilaine (35).
 Info: 9 place A-Jehanin, 35190 Bécherel. ✆02 99 66 75 23. www.becherel.com.
 Location: Take the N 137 then the D 20 from Rennes (35km/22mi N) or the D 68 from Dinan (23km/14mi).
 Timing: A guided tour followed by a walk around the bookshops.

ted with statues and other monuments inspired by history and mythology. It has been nicknamed the Versailles of Brittany.

Église des Iffs★

🌀*7km/2.4mi SW on D 27.* 🔊*Call for details of guided tours.* ✆*02 99 45 83 85.* Inside are nine lovely 16C **stained-glass windows**★ inspired by the Dutch and Italian Schools (16C).

Château de Montmuran★

🌀*800m/0.5mi N of Les Iffs.* 🔊*Guided tours (45min) Jun–Sept, Sun–Fri 2pm –7pm.* ◉*5€.* ✆*02 99 45 88 88. www.montmuran.com.*

EXCURSIONS

Château de Caradeuc

🌀*1km/06mi W.* 🕐*Open May–Jun and Sept, Sat–Sun, hols 2pm–6pm, Jul–Aug, daily noon–6pm .* ◉*6€.* ♿. ✆*02 99 66 77 76.*
This château, the former home of a famous attorney-general, Louis-René, Marquis de Caradeuc de la Chalotais (1701–85), has a very fine **park**★ dot-

A drawbridge across the moat leads to the narrow gateway framed by two massive round machicolated towers. Behind the entrance fort an external staircase leads to the chapel where Du Guesclin was knighted in 1354 after a skirmish with the English.

From the top of the castle towers, you can admire the vast panorama extending as far as Hédé and Dinan.

Château de Hac

▶ *8km/5mi N on D 68, D 26 and D 39.*
◁ *Guided tours (45min) Aug–Sept, Sun–Thu 1pm–7pm.* ⊜*5€.* ℘*02 96 83 43 06.*

This large manor house, a 14C seigneurial residence, has survived without any major alterations. The large rooms house Gothic and Renaissance furniture; in particular an interesting collection of chests, for the most part Breton.

Tinténiac

▶ *8km/5mi E of Bécherel on D 20.*

The **Musée de l'Outil et des Métiers** (🕐*open Jul–Sept, Tue–Sun 10am–noon, 3–6pm; Sun 3–6pm;* ⊜*2€;* ♿ ℘*02 99 23 09 30*), brings old trades back to life in a wooden building near the canal.

♟ Médréac

▶ *10km/6.25mi SW of Bécherel, by the D 20 then D 220.*

On the old railway line from La Brohinière to Dinan-Dinard, la Gare de Médréac offers trips by vélo rail to explore the surrounding countryside (🕐*Jun–Sept daily 10am–6pm;* ⊜*6/8 € (3/6 € under 8 years)*). Choose to ride a bicycle along the rails for 6km/3.7mi return (1h), 14km/8.7mi return (2h), or from 10am–2pm, 4h return, ideal for having a picnic.

Hédé

▶ *5km/3mi S of Tinténiac in the tiny village of La Madeleine. After the bridge over the canal, bear left to the car park by the lock keeper's house.*

There are 11 locks, the **Onze Écluses**, three before and eight after the bridge, to negotiate a drop of 27m/88.5ft on the Ille-et-Rance Canal. The towpath offers a pleasant walk in a pretty setting.

Bookshop in Bécherel

Franck Hamon/Office de Tourisme du pays de Bécherel

ADDRESSES

🛏 STAY

⊜⊜**Chambre d'hôte Les Effourneaux** – *Les Effourneaux - 22630 St-Juvat. 14km/8.75mi from Bécherel by the D 20, D 220 and D 12.* ℘ *02 96 88 17 52. www.leseffourneaux.com.* 🍽 *3 rooms.* 🍴*.Near the village of St-Juvat this recently renovated limestone 19C house is typical of the local architecture: a pleasant mixture of sobriety and elegance. Brioches and salted butter for breakfast.

🍴 EAT

⊜⊜ **La Vieille Auberge** – *Rte de Tinténiac, 35630 Hédé. 14km/8.75mi W of Bécherel by the D 27 and D 80.* ℘ *02 99 45 46 25. www.lavieilleauberge35.com. Closed mid Aug–early Sept, mid Feb–early Mar, Sun eve and Mon .* 17C mill with rustic décor, bucolic charm and a shady terrace next to the establishment's private lake in a small garden. Family atmosphere and mouthwatering seasonal cuisine of fresh local produce, such as homemade bread, oysters from Cancale and lamb raised on the premises.

Combourg★

This picturesque old town stands at the edge of Lac Tranquille, a large lake, and is dominated by an imposing feudal castle. The Tourist Office is on Place Albert-Parent, inside the restored 16C Maison de la Lanterne. Those who want to take only a quick look at the castle from the outside should walk along the local road that branches off the Rennes road and runs beside the lake.

▶ **Population:** 4,850.
Michelin Map: Local map 309 Ille-et-Vilaine (35).
Info: pl. Albert-Parent, 35270 Combourg. ℘02 99 73 13 93. www.combourg.org.
Location: North of Rennes on the N 137.
Kids: Cobac amusement park, Villecartier mini boats.
Timing: Combine your visit with a trip to Mont-St-Michel.
Don't Miss: The Château de Combourg.

CHÂTEAU★

⏱Open Apr–Oct Sun–Fri daily Jul–Aug. Park 9.30am–12.30pm, 2pm–6pm; Oct 10am–noon, 2–5pm. Guided château tours Apr–Jun and Sept 2pm–5.30pm, Jul–Aug 10.30, 11.15am & 2pm–5.30pm, Oct 2–5pm. ⌐7€. ℘02 99 73 13 93. www.combourg.net.

The exterior of the castle looks like a powerful fortress with its four massive towers, pepper-pot roofs, crenellated parapet walk and thick walls slit by narrow openings. The tour takes in the chapel, the drawing room (now divided in two), the Archives, where souvenirs of Chateaubriand are displayed, and François-René's austere bedroom in Cat Tower. From the parapet walk there are views of the locality, the lake and the pretty, sweet-smelling park.

EXCURSIONS

Cobac Parc

▶Le Bois de Cobac, Lanhélin. Follow the signs for Parc de Loisirs.

⏱Open Apr–May weekends & public holidays 11am–6pm, Jun Tues–Sun 11am–6pm, Jul–Aug daily 11am–6pm (11 Jul–22 Aug 10.30am–6.30pm), Sept first & second Weds & weekends 11am–6pm. ⌐16€ (children 13.50€), two-day and season tickets available. ℘02 99 73 80 16. www.cobac-parc.com.

This open-air park, covering 10ha/25 acres, is a family recreation area with more than 30 leisure attractions, including a swimming pool with giant slide, quads, a small train and merry-go-rounds. There is a picnic area and a restaurant. Check out the package deals that include attractions in St-Malo, cruises, hotel discounts, etc.

Bazouges-la-Pérouse

▶8km/5mi SW of Antrain on D 313, which intersects D 155.

This pleasant village is an artists' haven, where work is displayed and workshops organised in summer.

Château de la Ballue

⏱Open 15 Mar–1 Nov daily 10.30am–6.30pm. Guided tours (1hr). ⌐9€. ℘02 99 97 47 86. www.laballue jardin.com.

Château de Combourg

Liliane Lawrence/Office de Tourisme de Combourg

Chateaubriand at Combourg

The château, which was built in the 11C, was enlarged in the 14C and 15C and restored in the 19C. It belonged first to the Du Guesclin family, and then in the 18C to the Count of Chateaubriand, father of François-René, the Romantic writer.

In his Memoirs, Chateaubriand recalled the two years he spent at Combourg in his youth. The Count, a sombre and moody man, lived very much in retirement; when the family met he would walk up and down for hours in the drawing room, in silence, while no one dared to speak. The Countess, who was unwell, kept only a distant eye on the children. Months passed without a visitor. Left to themselves, the young Chateaubriand and his sister Lucile grew close, sharing their boredom, their dreams and their fears.

The old castle, almost deserted, was gloomy; the lake, the woods and the surrounding heath exuded melancholy. The Cat Tower (Tour du Chat), in which François-René had his lonely room, was haunted; a former Lord of Combourg was said to return there at night in the form of a black cat, which the boy anxiously watched for. The owls fluttering against the window, the wind rattling the door and howling in the corridors made him shiver.

It was from this gloomy environment that the dreamy and melancholy soul of one of the great Romantic writers was formed.

In the eyes of some Romantic writers, this residence symbolised the royalist rebellion, and for this reason was visited by Musset, Balzac and Hugo. Don't miss the pretty **garden**★.

Château de Bonnefontaine

◐ *1.5km/1mi S of Antrain via rue Général-Lavigne & rue Bonne-Fontaine.*
◷ *Open Apr–Oct, daily 11am–6pm.*
◉ *5€. ℘02 99 98 31 13. www.bonne fontaine.com.*
Built in 1547 as a feudal manor-house and remodelled in the 19C, this castle rises in the centre of a beautifully maintained park (only the park is open to visitors). The elegant turrets adorning the massive main range, the tall windows and the carved dormer windows balance the severity of the squat, machicolated pepper-pot towers.

Antrain

◐ *21km E of Combourg on D 796 and D 313.*
High on a promontory, Antrain is a market town with steep little streets and 16C and 17C houses. **Église St-André** (for the most part from the 12C) hosts an imposing 17C bell-tower, topped by a dome with lantern turrets.

ADDRESSES

⌂ STAY

◉◉ **Hôtel du Lac** – *pl. Chateaubriand. 02 99 73 05 65. www.hotel-restaurant-du-lac.com. Closed Feb. 28 rooms. Restaurant.* Traditional house with practical, cool rooms, two dining rooms, a veranda that overlooks the water and an attractive garden.

⸮ EAT

◉◉ **L'Écrivain** – *20 Place St-Gilduin. ℘02 99 73 01 61. Closed Wed eve, Thu and Sun eve off season, Feb and Nov school holidays.* Light and flavourful traditional cuisine with a contemporary flair.

◉◉ **Auberge de la Tourelle** – *1 Place de la Mairie, Sens-de-Bretagne. ℘02 99 39 60 06. Open lunchtimes. Closed Sun, Mon and Tue eve.* Enjoy simple but delicious regional cuisine in a rustic setting.

◉◉ **Hôtel Restaurant du Château** – *1 pl. Chateaubriand. ℘ 02 99 73 00 38. www.hotelduchateau.com. Closed Sun eve off season, Sat noon, Mon Oct–Apr, a week in Apr and 20 Dec–20 Jan.* Rustic and comfortable setting for high-quality classic cuisine. Rooms available.

CÔTE D'ÉMERAUDE

In the late 19C, the stretch of coast from Pointe du Grouin and Le Val-André came to be known as La Côte d'Émeraude – the Emerald Coast. The area includes some famous beaches, the smart resort of Dinard, stunning Moont-St-Michel, as well as the city of the privateers, St-Malo. Rocky, heavily indented and very picturesque, the Côte d'Émeraude is a series of points with fine panoramican views, principally from Pointe du Grouin and Cap Fréhel. The coast is bisected by the Rance estuary on which a boat excursion between Dinan and St-Malo can be enjoyed. For beach lovers, there is a wide choice, which includes St-Lunaire, Sables d'Or-les-Pins and Val André.

Highlights

1 Walking the **ramparts** of St-Malo (p125)
2 Riding in the submarine at St-Malo's **Grand Aquarium** (p132)
3 **Birdwatching** at Cap Fréhel (p141)
4 Strolling Dinan 's **old town** (p143)
5 Approaching **Mont-St-Michel** across the bay on horseback (p168)

A Bit of History

The Côte d'Emeraude takes its name from the colour of the sea along the coastline of the Côtes-d'Armor and Ille-et-Vilaine *départements* in the northeast of Brittany.

The territory covered by this section of the Guide stretches from the border with the Manche *département* of the Normandy Region in the east, to Cap Fréhel in the west.

Its northern frontier is defined by the English Channel where the mighty Atlantic Ocean rushes in, helping to create this splendid coastline.

The economy of the coastal region relies heavily on tourism and the fishing industry while the inland area is mainly agricultural. St-Malo has a direct TGV link with Paris and has attracted much new industry including marine biotechnology to add to its activities as a port.

The main city of this coastal region is the renowned walled stronghold of the Corsaires, St-Malo in the Ille-et-Vilaine, named after the Celtic holy man who brought Christianity here in the 6C.

An ideal base from which to explore the area, St-Malo has a great deal of interest for the visitor, such as its splendid ramparts which provide views of both the city and the sea, and the aquarium.

Along the Emerald Coast

The old Port of Dinan, associated with the medieval Breton hero Du Guesclin whose heart is buried in the St-Sauveur Basilica, can be reached using either the left or the right bank of the river Rance. Driving itineraries for each side are included in this chapter (🔊 *see p148*) as well as for coastal routes heading east and west: from oyster producing Cancale to St-Malo (🔊 *see p155*), from grand Cap Fréhel to the sandy beaches at le Val André (🔊 *see p169*) and from Dinard to Cap Fréhel (🔊 *see p137*).

All of these routes along the coast allow the visitor to explore fully this delightful shore, its fascinating inlets and picturesque ports. Just south of the coast is the small town of Dol-de-Bretagne which, until early medieval times, was actually on the seaside and is now the capital of the marshy Marais de Dol, which is land reclaimed from Mont-St-Michel Bay. From here another itinerary explores the fertile plain just to the south of Dol (🔊 *see p158*).

For many, the most spectacular and memorable attraction of the entire Côte d'Émeraude is undoubtedly the UNESCO World Heritage site of Mont-St-Michel. Strictly speaking it is not actually in modern Brittany, being about 4km/2.5mi into Normandy, but nevertheless it is a significant part of the heritage of the region.

This unique abbey church was dedicated to the Archangel Michael. Together with its associated buildings, all built

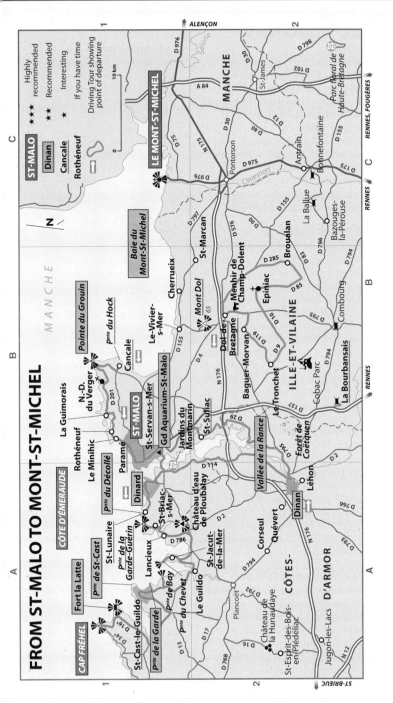

FROM ST-MALO TO MONT-ST-MICHEL

on a rocky tidal island and surrounded by sea, sand and grassy flats, the abbey and its spire are visible for many miles and makes a striking image particularly at dawn and dusk, with the sun glinting off the golden statue of St-Michael.

St-Malo★★★

St-Malo, St-Servan, Paramé and Rothéneuf have joined together to form the municipality of St-Malo. The site★★★ is unique in France and makes it one of the great tourist centres of Brittany.

Almost entirely destroyed during World War II, the carefully restored old town has regained the atmosphere of the once famous privateer stronghold. This part of town is now a pedestrian zone.

A BIT OF HISTORY

Origin – St-Malo, returning from Wales in the 6C, converted the Gallo-Roman settlement Aleth (St-Servan) to Christianity and became its bishop. The neighbouring island, on which the present town of St-Malo is built, was then uninhabited. Later, people settled there because it was easy to defend from the Norsemen, and it became important enough for the Bishopric of Aleth to be transferred to it in 1144. It took the name of St-Malo, while Aleth put itself under the protection of another local saint, St-Servan.

The town belonged to its bishops, who built its ramparts. It took no part in provincial rivalries. At the time of the League, St-Malo declared itself a republic and was able to keep its independence for four years. This principle was reflected in the saying: *"Ni Français, ni Breton, Malouin suis"*("I am neither French nor Breton but a man of St-Malo").

Famous men of St-Malo

Few towns have had as many famous sons as St-Malo over the centuries.

Jacques Cartier left in 1534 to look for gold in Newfoundland and Labrador; instead he discovered the mouth of the River St-Lawrence, which he took to be the estuary of a great Asian river. As the word Canada, which means 'village' in the Huron language, was often used by the Indians he encountered, he used the word to name the country. Cartier took possession of the land in the name of the

- ▶ **Population:** 49,661.
- **Michelin Map:** Local map 309 J3 – Ille-et-Vilaine (35).
- **Info:** Esplanade St-Vincent, 35400 St-Malo. ℘08 25 13 52 00. www.saint-malo-tourisme.com.
- **Location:** North of Dinan (35km/22mi) and Rennes (75km/46.5mi). Its fortified old town, called Intra-Muros, is confined to a presqu'île.
- **Kids:** The Grand Aquarium.
- **Timing:** Intra-Muros in the morning, the beach in the afternoon and a galette near the cathedral in the evening – a day should suffice. Enquire about tide times as certain sites are only accessible at low tide.
- **Parking:** Few cars enter the old town. In summer, the car parks in the centre fill up quickly. Better to leave your car in one of the car parks on the outskirts, then take the shuttle bus into the centre.
- **Don't Miss:** A walk around the ramparts for the view over St-Malo and the sea.

King of France in 1534, but it was only under Champlain that the colonisation of Canada began and that Quebec was founded (1608).

René Duguay-Trouin (1673–1736) and **Robert Surcouf** (1773–1827) are the most famous of the St-Malo privateers. These bold seamen received 'letters of marque' from the king, which permitted them to attack warships or merchantmen without being treated as pirates, that is, hanged from the main yard. In the 17C and 18C, privateers inflicted heavy losses on the English, Dutch and Spanish.

Duguay was the son of a rich shipowner and had been destined for the priesthood; but by the time he was 16 the only

GETTING AROUND

BY BUS – Map of the bus network at the **Infobus** kiosk, *espl. St-Vincent, terminal du Naye.* ℘*02 99 56 06 06.*

BY TOURIST TRAIN – Departs porte St-Vincent every 30min. ℘*02 99 40 49 49. www.lepetittrain-saintmalo.com.* Adults 5.50€ (children 4€).

BY BIKE – **Les Vélos Bleus** – *19 rue Alphonse Thébault.* ℘*02 99 40 31 63. www.velos-bleus.fr. Closed Nov–Mar. From 10€ for half a day.*

TOURS

Guided tours of Intra-Muros – from early Jun–late Sept leaving from the Tourist Office. 1hr 30. 6€. Enquire within.

Audio-guide – Voyage Corsaire – *Maison de Corsaire, 5 rue d'Asfeld.* ℘*02 99 56 09 40. www.saint-malo-tourisme. com.* Rental of audio-guides: 12€ for two hours for two people. Discover the old town at your own pace via an audio tour narrated by actors in a lively style.

---

way to put an end to his wild living was to send him to sea. His gifts were such that, at 24, he entered the so-called Great Corps of the French Navy as a commander, and at 36 he was given a peerage. When he died, he was a Lieutenant General in the seagoing forces and a Commander of the Order of St-Louis. Surcouf's history is completely different, but just as outstanding. He answered the call of the sea when very young and soon began a prodigious career of fabulous exploits. First as slaver, then as privateer, he amassed an enormous fortune. At 36 he retired, but continued to make money by fitting out privateers and merchantmen.

François-René de Chateaubriand (1768–1848) was the tenth and last child of a very noble Breton family who had fallen on bad times. His father went to America in search of fortune and was able, on his return, to set up as a shipowner at St-Malo. In a room on the second floor of a modest town house (*Maison Natale de Chateaubriand,* which gives onto the courtyard of the Hôtel France et Chateaubriand and is near the Tour Quic-en-Groigne) René was born. From its window he could look out to sea beyond the ramparts and dream... The future poet spent his early years roaming about the port, then went in succession through schools at Dinan, Dol, Rennes and Brest, dreaming sometimes of the priesthood, sometimes of the sea. He spent two years in exile at Combourg with his father, mother and

sister Lucile. It was through the profession of arms that he began, in 1786, the adventurous career which ended in 1848 in the solitary grandeur of Grand Bé.

Frédéric de La Mennais (1782–1854), another St-Malo shipowner's son, also had a place in the Romantic Movement. He became an orphan at a very young age and was brought up by an uncle at the castle of Chesnaye, near Dinan. At 22 he taught mathematics in the College of St-Malo before entering the seminary of that town. He was ordained a priest in 1816 and had a great influence on Lacordaire and Montalembert. His writings and violent quarrels got him into trouble with Rome, which led him to renounce the Church.

He retired to Chesnay, and published the famous *Paroles d'un croyant (Words of a Believer)* in 1834. Owing to his advanced political ideas, he was sentenced to a year's imprisonment in 1840 but won a seat in the National Assembly in 1848.

🕬 WALKING TOURS

② THE RAMPARTS ★★★

Allow 2hr. Start from esplanade St-Vincent.

St-Malo and the surrounding area were turned into an entrenched camp by the Germans and became the prize for which a merciless battle raged from 1–14 August 1944. The town was left in ruins. With a great sense of history, its restorers were determined to bring the old city back to life. They have been completely successful in their quest.

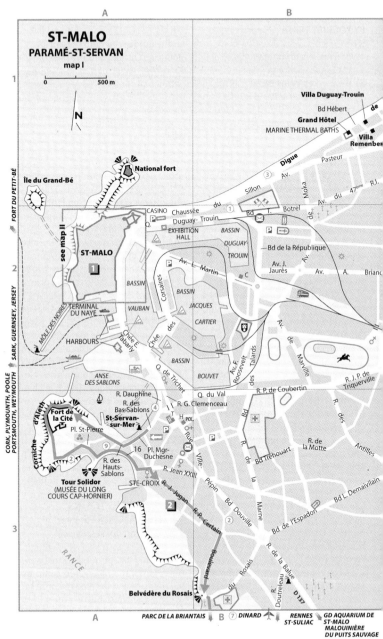

ST-MALO
PARAMÉ-ST-SERVAN
map I

0   500 m

N

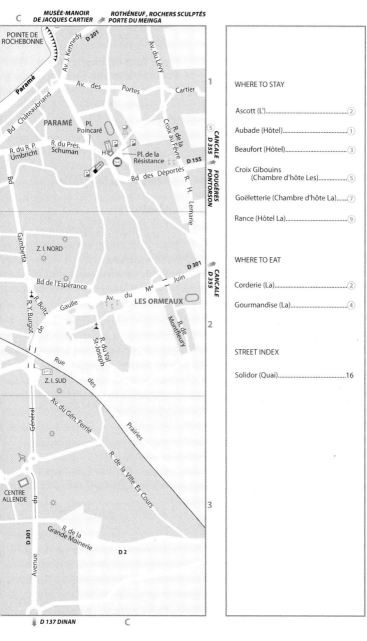

WHERE TO STAY

Ascott (L')..②

Aubade (Hôtel)......................................①

Beaufort (Hôtel)....................................③

Croix Gibouins
(Chambre d'hôte Les)....................⑤

Goëletterie (Chambre d'hôte La).......⑦

Rance (Hôtel La)....................................⑨

WHERE TO EAT

Corderie (La)..②

Gourmandise (La)..................................④

STREET INDEX

Solidor (Quai)...16

The statue near the esplanade, at the entrance to the Casino garden, portrays Chateaubriand by Armel Beaufils. It was erected in 1948 on the centenary of his death.

◯ Pass under Porte St-Vincent which consists of twin gates; then take the staircase to the right leading to the ramparts.

The ramparts, started in the 12C, were enlarged and altered up to the 18C and survived the wartime destruction. The rampart walk commands magnificent views, especially at high tide, of the coast and islands.

From Porte St-Vincent to Bastion St-Louis
Directly after Grande Porte (Great Gate), which is crowned with machicolations, the view opens out over the narrow isthmus which joins the old town to its suburbs, the harbour basins and, in the distance, St-Servan.

From Bastion St-Louis to Bastion St-Philippe
The rampart skirts the houses where the rich shipowners of St-Malo lived; two, near the Bastion St-Louis, are still intact but the following walls and façades are reconstructions of carefully dismantled buildings. This fine group of houses with their high roofs, surmounted by monumental chimneys rising from the ramparts, enhances this part of town's old look.
The view extends over the outer harbour; to Rocher d'Aleth, crowned by Fort de la Cité, and the mouth of the Rance estuary; to Dinard, with Prieuré Beach and Pointe de Vicomté.

From Bastion St-Philippe to Tour Bidouane
A very fine view of the Côte d'Émeraude west of Dinard, and of the islands off St-Malo. To the right of Pointe du Moulinet you can see part of the beach at Dinard, Pointe des Étêtés separating Dinard from St-Lunaire, Pointe du Décollé, the Hébihens Archipelago, Pointe de St-Cast

and Cap Fréhel; nearer, on the right, are the Île Harbour and, further to the right, Grand Bé and Petit Bé Islands; then, in the background, Île de Cézembre and Fort de la Conchée. Near Tour Bidouane stands a statue of Surcouf.

From Tour Bidouane to Porte St-Vincent
Having skirted the *École nationale de la Marine Marchande*, you can see the Fort National and the great curve which joins St-Malo to Pointe de la Varde, passing through the beaches of Paramé, Rochebonne and Le Minihic.

1 THE WALLED CITY★

Château★★
You can enter the courtyard and see the façades of the former 17C–18C barracks (now the town hall), the well, the keep and the gatehouse.
The little keep was built as part of the ramparts in 1395. The great keep (1424) dominates the castle: from the keep's watchtower, you will admire an impressive **panorama**★★ of the town; the corner towers were constructed in the 15C and 16C. The chapel and the galley date from the 17C.

Musée d'Histoire de la Ville et d'Ethnographie du Pays Malouin★
Allow 1hr 30min.
◯*Apr–Sept, 10am–12.30pm, 2pm–6pm, rest of the year Tue–Sun 10am–noon, 2pm–6pm.* ◯*Closed 1 Jan, 1 May, 1 and 11 Nov and 25 Dec.* ◉*5.40€.* ✆*02 99 40 71 57.*
The museum, which is installed in the great keep and gatehouse, records the development of the city of St-Malo and its celebrities (Jacques Cartier, Duguay-Trouin, La Bourdonnais, Surcouf, Chateaubriand, Lamennais and the mathematician Maupertuis). Documents, ship models, paintings and arms trace St-Malo's sea-faring tradition.
To end the visit climb up to the keep's watchtowers, from where you can admire an impressive panorama of the town, harbour, coast and sea.

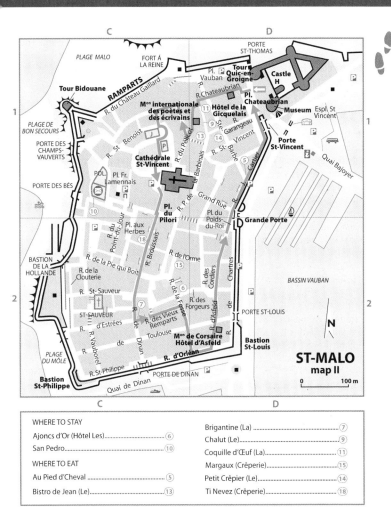

ST-MALO
map II

0   100 m

A passage leads from the old chapel to the Tour Générale. This tower contains an exhibition laid out on three floors devoted to the economy (commercial fishing, shipbuilding), way of life (headdresses, furniture) and significant historical events in the St-Malo region.

Tour Quic-en-Groigne★

This tower (65 steps), which is located in the left wing of the castle, bears the name Quic-en-Groigne from an inscription Queen Anne had carved on it in defiance of the bishops of St-Malo: *"Qui-qu'en-groigne, ainsi sera, car tel est mon bon plaisir"* ("Thus it shall be, whoever may complain, for that is my wish").

Place Chateaubriand

As a child, Chateaubriand lived at number 2 (hôtel White). The 18C façade has been restored exactly as it was. He was born at number 3 rue Chateaubriand, the 17C Hôtel de La Gicquelais.

◔ *Take the rue Chateaubriand.*

Cour La Houssaye

The 15C tower in this small courtyard is part of a house said to belong to **Duchess Anne.** It is a typical "Malouin' housethat gives an idea of how the town loked at the end of the middle ages.

Take rue du Pelicot on the left.

From cour La Houssaye to the Cathedral

On Rue du Pélicot you will pass in front of some wood and glass façades belonging to the Maison International des poetes et ecrivains. At the intersection with the rue du College, turn right into the rue Mahe de la Bourdonnais. La Bourdonnais became the Governor of the Isles of Mauritious and of La Reunion (1699-1753) and lived for a while at number 2. Note the sculpted wooden Renaissance door (1652). At the end of the street, there is a fine view of the Fort National.

Turn right into rue de la Victoire.

In the rue de la Victoire, beside the façade of number 8 (17C), there is the old Chapelle des Benedictines (1622) and further on, L'École Nationale de la Marine Marchande.

By the rue Maclow, go back to la place Jean-de-Châtillon and the Cathedral.

Cathedral St-Vincent

Pl. Jean-de-Chatillon.

Ⓞ*Open 8am–6.30pm.*

The building, started in the 11C and completed in the 18C, was topped by a pierced spire in the 19C, replacing the quadrangular roof.

The nave is roofed with quadripartite vaulting typical of the Angevin style; dark and massive it contrasts with the slender 13C chancel. Lit by magnificent **stained-glass windows**★ by Jean Le Moal, the chancel becomes a kaleidoscope of colours. In the transept, restored in the 17C style, the stained-glass windows are muted in colour while in the side aisles the windows by Max Ingrand are brighter (Chapel of the Holy Sacrament). The north side aisle has preserved its original vaulting.

A 16C Virgin, Notre-Dame-de-la-Croix-du-Fief, which comes from a medieval house, is kept in the second chapel north of the ambulatory together with the remains of Duguay-Trouin. The neighbouring chapel houses the head reliquary of Jacques Cartier.

Continue by the rue Broussais and the rue des Vieux Ramparts to the left, then turn right into rue Feydeau leading back to the rue d'Orleans with some beautiful façades of 18C shipowners houses. Turn left and left again into rue d'Asfeld.

Maison de Corsaire – Hôtel d'Asfeld

5 rue d'Asfeld. ⤜*Guided tours (1hr) Jul–Aug and school holidays Tue–Sun 10am–11.30am, 2.30pm–5.30pm; rest of the year Tue–Sun 2.30pm–5.30pm.* ⤜*5.50€ (age 7–12, 4€). ℘02 99 56 09 40. www.demeure-de-corsaire.com.*
Saved in 1944, this 18C dwelling is now classed as an Historic Monument. It belonged to François Auguste Magon de La Lande, the King's Corsair, Director of The India Company and a very influential *malouin* (native of St-Malo). Visit the collection of arms and chests.

COASTAL DEFENCE SYSTEM
🏰 Fort National★

Access by Plage de l'Éventail at low tide, 15min on foot there and back. ⤜*Guided tours (45min) Easter, Whitsun, Jun–Sept, daily at low tide (variable times).* Ⓞ*Closed during high tide (check with the Tourist Office).* ⤜*4€. ℘02 99 85 34 33.*
Built by Vauban in 1689, the Royal Fort became the National Fort after the Revolution (1789), and then private property. Built on the rock, this stronghold assured the protection of the city. The **view**★★ from the ramparts is remarkable. The fort commands extensive views of the coast and the islands: St-Malo, St-Servan, the Rance estuary, Dinard, the Île du Grand Bé, Île du Petit Bé, Île Harbour, the Grand Jardin Lighthouse, the Fort de la Conchée and in the distance the Îles Chausey.

During the tour, one of the events recorded is the fort's resistance in 1692 against the English and Dutch fleet, and Surcouf's memorable duel in which he

Fort National at low tide

R. Mattes/MICHELIN

defended the honour of France against 12 opponents, of whom he spared the last to testify to his exploit. The dungeon is worth visiting.

🚶 Île du Grand Bé

Allow 45min on foot there and back. Only at low tide.
Leave St-Malo by Porte des Champs-Vauverts and cross the beach diagonally to the causeway. Follow the road that skirts the right side of the island.

Chateaubriand's tomb is on the seaward side; it is a plain, unnamed flagstone surmounted by a heavy granite cross. From the highest point on the island there is a beautiful **panorama**★★ of the entire Côte d'Émeraude.

  Cross the open space, go down a few steps and turn left along a road leading back to the causeway by which you came.

Le Petit-Bé

Access on foot or by boat (depending upon tides) departing from Grand Bé. 5 € (child 3 €). ✆06 08 27 51 20 . www.petit-be.com.
Situated after Le Grand Bé, the island has a remarkable fort constructed in1693 by Vauban and now restored. The guided visit demonstrates the fortifications of the Bay of St-Malo and the phenomenon of the tides.

The port

Located in the centre of the large roadstead, which once divided the privateer's encampment (St-Malo-de-l'Isle) from the continent (St-Servan, Paramé), the port is developing a wide range of activities.

It has four wet docks (Vauban, Duguay-Trouin, Bouvet and Jacques-Cartier) sheltered by a lock, where handling of goods and fish are concentrated. Imported products hold an important position: fertilisers, timber and wood. Its outer harbour is equipped with two shipping terminals for **car ferries** and **boat services**; there are daily services between St-Malo and Portsmouth and St-Malo and the Channel Islands (Jersey and Guernsey).
Pleasure boating has not been forgotten: you can board at the foot of the ramparts and at Bas-Sablons near the Corniche d'Aleth.

EXCURSIONS
St-Servan-Sur-Mer Resort★

 3.6km/2mi SE of St-Malo.
The resort of St-Servan-sur-Mer is cheerful with its many gardens, in striking contrast to the walled town of St-Malo. Its main beach is formed by Sablons Bay, although there are also smaller beaches along the Rance.
The town has three ports: the Bouvet dock (**Bassin Bouvet**), a trading and a fishing port, linked with that of St-Malo,

the Solidor, a former naval base, and that of St-Père.

Corniche d'Aleth★

2.8km/1.7mi W along rue d'A'eth. Leave your car in place St-Pierre, by the ruins of the former cathedral of Aleth.

Fort de la Cité, the City Fort, (*guided tours (1hr) Jul–Aug, 10.15am, 11am and 2pm, 3pm, 4pm, 5pm, Apr–Jun and Sept, Tue–Sun 2.30pm, 3.15pm, 4.30pm, Oct, Thur–Sun 10am, 3.15pm, 4pm, Tue–Wed 3.15pm and 4pm; 5.40€; 02 99 82 41 74)* was built in 1759 and considerably altered by the Germans during World War II. Around the inner courtyard is a chain of blockhouses joined by over 2km /1.2mi of underground passages.

Port St-Père

Opposite Dinard, this little harbour backing on to the presqu'île d'Aleth, is framed by the *marégraphe* (machine which registers the height of the tides) and the Tour Solidor.

Follow the beach to reach quai Solidor. At the end of the creek, turn left into rue La Fontaine. Look left into rues Duport-du-Tertre and de l'Étoupe: they have the best-preserved houses in the old town.

Tour Solidor★

This tower (27m high), which commands the Rance estuary, was built in 1382 and restored in the 17C. It now houses the **Musée International du Long Cours Cap-Hornier**★(*open Apr–Sept, daily 10am–12.30pm, 2pm–6pm, rest of the year daily (except Mon and holidays) 10am–noon, 2pm–6pm; closed 1 Jan, May, 1 and 11 Nov, 25 Dec; 5.40€; 02 99 40 71 58)*, a museum devoted to Cape Horn Vessels. Visitors can study the exhibits on their way up to enjoy the **view** from the the top of the tower, making the climb easier.

Belvédère du Rosais★

The viewpoint is near the little marine cemetery on the side of a cliff overlooking the Rance which contains the tomb

of the Count and Countess of Chateaubriand, the writer's parents. **View**★ of Rance Dam, the Rocher Bizeux with a statue of the Virgin on top of it, Pointe de la Vicomté and Dinard.

Parc de la Briantais★

Towards Quelmer, Rance dam. Open Jul–Aug, 9am–7pm; rest of the year, 2pm–5pm exc. Sat–Sun and hols 9am–5pm. 02 99 81 83 42.
This large estate has stunning views over St-Servan. The château (1850) replaced a manor (17C) and hosts temporary exhibitions.

Paramé Resort

Paramé, a much-frequented seaside resort, possesses a salt-water thermal establishment. It has two magnificent beaches extending for 2km/1.2mi: Casino Beach, which continues that of St-Malo, and Rochebonne Beach. The splendid seafront promenade 3km/1.8mi long is the chief attraction for the passing tourists.

SOUTH OF TOWN
Grand Aquarium★★

Leave St-Malo on the D 137, the follow the signs. Av. du Général-Patton. Open mid Jul–mid Aug, 9am–10pm; first two weeks Jul and last 2 weeks Aug, 9.30am –8pm; Apr–Jun and Sept, 10am–7pm; rest of the year 10am–6pm (last entry 1hr before closing). Closed 3rd week Jan, 16–27 Nov (open Sat–Sun in Nov and Dec). 15.50€ (age 4–14 9.50€). 02 99 21 19 00.
www.aquarium-st-malo.com.
This is one of the region's most popular attractions, with eight large rooms on two storeys, much of the space devoted to the great navigators from St-Malo. The aquariums include a hands-on area which is a miniature reproduction of Brittany; the 'sunken ship' gives visitors the strange sensation of being at the bottom of the sea; the **Shark Ring** puts you right in the middle of the action. Ride in a four-place submarine, the **Nautibus**, in the giant tank where you navigate amid tropical fish and Celtic statues; you can discover a sunken city

and an abyss inhabited by strange creatures. There's also an area for children to pet fish such as rays.

Rothéneuf Resort

This seaside resort has two beaches, which differ greatly. That of Le Val is wide open to the sea, while that of Le Havre lies on an almost landlocked bay like a large lake surrounded with dunes, cliffs and pines.

Manoir de Jacques Cartier Limoëlou★

Rue David Macdonald Stewart, Rothéneuf. ✎ *Guided tours (1 hour) Jun–Sept, daily 10am–11.30am, 2.30pm–6pm; Oct–May, Mon–Sat 10am and 3pm.* **Ⓞ** *Closed public holidays.* ✆ *5€.* ✆ *02 99 40 97 73. www.musee-jacques-cartier.com.*

After his expeditions to Canada, the explorer, Jacques Cartier, bought a farm which he extended and called *Limoëlou* (bald hillock). This 15C–16C house and its 19C extension have been restored and furnished in the style of the period. The tour includes an audio-visual presentation on the explorer's expeditions and of the colony 'Nouvelle France' otherwise known as Canada.

⚑ Walk

Take rue St-Pierre at the east end of the church and follow the coastal pathway on the left.

This walk offers magnificent **views★★**. First comes a remarkable view of St-Malo. On a clear day you can then make out the Petit Bé, the Grand Bé and Cézembre Islands to the left.

Bear left and skirt the seashore then go round the fort; the whole harbour is now visible: to the right of the Île de Cézembre, in the distance, is the fortified Île de la Grande Conchée; on the left, the Grand Jardin Lighthouse, Île Harbour and its fort and, in the distance, Cap Fréhel and Pointe du Décollé, followed by a maze of reefs.

Finally take a steep downhill path to the right to enjoy a very fine view of the Rance estuary, barred by the Rocher Bizeux, on which stands a statue of the Virgin, and beyond, of the Usine Marémotrice de la Rance.

ADDRESSES

🛏 STAY

INTRA-MUROS

🛏 **Hôtel San Pedro** – *1 rue Ste-Anne.* ✆ *02 99 40 88 57. www.sanpedro hotel.com. 12 rooms.* 🍽 *8€. Closed mid Nov–late Feb.* A short hop from Bon Secours beach, this great budget choice offers a warm welcome, decently equipped, small rooms and a delicious breakfast.

🛏🛏 **Hôtel Les Ajoncs d'Or** – *10 rue Forgeurs.* ✆ *02 99 40 85 03. www.st-malo-hotel-anjoncs-dor.com. 22 rooms.* 🍽 *12€. Closed Dec & Jan.* In a peaceful street in the old town, this establishment offers nicely kept rooms and a breakfast room decorated with engravings.

EXTRA-MUROS

🛏🛏 **Hôtel La Rance** – *15 quai Sébastopol.* ✆ *02 99 81 78 63. www.la rancehotel.com. 11 rooms.* 🍽 *7.5€.* This lovely, small hotel, located in the shadow of the Solidor tower, offers pleasant rooms, some of which have balconies overlooking the sea.

🛏🛏🛏 **L'Ascott** – *35 rue Chapitre.* ✆ *02 99 81 89 93. www.ascotthotel.com. 10 rooms.* 🍽 *10€.* Contemporary and classic details in a quiet residential neighbourhood.

🛏🛏🛏 **Hôtel Aubade** – *8 place Duguesclin.* ✆ *02 99 40 47 11. www. aubade-hotel.com. 20 rooms.* 🍽 *11€. Closed 31 Jan–9 Feb.* Homely place where each floor is decorated in a different colour scheme.

🛏🛏🛏 **Hôtel Beaufort** – *25 chausée du Sillon.* ✆ *02 99 40 99 99. www.hotel-beaufort.com. 22 rooms.* 🍽 *13€.* Colonial-style rooms behind a mustard coloured façade. Avoid the noisier rooms overlooking rue du Sillon.

NEARBY

🛏🛏 **Chambre d'Hôte Les Croix Gibouins** – *6km/3.7mi E of St-Malo on the D 301 rte de Cancale and D 155 rte de*

St-Méloir-des-Ondes. ☎*02 99 81 12 41. www.les-croix-gibouins.com.* 🍴. *3 rooms.* 🛏. Don't worry about the road that passes near this lovely 16C gentleman's residence as its thick walls guarantee calm inside. The comfortable, restored rooms overlook a meadow.

🍽🍷**Chambre d'Hôte La Goëletterie** – *20 rue Goëletterie, quartier Quelmer. 5km/ 3mi from St-Malo towards Dinard then Quelmer.* ☎*02 99 81 92 64.* 🍴. *Closed 15 Dec–15 Feb. 5 rooms.* 🛏.This pretty farm overlooking the Rance offers tranquillity aplenty. Rooms have been recently renovated. Friendly welcome.

🍴EAT

INTRA-MUROS

🍽**La Brigantine** – *13 rue de Dinan.* ☎*02 99 56 82 82. Closed Tue and Wed off season except school holidays.* Galettes and crêpes made from organic products are the order of the day in this bright dining room, which takes its name from the sail behind the old riggings.

🍽**Ti Nevez** – *12 rue Broussais.* ☎*02 99 40 82 50. Closed Jan and Tue–Wed except school holidays.* Traditional *crêperie* with a rustic setting, well-known for its flat cake, egg-cheese-andouille and its crêpe Québécoise with maple syrup.

🍽**Au Pied d'Cheval** – *6 rue Jacques Cartier.* ☎*02 99 40 98 18. Closed 15 Nov–30 Mar.* The Le Moal family raise their own shellfish in nearby Cancale, and serve a delicious variety in their nautically decorated restaurant.

🍽**Crêperie Margaux** – *3 place du Marché aux légumes.* ☎*02 99 20 26 02. Closed Tue & Wed, except for school holidays.* Enjoy freshly-made *crêpes* on a lovely terrace in fine weather. Tea room serving ice cream in the afternoon.

🍽**Le Petit Crêpier** – *6 rue Ste. Barbe.* ☎*02 99 40 93 19. www.lepetitcrepier.fr. Closed Jan, 15 days in Nov, Tue & Wed, except for school holidays.* Traditional *crêpes* and some fillings too in a maritime-themed atmosphere.

🍽🍷**La Coquille d'Oeuf** – *20 rue de la Corne-de-Cerf.* ☎*02 99 40 92 62. Closed Mon.* Yellow walls decorated with paintings, parquet floor, little armchairs … the contemporary style of this restaurant in the town centre is

lovely. Add to the mix great service and delicious food and you'll understand why it makes a good pit stop.

🍽🍷🍷**Le Chalut** – *8 rue de la Corne de Cerf.* ☎*02 99 56 71 58. Closed Mon and Tue. Reservations obligatory.* Well-known address for its fish, seafood and lobsters, this cosy setting fittingly evokes the sea and its ships. Excellent value for money.

EXTRA-MUROS

🍽🍷**La Corderie** – *Cité d'Aleth, 9 chemin de la Corderie, St-Servan-sur-Mer.* ☎*02 99 81 62 38. www.lacorderie.com. Closed Mon except public holidays.* Perched above the Solidor tower, this villa offers fine views over the Rance and its dam. Famous for its fish specialities, there's a terrace for fine days and two dining rooms with panoramic windows.

🎭 NIGHTLIFE

L'Aviso – *12 rue du Point-du-Jour.* ☎*02 99 40 99 08.* More than 300 specialities of beer await lovers of a good brew. Snacks and summer musical nights.

Le Cancalais –*1 quai Solidor.* ☎*02 99 81 15 79. Closed Mon off season.* Pleasant terrace on the Solidor dock, where many generations intermingle when it's time for an aperitif. Quick snacks, internet access and summer concerts.

Cuningham's Bar – *2 rue des Hauts-Sablons.* ☎*02 99 81 48 08. www.st-malo-hotel-cunningham.com.* This warm bar-pub, decorated as a steerage deck, offers good views over the beach and organises regular entertainment evenings with Jazz and Brazilian music.

Casino Barrière – *2 chaussée du Sillon.* ☎*02 99 40 64 00.* Fruit machines, roulette, bar and restaurant.

🏃ACTIVITIES

Diving – Club Subaquatique de la Côte d'Émeraude – *terre-plein du Naye.* ☎*02 99 19 90 36. www.saintmalo plongee.com. Open all year.* Full range of dives on the Côte d'Émeraude: introductory dives, thematic diving (biology, archaeology), fishing lessons.

Kayak – Corsaires Malouins – *4 rue des Bouchers.* ☎*02 99 40 92 04.* Lessons, trips on the Rance estuary and introductory tours for age 10 and up.

Sailing – Société Nautique de la Baie de St-Malo (SNBSM) – *quai du Bajoyer. ✆02 99 18 20 30. www.snbsm.com. Based at the beaches of Bon Secours and Havre de Rothéneuf. Closed Dec–mid-Apr.* Lessons or equipment rental.

Surf School – *2 av. de la Hoguette. ✆02 99 40 07 47. www.surfschool.org. Open 9am–12.30pm, 1.30pm–6pm.* On Hoguette beach, this club offers lessons in windsurfing, fun board and catamaran, as well as trips on old ships.

Thalasso – Thermes Marins – *Grande Plage du Sillon. ✆02 99 40 75 00. www. thalassotherapie.com. Closed first half of Jan.* Seaweed, showers, jets, pool, sauna, restaurant: a great place on a rainy day.

BOAT TRIPS

Étoile Marine Croisières – *41 quai Duguay-Trouin. ✆02 99 40 48 72. www. etoile-marine.com.* For a day, a weekend or a week, you can sail on a sailing ship towards Chausey and Morbihan.

Le Renard – *Tour Ouest, Grande Porte, ✆02 99 40 53 10. www.cotre-corsaire-renard.com.* In summer, set sail on board a privateer's ship where you can participate in the operations on board.

FESTIVALS

Étonnants Voyageurs – *✆02 99 31 05 74. www. etonnants-voyageurs.com.* Pentecost literary festival at the Palais du Grand Large; **Solidor en Peinture** – *✆02 99 81 96 80. www.solidorenpeinture. com.* Last weekend of June, near the Solidor tower. Professionals or amateurs paint the tower or the port; **La Route du Rock** – *✆02 99 54 01 11. www.laroute durock.com.* Three days of music in August from international rock bands, with around 25 000 festival-goers.

Dinard ♨♨♨

This smart resort, which lies in a magnificent setting on the estuary of the Rance, opposite St-Malo, is frequented by the international set and in particular by the British and Americans. The place was 'launched' about 1850 by an American named Coppinger and developed by the British. Before that it was a small fishing village and an offshoot of St-Énogat.

THE NORTH
Pointe du Moulinet★★
A walk round this point starting from Grande Plage offers a series of magnificent views of the coast from Cap Fréhel on the left, to St-Malo on the right and, a little further on, of the Rance estuary.

Grande Plage (Plage de l'Écluse★)
This beach of fine sand, bordered by luxurious hotels, the casino and convention centre (Palais des Congrès), extends to

▶ **Population:** 10,644.
◔ **Michelin Map:** Local map 309 J – Ille-et-Vilaine (35)E.
Info: 2 blvd. Féart, 35802 Dinard. ✆02 99 46 94 12. www.ot-dinard.com.
◔ **Location:** On the left bank of the Rance estuary, across from St-Malo.
◔ **Timing:** This popular resort is especially enjoyable in late spring. Allow 2hr for a walk around town, then walk along the coast towards St-Lunaire.
Parking: St-Énogat car park has 500 spaces in the centre of town.

the end of the cove formed by Moulinet and Malouine Points.
Following the promenade along the beach to the left you will reach a terrace from which you can see St-Malo.

GETTING AROUND

Cycles Duval – 53 rue Gardiner. 𝒞02 99 46 19 63.
Breizh Cycles – 8 r. St-Énogat. 𝒞02 99 46 27 25. www.breizhcycles.com.

TOURS

Dinard is a designated "Ville d'art et d'histoire" and offers guided tours *(1hr 30)* from Jun–Sept. Enquire at the Tourist Office.

THE EAST

Promenade du Clair de Lune and Plage du Prieuré★

This walk *(pedestrians only)* lies along a sea wall which follows the water's edge and offers pretty views over the Rance estuary. Lovely multicoloured flower beds and remarkable Mediterranean vegetation embellish the promenade. The **Plage du Prieuré** is at the end of the Promenade. It owes its name to a priory founded here in 1324.

Pointe de la Vicomté★★

The Vicomté, a fine estate divided into lots, is becoming one of Dinard's most fashionable quarters.
Walk along the circular road (chemin de Ronde), which starts at Avenue Bruzzo and offers splendid vistas towards the roadstead, the Rance estuary and the Usine marémotrice de la Rance.

🚗 DRIVING TOUR

From Dinard to Cap Fréhel

73km/45mi – allow 4hr.

Dinard⚐⚐⚐

Though the road does not follow all the indentations of the coast between Dinard and Cap Fréhel, it has interesting overhanging sections and opens up fine panoramas and remarkable scenery. Many fashionable and family resorts lie along the coast.

St-Lunaire⚐⚐

4km/2.5mi along D 786.

This smart resort, not far from Dinard, has two fine beaches: St-Lunaire to the east, which is the more frequented as it faces St-Malo, and Longchamp (the larger of the two that face Cap Fréhel) to the west.

Pointe du Décollé★★

The point is joined to the mainland by a natural bridge crossing a deep fissure and is known as the Cat's Leap (Saut du Chat); the Décollé promenades are laid out beyond the bridge.

To the left of the entrance to the Décollé Pavilion, take the road leading to the point, where there is a granite cross.

From here the vantage point affords a very fine **view**★★ of the Côte d'Émeraude, from Cap Fréhel to Pointe de la Varde.

Grotte des Sirènes★

From the bridge crossing the cleft through which it opens to the sea, you can see the bottom of the grotto. The wash of the sea at high tide is spectacular.

Vieille église St-Lunaire

🕐*Open Easter–Oct, 9am–7pm.*
𝒞02 99 46 30 51 (Town Hall).
The church stands among the trees in a former cemetery. The nave is 11C; the side aisles and canted chancel were rebuilt in the 17C. In the middle of the nave lies the tomb of St-Lunaire with the recumbent figure of the saint (14C) resting on a Gallo-Roman sarcophagus. The transept contains seven tombs; in the Chapelle des Pontbriand in the north arm, note the tombs of a squire and a lady (15C), and in the Chapelle des Pontual in the south arm, the tomb of a lady of the Pontual family (13–14C), richly carved in high relief.

🚶 Pointe de la Garde Guérin★

15min on foot there and back. 🅿
After crossing the point at its base, turn right onto a road as it descends to the

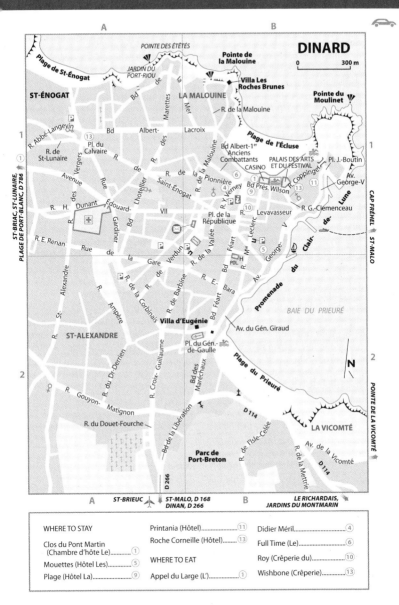

WHERE TO STAY		
Clos du Pont Martin (Chambre d'hôte Le)	1	
Mouettes (Hôtel Les)	5	
Plage (Hôtel La)	9	
Printania (Hôtel)	11	
Roche Corneille (Hôtel)	13	
WHERE TO EAT		
Appel du Large (L')	1	
Didier Méril	4	
Full Time (Le)	6	
Roy (Crêperie du)	10	
Wishbone (Crêperie)	13	

foot of the hill, which is honeycombed with casemates. Climb on foot to the top of the promontory, from which a fine **panorama**★★ extends from Cap Fréhel to Pointe de la Varde.

The road crosses Dinard golf course (60ha/148.3 acres).

St-Briac-sur-Mer⌂

This pleasant resort with its picturesque and varied sites, has a fishing harbour, a marina, and many good beaches. There are good views of the coast from the Balcon d'Émeraude (Emerald Balcony) and the Croix des Marins (Sailors' Cross) which is accessed from the Emerald Balcony by a path on the left, just before a bridge.

◯ *As you come out of St-Briac cross the Frémur river on a bridge 330m long.*

137

Lancieux

This village has a very extensive beach of fine sand, from which there is a lovely view of Ebihens Island and the advanced points of the coast: St-Jacut-de-la-Mer, St-Cast and Cap Fréhel. In the centre of the village stands the old bell-tower of the former church. The square tower is capped by a dome and its lantern turret.

Château d'eau de Ploublay

Enquire about opening times.
℘02 96 27 36 98.
Its 54m-high circular terrace gives a splendid view of the horizon taking in Ploublay and Dinan, the river Frémur, St-Jacut, St-Cast, St-Malo and, on a clear day, the Îles Chausey.

In Ploubalay take the road towards Dinard and 800m further on turn left.

St-Jacut-de-la-Mer

The road follows a long peninsula and goes through St-Jacut-de-la-Mer, a small fishing port and seaside resort. After skirting the beach of Le Rougeret, you will reach the high and picturesque cliff of the **Pointe du Chevet**. Opposite there is a fine **view** of the Île Ebihens and its tower, of the Bay of Arguenon (note the upstanding poles – *bouchots* – where mussels mature) to the left, and of St-Cast, to the right of the Bay of Lancieux.

Le Guildo

This village lies in a picturesque setting on the shore of the Arguenon estuary. From the bridge across it you will see the ruins of Le Guildo Castle on the east bank. In the 15C this was the seat of Gilles de Bretagne, a carefree and gallant poet, who led a happy life at Le Guildo. However, Gilles was suspected of plotting by his brother, the reigning duke, and was thrown in jail. As he did not die quickly enough, he was smothered. Before Gilles died he summoned his brother to the judgement of God. A short time later the Duke died, supposedly of remorse.

Les Pierres Sonnantes

Opposite the ruins of the castle *(to the right, on the far bank)* you will find a pile of rocks known as "the ringing stones" which emit a metallic note when you strike them with a stone of the same type. This resonance is due to the perfectly even grain of the rocks.

Go towards St-Cast on the coast road.

Pointe de Bay

A good road on the right leads to a large car park. The **view** includes the Arguenon estuary with its lines of mussel poles and the Presqu'île de St-Jacut, as well as the Île Ebihens. The road skirts the fashionable, sandy beach of **Pen-Guen**.

Pointe de la Garde★★

At the end of this point there is a very fine **view**★★ of the beaches of St-Cast and Pen Guen and the coast as far as Pointe de la Garde; also a statue of Notre-Dame-de-la-Garde by Armel Beaufils. A scenic path goes round the point by way of the Corniche de la Plage near the Hôtel Ar Vro, passes beside the oratory, follows the cliff along the point and, on the south shore, joins the road leading to the slipway near the oratory.

Church

At Le Bourg.
The modern church, built between 1897 and 1899, contains a 12C stoup and some 17C statues of St-Clément and St-Cado. The latter, very popular in Wales, is called Cast in Breton. He can be found elsewhere in Brittany, notably St-Cado and Pleucadec.

St-Cast-le-Guildo

West of Dinard (25km/15.5mi) and St-Malo (32km/20mi), St-Cast is reached by the D 786, D 13 or D 19. See Michelin map 309 I3 – Côtes-d'Armor (22).
This seaside resort (population 3,187) is formed by three settlements: Le Bourg, L'Isle and Les Mielles. The port shelters a small fishing fleet which specialises in scallops and clams. Paths lead to Pointe St-Cast and Garde for their views.

Chapelle Ste-Blanche
At L'Isle.
Above the high altar is an old statue of St-Blanche – the mother of St-Guénolé, St-Jacut and St-Venec – which is the object of great veneration.

Pointe de St-Cast★★
There is a superb **view**★★ of the Côte d'Émeraude from here. A viewing table – *table d'orientation* – beside the signal station indicates local sites of interest, including, on a fine day, Jersey, 100km/62mi away.
At the tip of the point a monument to the Escaped Prisoners of France *(Monument aux Évadés)* can be reached by a cliff path which follows the shore, passes another monument dedicated to the crew of the frigate *Laplace*, mined in 1950, and rejoins the St-Cast road at La Mare Beach *(Plage de la Mare)*.

After Trécelin, take teh D 16A to the entrance of the fort, where you will find parking.

Fort La Latte★★
Open 7 Jul–26 Aug, 10am–7pm; Apr–Jun, 10am–12.30pm, 2pm–6pm; Oct–Mar, Sat–Sun 2pm–6pm. Guided tours (50min). 5€ (children 2.80€). 02 96 41 57 11. www.castlelalatte.com. This stronghold, built by the Goyon-Matignons in the 14C, remodelled in the 17C and restored in the early 20C, has kept its feudal appearance. It stands on a spectacular **site**★★, separated from the mainland by two gullies, which are crossed by drawbridges.
A gate marks the entrance to the park. Follow the lane to the fort; you will pass a menhir known as Gargantua's Finger. You will visit in succession: the two fortified enclosures, the inner courtyard, around which are located the guardroom, the Governor's living quarters, the cistern and the chapel. Cross the thick walls made to shield the defender from cannon-balls and go to the Échauguette Tower *(Tour de l'Échaugette)* and the cannon-ball foundry. A look-out post takes you to the keep. From the parapet walk, there is a **panorama**★★ of Sévignés Cove, Cap Fréhel, the bay of La Frênaye, Pointe de St-Cast, the Hébihens archipelago, the resorts of St-Briac and St-Lunaire, Pointe du Décollé, St-Malo, Paramé and Rothéneuf, the Île de Cézembre, the Pointe du Meinga and the walls of the fort. It is possible to walk up to the top of the tower *(difficult steps)*.

ADDRESSES

STAY
DINARD
Hôtel Les Mouettes – *64 av. George V.* 02 99 46 10 64. 9 rooms. 8€. Unpretentious away from the bustle of the town centre, but near the coast. Rooms are on the small side, but they are soundproofed, and welcome is extremely warm.

Chambre d'hôte Le Clos du Pont Martin – *35 800 St-Briac-sur-Mer.* 02 99 88 38 07/06. www.briac.com. 3 rooms. Cosy welcome at this modern house 5mins from the beach. During winter, breakfast is served next to a roaring fire.

Hôtel La Plage – *3 blvd Féart.* 02 99 46 14 87. www.hoteldelaplage-dinard.com. 18 rooms. 10€. Breakfast is served on terrace overlooking the beach at this charming hotel. Renovated rooms ensure a restful night.

Hôtel Printania – *5 ave. Georges V.* 02 99 46 13 07. www. printaniahotel.com. 57 rooms. Closed 20 Nov–20 Mar. 9.50€. The communal areas are very well decorated with furniture, faiences and paintings evoking Brittany. Guest rooms have a view over the sea or over the avenue. Breakfast on a pleasant veranda.

Roche Corneille – *4 rue G. Clemenceau.* 02 99 46 14 47. www. dinard-hotel-roche-corneille.com. 28 rooms. 13€. Late 19C villa elegantly furnished, with mod cons such as Wi-Fi. Restaurant specialises in market fresh "surf and turf".

MATIGNON

Hôtel Restaurant de la Poste – *11 pl. Gouyon, 22550 Matignon. 5km/3mi SE on the D 13.* ℘*02 96 41 02 20. www. hoteldelaposte.pays-de-matignon.net. Closed 2 weeks in Jan, 2 weeks in Oct, Sun eve and Mon. 13 rooms.* ⌑*8€. Restaurant*. This welcoming auberge dating from 1900 has comfortable, well-kept rooms. The dining room opens onto a covered terrace.

ST-LUNAIRE

La Pensée – *35 rue de la Grève.* ℘*02 99 46 03 82. www.la-pensee.fr.* ⌑. Tastefully decorated rooms overlooking an English garden along the sea.

LA RICHARDAIS

Le Berceul – *24 rue de la Théaudais.* ℘*02 23 17 06 00. www.berceul.com. 3 rooms.* ⌑*.18C shipowners' house and garden. Elegant country setting. Family accommodation for four people in duplex.

⟡EAT

DINARD

Crêperie Wishbone – *8 Place du Calvaire, St-Énogat.* ℘*02 99 46 94 92. Closed Jan, Mon and Tue off season.* Traditional crêpes served under exposed beams or on the terrace.

Le Full Time – *2 blvd Albert 1er.* ℘*02 99 46 18 72. Closed Oct–Mar.* Sandwiches and ice cream.

Crêperie du Roy – *9 blvd Féart.* ℘*02 99 46 10 52. evelynepeda@wanadoo.fr.* Huge range of homemade *crêpes* and galettes surrounded by model boats.

Castor-Bellux – *5 rue Winston Churchill.* ℘*02 99 46 25 72. www.hotel-altair-dinard.com. Closed Tue and Wed off season.* Pizzas, mussels and mixed salads in a lively atmosphere.

L'Appel du Large – *4 blvd Wilson.* ℘*02 99 16 30 30. www.lucienbarriere.com. Closed second week of Jan, first week of Feb, Mon & Tue except Jul & Aug.* Wonderful views of Dinard beach. Classic brasserie menu with good seafood served amid cruise liner decor.

Didier Méril – *1 place Géneral de Gaulle,* ℘*02 99 46 95 74. www.restaurant-didier-meril.com Closed 17 Nov–2 Dec.* Traditional cuisine in modern surroundings. Rooms () available.

MATIGNON

Crêperie St-Germain – *St-Germain-de-la-Mer.* ℘*02 96 41 08 33. Open from Easter.* ⟡*Reservations obligatory off season.* Well known for its famous salmon galette. Rustic interior with fireplace.

ST-LUNAIRE

Le Décollé – *Pointe du Décollé,* ℘*02 99 46 01 70. www.restaurantdu decolle.com Closed Mon and Tue off season, Mon in Jul–Aug and 12 Nov–1 Feb.* Superb seafood and wonderful views over St-Malo bay.

♥ ENTERTAINMENT

Yacht Club de Dinard – *9 promenade du Clair de Lune.* ℘*02 99 46 14 22. www.yacht-club-dinard.fr.* Open to everyone for a drink or a lunch in a moderately formal atmosphere.

L'Escale à Corto –*12 av. George V.* ℘*02 99 46 78 57. Closed Mon off season.* Step into the world of Corto Maltese and enjoy the hip atmosphere of this pub-restaurant.

Casino de Dinard – *4 blvd Wilson.* ℘*02 99 16 30 30. www.lucienbarriere.com.* Slot machines, seafood restaurant and pub on Écluse beach.

La Chaumière – *pointe du Décollé.* ℘*02 99 16 61 12. From midnight to daybreak, daily in summer, weekends off season.* Perched above the waves, the only nightclub in the area.

⟡ACTIVITIES

Beaches – Bathing is supervised (*10am–1pm and 3pm–7pm*) on **Prieuré and Écluse beaches** (the busiest beaches) and at **St-Énogat** and **Port-Blanc**. **Best beaches:** Grande Plage, Pen-Guen; the wilder La Frênaye and La Pissotte.

Boat Trips – up the Rance and to the Discover the little creeks and fine sandy south-facing beach of the Île de Cézembre. Enquire at the Tourist Office.

Diving – Club subaquatique Dinardais – *25 rue Barbine, ☎02 99 46 25 97. Apr–Oct and weekend.* Level 1 and equipment required *(17P/diving).*

Horse-riding – Centre Hippique de DInard – *20 rue du Val Porée. 02 99 46 23 57. www.dinard-equitation.com. Open daily 10am–noon, 2pm–6pm during the season. Closed Sept and Mon off season.* This equestrian centre organises lessons and treks. International showjumping competition in August.

Sea kayak and windsurf – Centre nautique de Port-Blanc – *rue Sergent-Boulanger. ☎02 99 88 23 21, www.voile dinard.com.* Windsurfing lessons for children from 7 years old; kayaks and windsurfer rentals. **Wishbone Club** – *plage de l'Écluse ☎02 99 88 15 20. www. wishbone-club-dinard.com)* Lessons for children from 6–15 years old from Mar–Dec Mon–Sat.

Sea water swimming pool- *Digue de l'Écluse. ☎02 99 46 22 77.* All year, open-air, heated swimming pool, sauna.

Thalassotherapy – Thalasso Dinard – *1 ave. du Château Hébert. ☎02 99 16 78 10. www.novoteldinard.com. Open 9am–1pm and 2pm–6pm. Closed 5–26 Dec.* Opened in 1990, this modern building has great views over St-Malo.

FESTIVALS AND EVENTS
La Promenade du Claire de Lune – From Jul–Sept there are *son et lumière* spectacles in town.

Festival du Filme Britannique de Dinard (Dinard British Film Festival) – *Palais des Arts et du Festival, 2, boulevard Féart , 35800 Dinard. ☎299 49 19 04.* This annual film festival takes place in October. Visit *www.festivaldufilm-dinard. com* for more information.

SHOPPING
There's a **market** on *place Crolard* on Tue, Thu and Sat mornings. It is well-known throughout the region and its loyal clients come from miles around.

Cap Fréhel★★★

The site of this cape is one of the grandest on the Breton coast. Its red, grey and black cliffs rise vertically to a height of 70m/230ft and are fringed with reefs on which the swell breaks heavily.

BACKGROUND
Overlooking the English Channel, legend has it that in ancient times you could walk to the UK from here! Of course, scientists have since proved otherwise. This wild, protected site covers 400ha/988.4 acres of heathland and includes an ornithology park. Many bird species nest on the rocks.

PANORAMA
Open May–Sept, daily exc Tue; Mar–Apr exc Tue and Wed 2pm–6pm. ☎02 96 41 43 06. (2€).
The coastal panorama is vast in clear weather: from the Pointe du Grouin, on the right, with the Cotentin in the back-

- **Michelin Map:** Local map 309 I2 - Côtes-d'Armor (22).
- **Info:** place de Chambly, 22240 Fréhel. ☎02 96 41 57 23. www.paysde frehel.com.
- **Location:** Between St-Brieuc and Dinard, on the Emerald Coast.
- **Kids:** Fort La Latte.
- **Timing:** Be around for high tide when the waves crash on the rocks.
- **Don't Miss:** Fort de la Latte and the coastal walks.

ground, to the Île de Bréhat, on the left. The famous outline of Fort la Latte is visible on the right.

TOUR DU CAP
30min walk.
At the extremity of the headland stands the **lighthouse** built in 1950 and lit

Cap Fréhel

Y. Tierny/MICHELIN

automatically nowadays by a xenon flash lamp; the light carries only 200m in foggy weather but it can be seen 120km/75mi away when it is clear. From the gallery at the top of the tower, there is an immense view of the horizon: you may see Bréhat to the west, Jersey to the north, Granville, a part of the Cotentin Peninsula and the Îles Chausey to the northeast. At a point 400m from the lighthouse a siren mounted in a shelter gives two blasts every minute in foggy weather.

After passing the furthest point where the siren stands, you can look down on the **Fauconnière rocks**, crowded with seagulls and cormorants; the contrast between the mauvish-red of the rocks and the blue or green of the sea is striking. Near the Restaurant de la Fauconnière, take a steep path on the right; halfway down it reaches a platform from which there is another fine view of the Fauconnière rocks and the sea.

ADDRESSES

⍩/ EAT

⊜⊜ **La Fauconnière** – *À la Pointe, 22240 Fréhel.* ℘*02 96 41 54 20. Closed Oct–Mar.* You have to go on foot to reach this restauant which has been built on the rocks in a wild setting and offers excellent views over the sea and the coast. Perfect for tourists, the chef offers a choice of menus at good prices.

⊜⊜ **Le Victorine** – *Pl. de Chambly, 22240 Fréhel.* ℘*02 96 41 55 55.* Family restaurant serving traditional dishes

⍨⍨ ACTIVITIES

Nature Walks – *Syndicat des Caps, rue Notre Dame, 22240 Plévenon.* ℘*02 96 41 50 83.* This organisation offers guided walks to explore the rocks, observe birds, cross dunes and marshes, admire the caves by kayak, follow in the footsteps of the Templars, help at the fish auction. You'll need to speak French!

BOAT TRIPS

Boats leave St-Malo, St-Cast and Dinard allowing you to view Cap Fréhel from the sea.

Compagnie Corsaire – ℘*0825 138 035. www.compagniecorsaire.com.* Trip with commentary *(2hr 30)* from St-Malo *(cale de Dinan)* and Dinard; explore the west coast to Fort La Latte and Cap Fréhel The return boat stops at St-Cast during July and August.

Dinan★★

Dinan's old town is a small gem; its old houses and streets are surrounded by ramparts and guarded by an imposing castle. Enhanced by trees and gardens, it stands on a plateau overlooking the Rance and the marina 75m/ 230ft below.

A BIT OF HISTORY

Du Guesclin against Canterbury

In 1357 the Duke of Lancaster besieged Dinan, which was defended by Bertrand Du Guesclin and his brother Olivier. After several encounters with the superior English forces, Bertrand asked for a 40-day truce, after which, he promised, the town would surrender if it were not relieved. In violation of the truce, Olivier, who had gone out of the town unarmed, was made prisoner by an English knight, Canterbury, who demanded a ransom of 1 000 florins. Bertrand challenged the Englishman to single combat. The encounter took place at a spot now called place du Champ; a stele marks the spot. Lancaster presided. Canterbury lost and had to pay Olivier the 1,000 florins he had demanded and surrender his arms to Bertrand. He was also discharged from the English army.

Du Guesclin's tombs

After more than 20 years of campaigning for the King of France, Bertrand du Guesclin died on 13 July 1380, at the gates of Châteauneuf-de-Randon, to which he had laid siege. He had asked to be buried at Dinan. The funeral convoy, therefore, set out for that town. At Le Puy the body was embalmed and the entrails buried in the Jacobins' church (now the Église St-Laurent).

As the embalming was inadequate, the remains were boiled at Montferrand and the flesh was removed from the skeleton and buried in the Franciscans' church (destroyed in 1793). At Le Mans an officer of the King brought an order to bring the body to St-Denis; the skeleton was then handed over to him. Only the heart

- ▶ **Population:** 11,235.
- 🖍 **Michelin Map:** Local map 309 J4 – Côtes-d'Armor (22).
- 🗊 **Info:** 9 rue du Château, 22105 Dinan. ✎02 96 87 69 76. www.dinan-tourisme.com.
- ◖ **Location:** About 30km/ 18mi S of St-Malo.
- 👥 **Kids:** The zoo at Château de la Bourbansais.
- ◷ **Timing:** Allow a day to explore the old town and an afternoon for a trip on the Rance river.
- ◉ **Don't Miss:** Rue du Jerzual.

Château de Dinan

A. de Valroger/MICHELIN

arrived at Dinan, where it was deposited in the Jacobins' church. It has since been transferred to the Église St-Sauveur. So it was that, while the kings of France had only three tombs (for the heart, entrails and body), Du Guesclin had four!

🐾WALKING TOUR

Vieille Ville ★★

A medieval atmosphere can be felt as you walk through Dinan's old streets with their beautifully restored, picturesque half-timbered houses.

GETTING AROUND

Dinan can be explored on foot. Ask for the car park list at the Tourist Office.

Guided Tours – Dinan is a designated 'Ville d'art et d'histoire' and the Tourist Office offers several themed tours *(1hr 30min)*. See *www.dinan-tourisme.com.*

Tourist train – Guided tours of the town *(45min)*. Departures from the *Théâtre des Jacobins, place Duclos* and from the marina. *Easter–Oct, daily 9am–7pm.* ⌑6€. ℘02 99 88 47 07.

Rent a bike – **Cycles Gauthier**, *15 rue Déroyer.* ℘02 96 85 07 60. Be careful on the many cobbled streets of Dinan!

Place Du-Guesclin

In this square, bordered with 18C and 19C town houses, stands the equestrian statue of Du Guesclin; the square, with *place du Champ*, served as a fairground during the Middle Ages.

> *Bear right on rue Ste-Claire, then left on rue de l'Horloge.*

Hôtel Kératry

This attractive 16C mansion with three granite pillars, houses the Tourist Office.

Maison du Gisant

During the restoration of this 17C house, the 14C recumbent figure (exhibited outside) was found.

Tour de l'Horloge

⏱*Open Jun–Sept, 10am–6.30pm, Apr–May 2pm–6pm* ⌑*2.95€.* ℘02 96 87 02 26. Exhibition on Anne of Brittany. Exhibited in the belfry is the clock, bought by the town in 1498. From the top of the Clock Tower (158 steps), there is a vast **panorama**★★ of the town and its principal monuments and the surrounding countryside.

Place des Merciers★

The old well and lovely old triangular-gabled houses with wooden porches paint a pleasant scene. Different types of half-timbered houses, characteristic of 15C to 17C Dinan architecture, can be seen in rue de l'Apport: houses with the upper floor resting on thick wooden pillars, under which the merchants and tradesmen exposed their wares, houses with overhanging upper storeys and houses with large projecting display windows.

Glance into nearby rue de la Cordonnerie and rue du Petit-Pain lined with corbelled houses. At number 10 rue de la Mittrie, Théodore Botrel (1868–1925), the songwriter, was born.

> *Cross place des Cordeliers and take the Grande Rue on the left to reach St-Malo Church.*

Église St-Malo

This Flamboyant Gothic church was begun in 1490 and finished in the 19C. The late-15C transept, chancel and chevet make a striking impression. The **stained-glass windows** date from the 20C and depict life in the various districts of Dinan during major religious festivals.

> *Walk back along Grande-Rue and continue along rue de la Lainerie*

Rue du Jerzual★

This lovely cobbled street slopes steeply downhill. The 15C and 16C **shops** lining the street are now occupied by artists: glass-blowers, sculptors, weavers etc. This was once the main street leading down to the port; imagine the constant comings and goings of the bourgeois, the hawkers with their overflowing carts and the tradesmen and apprentices running about.

Maison du Gouverneur

24 rue du Petit-Fort.

This is a fine 15C mansion in which a weaving and high-warp tapestry workshop has been installed.

Walk down the street to the marina. On your way back, take the pretty walk along the watch-path of the ramparts

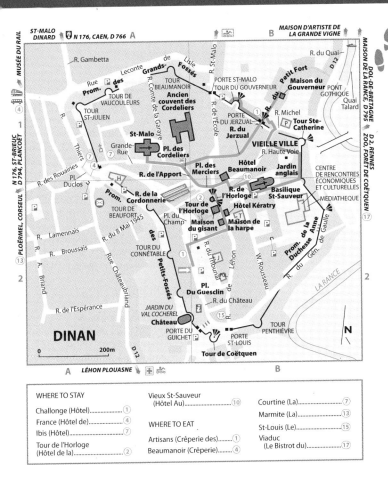

(stairs by the Porte de Jerzual). The walk leads past Tour due Gouverneur, which offers a lovely **view**★★ of the Rance Valley.

▷ *Walk up rue Michel then rue du Rempart to the Jardin Anglais.*

Jardin Anglais

The terraced garden offers a good overall **view**★★, especially from Tour Ste-Catherine, of the River Rance, the port, the enormous viaduct, 250m/820ft long and 40m/131ft high, and the ramparts.

Basilique St-Sauveur★

This basilica features a Romanesque porch surmounted by a Flamboyant Gothic gable opening off the façade. Construction stretched from the 12C

(the wall to the right) to the 16C. The original dome of the tower, which was destroyed by lightning, was replaced in the 18C by a timber steeple covered with slate.

Inside, the building's lack of symmetry is striking; the south side is Romanesque, while the north side, the transept and the chancel are Flamboyant Gothic. In the north transept, the heart of Du Guesclin is preserved behind a 14C tomb stone incorporated in a 19C tomb. The modern stained-glass windows were made in the Barillet workshop.

As you leave the basilica on place St-Sauveur, there is a house with pillars on the left, in which Auguste Pavie, diplomat and explorer of Indochina, was born in 1847.

145

Ancien Hôtel Beaumanoir

A beautiful Renaissance porch, called the Pelican, adorns the entrance of this old mansion. In the courtyard, note the decoration of the windows and a 16C turret, which houses a lovely staircase.

THE RAMPARTS

Promenade de la Duchesse-Anne

From this promenade along the ramparts, there is a lovely **view**★ of the Rance, the viaduct and the port.

Promenade des Petits-Fossés

This promenade skirts the outside of the 13C–15C ramparts. Looming above are the castle, and the Connétable and Beaufort Towers.

Promenade des Grands-Fossés

This magnificent avenue is embellished by the St-Julien, Vaucouleurs and Beaumanoir Towers and the Porte St-Malo.

Banks of the Rance

Allow 1hr on foot. Go down to the Rance and cross thePont Gothique (Gothic bridge).
On the right, take the old towpath which passes under the viaduct and follows the river. Green and sheltered, this is a pleasant place to stroll.

ADDITIONAL SIGHTS

Musée du Rail

In the left wing of Dinan station.
Open Jun–mid-Sept, 2pm–6pm.
4€. ℰ02 96 39 81 33.
www.museedurail-dinan.com.
The railway museum contains two model railway networks and a Vignier signal box dating from 1889. Railway enthusiasts will love the posters, clocks, lamps, engine plates, etc.

Ancien Couvent des Cordeliers

Open Jul and Aug, Mon–Fri 10am–6pm. ℰ02 96 85 89 00.
The 15C Gothic cloisters and the 13C turreted (pepper-pot roofs) main courtyard are all that remain of the monastery.

EXCURSIONS

Léhon

2km/1.25mi to the south.
In this little town nestling in the valley of the River Rance, you will find the prieuré de St-Magloire, built in the 12C. 45min visit.

The abbey **church** (abbatiale) (*open Jul–Aug, 10.30am–12.30pm, 2.30–6.30pm, Sun 2.30–6.30pm; guided tours available; 4€ (12-18 years, 3€); ℰ02 96 87 40 40*) was rebuilt in the 13C and restored in the late 19C. The nave, with its rounded, ribbed ceiling vault in the Angevin style, contains funerary

Marina on the River Rance

G. Targat/MICHELIN

monuments to the Beaumanoir family and a 13C font. At harvest time, people used to come to sharpen their sickles on the edge of the font in the hope of a good harvest.

A small stonework museum (musée lapidaire) in the **abbey buildings** contains capitals from the old Romanesque cloister. The 13C refectory is the oldest room in the abbey and has been nicely restored. Highlights include the pulpit with its staircase and platform and the open-work Gothic façade. Some objects from the abbey treasure, including a reliquary containing the relics of St-Magloire, are kept in the dormitory.

Upstairs, visitors can admire an impressive roof frame reminiscent of an inverted ship's hull, and some strange box structures that were built for the filming of a French television series, Les Compagnons du Nouveau Monde. Excavations in the **gardens** have revealed a covered canal linking the abbey to the River Rance below.

Quévert

▶ 3.5km/2.2mi NW. Access via the D 68.
The village is well-known to gardening enthusiasts for its wonderful flowers, especially roses, thanks to its scented garden, the **Courtil des senteurs★**. The garden (pl. de la Mairie, ℰ 02 96 85 81 80) contains over 700 varieties of roses, perennials and scented bulbs. Its sights and smells are a delight for the senses, particularly in late spring or early summer.

The **garden** is also the starting point for several themed walks: rose bushes, rocks or fruit trees (walks leave from the garden entrance, in front of the town hall. Duration, 1h, 2hrs or 3hrs - accessible to all).

Forêt de Coëtquen

▶ 10km/6.25mi to the east. Take the D 68 S or the VC 3 from St-Hélen.
This 557-hectare forest consisting mainly of broad-leafed trees offers lovely walks. Several paths have been signposted and trips are organised by the Maison de la Rance in Dinan (see p. 148).

Corseul

▶ 11km/7mi W. Leave Dinan towards St-Brieuc, then bear right onto D 794 to Plancoët.
Already known to the Celts, Corseul was conquered and extensively modified by the Romans, as was most of the Armor area. Many artefacts from those periods are gathered here, notably in the Garden of Antiquities (Jardin des Antiques), and in the **Musée de la Société Archéologique de Corseul** (◷ open Mon–Fri 10am–noon, 2pm–5.30pm, Sat 10am–noon; ◉2€; ℰ 02 96 82 73 14). On the second floor of the town hall are fossils from the Falun Sea, polished and dressed stones, funerary urns, coins, Roman murals and everyday implements from Gallo–Roman times. The most remarkable vestige is the **Temple du Haut-Bécherel**, said to be the Temple of Mars (1.5km/1mi on the road to Dinan and right on an uphill road). It is a polygonal tower with masonry in small courses, dating from Emperor Augustus' reign.

Château et Parc Zoologique de la Bourbansais★

▶ 14km/8.7mi SE. Guided tours of the château (50min), Apr–Sept 11.15am, 2pm, 3pm, 4pm, 5pm, Oct Sun only 3pm and 4pm. ◉17.00€ (children 12.50€). Combined ticket for Park and Château ◉21.00€. ℰ 02 99 69 40 07. www.labourbansais.com.
Standing in an immense park, this impressive late-16C building was embellished by three generations of the Huart family, counsellors to the Breton Parliament.

Château exterior

The main building is flanked by pinnacled turrets and saddleback-roofed pavilions characteristic of the 18C. The 13C Porte du Guichet is framed by towers pierced with arrow slits. The 14C dungeon, with its bold machicolations, houses a **museum** of the history of Dinan from prehistoric times to the early 20C. It also contains exhibits of local crafts. The top room displays works by painters who have drawn inspiration from the town and surrounding area, and by late 19C sculptors who worked in Dinan. From the terrace overlooking the watch-path there is a lovely **panorama**★ of the region. The Tour de Coëtquen, the old artillery tower, exhibits tombstones in a ground-floor room.

Château interior

On the ground floor the rooms are decorated and furnished in the 18C style and contain 17C Aubusson tapestries and a fine collection of porcelain from the Dutch India Company. In the peristyle, there is a display of documents, archives and personal objects belonging to the past owners that evoke the château's history.

Parc Zoologique et Jardin

⏱ *Daily Apr–Sept, 10am–7pm; Oct, 1.30pm–5.30pm..* ⚌17.00€ *zoo and gardens (3-12yrs 12.50€). Combined ticket for park and château 21.00€.* ♿
The zoo houses more than 500 animal species from the five continents. Entertainment several times a day, such as falconry displays and animal feeding. From July to September there's a maze made from corn in which to play hide and seek. Picnic area and restaurant.

🚗 DRIVING TOURS

VALLÉE DE LA RANCE★★

The Rance estuary, lying between St-Malo and Dinard, is one of the most popular spots in Brittany. Upstream, Dinan is a typical old inland town. The Rance is a perfect example of a Breton river. It forms a deep gulf between Dinan and the sea, flowing with many branches and inlets over a level plateau. This curious gulf is due to the marine flooding of an ordinary but steep-sided valley: the stream itself and the bottom of the valley have been 'drowned' by a mass of tidal water.
All that remains visible of the original valley is its steep sides, sloping into the sea. The Rance proper is a small river

without much water, which winds along above Dinan.

Boat Trip★★

Allow 5hr there and back – not counting the stop and tour of Dinan.
🗊 *For information, ask at the Tourist Offices of St-Malo, Dinard or Dinan.*
The boat follows the Noires breakwater (*Môle des Noires*) and crosses the Rance estuary for a brief stop at Dinard. It enters the Rance, leaving the Corniche d'Aleth on the left (St-Servan), passes in front of Pointe de la Vicomté and Rocher Bizeux and then enters the lock of the Rance dam. You will go up the river, between its great banks, through a series of narrow channels and wide pools. After Chatelier Lock (*Écluse du Chatelier*), the Rance gets narrower and narrower and becomes a mere canal just as you come within sight of Dinan, perched on its ridge.
Your boat will stop for a longer or shorter time according to the tide – from 8hr to only 15min.

1 RIGHT BANK: FROM DINAN TO ST-MALO

87km/54mi – allow one day.

Maison de la Rance

Quai Talard, on the port. ⏱*Open Jul– Aug, 10am–7pm; Apr–Jun and Sept– Nov Tue–Sun 2pm–6pm.* ⚌*3.90€.* ♿
📞*02 96 87 00 40.*
The Rance estuary is popular with recreational boaters. But the River Rance has a long and interesting history, as this exhibit shows. Interactive displays help visitors learn about the flora and fauna of this ecosystem.

Lanvallay

A remarkable **view**★ of the old town of Dinan, its ramparts and its belfries from here.

▷ *At Lanvallay, take the D 676 for 6km/3.7mi then the D 29 in the direction of Pleudihen-sur-Rance. 300m/328yds after La Vicomté-sur-Rance, there is a car park on the left . 500m/547yds on foot.*

Moulin du Prat

Open Jul–Aug 10am–
noon, 3pm–7pm; May–Jun
and Sept, Sat–Sun and public
holidays 2.30pm–6pm; rest
of the year Sun and public
holidays 2.30pm–6pm. 3€
(children no charge).
02 96 83 21 41.
This restored 15C mill is the
only functioning one that can
be visited in the area. There's
an exhibition on the evolution of mills and wildlife to be
seen in the grounds (herons,
egrets). If you're lucky, you'll
spy the seal who has made his
home in the creek.

Rejoin the D 29 for
1km/0.6mi then turn left in
the direction of Mordreuc.

Cale de Mordreuc

From this lovely spot there are
good views of Pont St-Hubert
downstream, the deepening
valley upstream and the ruins
of an old castle on an opposite promontory.

From Mordreuc, follow
the D 48 for 1km/0.6mi.

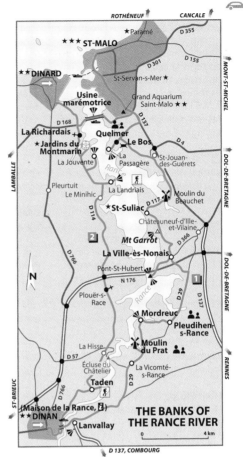

THE BANKS OF
THE BANKS OF THE RANCE RIVER

Pleudihen-sur-Rance

The farm's outbuildings house the
Musée de la Pomme et du Cidre
(Apple and Cider Museum: open
Jul–Aug, daily 10am–7pm; Apr–Jun
and Sept–15 Oct, Mon–Sat 2pm–7pm;
3.50€; 02 96 83 20 78).

Tidal Power

The use of tidal power is nothing new to the Vallée de la Rance. As early as the
12C, riverside dwellers had thought up the idea of building little reservoirs
which, as they emptied with the ebb tide, drove mill wheels. To double the
output of a modern industrial plant, it was tempting to try to work out a means
of using the flow as well as the ebb tide. The French electricity board (EDF),
therefore, searched for new technical methods of producing electricity and
successfully set up, between the headlands of La Briantais and La Brebis, a usine
hydro-électrique (hydroelectric power station) operated by both the flow and
ebb of the tide. A 750m/820yd-long dam extends across the Rance estuary; it
forms a rservoir covering 22sq km/8.5sq mi. The road linking St-Malo and Dinard
runs along the top of the dam and across the 65m/213ft-long lock which allows
ships through.

Before visiting the museum stop by the orchard planted with different varieties of apple trees. Inside the museum, the apple, its origin, the different varieties, diseases, cultivation and picking are explained.

A film illustrating the different apple-related trades (e.g. cooperage) and a tasting end the tour.

Take the D 29 for 7km/4.3mi and turn left onto the D 366 in the direction of la Ville-ès-Nonais ; go through the town continue until the pont St-Hubert.

Pont St-Hubert

From the suspension bridge there is a beautiful view of the Rance, the slipway of Port St-Jean and on the other rocky bank, the slipway of Port St-Hubert.

From Ville-ès-Nonais, take the D 407 then the D 7 in the direction of St-Suliac and turn left onto the route du Mont-Garrot. Leave the car near the crenelated watch tower, about 1km/0.6mi before St-Suliac.

Mont Garrot

Allow 15min on foot there and back. A path to the right leads to the point, passing behind a farm. Notice the views of the Vallée de la Rance on the way.

Continue along the route du Mont Garrot for 1km/0.6mi.

St-Suliac

This charming fishing village has retained a number of old granite houses along its meandering streets overlooked by the massive bell-tower of the church (13–17C).

Note the fine **parish close** nearby. A steep street leads down to the bank of the Rance where the local sailing school is active in fine weather.

At St-Jouan-des-Guérets, take the C 2 in the direction of the plage du Vallion then Le Fougeray. Follow on for 1km/0.6mi and notice on the left the Chàtea de Bos.

From the foot of the tower, there is a wide **panorama**★ of St-Suliac Cove, St-Malo, the Dol countryside, the River Rance and Pont St-Hubert.

Château du Bos

Not open to the public.
An example of a St-Malo mansion once the country home of merchants or corsaires.

Continue to the crossroad. Turn left at the chapelle du Bos.

Quelmer

The itinerary continues in front of the old house of Commandant Charcot (private) and leads to the slipway of la Pasagere which gives a pretty view of the Rance. Be careful: bathing is dangerous due to the proximity of the barrage. Not far away, the boat cemetery presents a nostalgic image.

The **Labyrinthe du corsaire** maze is comprised of tall maize plants (*Rte Quelmer la Passagère, 35 400 St-Malo; daily 7 Jul–29 Aug, 10.30am–7pm; 7.50€; ℘02 99 81 17 23. www.labyrinth educorsaire.com*).

Return to St-Malo by the D137.

St-Malo★★★ – See ST-MALO.

Return to the other bank of the Rance along the crest of the dam in the direction of Dinard.

2 THE LEFT BANK: FROM DINARD TO DINAN

28km/17.5mi – allow half a day.

Usine Marémotrice de la Rance

Open Apr–Sept, 10am–12.30pm, 1.30pm–6pm; school holidays (Feb, Nov, Dec), Wed–Sun 10am–12.30pm, 1.30pm –6pm. ℘02 99 16 37 14.

The **power station** is in a huge tunnel nearly 390m long in the very centre of the dam. In this room, are the 24 AC generators of a combined capacity of 240 000kW which can produce 600 million kWh per year (equal to the annual consumption of a city comparable to Rennes and its outskirts). The **view**★ from the platform atop the dam extends over the Rance estuary as far as Dinard and St-Malo. The dam lies between the power station and the right bank with its centre on the small island of Chalibert. There are six sluice-gates at the eastern end that regulate the emptying and filling of the reservoir, thus controlling the water supply to the power station.

 ▷ *Continue for 3km/1.75mi. At the entry to La Richardais there is a view over the l'Usine Marémotrice and the estuary of the Rance.*

La Richardais

The **church** (◔ open mid-Jun–mid-Sept, Sun–Fri 2pm–7pm; Apr–May and mid-Sept–Oct, Sun–Fri 2pm–6pm; ℘02 99 88 58 79) is dominated by its pierced tower and the calvary surmounting it. On the walls of the nave runs a fresco (1955) depicting the Stations of the Cross by Xavier de Langlais. In the transept is a fresco illustrating the arrival of St-Lunaire and St-Malo on the Breton coast. From the fine wood vaulting resembling the upturned keel of a ship, four lamps in the form of wheels hang down. Five stained-glass windows are by Max Ingrand.

On nearby rue du suet is the Atelier Manoli (9 rue du suet; ◔open daily Jul–Aug, 10.30am–12pm, 3pm–7pm; Apr–Jun and Sept–Oct, weekends and public holidays 3pm–7pm; •–•guided tours available on request, phone 5 days in advance; ▨4€, under 12yrs, free; ℘02 99 88 55 53), where you can see more than 300 of the sculptor's works in his studio and garden. On leaving La Richardais by the north, you get a **view** of the tidal power scheme and the Rance estuary.

 ▷ *Follow the D114 for 500m/547yds and turn left.*

Jardins du Montmarin

500m/547yds on the right by the D 114. ◔*Open Apr–Oct Sun–Fri 2pm–7pm.* ◑*Closed public holidays.* ▨*6€.* ℘*02 99 88 58 79. www.domaine-du-mont marin.com.*

An elegant 18C house whose gardens descend in terraces to the river. The paths offer wonderful views. Nursery.

 ▷ *Continue on the D114 and take the next left.*

Cale de la Jouvente

Opposite La Passagère.
There is a nice view of the Rance and the Île Chevret.

 ▷ *Rejoin the D114 for 1km/0.6mi and turn to the left.*

La Landriais

The port contains naval dockyards. The walk along Hures Promenade (▮on foot take Chemin de ronde des Douaniers) starts from the car park and skirts the Rance for 2km/1.2mi affording fine views.

 ▷ *Rejoin the D114 then the D12 until Taden.*

▮ Taden

When you cross the village towards the slipway, glance at the porch and keep, which are flanked by a 14C turret. The towpath, which used to link Dinan to the Écluse du Chatelier, is a favourite spot for fishermen and a pleasant place to stroll (7km/4.5m). Taden Plain is the home of a number of aquatic birds: black-headed gulls, herring gulls, coots, etc.

ADDRESSES

⌂ STAY

DINAN

⌂ **Hôtel Au Vieux St-Sauveur** – *19 pl. St-Sauveur.* ℘*02 96 85 30 20. www.hotel pubsaintsauveur.com. 6 rooms.* ▭ *6€.* This residence in the historic quarter, dates from the 15C. The bar gives a warm welcome to customers until 2am in summer. There are small unpretentious but pretty rooms on all floors.

⌂⌂ **Le Hôtel Challonge** – *29 Place Du Guesclin.* ℘*02 96 87 16 30. www.hotel-dinan.fr. 18 rooms.* ▭ *8€.* Comfortable establishment in town centre with a classical façade. Comfortable well soundproofed rooms with green and ochre walls, some of which have views over the square.

🛏🍽 **Hôtel La Tour de l'Horloge** – *5 r. de la Chaux. ☎02 96 39 96 92. www. hotel-dinan.com. 12 rooms. ☐ 7€.* An 18C house in the heart of the historic quarter, this hotel offers individually decorated rooms and a very warm welcome.

🛏🍽 **Hôtel de France** – *7 Place Du 11 Novembre. ☎02 96 39 22 56. 14 rooms. ☐ 7.50€.* This practical well situated old establishment near the Château offers spacious well soundproofed and air-conditioned rooms. The redecorated dining room has an attractive veranda.

🛏🍽 **Hôtel Ibis** – *1 place Duclos. ☎02 96 39 46 15. h5977@accor.com. 62 rooms. ♿ ☐ 8€.* Functional, spacious rooms with air-conditioning. Well situated between the ramparts and the château.

VALLÉE DE LA RANCE

🍽🛏 **Chambre d'hôte Les Mouettes** – *17 Grande-Rue, 35 430 St-Suliac. ☎02 99 58 30 41. www.les-mouettes-saint-suliac. com. 5 rooms. ☐☐.* This 19C building in the heart of the village with very pretty rooms, adorned by paintings chosen by the young manageress and a pleasant small garden make for a very nice stay.

🛏🛏🛏🛏 **Hôtel Manoir de St-Meleuc** – *St-Meleuc, 22690 Pleudihen-sur-Rance. 11km/6.9mi NW of Dinan by the D 795 then D 29. ☎ 02 96 83 34 26. www.manoir-de-saint-meleuc.com. 4 rooms. ☐.* A small, well renovated 15C manor house in the heart of a large park of 2.5 hectares/ 6.2 acres. Traditional style bedrooms. Breakfast is served in a large dining room with exposed beams and stonework.

♈/EAT

🍽 **Crêperie des Artisans** – *6 r. Petit-Fort. ☎02 96 39 44 10. www.creperie-des -artisans.com. Closed end Sept–Palm Sunday and Mon.* This restaurant is situated near the port in the old town

where you can enjoy traditional crêpes and farm products. There is also an amazing collection of percolators and cafetières for your perusal.

🍽 **Crêperie Beaumanoir** – *4 pl. Duclos ☎02 96 39 33 91. Closed 1 week in Apr, Tue eve from Sept–Jun, Mon eve and Sun.* Small restaurant with renovated granite walls situated opposite the the Town Hall serving salads, crêpes, galettes and the house specialities of *roules bretons* and *galichons*.

🍽 **La Marmite** – *91 r. de Brest. ☎02 96 39 04 42. http://marmitedinan.fr.st. Closed Sat eve and Sun.* This restaurant was recently renovated and has a warm relaxed atmosphere with mimosa coloured walls, ash panelling and rooms with a personal touch.

🍽🍽 **La Courtine** – *6 r. de la Croix. ☎02 96 39 74 41. Closed 1-15 Nov, Tue eve, Wed eve, Sat lunch and Sun eve (in summer : closed Sun) 15–30 Mar, 12–19 Jul.* Granite walls and wooden beams create a warm atmosphere within this picturesque house built in 1832. Just the setting to enjoy traditional cooking and fish dishes. Excellent service.

🍽🍽 **Le St-Louis** – *R. du Lion-d'Or. ☎02 96 39 89 50. Closed Wed in winter.* Revealed stone walls, a granite chimney decorated with the paintings of regional artists give a rustic feel to this restaurant. Plentiful traditional cooking with copious buffets of *hors-d'oeuvre* and desserts.

🍽🍽 **Le Bistrot du Viaduc** – *22 rue du Lion d'Or. ☎02 96 85 95 00. www.lebistrot duviaduc.com. Closed 15 Jun–1 Jul, 20 Dec –15 Jan, Sat noon, Sun evening, Mon.* Enjoy the beautiful view of the ramparts of Dinan from this restaurant located at the entrance of the Rance viaduct. Generous helpings of traditional cuisine made with fresh regional produce in the retro surroundings of the dining room.

VALLÉE DE LA RANCE

🍽🍽 **La Ferme du Boucanier** – *2 r. de l'Hôpital, 35 430 St-Suliac. 25km/15.75mi NW of Dinan by D 795 then D 137 and D 117. ☎02 23 15 06 35. Closed Tue, Wed exc eve from May– Sept, Thu lunch low* season and end Dec–early Jan. Two restaurants in one here. In summer, a room decorated in retro style serves food seasoned with spices; in the winter, traditional regional décor with a fireplace (where meat is roasted) creates warm surroundings where rustic food is served.

NIGHTLIFE

La **rue de la Cordonnerie**, is the centre of nightlife in Dinan. In **À la Truye qui file** (n° 14, ℰ02 96 39 72 29), the owner, known to regulars as 'Nounours' (teddy bear), sometimes seranades clients with a song. In the same street, **La Lycorne** and **Le Saut de la Puce** are popular with a younger crowd. **Le Poche Café** (1 bis rue Haute-Voie, ℰ02 96 39 98 60) is home to a bookstore with 8 000 paperback books, a pub and an exhibition gallery. Thematic nights organised one Sat each month. On the port, the **Rive Gauche** is a cool place to savour a late-night cocktail.

ACTIVITIES

BOAT TRIPS

La Compagnie Corsaire (ℰ08 25 13 81 20 (0.35€/min), www.compagniecorsaire. com) organises guided cruises (2hr 45min, 29.50€) on the River Rance to St-Malo. Departures from Apr–Sept daily in accordance with the tides. In Jul–Aug, this company provides a return trip by bus from St-Malo. Off season, you'll have to take a regular bus or the train. They also run 1hr tours (8€) up the Rance to La Hisse.

Le Jaman IV (ℰ06 07 87 64 90 or ℰ02 96 39 28 41, www.vedettejamaniv.com) takes you on a cruise (1hr) to Léhon and the St-Magloire abbey. Departures Jul–Aug, daily 11am, 2.30pm, 4pm and 5.30pm; rest of the year, enquire at the company. 11€. **Danfleurenn Nautic** (rue du Quai, ℰ06 07 45 89 97) hires out boats without a licence for 4–8 people, Easter–Nov. 29–35€/hr or 129–146€/day.

Canoë-kayak – Maison de la Rance (quai Talard, ℰ02 96 87 00 40) – Guided trips on the Rance.

EVENTS

Rencontres Internationales de la Harpe Celtique – ℰ02 96 87 36 69. www.harpe-celtique.com. Dinan pays homage to the Celtic harp each July with concerts across the town, workshops and lessons.

Festival des Terre-Neuvas – Beginning of July at Bobital, 8.3km/5mi SW of Dinan. ℰ02 96 87 69 76. www. festival-terre-neuvas.com. Created in 1998, the festival has become the incontrovertible rendezvous of all kinds of music from rock, reggae and techno to salsa and chanson française.

Fête du Blé (celebration of wheat) – Pleudihen-sur-Rance, early Aug, ℰ02 96 83 35 43, www.fete-du-ble.com. Hundreds of volunteers give life to the old rural jobs and the old traditions.

SHOPPING

Market – Markets take place Thursday mornings on rue du Petit-Pain, promenade des Petits-Fossés and rue de l'Espérance. The rest of the week, you can find regional products at the halles.

Culinary specialities – **Le Rucher Fleuri** – 16 rue de l'Horloge. ℰ02 96 85 92 01. Tue–Sun 10am (11am Sun) to 12.30pm, 2.30pm–7pm; Jul–Aug, daily 10am–7.30pm. Closed Jan–Mar. Products from the beehive and Breton cakes.

Boulangerie-pâtisserie Monnier – The port. ℰ02 96 85 03 12. Closed Wed. Home-made shortbread with plums, Dinan pave, apple far and kouign amann, a rich, crusty Breton cake made with butter and sugar.

Arts and crafts – Old Dinan is full of workshops of all kind. The **Circuit des artistes et des artisans d'art** is a map showing their locations (rue Jerzual is a good place), available at the **Tourist Office**. The association **Art Di** (ℰ09 50 39 11 48; http://mon-guide.info/art. di.carte) organises guided tours of the workshops during the summer.

Cancale★

To get a good view of Cancale's picturesque setting, take the tourist road (route touristique – one-way) that branches off D 76 to the right 2.5km/1.5mi after the Portes Rouges crossroad. As you drive into Cancale the views★ of the resort and Mont-St-Michel Bay are splendid. The town derives its gastronomic reputation from the oysters that flourish in the beds in the bay (parc à huîtres), which oyster lovers come to eat in the cafés and restaurants around the port.

▶ **Population:** 5,285.
◉ **Michelin Map:**
    Michelin local map 309
    K2 - Ille-et-Vilaine (35).
▢ **Info**: 44 rue du Port, 35260 Cancale. ℘02 99 89 63 72. www.ville-cancale.fr.
◗ **Location**: On the coast between St-Malo and Mont-St-Michel.
👥 **Kids:** The oyster farm and museum.
◎ **Don't Miss:** The oysters, coastal path and views from the Pointe du Grouin.

SIGHTS
Port de la Houle★

A bustling, animated area, the quays along the port teem with people unloading oysters, repairing nets, cleaning boats or just waiting for the arrival of the fishing fleet at high tide.

Go to the Fenêtre jetty for a view of the bay and, at low tide, of the oyster beds. The port is surrounded by a picturesque district where sailors and fishermen lived. A street, the *Vaubaudet* or *Val du Baudet*, was the only link with the town of Cancale, the upper district, where the landsmen and traders lived.

Bisquines were traditional fishing boats used in the area until the beginning of the 20C. Today visitors can take a trip round the bay aboard one of these boats, **La Cancalaise**.

Famous Cancale Oyster

Cancale is famous for oyster-farming and you can sample the local oysters in many of Cancale's eateries. A mysterious disease decimated the native spat (oyster spawn) around 1920, so young oysters were brought from Auray for cultivation in the bay. Since then, the spat has flourished in Cancale's immense sea beds. Oysters here have developed a particular local flavour due to the richness of the plankton of Mont-St-Michel bay.

Sentier des Douaniers★

This former customs officers' watch-path branches off *rue du Port* (after some steps) and along the coast for 7km/4.3mi to the Pointe du Grouin. From the war memorial there is already a fine view of Mont-St-Michel Bay and Mont-Dol. Farther on, the **Pointe du Hock** affords an extensive **view**★ over Cancale Rock (*Rocher de Cancale*), Mont-St-Michel Bay and the mount itself; below on the right, at the foot of the cliff, are the oyster beds. On either side of Pointe du Hock, the Sentier des Douaniers overlooks the shore. If you follow the coastline as far as Port-Mer, you will get a splendid view of Pointe de la Chaîne opposite Cancale Rock.

Église St-Méen

Apply to the Tourist Office. ◷*Open daily in summer; Mon–Sat in winter.* ◷*Closed Christmas and New Year holidays.*

From the church tower's upper platform *(189 steps)*, where there is a viewing table, you can enjoy a wide panoramaa of Mont-St-Michel Bay, Granville and some 40 belfries. In clear weather you can see the Îles Chausey.

👥 La Ferme Marine: Musée de l'Huître et du Coquillage

S of the town centre on the coast road. 🚶*Guided tours (1hr) Jul–mid-Sept 11am, 3pm, 5pm; mid-Feb–mid-Jun, mid-Sept–end Sept, Mon–Fri at 3pm.*

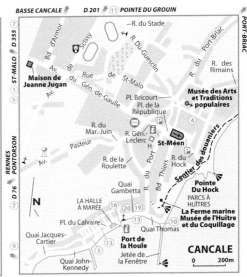

⌖€6.80 (children 3.10€). ◷Closed 1
Jan, 1 May, 25 Dec. ℘02 99 89 69 99.
www.ferme-marine.com
Located in St-Kerber, at the heart of an
oyster-breeding farm, with displays on
the evolution of oyster-breeding techniques as well as the activities of oyster
farmers through the centuries. There is
a lovely collection of shellfish.

Musée des Arts et Traditions Populaires

◷Open Jul–Aug, daily 10am–noon
(except Mon morning), 2.30pm–6.30pm;
Jun and Sept, Fri–Mon 2.30pm–6.30pm.
⌖3.50€. ♿℘02 99 89 71 26.
Housed in the old Église St-Méen (1714,
now deconsecrated), the museum is
devoted to the popular arts and traditions of the Cancale region (fishing,
oyster-breeding, farming, costumes and
furnishings) and to the life of Jeanne
Jugan, founder of the Petites Soeurs
des Pauvres (1792–1879) order. There
is also a presentation relating to the
sailing school (École de Navigation des
Rimains), which has been located in the
town for over 100 years.

EXCURSION
⚑Pointe du Grouin★★
4.5km/3mi N by the D 201.
About 30min.

▶ Leave Cancale by rue du Stade, then
turn right onto the road that leads
straight to the Pointe du Grouin. At the
end of the road, after the Hôtel de la
Pointe du Grouin, leave your car in a
vast parking area and take a path, to the
right of the signal station, which leads
directly to the point.

This wild, rocky headland overlooks
the sea from a height of 40m/130ft
and affords a great **panorama**, which
stretches from Cap Fréhel to Granville
and Mont-St-Michel Bay with, in the distance, the Îles Chausey. At low tide one
can take a path to a cave in the cliffside
(height 10m/33ft, depth 30m/100).
The Île des Landes, opposite, is an
island with a bird sanctuary and nature
reserve. Housed in the blockhouse is an
exhibition on sea birds.

🚗 DRIVING TOUR

From Cancale to St-Malo
23km/14mi – allow 5hr.

The scenic road along the Emerald Coast
is a major tourist attraction of Brittany's
north coast. Although it does not hug
the coastline all the way, it offers many
excursions, enabling the visitor to enjoy

spectacular sites with views and panoramas typical of this jagged coastline.

▷ *Leave Cancale along rue du Stade, turn right towards Pointe du Grouin 300m further on.*

Pointe du Grouin★★ – *See above.*
The coast road follows the cliffs as far as Le Verger and offers lovely views.

▷ *Bear right towards the beach.*

Chapelle Notre-Dame-du-Verger
This small chapel, rebuilt in the 19C, is venerated by the sailors of Cancale (*pardon* 15 August). There are models of different kinds of sailing vessels: sloops, three-masted ships, schooners, etc.

La Guimorais
Chevrets Beach stretches between Pointe du Meinga and the Presqu'île Bénard near this quiet seaside resort. The road skirts the harbour of Rothéneuf, where low tide almost completely empties the harbour.
On the right, note the elegant 17C **Château du Lupin**, a malouinière built by a wealthy St-Malo shipowner.

Rothéneuf and Le Minihic – *See ST-MALO: Rothéneuf.*
The road here offers fine glimpses of the Bay of St-Malo.

▷ *You can continue the tour by going to Paramé and on to St-Malo.*

ADDRESSES

🛏 STAY

🍽 **Hôtel Le Chatellier** – *Quatrevais 1km/0.6mi via D 355.* ☎ *02 99 89 81 84. www.hotellechatellier.com . Closed Dec–Jan 13 rooms.* ⌂*8.50 €.* Charming family run hotel with attractive rooms situated in pretty countryside with garden.

🍽 **Hôtel le Victor-Hugo** – *20 r. Victor-Hugo,* ☎*02 99 89 92 81. www.le-victor-hugo.com. Closed 12 Nov–Mar. 5 rooms.* ⌂*6 €.* Converted fishermen's house in the heart of the attractive area surrounding the Port de la Houle. Small, comfortable, well maintained rooms.

🍽 **Chambre d'hôte La Pastourelle** – *Les Nielles, 35 350 St-Méloir-des-Ondes.* ☎*02 99 89 10 09. www.baie-saintmichel.com. Closed 15 Dec–15 Jan.* ⌂*5 rooms.* ⌂.
The immaculate rooms are spacious and soundproofed with attractive bathrooms. On the ground floor is a sitting area plus the restaurant, which has old beams and stone walls. Delightful garden.

🍽 **Auberge de la Motte Jean** – *2km/1.2mi via D 355.* ☎*02 99 89 41 99. www.hotelpointedugrouin.com. Closed 1 Dec–31 Jan.* ⌂ *8 €.* Converted old farm building in the Cancalaise countryside. Very quiet with a well cared for garden

and a pool. The rooms are individually styled and have antique furniture.

🍽 **Chambre d'hôte Le Manoir des Douets Fleuris** – *1.5km /1mi from Cancale on the D 365.* ☎ *02 23 15 13 81. www.manoirdesdouetsfleuris.com.* 📷 *10 rooms.* ⌂*12€.* 17C manor with well-kept garden. Splash out on the suite, which has a canopied bed and granite fireplace.

🍽 **Duguay Trouin** – *11 quai Duguay-Trouin.* ☎*02 23 15 12 07. www. hotelduguaytrouin.com.* ♿*.7 rooms.* ⌂ *8 €.* This hotel located in the fishing port has recently been renovated. The rooms are decorated with fishing and coastal scenes.

🍽 **Hôtel Pointe du Grouin** – ☎*02 99 89 60 55. www.hotelpointedu grouin.com. Closed 16 Nov–31 Mar. 16 rooms.* ⌂ *€8.50.* The location of this charming hotel is exceptional: its views extend over the coast and to Mont-St-Michel.

℗ EAT

🍽 **Crêperie du Port** – *1 pl. du Calvaire (in the port).* ☎*02 99 89 60 66. creperie-du-port@wanadoo.fr. Closed 15 Nov–15 Dec and Tue exc school hols.* Seaside feel to this *crêperie* which has a terrace facing the port and a ceiling decorated with a fresco.

Le Marché aux Huitres – *at the end of quai Thomas at Cancale port.* Where better to enjoy fresh oysters than at the fish market, as soon as they are landed?!

Au Pied d'Cheval – *10 quai Gambetta. ℘ 02 99 89 76 95. www.au-pied-de-cheval.com. Closed from mid Nov–Mar and Tue–Wed exc Jul.* Owned by a local oyster farmer this restaurant is dedicated to tasting oysters and sea food from the bay of Mont-St-Michel.

Crêperie La Cancalaise – *3 r. Vallée-Porçon (near the church) ℘ 02 99 89 71 22. lacancalaise@wanadoo.fr. Closed 1st week Mar, 1st week Jun, 3 weeks end Nov, eve except Fri and Sat and Jul–Aug.* Crêpes and galettes are served garnished with regional products. Deserving of its excellent reputation.

Surcouf – *7 quai Gambetta. ℘02 99 89 61 75. Closed 3 Jan–4 Feb, 22 Nov–17 Dec, Wed (except 10 Jul–22 Aug) and Thu.* Here food lovers can enjoy themselves without breaking the bank. Served on the terrace or in the dining room, the menus are based around seafood and fresh, regional produce.

Le Troquet – *19 quai Gambetta. ℘02 99 89 99 42. Closed mid Nov–late Jan, Thu & Fri except Aug.* Cancale oysters and other top-quality seafood in a charming little bistro.

ACTIVITIES

École de Voile – *Port-Mer ℘02 99 89 90 22. Open daily Mar–Nov.* Lessons and little boats or surfboards for hire. They also arrange half-day outings in a traditional boat.

Walks – One of the most beautiful parts of the **GR 34**, called **'The Customs Officers' Path'**, snakes 11km/6.9mi between Cancale and the pointe du Nid, going by the pointe du Grouin, affording views of the island of Rimains and the bay of Mont-St-Michel. Not advisable if you have young children. In season, a shuttle bus goes to the pointe du Grouin (contact Tourist Office).

SHOPPING

MARKETS – Sat morning near the church. At the same place, Summer Flavours, in *Jul–Aug, 5pm–9pm.*

OYSTERS AND SEAFOOD PRODUCTS – **On the port**, along quai Thomas, a farmers' market is held daily in season.

Dol-de-Bretagne★

Dol, a former bishopric and proud of its fine cathedral, is now the small capital of the "Marais" (marsh) district. It stands on the edge of a cliff, about 20m/65ft high, which was washed by the sea until the 10C, when marine deposits began forming. This enabled the construction of the sea dyke, now a section of the Pontorson-St-Malo tourist road.

SIGHTS

Cathédrale St-Samson★★
Allow 30min.
The cathedral is a vast structure, built of granite in the 12C and 13C and completed during the next three centuries. It gives an idea of the importance that the bishopric of Dol then enjoyed.

▶ **Population:** 4,760.
◔ **Michelin Map:** Local map 309 L3 - Ille-et-Villaine (35).
▯ **Info:** 5 place de la Cathédrale, 35120 Dol-de-Bretagne. ℘02 99 48 15 37. www.pays-de-dol.com
▶ **Location:** Off the N 176, half way between Mont-St-Michel and St-Malo.
▲ **Kids:** Cathédraloscope
◔ **Don't Miss:** The cathedral and the view from Mont Dol.

On the outside, the most interesting part is the south wall, which includes two porches: the splendid **great porch**★ (14C) and the little porch (13C) with its fine pointed arcade. Seen from the north, the cathedral looks like a fortress;

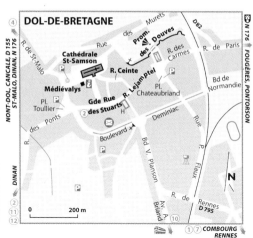

DOL-DE-BRETAGNE

WHERE TO STAY

Baillage
(Chambre d'hôte Le)......(2)

Croix Gaillot
(Chambre d'hôte La)......(4)

Ferme de la Haute Lande
(Chambre d'hôte)..........(7)

Golf & Country Club.........(11)

Grand Hôtel
de la Gare.....................(10)

Mesnil des Bois (Le)..........(12)

WHERE TO EAT

Cour Verte
(Auberge de la)................(1)

Food Shop...........................(2)

its crenellated parapet was linked to the old fortifications of the town.

The interior, 100m/328ft long, is impressive. The chancel has numerous interesting features: the medallion-glass **window**★★ (13C restored); eighty stalls (14C); a carved wood Bishop's throne (16C); and, above the high altar, a 14C wooden Statue of the Virgin, coloured in 1859. In the north arm of the transept is the tomb of Thomas James, Bishop of Dol (16C); it is the work of two Florentine sculptors, Antoine and Jean Juste. In the north aisle note the Christ Reviled.

👥 Médiévalys★

🕐 Open Jul–Aug, 10am–8pm. Sept–Jun, 10am–7pm. ⬟7.50€ (children 4.90€). ♿ ☎02 99 48 35 30.
This exhibit, installed in the former residence of the bishops of Dol, is devoted to the subject of cathedrals, and is especially attractive to children. In a modern and uncluttered setting, which lends itself to contemplation, various models of cathedrals and the machines used to build them are on display, as well as items relating to the craftsmanship of stained-glass windows and sculpture.

Promenade des Douves

This public garden (also known as Promenade Jules Revert) has been traced along the northern part of the old ramparts. One of the 12 defence towers, the large Tour des Carmes, can still be seen.

Its offers a fine **view**★ of the Mont Dol and the Marais de Dol.

The streets near the cathedral precincts have interesting old half-timbered houses, town houses, and shops.

Number 17 **Grande-Rue des Stuarts** dates from the 11C and 12C and has Romanesque arcading; number 27 (antique-dealer) is 13C; number 33 is a dwelling (1617) with fine dormer windows; number 18, a former Templars' inn with a 12C vaulted cellar, is now transformed into a bar-crêperie; a charming 16C courtyard is at number 32.

Number 31 **Rue Le-Jamptel** (now a hardware store) dates from the 12C or 13C; number 27 is a 15C house decorated with pillars.

Rue Ceinte formerly claimed home to the chapter-house. Number 1, an old shop with a granite counter, and number 4, now a crêperie, are both 15C; number 16 dates from 1668.

🚗 DRIVING TOURS

1 MONT DOL★

◯ *Leave Dol-de-Bretagne heading for Cancale (2km/1.2mi).*

This granite mound, though only 65m high, overlooks a great plain and resembles a small mountain. The remains of many prehistoric animals– mammoth, elephant, rhinoceros, reindeer – and flint implements have been unearthed on its slopes. *It is possible to go around the mound by car on the surface road.*

Panorama★

To the north, from the top of the tower there is a view of the Îles Chausey and Cancale and Grouin Points; to the northeast, Mont-St-Michel, Avranches and Granville. From the calvary, to the south, on the edge of the Dol Marsh, Dol and its fine cathedral can be seen with the Hédé heights in the background; and below, the Dol Marsh.

Petit-Mont-St-Michel – *See MONT-ST-MICHEL*

Le Vivier-sur-Mer and Cherrueix – *See MONT-ST-MICHEL*

2 THE MARAIS DISTRICT

30km/18.5mi – allow 1hr 45min.

Leave Dol SE of the town plan on D 795. Leave the road to Épiniac on your left; 600m/650yds further turn left then turn right onto a tarmac road.

Menhir de Champ-Dolent

The dolmen, one of the finest in Brittany, stands 9.5m/30ft high (8.7m/28ft wide). The granite comes from Bonnemain located 5km/3mi south. The name Champ-Dolent (Field of Pain) refers to a legendary struggle which is supposed to have taken place here.

Return to the road to Combourg.

♟ Baguer-Morvan – Musée de la Paysannerie

Open mid Jul–mid Sept, 10am–7pm exc Sat 2pm–7pm. ∞5€ (children 3€). ℘02 99 48 04 04.

Housed in three large buildings. This museum retraces the past 100 years in the life of the peasant farmer: reconstructed furnished interiors, photographs and postcards, farming equipment (tractors, threshers, harvesters) and tools (rakes, knives, hammers). Cider tasting is offered at the end of the tour.

Take the D 119 to Tronchet.

Le Tronchet

In the village, see the cloister of the **Abbaye Notre Dame de Tronchet,** constructed in the 17C on the ruins of a 12C Benedictine monastery.

Follow the signs to Fôret du Mesnil to leave the village on the D 9 then follow signs to Maison des Fées. Park in the car park.

La Maison des Fées

This is a megalithic alley covered with eight large slabs. The sculptures of breasts and necklaces on the ruins of the burial chamber symbolise the goddess cult, which gives the chamber its name.

Go back to Tronchet and then take the D 795 and then left towards Épiniac.

Marais de Dol

This is the name given to land reclaimed from the marshes and the sea in Mont-St-Michel Bay. Seen from the mound, the countryside looks strange and monotonous; it extends for about 15,000ha/37,065 acres from the mouth of the River Couesnon to near Cancale. The old shoreline ran through Cancale, Châteauneuf, Dol and St-Broladre and along the stretch of road between Pontorson and St-Malo.

Some 12 000 years ago the sea covered the Marais de Dol; it then receded, uncovering a large part of the bay. Bit by bit, forest and vegetation took possession of the land. Drainage went on for centuries and today the marais is fertile plain devoted to mixed agriculture.

Épiniac

In the north aisle of the **church**, on the altar, is a 16C polychrome high relief representing the Dormition of the Virgin.

 Follow D 85 then bear left onto D 285.

Broualan

In the centre of the village near a small yet remarkable calvary stands a 15C church, enlarged in the 16C. The east end is decorated with pinnacled buttresses and lovely Flamboyant windows. The small columned bell tower rests on the large arch which separates the nave from the chancel.

 Via La Boussac return to Dol-de-Bretagne.

ADDRESSES

STAY

Grand Hôtel de la Gare – *21 av. Aristide-Briand.* ℘*02 99 48 00 44. hoteldelagaredoldebretagne@orange.fr. Closed 8 –21 Mar and 18 –24 Oct. 13 rooms* ⌑ *6 €.* Recently renovated small hotel with pleasantly decorated small rooms, benefiting from good soundproofing.

Chambre d'hôte Ferme de la Haute Lande – *3km/1.8mi from Dol-de-Bretagne on the Rennes road, then head towards Épiniac.* ℘ *02 99 48 07 02. www. lahautelande.fr .Closed 1 week in winter.* ⌑*. 3 rooms.* ⌑*. 1 gîte.* Enjoying a perfectly isolated situation, this stone built dairy farm is the ideal address for a quiet rest. Sleep in clean simple rooms accessed by a beautiful 17C wooden staircase.

Chambre d'hôte La Croix Gaillot – *35 120 Cherrueix. 8km/5mi N of Dol along the D 82 towards Cherrueix then right on the D 85 towards Baguer-Pican.* ℘ *02 99 48 90 44. www.la-croix-galliot.fr. Closed Jan.* ⌑*. 5 rooms.* ⌑*.* This old cereal farm has comfortable quiet rooms and a sitting area opening on to the garden. Two gîtes and six camping pitches are also available.

Chambre d'hôte Le Baillage – *Le Baillage, 35 540 Le Tronchet. 10km/ 6.25mi SW by D 676 and D 119.* ℘ *02 99 58 17 98. www.lebaillage.com. 5 rooms.* ⌑*.* This characterful residence is situated in a garden within an arboretum. Comfortable rooms with elegant bathrooms. There is also a family suite on an upper level. Private sitting area and hall. Peace guaranteed.

Golf & Country Club – *Domaine St-Yvieux, 35 540 Le Tronchet. 11km/6.9mi SW by D 119 then D 75.* ℘ *02 99 58 98 99. www.saintmalogolf.com. Closed 20 Nov– 1 Mar. 29 rooms.* ⌑ *12 €.* Located on a golf course, this old 19C abbey has large rooms in a loggia with a mini-terrace. The restaurant looks on to a pool and the greens .

Le Mesnil des Bois – *35 540 Le Tronchet. 11km/6.9mi SW by D 119 and D 75, then 2km/1.2mi SW from Le Tronchet by the D 9 and D 3.* ℘ *02 99 58 97 12. www.le-mesnil-des-bois.com. Closed mid Nov–in Feb. 5 rooms.* ⌑*.* This beautiful 16C farm/manor house stands on the edge of a forest. Pretty rooms with antique furniture.

EAT

Auberge de la Cour Verte – *Rte de Rennes.* ℘ *02 99 48 41 41. Closed Mon.* This restaurant located on a farm built in 1640 has a reputation for meat grills. The dining room is truly rustic with a stone chimney. The menu has Belgian specialities and crêpes.

Food Shop – *43 Grande-Rue-des-Stuarts.* ℘ *02 99 48 01 54. www.food shop.fr. Closed Sun Mon.* In this contemporary bistro the cooking of bright colourful exotic meals is centred on olive oil and spices. You will receive a friendly welcome by the patron who is full of bonhommie.

Mont-St-Michel★★★

Mont-St-Michel has been called "the Marvel of the Western World", owing to its island setting, its rich history and the beauty of its architecture. The dramatic silhouette of the abbey atop a mass of granite and surrounded by the immense bay leaves an indelible impression in any season. Up close, it is even more fascinating. It was among the first sites to be included on UNESCO's World Heritage List (1979).

A BIT OF HISTORY

Geography – As the bay is already partially silted up (*see DOL-DE-BRETAGNE: Marais de Dol*), the mount is usually to be seen surrounded by huge sand banks which shift with the tides and often reshape the mouths of the neighbouring rivers.

The course of the Cousenon, which used to threaten the dykes and polders with its wandering, has been canalised and the river now flows straight out to sea to the west of the mount. Its former course, northwest from Pontorson, used to mark the frontier between the Duchies of Normandy and Brittany.

Foundation – The abbey's origin goes back to the early 8C, when the Archangel Michael appeared to Aubert, Bishop of

▶ **Population:** 72.
Michelin Map: Local map 59 303 C8 - Manche (50).
Info: Corps de garde des Bourgeois, 50116 Le-Mont-St-Michel. ℰ02 33 60 14 30. www.ot-montsaintmichel.com.
Location: The Mount is at the extreme north end of the D 976.
Timing: Get information on the tide times.
Parking: The public car parks (4€/day) are 2km/1.2mi away. If you arrive early enough, there are four car parks 500m from the Mount.
Don't Miss: The panorama of the bay from the ramparts of the abbey.

Avranches, who founded an oratory on the island, then known as Mont Tombe. In the Carolingian era, the oratory was replaced by an abbey and from then until the 16C a series of increasingly splendid buildings, in the Romanesque and then the Gothic styles, succeeded one another on the mount which was subsequently dedicated to the Archangel. The well-fortified abbey was never captured.

Mont-St-Michel

Office de Tourisme du Mont Saint-Michel/www.ot-montsaintmichel.com

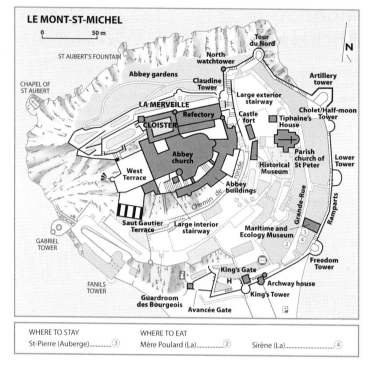

LE MONT-ST-MICHEL

0 ——— 50 m

Tour du Nord
ST AUBERT'S FOUNTAIN
North watchtower
Abbey gardens
Claudine Tower
Artillery tower
CHAPEL OF ST AUBERT
Large exterior stairway
LA-MERVEILLE
Refectory
Castle fort
Cholet/Half-moon Tower
CLOISTER
Tiphaine's House
Abbey church
Parish church of St Peter
Lower Tower
West Terrace
Historical Museum
Chemin de Ronde
Grande-Rue
Ramparts
Abbey buildings
Saut Gautier Terrace
Large interior stairway
Maritime and Ecology Museum
GABRIEL TOWER
Freedom Tower
King's Gate
FANILS TOWER
Archway house
King's Tower
Guardroom des Bourgeois
Avancée Gate

WHERE TO STAY	WHERE TO EAT	
St-Pierre (Auberge)...........③	Mère Poulard (La)............②	Sirène (La).............④

Pilgrimages – Even during the Hundred Years' War, pilgrims flocked to the mount. The English, who had possession of the area, granted safe conduct to the faithful in return for payment. People of all sorts made the journey: nobles, rich citizens and beggars, who lived on alms and were given free lodging by the monks. Hotels and souvenir shops flourished even then. The pilgrims bought medals bearing the effigy of St-Michael and amulets, which they filled with sand from the beach.

Of the many thousands of people crossing the bay, some were drowned and others were lost in quicksand. This gave rise to the longer dedication: St-Michael in Peril from the Sea.

Decline – In the 17C, the Maurists, monks from St-Maur, were made responsible for reforming the monastery. They made only deceptive architectural changes, tinkering with the stonework. Used as a local facility before the Revolution, the abbey suffered further when it became a national prison in 1811 and took in political prisoners including Barbés and Blanqui. In 1874, the abbey and the ramparts passed into the care of the Historic Monuments Department (Service des Monuments Historiques). Since 1969 a few monks have again been in residence, conducting services in the abbey church.

Stages in the abbey's construction – The construction is an amazing achievement. The blocks of granite were transported from the Îles Chausey or from Brittany and hoisted up to the foot of the building. As the crest of the hill was very narrow, the foundations had to be built up from the lower slopes.

Romanesque Abbey – 11C–12C. Between 1017 and 1144 a church was built on the top of the mount. The previous Carolingian building was incorporated as a crypt – Our Lady Underground (Notre-Dame-sous-Terre) – to support the platform on which the last three bays of the Romanesque nave were built.

Other crypts were constructed to support the transepts and the chancel, which projected beyond the natural rock.

The conventual buildings were constructed on the west face and on either side of the nave. The entrance to the abbey faced west.

Gothic Abbey – 13C–16C. This period saw the construction of: the magnificent Merveille buildings (1211–1228) on the north side of the church, used by the monks and pilgrims and for the reception of important guests; the abbatial buildings (13C–15C) on the south side comprising the administrative offices, the abbot's lodging and the garrison's quarters; the fort and the outer defences (14C) on the east side, which protected the entrance, moved to this side of the mount.

The chancel of the Romanesque church had collapsed and was rebuilt more magnificently in the Flamboyant Gothic style (1446–1521) above a new crypt.

Alterations – 18C–19C. In 1780 the last three bays of the nave and the Romanesque façade were demolished.

The present bell-tower (1897) is surmounted by a beautiful spire which rises to 157m and culminates in a statue of St-Michael (1879) by Emmanuel Frémiet.

THE TOWN

Outer Defences

The Outer Gate is the only breach in the ramparts and opens into the first fortified courtyard. On the left stands the **Citizens' Guard-room** (16C), which presently houses the Tourist Office; on the right are the 'Michelettes', English mortars captured in a sortie during the Hundred Years' War.

A second gate leads into a second courtyard. The third gate (15C), complete with machicolations and portcullis, is called the **King's Gate** because it was the lodging of the token contingent maintained on the mount by the king in assertion of his rights; it opens into the Grande-Rue where the abbot's soldiers lodged in the fine arcaded house (right).

Grande-Rue★

This picturesque narrow street climbs steeply between old (15C–16C) houses, several of which have retained their original name – **Logis Saint-Etienne,**

Movement of the Tides

The movement of the tides in the bay is very great and the difference in sea level between high and low water can be over 12m/40ft, the highest in France. As the sea bed is flat, the sea retreats a long way exposing 15km/9mi of sand. The tide comes in very rapidly, not quite at the speed of a galloping horse, as has been said, but of a person walking at a brisk pace. This phenomenon, which is aggravated by numerous currents, can spell danger for the unwary.

Vieux Logis, Sirène, Truie qui file – and ends in a flight of steps. In summer it is lively and crowded with restaurants and the stalls of souvenir merchants, as it was in the Middle Ages at the height of the most fervent pilgrimages.

Ramparts★★

These are 13C–15C. The sentry walk offers fine views of the bay; from the North Tower the Tombelaine Rock, which Philippe Auguste had fortified, is clearly visible.

Musée de la Mer et de l'Écologie

🕐*Open Jul–Aug, 9am–7pm; rest of the year, 9.30am–6.30pm. Closed Jan– Feb and 11 Nov–20 Dec. ⌑9€ (under 25 yrs no charge), combined ticket with three other musuems 18€. ☏02 33 60 23 34.* Audio-guided visit showing films of the Mount's natural environment, the tidal range and the dangers of the bay as well as the sand issues. More than 250 old models of boats.

Église Paroissiale St-Pierre

The building, dating from the 11C, has been much altered. The apse spans a narrow street. The parish church contains a Crucifix and other furnishings from the abbey; the chapel in the south aisle contains a statue of St-Michael covered in silver; in the chapel to the right of the altar there is a 15C statue of the

Virgin and from the gallery hang numerous pilgrim banners.

Logis Tiphaine

🕐*Open Jul–Aug, daily 9am–7pm; Rest of the year, 9.30am–6.30pm.Closed Jan – Feb and 11 Nov–20 Dec.*✆*9€ (under 25 yrs no charge), 18€ combined ticket.* ✆*02 33 60 23 34.*

When Du Guesclin (ও *see DINAN*) was captain of the mount, he had this house built (1365) for his wife, Tiphaine Raguenel, an attractive and educated woman from Dinan, while he went off to the wars in Spain. Note the Constable's room (tester bed, chest), dining room (six-door sideboard, chimney bearing the arms of Du Guesclin, 17C copperware) and Tiphaine's room (cupboard, tester bed, wax figure).

Musée Historique

🕐*Open Jul–Aug, 9am–7pm; Rest of the year, 9.30am–5.30pm.Closed Jan– Feb and 11 Nov–20 Dec.* ✆*8€ (under 25 yrs no charge), 18€ combined ticket.* ✆*02 33 60 07 01.*

The museum traces 1 000 years of the Mount's history with a short *son et lumière* and display cases filled with collections of arms, paintings, pirates' chests and more. The visit ends in the dungeon.

THE ABBEY★★★

🕐*Open May–Aug, daily 9am–7pm; Sept–Apr, 9.30am–6pm (last entry 1hr before closing).* 🕐*Closed 1 Jan, 1 May and 25 Dec.* ✆*8.50€ (under 25 yrs no charge). Free 1st Sun of month or if attending a service.* ✆*02 33 89 80 00. www.monum.fr.*

The tour of the abbey does not go from building to building nor from period to period but from floor to floor through a maze of corridors and stairs.

Outer Defences of the Abbey

A flight of steps, the Grand Degré, once cut off by a swing door, leads up to the abbey. At the top on the right is the entrance to the gardens; more steps lead up to the ramparts.

Through the arch of an old door is a fortified courtyard overlooked by the fort, which consists of two tall towers shaped like mortars standing on their breeches and linked by machicolations. Even this military structure shows the builder's artistic sense: the wall is attractively constructed of alternate courses of pink and grey granite.

Beneath a pointed barrel vault, a steep and ill-lit staircase, known as the Pit Steps *(Escalier du Gouffre)*, leads down to the beautiful door which opens into the Guard-room, also called the Gatehouse *(Porterie)*.

Guard-room or Gatehouse

This hall was the focal point of the abbey. Poor pilgrims passed through on their way from the Merveille Court to the Almonry. The abbot's visitors and the faithful making for the church used the Abbey Steps.

Abbey Steps

An impressive flight of 90 steps rises between the abbatial buildings (left) and the abbey church (right); it is spanned by a fortified bridge (15C). The stairs stop outside the south door of the church on a terrace called the Gautier Leap *(Saut Gautier)* after a prisoner who is supposed to have hurled himself over the edge. The tour starts here.

The **West Platform** is a spacious terrace, which was created by the demolition of the last three bays of the church, providing an extensive **view**★ of the bay of Mont-St-Michel.

Church★★

The exterior of the church, particularly the east end with its buttresses, flying buttresses, bell turrets and balustrades, is a masterpiece of light and graceful architecture. The interior reveals the marked contrast between the severe and sombre Romanesque nave and the elegant and luminous Gothic chancel. The church is built on three crypts which are visited during the tour.

St-Michael's Mount, Cornwall

In the 4C BC ships came from the Mediterranean to the **Island of Ictis**, as they named it, to trade in tin, copper and gold; in AD 495, according to Cornish legend, fishermen saw St-Michael standing on a westerly ledge of the granite rock which rises high out of the sea, whereupon the island became a place of pilgrimage. By the 8C, it is said, a Celtic monastery had been founded upon it which endured until the 11C.

In AD 708 in France, St-Michael appeared three times in a vision to Bishop Aubert of Avranches, who then built an oratory to the saint on the island from then on known as Mont-St-Michel. By the time of the Battle of Hastings (1066), the oratory in France had developed into an important Benedictine community to which St-Michael's Mount passed as a dependency. The English house, always modest by comparison with the French monastery, was ultimately appropriated during the course of the Hundred Years' War by Henry V as alien property and was finally suppressed in 1535.

La Merveille★★★

The name, which means The Marvel, applies to the superb Gothic buildings on the north face of the mount. The eastern block, the first to be built between 1211 and 1218, comprises from top to bottom, the Refectory, the Guests' Hall and the Almonry; the western block, built between 1218 and 1228, consists of the cloisters, the Knights' Hall and the cellar.

From the outside the buildings look like a fortress although their religious vocation is suggested by the dignity and purity of their line. The interior is a perfect example of the evolution of the Gothic style, from a simplicity which is almost Romanesque in the lower halls, through the elegance of the Guests' Hall, the majesty of the Knights' Hall and the mysterious luminosity of the Refectory, to the cloisters which are a masterpiece of delicacy and refinement. The top floor comprises the cloisters and the Refectory.

Cloisters★★★

The cloisters seem to be suspended between the sea and the sky. The gallery arcades display heavily undercut **sculpture** of foliage ornamented with the occasional animal or human figure (particularly human heads); there are also a few religious symbols. The double row of arches rests on delightful slim single columns arranged in quincunx

Cloisters

G. Targat/MICHELINv

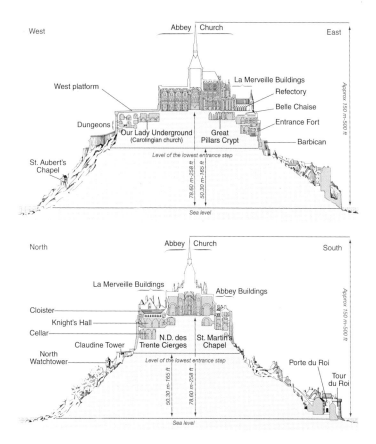

to enhance the impression of lightness. The different colours of the various materials add to the overall charm. The *lavatorium* (lavabo), on the right of the entrance, recalls the ceremonial 'washing of the feet' which took place every Thursday.

Refectory★★

The effect is mysterious; the chamber is full of light although it appears to have only two windows in the end wall.

To admit so much light without weakening the solid side walls which support the wooden roof and are lined with a row of slim niches, the architect introduced a very narrow aperture high up in each recess.

Old Romanesque Abbey

The ribbed vaulting of this former abbey marks the transition between Romanesque and Gothic. The tour includes the **Monk's Walk** *(Promenoir des Moines)* and part of the old dormitory.

Grande Roue

This huge wheel brings back the days in which the abbey served as a prison. Operated by five to six prisoners who would tread inside it, the wheel was used for hoisting provisions and pieces of equipment.

Crypts

The chancel and transepts of the church are supported by three undercrofts or crypts; the most impressive is the **Crypte des Gros Piliers**★ (Great Pillared Crypt) with its ten pillars 5m round, sculpted in granite coming from the Îles Chausey.

Guests' Hall★

Here the Abbot received royalty (Louis IX, Louis XI, François I) and other important visitors. The hall, which is 35m long, has a Gothic ceiling supported on a central row of slim columns.

At one time it was divided down the middle by a huge curtain of tapestries; on one side were the kitchen quarters (two chimneys) and on the other the great dining hall (one chimney).

Knights' Hall★

The name of this hall may refer to the military order of St-Michael which was founded in 1469 by Louis XI with the abbey as its seat.

The hall is vast and majestic (26 x 18m) and divided into four sections by three rows of stout columns. Functionally, the hall was the monks' workroom, where they illuminated manuscripts, and was heated by two great chimneys.

Cellar

This was the storeroom; it was divided in three by two rows of square pillars supporting the groined vaulting.

Abbey Gardens

ⓘ*Closed in winter and in bad weather.*
Allows visitors to see the west side of the Mount and the Chapelle St-Aubert.

MONT-ST-MICHEL BAY

The bay has been a UNESCO World Heritage site since 1979 and is fringed by around 100km/62mi of coastline. Its islands, cliffs, beaches and dunes form a succession of habitats harbouring a great variety of flora and fauna. The coastal route offers amazing **views**★ of Mont-St-Michel and pleasant walks between the polders and salt marshes.

Le télégraphe de Chappe St-Marcan

▶*21km/13mi to the west. At Pontorson, take the N 176, then the D 89 towards St-Marcan.* ⬝*Guided visit (1h30).* ⓘ*May–Sept Wed–Sun. 10am–12.30pm, 2–6.30pm.* ⬝*3€ (8–12 years 1€).* ✆*02 99 48 53 53.*

This telegraph system could transmit messages from Paris to Brest in just 20 minutes. Museum visit and manipulation of the reconstructed mechanism.

Cherrueix

▶*27km/16.5mi to the west on the D 82.*

Although almost all the windmills along the shore have lost their sails, wind is still very important to Cherrueix. These days, land yachting enthusiasts taking advantage of the magnificent expanses of sand are the centre of attention.

A garlic festival (July) celebrates this popular crop, which is also widely sold locally.

Le Vivier-sur-Mer

▶*35km/22mi to the west on the D 155.*

The posts stretching across the bay and the strange aluminium boats on wheels leave you in no doubt that the local business here is mussel farming. To find out more about the shellfish or the rich natural resources of the bay, head for the Maison de la baie with its permanent exhibition. ✆ *02 99 48 84 38. www.maison-baie.com. Jul-Aug, 9am–12.30pm,*

Returning Mont-St-Michel to the Sea

Mont St-Michel has been silting up for several decades. Every year, the sea deposits tonnes of sediment in the bay. In part, this can be blamed on man, since between the mid-19C and 1969 a number of regional building initiatives were taken that accelerated the formation of polders (canalisation of the River Couesnon, building of a dyke then a dam). A 1995 project was commissioned by the State and local authorities, intended to return the Mount to the sea. Ideally, this would make it possible to replace the dyke by a footbridge under which cross-currents could once again flow between the mainland and the island. It would also help restore the scouring action of the coastal rivers and streams.

2pm–6.30pm; Apr–Jun, 9am–12.30pm, 2pm–5pm but closed Sun; rest of the year, 9am–12.30pm, 2pm–5.30pm, but closed Sun and public holidays. ☁ Guided tours available (1.30pm) Closed Christmas holidays. ☞3 € (under 12 yrs free).

ADDRESSES

STAY

☕☕ **Hôtel La Tour Brette** – 8 r. Couesnon, 50 170 Pontorson. ☎02 33 60 10 69. www.latourbrette.com. Closed 14–22 Mar, 1–20 Dec and Wed exc Jul–Aug. 10 rooms. ☐ 7 €. This small centrally situated hotel gives it name to the tower which in the past protected Normandy from attack from the Duchy of Bretagne. Small, recently renovated rooms. Traditional cooking.

☕☕ **Chambre d'hôte Mme Gillet Hélène** – 3 Le Val-St-Revert, 35610 Roz-sur-Couesnon. ☎ 02 99 80 27 85. 15km/9.4mi SW from Mont-St-Michel, along the coastal St-Malo road (D 797). ☎02 99 80 27 85. 4 rooms. ☐. This family run 17C house dominates the bay with a beautiful view of Mont-St-Michel. Three sides facing the sea while the other has a terrace opening to the garden.

☕☕ **Hôtel Le Bretagne** – rue Couesnon, 50170 Pontorson. 4km/2.5mi S of the Mount on the D 976. ☎02 33 60 10 55. Closed 15–30 Jan. 13 rooms. ☐7€. Restaurant☕☕. Traditional regional house with 18C woodwork and a grey marble fireplace. Spacious, nicely furnished rooms.

☕☕ **Hôtel les Vieilles Digues** – Rte du Mont-St-Michel , 50170 Beauvoir. 3km/2mi S of Mont-St-Michel in the direction of Pontorson. ☎ 02 33 58 55 30. www.bnb-normandy.com. Closed Dec–Jan. 5 rooms. ☐. This attractive stone built hotel has large rooms, looking on to Mont-St-Michel. Pleasant half timbered breakfast room and country garden.

☕☕☕☕ **Auberge St-Pierre** – 50 116 Le Mont-St-Michel. ☎ 02 33 60 14 03. www.auberge-saint-pierre.fr. 21 rooms. ☐ 14 €. This 15C timber framed residence at the heart of the island has small, nicely decorated rooms. Choose

between a brasserie next door, a dining room or eating on the terrace, where French and Normandy cuisine are served.

EAT

☕ **La Gourmandise** – 21 rte du Mont-St-Michel, 50 170 Beauvoir. 4km/2.5mi S of Mont-St-Michel. ☎02 33 58 42 83. A Breton house transformed into a creperie gives a lively presence to this small locality. Crepes and galettes.

☕☕ **La Sirène** – Grande Rue. ☎02 33 60 08 60. Closed 10 Jan–2 Feb and 15 Nov –20 Dec. This former 14C inn, now a crêperie is reached by a spiral staircase.

☕☕ **Auberge de la Baie** – La Rive, 50 170 Ardevon. 3km/1.9mi SE of Mont-St-Michel in the direction of Avranches by D 275. ☎ 02 33 68 26 70. www.auberge delabaie.fr. Daily Apr–Nov; Rest of year closed Wed. The hotel/restaurant is a welcome stop for a weekend or a meal. The à la carte menu has traditional and regional dishes (salted lamb and seafood) and crêpes.

☕☕ **Pré-Salé** - 2km/1.25mi S of Mont-St-Michel by the D 976. ☎02 33 60 14 18. www.le-mont-saint-michel.com. Closed 12 Nov–6 Feb. The Hotel Mercure recently renovated its dining room, where you can try the famous salt meat dishes of Mont-St-Michel Bay.

☕☕☕☕ **La Mère Poulard** – Grande-Rue, 50 116 Le Mont-St-Michel. ☎02 33 89 68 68. www.mere-poulard.com. Don't miss the delicious omelettes prepared out in the open over a wood fire. Traditional cuisine in a rustic setting.

ACTIVITIES

Crossing the bay of Mont-St-Michel on foot or horseback is unforgettable but dangerous and should never be attempted without an authorised guide:

Atouts Baie (6 rue de la Métairie, 50170 Boucey; ☎02 33 60 68 00; www.mont-saint-michel-voyages.com) organises guided walks, as does **Chemins de la Baie** (34 rue de l'Ortillon, 50530 Genêts; ☎02 33 89 80 88. www.cheminsdelabaie. com; closed Nov–Mar). **La Tanière riding school** (La Grève, 50170 Moidrey; ☎02 33 58 13 53; www.randobaie.com) offers horse treks (2hr) across the bay.

Le Val-André♨♨

The resort, known officially as Pléneuf-Val-André, has one of the finest sandy beaches on the north coast of Brittany.

👣WALKS

🚶 Pointe de Pléneuf★

Allow 15min on foot there and back.
A path running at the foot of the cliff starts from the 🅿 car park at the port of Piégu. Take the stairs to rue de la Corniche.

It leads to a small viewpoint (bench) facing the **Île du Verdelet**, a bird sanctuary. Certain spring tides permit access on foot (*ask at the Poste des Sauveteurs on the pier or at the Tourist Office*).
By skirting Pointe de Pléneuf it is possible to reach Plage des Vallées (*30min on foot*) and further on to Ville Berneuf (*45min on foot*). This very pretty walk, on a cliff path overlooking the sea, affords superb **views**★★ of St-Brieuc Bay and the beach and resort of Le Val-André.

🚶 Promenade de la Guette★

Allow 1hr on foot there and back.
At the southwest end of the quay at the juncture with rue des Sablons, two arrows point the way to the Guette pathway (Chemin de la Guette), the Corps de Garde and the Batterie.

Go round the stairs (Anse du Pissot), which go down to the beach, and along the Corps de Garde, which has recently been restored. Soon after, there is an extensive **view**★ of St-Brieuc Bay. From the statue of Our Lady of the Watch go down to **Dahouët**, a fishing port and pleasure boat harbour.
In 1509, seamen drom Dahouët were the first to fish off the coast of Newfoundland discovered just 12 years earlier by the Venetian explorer John Cabot.

⟳ *Follow Quai des Terre-Neuvas and take the Mocquelet Path to Val-André Quay.*

▶ **Population:** 3, 695.
⚲ **Michelin Map:** Local map 309 G3 – Côtes-d'Armor (22).
🛈 **Info:** 1 rue Winston Churchill, BP 125, 22370 Pléneuf-Val-André. ☎02 96 72 20 55.
◑ **Location:** 20km/12.5mi NE of St-Brieuc on the D 786.
⏱ **Timing:** Two days to enjoy this resort.

🚗 DRIVING TOUR

The Emerald Coast (Côte d'Émeraude)

⚲*See map p123.*

34km/21mi – about 2hr 30min

The tourist road, which twists and turns in the moor, affords striking **views**★★ of the sea, cliffs and golden beaches. The road also goes through a pine forest.

Château de Bienassis

👣*Guided tour (50min) for interior visits of the château.* ◑mid-Jun–mid-Sept, 10.30am–12.30pm, 2pm–6.30pm, Sun and public holidays 2pm–6.30pm. ⬡5€. ☎02 96 72 22 03. *www.chateau-bienassis.com.*

The crenellated walls date from the 15C whereas the towers date from the 17C. On the ground floor there is porcelain from China and Japan and some furniture. The garden façade has two towers dating from the 15C.

⟳ *Rejoin the D 786.*

Erquy☨

In the 19C, a number of historians believed that Erquy was located on the alleged site of Reginea, a former Gallo-Roman settlement. It now appears they may have been mistaken. However, due to this misunderstanding, the inhabitants of Erquy have retained the charming name of Réginéens.

Set against a backdrop of rugged cliffs, this busy fishing port (2,000t of scallops in 1993) is gradually extending its influence. Its fishing fleet is made up of around 80 boats specialising in coastal fishing: fish (sole, turbot, gurnard, John Dory) and shellfish (scallops, clams and queen scallops). Among the many beaches, that of Caroual stands out on account of its **view** of the bay. Cap d'Erquy's natural topography ensures safe bathing for children.

At the edge of the road leading to Cap d'Erquy stand two small guard-rooms (the vestiges of Vauban's fortifications) along with a curious-looking cannon-ball foundry; its purpose was to manufacture cannon-balls for the batteries of artillery to fire at the approaching English, sailing forth in their 17C wooden ships.

As you enter Erquy go towards the cape.

Cap d'Erquy★

30min on foot there and back.

From the end of the road there is an extensive view of grey-pink shingle beaches lapped by clear waters, opposite Caroual Beach, Vallées seashore, the Pointe de Pléneuf and Verdelet Islet and beyond St-Brieuc Bay, the Pointe de l'Arcouest and the Île de Bréhat.

Pleasant footpaths bordered by bracken cross the heath dotted with patches of yellow and mauve and afford glimpses of the reefs. Guided tours of this area are organised in July and August.

Leave Erquy by the NE, then go through les Hôpitaux.

Sables-d'Or-les-Pins⚓

This seaside resort, created in 1922 and immediately fashionable, boasts opulent villas and Anglo-Norman-style hotels. The channel can be seen through the pine forest. From the vast sandy **beach★**, one of the finest in Brittany, a group of small islands can be distinguished, especially that of St-Michel and its chapel.

After the Plurien intersection, the St-Quay coastline comes into view across St-Brieuc Bay.

Pléhérel-Plage

The beach is on the right after a forest of conifers. A scenic view of Cap Fréhel and, in the foreground, a succession of tiny coves carved into the dunes may be enjoyed.

Take the D34A to continue to Cap Fréhel (See CAP FRÉHEL)

ADDRESSES

STAY

Grand Hôtel du Val André – *rue Amiral-Charner.* ℘*02 96 72 20 56. www.grand-hotel-val-andre.fr. Closed 2 Jan–13 Feb. 39 rooms.* ⚏*9.50€. Restaurant.* A seaside hotel from the turn of the 20C. The panoramic restaurant and modern rooms look out onto the beach.

EAT

Au Biniou – *121 rue Clémenceau.* ℘*02 96 72 24 35. Closed Feb, Tue eve and Wed except in summer.* In a small house in the centre of town, this restaurant serves tasty food in its small dining rooms and specialises in seafood.

ERQUY

Crêperie Bellevue – *near Château de Bienassis.* ℘*02 96 72 47 93. Closed Dec–Feb.* An assortment of delicious crêpes with a pleasant terrace and space for children to play.

Saint–Aubin – *22430 Erquy.* ℘*02 96 72 13 22. www.relais-saint-aubin.fr.* This 17C country house has an attractive dining room, nice terrace and garden.

SHOPPING

Markets – Tue morning at Pléneuf and Fri morning at Val-André.

St-Brieuc and Trégor are two of the original regions of Brittany although nowadays they are both part of the Côtes-d'Armor *département*. The coastline of the Côtes-d'Armor is heavily indented much like the coasts of its neighbours. Several islands, notably the lovely, car-free Île de Bréhat and the virtually uninhabited Les Sept Îles just north of the Pink Granite Coast, can be visited from the mainland. There are fine beaches too, notably at Trégastel Plage and St Guirec, which are near the lively resort of Perros-Guirec. Inland, the landscape is best exemplified by the forest, hills and ravines around Belle-Isle-en-Terre, from which many picturesque areas and towns can be explored.

A Bit of History

The Côtes-d'Armor *département* is located in the north of Brittany between the *départements* of Ille-et-Vilaine in the east and Finistère in the west. In the north, the waters of the English Channel pound the rocky coastline while to the south the land rises up to 300m/1,000ft where it borders with the Morbihan. It is often referred to as "mountainous" by those who live on the coast as it can be barren, desolate and windy even though it is not very high.

The economy relies heavily on tourism and fishing, particularly on the coast, while inland there are still strong agricultural and livestock-raising traditions, especially pork breeding. At Lannion and St-Brieuc, telecommunications and other high-tech research programmes represent the future prosperity of the region.

The main city of St-Brieuc is also the *préfecture* of the Côtes-d'Armor. It gives its name to the bay just to the north, which has one of the biggest tidal ranges in the world. The tide can recede around 7km/4.4mi, revealing in excess of 70 species of native shellfish native. An interesting town with many half-timbered houses in the area to the north of the cathedral, St-Brieuc is named, like many Breton settlements, after a 6C Celtic monk. It is well worth exploring, as are the other major towns of Lannion, Paimpol and Guincamp.

Inland towards the south of the *département* and in the heart of the Argoat can be found the Lac de Guerléden, a reservoir formed by the damming of the River Blavet which has created a recreational area for a wide variety of water sports and activities such as cruises, some of which include dinner.

Highlights

1 Picnicking on car-free **Île de Bréhat** (p185)

2 Wandering the cloisters of **Cathédrale St Tugdual** in Tréguier (p187)

3 Exploring the romantic **Jardins de Kerdalo** in Trédarzec (p189)

4 Driving along the **Côte de Granit Rose** (p205)

5 Taking a leisurely boat trip on **Lac de Guerléden** (p219)

While there is a great deal to be enjoyed in the interior of the Côtes-d'Armor, many of the attractions in this section of the Guide are located on or near to the coast. In addition to many superb beaches, there are the beautiful rock formations of the Pink Granite Coast or *Côte de Granit Rose* which assume such amazing shapes that the locals have christened them with imaginative names such as "Napoleon's Hat" "the Elephant" and "the Corkscrew". Between Perros-Guirec and Trébeurden the driving itinerary (&see page 205) takes in the splendours of this coastline, making for a perfect day out with the added bonus of magnificent views of the Les Sept Îsles and numerous other islands: Île Grande (which can be reached by a bridge) with its traces of prehistoric remains; Île Milliau (accessible on foot at low tide) resplendent with its many species of flora; and the huge prehistoric standing stone known as the Menhir de St-Uzec, embellished with some 17C Christian stone carving and a cross.

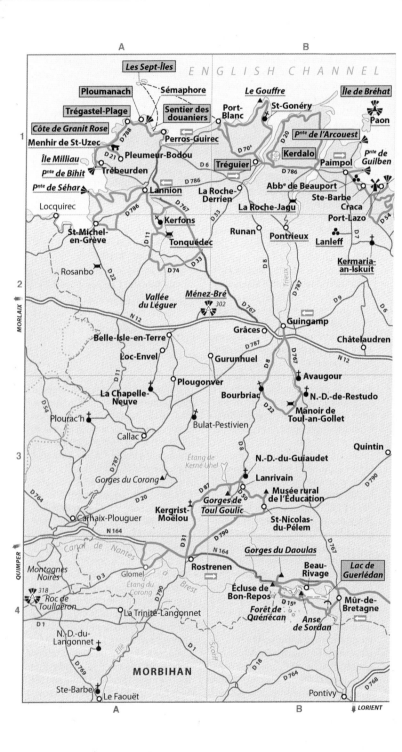

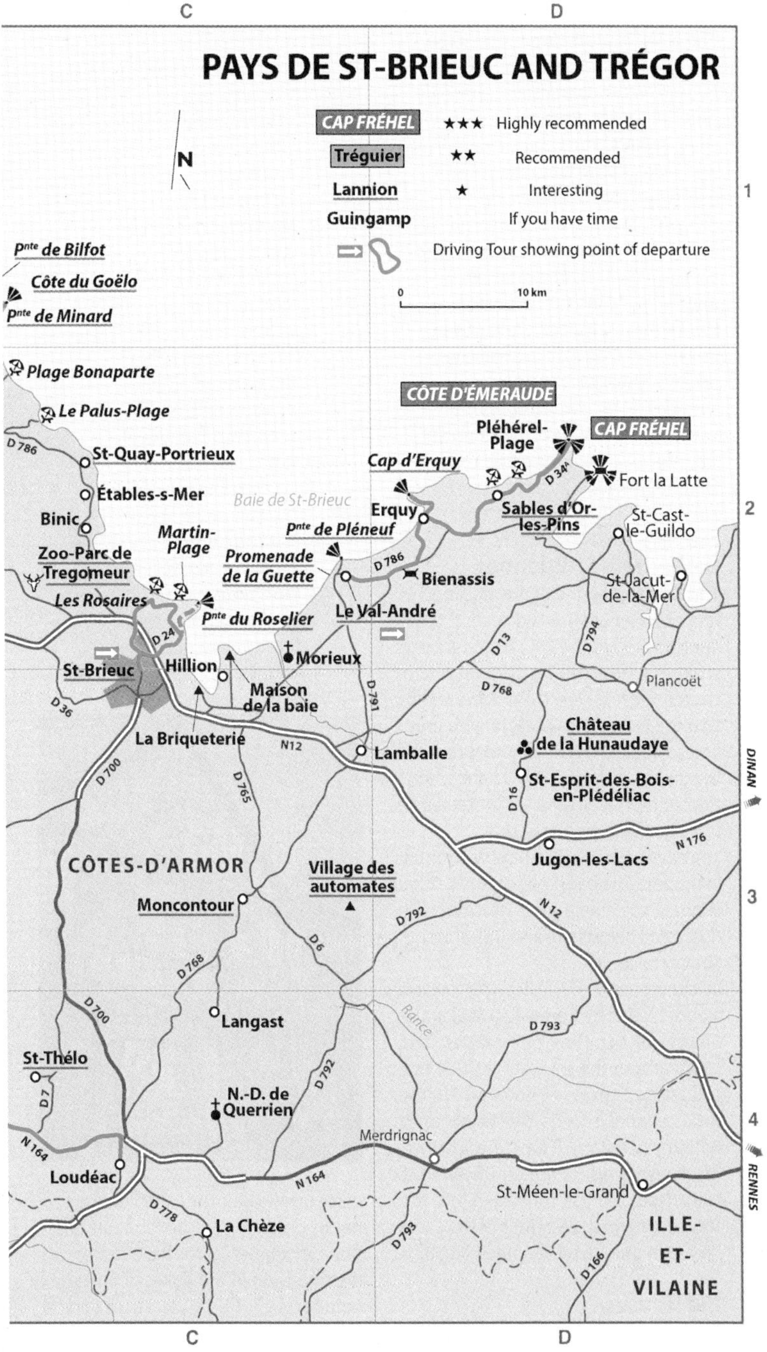

PAYS DE ST-BRIEUC AND TRÉGOR

N

CAP FRÉHEL	★★★	Highly recommended
Tréguier	★★	Recommended
Lannion	★	Interesting
Guingamp		If you have time
⇨		Driving Tour showing point of departure

0   10 km

P^nte de Bilfot
Côte du Goëlo
P^nte de Minard

Plage Bonaparte

Le Palus-Plage

D 786

St-Quay-Portrieux

Étables-s-Mer

Binic

Zoo-Parc de
Tregomeur

Les Rosaires

St-Brieuc

D 24

Hillion

D 36

CÔTE D'ÉMERAUDE

Pléhérel-
Plage

Cap d'Erquy

Baie de St-Brieuc

Martin-
Plage

Promenade
de la Guette

P^nte de Pléneuf

Le Val-André

P^nte du Roselier

Morieux

Maison
de la baie

Erquy

D 786

Bienassis

Sables d'Or-
les-Pins

CAP FRÉHEL

D 34

Fort la Latte

St-Cast-
le-Guildo

St-Jacut-
de-la-Mer

D 794

Plancoët

La Briqueterie

N12

Lamballe

D 791

D 768

D 13

Château
de la Hunaudaye

St-Esprit-des-Bois-
en-Plédéliac

DINAN

D 700

D 765

CÔTES-D'ARMOR

Moncontour

Village des
automates

D 792

D 16

Jugon-les-Lacs

N 176

N 12

D 6

D 768

D 700

Langast

Rance

D 793

St-Thélo

D 7

N.-D. de
Querrien

D 792

Merdrignac

RENNES

N 164

Loudéac

N 164

St-Méen-le-Grand

ILLE-
ET-
VILAINE

D 778

La Chèze

D 793

D 166

St-Brieuc★

The town is built 3km/1.8mi from the sea on a plateau deeply cleft by two water courses: the Gouëdic and the Gouet. Bold viaducts span their valleys. The Gouet is canalised and leads to the commercial and fishing port of Légué. St-Brieuc is the administrative, commercial and industrial centre of the *département* (Côtes-d'Armor). The markets and fairs of the town are much frequented, especially the Fair of St-Michael (Foire de la St-Michel) on 29 September. On Saturdays, a market is held in front of the cathedral. The peaceful provincial city has retained some fine timber-framed houses.

SIGHTS

Cathédrale St-Étienne★

This great cathedral of the 13C and 14C has been reconstructed several times and restored in the 19C; its mass bears striking witness to its original role of church fortress. The front is framed by two great towers complete with loopholes and machicolations and supported by stout buttresses. The two arms of the transept jut far out and are protected by towers with pepper-pot roofs.

The nave with its seven bays was rebuilt in the 18C. The harmonious three-sided chancel has an elegant triforium with quatrefoil balustrade and trefoil arches above the great arcades.

In the south aisle, note the carved wooden altar by Corlay (c. 1745) in the Chapel of the Holy Sacrament. The south arm of the transept is lit by fine 15C stained-glass windows and in the small chapel stands the tomb of St William (d. 1234). The stained-glass windows represent the Glorification of Mary. Note too the 16C organ loft, the 18C pulpit and the Stations of the Cross carved in granite by Saupique (1958).

Old Houses

The area to the north of the cathedral still retains many 15C–16C half-timbered and corbelled houses. Walk through

▶ **Population:** 46,437.

Michelin Map: Local map 309 F3 – Côtes-d'Armor (22).

Info: 7 rue St-Gouéno, 22000 St-Brieuc. ℘02 96 33 32 50. www.baiedesaintbrieuc.com.

Location: St-Brieuc is crossed by the N 12, which comes from Dinan (60km/37mi E) and goes to Brest (145km/90mi W). The D 786 follows the coast, serving the beaches and resorts of the Côte d'Émeraude.

Kids: A walk through the Galerie des Oiseaux at the Maison de la Baie.

Timing: Allow a day to visit the town and beaches.

Don't Miss: The exceptional views from pointe du Roselier.

Rue du Gouët

H. Le Gac/MICHELIN

place du Martray, rue Fardel (at the corner of place au Lin: the Ribeault mansion); at number 15, the house known as the "mansion of the dukes of Brittany"; numberss 17, 19, 27, 29, 31, 32 and 34 are also worth a look); rue Quinquaine (number 9) and rue de Gouët (numbers 6, 16, 22).

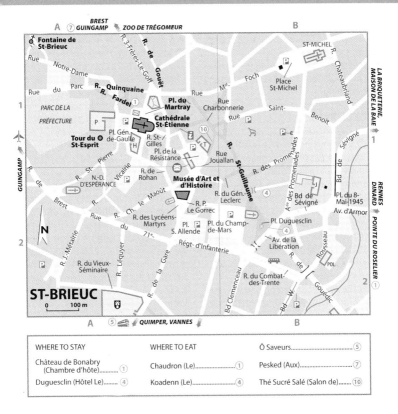

Tour du St-Esprit is an interesting Renaissance structure with a pepper-pot octagonal corner tower, and has been carefully restored.

Fontaine de St-Brieuc is sheltered by a lovely 15C porch, and stands against the east end of the Chapelle of Notre-Dame-de-la-Fontaine. Brieuc, the Welsh monk who came to the region in the 5C, is believed to have settled here.

Tertre Aubé★

The hill commands a fine view★ of the Vallée du Gouët, crossed by the viaduct which carries the road to Paimpol; also of the partly hidden port of Légué, below, and, to the right, of St-Brieuc Bay and the ruined tower of Cesson.

ADDITIONAL SIGHT
Musée d'Art et d'Histoire

Cours François Renaud, rue des Lycéens Martyrs. ⊙*Permanent exhibition open Tue–Sun 10am–noon, 1.30pm–6pm, Sun and public holidays 1.30pm–6pm.*

Temporary exhibitions 10am–6pm, Sun 2pm–6pm. ⊙*Closed Mon, 1 Jan, 1 May and 25 Dec.* ☏*02 96 62 55 20.*

Located in renovated rooms, the museum traces the history and development of the Côtes-d'Armor *département* (formerly Côtes-du-Nord) during the 19C, when traditional Brittany evolved into modern Brittany. Different themes – St-Brieuc Bay, heathland, cloth and

St Brieuc's Festivals

Festival Art'Rock – *first weekend of May.* www.artrock.org. Numerous concerts and entertainment in the town centre.

Nocturnes de St-Brieuc – *Jul–Aug, Thu & Fri evenings.* Street shows.

Quai en Fête – *alternate years in early July.* St Brieuc's Port du Légué hosts old riggings, music and other activities.

linen trade, village life – are covered, accompanied by models, equipment and tools used for fishing, navigation and husbandry, as well as costumes and furnishings.

EXCURSIONS
La Briqueterie

5km/3mi E on the N 12. Take the Langueux centre exit and follow signs to Site Boutdeville-École d'horticulture St-Ilan. ℘ 02 96 63 36 66. ⏱ Jul–Aug: Mon–Fri 10.30am–6.30pm, Sat– Sun and holidays 1.30pm–6.30pm ; Jun and Sept : Wed, Fri–Sun 2pm–6pm ; Oct–May: Wed, Fri–Sun 2pm–6pm. Guided visit Jul–Aug : Fri 2pm and 4pm. ⏱ Closed 5 weeks from 28 Dec. ⊚4 € (children 2.50 €).

At the former St-Ilan brickworks, you can discover the different activities that drove the economy of the bay of St-Brieuc in the 19C. The museum also recalls the era of local narrow-gauge trains in the Côtes-d'Armor, with a life-sized reconstructed station platform and a large-scale moving model of a train. Exhibition on the history of the building with its restored Hoffmann kiln (1870). Entrance includes a free booklet to help 8-12 year-olds discover the site, Sur la piste de Jean Fédébric (Tracking Down Jean Fédébric).

Hillion

14km/8.7mi E of St-Brieuc. Leave the town to the E and join the N 12 towards Yffignac. Take D 80 to Hillion. Follow the signs to Maison de la Baie.

👤 Maison de la Baie

10km/6.2mi E of St-Brueuc at Site de l'Étoile. ⏱ Open Jul–Aug, Mon–Fri 10.30am–6.30pm, Sat–Sun 1.30–6.30; Jun, Sept, Wed–Fri, Sun 2pm–6pm; Oct–May, Wed, Fri, Sun 2pm–6pm. ⊚3€. ℘02 96 32 27 98. www.cabri22.com/fr/maison_de_la_baie.php.

A visitor information centre for the marine environment presents exhibitions devoted to the environment and ecosystem of St-Brieuc Bay. Regular excursions are organised to discover the local bird life or the natural habitat.

👤 Zoo-Parc de Tregomeur

16km/10mi W of St-Brieuc. Take the express way N 12 to Morlaix. Take the exit for the D 6 towards Paimpol then follow the signs to Tregomeur. ℘ 02 96 79 01 07. www.zoo-tregomeur.com. ⏱ Apr–Sept : 10am–7pm (ticket office closed 1h30mins before closure) ; Oct–Mar : Wed, Sat–Sun, holidays: 1pm–5.30pm ; Nov and Feb school hols : 10.30am–5.30pm. ⏱ Closed 1 Jan & 25 Dec ⊚13.30 € (3-12 years 9,30 €).

The zoo is set in a valley of streams meandering past little islands, offering pleasant walks to the sound of birdsong. Everything is based on a Southeast Asian theme: the wooden buildings are reminiscent of Thailand or Indonesia, whilst the planting scheme favours bamboo and other exotics.

Visitors follow a circuit that leads them from the tiger's cage to less well-known animals, such as several species of lemur, binturongs, Bactrian camels, Przewalski's horses, gibbons and Manchurian cranes. Most of these animals of Asian origin are often overlooked by other zoos.

The site has been designed to appeal to children, who can finish off their visit at the adventure playground.

Quintin

At the crossroads of the D 7 and D 790, Quintin is 20km/12.5mi SW of St-Brieuc

In the past, Quintin was well known for its fine linen, which was used for headdresses and collars. In the 17C and 18C the industry expanded to the manufacture of Brittany cloth, which was exported to America, but decline set in with the Revolution. The old houses of Quintin rise in terraces on a hill; the River Gouët forms a fine stretch of water below.

There are fine 16C–17C corbelled houses lining picturesque Place 1830, rue au Lait (numbers 12, 13) and Grande Rue (numbers 37 and 43). In place du Martray, the Hôtel du Martray, the town hall and the house at number 1 date from the 18C.

Basilica (Basilique)

🕐*Open 9.30am–6.30pm.* ☞*For guided tours, ask at the Tourist Office.*

Built on the site of a collegiate church in 1887. The relics of St Thuriau and a piece of the Virgin's girdle, brought from Jerusalem in the 13C by a lord of Quintin (Geoffroy Botrel or Botherel), are kept in the basilica. There are also four stoups made of shells from Java and the old crowned statue of *Notre-Dame-de-Délivrance* (Our Lady of Safe Delivery), especially venerated by expectant mothers; a 14C font in the north transept and two 14C recumbent figures in the chancel.

At the east end of the basilica stands the 15C New Gate (*Porte Neuve*), all that remains of the ramparts that surrounded the town.

Château

Access via place 1830. ☞*Guided tours (1hr; last admission 30min before closing) daily Jul–Aug 10.30am–noon, 2pm–6pm; Jun and Sept 2pm –5.30pm; Jan and May 5–31, Oct–Dec, Sun and school hols 2pm–5pm.* ☜*5€.* ♿
♪02 96 74 94 79/04 63. www.chateau dequintin.fr

The château is made up of an older 17C building and a grand 18C building, flanked by a low-lying wing at right angles, visible once through the gate.

The **museum**, housed in the 18C part of the château, recounts Quintin's history and that of the chateau's previous owners. Displayed inside are hand-painted India Company plates, Meissen tableware, archives and Quintin linen. In the kitchen is an unusual piece: an 18C granite oven with seven holes (used for slow cooking).

Musée-atelier du Tisserrand et des Toiles

1 rue des Degrés. 🕐*Open Jun–Sept, Tue –Sat 1.30pm–6.30pm; Sun 10am–1pm.* ☜*3€.* *♪02 90 03 24 02.*

Already being made in the Middle Ages, Quintin linen developed greatly from 1650 to 1830. This model of a weaver's house presents the cloth's history and includes a weaving demonstration.

Menhir de Roche-Longue

800m/875yds farther on by the road beyond the calvary which skirts the lake. At the top of the hill, a 4.7m-high menhir stands in a field to the left.

🚗 DRIVING TOUR

Former Beaches

Round tour of 25km/15mi – 2hr.
◐ *Leave St-Brieuc N by Légué port, follow the quay on the north bank.*

On the right, the ruined tower of Cesson is outlined amid the greenery; as the road climbs there is a good view over the Pointe des Guettes at the far end of the bay and the coast as far as Cap d'Erquy.

🏛 Pointe du Roselier★

Take a path on the right of the telescope to go round the point. Fine **views**★ extend over St-Quay-Portrieux and the coast; the path passes near an old oven used for turning cannon-balls red-hot, and skirts a villa.

The view takes in the Pointe de Cesson, the far end of St-Brieuc Bay and the Pointe des Guettes with its mussel poles, and the coast towards Le Val-André. Paths cut in the cliffside lead back to the starting point.

◐ *Turn back and after 2km/1.2mi, bear right.*

Martin-Plage

This pretty beach lies between Pointe du Roselier and the Tablettes Rock (*Rocher des Tablettes*).

The road then climbs steeply and at Ville-Fontaine, bear right onto a pleasant little road descending between wooded embankments.

Plage des Rosaires

The beach is framed by wooded cliffs some 100m high. The **view** includes the whole of St-Brieuc Bay from St-Quay Point to Cap d'Erquy.

◐ *The road leads straight back to St-Brieuc.*

ADDRESSES

STAY

ST-BRIEUC

Hôtel Le Duguesclin – *2 Pl. Duguesclin.* $02 96 33 11 58. www.hotel-duguesclin.com. 17 rooms. 10€. Pub cuisine and seafood dominate the terrace and a comfortable upstairs dining room in this friendly brasserie.

HILLION

Chambre d'hôte Château de Bonabry – *22120 Hillion.* $02 96 32 21 06. www.bonabry.fr. Closed Nov –Apr. 4 rooms. Time seems to stand still in this noble coastal castle. The suites, which have canopy beds, family pictures and a fireplace, open on to the park and paths leading to the beach. To see: Le Columbier and Chapel of Rest.

QUINTIN

Hôtel du Commerce – *2 r Rochonen.* $02 96 74 94 67. www.hotel ducommerce-quintin.com. Closed Sun eve, Fri eve and Mon low season. 11 rooms. Restaurant. A skillful renovation has given all the comforts of modern living while preserving the rustic look of this 19C residence.

EAT

Le Bistrot Breton – *9 rue St-Guillaume.* $02 96 61 93 77. In these old stables with beams and exposed stones, you'll find a very cosy restaurant – especially if the fire is burning. On the menu are hot, fresh crêpes, generously filled with delicious local produce.

Salon de Thé Sucré Salé – *6 r. Jouallan.* $02 96 68 34 22. Closed 3 weeks Aug, 1 week Feb, Sun and Mon. Situated in a pedestrianised street, the Salon's window displays appetising patisseries and boxes of tea. Taste savoury tarts and sugar confectionery specialities.

Le Chaudron – *19 r. Fardel.* $02 96 33 01 72. http://lechaudron.info. Closed Mon except Jul–Aug, eve Jul–Aug. It's in a cobbled street in the old town that you'll find this half-timbered house. Fondues, raclettes and grills are on the menu in this 'old tavern' atmosphere. Savoyard-style interior and nice terrace.

Le Koadenn – *9 r. St-Guillaume.* $02 96 61 93 77. lekoadenn@hotmail.fr. Closed Sun. This old converted stable with its beams and revealed stones is cosy and has a roaring fire. Crêpes are always served piping hot and well garnished with top quality ingredients.

Ô Saveurs – *10 r. J.-Ferry -* $02 96 94 05 34. www.osaveurs-restaurant.com. Closed 2 weeks Aug, Jan, Sat lunch, Tue eve and Sun. Behind the station this restaurant is decorated in black and white. Seasonal menu. You can expect a warm welcome and good service.

Aux Pesked – *59 r. Légué.* $02 96 33 34 65. www.auxpesked.com. Closed 2–12 Jan, 26 Apr–3 May, 30 Aug–13 Sept, Sat lunch, Sun eve and Mon. The *pesked* (Breton for fish) have place of honour in this well-known restaurant. Dishes are given a Breton touch. Dining room overlooks the countryside.

NIGHTLIFE

Rollais – *26 r. du Gén.-Leclerc.* $02 96 61 23 03. Open Mon–Sat 10am–midnight. Closed two weeks in Aug. Handed from father to son since 1912, this wine bar is legendary. Literary and philosophical evenings (Thu) plus accordion concerts are held.

SHOPPING

Markets – Wed and Sat morning around the cathedral; Sun morning Croix-St-Lambert district; night market, Place du Martray, Thu and Fri evening Jul–Aug. Port du Légué Thu morning in summer. Craft market mid Aug near the cathedral. St Michael's Fair in Sept.

ACTIVITIES

St-Brieuc Équitation – *r. de Brezillet, 22440 Ploufragan.* $02 96 94 19 19. Open daily 9am–7pm. Closed last week Aug and Thur. As well as lessons, this riding school offers treks in the nature reserve.

Sailing and Windsurfing – Centre Municipal de Voile de St-Brieuc – *27 blvd. de Cornouaille, Les Rosaires, Plérin.* $02 96 74 51 59. Open year-round.

Swimming –Aquabaie – *Espace Brezillet.* $02 96 75 67 56. www.cabri22.com/fr/aquabaie.php. Olympic-sized pool with diving area, hammam, sauna.

St-Quay-Portrieux ⚌

St-Quay-Portrieux, a popular seaside resort, owes its name to an Irish monk, St Ké, who, legend has it, landed on this coast c. 472. Its beautiful beaches – Casino, Châtelet and Comtesse – are sheltered by a rocky fringe known as the Roches de St-Quay.

SIGHTS

The ports

The tidal port at Portrieux used to equip fleets bound for Newfoundland. Nowadays, it is the lively home of a fishing fleet which fishes for mackerel, pollack, bass and, from November to April in particular, scallops and shellfish. The new deep sea harbour, inaugurated in 1990, contains 950 berths for pleasure boats and 100 for fishing boats. There is a regular crossing to the Channel Islands during the summer, and also the opportunity to take a boat out to Île de Bréhat (see ÎLE DE BRÉHAT).

Chemin de Ronde

Allow 1hr 30min on foot there and back, preferably at high tide.

This former customs officers' path starts at Portrieux port, beyond the town hall, skirts Comtesse Beach, passes in front of the Viking stele and the signal sta-

- ▶ **Population:** 3,091.
- **Michelin Map:** Local map 309 F3 – Côtes-d'Armor (22).
- **Info:** 17 bis rue Jeanne d'Arc, 22410 St-Quay-Portrieux. ℘02 96 70 40 64. www.saintquay portrieux.com.
- **Location:** From St-Brieuc or Paimpol, you reach St-Quay by the D 786.
- **Timing:** You could spend two days here on the beach.
- **Don't Miss:** Kermarie-an-Iskuit chapel for its frescoes; the scallop festival in April.

tion, affording a fine **view**★ of St-Brieuc Bay, from Bréhat to Cap Fréhel. It then continues along the terrace overlooking Plage du Châtelet *(viewing table)*, round the sea-water pool and reaches Casino Beach. The walk may be extended as far as the Grève St-Marc *(add on about 2hr on foot there and back)*.

EXCURSIONS

Étables-sur-Mer

5km/3mi S. Leave St-Quay-Portrieux on D 786 in the direction of St-Brieuc.

The town, built on a plateau and possessing a fine public park, overlooks

Chemin de Ronde

S. Sauvignier/MICHELIN

179

the quiet family resort on the coast. The two parts of the town are linked by an avenue lined with villas. The two sandy beaches, Godelins and Le Moulin, are separated by the Pointe du Vau Burel.

Chapelle Notre-Dame-de-l'Espérance

◷Open Jul–Aug, 2pm–6pm.
☏02 96 70 65 41.
Built after the cholera epidemic of 1850, the restored Chapel of Our Lady of Hope, decorated with stained-glass windows in blue tones, two paintings by Jean Michau and a tapestry depicting the Virgin and Child by Toffoli, stands on Étables cliff, overlooking St-Brieuc Bay.

Binic ≈

▷7.5km/4.6mi S. from St-Quay Portrieux.
Binic is a delightful resort whose port used to shelter fishing schooners in winter. It is now used by pleasure craft and a few coastal fishing boats.
A small **museum** (◷open Jul–Aug, daily 2.30pm–6pm; Apr–Jun and Sept, Wed–Mon 2.30pm–6pm; ☞3.50€; ☏02 96 73 37 95) evokes daily life in Binic a century ago with a display of head-dresses, Breton costumes and various objects related to marine life and deep-sea fishing.
Jetée Penthièvre (pier), closing off the outer harbour, is reached by Quais Jean-Bart and Surcouf. From a belvedere on the jetty there is a pleasant view of the beach with its raised huts dominated by a pine-topped knoll and the port.

Le Palus-Plage

▷11km/6.8mi N. from St-Quay Portrieux.
A lovely cove. To the left of the beach, a stairway cut in the rock leads to an upper path from which there are good views of St-Brieuc Bay.

Plage Bonaparte

▷13km/8mi N. from St-Quay Portrieux.
From this beach at the bottom of Cohat Bay, reached by a tunnel cut through the cliff, Allied pilots brought down on French soil were taken back to Great Britain. To reach the commemorative monument, take the stairway to the

right of the beach car park, then the path up to the top of the cliff or, by car, drive along the road leading off to the right before the beach. Fine **view** of St-Brieuc Bay and Cap Fréhel, with Port-Moguer to the right and Pointe de Minard to the left.

Chapelle de Kermaria-an-Iskuit★

▷11km/6.8mi N. from St-Quay Portrieux via D 786, turn left on D 21.
◷Open 10am–noon, 2pm–6pm.
☏02 96 20 35 78.
The Chapelle de Kermaria-an-Iskuita (House of Mary who preserves and restores health) is a popular scene of pilgrimage (third Sunday in September). This former baronial chapel, in which a few of the bays of the nave are 13C, was enlarged in the 15C and 18C. In the archives, above the south porch, is the former 16C courtroom, which has a small balcony.
The walls over the arcades are decorated with 15C **frescoes**★. The best ones are preserved in the nave, and depict a striking dance of death: Death, in the shape of jumping and dancing skeletons and corpses, drags the living into a dance. Those depicted include pope, emperor, cardinal, king, constable, bourgeois, usurer, lover, lord, ploughman, monk. Above the high altar is a great 14C Christ. In the south transept are five alabaster **low-relief sculptures**★ of scenes from the Life of the Virgin. There are numerous wooden statues, including, in the transept, a curious 16C figure of the Virgin suckling her unwilling Child.

Lanleff

▷5.5km/3.5mi. Leave Kermaria W on D 21 to the left and after Pléhédel, bear left.
In the village, away from the road, stands the **temple**★, a circular building, a former chapel or baptistery built by the Templars in the 11C on the model of the Holy Sepulchre in Jerusalem. Twelve round-arched arcades connect the rotunda with an aisle set at an angle with three oven-vaulted apsidal chapels to the east.

Paimpol

Pierre Loti's novel *Pêcheur d'Islande* (Fisherman of Iceland, 1886) and Botrel's song *The Paimpolaise* brought literary fame and popularity to Paimpol. The cliff mentioned in *The Paimpolaise* is actually located near the town, towards the Pointe de Guilben. However, life has changed a great deal since those days when deep-sea fishing was done off the banks of Iceland. The fishermen now tend to fish along the coast; the port, large and impersonal, contains mostly pleasure boats. Oyster farming has brought wealth to the region, while the town prospers from the sale of early spring vegetables.

VISIT

Place du Martray

In the centre of the town, the square retains fine 16C houses; note at the corner of rue de l'Église the house with a square corner turret where Loti used to stay and where Gaud, the heroine of *Pêcheur d'Islande,* lived.

Square Théodore-Botrel

In the square stand an isolated 18C bell-tower, all that remains of a former church, and a monument to the popular singer Théodore Botrel, who died in Pont-Aven in 1925.

Musée de la Mer

Rue de la Benne. Open mid-Jun–Aug, daily 10.30am–12.30pm and 2pm–6.30pm; mid-Apr–mid-Jun and first half of Sept 2pm–6pm. 4.70€. 02 96 02 19. www.museemerpaimpol.com. Paimpol's seafaring activity, from the time of the Icelandic fishing expeditions to the present day, is recalled by models, photographs and navigational instruments.

La Vapeur du Trieux

Ave du Général-de-Gaulle. Open May–late Sept: 1 or 2 departures daily (sometimes does not operate on Mon or Tue). 22€ (children 11€). 08 92 39 14 27. www.vapeurdutrieux.com.

- **Population:** 7,788.
- **Michelin Map:** Local map 309 D2.
- **Info:** Rue Pierre-Feutrun, 22500 Paimpol. 02 96 20 83 16. www.paimpol-goelo.com.
- **Location:** Paimpol is 15km/9mi E of Tréguier on the D 786.
- **Kids:** The Vapeur du Trieux and the Labyrinthe Végétal.
- **Parking:** Avoid the centre on Tuesday mornings (market day). You'll find several car parks in the centre, notably place de la République.
- **Don't Miss:** The sight of Bréhat from the pointe de l'Arcouest.

The whistle blow of this old steam locomotive gives a real blast from the past. The train carries passengers on a round trip (4hr 30min) from Paimpol to Pontrieux and back (one-way trips also possible) along the Trieux estuary.

Choose the option *avec halte* and stop for 40 minutes at the Manoir de Traou Nez for cider and crêpes and some local colour (music, art exhibits).

The website is informative and available in English.

EXCURSIONS

Labyrinthe Végétal

In Plourivo. 2km/1.2mi SW along D 15. Open Jul–Aug, Tue–Sun 1.30pm–8pm (last entry, 6.30pm). 6€ (children 4.50€). 02 96 20 44 06.

"Get lost" takes on new meaning here. A maze laid out in a 6ha/15-acre corn field provides ample opportunity for adventure.

Every year the theme of the maze varies, with new enigmas to solve, clues to find and actors to make the experience complete (and to help find your children before closing time).

Tour de Kerroc'h

This tower stands in a pretty wooded setting. From the first platform there is a fine **view**★ of Paimpol Bay.

Ploubazlanec

In the cemetery is a wall on which the names of men lost at sea are recorded.

Pointe de l'Arcouest★★

On the way down to the creek of Arcouest there are remarkable **views** of the bay and of the Île de Bréhat at high tide. Each summer the place is invaded by a colony of artists and men of science and letters. A monument – two identical pink blocks of granite set side by side – has been erected to the memory of Frédéric and Irène Joliot-Curie, who were frequent visitors to Arcouest (below the car park, before the point's larger car park).

Loguivy-de-la-Mer

▶ *5km/3mi N. Leave Paimpol towards the Pointe de l'Arcouest, then take D 15.*
This fishing port, the second in the Côtes-d'Armor *département*, is simply a creek in which boats are grounded at low tide. Climb the promontory that encloses the creek on the left to get a view of the mouth of the River Trieux, Bréhat and the many islands.

🚗 DRIVING TOUR

La Côte du Goëlo★

Round trip of 47km/29mi – 4hr.

▶ *Take D 786 S towards St-Quay-Portrieux. On leaving Paimpol, turn left.*

Pointe de Guilben

This is the cliff mentioned in the song by Botrel. Enjoy the lovely view of the coast from the tip of the tongue of land that cuts the cove of Paimpol in two.

▶ *After Kérity, a road to the left leads to the Abbaye de Beauport.*

Abbaye de Beauport★

🕐 *Open mid-Jun–mid-Sept 10am–7pm; mid-Sept–mid-Jun 10am–noon, 2pm–5pm.* 🚶 *Guided tours (1hr) mid-Jun–Sept.* 🕐 *Closed 1 Jan, 24, 25, 31 Dec.* ⊜6€. 📞*02 96 55 18 58. www.abbaye-beauport.com.*
Founded in the 13C by the Premonstratensians, the abbey was seen as an important spiritual and economic centre for the St-Brieuc diocese. Of the 13C and 14C church, only the façade, open-air nave, north aisle and north arm of the transept remain. The long chapter-house with its polygonal apse, lying to the east of the cloisters, is an excellent example of the Anglo-Norman Gothic style, in the pure Mont-St-Michel tradition.

In the northwest corner of the cloisters, to the right of the three fine depressed arches that stood above the lavabo, is the elegant entrance to the large refectory, which looks out over the sea. Pass into the lower court overlooked by the Duc building, a huge hostelry for receiving the pilgrims, and the cellar underneath the refectory, whose groined vaulting rests on eight massive granite columns.

The tour ends with the almonership, the room in which the monks collected the tax on salt and cereals, and the visitor's hostel, with its two naves, where you can see an unusual box bed open on two sides.

The *Conservatoire du Littoral*, a national body in charge of preserving France's coastal heritage, has acquired the abbey estate and implemented a programme aimed at protecting the premises and organising guided tours for visitors.

▶ *Return to the St-Quay road, turn left and past the pool, turn left again onto an uphill road.*

Ste-Barbe

The sea can be seen from the small square of the chapel, the portico of which is decorated with a statue of St Barbara. A path (🅿), 250m/273yds further on takes you to a viewing table from where one can see beyond the meadow, Paimpol Bay and its nearby islands, the oyster beds, Port-Lazo and Mez du Goëlo Lighthouse.

LA CÔTE DU GOËL

At Plouézec, turn left and at St-Riom left again to Port-Lazo. At the end of the road there is a view of Paimpol Bay.Return to St-Riom; bear left.

Pointe de Bilfot★
From the viewing table, the **view** extends westwards to the Île de Bréhat and eastwards to Cap Fréhel.
Between the small lighthouse at Mez du Goëlo nearby and Paon Lighthouse at Bréhat in the distance, the bay is studded with rocks.

Turn back and at the entrance to Plouézec, bear left (D 54C).

Pointe de Minard★★
Make for this rocky platform, which affords a wide view over St-Brieuc Bay and Cap d'Erquy, the Paimpol Cove and the Île de Bréhat.

After a picturesque run along the coast to Le Questel, bear left twice after the hamlet. Make a detour via Pors Pin, a small creek with rocks curiously shaped by erosion, then return to the first junction and make a left turn.

The road runs along the edge of the bare cliff offering glimpses of St-Brieuc Bay and leads to a **viewpoint** ( ).
The **view**★ extends over the site of Bréhec-en-Plouha, Pointe de la Tour, St-Quay rocks and the coast from Erquy to Le Val-André.

Bréhec-en-Plouha
A small harbour sheltered by a dyke and a modest seaside resort at the bottom of a cove bounded by the Pointe de la Tour on the right and the Pointe de Berjule on the left. St Brieuc and the first emigrants from Britain landed at Bréhec in the 5C.

Go up the green valley of the Kergolo stream.

Lanloup
The 15C–16C church has an interesting south portico flanked by buttresses with niches and with St Lupus and St Giles standing on the pediment.
The 12 Apostles, carved in granite, on ornate corbels precede the doorway topped by a 14C Virgin. In the cemetery are a cross (1758) and the tomb of the composer Guy Ropartz (1864–1955) in an alcove to the right of the porch.

Return to Paimpol via Plouézec.

ADDRESSES

🛏 STAY

Hôtel Berthelot – *1 rue du Port, Paimpol.* 📞*02 96 20 88 66. 12 rooms.* 🍴 *5.50€.* Recently renovated and well-kept. Seven bedrooms have a shower and toilet, the rest have just a toilet. Double glazing, good prices and a nice welcome.

Hôtel L'Origano – *7 bis rue du quai, Paimpol.* 📞*02 96 22 05 49. Closed Easter and 15 Nov–31 Mar. 9 rooms.* 🍴 *6€.* The mistress of this establishment was born in this pretty Breton house. The bedrooms are charming and all different – one of the biggest has its own fireplace and garden.

Hôtel Goëlo – *Quai Duguay-Trouin, Paimpol.* 📞*02 96 20 82 74. www.legoelo.com. Closed 15–30 Nov. 32 rooms.* 🍴 *7€.* Renovated building on the *port* with small, comfortable rooms.

Chambre d'hôte La Maison des Îles – *29 rte de la Vieille Côte, pointe de l'Arcouest. 3km/1.8mi NE of Ploubazlanec on the D 789.* 📞*02 96 55 87 01. 4 rooms and 1 gîte. Meal* 🍴. A stone's throw from the embarcation point, this stone house has regained its lustre thanks to a significant renovation project. Contemporary décor with some antique furniture. Seafood specialities at dinner (reservations only).

Les Korrigann'ès – *10 rue des Fontaines, Pontrieux.* 📞*02 96 95 12 46. http://monsite.wanadoo.fr/korrigannes. 5 rooms.* The refined setting of this spacious house owned by artists is a blend of rustic and eastern influences. Tea room and lovely garden.

Hôtel du Relais Brenner – *Rue St-Julien. 5km/3mi rte de Tréguier, at pont de Lézardrieux.* 📞*02 96 22 29 95. www.relais-brenner.fr. Closed Nov–Mar. 18 rooms.* 🍴 *7€.* Entirely renovated, this characterful inn has spacious and comfortable rooms. There's a lovely view of the estuary from the lounge.

🍴 EAT

Crêperie Morel – *11 Place du Martray, Paimpol.* 📞*02 96 20 86 34. Closed one week in Feb, one week in Jun, three weeks in Nov, Tue off season and Sun.* Try this rustic place to savour crêpes and galettes made in the Breton tradition. Eat outdoors on sunny days.

Ferme de Kerroc'h – *14 rte de Bréhat, 22620 Ploubazlanec. 3km/1.8mi N of Paimpol on the D 789.* 📞*02 96 55 81 75. Closed Sun eve and Tue lunch Sept–Jun.* The stone façade and attractive tiled roof of this century-old farm catch the eye. Rustic dining room arranged around a fireplace where meat is grilled. Summer terrace.

🛒 SHOPPING

Markets – Paimpol, Tue morning, beautiful stands of seafood products; **Plouézec,** Sat morning; **Ploubazlanec,** Sun morning.

The **halle aux poissons** (fish market) displays the catch of the day from the local ports. At the end of Aug, the other speciality is the *coco de Paimpol,* string beans.

🏃 ACTIVITIES

Beaches – Near the yachting harbour of Paimpol, **La Tossen** is supervised and offers a sea water swimming-pool.

Cycling - Cycles du Vieux Clocher – *Place de Verdun.* 📞*02 96 20 83 58.*

Diving – Association Subaquatique Paimpolaise – 📞*06 96 20 56 98. Open Apr–Nov.* Explorations and lessons around the island of Bréhat.

Sailing – Initiation to sailing and fishing, on board the Eulalie, an old sardine boat (*39€/day; 42€ Jul–Aug*). Dominiuque Sicher, 38 chemin François Ollivier, 22860 Plourivo. 📞*02 96 55 99 99. www.eulalie-paimpol.com.*

Walks – The **GR 34 boasts wonderful landscapes between the** pointe de l'Arcouest, Loguivy-de-la-Mer and the mouth of the Trieux. Information at the Tourist Office.

Windsurf and sea kayak – Centre Nautique du Trieux – 📞*02 96 20 92 80. www.pole-nautique-paimpol.com.* Lessons and initiation. **Force 8** – *rte de Lézardrieux.* 📞*02 96 22 03 31. www.force8-paimpol.com* Rental of kayaks and windsurfing equipment.

Île de Bréhat★★

Bréhat is a much-frequented holiday resort. Its pink rocks stand out against the sea. Cars are not allowed; tractors are used for transportation.

A BIT OF HISTORY

A mild climate – Bréhat, which is about 3.5km/2mi long and 1.5km/0.9mi wide, consists of two islands joined in the 18C by a bridge built by Vauban. The coast, very broken and indented, is surrounded by 86 islets and reefs. Thanks to its mild climate (winter average 6°C/43°F), mimosa, eucalyptus and fig trees grow out in the open and the façades are bedecked with geraniums. There is little rain, the clouds generally passing over the flat island to condense over the mainland. The island's interior is a labyrinth of paths lined with honeysuckle or flower-covered dry stone walls, low houses with masses of hydrangea bushes, villas with vast gardens, a couple of cows in a tiny field or sheep on the heath. Its southern part is more welcoming than the rugged north.

A varied history – Bréhat owes its name (Breiz Coat: Brittany of the Woods) to an Irish monk, St Budoc, who landed on Lavrec Island in AD 470. A medieval fortress facing this island was destroyed by the English in 1409 and local people were hanged on the sails on Crec'h ar

▶ **Population:** 421.

⚐ **Michelin Map:** Local map 309 – Côtes-d'Armor (22).

▯ **Info:** Le Bourg, 22870 Île-de-Bréhat. ✆02 96 20 04 15.

◗ **Location:** Opposite the Point d'Arcouest, north of Paimpol.

◔ **Timing:** Prepare a picnic and make a day trip.

☝ **Don't Miss:** The view from the Chaise de Renan; Le Bourg; Paon lighthouse.

ACCESS

Les Vedettes de Bréhat (✆02 96 55 79 50; www.vedettesdebrehat.com) carry passengers to the island from Arcouest. The company also organises day trips from Erquy, Val-André, St-Quay-Portrieux, Binic and Perros-Guirec (from about 21€).

Transport

Bikes can be rented from the town or the landing stage. Some are equipped with child seats. However, given the number of visitors during the high season, cycling is not recommended. Several paths are barred to cyclists. As the island is a mere 3.5km/2mi long it is easier to explore on foot.

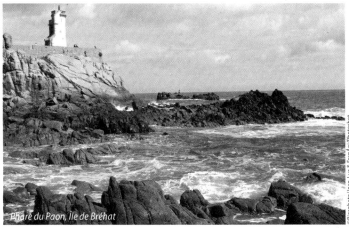

Phare du Paon, Île de Bréhat

©Biosphoto/Jean-Luc & FranAoi/Photoshot

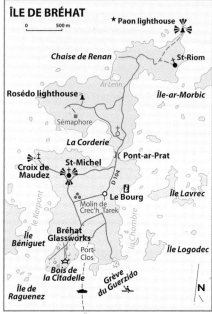

ÎLE DE BRÉHAT

0 — 500 m

★ Paon lighthouse

Chaise de Renan

✝ St-Riom

Ar Lenn

Rosédo lighthouse

Île-ar-Morbic

Sémaphore

La Corderie

✝ Pont-ar-Prat

St-Michel

Croix de Maudez

D 104

Le Bourg

Île Lavrec

Molin de Crec'h Tarek

la Chambre

le Kerpont

Île Béniguet

Bréhat Glassworks

Port-Clos

Île Logodec

Bois de la Citadelle

Grève du Guerzido

Île de Raguenez

N

POINTE DE L'ARCOUEST ST-QUAY-PORTRIEUX, PAIMPOL

Pot mill on North Island. La Corderie Bay, on the west coast, was used as anchorage. According to local tradition, it was a sea captain from Morlaix, Coatanlem, living in Lisbon, who revealed the existence of the New World to Christopher Columbus in 1484 – eight years before its official discovery – and showed him the course taken by the island's fishermen, already familiar with Newfoundland waters. In the 19C, the island was frequented by privateers and during the last war, it was occupied by German troops until 4 August 1944.

SIGHTS

The island is criss-crossed by paths with arrows at ground level showing the way. The houses of the island's capital, known as **Le Bourg,** are grouped around a small square lined with plane trees.

Chapelle St-Michel

High on a mound (26m; 39 steps), this chapel serves as a landmark for ships. There is an extensive **view**★★ over the Île Sud, the Kerpont channel and the Île Béniguet, Birlot Pool overlooked by the ruins of a once tide-operated mill, La Corderie Bay and the Île Nord.

Croix de Maudez

Erected in 1788 amid the heather and facing the ocean, the cross evokes the memory of a monk named Maudez who founded a monastery in AD 570, on a neighbouring island. There is a fine **view**★ of the islands of Béniguet to the left and Maudez to the right and the reefs.

North Island Lighthouses

Dating from 1862, the **Phare du Rosédo** stands inland, whereas the **Phare du Paon**★, was rebuilt in 1949 at the tip of North Island. The paved platform at the foot of the lighthouse affords a remarkable view of the rugged coastline, the chasm, the pink rocks and the shingles. This is the wildest part of the island.

BOAT TRIPS

Estuaire du Trieux★

Sail along the Trieux Estuary, whose banks are sheer, rocky, wooded and at times low-lying and cultivated, offers views of the pretty site of Lézardrieux with its suspension bridge. The river flows at the foot of Château de la Roche-Jagu, which can be reached via a fairly steep path through woodlands.

Tour of the Island★★

The tour allows visitors to admire the changing aspects of the coast: the beauty of the northern rocks and cliffs, the Mediterranean charm of the eastern shore and the ever-changing colour of the sea, which is often a deep blue.

Tréguier★★

The town (evangelised in the 6C by St Tugdual), a former episcopal city, was built in terraces on the side of a hill overlooking the wide estuary of the River Jaudy and River Guindy. The port, which provides a magnificent anchorage for yachts, can receive large ships.One of the great Breton *pardons* takes place in the town of St Yves on the third Sunday in May. This is the *pardon* of the poor, as well as that of advocates and lawyers. The procession goes from the cathedral to Minihy-Tréguier.

▶ **Population:** 2,676.

♿ **Michelin Map:** Local Map 309 C2 – Côtes-d'Armor (22).

ℹ **Info:** 67 rue Ernest-Renan, 22220 Tréguier. ℘02 96 92 22 33. www.ot-cote desajoncs.com.

▶ **Location:** Halfway between Lannion and Paimpol on the D 786.

🕐 **Timing:** Allow two days to explore the area.

👁 **Don't Miss:** The cloister of St-Tugdual cathedral, the gardens in the château Roche-Jagu.

SIGHTS
The Port
This magnificent expanse of water provides ample anchorage for yachts, but can also accommodate large coasters.

▶ *Leave the car in the harbour car park and enter the town along rue Ernest-Renan, which is lined with tall half-timbered houses. The two great square towers once framed the town gate.*

Maison d'Ernest Renan
🕐*Open Jul–Aug, daily 10am–noon, 2pm–6pm; Apr–Jun and Sept, Daily exc Sat 10am–noon, 2pm–6pm, Sun and public holidays 2pm–6pm.* 🕐*Closed 1 Jan, 1 May, 1 and 11 Nov, 25 Dec.* ⊙*3€. ℘02 96 92 45 63.*

This 16C half-timbered house contains memorabilia of the writer Ernest Renan (1823–92). Visitors can see the room in which he was born, a reconstruction of his study and library at the Collège de France and, on the top floor, the two tiny rooms in which, as a child, he liked to shut himself away to work (lovely view of the town).

Cathédrale St-Tugdual★★
🕐*Open Jun–Sept, 8am–7pm; Oct–May, 9am–noon, 2pm–6pm. ℘02 96 92 30 51.* The cathedral, which dates from the 14C–15C, is one of the finest in Brittany. The transept is surmounted by three towers; the tower of the south arm,

Cloisters, Cathédrale St-Tugdual

J. Malburet/MICHELIN

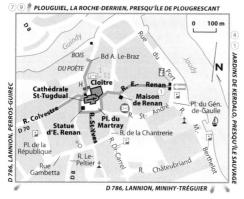

TRÉGUIER

WHERE TO STAY

Manoir de Troézel Vras
(Chambre d'hôte)...................① 1

WHERE TO EAT

Crustacé (Le)..........................⑨ 9
J.-P. Moulinet
(La poissonnerie)...................① 1
Moulin à Mer (Crêperie du)......④ 4
Pesked (Café)..........................⑦ 7

topped by an 18C pierced spire, rises 63m. At its base is a porch (1438) under a fine Flamboyant **window**★. The Gothic tower of the sanctuary, uncompleted, rises above the crossing. The Romanesque Hastings Tower is all that is left of the 12C church.

◯ *Enter through the main porch.*

Steps lead down towards the luminous nave with its Gothic arches worked delicately in granite. A sculpted frieze runs under the triforium. The ribbed vaulting in the Tudor style is lit by clerestory windows. The modern stained-glass windows, the work of the master glazier Hubert de Ste-Marie, portray biblical themes (to the left scenes from the Old Testament, to the right scenes from the Gospels).

◯ *Start from the north aisle.*

The **tomb of St-Yves** is an 1890 copy of the monument built by Jean V, Duke of Brittany, in the 15C. The recumbent figure of Jean V, sculpted in 1945, is located in the Duke's Chapel, lit by stained glass donated in 1937 by American, Belgian and French lawyers. The north arm of the transept is cut off by the Hastings Tower. The doors of the sacristy and cloisters open under handsome Romanesque arches which rise above a heavy pillar, coupled by columns with sculpted capitals and surmounted by an arcature. In the ambulatory, the third chapel houses a 13C Christ carved in wood. The chancel with slender columns has

15C painted vaulting. It holds 46 Renaissance **stalls**★.

The **stained-glass window**★ brightens the south transept. It recounts the story of the Vine (symbol of the Church), which winds round the founders of the seven Breton bishoprics (among them St Tugdual), around the saints of the land and around the Breton trades. Near the south doorway an interesting 15C **carved wooden group** represents St Yves between the Rich and the Poor. In the south aisle, note the 15C **recesses** sculpted with knights in armour.

Treasury

◯ *Open Jun–Sept, daily 10am–6pm, Sat 10am–noon.* ◉*4€ combined ticket with the Cloisters.* ℘*02 96 92 30 51.*
The sacristy contains the treasure, which includes the head reliquary (19C) of St Yves in gilded bronze placed against the foundation wall of the Hastings Tower (c. 11C).

Cloisters★

◯ *Open Jun–Sept, daily 10am–6pm; Oct–May, 10am–noon, 2pm–6pm.* ◉*4€ combined ticket with the Treasury (Oct–Mar, no charge).*
The 15C cloisters abut the former bishop's palace and the cathedral chevet cuts across the north gallery. The Flamboyant arches in Breton granite, roofed with slate, frame a cross rising on a lawn. Under the wooden vaulting with its sculpted purlin, there are 15C to 17C recumbent figures in the ambulatory. On Fridays during the summer, entertainment such as storytelling takes place.

Place du Martray

The shaded square, in the heart of the town, still features picturesque old houses. It contains a **statue** of Ernest Renan, commemorating the writer's birth in Tréguier and his attendance at the local college.

Rue St-Yves

A small tower in this pedestrian street gives a view of **La Psalette**, a residence for young singers in the cathedral, which was built in 1447.

Monuments aux Morts

North of the cathedral.

This war memorial is a sober and moving work by F Renaud, depicting a grieving Breton woman wearing a cape of mourning.

Take **rue Colvestre**, almost opposite, which features some lovely old houses and, more particularly, Duke Jean V's house, the Hôtel de Kermorvan and the Hôtel de Coetivy. Turn back and go down, beneath the old bishop's palace, to the **Bois du Poète**, overlooking the River Guindy and containing a monument to the writer Anatole Le Braz. This makes for a pleasant walk.

Notice also the **Calvaire de la Protestation** (Calvary of Protest) by the sculptor Yves Hernot, put up in 1904 to reflect the Catholics' objections to the erection of the statue in honour of Ernest Renan in the *place du Martray.*

EXCURSIONS

Jardins de Kerdalo★★

To the E. In the village of Trédarzec. Take the D 20 towards Kerbors then the first left and left twice again. Open Apr–Jun and Sept, Mon and Sat 2pm–6pm; Jul–Aug, Mon–Sat 2pm–6pm. 8€. 02 96 92 35 94. www.apjb.org/fr/parcs/kerdalo.html.

Created by Peter Wolkonsky in 1965, these botanic gardens can be found in a romantic setting of 18ha/44.5acres. The paths wind through the majestic trees, woods and perfumed areas. Flower-filled borders, perfectly cut lawns, an Italian grotto, a Chinese pagoda… it's a truly sensorial experience. Waterfalls tumble to the Trieux down below. Lovely **view**★ over the port of Tréguier.

Jardins de Kerdalo

©Isabelle Vaughan/Jardins de Kerdalo

Minihy-Tréguier

1km/0.6mi S. Leave Tréguier towards La Roche-Derrien. On leaving the town, turn left.

The birthplace of St Yves is the scene of a *pardon* on the third Sunday in May. This is called locally "going to St-Yves"; the local priest is even known as the Rector of St-Yves. The 15C church is built on the site of the former chapel of the manor of Ker-Martin, where Yves Helori was born and died (1253–1303). His will is written in Latin on a painted canvas kept in the chapel.

A 13C manuscript kept in the presbytery is called the *Bréviaire de St-Yves* (Breviary of St-Yves). In the cemetery is a 13C monument pierced in the middle by a very low archway, under which the pilgrims pass on their knees. This is called the *Tombeau de St-Yves* (tomb of St-Yves), but is probably an altar belonging to the original chapel.

La Roche-Derrien

6.5km/4mi SW on the D 8.

This old strategic point was the setting for an important battle during the Wars of Succession in 1347. It owed its prosperity to linen trading and today is a pleasant spot in the Jaudy valley.

The **church** owes its unusual form to the addition of a large chapel by Roland de Kersaliou in 1376. A window installed in 1927 depicts the famous battle when Charles de Blois was taken prisoner.

Château de la Roche-Jagu

R. Mattes/MICHELIN

Château de la Roche-Jagu★

◐ *13km/8mi SE via D 786 and D 787.*
◷ *Open Jul–Aug, daily 10am–7pm;
Easter–Jun and Sept–Oct, 10am–12pm,
2pm–6pm.* ◌ *Guided tours of the
gardens available, Jul–Aug including
shows.* ◌ *4€ château, garden no charge.*
☎ *02 96 95 62 35.*

The **castle** was built in the 15C at the
top of the steep wooded slopes which
form the west bank of the River Trieux.
It was restored in 1968. Together with
other fortresses, no longer extant, it
commanded the river and thus retains
its defensive aspect. On the west façade,
note the corbels which supported the
former wall-walk and its five doors. The
tour includes several rooms with French-
style ceilings and large chimneys, the
small chapel and its two oratories. There
is a magnificent view of the **setting**★ of
the Trieux from the covered wall-walk in
front of the east wall. The river forms a
steep-sided loop at the foot of the castle
which can be reached by a footpath to
the right.

During the summer, exhibitions and
displays take place in the castle.

Park – After the terrible storm of 1987, a
modern park was created. The gardens
recall the landscapes of Brittany, but also
feature palm trees and the remains of a
linen workshop.

Runan

◐ *13km/8mi S via D 8.*
Runan, which stands on a plateau in
the Tréguier region, has a large church

which belonged to the Knights Templar
and then to the Hospitallers of St John
of Jerusalem.

The 14C–15C **church** is richly decorated. The south side has four gables
pierced with broad windows and
emblazoned façades. The porch gable
is adorned with a sculpted lintel depicting the Annunciation and a Deposition.
The superimposed figures of the 12
Apostles join to form the keystone of
the vaulting.

Inside, the building is roofed with panelled vaults resting on multicoloured
purlins: signs of the Zodiac to the left
of the nave, animals on the right.

The mid-15C altarpiece of the font
chapel includes exceptionally delicate
figures (five scenes from the lives of
Christ and the Virgin) made of bluish
Tournai stone.

🚗 DRIVING TOURS

1 PRESQU'ÎLE DE PLOUGRESCANT

Round tour of 37km/23mi – about 2hr.

◐ *Leave Tréguier on D 8 to the N and
at Plouguiel, bear right.*

La Roche-Jaune

A small port on the Jaudy Estuary with
Oyster farms. On leaving La Roche-Jaune
in the direction of St-Gonéry, you will
enjoy a good view of the Jaudy estuary,
the oyster-beds and the islands.

Chapelle St-Gonéry★

Guided tours on request from the Association Art, Culture et Patrimoine, 22 rue Renan. Mid-Jun–mid-Sept and school holidays, 3pm–6pm. 2.50€. 02 96 92 27 54.

The chapel has a curiously leaning lead steeple (1612) on a 10C tower.

Inside, the painted wood vaulting depicts scenes from the Old and New Testaments; these **paintings**, which date from the late 15C, were restored in the 18C and 19C.

In the chapel on the right of the chancel, there is a 16C **reliquary cupboard**★, a finely carved canopied type of chest. The left chapel contains the 16C **mausoleum**★ of a bishop of Tréguier; the recumbent figure rests on a great marble slab decorated with mouldings and supported on four lions.

▷ *At St-Gonéry, take the road to Pors-Hir.*

Pors-Hir

A small harbour built between immense rocks near a little cove.

The road follows the coastline in a beautiful setting; houses built against huge rocks or nestling between tall boulders add a fairy like touch.

Pointe du Château, Presqu'île de Plougrescant
©Photononstop/Tips Images

Pointe du Château

From the tip of the headland, there are beautiful views over the Îles d'Er, the Heaux Lighthouse and Sept-Îles.

Le Gouffre★

Allow 15min on foot there and back.
A deep cleft in a mass of rocks into which the sea roars furiously.

▷ *Turn back and follow the road along the bays, then bear right three times.*

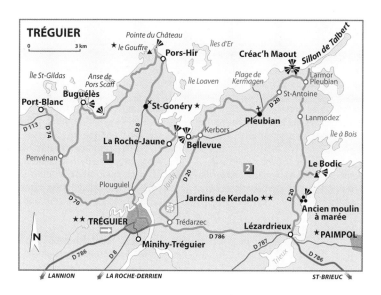

From Le Roudour, you can make for **Anse de Pors Scaff** bristling with islands, then head for **Buguélès**, a small resort fringed by islands, all inhabited.

After Le Roudour the coastal road affords lovely views.

Port-Blanc⌂
A small fishing port and seaside resort. Under the dunes of the main beach are traces of memorial stones (covered), which suggest the existence, at one time, of a necropolis.

Go to the great esplanade by the sea, turn left before a group of houses built on the rocks (🅿) At the left corner, take an uphill path and a stairway (35 steps).

The 16C **Chapelle Notre-Dame-de-Port-Blanc** (🕐*open Jul–Aug, daily 10.30am–noon, 3pm–6pm*) has a roof that comes down to the ground. Every year, the small **Île St-Gildas** hosts the *pardon aux chevaux*, also known as *pardon de St-Gildas*.

Return to Tréguier by Penvénan.

② PRESQU'ÎLE SAUVAGE
Round tour of 49km/30.5mi – 3hr

Leave Tréguier towards Paimpol.

Lézardrieux
The town is built on the west bank of the Trieux, which is spanned by a suspension bridge. The 18C church has an elegant gabled belfry flanked by two turrets and topped by a pinnacle pierced with arcades containing the bells. This particular type of belfry is to be found throughout the peninsula.

Make for the Talbert Spit (Sillon de Talbert), skirting the large marina on the Trieux. After 3km/1.8mi bear right onto a downhill road.

Ancien Moulin à Marée
The ruined mill was driven by water from a small reservoir upstream. From the dyke, there is a good view over the mouth of the Trieux.

Return to Talbert Spit and turn right.

🄺 Phare du Bodic
This small lighthouse commands the mouth of the Trieux.
A path on the left leads through fields to a look-out point from which the **view**★ extends over the Trieux estuary and the Île à Bois in the foreground and the Île de Bréhat in the distance.

The road then passes near Pommelin Bay, crosses Lanmodez and Larmor-Pleubian. This stretch of coast (Port-Blanc – Paimpol) can also be explored on foot along the long-distance footpath GR 34.

Sillon de Talbert
This long (3km/1.8mi), narrow tongue of land, surrounded by reefs, consists of sand and shingle washed by the currents of the Trieux and the Jaudy; it is possible to go round on foot. Seaweed is collected (the annual local production is estimated at 8 to 10 000t of algae) and dried on the spot and then sent to a factory nearby for processing. The Sillon de Talbert is now a national preserved site, placed under the protection of the *Conservatoire du Littoral*.

Return to Larmor-Pleubian and bear right towards Pors-Rand Beach.

Créac'h Maout viewing table
From the viewing table in front of the war memorial and the signal station, there is a wide **panorama**★ over Pointe de l'Arcouest, Île de Bréhat, Sillon de Talbert, Heaux Lighthouse (built in 1836–9, 56m high, average range 35km/22mi), Pointe du Château and the Jaudy estuary.

Go through St-Antoine to the entrance of Pleubian and bear right.

Pleubian

On the north side of the church with its characteristic belfry, is a fine 16C round **pulpit**★ surmounted by a cross and decorated with a frieze depicting the Last Supper and scenes from the Passion: Judas's Kiss, the Flagellation, Christ bearing the Cross.

At Pleubian, take the direction of Kerbors by the coast road.

The road passes near the covered alleyway at Men-ar-Rompet, partly hidden in the greenery, and by the Île à la Poule.

At Kerbors, turn right before the church.

Bellevue

It is located on the bank of the Jaudy. On the right the view extends over the Jaudy estuary, on the left over the valley and site of Tréguier dominated by the cathedral towers; opposite, La Roche-Jaune rises in terraces. There are trout and salmon farms along the Jaudy, which is tidal. Fish farming is developing in the region.

The road winds through fields growing early vegetables and descends towards the Jaudy Valley and Tréguier.

ADDRESSES

STAY

Chambre d'hôte du Manoir de Troézel Vras – *22610 Kerbors. 9km/5.5mi NE of Tréguier rte de Paimpol, towards Pleumeur-Gautier. http://troezel.vras.free. fr/troezel/anglais/default.htm. 02 96 22 89 68. 5 rooms. Closed Oct–Mar. Restaurant (eve only).* Flagstone floors, original engravings on the walls, old and new furniture: eclectic style and lovely rooms in a 17C manor. A charming place.

Chambre d'hôte du Penquer – *Minihy-Tréguier. 02 96 91 57 03. 4 rooms.* In the countryside, a block of stone buildings form two family units with rooms in blue and yellow tones. Good breakfast with 10 varieties of homemade jam! Kitchen area.

Hôtel Aigue Marine – *Port de Plaisance. 02 96 92 97 00. www.aiguemarine-hotel.com. 48 rooms. 13.50€. Closed Jan–Feb. Restaurant.* Comfortable rooms with views overlooking the port or the swimming pool and garden.

EAT

Crêperie du Moulin à Mer – *11 rue du Moulin à Mer. 11km/7mi E of Tréguier at Lézardrieux. 02 96 20 19 49. Closed Sat eve & Sun Sep–Easter.* Very popular *crêperie* in a 17C manor house.

La Poissonnerie Moulinet – *2 rue Ernest Renan. 02 96 92 30 27. Open Jul–Sept.* This fishmonger has two dining rooms above his shop where you can enjoy fresh sea produce at good prices. A children's menu introduces little ones to fishy delights.

Café Pesked – *21 rue du Port, Plouguiel. 02 96 92 01 82. Phone for opening times.* Wide selection of fresh seafood in a charming Breton house.

Le Crustacé – *2 rue de la Poste, Penvénan, 8km/5mi W of Tréguir. 02 96 92 67 46. Closed Mon in Jul–Aug, Sun eve, Tue eve & Wed Sep–Jun.* Family-run restaurant opposite the church serving traditional dishes and seafood.

SHOPPING

Markets – Tréguier, Wed; **La Roche-Derrien**, Fri; **Lézardrieux**, Fri; **Penvénan**, Sat; **Pleubian** Sat; **Port-Blanc**, Thu morning in summer; **Trévou-Tréguignec**, Tue in summer.

Boulangerie Muzard – *Place de l'Église, Pleudaniel. 02 96 20 14 73. Open*

Tue–Sat. Breads and other culinary specialities.

Sea Grocery – *Lanmodez.* ℘*02 96 22 95 94. Open Mon–Fri.* Noodles, canned food, and smoked fish in season.

Oysters – M. Rouzès, *in Lanmodez (*℘*02 96 22 85 91)* and **David Percevault**, *on the port of La Roche-Jaune (*℘*02 96 92 57 88)* sell high quality products.

FESTIVALS AND EVENTS

Every Wed evening, mid-Jul to mid-Aug, concerts and a nocturnal market animate the centre of Tréguier.

During the same period, **Festivals en Trégor** offers classical concerts in the churches of the region (information at the Tourist Office of Tréguier).

The more contemporary, **Les Irréducktibles** is for lovers of rock, songs and theatre, takes place in Plougrescant the first weekend of Aug.

Les **Régates de La Roche-Jaune**, a maritime festival with sailing competitions, sea shanties and a musical evening, takes place in Aug in Plouguiel.

Le grand *pardon* **de St-Yves**, 15 May in Tréguier, and Le grand *pardon* de **St-Gildas**, in Penvénan, (end May–beginning of June) are traditional events. The latter is the "*pardon* of horses".

The **Festival Gospel in the Peninsula** takes place in the chapels of the Peninsula Sauvage in Mar and Apr.

🗓 *Contact the Tourist Office for details of all events.*

ACTIVITIES

Bike rental – Bar Les Plaisanciers – *le port, Tréguier.* ℘*02 96 92 49 69.*

Camping Le Gouffre – *between Le Gouffre and Pors-Hir.* ℘*02 96 92 02 95. www.camping-gouffre.com.*

Horse-riding – Poney-Club de Port-Blanc – *Kerelguen.* ℘*02 96 92 79 73.* Easy ride (2hr) all year and all day Sat in summer for ages 4 and up. **La Ferme du Syet** – *Minihy-Tréguier (*℘*02 96 92 31 79,*

www.la-ferme-du-syet.com), half-day rides and full-day rides in the forest or along the sea in accordance with the season.

La Marie-Georgette – 9m/29ft half decked sloop available for day trips (6hrs) from Apr–Oct . Information at Le Gavroche pub in Plougrescant. ℘*02 96 92 09 15* or ℘*02 96 92 52 83.*

Walks – The **GR 34** follows the edge of the two peninsulas. The Tourist Office of the peninsula of Lézardrieux (Sauvage) sells a **guide** offering 17 tours. You will also find information on several hikes on the peninsulas in *Balades en pays de Trégor et Goëlo*, available at the *Pays Touristique, 9 Place de l'Église, La Roche-Derrien.* ℘*02 96 91 50 22. www. tregorgoelo.com* or at the *Conseil Général des Côtes-d'Armor (*℘*02 96 62 27 64).*

Windsurf and kayak – Centre nautique de Port-Blanc – *bd de la mer.* ℘*02 96 92 64 96. www.cnportblanc.fr.* Windsurfing and kayak lessons.

Plougrescant Kayak de Mer – ℘*02 96 31 51 48. Open Jul–Aug.* Kayak 10 yrs old and up: lessons and trips between the peninsulas.

Rocky coast to Plougrescant

R. Mattès/MICHELIN

Lannion★

Lannion, spread out on both banks
of the River Léguer, has retained its
typical old Brittany character. From
the bridge, there is a good view of
the port and of the vast Monastère
Ste-Anne. The Centre de Recherches
de Lannion and the Centre National
d'Études des Télécommunications,
where research is undertaken in
telecommunications and electronics,
have been built 3km/1.8mi north
of Lannion at the crossroads of the
road to Perros-Guirec and that of
Trégastel-Plage. Lannion's annual
organ festival takes place in Église
St-Jean-du-Baly (16C–17C).

SIGHTS
Old Houses★
The beautiful façades of the 15C and 16C
houses, half-timbered, corbelled and
with slate roofs, may be admired especially at *place du Général Leclerc* (n°s 23,
29, 31, 33), *rue des Chapeliers* (numbers
1–9), *rue Geoffroy-de-Pont-Blanc* (numbers 1 and 3) and *rue Cie-Roger-de-Barbé*
(numbers 1 and 7).
At the corner of the latter, on the left,
a granite cross has been sealed in the
wall at the spot where the *Chevalier de
Pont-Blanc* distinguished himself in the
heroic defence of the town during the
War of Succession.

Église de Brélévenez★
Escalier de la Trinité (140 steps).
Open 10am–6pm. 0.20€.
The church was built on a hill by the
Templars in the 12C and remodelled in
the Gothic period.
Before entering look at the curious
Romanesque apse which is decorated
with engaged round pillars, carved capitals and modillions.
The bell-tower, crowned by a granite
spire, dates from the 15C. From the terrace, there is an attractive view of Lannion and Léguer Valley.
Under the chancel, the Romanesque
crypt, which was remodelled in the
18C, contains a marvellous 18C **Entomb-**

- **Population:** 19,459.
- **Michelin Map:** Local map
  309 B2 - Côtes-d'Armor (22).
- **Info:** 2 quai d'Aiguillon,
  22300 Lannion. 02 96 46
  41 00. www.ot-lannion.fr.
- **Location:** The town is
  crossed by the D 786 which
  links Morlaix (38km/
  23.5mi W) and Paimpol
  (35km/22mi E), passing
  by Tréguier.
- **Timing:** Explore old
  Lannion in the morning
  and the outskirts in
  the afternoon.
- **Parking:** Ursulines car
  park is free all year.
- **Don't Miss:** The medieval
  old town, the market on
  Thursday morning and
  Séhar point for the views.

ment★, in which the subjects, carved
in polychrome stone, are depicted
life-size.

DRIVING TOURS

1 CASTLES AND CHAPELS
Round trip of 50km/31mi – 3hr.

Leave Lannion on the D 11 heading S,
the road to Plouaret. 1.5km/0.9mi after
Ploubezre, bear left at a fork where five
granite crosses stand and 1.2km/0.7mi
further on, turn left.

Chapelle de Kerfons★
Open mid-Jun–mid-Sept Wed–Mon
10.30am–noon,2pm–6.30pm.
Guided tour 2€. 02 96 47 15 51.
This chapel is surrounded by chestnut
trees in front of an old calvary. Built in
the 15C and 16C, it has a flat east end, a
modillioned cornice along the south wall
and a pinnacle turret decorated with
telamones crowning the gabled south
transept. It contains a late-15C carved
rood screen★.

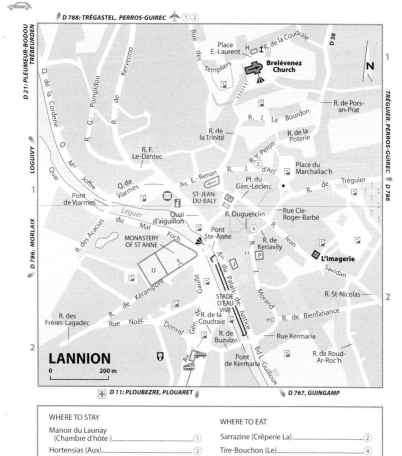

LANNION

0 — 200 m

WHERE TO STAY		WHERE TO EAT	
Manoir du Launay (Chambre d'hôte)	①	Sarrazine (Crêperie La)	②
Hortensias (Aux)	②	Tire-Bouchon (Le)	④

▷ *Turn back and take the road on the left.*

Soon the road starts to wind downhill providing good views over the ruins of Tonquédec in the Léguer Valley. After crossing the swiftly flowing river you will see the castle on the left (P).

Château de Tonquédec★

⏱ *Open 21 Jun–21 Sept 10am–7pm; Apr–20 Jun and 22–30 Sept 2pm–6pm; Oct and Nov school hols, Sat–Sun 2pm–5.30pm.* *Guided tours (30min).* ☏ *02 96 54 60 70. www.chateau-tonquedec.com.* *5€.*

The ruins of the castle stand in very fine surroundings at an elevation overlook-ing the Léguer Valley. The castle, which was built in the early 13C, was disman-tled by order of Jean IV in 1395; rebuilt at the beginning of the 15 C, it was again razed by order of Richelieu in 1622.

The entrance gate is opposite a pool now run dry. Enter a fortified outer courtyard. On the right, two towers connected by a curtain wall frame the main entrance to the second enclosure. Pass through a postern into the second courtyard. Opposite, standing alone, is the keep with walls over 4m thick. Go up a stairway *(70 steps)* to a platform to admire the plan of the castle and the local countryside: a wide, fertile and populous plateau intersected by deep, wooded valleys.

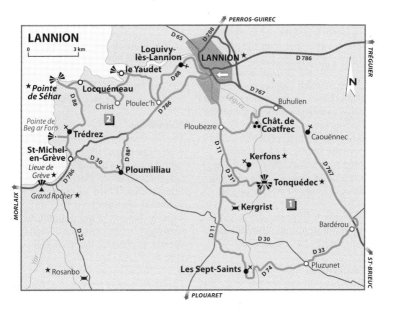

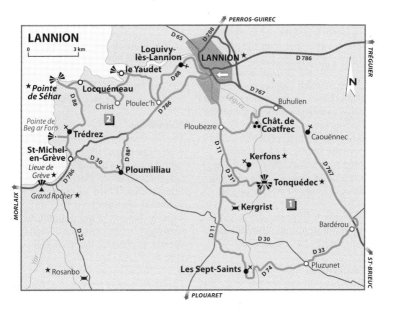 *Turn back and at the first crossroads bear left to join the road to Plouaret, then turn left again; and after 1km/0.6mi turn left.*

Château de Kergrist

Guided tours (30min) of the interior by reservation. Easter–Oct 11am–6.30pm; Combined ticket château and gardens ⊜10€, gardens only ⊜5€. ℘02 96 38 91 44.

One of the principal attractions of the château lies in the variety of its façades. The north façade is Gothic with dormer windows set in tall Flamboyant gables; the main building, which belongs to the 14C and 15C, nevertheless features an 18C façade on the opposite side, while the wings running at right angles, which were built at an earlier date, have Classical fronts overlooking the gardens. The formal French gardens extend as far as the terrace which overlooks a landscaped English garden and the woods.

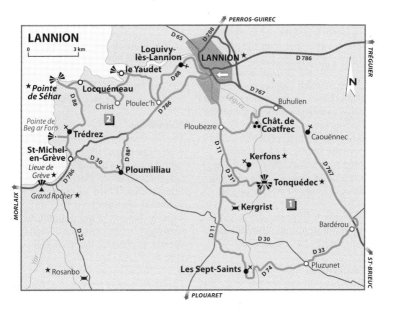 *Return to the Plouaret road and bear left; after 2.2km/1.3mi, turn left.*

Chapelle des Sept-Saints

Open 8am–7pm. ℘02 96 38 90 08.

This 18C chapel, surrounded by greenery, is unusual in that it is built in part on top of an imposing dolmen. From the outside, a small door in the south arm of the transept leads under the dolmen, which has been turned into a crypt for the cult of the Seven Sleepers of Ephesus. According to legend, seven young Christians walled up in a cave in the 3C woke up 200 years later. Every year, an Islamic-Christian pilgrimage (*see Calendar of Events*) is held in this Breton chapel.

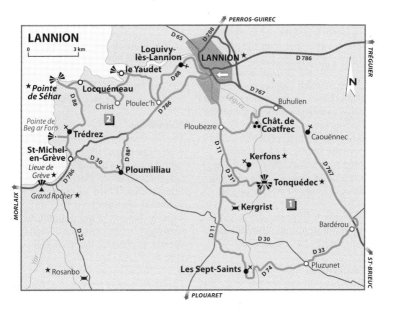 *Via Pluzunet and Bardérou you will reach the road to Lannion, then bear left. Drive past Caouënnec-Lanvézéac and continue towards Lannion and at Buhulien bear left in the direction of Ploubezre and 100m after a farm at Pont-Keriel, turn left onto an unsurfaced path through the woods.*

Château de Coatfrec

There are fine ruins of this large 16C mansion.

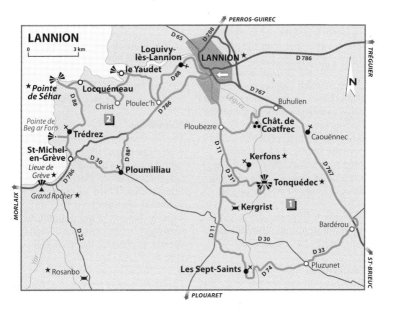 *Make for Ploubezre and turn right to Lannion.*

197

② TOWNS IN THE LÉGUER ESTUARY

Round trip of 32km/20mi – 2hr.

▷ Leave Lannion by Quai du Maréchal-Foch.

The south bank of the River Léguer is picturesque, especially at high tide.

Loguivy-lès-Lannion

This town on the outskirts of Lannion clings to the hillside in a pleasant setting. The **church**, nestled in a verdant landscape along the banks of the Léguer, is 15C. A curious outdoor stairway leads to the wall-belfry (1570).

Inside the church, in the chapel to the right of the chancel, there is a 17C wooden **altarpiece** depicting the Adoration of the Three Wise Men with shepherds in Breton costume playing the bagpipes and the bombardon. The fine wooden balustrade in the chancel dates from the same period.

In the cemetery, a granite fountain, dating from 1577, plays beneath yew trees which are several centuries old.

Le Yaudet

This hamlet, in its beautiful setting, was the episcopal seat in the early centuries of our era and was destroyed by the Danes (c. AD848); it has remains of Roman walls and an interesting **chapel** (⏱ *open year-round 9.30am–6.30pm*) overlooking the bay. Inside, above the altar, is a curious sculpted panel depicting the Trinity: a recumbent figure of the Virgin with the Infant Jesus at her side; God the Father is sitting in an alcove at the foot of the bed over which hovers a dove symbolizing the Holy Spirit.

From the car park, the *Corps de Garde* footpath leads to a viewpoint, which affords a lovely **view** of the Léguer.

▷ Return to the centre of Le Yaudet and turn right. At the village of Christ, bear right towards Locquémeau.

Locquémeau

The town overlooks the beach and the fishing harbour which are reached by a corniche road to the left at the entrance to the town.

Pointe de Séhar★

Leave your car near the Locquémeau port and make for the point.
The **view**★ extends westward as far as the Pointe de Primel and eastward to the resort of Trébeurden.

Trédrez

St Yves was Rector of Trédrez from 1284–1292. The **church** (👄 *guided tours by the town hall Jul–Aug, 10am–noon, 5pm–7pm; ℘02 96 35 74 52*) was completed in 1500 by Philippe Beaumanoir to whom we owe many of the region's churches, with their characteristic wall belfries. Note inside the 14C granite font crowned with a beautifully carved wood canopy (1540).

▷ Leave Trédrez by the road going towards Kerbiriou and follow the road that leads to the Beg-ar-Forn headland.

Shortly before the car park there is a good view of the bay and the Lieue de Grève.

▷ Turn round and at the second junction turn right towards St-Michel-en-Grève.

St-Michel-en-Grève

👟 *See Côte des BRUYÈRES.*

▷ Take the road to Lannion on leaving St-Michel-en-Grève, then bear right.

Ploumilliau

The 17C **church** (⏱ *open Jul–Aug; ℘02 96 35 45 09*) contains, in the south transept, 13 wooden **panels**, carved and polychrome, which illustrate scenes from the Life of Christ (Last Supper, the Passion, the Resurrection).

There is also, on the wall opposite the sacristy, a curious portrayal of Ankou (Death), so often mentioned in Breton legend.

▷ Return to the Morlaix-Lannion road to the N; turn right towards Lannion.

ADDRESSES

STAY

Aux Hortensias – *Rte de Perros-Guirec.* ℘*02 96 48 75 39. 16 rooms.* ⌖ *€7.50.* Standard rooms or studios equipped with a small kitchen.

Chambre d'hôte Manoir du Launay – *Chemin de Ker-Ar-Faout. On the D 21 rte de Pleumeur-Bodou.* ℘*02 96 47 21 24. www.manoirdulaunay.com.* ⌖. *5 rooms.* ⌖. This superb little manor house dates from the 17C but it was entirely rebuilt after WWII using original materials. The charming interior has beautiful furniture and fireplaces, individually decorated rooms and modern bathrooms.

EAT

Crêperie La Sarrazine – *13 rue Jeanne-d'Arc.* ℘*02 96 37 06 48. alicia.huet@wanadoo.fr. Closed Wed lunchtime.* Enjoy traditional *crêpes* in a homely room or, in fine weather in the garden behind the house.

La Légende – *18 rue Jean Savidan, Lannion.* ℘*02 96 37 19 59. www.restaurant-lalegende.com.* The décor has an automotive theme. One of the region's best restaurants in this price range.

Le Tire-Bouchon – *8 rue Keriavily.* ℘*02 96 37 10 43. Closed first week Jun, two weeks late Oct, 1 week at Christmas, Mon & Sat lunchtime, Sun.* ⌖. Flavourful, traditional food served with charm in a convivial atmosphere.

La Flambée – *67 rue Georges Pompidou, Lannion.* ℘*02 96 48 04 85. www.restaurant-laflambee.fr. Closed Mon off season.* Fish specialities prepared with all kind of sauces, served in a traditional setting.

Hôtel-restaurant de la Baie – *Trédrez-Loquemeau, in the village.* ℘*02 96 35 23 11. www.hotel-delabaie.com.* A cosy restaurant where you will be served regional meals and copious seafood sauerkraut. Also offers some basic rooms.

Les Filets Bleus – *pointe de Séhar, 6km/3.7mi W of Ploulec'h.* ℘*02 96 35 22 26. www.lesfiletsbleus.fr. Closed Mon–Wed except Jul–Aug.* Fabulous views over the sea from the dining room. Seafood menu.

La Ville Blanche – *5km/3mi towards Tréguier by the D 786.* ℘*02 96 37 04 28. Closed Sun evening and Wed except Jul–Aug, Mon all year, and 28 Jun–7 Jul and 20 Dec–29 Jan.* Top quality cuisine made with seasonal Breton produce in an elegant setting.

NIGHTLIFE

Les Valseuses – *opposite the church of Brélévenez.* ℘*02 96 48 75 19. www.lesvalseuses.net. Closed Mon. Open until 1am (2am in summer).* Concerts two Thursdays per month, and theatrical improvisations. Breton beers, parlour games and good atmosphere.

Le Flambart – *7 Place du Gén. Leclerc.* ℘*02 96 37 40 72.* Good choice of Breton beers and lively atmosphere during the weekend with some live music nights.

SHOPPING

Le Fournil d'Hubert – *16 pl. du Gén Leclerc.* ℘*02 97 37 60 65. www.pain-tregor.fr. Open Tue–Sun 7.30am–8pm.* Twenty varieties of breads, pure-butter pastries and *kouign amann.*

Distillerie Warenghen – *rte de Guingamp.* ℘*02 96 37 00 08. www.distillerie-warenghem.com. Closed 1 Oct–14 Jun.* Cream liqueurs, Breton whisky, beers and guided tours.

ACTIVITIES

Kayak – Base de canoë-kayak – *rue St-Christophe.* ℘*02 96 37 43 90. www.ville-lannion.fr. Open daily 9am–5.30pm in summer.* Kayak and raft on the river all year. Sea kayak in the bay of Lannion in Jul–Aug.

Walks – The Tourist Office of Lannion has maps showing trails. From the **Château de Tonquédec**, there is a beautiful 11km/7mi walk (half a day).

TOURS

The Tourist Office organises guided tours and heritage days throughout the year.

Perros-Guirec ♨♨

This much-frequented seaside resort (with casino and seawater therapy centre), built in the form of an amphitheatre on the Pink Granite Coast, overlooks the fishing and pleasure boat harbour and the two gently sloping fine sand and sheltered beaches of Trestraou and Trestignel.

SIGHTS
St-Jacques Church

⏱ *Open Mon–Fri 9am–noon, 2pm–6pm. Presbytère de Perros-Guirec* ✆ *02 96 23 21 64.*

A porch with delicate trefoil arches abuts onto the massive 14C belfry topped by a dome (1669) crowned by a spire.

Go into the **Romanesque nave**★ – all that remains of the first chapel built on the spot. Massive pillars, cylindrical on the left and with engaged columns on the right, support capitals which are either historiated or adorned with geometrical designs.

A diaphragm arch from the Gothic nave was built in the 14C at the same time as the chancel. In this arch is a rood beam on which Christ is surrounded by the Virgin and St John.

The church has a 12C granite stoup decorated with small figures and several old statues: an Ecce Homo (15C), St Lawrence and St Catherine (16C), St James, patron of the parish (17C). The round-arched south porch is richly ornamented.

Viewing Table (Table d'orientation)

A splendid **view**★ of the Pointe du Château, Trestrignel Beach, Port-Blanc, Trélevern, Trévou, the Île de Tomé, Sept-Îles and of the rocks below.

Pointe du Château

From this steep little viewpoint, there is a lovely **view**★ over the site of Perros-Guirec, Sept-Îles, the Île Tomé and the coast as far as Port-L'Épine.

▶ **Population:** 7,369.

⚙ **Michelin Map:** Local map 309 B2 – Côtes-d'Armor (22).

ℹ **Info:** 21 pl. de l'Hôtel-de-Ville, 22700 Perros-Guirec. ✆02 96 23 21 15. www.perros-guirec.com.

▶ **Location:** Perros-Guirec can be reached from Guingamp (45km/28mi SE) by the D 767 and from Lannion (13km/8mi S) by the D 788.

🕐 **Timing:** A full day on the Sept-Îles and another at Perros-Guirec.

🅿 **Parking:** Spaces are easy to find and parking is free.

👁 **Don't Miss:** The coastal path at high tide to see the waves on the rocks; the pink rocks of Ploumanach.

Musée de Cire Chouannerie Bretonne

51 bd. du Linkin. ⏱*Open Jul–Aug, 9.30am–6.30pm; Apr–May and Sept, 10am–12.15pm, 2pm–6pm.* ⏴*3€.* ✆*02 96 91 23 45.*

This wax museum has reconstituted historical scenes with figures dating from La Chalotais to Auguste Renan. Note the collection of regional headdresses from Lower Brittany.

EXCURSIONS
La Clarté

▶ *3km/1.8mi W. of the town centre.*

The pretty rose granite **Chapelle Notre-Dame-de-la-Clarté**★ stands 200m back from the road. In the 16C the Lord of Barac'h, whose ship was in danger in fog off the coast, vowed to build a chapel to Our Lady at whatever spot on the coast that first emerged from the fog. The promised chapel was built on the height that enabled him to take his bearings; to commemorate the circumstances, it was called Our Lady of Light (*Notre-Dame-de-la-Clarté*). The south doorway is adorned with sculptures in

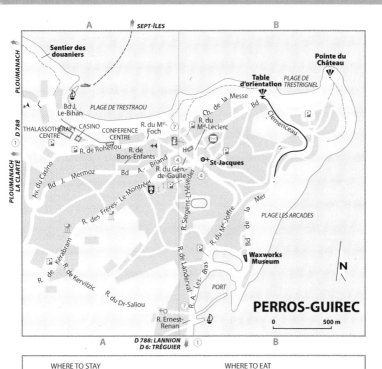

PERROS-GUIREC

WHERE TO STAY		WHERE TO EAT	
Ferme de l'Étang (Chambre d'hôte La)	①	Clarté (La)	①
Hermitage (Hôtel)	④	Crémaillère (La)	④
Levant (Hôtel Le)	⑦	Gulf Stream (Hôtel restaurant Le)	⑦

low relief: on the lintel, an Annunciation and *Pietà*; two coats of arms and a Virgin and Child frame the mullioned window in the registry; under the porch are two 17C wood statues and 16C door panels. The tall nave includes three bays decorated with carved roses and foliage; the three Moorish heads and the Stations of the Cross by Maurice Denis (1931) are noteworthy. A *pardon* is held every year (🕭 *see Calendar of Events*). Take *Rue du Tertre* which starts on the north side of the chapel, leading to the top of a rocky knoll which affords a good **view**★.

Sémaphore★★ (Signal Station)
◯ *3.5km/2mi W. of the town centre.*
From the roadside look-out point the **view**★ extends to the rocks of Ploumanach, seawards to Sept-Îles and behind to the beaches of Perros-Guirec, and in the distance along the Port-Blanc coastline.

🥾 Le Sentier des Douaniers★★
3hr on foot there and back.
⏱*The best time to go is in the morning, and if possible, at high tide.*
Follow the edge of the cliff as far as Pors-Rolland to reach the lighthouse via the Pointe de Squéouel, the Ploumanac'h

Le Sentier des Douaniers

R. Mattès/MICHELIN

lighthouse and the *Maison du Littoral* information centre. Bring your camera.

Ploumanac'h★★

This little fishing port on the Pink Granite Coast, belonging to the municipality of Perros-Guirec and well situated at the mouths of the two picturesque Traouiéros valleys, has become a well-known seaside resort, famous for its piles of **rocks**★★. You will get a good

view of them by going to the lighthouse. The **Parc Municipal**★★ extends from Pors-Kamor, where the lifeboat is kept, to Pors-Rolland. It is a sort of reserve where the rocky site is kept in its original state. The most interesting feature is the Pointe de Squewel, formed of innumerable rocks separated by coves. The Devil's Castle (*Château du Diable*) also makes a fine picture.

The park is studded with curiously shaped rocks: note a turtle by the sea, and inland, a mushroom and a rabbit.

Maison du Littoral

◯ *Open mid-Jun–mid-Sept, Mon–Sat 10am–1pm, 2pm–6pm; rest of the year and school hoiidays Mon–Fri 2pm–5pm.* ◯ *Closed public holidays.* ♿ *℘02 96 91 62 77. No charge.*

This information centre has a variety of exhibits related to the formation of

granite and the different methods for extracting and using this stone. The centre also organises walks in summer.

Beach

The beach lies in the bay of St-Guirec. At the far end on the left, on a rock washed by the sea at high tide, stands the oratory dedicated to St Guirec, who landed here in the 6C. A granite statue of the saint has taken the place of the original wooden effigy which had suffered from a disrespectful tradition: girls who wanted to get married stuck a pin into his nose. Opposite here is the Île de Costaérès and its château (private).

Vallée du Traouïero

⚑ *Allow half a day. Sturdy shoes recommended.*

Behind the mills at the port, the little and large Traouïero are two wild valleys bathed in legend. The vegetation is dense and the paths wind in and out of the pink granite rocks.

Les Sept-Îles

Access to the islands: Apr–Sept, 8.30am–6.30pm. Discovery of the Sept-Îsles ◉16€ (children 10€) and excursions led by the LPO (Ligue pour la Protection des Oiseaux/ Bird Protection League). Jul–Aug sea fishing departure 8.30am. ℘02 96 91 10 00. www.armor-decouverte.fr.

This archipelago has been an ornithological centre since 1912. You can observe more sea birds in the morning and in the evening: choose the first or the last departure. Four companies use the central reservation system at the *gare maritime de Trestraou*. They offer guided tours of the archipelago, the largest natural reserve of marine birds in France (20 000 pairs).

Île Rouzic

☺*Landing forbidden.*

The boat goes near the island, also known as Bird Island, where a large **colony**★ of northern gannets, some 12 000 pairs, settle from February to

Puffins nest in colonies on cliffs and grassy islands

M. Janvier/MICHELIN

September; they can be observed from Grande Island's ornithological centre via CCTV. One can see guillemots, razorbills, lesser and great black-backed gulls, puffins, crested cormorants, black-legged kittiwakes, oyster catchers and petrels all of which reproduce in March and leave at the end of July.

Another interesting feature is the presence of a small colony of grey seals. The boat then skirts Malban and Bono Islands.

Île aux Moines

The boat stops at the island *(1hr)* where you may visit the old gunpowder factory, the **lighthouse** *(83 steps; range 40km/25mi;* ⏲ *open depending on the availability of the lighthousekeepers; call for information;* ☎*02 96 23 92 10)*, which offers a fine panorama of the islands and the coast, the ruined fort erected by Vauban on the far tip and below the former monastery with its tiny chapel and well.

On the return journey, the curious pink granite rocks at the Pointe de Ploumanach come into view.

ADDRESSES

🛏 STAY

🍽🛏 **Chambre d'hôte La Ferme de l'Étang** – *Le Launay, 22660 Trélevern. 9km/5.6mi from Perros on the rte de Paimpol then the D 73 towards Tréleven.* ☎*02 96 91 70 44.* ⚐. *3 rooms.* The ducks paddle on the lake or preen themselves

on the lawn of this 19C longhouse where guests appreciate the rustic charm, quiet and large lounge.

🍽🛏 **Hôtel Hermitage** – *20 rue des Frères-le-Montréer.* ☎*02 96 23 21 22. www.hotelhermitage-22.com. Closed 29 Sept–31 Mar. 23 rooms.* ⚐ *6.50€. Restaurant*🍽🛏. An old building, with garden, in the centre of town. Rooms are small but clean. Friendly welcome and atmospheric.

🍽🛏 **Hôtel Le Levant** – *91 r. E.-Renan.* ☎ *02 96 23 20 15. www.le-levant.fr. 19 ch.* ⚐ *6 €. Restaurant* 🍽🛏. This new hotel is popular with businessmen. Small functional rooms each having a balcony or a terrace looking onto the port de plaissance. The dining room has a sea related décor and enjoys a view of the harbour. Traditional seafood meals.

🍽🛏 **Hôtel du Parc** – *174 pl. St Guirec, 22700 Ploumanac'h.* ☎*02 96 91 40 80. www.hotelduparc.com. Closed 11 Nov–20 Dec; Sat lunch, Sun eve, exc. school hols. 10 rooms.* ⚐*8€. Restaurant*🍽🛏. In the centre of the village known for its beach and rocks, this pink granite family home has clean, welcoming rooms. Seafood served on the terrace or in the airy dining room.

🍽🛏🛏 **Le Beauséjour** – *plage du Coz-Pors.* ☎*02 96 23 88 02. www.beause joursarl.com. 16 rooms.* ⚐*10€. Restaurant*🍽🛏🛏. *Closed 5 Jan–mid-Feb, 15 Nov–18 Dec.* Rooms of variable sizes, decorated in a maritime theme, boast views of the water or use of a terrace. Rooms st the back are simpler with a view of the rocks. Pleasant restaurant serving traditional cuisine.

🍴 EAT

🍽🛏 **Hôtel Restaurant Le Gulf Stream** – *26 rue des Sept-Îles.* ☎*02 96 23 21 86. www.gulf-stream-hotel-bretagne.com. Closed 4 Jan–5 Feb, 15 Nov–15 Dec.* Seasonal fare with lots of seafood on the menu, served in a panoramic dining room. Good but expensive wine list. Rooms available.

🍽🛏 **La Crémaillère** – *Place de l'Église.* ☎*02 96 23 22 08. Closed Sat lunch and Mon lunch except Jul and Aug.* Dine on inventive regional cuisine (the grills are good) and seafood under the beams of this rustic (think stone and wrought iron) 19C house.

🍽🍴🛏 **La Clarté** –*24 rue Gabriel-Vicaire. ℘02 96 49 05 96. www.la-clarte.com. Closed 13 Dec–5 Feb, Wed eve, Sun eve except 15 Jul–26 Aug and Mon.*
On the outskirts of Perros towards Ploumanac'h, this restaurant offers daily specials in a warm setting.

🍽🍴 **Les Blés Noirs** – *105 av. du Casino. ℘02 96 91 19 47.* Set back from the beach of Trestraou, a crêperie well-known for its culinary skill. Terrace and room with a maritime setting.

🍽🍴 **La Bonne Auberge** – *Place de la Chapelle, La Clarté. ℘02 96 91 46 05.* www.la-bonne-auberge.com. The freshness of the seafood is guaranteed by the owner (a fish merchant).

🕯 NIGHTLIFE

Casino de Perros-Guirec – *plage de Trestraou. ℘02 96 49 80 80.* Games of chance begin at 9.30pm.

🛒 SHOPPING

Markets – Fri in **Perros-Guirec** and Tue in **Trébeurden**.

Honey – Lossouarn – *20 rue du Mar. Joffre. ℘02 96 23 14 43.* Honey of heather, chestnut tree, bramble and other flavours of Brittany.

🏃 ACTIVITIES

👪 **Perros-Guirec** has excellent facilities for its young visitors, including three **beach clubs** for 2–11 year olds.

Diving – Lodan Glaz – *Barnabanec, Perros-Guirec. ℘06 80 45 81 93. Open Easter–Nov.* Trips and explorations on Ploumanach and the reserve of the Sept-Îles. **Centre Activités Plongée de Trébeurden** – *54 corniche de Goas Treiz. ℘02 96 23 66 71. www.plongeecap. com. Open Apr–15 Nov.* Explore between Trébeurden and Trégastel (14yrs or over).

Horse Riding – Poney-Club de Rulan – *rte de Lannion, Trégastel. ℘02 96 23 85 29. Closed Sept.* Ponies and horses for all levels (1hr – full day available).

Old Riggings – Participate as a crew member on board the Sant C'hireg, *℘06 85 92 60 61, 22€/36€* day.

Le Centre Nautique de Perros-Guirec also offers trips along the Côte de Granit Rose on board the Argentilez.

Thalasso – Thermes Marins de Perros-Guirec – *plage de Trestraou, ℘02 96 23 28 97. www.france-thalasso.com.* Stress therapy, sauna, Jacuzzi.

Forum de Trégastel – *℘02 96 15 30 44.* Water games, paddling pools and warm sea-water swimming pool.

Walks and hikes –The Perros-Guirec Tourist Office publication details three easy walking itineraries in the area, as well as a 23km/14mi of marked circuit for all terrain vehicles. Guided walks on the path between Perros-Guirec and Ploumanach are organised by the *Maison du Littoral* in Ploumanach, 15 Jun–15 Sept: Mon–Sat.

Water sports – Centre Nautique de Perros-Guirec – *plage de Trestraou. ℘02 96 49 81 21. www.perros-guirec.com. Open 9am–7pm. Closed Dec and Jan.* Windsurfing lessons and rentals at the Point Passion Plage in summer. Trips and individual kayaking lessons.

Base Nautique de l'Île Grande – *Pors Gelen. ℘02 96 91 92 10. http://bnig.free.fr. Open Mar–Nov.*

Club Nautique de Trégastel – *La Grève Rose. ℘02 96 23 45 05. www.cntregastel. com.* Learn to pilot an Optimist and sailer (min. 5 yrs); windsurf rental, funboards, kayaking trips from 1 hour to a day (min. 14yrs); lessons Jul–Aug.

Surf – Seven Island Surf Club – *Perros-Guirec, plage de Trestraou. ℘02 96 23 18 38. www.7islandsurfclub.com. Closed Dec and Jan.* Surf, bodyboard and longboard lessons.

Côte de Granit Rose★★

The scenic Breton coast road that joins Perros-Guirec and Trébeurden, following the Pink Granite Coast from Pointe de l'Arcouest, is one of the most interesting drives in Brittany.

🚗 DRIVING TOUR

From Perros-Guirec to Trébeurden

27km/16.5mi – about 6hr.

This tour begins in the bustling resort town of Perros-Guirec (💰 see p200).

▷ *Leave Perros-Guirec heading W. You can stop off at Chapelle Notre-Dame-de-la-Clarté, then Ploumanac'h★★ (💰 see Perros-Guirec).*

Trégastel-Plage⌂⌂ –
💰 *See TRÉGASTEL-PLAGE.*
As you leave the village, on the right, at the end of a short rise, look behind you to admire the view of Sept-Îles.

🕑 **Michelin Map:** Local map 309 A/B 2 Côtes-d'Armor (22).

ℹ️ **Info:** ☎02 96 23 21 15. www.perros-guirec.com.

👪 **Kids:** The Planetarium at Plumeur-Boudou and the 'bird hospital' on Île Grande.

🕐 **Timing:** Allow three to four hours to walk the path between Perros and Trégastel.

👁️ **Don't Miss:** The blocks of pink granite that dot the coastal path.

▷ *At Penvern, bear left after the Café du Menhir, and take the road to Pleumur-Bodou.*

Menhir de St-Uzec★
A giant standing stone is surmounted by a Crucifixion with Instruments of the Passion *(Arma Christi)* surrounding the figure of a praying woman.

▷ *Take the road below the menhir to rejoin the Pleumur-Bodou road, then*

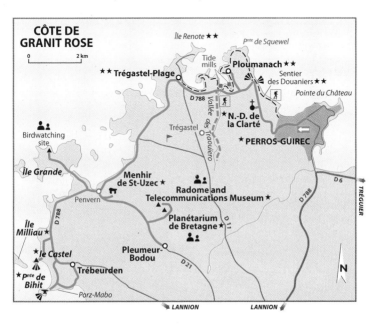

COTE DE GRANIT ROSE

0   2 km

Île Renote ★★   Pᵗᵉ de Squewel

Tide mills   Ploumanach ★★

★★ Trégastel-Plage   Sentier des Douaniers ★★

D 788   Vallée des Traouïero   Pointe du Château

Trégastel   ★ N.-D. de la Clarté

Birdwatching site   ★ PERROS-GUIREC

Île Grande

Menhir de St-Uzec ★   D 6   TRÉGUIER

Penvern   Radome and Telecommunications Museum ★

D 788   Planétarium de Bretagne ★   D 11

Île Milliau ★

★ le Castel   Pleumeur-Bodou   D 21

★ Pᵗᵉ de Bihit   Trébeurden

Porz-Mabo   LANNION   LANNION

N

Sailing along La Côte de Granit Rose

B. Pérousse/MICHELIN

Granite Rose

The aptly named Côte de Granit Rose, the Pink Granite Coast, in northern Brittany boasts a remarkable stretch of pink-coloured rocky coastline between Trégastel and Trébeurden. While there are many places in the world that have pink or red rock – such as the Esterel Massif in southern France which is composed of red porphyry rock and similar to granite in its composition – there are only two other places that have the same type of pink granite found at the northern Brittany coast: the Bavella range of mountains in southeast Corsica, and in southeast China. Due to the fragility of this spectacular environment, the Pink Granite Coast has been designated a conservation area with dedicated footpaths to protect the rock from the impact of erosion created by human activity. It's well worth visiting at sunset, when the light picks out the dozens of orange and pink hues from various minerals in the rock.

Granite is composed of quartz, mica and feldspar. With the passage of time, the feldspar turns into kaolin (china clay), which is washed away by water. The residue of the quartz grains makes sand, which is carried away by rain and waves. Little by little, the stone changes shape and takes on surprising forms: almost perfect spheres. Erosion at the northern Brittany coast has been severe because the rocks are coarse-grained and easily broken.

It's not just the vivid pink and orange tints that are spectacular along the Côtes-d'Armor's Pink Granite Coast; wind, rain and the tide have carved the rocks here into extraordinary shapes. Local imagination has given names to many of the rocks dotted along the shore, such as Napoleon's Hat, the Gnome, the Witch, the Elephant, the Whale, the Ram, the Rabbit, the Tortoise and the pile of crêpes.

Rocks of Ploumanac'h

R. Mattès/MICHELIN

turn left and 400m further on, left again.

Pleumeur-Bodou

This village, located between Lannion and Penvern, has given its name to the radar dome, near which a telecommunications museum and planetarium have been set up.

👤👤 Cité des Télécoms★

Site Cosmopolis, Plemeur-Bodou. 🕐*See website for varying opening times.* 🕐*Closed 11 Nov and 25 Dec.* 👜*7€ (children 5.60€).* ♿ *☎02 96 46 63 80. www.cite-telecoms.com.*

The Pleumeur-Bodou telecommunications centre, inaugurated in 1962, is the historic site of the first transatlantic communication between France and the United States (Andover), via the **Telstar** satellite, on 11 July 1962.

The **Telecommunications Museum**, in a building shaped like an immense Delta wing, retraces one and a half centuries of inventions, progress and continuously updated technology.

👤👤 Planétarium du Trégora

🕐*Closed 24, 25 and 31 Dec. By arrangement. Closed Sat (Sept–Jun), Jan 24–25 and 31 Dec.* 👜*7€ (children 5.80€).* ☎*02 96 15 80 30/32. www.planetarium-bretagne.fr.*

Beneath a dome (20m in diameter) the visitor travels through the universe. In the entrance hall is an exhibition on astronomy and astrophysics.

Île Grande

(across the bridge)

The island offers a landscape of heath bordered by blue granite shores. This granite was used for building as far away as London and Antwerp. There are megalithic vestiges, in particular a passage tomb *(allée couverte)* northeast of the village.

A sort of hospital for seabirds, the 👤👤 **Station Ornithologique** (☎*02 96 91 91 40; www.lpo.fr)* presents different bird species (Guillemot, Herring Gull, Black-Headed Gull, Puffin, Northern Gannet and Razorbill) on Sept-Îles.

◐ *Return to the coast road and turn right towards Trébeurden.*

Trébeurden⚓

This seaside resort has several beaches. The two main ones are well situated and separated by the rocky peninsula of Le Castel: Pors-Termen Beach is opposite the harbour; Tresmeur Beach is larger and more popular.

🚶 Le Castel★

Allow 30min on foot there and back.

Follow a path along the isthmus (🅿) between the two beaches of Trozoul and Tresmeur. Le Castel commands an extensive **view**★ of the coast.

Île Milliau

Access on foot at low tide from the peninsular at Castel. The Tourist Office at Trébeurden can provide tide tables. It is possible to stay overnight in a 'gîte d'étape', a 16C farmhouse.

As you walk across sand and pebbles from the mainland to this island, note how the rocks change in colour from pink to grey. This prehistoric islet is home to 280 species of flora, including bracken, gorse and brambles. There is a lovely panoramic view from the far end of the island.

The ruined house was once inhabited by Nobel Peace Prize winner and eleven-time Prime Minister of France, Aristide Briand.

Pointe de Bihita

Round trip of 4km/2.5mi.

The Porz-Mabo road overlooks Tresmeur Beach and offers views of Grande, Molène and Milliau Islands.

◐ *Take the road to the right.*

From the viewing table there is a fine **view**★ of the coast from Île de Batz and Roscoff right over to Île Grande and Triagoz lighthouse.

Trégastel-Plage ☼☼

The resort of Trégastel rivals the neighbouring locality of Ploumanach for the beauty and strangeness of its **rocks**★★, which are characteristic of the Corniche Bretonne. Walkers will appreciate the charm of the path at île Renote.

SIGHTS

☺ Aquarium Marin

🕐 *Open Apr–Jun and Sept, Tue–Fri 10am–6pm, Sat–Sun 2pm–6pm; Jul–Aug, daily 10am–7pm; Mar, Oct and school holidays, Tue–Sun 2pm–5pm. Call if unsure. ☞ Guided tours available (1€ extra). ☞ 7.50€ (children 5€). ☎ 02 96 23 48 58. www.aquarium-tregastel.com.*

The aquarium is located in caves, which housed a church in the 19C under a mass of enormous rocks known as the Turtles. In three rooms varieties of fish from Breton waters and tropical seas are exhibited, along with stuffed birds including puffins, guillemots, penguins and gannets, all from Sept-Îles.

At the exit, a stairway *(28 steps)* leads up to a statue of the Eternal Father *(Père Éternel)*. From the look-out point, there is a good view of the mass of **rocks**★★ and the Pink Granite Coastline.

Trégastel-Plage rock formations

©Photononstop/Tips images

- ▶ **Population:** 2,234.
- ⛰ **Michelin Map:** Local map 5309 B2 – Côtes-d'Armor (22).
- 🛈 **Info:** 5 pl. Ste-Anne, 22730 Trégastel. ☎ 02 96 15 38 38. www.ville-tregastel.fr.
- ▷ **Location:** 13km/8mi N of Lannion on the D 11.
- ☺ **Kids:** Aquarium.
- 🕐 **Timing:** Allow a day for walks around the beaches.
- 👁 **Don't Miss:** Île Renote for its pink granite rocks.

🏊 Plage de Coz-Porz

This sandy beach is lined with rocks bearing names such as the Turtles and the Witch. At the north end of the beach, beyond the jetty, make for a small beach near two rocks, the **Tête de Mort** (Death's Head) and the **Tas de Crêpes** (Pile of Pancakes), both on the right. This last rock, which appears to lie in folds, is a good example of wind erosion. Beyond a sandbank there is a mass of rocks, among which is the **Dé** (Thimble).

EXCURSIONS

🏊 Grève Blanche★

Allow 1hr on foot there and back.

The path, which starts from the left end of this beach (Plage de Coz-Porz), follows the cliff edge around a promontory from the end of which can be seen the White Shore, Rabbits' Island (Île aux Lapins) and, out at sea, the Triagoz Islands. The path continues near the foot of a rock called the **Tire-Bouchon** (Corkscrew) and reaches the end of the White Shore, dominated by a great rock, **Roi Gradlon** (King Gradlon) on account of its resembling a crowned head.

Viewing table

A telescope gives a circular **view**★ of the coast: the White Shore, Île Grande, the Triagoz Lighthouse, Sept-Îles and the hinterland (when weather permits): Clarté, Pleumeur-Bodou (with its distinctive Radôme) and Trébeurden villages.

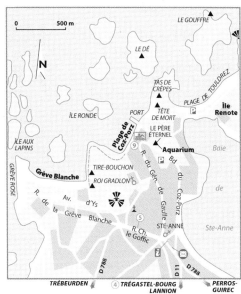

TRÉGASTEL-PLAGE

WHERE TO STAY

Résidence d'Arvor
(Hôtel de La).....................④

WHERE TO EAT

Iroise (Crêperie L')..............⑤
Triagoz (Les).........................⑨

Île Renote★★

Leaving the sand bar behind, you will see opposite Renote Island, formed of huge blocks of granite and now connected with the mainland.

Following the road that crosses the island, you pass Plage de Touldrez on your left and approach the Chasm (Le Gouffre), a cavity in the middle of a mass of rocks which can be reached at low tide. As you walk amid the rocks to the very tip of the peninsula, you get good views of the horizon out to sea and of the Sept-Îles looking north; of the Ploumanach coast to the east and the Baie de Ste-Anne to the south. In 1977 the island was classified a "site pittoresque", and has since benefitted from protection from development.

Trégastel-Bourg

▶ *3km/1.8mi S towards Lannion.*
The 13C church was remodelled in the 14C and 18C. To the right of the south porch stands a semi-circular 17C ossuary adorned with balusters and crowned with a domed turret.

ADDRESSES

🛏️STAY

🍽️🛏️ **Hôtel de La Résidence d'Arvor** – *52 rte des Traouïeros.* 📞 *02 96 15 31 90. www.residencedarvor.com. 9 rooms.* 🚇. A choice of accommodation available, recently renovated rooms, some with kitchenette, also a furnished house for long family stays. All pleasant and well kept. Cooking equipment is available to residents, as well as Wi-Fi.

🍽️EAT

🍽️ **Crêperie L'Iroise** – *29 rue Charles-le-Goffic.* 📞*02 96 15 93 23. Closed mid-Nov–Jan and Thu except school holidays.* As well as crêpes, this restaurant offers traditional dishes and as mussels.

🍽️ **Les Triagoz** – *Forum de Trégastel, plage du Coz-Porz.* 📞*02 96 15 34 10. Closed Jan and 1–20 Dec.* On the terrace near the beach, opposite the famous rocks, or in the dining room with large windows, you're ideally positioned to watch the sunset. The menu has a marine emphasis.

Belle-Isle-en-Terre

Belle-Isle-en-Terre is a perfect example of inland Brittany's beauty: a picturesque region of forests, hills and ravines, favourable for walking, fishing, canoeing or kayaking.

SIGHT

Centre régional d'initiation à la rivière

Daily 2pm–6pm during school hols, Wed and Sun May–Sept. 3 € (under 8s free). 02 96 43 08 39. http://educatif. eau-et-rivieres.asso.fr.

The Centre, housed within the Chateau in the centre of the town, organises 3hr themed walks of during the school holidays, designed with children in mind. There is an aquarium, touch tanks and an area to find out more about the fish.

Locmaria

1km/0.6mi N. of the town signposted from the centre of Belle-Isle.

The chapel of Locmaria has a beautiful 16C rood screen in multi-coloured wood supported by four cabled columns decorated with vine leaves and grapes. The altar side of the Rood Screen has celtic inspired decoration while the side facing the Nave shows the Apostles.

Fontaine de Pendréo

Visible from the road on the left descending to Locmaria.

The fountain can be found on the wooded hill which overlooks the southern edge of the town. Accessible by 110 steps (care should be taken as the steps can be slippery). Until 1920 mothers brought their children suffering from whooping cough hoping that the water from the fountain would cure them.

EXCURSIONS

Loc-Envel

4km/2.5mi S. Leave on the Callac road, D 33, and then right.

The Flamboyant Gothic style **church** of Loc-Envel rises from the top of a mound and dominates the village. To the left

- **Population:** 1, 050.
- **Michelin Map:** Local map 309 B3 – Côtes-d'Armor (22).
- **Info:** 15 rue Crech-Ugen, 22810 Belle-Isle-en-Terre. 02 96 43 01 71. www.belleisleenterre.com.
- **Location:** 18km/11mi W of Guingamp, where the N 12 meets the D 33.
- **Timing:** Allow a day and bring a picnic.

of the belfry-porch, note three small semicircular openings through which lepers followed the services. Inside, particularly striking features are the Flamboyant **rood screen**★ and the rich decoration of the wood-panelled **vaulting**★: carved purlins and tie-beams, polychrome hammerbeams and the two hanging keystones.

Plougonver

7.5km/4.6mi S on the D 33.

St-Pierre church houses an interesting baptistery with two fonts (15C).

Menez-Bré★

9km/5.6mi NE along the D 116. 2.5km/1.5mi after Louargat, turn left onto the steep uphill road.

The Menez-Bré and its *Chapelle de St-Hervé*, commands a wide **panorama**★ over the Trégorrois Plateau: to the north, the plateau slopes gently towards the sea, to the south over the maze of hills and valleys of Cornouaille; and southwest towards the Monts d'Arrée.

Gurunhuel

9km/5.6mi SE on D 22.

Near the 16C church stands a calvary of the same period. From the base rise three columns: the central one bears a Crucifixion with Christ between the Virgin Mary and St John on one side and a Virgin of Pity on the other. The other two crosses show the robbers: their souls are being received by an angel (the good robber) and a demon (the bad robber).

Guingamp

Located on the edge of Armor and Argoat, Guingamp is a commercial and industrial town that has greatly developed in recent years. Guingamp comes from the Breton *guen gamp* meaning "white camp" or "favoured camp", highlighting the privileged status of the town. It has a mild coastal climate, making it ideal for a leisurely stroll of its streets.

▶ **Population:** 8,008.

Michelin Map: Local map 309 D3 - Côtes-d'Armor (22).

Info: pl. du Champ-au-Roy. ℘02 96 43 73 89. www.ot-guingamp.org.

Location: Between Morlaix and St-Brieuc.

Timing: You can explore the town in half a day.

Parking: There are car parks in the centre and near the station.

Don't Miss: July's *pardon*.

SIGHTS

Basilique Notre-Dame-de-Bon-Secours★

This church was built in the Gothic style in the 14C (a Romanesque part remains at the transept crossing); but two centuries later the south tower collapsed, demolishing the nave's south side. The town asked several architects to plan its reconstruction.

A young man named Le Moal submitted plans in the Renaissance style, something almost unknown in Brittany at that time. Quite unexpectedly the people of Guingamp awarded the prize to the innovator. Since then the church has had the unusual feature of being Gothic on the left and Renaissance on the right. Inside, the church is unusual, with numerous pillars and graceful flying buttresses in the chancel. The triforium is adorned with trilobed arches while lower down the nave has striking Renaissance decoration.

A great *pardon* draws thousands of pilgrims each year. After the torch-lit procession three bonfires are lit on **Place du Centre** in the company of the bishop, who also presides over the ceremony. There are a few old houses on the square (numbers 31, 33, 35, 39, 48) and at the corner of rue St-Yves and rue du Cosquet. The fountain called **la Plomée**, with three lead and stone basins, is Renaissance.

Hôtel de Ville

Open Mon–Fri 8.30am–noon, 1.30pm–5.30pm, Sat 8.30am–noon. ℘02 96 40 64 40. www.guingamp.fr.

The town hall (1699) housed in the old hospital (Hôtel-Dieu), was formerly an Augustinian monastery. The cloisters, great staircase and fine Italian-style chapel (1709) are open to the public. Among the permanent collection are paintings by Sérusier and the Pont-Aven School.

Ramparts

Standing on place du Vally is all that remains of the castle (1438–42). Ruins of the fortifications that once surrounded the town can be seen not far from rue du Maréchal-Joffre and place St-Sauveur.

EXCURSIONS

Grâces

3.5km/2mi. Leave Guingamp on D 54, W on the town plan. Turn right after 2km/1.2mi; in the village centre is the large church.

Originally **Église Notre-Dame** would appear to have been a pilgrims' chapel, probably founded by Queen Anne. Built in the 16C, it was slightly altered in the 17C and restored in the 19C. The four gables of the single aisle give it a sawtooth silhouette from the south.

Inside, note the nave's tie-beams and the superb carved purlins. A satirical picture of drunkenness is the main theme; but there are also hunting scenes, monsters, and a poignant Holy Face surrounded by little angels.

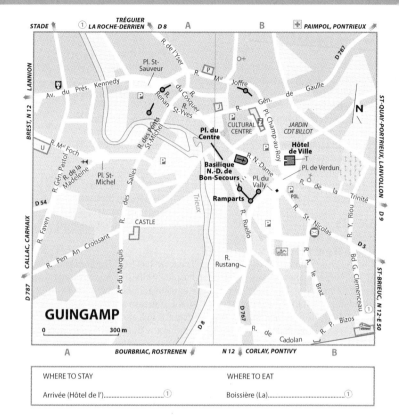

GUINGAMP

0   300 m

WHERE TO STAY	WHERE TO EAT
Arrivée (Hôtel de l')............................①	Boissière (La)............................①

Châtelaudren

▶ *14km/8.6mi E along N 12.*

This little town stands on a bend of the Aulne, in the green and deep valley through which the river canal flows decorated by two lines of shady quays. Camping and fishing facilities replaced the former fortifications by the lake. Perched on a hill, the **Chapelle-Notre-Dame-du-Tertre** (built in the 14C–17C) is in an eclectic style. 96 panels from the 15C decorate the vaulted choir and depict scenes from the Old and New Testaments (*by car from place des Sapeurs-Pompiers via rue Arbirart and rue Notre-Dame*).

🚗 DRIVING TOUR

Valleé du Trieux

Round trip of 39km/24mi– 2hr.

▶ *Leave Guingamp on the D 8.*

Bourbriac

The church rises in the centre of the town, surrounded by gardens with its soaring bell-tower 64m high. There have been several buildings erected on the site: of the first there remains a crypt probably of the 10C or 11C; of the Romanesque church which followed, there is the very high transept crossing – the tower above it was burnt down in the fire of 1765 and has been replaced by a pinnacle. In 1535 building on the west tower began; a remarkable example of the style that was to come. While the big pointed arched porch and all the lower floor are in the Flamboyant style, the remainder of the tower is Renaissance. The spire was added in 1869. Inside, the sarcophagus of St Briac, dating from Merovingian times, is invoked as a cure for epilepsy.

▶ *Go towards Plésidy and then in the direction of St-Péver.*

After 2km/1.2mi, note on the left below the road the small Manoir de Toul-an-Gollet, with a pepper-pot turret.

▷ *Turn left at the crossroads and before the bridge over the Trieux, take a small road to the right.*

Chapelle Notre-Dame-de-Restudo
🕐*Visits by appointment – key at the Town Hall in St-Péver (Mon, Tue, Thu and Fri).* 📞*02 96 21 42 48.*
This 14C–15C chapel retains traces of 14C frescoes depicting the Last Supper and chivalric scenes. A *pardon* is held on 30 June in honour of St Eligius.

▷ *Turn back and take the road back to Guingamp.*

The Trieux Valley offers varied scenery.

▷ *After 2km/1.2mi bear right to Avaugour.*

Chapelle d'Avaugour
🕐*Visits by appointment – key at the Town Hall in St-Péver (Mon, Tue, Thu and Fri).* 📞*02 96 21 42 48.*
The chapel stands in an attractive setting and contains a finely carved wood sacrarium (shrine) of the 16C.

▷ *Return to Guingamp along D 767.*

ADDRESSES

STAY
▭▨ **Hôtel de l'Arrivée** – *19 bd Clemenceau, Guingamp.* 📞*02 96 40 04 57. www.hotel-arrivee.com. 27 rooms.* ▭*8€.* Near the train station: renovated, functional and well kept rooms make this a good place for early arrivals or departures.

EAT
▭▨ **La Boissière** – *90 rue de l'Yser, Guincamp.* 📞*02 96 21 06 35. Closed 1–14 Mar, 17 Aug–6 Sept, Sun eve (except Jul and Aug), Sat lunch, Sun eve and Mon.* Nice bourgeois house in a park setting. Two pleasant dining rooms serve traditional cuisine that changes with the seasons.

TOURS
The Tourist Office organises free guided tours of the town in July and August and you can follow a 'medieval and renaissance circuit' around town.

NIGHTLIFE
Campbell's Pub – *14 place St-Michel.* 📞*02 96 43 85 32.* The most animated café in town is open late at night.

ACTIVITIES
Walks – a guide to walks in the area is available from the Tourist Office for *2.50€.*

▨▮ **Armoripark** – *22140 Bégard. 10km/6mi from Guingamp towards Lannion.* 📞*02 96 45 36 36. www.armoripark.com.Daily Apr–Sept, see website times.* ▭*8€.* Water-based fun and a pets' corner.

EVENTS
July: Le Pardon N.-D.-de-Bon-Secours on the first Sat of Jul, is dedicated to the Black Virgin, patron saint of the Basilica. The procession takes place at night by torchlight. Afterwards, fires of joy are lit in *place du Centre*, in the presence of the bishop.

The **Bugale Breizh** sees 1 000 children from across Brittany gather to take part in Breton dances held on the first Sun.

Les Jeudis de Guingamp – Music, street entertainment and open-air cinema on Thursdays.

August: Le Festival de la Danse Bretonne et de la St-Loup (📞*02 96 43 73 89; www.dansebretonne.com*) sees thousands of Breton dancers gather for this annual festival and competition.

Rostrenen

This pretty little town is situated on a hillside in the Fisel countryside – the prefix "Roz" is Breton for "hill". An important dance competition is organised by the local Celtic society every year in August. Due to its location in the centre of the region, there is not a better point from which to explore the Breton interior. The nearby Nantes-Brest Canal also provides several walking opportunities in the area.

▶ **Population:** 3,397.

Michelin Map: Local 309 C5 – Côtes-d'Armor (22).

Info: 5 pl. de la République, 22110 Rostrenen. 02 96 29 02 72.

Location: In the heart of Brittany, Rostrenen is situated on the N 164.

Kids: The Musée Rural de l'Éducation.

Timing: Allow half a day to explore the area.

Don't Miss: The Gorges de Toul Goulic.

SIGHTS

Église Notre-Dame-du-Roncier

Open 9am–5pm (on request). 02 96 29 01 55.

The church was once the castle chapel, which was set on fire during the time of the League in 1572. It was built in the 14C and remodelled in the 18C and 19C, and has a beautiful transitional Gothic-Renaissance porch. Near the church is an interesting fountain from the 17C. There is a *pardon* at the church on 15 August.

DRIVING TOURS

1 FISEL COUNTRY

Round trip of 45km/28mi – 3hr.

Leave Rostrenen NE by D 790 in the direction of St-Brieuc.

St-Nicolas-du-Pélem

The town includes a 15C – 16C **church** (*open Jul–Sept, Mon–Fri 2pm–6pm*) with two fine stained-glass windows depicting the Passion (1470) at the flat east end. Go round the north side of the church to see the 17C fountain of St-Nicolas that abuts onto a house.

Proceed to Lanrivain and follow signs for Musée-École de Bothoa.

Musée Rural de l'Éducation

Bothoa. Open May–Jun Sun 2pm–6pm; Jul–15 Sept, Easter and Nov holidays Tue–Sun 2pm–6pm. 4€ (children 6–14, 2€). 02 96 29 73 95.

A reconstruction of a 1930s school in an old schoolhouse, with desks, quill pens and violet ink. Exhibition with photos.

Lanrivain

In the cemetery stands a 15C ossuary with trefoil arches. To the right of the church , the 16C calvary is decorated with figures of Kersanton granite.

Chapelle Notre-Dame-du-Guiaudet

1.5km/0.9mi N by the road towards Bourbriac. At the entrance to the hamlet of Guiaudet take an alleyway marked by two granite pillars on the right. Open Easter–Nov 10am–6pm.

The chapel, which dates from the late 17C, has over the high altar a sculpted scene representing a recumbent Virgin holding the Infant Jesus in her arms.

Continue to Trémargat and after 1.5km/0.9mi bear left.

Gorges de Toul Goulic★

15min on foot there and back.

At the far end of the car park overlooking the wooded valley of the Blavet, take the steep path leading downhill through the woods to the cleft in which the Blavet disappears. The river is still full at the beginning of the cleft (north side), but has completely vanished by the time you reach the middle of the

Countryside near Rostrenen

© Peter Dean/Agripicture Images/Alamy

cleft, where it flows, rumbling, beneath a mass of huge rocks.

◯ *Turn back and bear left.*

Between Trémargat and Kergrist-Moëlou, the landscape is studded with enormous boulders.

Kergrist-Moëlou

On the church square, shaded by fine old yew trees, stands a **calvary** (1578) with some 100 figures in Kersanton granite resting on its octagonal plinth. The figures were damaged during the Revolution and have been replaced haphazardly.

◯ *Via St-Lubin return to Rostrenen.*

2 **NANTES CANAL TO BREST**

Round trip of 20km/12.5mi – 2hr 30min.

◯ *Leave Rostrenen on the road towards Carhaix-Plouguer and after 3.5km/2mi, turn left onto the Gourin road.*

The road reaches the canal, built between 1823 and 1834, at the summit level (alt 184m). Walk along the towpath for a view of the 44 locks through which boats climb or descend 120m/393ft over 17km/10.5mi to Carhaix-Plouguer.

◯ *Proceed to Glomet and then turn right onto the road towards Paule; after 1.8km/1mi, bear right.*

On the canal banks, the former lock-keeper's house stands on a pretty **site**★. There is a pleasant walk along the towpath.

◯ *Return to the main road and turn right back to Rostrenen.*

ADDRESSES

⊘ EAT

◯⊘ **L'Éventail des Saveurs** – *3 pl Bourg-Coz. ℘ 02 96 29 10 71. leventail-des-saveurs@wanadoo.fr. Closed 26 Jun–18 Jul, Tue eve, Sept–May Sun eve, Wed and Mon.* A charming restaurant with a good selection of tasty regional recipes and pleasant décor.

⊛ ACTIVITIES

FESTIVALS

In August the **Festival Fisel**, organised by the local Celtic circle, is a celebration of local music and dance over a long weekend *(www.fisel.org).*

Lac de Guerlédan★★

At the heart of the Argoat, the waters of the River Blavet form a winding reservoir known as Guerlédan Lake, a magnificent stretch of water surrounded by trees. It is one of the finest sights of inland Brittany and a lovely place for water sports.

🚗 DRIVING TOUR

Tour of the Lake

Round trip of 44km/27mi starting from Mûr-de-Bretagne – allow 3hr 30min.

Mûr-de-Bretagne
This is one of the liveliest towns in the interior of Brittany.
Chapelle Ste-Suzanne stands to the north of the town in a very pretty wooded setting. The splendid oak trees that surround it are several centuries old and inspired the painter Corot (1796–1875). The chapel's elegant **belfry-porch** dates from 1760. Inside, the

- **Michelin Map:** Local map 309 D5- Côtes-d'Armor (22).
- **Info:** 1, pl. de l'Église, 22530 Mûr-de-Bretagne. ☏02 96 28 51 41. www.guerledan.fr.
- **Location:** On the edge of the forest of Quénecan, the lake extends to the west of Mûr-de-Bretagne (3km/1.8mi) and south to the Rostrenen road.
- **Kids:** The preserved village of Forges-les-Salles and a boat trip.
- **Timing:** Book accommodation well in advance in summer.
- **Don't Miss:** A boat trip on the lake.

remarkable 18C **painted ceiling**★ is dedicated to St Suzanne.
In the village, a road to the right leads to a roundabout, which affords a lovely **view**★ of Guerlédan Lake and dam.

▷ *Take D 35 SW and after crossing two bridges over the canal and the Blavet, turn right.*

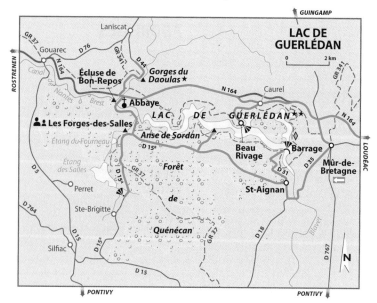

St-Aignan

In the charming 12C **church** note in particular a beautiful carved wooden image of the Tree of Jesse to the north of the chancel and a depiction of the Trinity surrounded by Evangelists, in the same medium, to the south. There is also a statue of St Mark and a Pietà.

Barrage de Guerlédan

A viewpoint overlooks this dam (45m/49yds high, 206m/225yds long along the top and 33.5m/36yds thick at the base), which created the lake, submerging 400ha/988 acres over 12km/7.4mi of the Blavet Gorges.

Make an about turn, then go right. At the entrance to the forest of Quénécan, turn right.

Anse de Sordan

Pleasant sheltered cove in a pretty peaceful place with a number of pleasure boats. Opposite the lake is a restaurant-bar.

Come back by the same road and bear right. Before entering the Forêt de Quénécan bear right.

Les Forges-des-Salles

Open daily Jul–Aug 2pm–6.30pm; Easter–Nov Sat–Sun 2pm–6.30pm. Guided tours (1hr). 5€ (children over 10, 3€). 02 96 24 90 12. www.lesforgesdessalles.info.

Les Forges hamlet, tucked at the bottom of a wooded valley, was an iron and steel industry site in the 18C and 19C. The setting itself is charming, quite apart from the site's remarkable testimony to a complete period of industrial history. This collection of well-designed buildings has not been altered since the mining and processing of iron ore was stopped in 1880.

The buildings of schist, which are arranged around the ironmaster's house, include some that are open to visitors; these are the former homes of blacksmiths (arranged as exhibition rooms). Some houses have been furnished according to their original style and function: the school, the accounts office, the canteen, the chapel, the joiner's workshop and a small smithy.

East of the castle, at the top of the terraced pleasure garden (the **Thabor**), there is a lovely view over the valley and the various stretches of water in it.

Forêt de Quénécan

The forest of 2,500ha/6,177 acres stands on an uneven plateau overlooking the Blavet Valley. Apart from beech and spruce around Lake Fourneau (Étang du Fourneau) and Les Forges des Salles, the forest, abounding in game (deer, wild boar), consists of pine, scrubland and heath.

The GR37 passes near to the steel manufacturing village of Forges-des-Salles and crosses the forest diagonally offering a number of walks.

Continue in the direction of Ste Brigitte to take a small detour allows a good glimpse of the étang des Salles. By Les Forges-des-Salles return to the big crossroad and turn left. Leave the car in the car park in front of the bridge on the left.

Écluse de Bon-Repos

A pretty picture is formed by the lock on the River Blavet, the old corbelled bridge, the former lock keeper's house and the overflow.

Cross over the bridge, on the right, follow the Chemin de Halage.

Abbaye de Bon-Repos

Open daily mid-Jun–mid-Sept 11am –7pm, Mar–mid-Jun and mid-Sept–Oct, 2pm–6pm. 3.50€. 02 96 24 82 20.

This 12C Cistercian abbey, a dependency of the Abbaye de Boquen, was rebuilt in the 14C and embellished in the early 18C. It was later sacked and destroyed during the Revolution. The fine façade of the abbot's lodging, the sober architecture of the conventual buildings and the vast size of the church may still be admired.

▷ *Rejoin the N 164 and turn left towards Gouarec; immediately after the bridge bear right to Daoulas Gorges.*

Gorges du Daoulas★

The fast-flowing waters of the Daoulas run in a narrow, winding valley with steep sides covered with gorse, broom and heather. To join the Blavet, which has become the canal between Nantes and Brest, the river has made a deep cut through a belt of schist and quartzite. The slabs of rock rise almost vertically; some end in sharp needles.

▷ *At 2km/1.25mi, make an about-turn near Toulrodez. Take the N 164 towards Loudéac, travel for 5km/3.1mi and turn right.*

After dropping down into a small pine wood, the road provides a beautiful **view**★ of the Lac de Guerlédan.

▷ *At Caurel turn right towards Loudéac. At 3.5km/2.2mi, turn right to rejoin Mûr-de-Bretagne.*

EXCURSIONS
Loudéac

▷ *21km/13.3mi E of Mûr-de-Bretagne by the D 35 then turn right by the N 164.*
🄸 *Tourist Office at 1 rue St-Joseph (℘02 96 28 25 17; www.centrebretagne.com)*
This little town, at the heart of Brittany, still holds some large fairs and markets. The region specialises in intensive farming, mainly chicken and pigs, and the countryside is dotted with large hangars flanked by tall silos.
The town is particularly famous for its horse racing but also its wooded landscape, its fish-filled rivers and for developing 'green' tourism.

Hippodrome

Loudéac is well known for its race meetings. With the second-largest **race track** (rte de Pontivy; ◐ *open Mon–Fri 9am–noon, 2pm–5pm;* ➤ *guided tours available (30min);* ◐ *closed public holidays;*

&. ℘*02 96 28 30 47)* in western France, the town remains faithful to a history of horse breeding which began in the Middle Ages. The Rohan family kept a stud farm of about 100 fine horses here. Today, tourists can discover the unspoilt landscapes during one of the centre's pony treks.
◐*Races take place the Sunday two weeks before Easter, Easter Sunday and Monday and the following Sunday.*

Notre-Dame deQuerrien

▷ *11km/6.8mi E along N 164 then left on D 14 beyond Loudéac Forest.*
The little village of Querrien was the site of the miraculous apparition of the Virgin to a young shepherdess in the 17C. There is an annual pilgrimage in the sanctuary in honour of Our Lady of Infinite Succour *(Notre-Dame-de-Toute-Aide)*.

La Chèze

▷ *10km/6.2mi SE on the D 778.*
In this village, which has preserved the vestiges of a 13C castle, is the **Musée Régional des Métiers de Bretagne** (Breton Crafts Regional Museum).
The centre evokes the crafts and trades of yesteryear with reconstituted workshops of the slate roofer, harness-saddle maker, cartwright, wooden shoemaker and blacksmith. ◐*Daily exc Mon Jul–Aug, 9am–noon, 2pm–6pm, Sun 2pm–6pm* ◐*Closed public holidays.* ≈*3.60€.* &.℘*02 96 26 63 16.*

St-Thélo

▷ *11km/8mi NW.*
This little village has prospered in its time thanks to its linen industry. **La Maison des Toiles** (Cloth House), set in an old merchant's house (18C), gives an insight into this industry, widespread in the region.
An exhibition traces the history of Breton cloth from the 17C. ◐*Daily Jul–Aug, 10am–1pm, 2.30pm–6.30pm; Apr–Jun and Sept Tue–Sun 2pm–6pm; rest of the year by arrangement.* ◐*Closed Jan–Mar* ≈*3.70€.* &. ℘*02 96 56 38 26.*

ADDRESSES

STAY

Camping Nautic International – 22530 Caurel. 2km/1.2mi S of Beau Rivage on the banks of the lake. ℘02 96 28 57 94. www.campingnautic.fr. Open 15 May–25 Sept. Reservations advised. 120 places. Since the local area doesn't offer any traditional hotel accommodation, you can count on this pleasant campsite, which hires out mobile homes at reasonable prices.

Chambres d'hôte du Pont-Guern – Mûr-de-Bretagne. Take the Pontivy road, then follow the signage on the right. ℘02 96 28 54 52. http://tycanal.e-monsite. com. 3 rooms. Along the Blavet, picturesque farmhouses offer rustic rooms overlooking a beautiful garden.

Pear Blossom House – 14 rue de la Résistance, Mûr-de-Bretagne. ℘02 96 26 05 79. www.pearblossomhouse.com. 2 rooms. A big house whose rooms are decorated in the owner's English style.

EAT

Les Pêcheries – St-Aignan. ℘02 97 27 50 12. www.restaurantlespecheries.com Closed Thur and Sun evening. Family cuisine and atmosphere.

Restaurant La Chapelle – 37 rue Ste-Suzanne, Mûr-de-Bretagne. ℘02 96 26 05 67. Closed Nov–Mar, Sat off season. Big-eaters will have plenty to choose from with three buffets of starters, main courses and desserts.

Merlin – Anse de Sordan. ℘02 97 27 52 36. www.restaurant-merlin.fr. Take a seat either on the terrace above the lake or in the elegant dining room before deciding on tapas, salads or several traditional courses.

Le Beau Rivage – Beau Rivage. 2km/1.2mi S of Caurel. ℘02 96 28 52 14. Closed 2–24 Feb, 6–22 Oct, Sun eve and Mon exc Jul–Aug. The large bay windows of this modern house open onto the lake and a panoramic terrace. Traditional cooking.

TOURS

Heritage Tours – the Tourist Office organises 'discovery days' of the local area in high season.

ACTIVITIES

BOAT TRIPS

Vedettes de Guerlédan – Beau Rivage, Caurel. ℘02 96 28 52 64. http://pagesperso-orange.fr/guerledan/tout.htm. Boat trips and dinner cruises. Call for times and details.

MULTI ACTIVITIES

Base de Loisirs de Guerlédan – 22530 Mûr-de-Bretagne. ℘02 96 67 12 22. www.base-plein-air-guerledan.com. Kayaks, sailing, climbing, orienteering, archery, bike hire. Lessons from qualified instructors.

PEDALOS

Pedalo hire can be found at Beau Rivage, the anse de Sourdan and Mûr-de-Bretagne.

SWIMMING

Swimming is not supervised at Beau Rivage or the anse de Sordan. However, at Gouarec, the swimming pool is open year-round. 22570 Gouarec. ℘02 96 24 86 15.

WATER SKIING

Ski Club de Guerlédan – Beau Rivage, 22530 Caurel. ℘06 09 38 03 26. Open Jul –Aug 9.30am–12.30pm, 2.30pm–7pm; May–Jun and Sept, Sat–Sun. Closed Oct–Apr. Water-skiing and wakeboarding. Courses with accommodation in mobile homes available. Lessons from qualified instructors.

WALKS

Check out the IGN map série bleue n° 0818 (1: 25 000) for details on the walks around the lake. Another good option includes Balades en Pays du Centre Bretagne (on sale at the Tourist Office of Loudéac). For easy access to the **Guerlédan-Argoat region**, head to the train station, Gouarec, west of the lake. ℘02 96 24 85 83.

EVENTS

The **Abbaye Bon Repos** holds an impressive son et lumière in August. ℘02 96 24 82 20.

Lamballe

Lamballe, once the capital of the duchy of Penthièvre, is a picturesque commercial town built on the slope of a hill crowned by the church of Notre-Dame-de-Grande-Puissance. It is an important market centre, slightly off the tourist track.

VISIT

Collégiale Notre-Dame

Open Jul–Aug, Sun–Fri 10am–noon, 2.30pm–6.30pm; rest of the year key available from M. Lévêque at 22 rue de la Dehanne. 02 96 31 92 06.

This Gothic collegiate church has Romanesque features. On the south side of the church with its buttressed gables, there is a terrace, built in the 19C, which affords a fine view of the town and the Gouessant Valley. A shady esplanade is located left of the church.

In nearby **Place du Martray**, the most remarkable old half-timbered house on this square is the 15C Maison du Bourreau (Executioner's House), which now contains the Tourist Office and two museums.

The **Église St-Martin** was once the old priory of Marmoutier Abbey was remodelled many times in the 15C to the 18C. In front of the church is a small, shady square. On the right is an unusual little porch (11C–12C) with a wooden canopy (1519).

ADDITIONIAL SIGHTS

Musée du Pays de Lamballe

Ground floor of the Maison du Bourreau. Open Jun–Sept Tue–Sat 10am–noon, 2.30pm–6pm. Closed public holidays. 2€. 02 96 34 77 63.

Devoted to popular arts and traditions, displays of pottery from Lamballe, etchings of the old town, headdresses and regional costumes.

Musée Mathurin-Méheut

First floor of the Maison du Bourreau. Open daily Jun–Sept 10am–noon, 2.30pm–6pm; Apr, Mon–Sat 10am–noon, 2.30pm–5pm; May and Oct–Dec, Wed, Fri–Sat 2.30pm–5pm. Closed

- ▶ **Population:** 11,037.
- **Michelin Map:** Local map 309 G4 - Côtes-d'Armor (22).
- **Info:** pl. du Champ-de-Foire, 22400 Lamballe. 02 96 31 05 38. www.lamballe-tourism.com.
- **Location:** Lamballe is 20km/12.5mi SE of St-Brieuc on the N 12.
- **Kids:** The Ferme d'Antan in St-Esprit-des-Bois to find out about rural life long ago.
- **Timing:** The stud farm organises horse shows and races from mid-July to mid-August.
- **Don't Miss:** The national stud farm or Château de la Hunaudaye.

public holidays. 3€. 02 96 31 19 99.
This museum contains works by the local painter M Méheut (1882–1958).

Haras National★ (Stud Farm)

Pl. du Champ-de-Foire. Guided tour (1hr) from Jul–Aug, 10.30am–5pm; rest of year daily exc Mon at 3pm. Closed 1 May. 5.50€. 02 96 50 06 98.
Founded in 1825, the stud contains 70 stallions (draught horses). From the beginning of March to mid-July, all the stallions are sent out to breeding stands in the Côtes-d'Armor and the north of Finistère. The stud houses a dressage school (40 horses) and a riding centre (20 horses).

The visit includes the stables, blacksmith's shop, carriage house, harness room, riding school and main court. There are horse shows in July and August.

EXCURSIONS

Château de la Hunaudaye★

15km/9.3mi E along D 28 towards Pléven, then take the D 28E to the right. Guided tours (1hr) mid-Jun–mid-Sept 10.30am–6.30pm; Apr–mid-Jun and mid-Sept–Oct, Sun and holidays

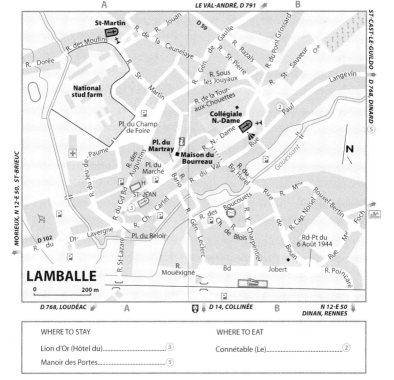

Map of LAMBALLE with scale 0 – 200 m. Surrounding road references: LE VAL-ANDRÉ, D 791; ST-CAST-LE-GUILDO, D 768, DINARD; MORIEUX, N 12-E 50, ST-BRIEUC; D 768, LOUDÉAC; D 14, COLLINÉE; N 12-E 50, DINAN, RENNES. Key sites: St-Martin, National stud farm, Collégiale N.-Dame, Pl. du Champ de Foire, Pl. du Martray, Maison du Bourreau, Pl. du Marché, ST-JEAN, Pl. du Beloir, Rd-Pt du 6 Août 1944.

WHERE TO STAY		WHERE TO EAT	
Lion d'Or (Hôtel du)	③	Connétable (Le)	②
Manoir des Portes	⑤		

2.30pm–6pm; Easter and Nov school holidays Sun–Fri 2.30pm–6pm.
⊜5€ Jul–Aug; 3€ Apr–Sept. ℘02 96 34 82 10. www.la-hunaudaye.com.

The ruins of La Hunaudaye Castle rise in a lonely, wooded spot. Still impressive and severe, they reflect the power of the great barons, equals of the Rohans, who built the castle.

Built in 1220 by Olivier de Tournemine, it was partly destroyed during the War of Succession. Rebuilt and enlarged by Pierre de Tournemine in the 14C, enriched in the early 17C by Sébastien de Rosmadec, husband of one of the Tournemine heiresses, it was dismantled at the time of the Revolution.

The shape is that of an irregular pentagon with a tower at each corner. The two smallest derive from the first building, the other three were built in the 14C–15C. A bridge, replacing the original drawbridge, gives access to a large rounded doorway surmounted by a coat of arms.

Tour de la Glacière – This 15C tower is north facing, hence its name (glacière meaning ice-house). Go up the spiral staircase to admire the elegant structure and chimneys, and the view of the moat.

Logis seigneurial –15C–16C. The walls and the splendid Renaissance stairway give some idea of the lay-out of this great manor house.

Donjon seigneurial – This 15C tower of this manorial keep with its spiral staircase (73 steps) is the best preserved. The monumental chimneypieces and loopholes in the walls are note worthy. This site is the setting for a performance, in period costume, of various aspects of life in a medieval castellany. The actors belong to the *Compagnie Médiévale Mac'htiern*.

♨♨ Ferme d'Antan

▶ St-Esprit-de-Bois-en-Plédeliac, beyond Plédéliac, 11km/6.8mi E along D 28, D 52A, D 52 and D 55.
⏱Apr–May 2pm–6pm exc Mon; Jun 10am–6pm, exc Sun and Mon am;

Jul–Aug 10am–6pm exc Sun and Mon am; Sept 2pm–6pm exc Mon; 24 Oct 2pm–6.30pm; non school hols 2pm–6pm exc Sun and Mon ⊜5€ (children, 3€). ℘02 96 34 80 77. www.ferme-dantan22.com.
This traditional farmhouse is surrounded by outbuildings with their usual implements. The living room is furnished in typical Breton style. The tour ends with a film projection illustrating the everyday life of a peasant family in this very farm at the beginning of the 20C.

Moncontour
16km/10mi SW on D 769, heading towards Loudéac.
Montcontour was built in the 11C on a rocky promintory, at the junction of two valleys. Picturesque **streets**★ and stairs lead to the gates built in the ramparts, partly dismantled by order of Richelieu in 1626. The Château des Granges, rebuilt in the 18C, stands on a hilltop north of the town.
Église St-Mathurin – The 16C church, considerably remodelled in the 18C, contains remarkable stained-glass windows: in the north aisle, they illustrate scenes from the life of St Yves, St Barbe and St John the Baptist; in the south aisle, they depict the Tree of Life and the life of St Mathurin.

Château de la Touche-Trébry
17km/10.5mi S along D 14, then D 25 right towards Moncontour just beyond Penguily. Open 15 Jul–29 Aug Tue–Sun 10am–noon, 2pm–6pm. Call in advance. ℘02 96 42 61 30. www.chateau-de-la-touche.com.
Although built at the end of the 16C, La Touche-Trébry looks like a medieval castle. It stands, facing a pond, protected by its defensive walls forming a homogeneous whole, unaltered in character by the restorations that have taken place.
The courtyard is regular in shape with the main building, with its symmetrical façade, at the far end. On either side,

at right angles, are the two wings with pointed roofs; next to them are the out-buildings, not as tall, extending all the way to the two entrance pavilions.

Jugon-les-Lacs
16km/10mi SE on N 12 then N 176 heading towards Dinan.
The town is near the dam forming the large Jugon reservoir, a 70ha/173-acre **lake** with sailing and water sports facilities. The church, partly rebuilt in the 19C, has retained a 12C porch and an intersting carved doorway on the south side. Note, in rue du Château, the **Hôtel Sevoy** (1634), built on rock.

ADDRESSES

STAY
⊜⊜ **Manoir des Portes** – *À La Poterie, 3.5km/2.25mi E of Lamballe. ℘ 02 96 31 13 62. www.manoirdesportes.com. Closed 22 Dec–5 Jan. ⊡8.50 €.15 rooms.* Near to an equestrian centre this 16C manor house has a pleasant flower garden which contains a potager and an orchard. The rooms are cosy and you are assured a peaceful night. The hotel has a rustic feel with wooden beams, exposed stones and a fireplace.

⊜⊜ **Hôtel du Lion d'Or** – *3 rue du Lion d'Or. ℘02 96 31 20 36. www.leliondor-lamballe.com. Closed 23 Dec–7 Jan. 17 rooms. ⊡8€.* This is a well-kept and traditional hotel with elegant, colourful rooms in a peaceful district.

EAT
⊜⊜ **Le Connétable** – *9 r. Paul-Langevin. ℘02 96 31 03 50. www.leconnetable-lamballe.com. Closed 2 weeks Jan, 2 weeks in Oct, Sun eve and Mon.* You would never guess that this residence was once a forge. Good service and menu a that showcases elaborate cooking styles using produce from the market and "terroir".

North Finistère covers more or less the same area as the old region of Léon in the northwest corner of Brittany, stretching from the Bay of Morlaix on the north coast around to the Presqu'île de Plougastel opposite the naval base of Brest in the southwest. Although the city of Brest is the largest in Finistère, it is not the *préfecture*. This distinction belongs to the smaller city of Quimper situated in the southern half of the *département*. This stretch of the the Brittany coastline is heavily indented, particularly in the northwest where the steep-sided Abers cut into the coast. Two islands – the Île de Batz, just off Roscoff in the north, and the Île de Ouessant, well out into the Atlantic in the west – are fascinating places to visit if time allows.

A Bit of History

Finistère is, as its name implies, at the very extreme western edge of Brittany, and indeed of France, jutting out into the Atlantic Ocean with the lighthouses which have saved the lives of countless seafarers over the years. North Finistère shares its border in the east with the Côtes-d'Armor *département* and for the purposes of this guide it covers that part of the Finistère *département* north of the Rade de Brest. Inland, the countryside is quite flat, cut into with Abers (Breton Fjords) in the north, it rarely rises above 100m/328ft and is largely agricultural. Not surprisingly, agriculture plays a major role in the economy as do food processing, fishing, especially on the north coast at Roscoff, and other light industries. The naval dockyards of the DCNS company at Brest employ nearly 13,000 workers who contribute significantly to the local economy.

The main city of north Finistère is Brest with over 210,000 Brestois residing in the city. Strategically very important, it was almost fully destroyed during WWII but was rebuilt shortly afterwards on a grid layout and, while some might be disappointed by the absence of an old town, there is much to see, especially if you are interested in naval matters. Also important is the ferry and fishing port of Roscoff in the northeast of the *département* and together with nearby St-Pol-de-Léon, these two towns have much to offer. St-Pol has arguably the two most striking buildings in Brittany, the Chapelle du Kreisker with its beautiful belfry and the Ancienne Cathédrale, whereas the port of Roscoff which was the home town of the "Onion Johnnies" who used to bring their produce to the

Highlights

1 Clamboring over the rocky coastline of **Les Abers** (p235)

2 Sailing to the **Île d'Ouessant** from Brest (p242)

3 Exploring the Gothic masterpiece of **Croaz-Batz Church** in Roscoff (p246)

4 Touring **Château de Kerjean** near St-Pol-de-Léon (p251)

5 Taking the **parish closes driving tour** (p260)

UK. Nowadays it is known mostly as a ferry port for visitors to Brittany.

A fascinating feature of the Breton countryside are Les Enclos Paroissiaux, the parish closes comprised of walled churchyards with cemeteries, calvaries and ossuaries. Though they appear all over Brittany, this section includes an itinerary (*see page 260*) starting from Morlaix in the north which presents some of the finest examples of these typically Breton landmarks.

The rocky northwest coast, known as the Côte des Légendes (Coast of Legends), is where long, deep channels snake in from the sea. A driving itinerary is provided (*see page 235*) so you can explore these so-called Breton Fjords. There are no major beaches in this area, but for many this is "real" seaside with a spectacular coastline and great walking opportunities. It was off this coast where the *Amoco Cadiz* supertanker broke up in 1978 after running aground on Portsall Rocks. Her anchor is displayed at Portsall to commemmorate this huge environmental disaster.

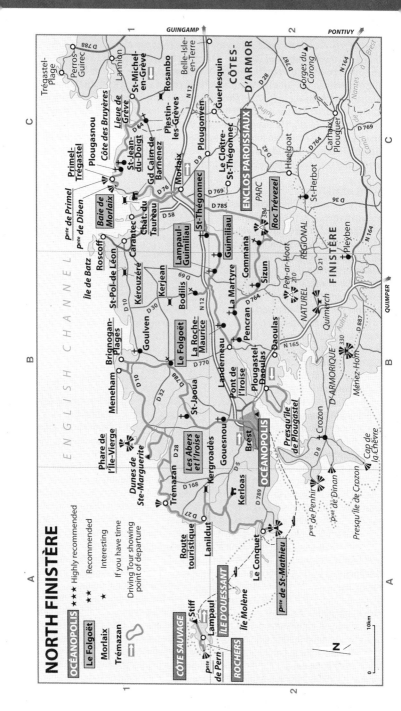

Brest★

Built on the shores of a magnificent, shallow roadstead, the city of Brest is almost an inland sea in itself. By tradition a naval port, today it welcomes ferries and cruise liners. Océanopolis, an impressive complex devoted to marine life, has opened near the marina and the entrance to the Elorn estuary. Every four years, the town welcomes some 2,000 traditional sailing ships from all over the world, a colourful gathering attended faithfully by over one million sailing enthusiasts. Brest is also Brittany's second university town and a major centre of oceanographic research.

▶ **Population:** 142,722.

Michelin Map: Local map 308 E4 - Finistère (29).

Info: 1 place de la Liberté, 29200 Brest. ✆02 98 44 24 96. www.brest-metropole-tourisme.fr.

Location: 243km/150mi W of Rennes, 71km/93mi N of Quimper.

Kids: The giant aquariums at Océanopolis.

Parking: Free parking in the port de commerce (15min walk from centre).

Don't Miss: The Fine Art Museum, the Naval Museum.

A BIT OF HISTORY

The English set foot in Brest (14C) – During the Breton War of Succession which began in 1341, Montfort, ally of the English, was rash enough to let them guard the town. When he became Duke of Brittany, he tried in vain to drive out the intruders. The king of France had just as little success in his turn. At last, in 1397, Charles VI persuaded the King of England, Richard II, who had married Charles's eldest daughter, Isabella, to restore Brest to the Duke.

The *Belle Cordelière* – On 10 August 1513, St-Laurence's Day, the English fleet of Henry VIII set out to attack Brest. The Breton fleet hurriedly set sail to meet it; however, under its panic-stricken commander it fled back to the Brest channel. The *Belle Cordelière,* the gift of Anne of Brittany to her Duchy and on which 300 guests were dancing when the order came to weigh anchor, covered the commander's retreat and bore the brunt of the attack. Fire broke out on board the *Cordelière* as she was fighting gun to gun with an English ship. The commander, Hervé de Portzmoguer, or as he was known in France, Primauguet, knowing that his ship was lost, exhorted his crew and his guests to die bravely with the words: 'We will now celebrate the Feast of St-Laurence who died by fire!' The two ships blew up together.

The work of Colbert (17C) – Colbert, the greatest minister the French Navy ever had, completed the task begun by Richelieu, making Brest the maritime capital of the kingdom. To obtain good crews he set up the *Inscription Maritime* (marine record and administrative office), which still exists today. After completing their military service, fishermen between the ages of 18 and 48 are placed on the French Naval reserve; the *Inscription Maritime* looks after them and their families throughout their lives. Colbert also founded a school of gunnery at Brest, a college of marine guards, a school of hydrography and a school for marine engineers. From this enormous effort a magnificent fleet developed. Ships reached a tonnage of 5 000 and carried up to 120 cannons; their prows and sterns were carved by such artists as Coysevox.

Duquesne improved the naval dockyard, built ramparts round the town and organised the defence of the channel (Le Goulet). Vauban, the military architect, completed the projects. Tourville improved mooring facilities in the roadstead laying down buoys to which ships could moor instead of dropping anchor.

The Belle Poule – In 1778, during the American War of Independence, the frigate *La Belle Poule* encountered the British *Arethusa* and forced her to retreat. This victory was very popular at court and all the ladies wore a new hairstyle, *La Belle Poule*, which included, perched on their tresses, a model ship in full sail.

The Surveillante – In 1779 a British captain, George Farmer, wagered that no French frigate could destroy his *Québec*. Du Couëdic, who commanded the frigate *Surveillante*, challenged the wager and a furious sea duel ensued.

After a spirited battle, north of Ushant, both ships were dismasted. The sails of the *Québec* fell across its guns, setting the ship on fire. Du Couëdic ordered rescue action. Later the *Québec* blew up with the wounded Farmer. Du Couëdic also died from his wounds. The *Surveillante* was brought back to Brest in triumph, and Du Couëdic was laid to rest in the church of St-Louis (destroyed in 1944).

Brest during World War II – In June 1940, when the impending arrival of the German forces was announced, the French naval and commercial authorities hastily cleared the port, destroying the installations and putting several bridges and buildings and four submarines undergoing repair work out of operation. Nonetheless, the port was immediately put to use by the German navy, which built a concrete shelter for submarines at **Laninon**. The port thus occupied a highly advantageous strategic position and represented a considerable threat to Allied forces sailing between the USA and Great Britain. As a consequence, the town was heavily bombarded for four years. When the Americans finally managed to enter the town in September 1944, after a siege of 43 days, they were greeted by nothing but ruins.

▲▲ OCÉANOPOLIS★★★

Allow half a day. ⓝ*Open Jul–Aug, daily 9am–7pm; May–Jun and Sept 9am–6pm, rest of the year 10am–5pm.* ⓝ*Closed 4–15 Jan 1 Jan and 25 Dec* ⓔ*16.50€ (children 11€) for all three pavilions.* ⓖ *℘02 98 34 40 40. www.oceanopolis.com.*

King penguins in Océanopolis

Océanopolis

The enormous crab-shaped complex of Océanopolis is located east of the commercial port (port de commerce) alongside the Moulin Blanc marina (port de plaisance). Take bus 7.

This scientific and technical centre on marine life provides a window on all the activities linked with oceanology. Researchers and the general public are brought into contact with each other. to foster understanding of the marine environment. Océanopolis expanded considerably in 2000: two new pavilions were added to the renovated *Pavillon Tempéré*, the *Pavillon Tropical* and *Pavillon Polaire*. Giant aquariums, containing some 10,000 animals (including sharks, penguins and sea lions) belonging to 1,000 different species, illustrate with spectacular results the variety of submarine life in each natural habitat.

Tidal movements and the swell of the sea are vividly recreated. Interactive terminals, models and films explain the history of the oceans and the extent of man's influence.

A restaurant (Vent d'Ouest) and a cafeteria (Atlantic Express) offer a pleasant break.

TOWN CENTRE

Allow 2hr.

After the full-scale destruction of the town during World War II, the centre of Brest was rebuilt on a geometrical (grid) layout. The main artery linking the naval base to the enormous *place de la Liberté* is the wide **rue de Siam**, once a tiny

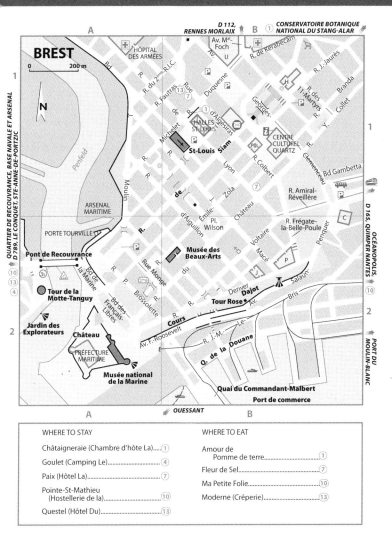

street named in honour of the visit to the town of three ambassadors of the King of Siam and their colourful retinue. Running at right angles to this artery are roads leading to the River Penfeld or the Cours Dajot, from which there are good views of the roadstead.

The **Église St-Louis**, built in 1957, was inspired by Le Corbusier's architectural style; the impression of height is increased by the vertical lines of the concrete bell-tower soaring above the rough-stone building. Inside, a stained-glass window by Paul Boni is devoted to St-Louis.

Cours Dajot

This fine promenade was laid out on the ramparts in 1769 by convicts from the naval prison. The Pink Tower, erected by the American Battle Monuments, commemorates the welcome offered by the people of Brest to the American troops during World War I. Destroyed in 1941, it was rebuilt in 1958.

View of the roadstead★★

From the viewing table at the east end of the promenade, you see the Brest roadstead from the mouth of the Élorn, and past the Ménez-Hom and the Pointe de

Roscanvel right over to Pointe de Portzic. The anchorage is vast (150sq km) and deep (12–20m/6–10 fathoms), and connected with many big estuaries. It communicates with the Atlantic through a channel with steep banks, 5km/3mi long and about 1,800m/1.21mi wide. This configuration explains why Brest has had such great military importance for more than 2,000 years.

To the left the Élorn estuary, spanned by the Albert-Louppe Bridge, makes a safe anchorage for yachts. In the foreground is the commercial port. Beyond lies the Île de Plougastel, hiding the southeast of the roadstead. On the south side of the roadstead, at Lanvéoc, is the Naval School; the nuclear submarine base is situated on nearby Île Longue.

On the horizon to the right you see the Presqu'île de Crozon and the opening of the channel between Portzic Fort and the Pointe des Espagnols. In front of the castle, the inner harbour, protected by its breakwater, serves as anchorage for the fleet.

Port de Commerce

This was established in 1860, once the Penfeld river became inadequate for accommodating both military and commercial shipping, for the use of the Brest Chamber of Commerce and Industry.

Traditional traffic is closely linked with the agricultural activities of west Brittany, and amounts to almost two million tonnes a year.

The commercial port imports oilseed and other products destined for livestock, as well as hydrocarbons and fertilisers; it exports mainly frozen poultry (for which it ranks as the world's number one port), potatoes and oils. The port is also an important centre for naval repair work and encompasses three types of dry dock. The most recent of these, built in 1980, has the capacity to accommodate the largest commercial ships yet made (over 500,000t). These installations, which include wet repair docks and a gas extraction station, make Brest the foremost French naval repair complex.

ADDITIONAL SIGHTS
Musée des Beaux-Arts

Open Tue–Sun 10am–noon, 2pm–6pm, Sun noon–2pm. Closed public holidays. 4€. *No charge 1st Sun of the month.* 02 98 00 87 96.

The Museum of Fine Arts' collections illustrate the Symbolist movement and in particular the Pont-Aven School (*By the Sea in Brittany* by Emile Bernard, *Green Corn at Le Pouldu* by Paul Sérusier and *Day in September* by Maurice Denis). Also well represented is 17C and 18C

Ships of the French fleet and Château de Brest

R. Mattes/MICHELIN

painting from the Italian, French and Dutch Schools (*Brest Harbour* by Van Blarenberghe, 1774). In addition, there are works by Orientalists such as Guillaumet and Fromentin, various seascapes and a noteworthy *Two Parrots* by Manet.

Château

The castle is the sole reminder of Brest's history. It was in the 11C that Brest's stronghold first put in an appearance at the mouth of the River Penfeld on a site which had already been fortified by the Romans. It was to fall victim to innumerable sieges over the centuries. Towers and fortifications were built from the 12C to the 17C. Richelieu, Colbert, Duquesne and Vauban, from 1683, were to strengthen the fortifications of the site. The curtain wall was restored after the last war. The museum and the ramparts are all that is open to the public; the castle houses the offices of the Harbour Police (Préfecture Maritime).

Musée de la Marine★

🕐*Open Apr–Sept, daily 10am–6.30pm; Oct–Mar, 1.30pm–6.30pm.* 🕐*Closed 1 May, 25 Dec.* ✍*5.50€.* ✆*02 98 22 12 39. www.musee-marine.fr.*

Access is through the Madeleine Tower (3C–15C), from the top of which there is a good view of the port and the roadstead. This museum is an offshoot of the Maritime Museum in Paris and displays valuable models of ships, navigation instruments and charts illustrating the feats of the navy sailing ships during the 18C. At the foot of the terrace there is a display of the 5622 pocket submarine, 11.87m long by 1.68m wide, and the taking aboard of the boat-people rounded up in the South China Sea by the teaching ship *Jeanne d'Arc* in 1988.

The tour continues along the watch-path of the Paradis Tower (15C) in which there is an exhibition on the history of the castle. Interesting exhibits of ship decorations are displayed throughout, in particular **figureheads** carved by unknown artists or by famous ones such as Antoine Coysevox who sculpted many statues of Louis XIV.

Musée national de la Marine Brest

Musée national de la Marine/M.Guilloud

Tour Tanguy

🕐*Open Jun–Sept, daily 10am–noon, 2pm–7pm; Oct–May, Wed–Thu 2pm–5pm, Sat–Sun, School hols, public hols, 2pm–6pm.* 🕐*Closed 1 Jan, 1 May and 25 Dec.* ✆*02 98 00 88 60.*

The tower stands opposite the castle, on the far bank of the Penfeld, overlooking the dockyard. This 14C construction, once the Quilbignon stronghold, houses the **Musée du Vieux Brest**, which depicts the most significant periods of Brest's history through dioramas, town plans, modles, coats of arms, etc.

Jardin des Explorateurs

On the banks of the Penfeld, on the same side as the Tour Tanguy. Access by rue de l'Église.

Typical of an international port that regularly welcomed naturalists returning with exotic plants, this garden reminds visitors of some of the great explorers (Bougainville, Commerson, La Billardière, Raoul), and is home to plants that are more often seen in distant lands, such as palm trees, giant ferns and Japanese anemones. There is a nice view of the château and the arsenal from the bridge.

Naval Base and Dockyard★ (Base Navale et Arsenal)

It was in 1631 that **Cardinal Richelieu** decided to turn the city of Brest into a harbour. In 1666, **Colbert** developed the infrastructure that already existed along the banks of the Penfeld: the meandering, enclosed estuary of this river was a perfect site, able to protect the boats from heavy storms. From 1740 to 1790, **Choquet de Lindu** undertook to build a huge dockyard and, as early as 1742, the first three dry docks of Pontaniou were built. In the late 19C a pier was erected, defining the boundaries of a vast roadstead; in 1970 two **jetties** able to accommodate large-tonnage vessels (aircraft-carriers, cruisers, frigates) were added onto the pier. **Docks** 8 (for careening only) and 9 (construction work) were built in 1918 and extended in 1953. Their huge size (300m/328yds long by 49m/53yds wide) enables them to receive the largest ships belonging to the French fleet, over 250m/273yds long and weighing more than 35,000t. At the same time, two other quays were built: **Quai de l'Armement** (555m/607yds long), designed to equip and repair ships, and **Quai des Flotilles** (752m/793yds long), which brings together most of the war vessels that make up the Atlantic fleet.

During the German Occupation in World War II, an underwater naval base was set up in Brest to protect the German submarines stationed in the Atlantic Ocean. As soon as the base became operational, it could accommodate up to 30 submarines. With a total area of 65,859sq m/78,766sq yds covered by a 4m/13ft thick slab, it was practically

invulnerable; during the bombing of 5 August 1944, the impact made by ten 6t bombs caused only minor damage. This base is still in service today.

Tour of the Dockyard

Access by Porte de la Grande Rivière by Pont de Recouvrance. ⌫⌫*Guided tours in French or English by appointment. Jul–Aug, daily 1.45pm–3.30pm; last 2 weeks Jun & first two weeks Sept 2.30pm and 3pm (rest of the year, call ahead for information).* ⏱*Identification required. No photographs. No charge.* ℘*02 98 22 06 12.*

The visit offers a tour of the submarine base built by the Germans during World War II and of one of the warships of the French Navy – whichever is available.

Mémorial des Finistériens

Allée Bir-Hakeim. Leave the town centre to the W by Recouvrance bridge in the direction of Conquet; Fort Montbarey is on the right. ⏱*Open Mon–Fri 9am–noon, 2pm–6pm.* ⌫⌫*Guided tours available (1hr 30min) on request.* ⏱*Closed public holidays.* ⊛5€. ♿ ℘*02 98 05 39 46.*

Fort Montbarey, built in 1784 on the orders of Louis XVI, bears the name of one of the king's ministers. Today it is a memorial site for the Finistère region. Visitors can see photographs, literature, objects and military equipment recalling the siege of Brest in 1944, escape routes to Braitain, deportation, etc. In the crypt is a list of local sons and daughters who died between 3 September and 19 December 1946. Several vaulted rooms have been reconstructed as the various garrisons for the fort (butcher's, baker's, chemist's shops).

♿♿ Conservatoire Botanique National de Brest★

E of the town by rue Jean-Jaurès, then by the road to Quimper. ⏱*Open Jul–Aug 9am–8pm; Apr–Jun and Sept–Oct, daily 9am–7pm; Nov–Mar, daily 9am–6pm. Greenhouses Wed–Sun 2pm–5.30pm.* ⊛*4.50€ (children 3€) for the tropical greenhouses.* ♿ ℘*02 98 02 46 00. www.cbnbrest.fr.*

Arsenal

G. Targat/MICHELIN

Greenhouse, Conservatoire Botanique National de Brest

©Loïc Ruellan/Conservatoire Botanique National de Brest

The *Vallon du Stang-Alar* houses one of the most prestigious botanical gardens in the world. As well as a beautiful public **garden** (22ha/54 acres) boasting a wide variety of both common and rare exotic ornamental plants, the **greenhouses** (1 000sq m) and other conservatories contain many species threatened with extinction. The role of this park is not only to preserve endangered varieties, but also to study them and to try to revive them in their natural environment. Thus attempts have been made to resuscitate the *Hibiscus fragilis,* the *Lobelia parva,* the *Narcissus triandrus capax* – which almost disappeared from the Îles de Glénan a few years ago – or the *Limonium dendroides,* of which only four specimens remained in the wild. Play areas for children and sports activities will delight nature lovers of all ages.

🚗 DRIVING TOURS

1 FROM BREST TO THE PRESQU'ÎLE DE PLOUGASTEL★

Round tour of 56km/35mi – about half a day.

▷ *Leave Brest along N 165 towards Quimper.*

Les ponts sur l'Élorn

You pass on the left the road leading to **Relecq-Kerhuon**, a resort nicely situated on the west bank of the Élorn.

Pont Albert-Louppe

Inaugurated by President Gaston Doumergue in 1930, this bridge crosses the Élorn estuary. It is 880m long and has three 186m spans. Four statues by the sculptor Quillivic stand at each end: a man and a woman from the Léon region on the Brest shore and a man and a woman from Plougastel on the opposite shore.

The bridge rises over 42m/137ft high above the river and offers a very fine **view**★ over the Élorn Valley and the Brest roadstead.

Pont de l'Iroise

Inaugurated in 1994, this bridge has a 400m/437yds-wide central span; it carries the main road between Brest and Quimper and is the first link of the major international highway E 60 which will eventually join Brest and the Black Sea via Switzerland, Austria and Hungary.

▷ *1km/0.6mi after the bridge bear right towards Plougastel-Daoulas.*
See Presqu'île de PLOUGASTEL for details of the rest of the drive.

Lighthouse, Pointe Saint Mathieu

© sc0p/Fotolia.com

2 COASTAL DRIVE TO POINTE DE ST-MATHIEU

56km/35mi tour – roughly 2hrs.

○ *Leave Brest heading W by Pont de Recouvrance and turn left onto rue St-Exupéry to reach the cliff road overlooking the naval dockyard. At 4-Pompes drive straight on; turn left at the entrance to Cosquer.*

Ste-Anne-du-Portzic

By the beach, in Ste-Anne Bay, a short walk on the coastal path offers fine views. Climb up the slope to reach the Pointe du Diable, opposite the strait (Goulet de Brest).

This extraordinary site overlooking the entrance to the roadstead is home to the **Technopole Brest-Iroise**, which comprises higher education institutions, businesses and research centres such as the French Research Institute for Exploitation of the Sea (IFREMER, www.ifremer.fr). The centre also specialises in biotechnologies, agribusiness, telecommunications and IT.

○ *Join the D 789.*

The road runs parallel to Trez-Hir beach, giving a good view of Bertheaume Bay, then goes through Plougonvelin.

Fort de Bertheaume

℘ 02 98 48 26 41. Jul–Aug : 10.30am–7pm ; Jun: Sat–Sun 2.30-6.30pm. ⊜2€. (under 11 years free).

This defensive structure at the entrance to the strait of Brest was fortified by the military architect Vauban and provides an opportunity for a walk along the coastal path.

St-Mathieu★★

St-Mathieu, which was an important town in the 14C, is now only a village known for the ruins of its abbey church, its site and its lighthouse.

The **lighthouse** (○ open Jul–Aug, 10am –7pm; May, Jun and Sept, weekends and public holidays 3pm–6.30pm; guided tour (20min); last admission 20min before closing; ⊜4€; ℘02 98 48 30 18; www.plougonvelin.fr) has a considerable system of lights; two auxiliary lights are reserved for air navigation. There is also a radio beam. The main light is served by a 600-watt halogenous lamp, giving it an intensity of about 5 million candlepower, with a range of 60km/37mi. From the top *(163 steps)* there is a superb **panorama★★**; spanning left to right – the mouth of the Brest Sound, Presqu'île de Crozon, Pointe du Raz, Île de Sein (in clear weather), Pierres Noires reef, and the Islands of Béniguet, Molène and Ouessant. Beyond Béniguet, 30km/18.5mi away, you can sometimes distinguish Jument Lighthouse.

The ruins of the **abbey church**★ are the remains of a Benedictine monastery (6C) which, according to legend, had as a relic the head of St Matthew.

The 13C chancel, which has pointed vaulting, is flanked by a square keep. The nave with rounded or octagonal pillars has a single aisle on the north side and two 16C aisles on the south side. The church has a 12C façade pierced by a round arched doorway and three narrow windows.

In front of the restored Chapelle Notre-Dame-des-Grâces, note the 14C porch, a relic of the former parish churchrooms

▷ *Go round the lighthouse enclosure to reach the tip of the point.*

Pointe de St-Mathieu

At the tip of the headland, a **column**, erected to the memory of the French sailors who died in WWI, is the work of the sculptor Quillivic. There is a magnificent **view** from the edge of the cliff. On the road back, 300m/327yds from St-Mathieu towards Plougonvelin, you will notice two Gallic **stelae** topped by a crosses (on the left, next to a house), which are known as the Monks' Gibbet (Gibet des Moines).

ADDRESSES

⌂STAY

⌂**Camping Le Goulet** – *Lanhouarnec. 6 km/3.75mi W by the D 789 rte du Conquet then left onto rte de Ste-Anne-du-Portzic.* ☏ *02 98 45 86 84. www.campingdu goulet.com.* ⊐⌂. *Reservation advised. 155 pitches.* Between country and coast this camp site allows you to visit Brest easily. There is space for tents, and mobile home and cottage rental. There is also a lake, a water park, games room and a snack bar.

⌂⊜**Chambre d'hôte La Châtaignerie** – *Keraveloc, 29490 Guipavas. E of the town, below the botanic gardens.* ☏*02 98 41 52 68. http://pagesperso-orange. fr/la-chataigneraie. 3 rooms.* ⊐⌂. ⊒. This large 1970s house perched on the heights of Stang-Alar enjoys a fabulous view of the bay of Brest in fine weather. Its rooms are spacious, comfortable and quiet. Lounge-library, games room and swimming pool (heated in summer).

⌂⊜**Hôtel Du Questel** – *120 r. F.-Thomas.* ☏*02 98 45 99 20. www.hotel-du-questel.fr. 36 rooms.* ⊒ *7.50 €.* A new hotel situated near to the north ringroad. Rooms are quiet, functional and well kept. Small snacks available.

⌂⊜▤**Hôtel La Paix** – *32 r. Algésiras -* ☏ *02 98 80 12 97. www.hoteldelapaix-brest.com. Closed 19 Dec–3 Jan. 29 rooms.* ⊒. *11€.* This small hotel in the centre of town has been completely redecorated in a modern style. Beautiful new rooms

well equipped and sound proofed. Large buffet breakfast.

⌂⊜▤**Hostellerie de la Pointe St-Mathieu** – *29217 La Pointe St-Mathieu.* ☏*02 98 89 00 19. www.pointe-saint-mathieu.com. 28 rooms.* ⊒ *12€. Restaurant*⌂⊜▤. This hotel-restaurant, neighbour of the lighthouses and abbey ruins, occupies an old house that was recently extended to provide accommodation. Enjoy a meal in the pretty vaulted dining room or the brasserie.

⍾EAT

⌂**Crêperie Moderne** – *34 r. Algésiras -* ☏ *02 98 44 44 36. Closed Sun lunch.* Built in 1922, this *crêperie* continues to serve the people of Brest who come to admire the dexterity of the crêpe makers.

⌂**Amour de Pomme de Terre** – *23 rue des Halles St-Louis.* ☏*02 98 43 48 51.* For love of the spud! This attractive and fun place serves every form of our favourite root vegetable: mashed, with cheese, baked, fried, etc. Meat, seafood and fish are grilled at your table.

⌂⊜**Ma Petite Folie** – *Plage du Moulin Blanc, Port de Plaisance.* ☏*02 98 42 44 42. Closed 1–10 Jan and Sun.* A beached fishing boat, the decks serves as dining rooms: this is a pleasant and amusing place to enjoy a seafood platter. Sit on the upper deck for a view of the beach.

⌂⊜▤**Fleur de sel** – *15 bis rue de Lyon.* ☏*02 98 44 38 65. www.lafleurdesel.com Closed 1–10 Jan, 1–22 Aug, Sat lunch and*

Sun. Excellent cuisine in an Art Deco dining room. The menu is inspired and creative, based on fresh produce and seafood. Good value for money.

NIGHTLIFE

Ayers Rock Café – *7 rue de l'Harteloire. 02 98 46 48 91. Open daily until the wee hours.* This chummy bar programmes concerts 365 days of the year. Happy hour from 8pm–11pm: 3 pints for the price of 2.

La Ronde des Vins – *31 rue Monge. 02 98 80 14 70. Open Tue–Sun 10.30am –midnight.* A pleasant wine bar, serving nice assortments of cold meats, oysters and salads.

Le Quartz – *Place de la Liberté. 02 98 33 70 70. www.lequartz.com. Closed Mon and holidays.* This fine national theatre welcomes more than 300,000 spectators yearly to plays, concerts and dance performances.

ACTIVITIES

Boat Trips – **Vedettes Azenor** *(port du Moulin Blanc; 02 98 41 46 23; www. azenor.com)* offers guided boat tours of the military harbour and the roadstead. Two or three departures daily Apr–Sept, Tue–Sun, Jul–Aug, daily 1hr 30min, 15.50€. With a meal on board: 3hr, from 47€.

Walking tours – The Tourist Office publishes a series of leaflets showing the footpaths in the area around Brest. You can also find them at www.brest-metropole-tourisme.fr.

Watersports – The Brest roadstead is like an inland sea and a great place to sail, windsurf, row, etc. Information from the **Station Nautique Rade de Brest** *(Port du Moulin-Blanc; 02 98 34 64 64; Open daily except Sun afternoon).*

Beaches – **Moulin-Blanc**, across from the marina, is the local favourite. The beach at **Ste-Anne-du-Porzic**, near the Brest-Iroise Technopôle, is a beautiful natural site.

SPECIAL EVENTS

Les Jeudis du Port – *www.mairie-brest. fr/jeudis-port.* Every Thursday evening in July and August, a free concert and street fair at the port.

Brest 2008 - maritime festival of Brest

©MAXPPP/Photoshot

Brest 2012 – Every four years, the Tall Ships come to Brest; the next rendez-vous is in July 2012. Concerts, events and tours of the ships.

Festival Européen du Film Court – *02 98 44 03 94. www.filmcourt.fr.* In early Nov, the Côte Ouest association organises a festival of short films.

SHOPPING

Markets – **Halles St-Louis**. The covered market is open every morning, but Sundays are most spectacular, with stalls spread out into the neighbouring streets. **Marché de Siam**, *rue de Siam*, Sun morning. This is the market where small local growers sell their wares, including cheese from the Monts d'Arrée; there is also a good selection of wine and clothing.

Chocolate – *Histoire de Chocolat, 60 rue de Siam. 02 98 44 66 09.www. histoiredechocolat.com. Open Tue–Sat 9.30am–7pm, Mon 2pm–7pm.* The chocolates are made on the premises and filled with praline, caramel, honey, salted butter and even algae!

Groceries – **Roi de Bretagne**, *12 quai de la Douane, port de commerce. 02 98 46 09 00. Open Mon–Sat 9.30am– 12.30pm, 1.30pm–7pm.* Specialising in products from Brittany, including beer, cider, potted fish, boating attire and celtic music.

Pastry shop – **Le Quéau**, *109 rue Jean Jaurès. 02 98 44 15 53. Open daily 9am–7.30pm.* This small shop is well known for its whipped cream – light and not too sweet. You can enjoy your treats in the old-fashioned tea room.

Les Abers★★

The low and rocky northwest coast of Finistère, still known as the Coast of Legends, offers a magnificent sight. Life is hard and the enormous anchor of the Amoco Cadiz is a reminder of the violence the elements can inflict on the region. No manicured beaches here, but lovers of romantic vistas, solitary coastal paths and the smell of seaweed will feel right at home.

🚗 DRIVING TOURS

1 FROM BREST TO BRIGNOGAN-PLAGES

50 km/31mi – Allow 4h with the visit to the basilica of Folgoët and the Musée du Léon.

▷ *Leave Brest heading N by the D 788 towards Roscoff.*

Gouesnou

The 17C Gothic and Renaissance **church** *(guided tours Jul–Aug, Tue, Wed, Thu 2pm–6pm)* has a polygonal chevet (1615) surmounted by three pediments. To the west, below the church, is a fine Renaissance fountain with an altar adorned with a statue of St-Gouesnou.

▷ *Take the direction of Lannilis (D 13) and, in Bourg-Blanc, turn right onto the D 38 in the direction of Plouvien.*

Chapelle St-Jaoua

At the centre of a large field, this chapel contains a tomb on which there is the recumbent effigy of St-Jaoua. The colourful panelling has been restored. In the parish church of **Plouvien** is a tomb in Kersanton granite dating from 1555. The recumbent figure rests on 16 little monks depicted at prayer, reading or meditating.

▷ *Leave Plouvien heading E by the road for Lesneven.*

🔧 **Michelin Map:** Local map 308 C/E 2/4 – Finistère (29).

🗎 **Info: Pays d'Iroise:** ℘02 98 84 41 15. www.vacanceseniroise.com. **Pays des Abers:** www.abers-tourisme.com. **St-Renan:** Pl. du Vieux Marché. ℘02 98 84 23 78. www.saint-renan.com. **Le Conquet:** Parc Beauséjour. ℘02 98 89 11 31. www.leconquet.fr.

▷ **Location:** The coastline from the Pointe St-Mathieu to Brignogan-Plages is wild and rugged, and is broken up by estuaries called "abers" (Aber-Wrac'h, Aber-Benoît, Aber-Ildut).

🕐 **Timing:** Make the most of the morning markets but try and stay to watch sunset from the rocks.

🏛 **Don't Miss:** A walk along the dunes of Ste-Marguerite at dusk; the breathtaking view of the rocks from the lighthouse at Île de Vierge.

St-Jean-Balanant

The 15C **chapel** *(for visits, ask at the town hall, ℘02 98 40 91 16)* was founded by the Order of St-John of Jerusalem and was a dependant of the La Feuillée Commandery in the Monts d'Arrée. To the right of the Chapel is a fountain.

▷ *Continue in the direction of Lesneven and, at the fourth crossroad, turn right towards Locmaria.*

Chapelle de Locmaria

In front of the 16C–17C chapel with its square belfry-porch, there is a fine **cross**★ with two crossbars adorned with figures.

▷ *By Le Drennec, go to Le Folgoët.*

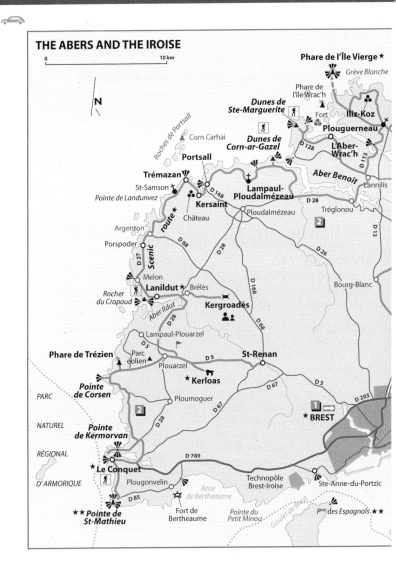

THE ABERS AND THE IROISE

Le Folgoët★★

N of Landerneau on the D 788 which links Brest (25km/15.5mi S) with St-Pol-de-Léon (35km/21.7mi E).

You should see this little village and its magnificent Basilica of Our Lady (Notre-Dame) during the *grand pardon* which takes place on the first Sunday in September. It is the best known in the Léon region of Finistère and one of the largest in Brittany. The *pardon* of St-Christopher with the blessing of cars is held on the fourth Sunday in July *(www.lefolgoet.fr)*.

Basilique★★

A great esplanade with inns on either side leads up to the basilica, but it is not wide enough to hold the crowd on *pardon* days. The **north tower**★ of the façade supports one of the finest bell-towers in Brittany.

The basilica is square in shape, which is unusual; the Chapel of the Cross, whose east wall is an extension of the flat east end, branches off the chancel. This chapel has a fine **porch**★. Salaün's fountain, where pilgrims come to drink,

North tower of the basilica, Le Folgoët

R. Mattes/MICHELIN

stands outside, against the east wall. The water comes from the spring under the altar.

Inside is a masterpiece of Breton art of the 15C, the admirably carved granite **rood screen**★★. Five 15C Kersanton granite altars stand in the east end. The Chapel of the Cross and the apse are adorned by fine rose windows. There is a 15C statue of Our Lady of Folgoët. Left of the basilica the little 15C manor house of Le Doyenné, though much restored, forms an attractive

group with the pilgrim's inn and the church. In the inn, a small **museum** (🕐 open mid-Jun–mid-Sept, Mon–Sat 10am–12.30pm, 2.30pm–6.30pm; Sun 2.30–6.30pm ⊛3€; ♿ ℘02 98 21 11 18) contains a collection of 15C, 16C and 17C stone statues, archives and 15C furnishings.

▷ *Head NE towards Lesneven.*

Lesneven
NE of Folgoët.
Lesneven was founded in the 5C by the Breton chief Even. There are several 17C and 18C granite houses. **The Musée de Léon** (🕐 open Jul–Aug, Wed–Mon 2pm–6pm; ⊛2.50€; ♿ ℘02 98 21 17 18), located in the Ursuline convent's chapel, is devoted to the history of the Léon region. Note the authentic decree signed by Louis XIV authorising the creation of an Ursuline convent in Lesneven.

▷ *Take the D 770 until Brignogan-Plages.*

Brignogan-Plages
Brignogan is a seaside resort lying deep inside Pontusval Bay, 11km from

Le Folgoët on the D 770 and framed by rock piles, some of which are curiously shaped. Take time to walk to the Pointe de Pontsuval to see the menhir Men Marz *(www.ot-brignogan-plage.fr)*.

2 THE COAST OF LEGENDS

170km/105mi – allow one day .

This tour offers the visitor the opportunity to go off the beaten track and to enjoy nature in its unspoiled state.

From Brignogan-Plages, take the D 770 towards Le Folgoët, turn right towards le Croazou and carry on until Meneham.

Meneham★

02 98 83 95 63.
This hamlet located on the coast behind impressive blocks of granite was home to a community of goémoniers (seaweed collectors) and has been restored to show their traditional living conditions. In 1685, a hidden guard-post was built in the rocks to keep watch over the coast. Later, a few houses were added for customs officers. The site was listed in 1975 and was bought by the municipality of Kerlouan in 1989 for restoration.

From Meneham, return to Kerlouan and take the D 10 until Plouguerneau.

Plouguerneau

The village **church** hosts an interesting collection of 17C wooden statuettes called the "little saints" which can be found near the baptistery on the left upon entering. Formerly carried in processions, these statuettes are the result of a wish made by villagers who had miraculously escaped the plague.

Take the D 32 towards St-Michel.

At the exit to the village, on the right, is the **Ecomusée de Plouguerneau et du Pays Pagan** (open Apr–Oct, Jul–Sept, Wed–Mon 2pm–6pm; May–19 Jun weekends only; 4€; 02 98 37 13 35; www.ecomusee-plouguerneau. fr). From the Vierge Island lighthouse to

the Koz Isle archaeological site by way of the Goemonniers and Algae ecological museum, the whole country can be explained through these natural and historic sites.

Life in former times and today for the people of North Finistère developed around the coast. Regional products, stories and legends, along with displays on the techniques of seaweed-gathering through the ages.

Go N on the D 32.

Ruines d'Iliz Koz

Open mid-Jun–mid-Sept, Tue–Sun 2.30pm–6.30pm; rest of year Sun only 2pm–5pm. 3€. 02 98 04 71 84.
These ruins of the church and the presbytery, which have been silted up since the early 18C, provide an excellent example of Breton funerary art at the end of the Middle Ages. A signposted route enables visitors to discover the most important elements of the site. Pay special attention to the tombs' ornamental motifs which describe the function of the tomb's occupant.

Phare de l'Île Vierge

Open Apr–Sept, daily 10am–4pm depending on tides. 2.50€. 02 98 37 13 35 / 02 98 04 74 94.
This is the tallest lighthouse in France (82.5m/271ft). From the top (397 steps) the **panorama**★ extends over the Finistère coast.

Follow the coast until the plage de St-Cava from where at low tide you can walk to the lighthouse at l'Aber-Wrac'h.

2km further on, the old road has become a lookout point (small calvary) affording a good **view**★ of l'Aber-Wrac'h.

In Lannilis, turn right.

L'Aber-Wrac'h

With its important sailing centre, l'Aber-Wrac'h is a very popular pleasure port. Its sailing school overlooks the village, and also livens up this seaside stay. The corniche road runs along the Baie des

Anges; past the ruins of the 16C convent of Notre-Dame-des-Anges.

Bear right towards Ste-Marguerite Dunes, then right again towards Cézon Fort.

From the platform by the roadside, there is an interesting view of l'Aber-Wrac'h estuary, the ruins of Cézon Fort on an island commanding the approach to the estuary, and the lighthouse on the Île Vierge.

Turn back and after Poulloc, bear right for the dunes.

Dunes de Ste-Marguerite

The footpaths through the dunes afford good views. Seaweed is left to dry on the dunes for two to three days and then is sent to the processing factories.

Make for the Chapelle de Brouënnou and turn left towards Passage St-Pabu. Go to Lannilis via Landéda and then take the Ploudalmézeau road.

Aber-Benoît

The road crosses the *aber* and runs along it for a while, giving good views of the pretty setting.

After 5km/3mi turn right for St-Pabu and after St-Pabu follow signs for the campsite to reach Corn-ar-Gazel Dunes.

Dunes de Corn-ar-Gazel

Beautiful **view** of Ste-Marguerite Peninsula, Aber-Benoît and its islets.

Turn round and follow the scenic road winding through the dunes and affording glimpses of the coast.

Lampaul-Ploudalmézeau

This modest village is home to a church in the Breton Renaissance style. Its north porch is a magnificent example of a bell-tower-porch (clocher-porche) topped by a dome with three lanterns.

Portsall

This small harbour is located in a bay sheltered by a chain of reefs called the Roches de Portsall, the rocks on which the oil tanker, *Amoco Cadiz*, ran aground in 1978. One of its two enormous anchors (20t) is fixed to the harbour breakwater in memory of the shipwreck, on which a legal settlement was not reached until 1992.

Kersaint

On your left, as you leave the village on the road to Argenton, are the ruins of the 13C Château de Trémazan.
Be warned that the ruins are very dangerous, but you can appreciate the majesty of the site from the viewing point.

Aber-Benoît

R. Mattes/MICHELIN

Trémazan

From the large car park past the village, the **view**★ extends over the Île Verte, the Roches de Portsall and Corn Carhai Lighthouse.

The **scenic corniche road**★ follows a wild coast studded with rocks; note the curious jagged **Pointe de Landunvez**. The road runs through several small resorts, Argenton, **Porspoder** and Melon.

▷ *Turn right at the entrance of Lanildut.*

Lanildut★

This is europe's foremost seaweed port. The Rumorvan quarter hosts several beautiful captain's houses from the 17C and 18C.

▷ *After Lanildut, the road follows the aber as far as Brélès.*

Château de Kergroadès

Guided tours (1hr) 9 Jul–26 Aug, 11am–noon, 2pm–6pm, Sun 2pm–6pm. Jun and Sept Thur 2.30pm. 4€. 02 98 32 43 93.

The main courtyard of this early 17C castle is closed by a crenellated gallery and is surrounded by an austere main building flanked by two round towers.

▷ *Return to Brélès and take D 28 to Plouarzel. Drive across town heading towards St-Renan, and about 1km/0.6mibeyond the outskirts, turn right towards the Menhir de Kerloas.*

Menhir de Kerloas★

This is the tallest standing stone in France, 9.5m tall, and is estimated to be 5,000 years old. The impressive menhir is nicknamed "The Hunchback" *(An Tor)* because of the two bumps, and has of course inspired many legends. A curious 19C tradition brought newlyweds here to rub their naked bodies on the bumps – the man in order to have sons, the woman in order to have authority in the home!

▷ *Follow the D 5 until St-Renan.*

St-Renan

This small town was founded in around 500 AD by the Irish hermit St-Ronan, and its history as the site of a ducal and then royal law court has left it with several fine half-timbered façades and a renowned market (*see Addresses below*). You can learn about St-Renan's rich history from the enamelled lavastone panels dotted throughout the town, and also at the **local history museum** (musée d'histoire locale), which displays traditional costumes, headdresses and furniture of the Léon region. It also tells the story of the tin mine that was discovered in 1957 and operated for around 15 years, and resulted in the nearby quarries that have been transformed into lakes. 16 r. St-Mathieu. *02 98 32 44 94. Jul–Aug, 3pm–6pm; mid-Jun to mid-Sept, Easter and Feb holidays, Tue–Fri 3pm–6pm, Sat 10.30am–12 noon, 3pm–6pm. Closed Sun and public holidays. 2 €.*

▷ *Return to Plouarzel and take the VC 4 towards Trézien.*

Along the way, you are bound to notice the **wind farm** built in 2000, with its huge turbines standing 60m/196ft tall and equipped with impressive rotors 47m/154 in diameter. Explanatory panel on site.

▷ *Continue towards Trézien. The village's 37m/121ft-high lighthouse has an average range of 35km/21mi. Head towards Porsmoguer Beach (Grève de Porsmoguer) and after some houses turn right.*

Pointe de Corsen

This 50m/165ft cliff is the most westerly point in continental France. There is a fine **view** of the coast and islands.

▷ *Go to Ploumoguer passing through Porsmoguer Beach, then turn towards Le Conquet. After 5km/3mi, bear right for the Pointe de Kermorvan.*

Pointe de Kermorvan

Its central part is an isthmus which gives a pretty view on the right of Blancs Sablons Beach and on the left of the **site**★ of Le Conquet. The Groaë footbridge gives pedestrians access to the point; at the very tip, to the left of the entrance to the lighthouse, the rocky chaos makes a marvellous lookout point.

Le Conquet ⚓

This town occupies a pretty **site**★, and affords a superb view of the Pointe de Kermorvan. This small fishing port is the departure point for the islands of Ouessant and Molène.

The harbour corniche road, the coastal footpaths and especially the Pointe de Kermorvan are pleasant walks offering good views of the port, the Four Channel, the Ouessant archipelago and its many lighthouses in the distance.

Site de la pointe St-Mathieu ★★

This wave-battered headland has been inhabited since ancient times. You will find several interesting buildings here: the former abbey, a lighthouse, a museum, a signal station occupied by the military, a monument to sailors who lost their lives at sea in the form of a woman dressed in mourning, and finally, a cenotaph dedicated to those who died at sea during wartime. A climb to the top of the lighthouse offers a superb aerial view of the whole site.

The **lighthouse** was built in 1835. It stands 37m/120ft tall and has a range of 50km/31mi. Visitors who tackle its 163 steps are rewarded with a superb **panorama**★★. From left to right, you can see the entrance to the sound (Goulet de Brest), the Crozon peninsula, the Pointe du Raz, the Île de Sein, and the Islands of Beniguet, Molène and Ouesssant. Beyond Beniguet, you can sometimes see the Jument lighthouse, 30km/18mi away. *℘02 98 84 41 15. www.vacances-en-iroise.com. Guided tour (20 min) to the top. Jul–Aug: 10am–7.30pm; May–Jun, weekends and public holidays 2pm–6.30pm; rest of the year, every day except Tue 2pm–6.30pm (apart from second fortnight of Sept)*

Closed Nov–Apr 3 € (under 4s free) combined ticket with museum.

The **abbey** is now in ruins. It was built by the Benedictines in the 11C. According to legend, the head of St-Matthew had been brought back from Egypt by local sailors and was kept as a relic here. You can still see the 13C choir, flanked by a square tower, and the nave, with its round and octagonal pillars. The monks had the right to collect driftwood and kept a signal fire burning on the tower, which has now been truncated. The **museum** next to the lighthouse explains the history of the site and its buildings through archives, a film and a model of the abbey. The **cenotaph** occupies a small fort built during the Second Empire. The crypt (*Jun–Sept 10am–6.30pm. Rest of year weekends, public holidays and school holidays; ℘02 98 84 41 15. www.vacances-en-iroise.com.)* contains photographs of sailors who lost their lives at sea during wartime.

The itinerary ends here, but you can reach Brest via the D 85 and the D 789, visiting the Fort de Bertheaume and Ste-Anne-du-Portzic on the way.

ADDRESSES

🛒 SHOPPING

St-Renan Saturday Market – *8am–2.30pm.* Local producers take over the medieval centre to sell regional specialities. Have a pitstop in *La Veuve Pochard*, a hostelry housed in a building dating from 1450.

🏃‍🏊 ACTIVITIES

Diving – **Aber Benoît Plongée** – *quai du Stellac'h, St-Pabu, ℘02 98 89 75 66.* Beginners' courses and underwater tours to see flora and fauna, plus, tours to wrecks of the Amoco Cadiz or the Elektra for advanced divers.

Sailing – **Centre de Voile de l'Aber Wrac'h** – *4 port de l'Aber Wrac'h, 29870 Llandéda. ℘02 98 04 90 64. www.cvl-aberwrach.fr.* Catamarans, cruisers or kayaks for hire.

Île d'Ouessant★★★

An excursion to the Île d'Ouessant by sea takes in the Brest Channel, Pointe de St-Mathieu, Four Channel, the famous Pierres Noires (Black Stones) and Pierres Vertes (Green Stones) reefs, the islands of Béniguet and Molène, and Fromveur Channel. The island itself is curious. On the way to Ouessant the boat usually anchors off and sometimes calls at Molène. There the pastures on the rare patches of earth in this archipelago are so small that, according to a local joke, a Molène cow stands in one field, grazes from another and fertilises a third.

A BIT OF HISTORY

Nature – Ouessant (Ushant in Breton) is famous in marine history for the danger of its waters due to frequent fog, strong currents (the Fromrust to the northwest and the Fromveur to the southeast) and countless reefs.

In winter the wind is the island's master and it hurls the waves against the broken and rocky shores with utmost fury for days on end. The scene is often sinister when the fog descends and the mournful howl of the foghorns mingles with the roar of the storm.

Few tourists know the island in this inhospitable guise, for the summer season brings a calm and quieter atmosphere, similar to that of Brittany's mainland coast. The climate is mild. In January and February, Ouessant has the highest average temperature in France. The colonies of sea birds that nest on the island's cliffs and on the neighboring islets are particularly numerous in the autumn when the migrants from Northern Europe fly in, attracted by the beams of the two lighthouses.

The people and their work – The majority of the island's population is made up of women and men who have retired from the Navy or the merchant navy. Their principal occupations are stock raising and food crops.

Vegetables and potatoes grow in beautifully maintained lots. The grain culti-

▸ **Population:** 857.

Michelin Map: Local map 308 A4 Finistère (29).

Info: Bourg de Lampaul, pl. de lÉglise, 29942 Ouessant. ℰ02 98 48 85 83. www.ot-ouessant.fr.

Location: 20km/12.5mi off the coast of Le Conquet, in the Iroise Sea. The island is 7km/4.3mi long and 4km/2.4mi wide and its highest point is 60m/196ft above sea level.

Kids: The Écomusée.

Timing: Reserve your boat trip and lodging in advance. It's best to explore the coast at high tide.

Don't Miss: The tour of the lighthouses and a walk around the coast.

ARRIVAL AND DEPARTURE

BY AIR – Finist'air – ℰ02 98 84 64 87. www.finistair.fr. Two flights per day (15min) between Ouessant and Brest airport. One-way ticket 65€ (children, 36€).

BY BOAT – Compagnie Penn Ar Bed – ℰ02 98 80 80 80. www.pennarbed.fr. In summer, three trips daily from Brest, four from Le Conquet (about 1hr). Round trip 30.20€. Bikes allowed on board. Reservations required 48 hours in advance.

vated on larger parcels of land is used as feed for poultry and also as a supplementary fodder crop for the cattle's diet.

The sheep – The livestock (sheep, dairy cows, horses) consists mainly of sheep with brown wool that graze on meagre tufts of salt grass; the result is meat with a splendid flavour, comparable to the famous *prés salés* of Mont-St-Michel Bay. They live in the open and take shelter from northwesterly or southwesterly gales behind low dry-stone walls built in a star formation, or in wood shelters.

Though from early February (a great cattle fair is held on the first Wednesday in February) before lambing to late September they are tethered in twos to a stake; they wander freely the rest of the year, their owner's mark being nicked on their ears.

The cultivation of algae and the raising of mussels has become a lucrative industry.

A rich natural heritage – Since 1988, Ouessant has been classified by UNESCO. The island has conserved a vast zone favorable for the observation of island flora and migratory birds. Of the 500 plants registered, some are protected such as the isoete fern and maritime centaurea. Ouessant welcomes more than 400 species of birds each year, including the rare chough, Siberian birds such as the pipit, seagulls and cormorants.

EXCURSIONS
Molène
Just noticeable as you cross from Ouessant, this little island (0.8km x 1.2km/874yds x 1,300yds), owes its reputation to the skill and courage of its sailors. It's easy to explore the island on foot but the beaches are rocky and it's dangerous to swim in the sea because of the currents. The island was the site of the shipwreck of the *Drummond Castle* in 1896.

Lampaul
This is the island's capital. Note the old houses; the shutters are painted in green or blue, the island's traditional colours. Its church (1860) has a bell that was presented by the British monarchy to thank the islanders for their help during the shipwreck of the *Drummond Castle* in 1896. The tiny port, west facing, is picturesque but can only be used at high tide and in calm seas, while the beach of Le Corz nearby extends south.

DRIVING TOUR

The roads from Lampaul lead to the best sites but visitors on foot will find many paths and tracks crisscrossing the island, fine cliffs, pretty little creeks, flora and marine fauna – such as herring gulls, cormorants, oyster catchers, puffins and terns.

La Côte Sauvage★★★

Leave Lampaul W by an uphill road; after 500m/546yds, bear right.

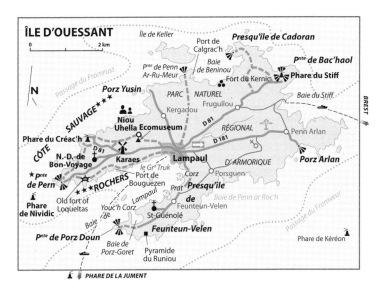

👥 Écomusée de l'île d'Ouessant

🕐 *Open Jun–Aug Tue–Sun 11am–6pm; rest of the year 11am–5pm.* 🎫*3.50€ (children 8–14, 2.20€).* ☎*02 98 48 86 37.*
At the hamlet of **Niou Uhella**, two traditional houses have been restored and rearranged by the *Parc Naturel Régional d'Armorique*. Visitors will see in one of them furniture typical of the island built of wood from wrecked vessels, painted in blue, a symbol of the Virgin's protection, and in the second a display of farm and domestic implements and costumes that depicts aspects of life on Ouessant.

▷ *Carry on towards the coast.*

Moulin de Karaes

This is the island's last mill (restored) with its round stone base. It was used to mill barley from which bread was still made at the beginning of the 20C.

Phare de Créac'h

This lighthouse, with that at Land's End, marks the entrance to the English Channel; it has two tiers of revolving beams. The light is cast by four lamps giving a total 20 million candlepower and an average range of more than 60km.
In the old machine room, there is a small **Centre d'Interprétation des Phares et Balises** (🕐*open Apr–Sept and school holidays, daily 10.30am–6.30pm; rest of the year, Tue–Sun 1.30pm–5.30pm;* 🎫*4.10€;* ☎*02 98 48 80 70*), which retraces the history of lighthouses from Antiquity to the present day. It shows how the original lighthouse was a tower, with, at its summit, a light fuelled by burning coal, wood or oil. The exhibit uses turbines, lens, lamps, beams and recounts the life of the lighthouse keeper.
Not far from here is a permanent centre for the study of migratory birds in France: the **Centre dÉtude du Milieu d'Ouessant** (🔍*guided tours 1hr 30 to 2hr;* 🎫*3.80€;* ☎*02 98 48 82 65*). In July and August they offer thematic nature visits: seabirds, flora and fauna of the north and coasts, migratory birds, algae and animals on the seashore.

▷ *Go around the lighthouse to the right to view the coast.*

The extraordinarily jagged **rocks**★★★ *(rochers)* are very impressive as they are pounded by the sea. A gangway in front of the lighthouse gives access to Pointe du Créac'h where the foghorn stands. Cargo boats and oil tankers can be seen on the horizon; some 300 ships pass daily in the area that is patrolled day and night by the French Navy.

▷ *Turn back and bear right towards Pointe de Pern.*

Chapelle Notre-Dame-de-Bon-Voyage

Also known as the Chapelle St-Gildas, after the English saint who came here in the 5C, this chapel was built at the end of the 19C. The people of Ouessant come to the chapel every year for the island's *pardon* on the first or second Sunday in September.

Pointe de Pern★

This, the western-most point of the island, extends into the sea in a series of rocks and reefs lashed by the rollers. In the distance is the unmanned Nividic Lighthouse (*Phare de Nividic*).

▷ *Leave Lampaul N by a road running past the island's electricity plant.*

Crique de Porz Yusin

The road passes several hamlets with white houses adorned with brightly coloured shutters and surrounded by small gardens, on the way to Porz Yusin, one of the few sheltered spots on the north coast.

▷ *At Lampaul, take the road skirting the cemetery.*

Presqu'île de Feunteun Velen

Pass near the small port of Lampaul, where some boats from Brest drop anchor. The jetty gives shelter to the fishing boats.

The road goes round the deep Lampaul Bay bounded by the Corz and Le Prat Beaches, with the Le Grand Truk and Youc'h Corz rocks in the centre, then descends gently towards the Pointe de Porz Doun. Note on the left the white pyramid of Le Runiou (*Pyramide du Runiou*), a landmark for shipping; on the right is the great cove of Porz Coret.

Pointe de Porz Doun
The cliff-lined point at the southern tip of the island affords a fine **view** over Lampaul, the Pointe de Pern and Jument Lighthouse (built from 1904–1912; unmanned) which reaches a height of 42m and houses a foghorn.

Leave Lampaul by the road running along the north side of the church.

Phare du Stiff
The road rises gently to the island's highest point (alt 60m/197ft), the **Pointe de Bac'haol.** The lighthouse, built by the military architect Vauban in 1695, comprises two adjoining towers, one containing a spiral staircase *(126 steps)* and the other three small superposed rooms. The light has a range of 50km/31mi thanks to a 1,000W lamp giving a total 600,000 candlepower. From the top a vast **panorama**★★ unfolds over the islands and the mainland from Vierge Lighthouse to the Pointe du Raz.

Paths lead to the tip of the **Presqu'île de Cadoran** (Cadoran Peninsula) from which may be enjoyed a pretty view of Beninou Bay, sometimes frequented by a seal colony, and Keller Island, favoured by nesting birds.

Leave Lampaul by the road skirting the cemetery, then turn left.

Crique de Porz Arlan
The road runs across the plateau, leaving on the right the 1863 Chapelle Notre-Dame-d'Espérance and on the left the airfield, before bearing right towards picturesque Porz Arlan.

In this creek nestle a tiny sandy beach and a small port sheltered by a jetty. From this charming site the beautiful **view** extends over the rocky coastline, Fromveur and Kéréon Lighthouse, and the Île de Bannec.

ADDRESSES

STAY

Le Keo – *Lampaul 29 242 Ouessant. 06 17 88 59 57. www.lekeo.com. Closed Jan & Feb. 5 rooms. 5€. Crêperie.* This large house has a tea-room, *crêperie* and interiors shop selling local designs.

Hôtel Roc'h-Ar-Mor – *Lampaul. 02 98 48 80 19. Closed 3 Jan–10 Feb and 15 Nov–15 Dec. 15 rooms. 10€. Restaurant.* On the edge of the village, opposite the bay, this large renovated building offers comfort and quality. Veranda and bright, modern rooms with sea views.

Ti Jan Ar C'hafé – *Kernigou. 02 98 48 82 64. 8 rooms. 10€. Closed 4 Jan–15 Mar, 12 Nov–22 Dec.* Tasteful and well laid-out rooms define this charming hotel. Take a break in one of the deckchairs on the veranda. Call ahead to announce your arrival.

EAT

Crêperie Ti Ar Dreuz – *Lampaul. 02 98 48 83 01. Open Apr –Sept and school holidays. Closed Sun eve and Mon exc Jul–Aug.* Delicious crêpes in an old house with a pretty garden.

Ty Korn – *Place de l'Église, Lampaul. 02 98 48 87 33. Closed 3rd week Jan and 2nd week Nov.* Savour local seafood, such as fresh bass, while seated with a view of an artist's rendition of the shore of Ouessant. Don't miss an opportunity to sample the fine variety of Breton beers.

Roscoff★

Roscoff is a much-frequented seaside resort and a popular destination for the seawater therapy treatment of thalassotherapy. It is also a fishing port for lobster and spiny lobster, has a marina, vegetable market and distribution centre. A pier to the east of Pointe de Bloscon closes off the deep-water harbour from which car ferries sail to and from Plymouth and Cork. The University of Paris and the Centre National de la Recherche Scientifique (CNRS) have a laboratory for oceanographic and biological research here.

▶ **Population:** 3,705.

Michelin Map: Local map 308 H2 – Finistère (29).

Info: Chapelle Ste Anne, 46 rue Gambetta, 29211 Roscoff. ✆02 98 61 12 13. www.roscoff-tourisme.com.

Location: Roscoff is situated 25km/15.5mi N of the bay of Morlaix.

Timing: Sail to the Île-de-Batz in the afternoon so that you can visit the Georges-Delaselle garden.

Don't Miss: The bell tower of Croaz-Batz church; the Jardin Exotique.

SIGHTS

Église Notre-Dame-de-Croaz-Batz★

This Gothic church was completed in 1545, funded by the privateers and merchants of the town. The church has a remarkable Renaissance **belfry**★ with lantern turrets, one of the finest examples of its type in Brittany. Inside, the **altarpiece** of the 17C high altar has six wreathed columns and is richly decorated with statues of the Evangelists and cherubs. In the church close are two chapel-ossuaries: that in the south-west corner dates from the 16C and has been dedicated to St-Brigitte; that in the northwest corner (early 17C) originally

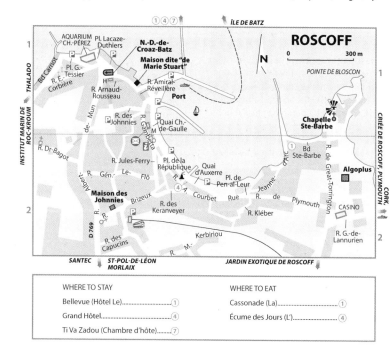

WHERE TO STAY		WHERE TO EAT	
Bellevue (Hôtel Le)	①	Cassonade (La)	①
Grand Hôtel	④	Écume des Jours (L')	④
Ti Va Zadou (Chambre d'hôte)	⑦		

Yucca, Opuntia and Aeonium garden, Jardin Exotique de Roscoff

Jardin Exotique de Roscoff

had no door at all, as it was used purely to store bones.

Chapelle Ste-Barbe

It is best to visit this chapel at high tide. Go round the fishing port and leave the car in the car park on the left. Viewing platform.

In the centre of a pretty little garden sits the tiny chapel dedicated to St-Barbara. Its white walls still serve as a landing mark to mariners. There is a beautiful view of the town, the port, the Île de Batz, Pointe de Primel and the deep-water harbour at Bloscon, which is the departure point for car ferries to Britain and Ireland.

Jardin Exotique de Roscoff★

Open Jul–Aug, 10am–7pm; April–Jun and Sept–Oct, 10.30am–12.30pm, 2pm –6pm; Nov–Mar, 2pm–5pm. 5€ (under 12s, no charge). 02 98 61 29 19. www.jardinexotiqueroscoff.com.

This extraordinary garden is wrapped around the Rocher de Roch-Hievec (or Rocher de Maison Rouge). Over 1 000 subtropical plant species thrive here, producing both blossom and fruit.

Maison des Johnnies et de l'Oignon Rosé

4 rue Brizeux. Guided tours (1hr) 19 Jun–17 Sept Mon–Fri 11am, 3pm, 5pm; Sun 3pm, 5pm. 4€ (under 10s, no charge). 02 98 61 25 48.

The Johnnies were Roscovites who spent 5–9 months in Britain each year selling their onions. First on foot, then on bikes, wearing strings of onions, they peddled their wares door to door. An exhibition traces their history.

EXCURSION
Île-de-Batz

The island of Batz (pronounced Ba), 4km/2.5m long and 1km/0.6m wide, is separated from the mainland by a narrow channel, notorious for its treacherous currents.

Largely treeless, the island has sandy beaches and a mild climate particularly suitable for market gardening. On Batz the men are either sailors or farmers and the women help in the market gardens or gather seaweed (www.iledebatz.com) An exotic 19C garden (*SE tip of the island; open 1 Apr–30 Jun & 1 Sep–1 Nov Tue –Sun 2pm–6pm; 1 Jul–31 Aug Mon–Sun 1pm–6.30pm; 4.60€; guided tours (1hr) Sun 3pm (7€), (2hr) Tue Jul & Aug (8€) 02 98 61 75 65; www.jardin-geogesdelasalle.fr) has a large collection of plants from around the world, including a renowned selection of palms.

Lighthouse

On the island's west side. 210 steps.

The 44m/144ft tall lighthouse stands on the island's highest point (23m/75ft).

ADDRESSES

🏠 STAY

🛏️🛏️ **Hôtel Le Bellevue** – Bd Ste-Barbe, Roscoff. ℰ 02 98 61 23 38. www.hotel-bellevue-roscoff.fr. Open mid Mar–mid Nov and 25 Dec–3 Jan. 18 rooms. 🍽️ 8 €. Most rooms very small and well kept. Some look on to a patio with flowers.

🛏️🛏️ **Grand Hôtel** – 29 253 Île-de-Batz. ℰ 02 98 61 78 06. Closed Dec–Jan. 35 rooms. 🍽️ 6 €. Seafood and family recipes in a pleasant setting and the view from the terrace is a delight. The rooms are simple but the view and quiet the hotel offers are worth the trip.

🛏️🛏️ **Chambre d'hôte Ti Va Zadou** – 29253 Île-de-Batz. ℰ02 98 61 76 91. Closed 15 Nov–1 Feb. Reservations advised. 🍽️ 4 rooms. A stone house with blue shutters

whose sign reads "the house of my fathers". The nicely decorated rooms have a fine view of the port.

🍴 EAT

🛏️🛏️ **L'Écume des Jours** – quai d'Auxerre, Roscoff. ℰ02 98 61 22 83. www.ecume-roscoff.fr. Closed 15 Dec–Feb, Tue (except Jul–Aug) and Wed. Lovely restaurant in an old Breton house near the light-house. Value-for-money menus and a warm atmoshpere.

🛏️ **La Cassonade** – 29253 Île-de-Batz. ℰ02 98 61 75 25. Closed Jan–Mar except school holidays and Tue in Jun. Reservations advised. Cassonade is the sweet speciality, with an apple base, of this welcoming little crêperie near the landing stage. The other speciality is baked potatoes with charcuterie and salad.

Côte des Bruyères★

This short section of the Channel coast, which is part of the Golden Belt and is also known as The Heather Coast, should be seen by all tourists who visit northern Brittany. The Lieu de Grève, a long, majestic stretch of sand, is backed by steep headlands skirted from a distance by the Armorican coast road.

🛢️ **Michelin Map:** 308 I/K 2/3– Finistère (29) and Côtes-d'Armor (22).

ℹ️ **Info:** place du Port, 29241 Locquirec. ℰ02 98 67 40 83. www.tourisme.morlaix.fr/.

📍 **Location:** This coastline stretches from Plestin-les-Grèves, in the bay of Lannion, to the Pointe de Diben, near the bay of Morlaix.

🕐 **Timing:** Allow a day to explore coast and churches.

🚗 DRIVING TOUR

From St-Michel-en-Grève to Pointe de Diben

38km/23.5mi– about 4hr.

St-Michel-en-Grève is a small seaside resort whose church is nicely situated near the sea.

📍 Join the coast road (D 786), and head W, with the sea on your right.

Lieue-de-Grève★

This magnificent beach, 4km/2.5mi long, lies in the curve of a bay which goes out

2km/1.2mi at low tide. Trout streams run into the sea through small green valleys. The road, which is very picturesque, follows the wooded coast and skirts the rocky mass of the Grand Rocher.

🧗 Climbing the Grand Rocher

45min on foot there and back.

A road to the left, just before the Grand Rocher, leads to a car park. From there, a path runs to the 80m/ 87yd-high belvedere which offers a fine **view**★ of the Lieu de Grève. At high tide especially, and on windy days, the sight

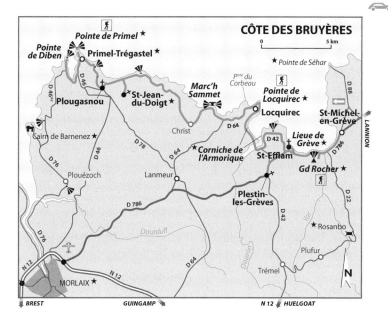

CÔTE DES BRUYÈRES

of the endless foaming waves breaking on the beach and dashing against the seawall gives an idea of the power of the sea.

Continue along the coast road.

St-Efflam

Next to the Chapelle St-Efflam, half-hidden by lush vegetation, there is a fountain, which is surmounted by a massive dome. Efflam, a hermit who came from Ireland, landed with seven companions in AD 470 on the beach of the same name.

Take the D 786 inland.

Plestin-les-Grèves

It was here that Efflam lived, founded a monastery and died in AD 512. The 16C **church**, which burnt down in 1944, has been restored; it contains the tomb of St-Efflam adorned with his recumbent figure (1576). In the south aisle, to the left of the altar, a statue shows him vanquishing a dragon, the symbol of paganism. Note the modern stained-glass windows.

Return to the coast road.

Corniche de l'Armorique★

Between St-Efflam and Locquirec, the road follows the indented coast. After *Pointe de Plestin* there is a fine view of the cove of Locquirec and its headland at high tide. Before reaching the village, you can see the *Côte de Granit Rose* in the distance, to the right.

Locquirec⌂

Built on a rocky peninsula, Locquirec is a small fishing port and marina as well as a seaside resort. There is a charming church with a Renaissance belfry.

Pointe de Locquirec

30min on foot there and back.
A walk starting near the church's east end offers fine views of Lannion Bay and the coastline.

Beyond the mill, Moulin de la Rive, take the coast road along the cliff.

Table d'Orientation de Marc'h Sammet

Built on a rocky headland, the viewing table commands splendid **views**★: to the east, the beaches of *Moulin de la Rive* and the *Sables Blancs*; to the north, the Île de Losquet; to the west, the Poul

Rodou Beach (access 800m/875yds below).

Go to the village of Christ and turn right. Follow the signposts to the scenic road (route touristique).

St-Jean-du-Doigt★

This picturesque village owes its name to a relic kept in the church since the 15C. It celebrates its *pardon*, which is attended in particular by those suffering from opthalmological problems, on the last Sunday in June.

The parish close has a 16C triumphal gateway and, on the left, a pretty Renaissance **fountain**★ dominated by God the Father blessing the baptism of His Son, as performed by John the Baptist.

Church★

St-John the Baptist's finger, which was brought to the Chapelle St-Mériadoc c. 1420, worked miracles. The construction of a great church was begun in 1440, but building went slowly and it was only finished in 1513 thanks to the generosity of Anne de Bretagne. Built in a Flamboyant style, the church has a flat east end. The bell-tower has lost its spire. At the base, abutting the buttresses, are two small ossuaries; one Gothic, one Renaissance.

The **treasury**★ contains several reliquaries, one of which holds the first joint of the finger of St-John the Baptist. There is also a **processional cross**★. The finest piece is a silver-gilt Renaissance **chalice**★★.

Plougasnou

At the centre of this small town, the church, which is mostly 16C, has a Renaissance porch opening on the square.

Take the road past the Tourist Office and at the third crossroads turn right.

Primel-Trégastel★

The beach of fine sand lies in a good setting near rocks comparable with those of Ploumanach and Trégastel.

☒ Pointe de Primel★

30min on foot there and back.

The headland is a jumble of pink rocks. From the central spur, there is a fine **panorama** extending from the Baie de St-Pol-de-Léon to the Trébeurden coast. Out at sea are the Île de Batz lighthouse and the Sept-Îles. The tip of the headland is separated from the rest of the peninsula by a fissure.

After 1km, turn right. The road passes near the fish ponds. At Le Diben, turn right in the direction of Les Vivier-le-Port; 100m/110yds further on, take the road opposite the port which leads to a dyke. Just before this, bear left onto a path leading to the Point de Diben.

Pointe de Diben

From here there is a fine view over the bay and of the Point de Primel.

EXCURSIONS

Château de Rosanbo

8.5km/5.2mi S of St-Michel-en-Grève via D 786 and D 22. *Open Jul–Aug, 11am–6.30pm; Apr–Jun and Sept, 2pm–5.30pm; Oct, Sun 2pm–5pm.* *Guided tours (45min) available.* *10€.* *02 96 35 18 77.*

The château stands on the foundations of an old 14C castle, overlooking the River Bô, hence its Breton name, meaning rock *(ros)* on the *(an)* Bô.

The different periods of construction can be seen as you enter the courtyard: the 15C manor house to the west, enlarged in the 17C (with mansard roofs) and 18C, and finally restored in the 19C.

Archive documents have enabled reconstruction of the most authentic rooms, namely the dining room and the 18C drawing room. The **library** contains over 8,000 volumes dating mainly from the 17C. The château is bordered by a **French-style garden**: the work of Achille Duchêne, the famous 19C landscape architect.

St-Pol-de-Léon★

This little town, which St-Paul, known as the Aurelian, made the first bishopric in Lower Brittany, offers the tourist two of the finest buildings in Brittany: the former cathedral and the Kreisker belfry. From January to September, during the cauliflower, artichoke, onion and potato season, St-Pol is extremely busy. Numerous lorries, vans and tractors with trailers arrive, bringing these famous Breton products to the market.

> **Population:** 7,068.
> **Michelin Map:** Local map 308 H2 – Finistère (29).
> **Info:** place de l'Évêché, 29250 St-Pol-de-Léon. ℰ02 98 69 05 69. www.saintpoldeleon.fr.
> **Location:** 20km/12.5mi from Morlaix on the D 58.
> **Kids:** Ferme-musée de Léon.
> **Timing:** A day should suffice for the town and environs.
> **Don't Miss:** The cathedral and Kreisker chapel.

WALKING TOUR

Chapelle du Kreisker★

Open daily Jul–Aug 10.30am– 12.30pm, 2pm–6pm, rest of year 10am –6pm. ℰ02 98 69 01 15.
This 14C–15C chapel used to be where the town council met; it is now the college chapel. What makes it famous is its magnificent **belfry**★★, 77m/250ft high. It was inspired by the spire of St-Peter's at Caen (destroyed during WWII – *see the Michelin Green Guide Normandy*) but the Breton building in granite surpasses the original. The Kreisker belfry has served as a model for many Breton towers.
The upper part of the spire is Norman in style, while the lower part with the squaring of its mullions and railing of the overhanging balcony recalls the English Perpendicular style.

> *Enter through the north porch.*

The church is roofed with wooden barrel vaulting. The only stone vault joins the four huge uprights which support the belfry at the transept crossing. In the south aisle is a vast 17C carved wood altarpiece (from the Chapelle des Minimes, no longer standing) depicting the Visitation.
You may climb the tower *(169 steps)*. From the platform you will get a superb circular **view**★★ of the town, Batz, the coast as far as the Corniche Bretonne and the Monts d'Arrée inland.

Rue Général-Leclerc

Note the slate-faced wooden façade at number 9; a Renaissance house with a corbelled turret at number 12; a mansion with a fine porch and ornate dormer windows (1680) at number 30.

> *Fllow Rue Général-Leclerc round to the cathedral.*

Ancienne Cathédrale★

Built on the 12C foundations, the former cathedral was erected in the 13C and 14C (nave, aisles, façade and towers) and in the 15C and 16C the side chapels, chancel, apse and remodelling of the transept.
The architects were inspired by the cathedral at Coutances and used Norman limestone to build the nave; the traditional granite was used for the façade, transept and chancel. The Breton influence can be found in the bell-turrets on the transept crossing and also in the porches.
The **façade** is dominated by two towers each 50m high. The terrace which surmounts the porch was used by the bishop to bless the people; the small door under the right tower was reserved for lepers. From a small public garden, on the north side between the church

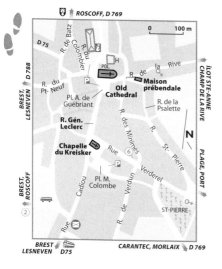

ST-POL-DE-LÉON

WHERE TO STAY

Coz-Milin Mme Moysan
(Chambre d'hôte).............................②

WHERE TO EAT

Pomme d'Api (Auberge La)..............⑥

and the former bishop's palace (now the town hall), is a view of the north transept wall with Romanesque characteristics. The **interior** has several remarkable features, including a Roman sarcophagus which serves as a stoup. Starting the tour from the right, note a Renaissance stained-glass window (1560) and in the transept the 15C rose window. The carved **stalls**★ of the chancel date from the 16C.

In wall niches against the chancel to the right of the ambulatory, 34 wooden reliquaries contain skulls.

▷ *Walk away from the eastern end of the cathedral across the small square.*

Maison Prébendale

This was the 16C residence of the canons of Léon. The façade is emblazoned. From rue de la rive, the **Champ de la Rive** makes for a pleasant shaded walk. Take the surfaced path on the right to reach the top of a hillock crowned by a modern calvary. From the viewing table there is a fine view of Morlaix Bay. As the road descends, there is a **view**★ over Morlaix Bay and its islands. Rue de l'Abbé-Tanguy and a dyke lead to **Île-Ste-Anne** and the Groux pleasure boat harbour. From the rock, which forms a remarkable viewpoint, the view extends from Roscoff as far as Pointe de Primel.

EXCURSIONS
Château de Kérouzéré★

▷ *8km/5mi to the W. Leave St-Pol-de-Léon via D 788 towards Lesneven, then the road to the right to Plouescat. At Sibiril, turn right towards Moguériec and after 500m/546yds left towards the castle.* ⌂★ *Guided tours (1hr) mid-Jul–Aug, 2.30pm, 4pm, 5.30pm; 1–14 Jul and 1–14 Sept, Wed and Sun at 5pm; mid-May–Jun and Oct, Wed at 5pm.* ⊕*4€.* ℘*02 98 29 96 05.*

This granite feudal castle is an interesting specimen of early 15C military architecture. Three of the massive machicolated corner towers remain standing, the fourth having been demolished in 1590 after a siege. A central stone staircase gives access to the three floors which were used by soldiers and include large bare rooms with deep window recesses and stone seats, a wall walk and a guard tower. The castle also retains pepper-pot roofs, oratory frescoes, tapestries and fine Breton furniture, all from the 17C.

Berven

▷ *13km/8mi SW on the D 788.*

The triumphal arch through which you enter the parish close is a fine specimen of Renaissance art with pilasters and three semicircular arches .

The 16C **church**★ has a façade surmounted by a square tower crowned with a dome with small lanterns and ornamented by balustrades; it was the first of its kind in Brittany (1573) and served as a model for many others.

A wooden rood screen stands before the fine chancel **enclosure**★, ornamented with small fluted columns of granite on the front, and wood at the sides.

Ferme-musée du Léon

200m/220yds after leaving Berven on D 788 towards Lesneven, take the little road towards Quéran. Open May–Sept, daily 10am–noon, 2pm–7pm, Mon 2pm–7pm; rest of the year Sat, Sun and public holidays 10.30am–noon, 2pm–7pm. 4.50€ (children 2€). 02 98 29 53 07.

The buildings of an old family farmhouse, in which the original furniture has been kept on display, house this small museum of agricultural tools and equipment and horsedrawn carts, which evokes the evolution over the course of a century of country life in Léon.

Château de Kerjean★

6km/3.7mi SW of Berven. Open Jul –Aug, daily 10am–7pm; Apr–May daily exc Tue 2–6pm; Jun and Sept, daily exc Tue 1–6pm; Oct, daily exc Tue 2pm–5pm; Nov–Mar, Wed and Sun 2pm–5pm. Closed Jan. 5€. 02 98 69 93 69. www.cheminsdupatrimoineen finistere.com

Half-fortress, half-Renaissance mansion, the château stands in a huge park, guarded by a moat and ramparts. Towards the mid 16C Louis Barbier inherited a fortune from his uncle, a rich abbot of St-Mathieu, and decided to build a castle which would be the finest residence in Léon. In 1710 part of the building burned down, later the castle was ransacked. The property of the State since 1911, it has since been restored except for the right wing. Enter the main courtyard via the old drawbridge.

A main building with two wings and a large portico enclose the main courtyard, which is adorned with a fine Corinthian-columned Renaissance **well**. The dwelling house contains a museum of Breton art with 17C and 18C **furnish-**

ings: box beds, chests and grain chests. The kitchen, a vast room with a 6m/20ft-high ceiling, has two massive chimneys, one of which was used as the bread oven, and a large copperware collection. On the courtyard's other side is the chapel, decorated inside with a wooden vault in the shape of a ship's keel, carved beams and purlins. The coach house wing once housed the stores, a forge and the servants' quarters, and has been restored. A door leads to an alley supported on a gallery with eight arches, which give a good overall view of the main courtyard and the buildings around it.

The **park** includes **French-style gardens** and a charming Renaissance **fountain**, consisting of a niche surrounded by four colonnettes, set into a little stone wall. The noise of the spring, mingled with the warbling of the birds, makes a pleasant background in which to meditate. On leaving, to the left of the central avenue, note the dovecote, a stone tower 9m/30ft in diameter.

Every year, temporary exhibitions devoted to contemporary art in spring, and the history of Brittany in summer are held. During July and August, evening theatre performances are on offer.

ADDRESSES

STAY

Chambre d'hôte Coz-Milin – *29233 Cléder. 10km/6mi W on the D 10. 02 98 69 42 16. www.gites-finistere. com/gites/cozmilin/indexgb.php. 2 rooms.* This attractive stone house is surrounded by a pretty flower-filled garden. Its rooms mix traditional with contemporary. There is also a 3-bedroom cottage ( ).

EAT

Auberge La Pomme d'Api – *49 rue Verderel. 02 98 69 04 36. yannick. lebeaudour@free.fr. Closed 12–30 Nov Sun eve, Tue lunch and Mon.* Delicious food served next to the old fireplace in a 16C stone house.

Baie de Morlaix★

The first thing the tourist will notice approaching Morlaix is its colossal viaduct. This structure bestrides the deep valley in which lies the estuary of the Dossen, commonly called the River Morlaix. The town is busy but the port, though it is used mostly by yachts, has only limited commercial activity (sand, wood, fertilisers).

OLD MORLAIX

Viaduc★

From place des Otages there is a good view of the viaduct, an imposing two-storeyed structure, 58m/190ft high and 285m/935ft long.

Église St-Mélaine

⊙*Open 10am–6pm.* ✆*02 98 88 05 65.* The present church, which dates from 1489, is in the Flamboyant Gothic style with an interesting porch to the south.

Viaduct and Église St-Mélaine
G. Targat/MICHELIN

Rue Ange-de-Guevrnisac

This street is lined with fine corbelled and half-timbered houses: the Hôtel du Relais de France at number 13, and the houses at numbers 9, 6 and 5 are of interest. Take a look in the picturesque alleyways, Venelle du Créou and Venelle au Son.

- ⚲ **Michelin Map:** Local map 308 H2- Finistère (29) – Local map see Les Enclos Paroissiuax p262.
- **Info:** Place des Otages, 29600 Morlaix. ✆02 98 62 14 94. www.tourisme. morlaix.fr.
- **Location:** Morlaix is crossed by the N 12 in the north, which comes from Guingamp (57km/35mi E) and goes to Brest (58km/36mi SW). The left bank of the bay is served by the D 769, which offers magnificent views.
- **Kids:** The Musée du Loup (Wolf Museum).
- **Timing:** Allow a day for a tour of the bay.
- **Don't Miss:** Morlaix's old town, the view from Pen-al-Lann.

Grand'Rue★

Here you will see picturesque 15C houses adorned with statues of saints and gro-tesques, and low-fronted shops with wide windows, especially at numbers 8 and 10. Originally these old houses, called **skylight houses**, comprised a large central area with skylights onto which opened the other rooms, linked by a spiral staircase supported by a lovely carved newel post. Queen Anne's House (⚲*see below*) has a fine collection and many illustrations of newel posts.

Maison de la Reine Anne

⊙*Open Jul–Aug, Mon–Sat 11am–6pm; May–Jun, Mon–Sat 11am–6.30pm (Thur 1.30pm–6pm; Sept, Mon–Sat 11am–6pm.* ⟵*Guided tours (20min).* ⊙*Closed public holidays.* ⟵*1.60€.* ✆*02 98 88 23 26. www.mda-morlaix.com.*
This 16C corbelled mansion, three sto-reys high, has a façade adorned with statues of saints and grotesques. With its courtyard lit by a skylight, the interior is a perfect example of the skylight house.

In one of the courtyard's corners, there is a magnificent spiral staircase, 11m high, carved from one piece of wood. The newel post is adorned with saints carved in the round: St-Roch, St-Nicholas, St-Christopher and St-Michael. Between the first and second floors, note the fine sculpture of an acrobat with his barrel. There is a monumental stone chimney piece opposite the staircase.

Musée de Morlaix – Couvent des Jacobins★

○Open Jul–Aug, daily 10am–12.30pm, 2.30pm–6.30pm; Apr–May and Sept, Wed–Mon 10am–noon, 2pm–6pm, Sun 2pm–6pm; Oct–Mar and Jun, Mon, Wed, Thu, Fri, Sat 10am–noon, 2pm–5pm. ⬤4.€. ⚙02 98 88 68 88. www.musee.ville.morlaix.fr.

The museum is housed in the former church of the Jacobins, which has a fine early 15C **rose window**★ at the east end. The exhibits include the finds from archaeological digs in the region, mementoes of Morlaix's famous citizens and of Old Morlaix with its skylight houses: 16C carved newel posts. Also on display are a large collection of 13C–17C religious statues, typical 17C furniture of the Léon region (chests, tester beds), household objects, farming and craft implements, and a collection of **modern paintings**★. On display is an old cannon from the privateer's ship *Alcida*, which sank at the mouth of the River Morlaix in 1747 (found in 1879).

Église St-Mathieu

The church was rebuilt in 1824 but the tower is 16C. Inside, it has a basilical plan and Doric columns supporting a pointed barrel vault. To the left of the high altar is an unusual wood statue of the **Virgin**★ (c. 14C) which opens. When closed it represents the Virgin suckling the Infant Jesus; open, it contains a group of the Holy Trinity.

EXCURSIONS
Plougonven★

○ 12km/7.5mi SE on D 9 towards Callac. This village, nestling at the foot of the Arrée Mountains, has an interesting parish close. The **calvary**★★ was built in 1554; the cross in two tiers, carries, above, the statues of the Virgin and St-John, and, below, two guards; the thieves' crosses stand on either side. At the foot of the main cross there is a Descent from the Cross. On the platform and around the base are scenes depicting various episodes in the life of Christ: the Temptation in the Desert, His Arrest etc. The charnel house presents a trefoil arcade and a basket-handle arched doorway. The **church**, built in 1523 and badly damaged by fire in the early 20C, is dominated by a graceful belfry with a balcony, a turreted staircase and striking gargoyles.

Le Cloître-St-Thégonnec

○ 13km/8mi S via Plourin-lès-Morlaix then along D 111.

≗≗ Musée du Loup

1 rue du Calvaire. ○Open Jul–Aug, 2pm–6pm; mid-Feb–Jun and Sept–mid-Dec, Sun 2pm–6pm. ⬤3.50€ (children over 7 yrs, 2.20€). ⚙02 98 79 73 45. www.museeduloup.fr.

This village's former school houses the Musée du Loup (Wolf Museum), which illustrates the lifestyle of wolves and the long struggle faced by the region's inhabitants at the turn of the 20C as they sought to chase this mythical beast from their presence. In 1885, an inhabitant of Le Cloître-St-Thégonnec was the last person to receive a bounty for killing a wolf in the Arrée hills.

Réserve des Landes de Cragou

⬤Walking tours leave from the car park across from the wolf museum. ○Open Jul–Aug, Mon and Fri 3pm (return 5pm). ⬤4€. ⬤Bring appropriate shoes and clothes. ⚙02 98 79 71 98. www.bretagne-vivante.asso.fr.

Buzzards are king in this nature reserve that is home to many bird species. The flora includes rare orchids and primitive ferns.

Guerlesquin

○ 26km/16mi E of Morlaix on the N 12. At Plouégat-Moysan, take the D 42.

This characterful little town is one of the entrances for the Parc Régional d'Armorique. Long and narrow, commercial activities have long been centred around the main square. The town is still known for its markets, including a cattle market on Monday mornings. Not to be missed is St-Jean chapel (17C), a remnant of the Dames Paulines convent; St-Ténéran church with its 16C belltower; the 17C prison built in Renaissance style; the 19C granite market *halles* and the many old granite houses around place du Martray, some of which date from the 16C, such as the.

🚗 DRIVING TOURS

1 FROM MORLAIX TO TÉRÉNEZ★

19km/11.8mi round tour NE of Morlaix.

◘ *Leave Morlaix on the D 786 but stick to the minor road beside the river when the D 786 bears right.*

The cliff road runs along the River Morlaix and gives views of the sand dredging port, the marina and the lock, the charming setting of the town, river and viaduct. After the bridge, it reaches the small oyster port of **Le Dourduff** where fish-merchants' boats are moored. Further on, the pleasant road goes through the picturesque Dourduff Valley.
The coast road offers glimpses of Morlaix estuary, the Château du Tareau and the peninsula topped by the Cairn de Bernenez.

The Maison à Lanterne

Unique to Morlaix, the 15C-16C "lantern houses" were built by the nobles who made their fortunes in the textile industry. They are constructed around a large, central space and boast at least three storeys. The interior reflected the wealth of its owner: a large, fireplace, a carved, oak staircase and galleries on each floor.

Grand Cairn de Barnenez

◷ *Open May–Aug, 10am–6.30pm; Sept–Apr, Tue–Sun 10am–12.30pm, 2pm–5.30pm; (last entry 45min before closing).* ◷ *Closed 1 Jan, 1 May, 1 and 11 Nov, 25 Dec.* ◈5€. ✆02 98 67 24 73. *www.monum.fr.*

This imposing tumulus on the Kernéléhen peninsula overlooks the bay of Térénenez and the estuary of the River Morlaix. Eleven funerary chambers were discovered under stone slabs between 1955 and 1968. The south-facing entrances are all preceded by a passage varying in length from 8m to 12m (26 to 39ft). The colour of the stones has revealed two distinct construction periods. The first cairn (46 000 BC) is built of dolerite, a green stone found in the area. The second cairn, located nearer the slope, is more recent by 200 years and is built of light granite from Stérec Island.

◘ *Turn back, then left as you leave St-Gonven.*

Térénez

This small, very pleasant and typically Breton port is a sailing centre.

2 FROM MORLAIX TO ÎLE CALLOT★★

14km/8.7mi round tour from Morlaix.

◘ *Leave Morlaix via N on the town plan.*

Carantec⌂

This family seaside resort lies on a peninsula between the estuary of the Penzé and the River Morlaix. There are several beaches suitable for bathing; the most important are Grève Blanche and Grève du Kélenn, the larger of the two.
A number of *pardons* are held at Carantec (🕯 *see Calendar of Events*). The apse of the modern **church** contains a fine silver **processional cross**★ (1652) and a less ornate one in front of the altar.

La Chaise du Curé

From this rocky platform, the **view**★ extends from left to right over the Porspol and Blanche Beaches with St-Pol-de

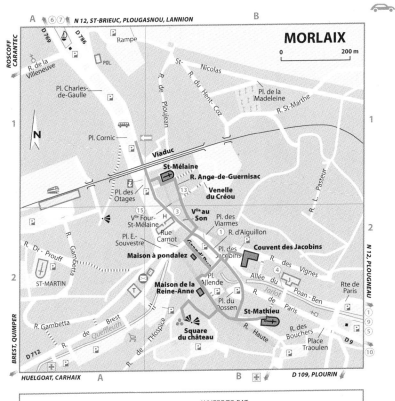

MORLAIX

A — 6 7 N 12, ST-BRIEUC, PLOUGASNOU, LANNION — B

0   200 m

ROSCOFF / CARANTEC

D 769 · D 786

Rampe

R. de la Villeneuve

POL.

Pl. Charles-de-Gaulle

St-Nicolas

R. de Plouian

R. du Hent-Coz

Pl. de la Madeleine

R. St-Marthe

Pl. Cornic

N

Viaduc

St-Mélaine

R. Ange-de-Guernisac

R. L. Pasteur

Pl. des Otages

Venelle du Créou

V^lle au - Son

V^lle Four-St-Mélaine

Pl. des Viarmes

R. d'Aiguillon

Couvent des Jacobins

R. Dr - Prouff

R. Gambetta

Rue Carnot

Pl. E.-Souvestre

Pl. des Jacobins

R. des Vignes

ST-MARTIN

Maison à pondalez

Allée du

Poan - Ben

Rte de Paris

Maison de la Reine-Anne

Pl. Allende

de

Paris

R. Gambetta

Brest

Pl. du Dossen

St-Mathieu

R. Gambetta · R. de Queffleuth

R. de l'Hospice

Square du château

R. Haute

R. des Bouchers

Place Traoulen

D 712

BREST, QUIMPER

HUELGOAT, CARHAIX — A — B — D 109, PLOURIN

D 9

N 12, PLOUGNEAU

9 · 5 · 10

ST-BRIEUC

View of the bay from Carantec

R. Mattès/MICHELIN

257

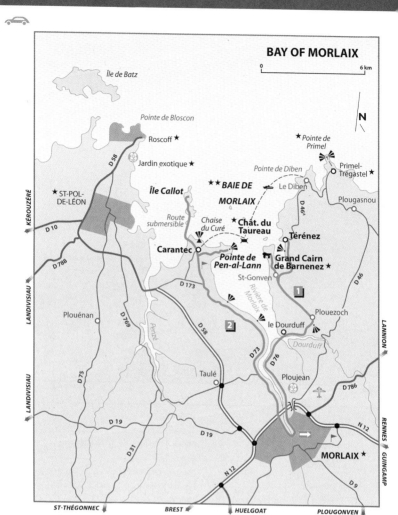

BAY OF MORLAIX

0   6 km

Île de Batz

Pointe de Bloscon

Roscoff ★

★ Pointe de Primel

Jardin exotique ★

Primel-Trégastel ★

Pointe de Diben

Plougasnou

★ ST-POL-DE-LÉON

Île Callot

★★ BAIE DE MORLAIX

Le Diben

Route submersible

Chaise du Curé

★ Chât. du Taureau

Térénez

Carantec

Pointe de Pen-al-Lann

Grand Cairn de Barnenez ★

St-Gonven

Plouezoch

Plouénan

le Dourduff

Taulé

Dourduff

Ploujean

MORLAIX ★

ST-THÉGONNEC   BREST   HUELGOAT   PLOUGONVEN

KÉROUZÉRÉ   LANDIVISIAU   LANDIVISIAU

LANNION   RENNES   GUINGAMP

-Léon and Roscoff in the background, as far as the Pointe de Pen-al-Lann.

⬛ Pointe de Pen-al-Lann

1.5km/0.9mi E, plus 15min on foot there and back.

Take rue de Pen-al-Lann and leave your car at the roundabout. Take the downhill path through pine trees to a rocky promontory.

The **view**★ extends along the coast from the Pointe de Bloscon, crowned by the Chapelle Ste-Barbe, near Roscoff, to the Pointe de Primel; opposite is the 1542 castle on **Taureau Island**, which guarded the mouth of River Morlaix from attacks by English pirates.

Louis XIV deemed it too costly to keep and had it made into a prison in 1660, after asking Vauban to restore it.

Île Callot

From Grève Blanche port you can reach the island by car (🅿) at mid-tide.

Pay attention to the tide times and 2hr is sufficient to visit.

The Chapelle Notre-Dame on the island was founded in the 16C and rebuilt in the 17C and 19C. Inside is a 16C statue of the Virgin and there is a *pardon* on the Sunday after 15 August

The island is excellent for fishing and has two lovely beaches: Park an Iliz and Park an Aod.

ADDRESSES

STAY

Chambre d'hôtes du Manoir de Lanleya – *in Lanleya, 29610 Plouigneau. 5km/3mi SE of Morlaix on the D 712 and D 64 towards Lanmeur.* ℘02 98 79 94 15. www.manoir-lanleya.com. 5 rooms. Due to the remarkable restoration, you wouldn't believe that this 16C manor was saved from a ruin. The rooms are little gems, the best one is done out in Louis XV style. A river runs at the bottom of the flower-filled garden.

Auberge Le Puits de Jeanne – *29650 Plouegat-Moysan.* ℘ 02 98 79 20 15. www.lepuitsdejeanne.com. 6 rooms. In this converted old cowshed you can taste le *Kig Ha Farz* and *le Bara Kig*, famous specialities of Brittany. Themed evenings.

Chambre d'hôte de Coat Amour – *Rte de Paris, Morlaix.* ℘02 98 88 57 02. www.gites-morlaix.com. 6 rooms. On the heights of Morlaix this 19C manor house, once owned by General Weygrand, is owned today by an English couple. Spacious rooms looking onto the park are furnished with antique furniture.

Chambre d'hôtes du Manoir de Roch ar Brini – *29600 Ploujean.* ℘02 98 72 01 44. www.brittanyguesthouse.com. 3 rooms. This 19C manor house surrounded by a wooded park has individually decorated bedrooms which are reached by a beautiful stone staircase. Elegant original dining room.

Hôtel d'Europe – *1 rue d'Aiguillon, Morlaix.* ℘02 98 62 11 99. www.hotel-europe-com.fr. Closed Christmas holidays. 60 rooms. 8€. Inside this 200-year-old building, the hall and stairway are decorated with sculpted woodworks. The rooms, regularly renovated and equipped with functional furniture, are less attractive but comfortable all the same.

EAT

Ar Bilig – *6 rue Au Fil, Morlaix.* ℘02 98 88 50 51. Closed Sun eve and Mon except Jul–Aug and school holidays. Reservations advised. You don't come here for the décor but to enjoy the crêpes, generously filled with produce from a nearby farm.

La Terrasse – *31 pl. des Otages, Morlaix.* ℘ 02 98 88 20 25. www.la terrasse-morlaix.com. Closed Sun. In a prestigious setting in a brasserie in the very centre of Morlaix the young owners offer a varied and inventive menu.

Les Bains Douches – *45 Allée du Poan-Ben, Morlaix.* ℘ 02 98 63 83 83. Closed Mon eve, Sat lunch and Sun. Traditional meals carefully presented in the wonderful setting of the former municipal baths. The atmosphere is like that of a Parisian bistro.

Crêperie Hermine – *35 r. Ange-de-Guernisac, Morlaix.* ℘ 02 98 88 10 91 - www.restaurantmorlaix.com. Closed 5 –14 Apr, 20–30 Sept, 1–15 Jan, Sun lunch and Wed. Beams, polished wooden tables and country objects make up the décor of this crêperie located in a pedestrian street. Specialities are galettes with fresh algae.

Le Cabestan – *At the port, 29660 Carantec.* ℘ 02 98 67 01 87. Closed 5 Jan–6 Feb, Tue. exc eve in Jul–Aug and Mon. Comes here to taste typical brasserie dishes. The décor of the dining room is rustic and upstairs there is a beautiful view of Callot island.

La Grange de Coatélan – *29640 Plougonven.* ℘02 98 72 60 16. www.la grangedecoatelan.com. Closed Feb school holidays and Christmas holidays. This collection of 18C buildings comprises three charming old weavers' cottages. The inn, decked out in blond wood and complemented by a bar in the shape of a boat's hull, is a friendly place. Rooms overlook the countryside.

NIGHTLIFE

Morlaix has plenty of old pubs and cafés such as *Café de l'Aurore*, *La Cabane* and the *pâtisserie Martin (29 pl. des Otages)*. Also of note is Coreff brewery (the first to brew Breton beer) and *La Maison des Vins*, in a 16C house.

Le Tempo – *quai de Tréguier.* ℘02 98 63 29 11. In front of the marina, this pub is a meeting place for old salts and landlubbers alike, who can share a drink or a daily meal (salads, stews, grills and quiches). Terrace in summer; exhibitions and musical evenings.

ACTIVITIES

Diving – Groupe Subaquatique Morlaix Trégor (GSMT) – *18 rue de Kernehelen, Plouezoc'h. ☏02 98 79 50 95. www.plongee-gsmp.fr.* Every day in summer. Evening dives are followed by a barbecue at the club.

Sailing – École de Voile de Terenez – *Plougasnou. ☏02 98 72 33 25. www. srtz.com.* In a small cove sheltered off the harbour of Morlaix, catamaran, day sailer and windsurfing lessons.

TOURS OF THE COAST

Le Léon à Fer et à Flots – *Place des Otages. ☏02 98 62 07 52. www.aferaflots. org. Closed Nov–Mar.* This association offers guided tours of the town and of the coast between Morlaix and Roscoff: on foot, on board a train or by boat. There are opportunities to explore sites that are usually off-limits to the general public, such as the first floor of the viaduct of Morlaix (spectacular view).

FESTIVALS

Festival des Arts de la Rue (FAR) – *☏02 98 46 19 46. www.artsdanslarue. com.* Twelve days in July and August. Street theatre from 7.30pm on Wednesdays.

SHOPPING

Bakery – Au Four St-Mélaine – *1 venelle Four St-Mélaine. ☏02 98 88 10 22. Daily 6am–7pm in Jul–Aug, Tue–Sun in May–Jun and Sept–Oct, Tue–Sat Nov–Apr.* One of the house specialities is the 'armoricain', cake without butter but with almonds.

Cider – Domaine de Kervéguen – *29620 Guimaëc. ☏02 98 67 50 02. www. kerveguen.fr. Open Aug, Mon–Sat 10am–7pm; Jul 10am–noon, 2–6.30; Apr–Jun and Sept, Mon–Sat 2.30pm–6pm; Oct–Mar, Sat 2.30pm–6pm.* Breton cider aged in oak vats, as drunk by the French President. Tastings and tours.

Market – *Place Allende and place des Otages.* A big market all day on Saturdays. Livelier in the morning.

Les Enclos Paroissiaux★★

Parish closes, which are a special feature of Breton art, are to be found mostly in lower Brittany. The route runs through the picturesque Élorn Valley and the foothills of the Monts d'Arrée and includes only a few of the more interesting ones. There are many others, especially that of Pleyben, further to the south.

🚗 DRIVING TOUR

Parish Closes of Brittany
130km/80mi – one day.

Morlaix★ –
👁 *See MORLAIX.*

◯ *Leave Morlaix SW along D 172*

- **Michelin Map:** Local map 308 F/I 3/4 - Finistère (29).
- **Info:** Park an Illiz, 29410 St-Théogonnec. ☏02 98 79 67 80. www.saint-the gonnec.fr.
- **Kids:** The Moulins de Kerouat ecomuseum.
- **Timing:** Allow a day for this circuit, especially if you want to have a wander around the Monts d'Arrée.
- **Don't Miss:** St-Théogonnec, Guimiliau and Lamapaul-Guimiliau as well as La Roche-Maurice and La Martyre.

St-Théogonnec★★

This village has a magnificent parish close, the ossuary and the church being the key features of this rich 16C–17C Renaissance group.

Enclos Paroissial★★

⬭ Enter the parish close via the place de l'Église to the south.

Porte Triomphale★
A rounded arch surmounted by small lantern turrets (1587).

Chapelle Funéraire★
🕐Open Jun–Aug, daily 9am–7pm; Apr, May and Sept 9am–6pm.
☎02 98 79 67 80.
The funerary chapel was built from 1676 to 1682. Inside is a 17C altarpiece (restored) with spiral columns. In the crypt is a **Holy Sepulchre**★ with figures carved in oak and painted (1699–1702), the work of a Breton sculptor, Jacques Lespaignol.
The treasury contains gold and silver plate including a silver gilt processional cross (1610).

Calvary★★
The calvary was erected in 1610. On the base are groups of figures depicting the Passion. Below, a small niche shelters St-Thégonnec with the wolf he harnessed to his cart after his donkey had been devoured by wolves.
The platform is surmounted by a double-armed cross bearing figures and two simple crosses for the thieves.
The **church**★ (*🕐Open Jul–Aug, daily 9am–7pm; Sept–Jun, daily 9am–6pm; ☎02 98 79 67 80*) has been remodelled several times and the only trace of the old building is the gable belfry (1563) on the left of the tower. The Renaissance tower is crowned with a dome with lantern and corner turrets.
A fire in June 1998 caused the roof to collapse and severely damaged the five chapels on the north side. An observatory enables visitors to admire some of the church's remarkable features, including the **pulpit**★★, **woodwork**★★ and Rosary **altarpiece**★.
An exhibition illustrates the history of the parish close.

⬭ Go round the east end of the church and bear left.

Guimiliau★★
The fame of the small village of Guimiliau is due to its remarkable parish close and to the magnificently ornamented furniture of its church.

Calvary★★
The calvary (calvaire), the most curious and one of the largest in the region, dates from 1581–1588 and includes over 200 figures. On the upper part stands a large cross with a thorny shaft bearing four statues: the Virgin and St-John, St-Peter and St-Yves. On the platform are 17 scenes from the Passion and a composition representing the story of Catell-Gollet above the Last Supper. The figures on the frieze are numerous and depict, in no chronological order, 15 scenes from the life of Jesus. The four Evangelists stand at the corners of the buttresses.

Church★
This 16C building was rebuilt in the Flamboyant Renaissance style at the beginning of the 17C.

South portico★★
The statuettes in the recessed arches give an interesting picture of the Bible and the Gospels. Above the portico's triangular pediment is the statue of St Miliau, King of Cornouaille and the area's patron saint. To the left is a small ossuary with sculptures depicting scenes from Christ's life.
The inside of the portico is a fine example of a common form of decoration in Brittany. Under the usual statues of the Apostles is a frieze ornamented with rose medallions, strapwork and scenes from the Old Testament. Note on the left side, near the date 1606, the Creation of Woman.

Interior
To the left of the entrance is a fine carved oak **baptistery**★★ from 1675. In the **organ loft** are three 17C **low-relief sculptures**★; on the nave side, David playing the harp, and St-Cecilia at the organ; opposite the baptistery, the Triumph of Alexander. The **pulpit**★, dating

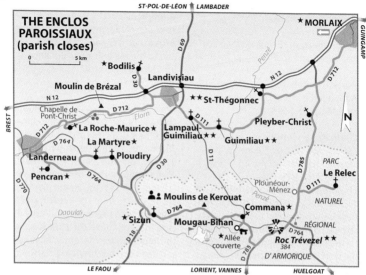

THE ENCLOS PAROISSIAUX (parish closes)

ST-POL-DE-LÉON LAMBADER

★ MORLAIX

GUINGAMP

★ Bodilis

Landivisiau

Moulin de Brézal

★★ St-Thégonnec

N 12

Chapelle de Pont-Christ

Pleyber-Christ

La Roche-Maurice ★

Lampaul-Guimiliau ★★

Guimiliau ★★

La Martyre ★

Landerneau

Ploudiry

Pencran ★

PARC

Le Relec

Plounéour-Ménez

NATUREL

Moulins de Kerouat

Commana ★

Sizun

Mougau-Bihan

RÉGIONAL

Allée couverte

Roc Trévezel ★★

D'ARMORIQUE

LE FAOU

LORIENT, VANNES

HUELGOAT

BREST

Elorn

Penzé

Daoulas

from 1677, is ornamented at the corners with statues of the four Sibyls.

The chancel with its central stained-glass window (1599) is enclosed by a 17C altar rail. Note from right to left: the colourful **altarpiece of St-Joseph,** on which can be seen St-Yves (the patron saint of barristers), set between a rich man and a poor one, and the blind St-Hervé with his wolf; the **altarpiece of St-Miliau,** representing scenes from the saint's life; and the **altarpiece of the Rosary**, with 15 mysteries, surmounted by a Trinity.

Chapelle Funéraire

🕑 Open daily 9am–6pm.

Guided visit possible.

The Renaissance funerary chapel dates from 1648 and has an outdoor pulpit set in one of the windows.

Lampaul-Guimiliau★

This village has a complete parish close. The church is especially noteworthy for its rich decoration and furnishings. If the calvary isn't as spectacular as some of the others in the area, the church makes up for it with its rich decoration.

Enclos Paroissial★

Recently restored, the parish close is entered via the **porte triomphale** (triumphal arch) surmounted by three crosses (1669). The **chapelle funéraire** (funerary chapel), a former ossuary (1667), abuts on the arch and has buttresses crowned with small lantern turrets. Inside is the altar of the Trinity, with statues of St-Rock, St Sebastian and St-Pol and his dragon. The **calvaire** (calvary), dating from the early 16C, is older than the rest.

Église★

The church is dominated by a 16C bell-tower, whose steeple was struck by lightning in the early 1800s. The apse, with a sacristy added in 1679, forms a harmonious whole in which the Gothic and Classical styles are blended. The porch on the south side dates from 1533. Under it are statues of the twelve Apostles.

Interior★★

A 16C **rood beam** spans the nave, bearing a Crucifix between statues of the Virgin and St-John. Both its faces are adorned with sculptures representing, on the nave side, scenes from the Passion and, on the chancel side, the twelve Sibyls separated by a group of the Annunciation. The pulpit dates from 1759. At the end of the south aisle is a **font** surmounted by a fine canopy dating from 1651. Higher up, on the right of the St-Lawrence altarpiece, is a curious stoup (17C) representing two devils writhing in holy water; above is the Baptism of Christ.

In the **chancel** are 17C stalls, and on each side of the high altar, carved woodwork: on the left, St-Paul on the road to Damascus and his escape; on the right, St-Peter's martyrdom and the divine virtues. The side altars have 17C altarpieces.

The altar of St-John the Baptist, on the right of the chancel, is adorned with low-relief sculptures of which the most interesting (left) represents the Fall of the Angels after Rubens. The altar of the Passion, on the left of the chancel, has an **altarpiece** in eight sections in high relief with lifelike figures and, on the top, the Resurrection. On either side are two panels showing the Birth of the Virgin (left), a rare theme in Brittany, and the Martyrdom of St-Miliau (right), King of Cornouaille beheaded by his jealous brother. In the north side aisle is a 16C **Pietà** with six figures carved out of a single piece of wood and also a 17C **banner**, embroidered in silver on a velvet ground (in an open cupboard). The impressive 1676 **Entombment** in polychrome tufa was carved by the naval sculptor Anthoine. Note the expression of the Christ figure in particular. The organ case is 17C. The sacristy contains a 17C chest.

Maison du Patrimoine

Open from mid Jun to mid Sept. Guided tour of the parish close (1hr) available by appointment. ℘02 98 68 76 67.

Facing the parish close, this old house built in the traditional regional style is a little museum featuring figures dressed in historical costumes, antique furnishings; in tourist season, there are exhibits of local artists' work.

Chapelle Ste-Anne

About 3km/1.8mi S. Guided tours available – ask at the town hall (℘02 98 68 76 67) or Mme Mingam (℘02 98 68 75 48, eve or weekend).

This little 17C chapel is dedicated to St-Anne of whom there are no fewer than three different representations (one of which was restored in 2005). There's also a rare depiction of Christ in a red robe on the cross.

Landivisiau

Landivisiau is a busy town. Its cattle fairs are among the largest in France. The **Église St-Thivisiau** (*Mon–Fri 9.30am–6pm*) is a modern church in the Gothic style, which still has the bell-tower and the fine granite **porch**★ of a former 16C church. Note the elegant canopies above the statues of the Apostles and the delicate ornamentation around the doors.

Chapelle Ste-Anne in middle of the churchyard was an ossuary in the 17C. The façade is adorned with six caryatids. Death is represented to the left of the west doorway.

In the village of **Lambader**, 8km/5mi north, the Chapelle Notre-Dame has a lovely rood screen in the Flamboyant Gothic style (1481).

Head towards Landerneau, then turn right via the intersection at La-Croix-des-Maltotiers.

Bodilis

The **church**★ (16C) is preceded by a Flamboyant bell-tower pierced with three openings at the base. The large 17C sacristy, jutting out from the north aisle, is very handsome, with a roof in the shape of an inverted hull, a richly decorated cornice and buttresses ornamented with niches. A porch opens on the south side. The interior has remarkable **decorations**★: purlins, tie-beams, hammerbeams, statues and gilded altarpieces. The font canopy is carved from Kersanton granite. There is also a colourful Entombment in high relief on the porch wall.

Rejoin the D 712 and bear right.

Moulin de Brézal

The mill, which has an interesting façade with a Flamboyant doorway, stands in a pleasant setting below a pool. On the opposite side of the road is the ruined Chapelle de Pont-Christ (1533).

3.5km/2mi further on, turn left to La Roche-Maurice.

La Roche-Maurice★

The village, situated on a hillside and dominated by the ruins of a castle, has a fine **parish close**, featuring three crosses with Christ and the thieves.

Church

Open daily 9am–6pm.
An elegant, twin-galleried belfry crowns the 16C building. The **south porch**★ is delicately carved with bunches of grapes and statuettes of saints. Inside, note the Renaissance **rood screen**★ decorated on the side facing the nave with 12 statues carved in the round, including nine Apostles and three Popes, and on the chancel side with low-relief sculptures of saints. Behind the high altar, a large **stained-glass window**★ (1539) illustrates the Passion and the Resurrection of Christ. Also of interest is the panelled ceiling adorned with angels and coats of arms, carved purlins and beams.

Ossuary★

This ossuary dates from 1640 and is one of the largest in Brittany. Above the outside font, Death is shown armed with an arrow, threatening small figures framed in medallions representing all social classes: a peasant, a woman, a lawyer, a bishop, St-Yves, a pauper and a rich man; an inscription reads "Je vous tue tous" ("Death comes to all").

Landerneau

Located between Léon and Cornouaille, this small port is an active market town; the Élorn abounds in salmon and trout, making Landerneau a paradise for anglers.

Pont de Rohan

Built in the 16C, this picturesque bridge, lined with houses with overhanging upper storeys, is one of the last inhabited European bridges.

Walk to the front of the town hall and enjoy the scene of the bridge and the slate-covered houses with overhanging upper storeys.

Old Houses

These are to be found mainly on the right bank of the River Élorn: number 9 place du Général-de-Gaulle, the turreted house (1664) known as the house of Duchess Anne; the façade at number 4 rue de la Fontaine-Blanche; at number 5 rue du Commerce, house with decorated turret and dormer windows (1667) and at the corner of the Pont de Rohan and Quai du Cornouaille is the so-called Maison des Rohan (Rohan House, 1639) with its sundial.

Église St-Houardon

The granite porch (1604) on the south side of this church served as a model for many parish closes along the Élorn Valley.

Walk across to the south bank.

Église St-Thomas-de-Cantorbéry

Guided tours (45min) Jul–Aug Tue and Thu 2pm–6pm.
This 16C church has a belfry-porch (1607) with three superimposed balconies. Inside, note the amusing decoration of the purlins in the north aisle and the great 18C altarpiece at the high altar. Note the **ossuary chapel** erected as an annexe to the church in 1635.

Leave Landerneau by the SE in the direction of Pencran.

Pencran★

Situated on the left bank of the river l'Élorn and at the side of a wooden hill this town possesses a 16C parish church. The Breton name signifies "a wooden head". The **porte triomphale** is decorated with three lanterns added in 17C. The large **Calvaire**★ has two cross pieces made from the crosses of thieves. The **Église** has an elegant double balcony bell tower and a **porch** built in 1553 with arches adorned with worshipping angels and musicians. On the pillars

Detail of the triumphal arch, parish close, Sizun

S. Sauvignier/MICHELIN

there are scenes from the Old testament under the elaborate sculpted canopy are statues of the apostles.

In the choir to the left of the main altar admire the remarkable **Descente de croix** (1517)

▷ *Leave Pencran in the direction of Kermaria then turn right towards Le Queff then rejoin the D 35.*

La Martyre★

This **parish close**★, the oldest in the Léon region, opens onto a triumphal arch with a Flamboyant balustrade and a small calvary. The ossuary (1619) is adorned with a curious caryatid and macabre motifs. The 14C–16C church has a fine historiated **porch**★ (c. 1450) on its south side. Inside, note the carved purlins, tie-beams, altarpieces and 15C chancel screen. The chancel is lit by 16C **stained-glass windows**★.

Ploudiry

The village, formerly the largest parish of the Léon region, has an interesting close. On the façade of the ossuary (1635), Death is depicted striking down men of all social classes. The church, rebuilt in the 19C, retains a fine south **porch**★ dating from 1665. The high altar, adorned with polychrome high-relief carvings and the side altars are good specimens of 17C Breton art. In

the chancel is a 17C window depicting the Passion.

▷ *After 8km/5mi, pass through Le Traon and turn left towards Sizun.*

Sizun★

Sizun, a village in the Léon region, has an interesting parish close, which was built from 16–18C. The village is a good location from which to explore the Monts d'Arrée and the Parc Naturel Régional d'Armorique.

Enclos Paroissial★

🕓 *Open daily, year round.*

🔖 *For guided tours, contact the Tourist Office.* 🞋 *02 98 68 88 40.*

The most interesting parts of the parish close are the triple triumphal **arch**★, decorated with Corinthian capitals and topped by a calvary, and the twin-arched ossuary-**chapel**★; both date from 1585 to 1588.

The ossuary-chapel houses a small local museum with box bed, dresser, headdresses, costumes and sacred art objects. The 16C **church**, remodelled in the 17C and 18C, is joined by a passage to the sacristy (late 17C) which stands alone. Inside, the decoration of the panelled vaulting is remarkable: there is a sculpted purlin with, in the transept and chancel, angels presenting the instruments of the Passion, crocodile-headed tie-beams, keystones and fluting. The organ loft, high altar, altarpieces and font canopy are all 17C. The **treasury** of religious art is the most important one in Brittany, with reliquaries and statues.

👥 Maison de la Rivière

1km/0.6mi W. Centre de Découverte, Moulin du Vergraon. ⏰*Open Jul–Aug, 10am–6pm; Sept–Jun, Mon–Fri 10am–noon, 2pm–5.30pm.* ⊘*Closed Christmas, 1 and 8 May.* 🎟*4€ (children 2.50€).* ✆*02 98 68 86 33. www.maison-de-la-riviere.fr.*

This small museum, located in Vergraon Mill, illustrates the importance of fresh water through various themes: fish and their habitat and angling (fishing tackle, flies used in salmon fishing). The exhibits are complemented by aquariums containing freshwater fish, explanatory panels, models and films. The Maison de la Rivière also organises guided rambles across the Monts d'Arrée, to the source of the Élorn, Drennec Lake or the Mougau peat bogs. Its annexe, the Maison du Lac (Fish-breeding Centre) located at the foot of the Drennec dam (*6km/3.7mi E*), is an information centre on the worldwide exploitation of rivers, lakes and fish farming.

⊙ *Go back to Sizun then take the D 764 in the direction of Carhaix-Plouguer.*

👥 Moulins de Kerouat

⏰*Open Jul–Aug, daily 11am–7pm; Jun, 10am–6pm, Sat–Sun 2pm–6pm; mid-Mar–May and Sept–Oct, Mon–Fri 10am–6pm, Sun and holidays 2pm–6pm.* 🎟*4.50€ (children 8–18 yrs, 2.10€).* ✆*02 9868 87 76. www.pnr-armorique.fr.*

Under the auspices of the *Parc naturel régional d'Armorique*, the 19C village of Kerouat has been revived and is now the **Écomusée des Monts d'Arrée**. You will see its mills, dwelling house, outbuildings (stable, barn) and bread oven; learn how a water mill functioned with its scoop wheel and mechanism (gears on the ground floor, millstone on the upper floor), and how the miller lived.

⊙ *Continue on towards Carhaix and at Ty Douar bear left.*

Commana★

The village stands on an isolated foothill of the Monts d'Arrée. Within the close is a 16C–17C **church**★ with a fine south porch. Inside, there are three interesting altarpieces. Note the **altar**★ to St-Anne (1682) in the north aisle and an Ecce Homo in wood on a pillar in the transept, to the right. The canopied font is ornamented with five statues: Faith, Hope, Charity, Justice and Temperance. In the summer there is an exhibit of sacred art in the charnel-house.

Mougau-Bian

Beyond the hamlet, to the right, is a **covered alleyway**★, 14m long; some of the uprights are carved on the inside with lances and daggers.

⊙ *Return to D 764 and turn right; 1km further on, take an uphill road to the right (D 11) to join the Morlaix road, and turn left onto D 785.*

Roc Trévezel★★ –

👣*See Monts d'ARRÉE*

⊙ *Near Plounéour-Ménez, turn right.*

Le Relec

Nestled in the valley, a 12C–13C church and the ruins of the monastery buildings, are all that remain of the former Cistercian abbey. It is a simple, austere building, although the façade was restored in the 18C. Concerts take place in the abbey on the Dimanches du Relec, from May to September, and during the Rencontres de Musique Vocale in August. The *pardon* of Notre-Dame-du-Relec is on 15 August.

Pleyber-Christ

In a small gothic and renaissance parish church, in front of a high triumphal gate constructed in 1921, the dead of WWI were consecrated. In the interior there are remarkable beams as well as the old stalls.

⊙ *Continue towards Ste-Sève. After 3.5 km/2.2m, the D 712 turn right back to Morlaix.*

ADDRESSES

STAY

Chambre d'hôte Ty-Dreux –
*29410 Loc-Eguiner-St-Thégonnec. 3.5km SE
of Guimiliau on the D 111.* 02 98 78 08 21.
5 rooms and 3 gîtes. Restaurant.
In the heart of the countryside, you'll
find this dairy farm where you can sleep
in renovated rooms and have breakfast
next to the 18C fireplace.

Hôtel des Voyageurs – *2 rue de
l'Argoat, Sizun.* 02 98 68 80 35. *Closed
11 Sept–3 Oct, Fri eve, Sun and Sat Oct–
Jun. 18 rooms.* 7.50€. *Restaurant*.

Near the church, this unpretentious,
family hotel is simple and pleasant in
style. The annexe has smaller rooms.

EAT

Restaurant de la Mairie – *9 rue de
la Tour d'Auvergne, Landernau.* 02 98
85 01 83. www.restaurantdelamairie.com.
Closed Tue eve. Two prettily decorated
dining rooms, traditional cuisine a good
wine list and a children's nursery..

Crêperie Steredenn – *6 rue de la
Gare, St-Thégonnec.* 02 98 79 43 34.
Closed Jan, Mon & Tue. Highly-regarded
sweet and savoury crêpes.

Presqu'Île de Plougastel★

Lying away from main roads,
Plougastel Peninsula is a corner of
the Breton countryside which may
still be seen in its traditional guise.
Narrow, winding roads run between
hedges, cutting farming country
up into squares. Apart from in the
occasional hamlets grouped round
their little chapels, there are few
houses. Here everything seems to
be hidden away: you are deep in
"strawberry country", but you will
not see the strawberries growing
in open fields unless you get out of
your car and look through the gaps
in the hedges .Vast glassed-in areas
shelter vegetables and flowers. In
May and June, however, when the
strawberries are picked, there is
plenty of life in this remote corner
of Brittany.

PLOUGASTEL-DAOULAS

Calvary★★

Open Jul–Aug, 9am–noon, 2pm–
6pm; Sept–Jun, 9am–noon.
Built in 1604 to commemorate the
end of the Plague of 1598, the calvary
is made of dark Kersanton granite and
ochre stone from Logonna. It is more
harmonious than the Guimiliau calvary
but the attitude of the 180 figures seems

- **Michelin Map:** Local map
  308 E4 Finistère (29).
- **Info:** 4 place du Calvaire,
  29470 Plougastel-Daoulas.
  02 98 40 34 98. www.
  mairie-plougastel.fr.
- **Location:** You reach the
  peninsula by the N 165
  from Brest (5km/3mi W).
- **Timing:** Try to be at the
  Pointe de Kerdéniel at
  the end of the day to
  watch the sun set over
  the bay of Brest.
- **Don't Miss:** The calvary.

more severe. On either side of the Cross,
the two thieves are surmounted by an
angel and a devil respectively. On the
calvary base an altar is carved under a
portico; above is a large statue of Christ
leaving the tomb.
The church is built of granite and reinforced concrete; inside it id decorated
in bright blues, greens, oranges and
violets.

Musée du Patrimoine et
de la Fraise

Open Jun–Aug, Mon– Fri 10am–
12.30pm, 2pm–6pm, Sat–Sun 2pm–
6pm; rest of the year, 2pm–5.30pm.
Closed Jan, first week of Feb and public
holidays. 4€. 02 98 40 21 18.

www.musee-fraise.net

This museum of local history, traditions and ethnology contains documents, objects, tools and items of furniture and clothing relating to everyday life from the 18C until the present. Displayed in more detail are the cultivation of the local crops of flax and **strawberries** *(fraises)*, and marine activities linked with their exportation, as well as trawling for scallops in Brest Bay.

Chapelle St-Jean
4.5km/2.8mi NE on D 29 towards Landerneau, and after crossing the Brest-Quimper motorway bear left then right.

The 15C chapel, remodelled in the 17C, stands in a verdant **site**★ on the banks of the Élorn.

🚗 DRIVING TOUR

Peninsula★
Round trip of 35km/21mi – allow 3hr.

🔘 *Leave Plougastel-Daoulas by a road to the right of the church; follow the signposts to Kernisi.*

Panorama de Kernisi★
At the entrance to the hamlet of Kernisi, leave the car and make for a knoll.
From here you will see a panorama of the Brest roadstead, the outer harbour

and town of Brest, the Élorn estuary and the Pont Albert-Louppe.

🔘 *Turn round and at the second main junction bear right towards Langristin.*

Drive past the 16C **Chapelle Ste-Christine** and its small calvary dating from 1587. From the **Anse du Caro** there is a fine view of Brest and Pointe des Espagnols.

🔘 *Go back in the direction of Plougastel-Daoulas and after 3km/ 1.8mi, turn right.*

Pointe de Kerdéniel★★
Allow 15min on foot there and back. Leave the car at the bottom of Kerdéniel and after the houses turn right and take the lane on the left (signposted) to the blockhouse.
The view extends, from left to right, over Le Faou estuary, the mouth of the Aulne, Ménez-Hom, Île Longue, Presqu'île de Crozon's east coast to Pointe des Espagnols and Brest Sound.

🔘 *Turn back and after 3km/1.8mi, bear right. Lauberlach fishing port and sailing centre is set in a pretty cove. Take the road on the right towards St-Adrien.*

From the hillside, the road gives fine glimpses of Lauberlach cove and passes the Chapelle St-Adrien (1549) on the right.

🔘 *Next turn right towards St-Guénolé. At Pennaster, go round Lauberlach Cove.*

The Chapelle St-Guénolé (1514) stands in a wooded setting to the left of the road.

🔘 *At the first junction beyond St-Guenolé, take an uphill road on the right; turn right, then left onto a stony lane.*

Keramenez Viewing Table★

An extensive panorama over the Presqu'île de Plougastel and the southern section of Brest roadstead.

▷ *Return to Plougastel-Daoulas by the fishing port of Tinduff, then Lestraouen and Lanriwaz.*

EXCURSION
Daoulas★

This small medieval town is located about 20km/12.5mi south of Brest on the banks of the river that shares its name which forms one of the many inlets in the Brest roadstead. The town owes its development largely to the presence of the abbey built here; the fates of both have been closely linked over the centuries. Daoulas has inherited many artistic features that bear witness to its past. Today, there are still some 15C and 17C houses along rue de l'Église.

Enclos paroissial★ (Parish Close)

The old abbey buildings are to the left. Opposite, and slightly to the right, a 16C **porch**★ leads into the cemetery. Both Gothic and Renaissance in style it is richly carved (note the remarkable vine). The **old abbey** church still has the original 12C west door, nave and north side aisle. In the east end the ossuary has been converted into a sacristy.

Ancienne abbaye

21 rue de l'Église. ○*Open May–Nov, 10.30am–6.30pm.* ↝*Guided tours available (1hr).* ⊛*6€.* ♿ *℘02 98 25 84 39. www.abbaye-daoulas.com.*

The abbey was founded around the year AD 500 and, until the 10C, played a major part in the history of Daoulas. It was razed by the Vikings, then rebuilt in the 12C by Augustinian canons, under whose care it flourished until the Revolution.

The abbey now belongs to the *Conseil Général de Finistère*, which has converted it into a cultural centre, more particularly a venue for international archaeological exhibitions.

Ancienne abbaye, Daoulas

R. Mattes/MICHELIN

The Romanesque **cloisters**, built in 1167 to 1173 (only three walls are still standing), is the only surviving example of this style of architecture in Brittany.

A path leads to a garden where herbs and medicinal plants are cultivated and to a fountain dating from 1550. Set back is the 16C **Oratoire Notre-Dame-des-Fontaines** with 19C additions.

ADDRESSES

SOUTH FINISTÈRE

South Finistère is the southwestern corner of the Breton peninsula and is surrounded on two sides by the Atlantic Ocean. There are two so-called mountain ranges, the Monts d'Arrée and the Montagnes Noires, although neither is very high. The main city is ancient Quimper with its renowned Gothic Cathedral. Like much of Brittany, the coast is fascinating: all the way from the Presqu'île de Crozon and the Pointe de Raz protruding into the Atlantic, down past the desolate Bay of Audierne and around the Pointe de Penmarch, to the south-facing shores which stretch along past Bénodet, numerous seaside resorts, pretty harbours and beaches can be discovered.

Highlights

1 Seeing sunlight shine through Quimper **Cathedral**'s stained glass windows (p274)

2 Taking in the view from the top of **Ménez-Hom** (p284)

3 Driving around the headlands of the **Presq'île de Crozon** (p285)

4 Walking the town walls of bustling **Concarneau** (p314)

5 Following the art trail in **Pont-Aven** (p319)

A Bit of History

South Finistère covers much the same territory as the ancient Breton region of Cornouaille and stretches from the treeless and barren Monts d'Arrée in the north to the shores of the Atlantic Ocean in the south. The Atlantic also washes the western shores of Finistère, whilst to the east a boundary is shared with the green and undulating *département* of Morbihan. The land is generally flat, especially in the coastal areas, although the uplands of the Monts d'Arrée and the Montagnes Noires rise to over 300m/1,000ft in places.

The main industries of the region are agriculture and fishing, with some small farmers on the coast doing a little of both. Douarnenez on the west coast and Concarneau on the south coast are amongst the largest fishing ports in France and there are several smaller active ports including Guilvanec, Lesconil and St-Guénole in the vicinity. Tourism, too, is vital to the region's economy with large numbers of British, Dutch and French visitors arriving each year.

Quimper is the main city and *préfecture* of Finistère, with nearly 65,000 Quimpérois in residence. Renowned for its faience pottery, there are workshops that open their doors to visitors as well as an excellent museum dedicated to the craft. The twin steeples of the 13C Cathédrale St Corentin, with the famous statue of folk hero and Cornishman King Gradlon, is an impressive sight especially when viewed along rue Kéréon.

Also of great interest is the old ville close (walled town) at Concarneau where you can walk around the ramparts of this unusual port. The pleasant towns of Pont-l'Abbé, capital of the Bigouden district, and Pont-Aven, with its Gaughin heritage, are also well worth visiting. There are many fine beaches such as at Beg Meil, Concarneau and Bénodet. If, however, you prefer to explore the interior, particularly the uplands, there are itineraries for both the Montagnes Noires (🕭 see p325) and the Monts d'Arrée (🕭 see p 335) which form a large part of the Parc National Régional d'Armorique.

The headlands of South Finistère jutting out into the Atlantic are similarly protected by the authorities. The Presqu'île de Crozon, with its crumbling forts and ruined gun batteries on the many headlands, is also part of the Parc National Régional d'Armorique.

There are three itineraries to help you make the most of the coves and cliff-top trails (🕭 see p 285) which all provide wonderful views. Just as well known is the rocky promontory of the Pointe de Raz on the south side of the Bay of Douarnenez, which provides a fine panorama of the Île de Sein and the treacherous Raz de Sein stretch of water lying between the two.

Quimper★★

The town lies in a pretty little valley at the junction (*kemper* in Breton) of the River Steir and River Odet. This used to be the capital of Cornouaille, and it is here, perhaps, that the traditional atmosphere of the province can best be felt. July's **Festival de Cornouaille**★ is an important folk festival.

FAMOUS RESIDENTS

The statue of **René-Théophile-Hyacinthe Laënnec** (1781–1826) commemorates the most illustrious son of Quimper – the man who invented the stethoscope.

Streets are named after Kerguelen, Fréron and Madec, three other famous men of Quimper: **Yves de Kerguelen** (1734–97) was a South Seas explorer; a group of islands bears his name. **Élie Fréron** (1718–76) was a critic, bitterly opposed to Voltaire and other philosophers. **René Madec** (1738–84) was a hero of adventure who, as a cabin boy in a ship of the India Company, jumped overboard and landed at Pondichéry. He served a rajah and became a successful man. The British found a relentless enemy in him. When he returned to France, enormously rich, the king gave him a title and the Cross of St-Louis, with a colonel's commission.

Quimper was also the birthplace of **Max Jacob** (1876–1944), a poet and illustrator and friend of Picasso.

A BIT OF HISTORY

A dynasty of faience makers – In 1690, a southerner, Jean-Baptiste Bousquet, a faience maker from St-Zacharie near Marseilles, settled on the site which was to become Locmaria, a suburb of Quimper on the banks of the Odet, where it has been revealed that potters were active as early as the Gallo-Roman era. Bousquet founded the first Quimper faience works, where he adopted his favoured style from Moustiers faience ware. His son Pierre succeeded him in 1708 and associated himself with a faience maker from Nevers, Pierre Bellev-

▶ **Population:** 64,902. (Agglomeration 120,441).

Michelin Map: Local map 308 G7 Finistère (29).

Info: pl. de la Résistance, 29000 Quimper. ℘02 98 53 04 05. www.quimper-tourisme.com.

Location: Quimper is 17km/10.5mi SE of Locranon.

Kids: A visit to Aquarive.

Timing: Allow a day to visit Quimper and its museums.

Parking: Use the central car parks: Providence in the north or the one behind the station.

Don't Miss: After visiting St-Corentin cathedral to see its windows, enjoy the view of the river Odet from Stangala.

GETTING AROUND

BY BUS – a ticket (1€) allows you travel for 45 minutes (you must use it within 45 minutes of buying it). A day ticket (3€) can be bought from the bus driver. ℘02 98 82 60 57.

TOURS

A *Ville d'Art et d'Histoire*, Quimper offers several guided tours (*1hr 30*) including evening tours, gardens and religious art. Full programme available from the Tourist Office.

eaux, and later on with a faience maker from Rouen, Pierre-Clément Caussy. Both of these were to play an important role in the evolution of Quimper faience: one by enriching it with new shapes, colours (yellow) and Nevers decorative motifs; the other by introducing rich iron red to the Quimper palette and adding some 300 decorative designs (tracings). It is this blend of expertise and working methods handed down to Quimper 'painters' over the centuries which has

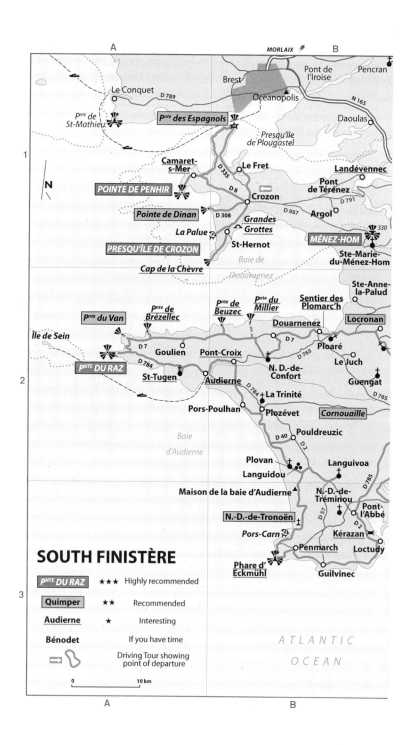

MORLAIX

A   B

Brest
Pont de
l'Iroise
Pencran

Le Conquet   D 789
Océanopolis

P^nte de
St-Mathieu

P^nte des Espagnols

N 165

Daoulas

Presqu'île
de Plougastel

1

Camaret-
s-Mer

Le Fret

Landévennec

POINTE DE PENHIR

D 355

D 8

Pont
de Térénez

D 791

Pointe de Dinan

D 308

Crozon

D 887

Argol

Grandes
Grottes

MÉNEZ-HOM   330

La Palue

St-Hernot

PRESQU'ÎLE DE CROZON

Baie de
Douarnenez

Ste-Marie-
du-Ménez-Hom

Cap de la Chèvre

Ste-Anne-
la-Palud

P^nte du Van

P^nte de
Brézellec

P^nte de
Beuzec

P^nte du
Millier

Sentier des
Plomarc'h

Locronan

Douarnenez

D 7

Île de Sein

D 7

Goulien

Pont-Croix

D 765

Ploaré

Le Juch

2

P^nte DU RAZ

D 784

St-Tugen

Audierne

N.-D.-de-
Confort

Guengat

D 784

La Trinité

D 765

Pors-Poulhan

Plozévet

Cornouaille

Baie
d'Audierne

D 40

Pouldreuzic

D 2

Plovan

Languidou

Languivoa

D 785

Maison de la baie d'Audierne

N.-D.-de-
Tréminou

Pont-
l'Abbé

D 57

D 2

N.-D.-de-Tronoën

Pors-Carn

Kérazan

SOUTH FINISTÈRE

Penmarch

Loctudy

Phare d'
Eckmühl

Guilvinec

P^nte DU RAZ   ★★★ Highly recommended

3

Quimper   ★★   Recommended

Audierne   ★   Interesting

Bénodet   If you have time

Driving Tour showing
point of departure

0   10 km

ATLANTIC

OCEAN

A   B

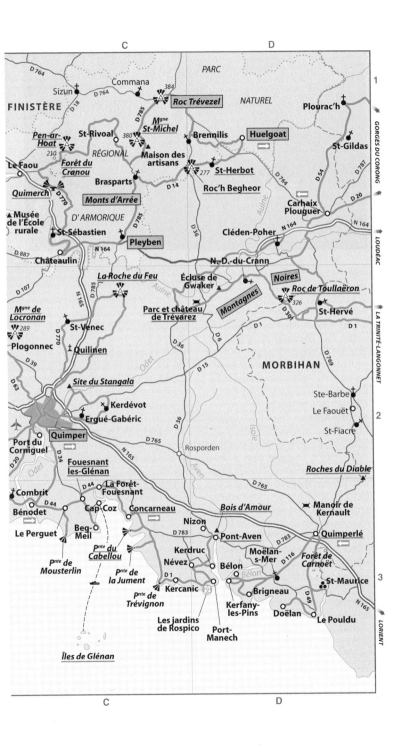

Interior, Cathédrale St-Corentin

© Colipicto/Dreamstime.com

made Quimper the seat of an artistic production distinguished by the diversity of style it encompasses.

Two more faience works were established in Quimper towards the end of the 18C: **Porquier** faience works, founded by François Eloury (c. 1772) and with which the name of **Alfred Beau** is linked in the 1870s; and **Dumaine** faience works, over which Jules Henriot assumed directorship in 1891.

Modern Artists – From 1920 onwards there was a long succession of artists. One of the first, **René Quillivic** (1879–1969), sculptor and ceramic painter, produced some striking works with designs based on woodcuts. The Odetta trademark, registered in 1922, produced works in sandstone, in dark tones made iridescent with enamel. Artists whose signatures adorn such work include Georges Renaud, René Beauclair, one of the most prolific, Louis Garin, Paul Fouillen and Jacques Nam.

The **Ar Seiz Breur** (Seven Brothers – a reference to seven Breton heros) movement was founded in 1923 by René-Yves Creston, Jeanne Malivel and Jorg Robin with the aim of modernising traditional Breton folk art by combining it with Art Deco and Cubism.

Many of the works produced by the artists who were members of this movement can be seen in exhibitions on this period.

CATHÉDRALE ST-CORENTIN★★

⏱Open daily 8.30am–noon, 1.30pm–6.30pm; Sun 9.30–noon, 2pm–6.30pm. (except Mass and fesitvals). ✆02 98 95 06 19.

This fine Gothic cathedral was built from the 13C (chancel) to the 15C (transept and nave). The two steeples were only erected in 1856, being modelled on the Breton steeple of Pont-Croix.

After seeing the north side of the building make for the façade. Between the spires stands the statue of a man on horseback: this is King Gradlon. Until the 18C, on 26 July each year, a great festival was held in his honour. A man would climb up behind him, tie a napkin round his neck and offer him a glass of wine. Then he drank up the wine himself, carefully wiped the King's mouth with the napkin and threw the empty glass down on the square. Any spectator who could catch the glass as it fell received a prize of 100 gold écus, if the glass was not broken.

Nave and chancel

Enter through the main door. On the right, note the 17C pulpit adorned with low-relief sculptures relating the life of St Corentin. The choir is quite out of line with the nave; this is due to the presence of a previous building. One theory is that in the early 13C, the cathedral craftsmen incorporated a small sanctuary set off to the left. The new chancel linked this chapel to the nave.

Side chapels

Visitors going round the fine 92m-long building will see in the side chapels' tombs (15C), altars, frescoes, altarpieces, statues, old (St John the Baptist, 15C alabaster) and modern **works of art** and, in the chapel beneath the south tower, an Entombment copied from that in Bourges Cathedral and dating from the 18C. The decoration of one of the chapels to the left of the chancel relates the legend of St Corentine, Quimper's first bishop (5C), who lived on the flesh of a single, miraculous fish.

Every morning he took half the fish to eat and threw the other half back into the river. When he came back the next day the fish was whole once more and offered itself to be eaten again.

Stained-glass windows★★

The cathedral has a remarkable set of 15C **stained glass**★★ in the upper windows, mainly in the nave and transept, depicting canons, lords and ladies surrounded by their patron saints. It is interesting to note the marked evolution from the stained glass decorating the chancel, which dates from the early 15C, and that adorning the nave and transept which was only completed at the end of the 15C, when artists had considerable skill in drawing and in the use of subtle colours.

OLD QUIMPER★

Allow half a day

The old district stretches in front of the cathedral between the Odet and the Steir. Rue du Parc along the Odet leads to Quai du Steir.

This small tributary has now been canalised and covered before its confluence with the Odet, to form a vast pedestrian precinct.

Rue Élie-Fréon

North of place St-Corentin. Walk up the number 22 to admire a 17C corbelled house with a slate roof, and a Renaissance porch at number 20. From here go to charming place au Beurre.

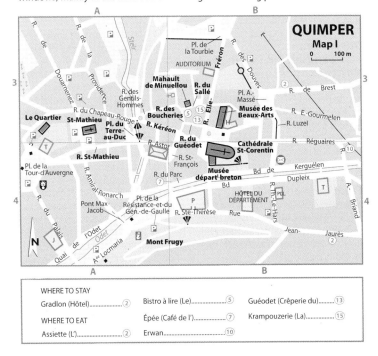

Rue Kéréon

R. Mattes/MICHELIN

Rue du Sallé

It was in the Middle Ages that the street of sausage and meat sellers got its name. Note the beautiful old house of the **Mahault de Minuellou** family at number 10.

Make a detour to the left via rue des Boucheries to **rue du Guéodet** where a house with caryatids and figures of men and women in 16C costume stands.

Rue Kéréon★

A busy shopping street and the most attractive in the town. It was once where the shoemakers were to be found (*kereon* in Breton – hence its name). The house at number 9, with its three polychrome figures, is rare in Quimper. The cathedral and its spires between the two rows of old corbelled houses make a delightful picture.

Place Terre-au-Duc

A picturesque square lined with old half-timbered houses. This was the lay town opposite the episcopal city and included the Law Courts, prison and the Duc de Bretagne market.

Take **rue St-Mathieu** which has some fine houses to reach **Église St-Mathieu**. This church, rebuilt in 1898, retains a fine 16C stained-glass window of the Passion half way up the chancel.

ADDITIONAL SIGHTS
Musée des Beaux-Arts★★

40 pl. St-Corentin. ◯*Open Jul–Aug, 10am–7pm; Rest of year, Wed–Mon 10am–noon, 2pm–6pm; Sun 2pm–6pm from Nov–Mar.* Guided tours available on Sat and daily in summer. ◯*Closed 1 Jan, 1 May, 1 and 11 Nov and 25 Dec.* 4.50€. &02 98 95 45 20. *www.musee-beauxarts.quimper.fr.*

This Fine Arts Museum contains a collection of paintings representing European painting from the 14C to the present. The museum has its own unique atmosphere, largely due to the mixing of natural and artificial lighting, in which it is possible to view the works in – quite literally – a new light.

On the ground floor, two rooms are devoted to 19C Breton painting: *A Marriage in Brittany* by Leleux; *A Street in Morlaix* by Noël; *Potato Harvest* by Simon; *Widow on Sein Island* by Renouf; *Flight of King Gradlon* by Luminais and *Fouesnant Rebels* by Girardet. One room is devoted to **Max Jacob** (1876–1944), who was born and grew up in Quimper.

His life and work are evoked through literature, memorabilia, drawings, gouaches, and in particular a series of portraits signed by his friends Picasso, Cocteau and others. At the centre of the first floor, the architect J P Philippon designed an area fitted in pale beech

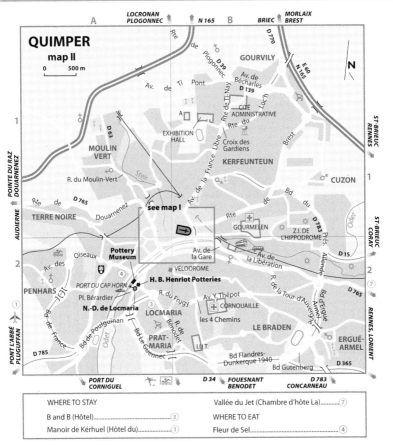

QUIMPER map II
0   500 m

wood to set 23 paintings from the dining room of the Hôtel de l'Épée, executed by the painter Lemordant (1878–1968). The area around the edges displays the work of different European Schools up to the contemporary period: Flemish (Rubens, Van Schriek); Italian (Bartolo di Fredi); Spanish; and French. Note in particular works by Boucher, Fragonard, Van Loo, *View of the Château de Pierrefonds* by Corot and *View of Quimper Harbour* by Boudin.

Musée Départemental Breton★

1 rue du Roi-Gradlon. ⏱*Open Jun–Sept, 9am–6pm; Oct–May, Tue–Sat 9am–noon, 2pm–5pm, Sun 2pm–5pm .* 👥*Guided tours available (1hr 30).* ⏱*Closed public holidays, 14 Jul and 15 Aug.* 💶*4€ (no charge on Sun Jan–May and Oct–Dec).* ♿ 📞*02 98 95 21 60.*

This museum, devoted to regional history (archaeology, ethnology, economy), occupies what used to be the episcopal palace, a large edifice built from the 16C to the 19C adjoining the cathedral.

After a brief display on prehistory, visitors enter the first rooms, devoted to the environment and way of life in one of the Gallo-Roman cities of the Osismes with such exhibits as coins, monumental mosaics, vases, funerary urns, silverware, and figurines of Venus and mother-goddesses.

There are two important pieces of **prehistoric jewellery**★ here: the Tréglonou necklace and the twisted belt from Irvillac.

One area of the medieval section displays a stone likeness of King Marc'h, Romanesque capitals and tomb stones, including the magnificently sculpted tombstone of Grallon of Kervaster.

The galleries of medieval and modern statues bring to mind the various religious cults that inspired this art form. The display includes two large 16C stained-glass windows.

The galleries which contain furniture retrace the history (17C–20C) of the domestic space occupied by folk furniture and the use to which it was put, from the grain and linen chests of Léon to the *petits meubles* mementoes by Plovézet. It is particularly interesting to see the role played by the cupboard in both the marriage ritual and in the attempt to create a 'modern Breton piece' between WW I and WW II.

The final section is devoted to Quimper faience and displays a rich collection of exhibits dating from the 18C to the present, illustrating the evolution of this decorative art form which reflects at once everyday life, creative spirit and perhaps even the dreams of an entire region.

Jardin de l'évêché

Between the cathedral and ramparts, the garden offers a good **view**★ of the cathedral chevet and spires, the Odet lined by the *préfecture* with its ornate dormer windows, the former Ste-Catherine hospital and Mont Frugy.

Some vestiges of the old ramparts can be seen in boulevard de Kerguélen and rue des Douves.

Musée de la Faïence★

14 rue Jean-Baptiste-Bousquet. ↻ *Closed - contact the* ⬛ *Tourist Office for information.* ♿ *℘02 98 90 12 72. www.quimper-faiences.com.*

This faience museum contains a rich collection of almost 2,500 items which it displays in rotation, retracing several centuries of the history of Quimper and its faience. The tour also explains the craft itself, giving details of techniques, artists and anonymous craftsmen (throwers, kiln-chargers and painters), to whom the museum pays homage in the form of a tall, colourful bas-relief.

The first two rooms are given over to the sequence of stages in the manufacturing process and to the tools and materials used. The marvellous works displayed in the following two rooms illustrate the blend of different styles from Rouen and Nevers.

The ground floor is reserved for 20C production concentrating on that from the period between the World Wars, which was particularly varied and prolific: from the shapes, colours and complex motifs by Quillivic or **Mathurin Méheut** to the highly refined ones of René Beauclair, or even the very original works by Giovanni Leonardi, to name but four artists.

The final gallery houses exhibitions on various themes.

Faïenceries de Quimper HB Henriot

Rue Haute. ↝ *Guided tours (35min). Call for details.* ⏱ *Closed Sat–Sun, all year, Christmas holidays and public holidays.* ≋*5€ (individual); 3€ (group tours).* ♿ *℘02 98 90 09 36. www.hb-henriot.com.*

The 300-year-old faience workshops were bought in 1984 by Paul Janssens, an American citizen of Dutch origin. Earthenware is still entirely decorated by hand with traditional motifs such as Breton peasants in traditional dress, birds, roosters and plants. A tour of the workshops enables visitors to discover in turn the various manufacturing stages, from the lump of clay to the firing process. A few concessions have been made to modern practices: the clay mixture is no longer prepared in house and the ovens are electrically heated. There is a shop on site.

Église Notre-Dame-de-Locmaria

This Romanesque church, rebuilt in the 15C and then later restored, is on the banks of the Odet. The plain interior contains, in the north side aisle, three tombstones dating from the 14C, 15C and 17C, and, on the rood beam, a robed Christ. In the south side aisle, a door leads to the garden of the old Benedictine priory (16C–17C) which has a cloistral gallery dating from 1669 and two 12C arches.

⚐ Mont Frugy

Allow 30min.

From place de la Résistance a path *(30min on foot there and back)* leads to the top of this wooded hill, 70m/75yds high. From the look-out point there is a good **view**★ of the city.

EXCURSIONS

Boat Trips down the Odet★★

Apr–Sept: up to five cruises daily (2hr 30min). Lunch cruises Tue–Sun. Possible stop-over in Bénodet, depending on the tide, or extended excursion to the Glénan Islands. Information at the ⚑ *Tourist Office or from Vedettes de l'Odet.* ℘02 98 57 00 58.

Baie de Kérogan★

The woods and castle parks lying along the river form a fine, green landscape. The Port du Corniguel, at the mouth of Kérogan Bay, adds a modern touch to the picture.

Les Vire-Court★★

The Odet here winds between high, wooded cliffs, a wild spot that has appeared in numerous legends. Two rocks at the narrowest point of the gorge are called Saut de la Pucelle (Maiden's Leap). Another rock is called theChaise de l'Evêque (the Bishop's Chair). Angels are said to have made it in the shape of a seat for the use of a saintly prelate of Quimper who liked to meditate in this lonely place. A little further on, the river bends so sharply that a Spanish fleet, coming up to attack Quimper, did not dare go through. Having taken on water at a fountain now called the Spaniards' Fountain, the ships turned back. On the west bank, before Le Perennou, ruins of Roman baths can be seen.

🚗 DRIVING TOURS

1 FROM THE BANKS OF THE JET TO THE ODET

Round trip of 27km/16.5mi – 2hr 30min.

▷ *Leave Quimper on avenue de la Libération, at the first major*

roundabout, turn left on the road to Brest and take the second road to the right to Coray. 700m/765yds further on, take the road towards Elliant.

The road runs beside the River Jet and offers views of the wooded countryside and pastureland.

Église d'Ergué-Gabéric

In the chancel of the early 16C church there is a stained-glass window depicting the Passion (1571) and a 17C group of the Trinity. The organ loft dates from 1680.

▷ *Bear right after the church towards the Chapelle de Kerdévot.*

Chapelle de Kerdévot

🕐*Open Jul–Sept, Tue–Sat 2.30–6.30pm, (Wed 3.30pm–6.30pm); Jun, Sun and hols 2.30pm–6.30pm.* ℘02 98 66 68 00.
The 15C chapel stands in an attractive setting near a calvary, which is of a later date and unfortunately somewhat damaged. Inside, a late 15C Flemish **altarpiece**★ standing on the high altar depicts six scenes from the life of the Virgin. There is a 17C statue of Our Lady of Kerdévot in painted wood in the nave.

▷ *Leave Kerdévot by the road on the left of the chapel, then turn left towards Quimper. After 3km/1.8mi turn right towards the hamlet of Lestonan. Go through Quéllénec, turn right onto a partly surfaced road 600m to the Griffonès car park.*

⚐ Site du Stangala★

After crossing an arboretum (red oak, copper beech), bear left through woodland to reach two rocky platforms. The site is a remarkable one: the rocky ridge overlooks the Odet from a height of 70m as the river winds between wooded slopes. Opposite and slightly to the right, the hamlet of Tréouzon clings to the slopes. Ahead, in the distance, to the left of the television tower, Locronan Mountain, with its characteristic outline and the chapel perched on its summit, can be picked out easily.

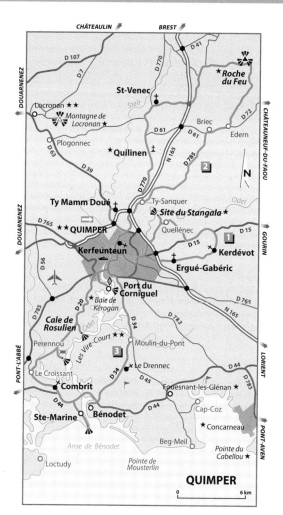

QUIMPER

On the way back to the car park, a road to the left leads down to the bank of the Odet *(30min there and back)*.

▷ *To return to Quimper, leave Quellénec W along Rte de Squividan, cross the N 165 (E 60) and follow signs for Quimper.*

2 CHAPELS AND CALVARIES

Round trip of 57km/35.5mi – 3hr.

▷ *Leave Quimper on rue des Douves. Shortly after a cemetery at the entrance of Kerfeunteun, turn right.*

Église de Kerfeunteun

Guided tour (Mon–Fri) on request from 76 blvd. des Frères-Maillot, Quimper. *02 98 64 30 46.*

A small square belfry with a stone spire surmounts the west façade.

The church was built in the 16C and 17C but the transept and chancel were rebuilt in 1953. It has kept a beautiful stained-glass window (16C) above the high altar, depicting a Tree of Jesse with a Crucifixion above.

▷ *Go down the av. France-Libre. At the second roundabout, take the road for Plogonnec. The first right is chemin de Ty Mamm Doué.*

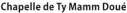

Chapelle de Ty Mamm Doué

Guided tours Jul–Sept, Thu and Sat 2pm–6pm. ✆02 98 95 81 38 (M. Duval). Built between 1541 and 1592, *Ty Mamm Doué* (House of the Mother of God) sees the introduction of the Renaissance style in Brittany. Note to the south the Gothic door with twisted columns, decorated with bee hives at the bottom. Inside, a unique nave, choir and 19C furniture.

> *Continue 800m/0.5mi further on, turn right towards Brest, then left in the direction of Briec and at Ty-Sanquer, left again.*

Calvaire de Quilinen★

Guided visits. Jul–Aug, Open May–Sept, 9am–7pm. ✆02 98 57 90 44. Near the main road, hidden by the trees, stands the **Chapelle Notre-Dame-de-Quilinen** with its unusual calvary. Built c. 1550 on two superposed triangular bases with the points opposite one another, the calvary reveals a rough and naïve style. As the Cross rises to the figure of Christ above the two thieves who are placed close together, the statues become ever more slender. The other side of the Cross represents Christ resurrected. The south portal of the 15C chapel is decorated by a graceful Virgin between two angels.

> *Return to the main road and bear right; after 5km/3.1mi, turn right towards the nearby Chapelle de St-Venec.*

Chapelle de St-Venec

Visit by appointment, ask at the 🛈 Tourist Office. ✆02 98 57 74 62. In Gothic style, this chapel portrays in stone St-Gwen and her triplets: St-Guénolé, St-Jacut and St-Venec. St-Blanche (called Gwen here), had three nipples: one to suckle each of her triplets. In front of the chapel is a calvary (1556) on a triangular base similar to that of Quilinen, and on the other side of the road stands a charming 16C fountain.

> *Take the chapel road, pass under the Quimper-Brest dual carriageway and turn left towards Chaelle Notre-Dame-des-Trois Fontaines. Proceed to the Gouézec road and turn right.*

🏃 La Roche du Feu★ (Karreg an Tan)

30min on foot there and back. From the car park, take a path to the summit (279m/915ft): an extensive **panorama**★ over the Montagnes Noires, Ménez-Hom and the Aulne Valley.

> *Return to Quimper via Edern and Briec.*

③ ALONG THE BANKS OF THE ODET

Round trip of 48km/30mi – 2hr 30min.

> *Leave Quimper on blvd. de Poulguinan to Pont-l'Abbé. After the roundabout, uphill, bear left.*

Port du Corniguel

This is the port of Quimper from which wine, timber and sand are exported. Fine view of the Odet and the Baie de Kérogan.

> *Return to the Pont-l'Abbé road, and then turn left towards Plomelin. At the next junction, bear left towards the Cale de Rosulien.*

Cale de Rosulien

Road unsurfaced at the end. A ruined mill stands on the right. From the dock, there is a good view of the **Vire-Court**★★.

> *Return to the junction, turn left and after the entrance to Perennou Castle, bear left towards the Odet (signposts).*

From the car park 🅿, take a path (🏃 *15min on foot there and back)* to the banks of the Odet with good views of the river. Before the Croissant junction where you bear left for Combrit, the road crosses the deep Combrit Cove, which presents a fine sight at high tide. The 16C **church** at **Combrit** has a square domed belfry flanked by two turrets.

An ossuary (17C) stands next to the south porch.

Parc Botanique de Cornouaille

⊙ *Open Jul–Aug, 10am–7pm; rest of the year 10am–noon, 2pm–7pm.* ⊙ *Closed 20 Sept–15 Oct and 15 Nov–15 Mar.* ⊙ *6.50€.* ℘ *02 98 56 44 93. www.parcbotanique.com.*

After you have visited this very beautiful 4ha/10-acre park, which constitutes one of the most important botanical collections in Brittany, you can buy bedding plants in the nursery, located at the entrance, where some of the 3,500 species of plants found in the garden are for sale. This is a magical place in March, when 550 varieties of camellias and 85 kinds of magnolias are in full bloom.

▷ *Proceed in the direction of Bénodet, then bear right for Ste-Marine.*

Ste-Marine

This small resort on the west bank of the Odet has a good sandy beach with a fine view over Loctudy and Pointe de Lesconil, the Île aux Moutons and the Îles Glénan, and a small pleasure boat harbour, from which you can enjoy a lovely view of Bénodet and the Odet (ⓒ *see BÉNODET). From July to August (10am–12.30pm, 1.50pm–7.15pm, Sat-Sun 1.50pm–7.15pm;* ⊙ *2€;* ℘ *06 81 66 78 67), a ferry for pedestrians links Ste-Marine and Bénodet.*

▷ *Go over the Pont de Cornouaille.*

Bénodet ⌂⌂ – ⓒ *See BÉNODET.*

The return road (*D 34*) is further inland from the east bank of the Odet and runs through **Le Drennec**. Standing in front of the chapel, beside the road, is a charming 16C fountain.

▷ *Pass through Moulin-du-Port to return to Quimper.*

ADDRESSES

🛏 STAY

🍽 **B and B** – *131 rue de Bénodet, Quimper.* ℘ *08 92 78 80 85. www.hotel bb.com. 72 rooms.* ⊡ *6 €.* Relatively near to the town centre and its shops, this hotel is, however, not typical of chain hotels. Of modern construction with large windows it has spacious well equipped rooms some of which are suitable for families having four to five beds.

🍽 **Hôtel Gradlon** – *30 rue de Brest, Quimper.* ℘ *02 98 95 04 39. www. hotel-gradlon.com. Closed 12 Dec–11 Jan.* ⊡ *12€. 22 rooms.* One of the nicest hotels in town, the Gradlon features distinctive rooms with antique furniture as well as a generous breakfast served in the tranquil courtyard.

🍽 **Chambre d'hôte La Vallée du Jet** – *Kervren, 29140 St-Yvi. 14km/8.7mi SE of Quimper on the D 765 rte de Rosporden.* ℘ *02 98 94 70 34. Closed Feb.* ⊡ *. 5 rooms. 2 gîtes.* This 19C longhouse overlooks the Jet valley. Rooms are quiet and have a terrace overlooking the large garden. Children will love the farmyard and sheep.

🍽 **Hôtel du Manoir de Kérhuel** – *29720 Plonéour-Lanvern. 12km/7.4mi S of Quimper on the D 785 rte de Pont l'Abbé then D 156 rte de Plonéour-Lanvern.* ℘ *02 98 82 60 57. http://manoirdekerhuel.com. Closed Jan–Easter, 11 Nov–27 Dec.* ⊡ *10€. Restaurant* 🍽. *26 rooms.* A long tree-lined drive leads to this 15C manor, situated in a pretty, flower-filled park. Charming, restful rooms.

🍴 EAT

🍽 **Le Bistro à Lire** – *18 rue des Boucheries.* ℘ *02 98 95 30 86. Closed Sun and Mon off season.* Since 2001, this bookshop-restaurant in the heart of the pedestrian area marries a love of books with the delights of eating. Events around crime novels each month.

🍽 **Crêperie du Guéodet** – *6 r. du Guéodet.* ℘ *02 98 95 40 38 - Closed Sun, Mon exc school hols.* Very small *crêperie* much frequented by locals who appreciate galettes made from organic flour. Cheerful décor with pottery and the atmosphere is friendly. If full, take a tour of old Quimper and try again.

La Krampouzerie – *9 rue du Sallé (Place au Beurre). 02 98 95 13 08. Closed Sun and Mon off season.* Savour unexpected specialities such as crêpes with algae from Ouessant or with onion jam from Roscoff, paired with caramel and ginger. Leave room for a dessert of Basque sheep's cheese and black-cherry jam.

L'Assiette – *5 bis rue Jean-Jaurès. 02 98 53 03 65. Closed 24 Aug–7 Sept and Sun.* Madame does front of house, Monsieur is at the stove and Junior makes the appetising desserts. The dining room is half-brasserie, half-bistrot; the traditional cuisine pays homage to the sea.

Café de l'Épée – *14 rue du Parc. 02 98 95 28 97. www.quimper-lepee.com.* Artists of stage and screen, writers and politicians have frequented this local institution. The brasserie offers seafood menus, fish and meat dishes.

Erwan – *3 r. Aristide-Briand. 02 98 90 14 14. www.erwan-restaurant.com.* Erwan is the owner of this friendly restaurant located near St-Corentin Cathedral. Breton furniture and décor in black, yellow and orange is the setting for Breton cuisine of simple small dishes taken from grandmothers' recipe notebooks.

Fleur de Sel – *1 quai Neuf. 02 98 55 04 71. www.fleur-de-sel-quimper.com. Closed 24 Dec-2 Jan, Sat lunch and Sun.* Situated in a picturesque quarter of Quimper on the Quai neuf, this restaurant serves traditional dishes.

NIGHTLIFE

Ceili – *4 rue Aristide Briand. 02 98 95 17 61. Open Mon–Sat 10.30am–1am, Sun 5pm–1am.* This Celtic pub organises year-round concerts: the perfect occasion to share a Breton beer with your neighbour and listen to bagpipes.

ACTIVITIES

Aquarive – *159 bd. de Creac'h Gwen. 02 98 52 00 15. Open Mon–Sat 10am–8pm during holidays.* Water complex with a wave machine, 60m slide, jacuzzis, sauna and hammam.

Hikes – I.D. or *Itinéraires Découverte* are available at the Tourist Office and are a helpful compilation of the hikes on the 225km of paths in the region.

Kayak to Bénodet – Discover the Odet by taking a kayaking class with

Club Canoë-kayak – *rue du Chanoine Moreau (at the yachting marina of Locmaria, behind the Faïenceries H.B. Henriot). 02 98 53 19 99. www.kayak-quimper.org . Closed Sept–Jun.*

FESTIVALS AND EVENTS

Festival de Cornouaille – *02 98 55 53 53. www.festival-cornouaille.com.* This established festival celebrates Breton culture over nine days in July and welcomes around 300 000 visitors.

Summer events – from mid-Jun–mid-Sept there are music and dance concerts in the bishop's garden on Thursdays at 9.15pm.

SHOPPING

Biscuiterie Quimper-Styvel – *8 rue du Chanoine-Moreau. 02 98 53 10 13. Closed Sun off season.* All kinds of regional products are sold in this shop including jam and pottery but they also make their own cakes and crêpes which you can enjoy straight from the oven.

Manoir du Kinkiz – *75 chemin du Quinquis, Ergue-Armel. 02 98 90 20 57. Closed public holidays.* Award-winning cider producer where you can visit, taste and buy.

Distillerie Artisanale du Plessis – *77 chemin du Quinquis, Ergue-Armel. 02 98 90 75 64. Closed Sun.* This distillery continues to make traditional products such as *pommeau*, cider, apple juice and liqueur. There are innovative new products too such as seaweed aperatifs. Don't miss a visit to the museum which ends with a tasting.

Ménez-Hom★★★

Ménez-Hom (alt 330m/1,083ft), a detached peak at the west end of the Montagnes Noires, is one of the great Breton viewpoints and a key position commanding the approach to the Presqu'île de Crozon. On 15 August a folklore festival is held at the summit.

SIGHTS

Panorama★★★

Viewing table.

In clear weather there is a vast panorama. You will see Douarnenez Bay, bounded on the left by the Cornouaille coast as far as the Pointe du Van, and on the right by the coast of the Presqu'île de Crozon as far as Cap de la Chèvre. To the right the view extends to the Pointe de St-Mathieu, the Tas de Pois Rocks, the Pointe de Penhir, Brest and its roadstead, in front of which you will see the Île Longue on the left, the Île Ronde and the Pointe de l'Armorique on the right. The nearer valley – that of the Aulne – follows a fine, winding course, spanned by the suspension bridge at Térénez. In the distance are the Monts d'Arrée, the Montagne St-Michel crowned by its little chapel, the Châteaulin Basin, the Montagne de Noires Montagnes, Locronan, Douarnenez and Tréboul. The slopes facing northeast were burnt in June 2006, losing 300ha/742 acres of protected heathland and peat bogs.

View over the Aulne from Ménez-Hom

R. Mattes/MICHELIN

- ⓘ **Michelin Map:** Local map 308 F5 - Finistère (29).
- ⓘ **Info:** ℰ02 98 27 93 60 or www.camaretsurmertourisme.com
- ⓘ **Location:** Travelling from Châteaulin towards Crozon along the D 887 and D 83, you can see the mount above you. The final 2km/1.2mi climb is along a road which branches off, 1.5km/1mi after the Chapelle Ste-Marie-du-Ménez-Hom.
- ⓘ **Kids:** The Musée de l'École Rurale en Bretagne – a reconstruction of an old schoolhouse.
- ⓘ **Timing:** Watch the sun set over the ocean in the evening.
- ⓘ **Don't Miss:** The panorama from the viewing table at the top.

⌖Go as far as the mark of the Geographical Institute *(Institut géographique)* to get a view of the horizon from all sides.

Chapelle Ste-Marie-du-Ménez-Hom

ⓘ*Open Apr–Sept, 10am–6pm. In the event that it is locked, ask at the Town Hall. ℰ02 98 81 59 43.*

The chapel stands in a small parish close at the entrance to Presqu'île de Crozon. The close has a very plain rounded doorway, dated 1739, and a calvary with three crosses rising from separate bases. The chapel, which has a twin-gabled façade, is entered through a doorway beneath the elegant galleried belfry, topped by a cupola which gives an upward sweep to the massive building. Inside, the ornate **altarpieces**★ take up the whole of the east wall, without covering over the window apertures. While both the central altarpiece, with The Family and Life of The Virgin as its theme, and the north altarpiece, depicting the saints, have figures which are rather heavy and expressionless. The figures of the

Apostles on the south altarpiece show life and elegance. The skill with which they were carved marks a step forward in Breton sculpture. The lovely purlins in the north transept, adorned with animals and various scenes, a remarkable St Lawrence and a graceful St Barbara in wood, are also noteworthy.

Trégarvan – Musée de l'École Rurale en Bretagne

7km/4.3mi N of Ste-Marie-du-Menez-Hom. Open Jul–Aug, 10.30am–7pm; mid-Jan–Jun and Sept, Sun–Fri (and Sat in Sept) 2pm–6pm; Oct–Nov, Sun–Fri 2pm–5pm; Dec–mid-Feb, Mon–Fri 2pm –5pm. *Closed 1 Jan, 1 Nov and 25 Dec.* 4€ (children 2.30€). 02 98 26 04 72.

From the Sky

ULM – *29550 Plomodiern.* 02 98 81 28 47. *Flights along the coast in a microlight aircraft. Lessons available.*

Paragliding – *29550 Plomodiern.* 02 98 81 50 27 *or* 06 80 32 47 34. *www.vol-libre-menez-hom.com. Closed mid-Sept–Mar.*

This museum, set up by the *Parc Naturel Régional d'Armorique*, recreates the atmosphere of an early 20C country schoolhouse. It includes a large classroom and the schoolmaster's living quarters.

Presqu'île de Crozon★★★

The Crozon Peninsula affords many excursions typical of the Breton coast. Nowhere else, except perhaps at Raz Point, do the sea and coast reach such heights of grim beauty, with the giddy steepness of the cliffs, the colouring of the rocks and the fury of the sea breaking on the reefs. Another attraction is the variety of views over the indentations and estuaries of the Brest roadstead, the Goulet, the broken coast of Toulinguet, Penhir, Dinan Castle, Cap de la Chèvre and Douarnenez Bay. All this can be seen in an immense panorama from the summit of the Ménez-Hom.

Michelin Map: Local map 308 E5 - Finistère (29).

Info: Bd. de Pralognan, 29160 Crozon. 02 98 27 07 92. www.crozon.fr.

Location: The peninsula sprawls into the sea between the Brest roadsteads and the Douarnenez Bay.

Kids: The Grandes Grottes caves.

Timing: Enjoy walks, bike rides and time on the beach.

Don't Miss: Sunset viewed from the Pointe de Penhir.

is modern. The altar to the right of the chancel is ornamented with a large 17C **altarpiece**★ depicting the martyrdom of the Theban Legion on Mount Ararat during the reign of Emperor Hadrian.

DRIVING TOURS

1 POINTE DE PENHIR TO POINTE DESESPAGNOLS★★★

Driving tour starting from Crozon – 45 km/28mi – 2hr 30min.

Crozon

The town stands in the middle of the peninsula of the same name. The **church**

Leave Crozon by the D 8, W of town and make for Camaret.

Camaret-sur-Mer
An important spiny lobster port, Camaret is also a quiet, simple seaside resort, close to impressive sheer cliff and facing the entrance to the Brest Channel,

Coastline at Crozon

R. Mattès/MICHELIN

65km north of Quimper. On the shore, to the left of the *Sillon*, a natural dyke which protects the port, is Corréjou Beach *(www.camaretsurmer-tourisme.fr)*.

Chapelle Notre-Dame-de-Rocamadour

This chapel stands at the end of the dyke. It was built between 1610 and 1683 and restored after a fire in 1910. It was originally a pilgrimage chapel on the pilgrims' route to Rocamadour in Quercy; from the 11C the pilgrims from the north, who came by sea, used to disembark at Camaret to continue the journey by land. A *pardon* is held on the first Sunday in September.

Château Vauban

A massive tower surrounded by walls was built by the military architect Vauban at the end of the 17C on Sillon Point. It now houses temporary exhibitions from time to time. There are fine views of the Brest Channel, Pointe des Espagnols and the port and town of Camaret.

Alignements de Lagatjar

This fine group of megaliths, whose name means hen's eye, includes 143 menhirs discovered in the early 20C. An isthmus bounded by Pen-Hat Beach leads to the **Pointe du Toulinguet** on which a French Navy signal station

stands. There is a view of the Pointe de Penhir to the south.

◯ Return to the entrance to Camaret and bear right.

Pointe de Penhir★★★

Penhir Point is the finest of the four headlands of the Presqu'île de Crozon. A memorial (150m off the road) to the Bretons of the Free French Forces has been erected on the cliff.

◯ 45min. Leave the car at the end of the surfaced road. Go onto the platform at the end of the promontory for a view of the sea 70m/336ft below (telescopes).

The setting is magnificent as is the **panorama**: below are the great isolated rocks called the **Tas de Pois** (literally, pile of peas!); on the left is the Pointe de Dinan; on the right, Pointe de St-Mathieu and Pointe du Toulinguet, the second with its little lighthouse, and at the back the Ménez-Hom. In the distance, the Pointe du Raz and the Île de Sein can be seen on clear days to the left, and Ouessant over to the right.
If you enjoy scrambling over rocks, you should take a path going down to the left of the platform and monument. Halfway down the sheer drop of the cliff there is a view of a little cove. Here take the path on the left that climbs towards a cavity covered with a rock beyond which is the **Chambre Verte,** a grassy strip. From here there is an unusual view of the Tas de Pois rocks and the Pointe de Penhir.

◯ Return to the car and take the Camaret road again. Turn right after 1.5km/0.9mi towards Crozon, to avoid the town; then take the road to Roscanvel, once a strategic road.

The view opens out to show Camaret Bay on the left and, on the right, the Brest roadstead. The road enters the walls that enclose the Presqu'île de Roscanvel before Quélern. These fortifications date from the time of Vauban and the Second Empire.

Tas de Pois, Pointe de Penhir

R. Matès/MICHELIN

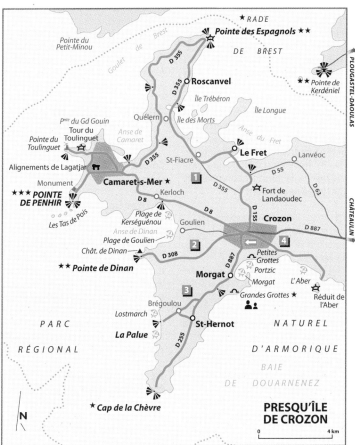

The road running west is picturesque. The curious contrast between the slopes on either side of the peninsula is striking: the western slope, facing the west wind and the sea, is moorland and lacks vegetation; the eastern slope is covered with trees and meadows.

Pointe des Espagnols★★

From here one can see a remarkable **panorama** that includes the Brest Sound, the town and harbour of Brest, the Elorn estuary, the Pont Albert-Louppe, the Presqu'île de Plougastel, and the end of the roadstead. The point owes its name to the Spanish garrison that occupied the area for a brief period in 1594 and built a fort on the headland.

Roscanvel

The church was rebuilt after a fire in 1956 and now possesses fine dark stained-glass windows by Labouret, and a coloured terracotta Stations of the Cross by Claude Gruher. Note the hedges of fuschia between the gardens.

The road, which to the south of Roscanvel goes round the end of the roadstead, affords fine views of Île Longue (*no entry, nuclear submarine base*), and in the foreground, of the two smaller islands, Trébéron and Morts. You leave the peninsular territory once more by the ruined fortifications.

About 500m/545yds beyond St-Fiacre, turn left.

Le Fret

This small port provides a regular boat service to and from Brest and has a view of the Presqu'île de Plougastel from the jetty.

The road runs along the jetty bordering Le Fret Bay.

When you come to a fork, leave the Lanvéoc road on your left and turn right to Crozon.

Enjoy a last look back at the roadstead.

② FROM CROZON TO POINTE DE DINAN★★

6km/3.7mi – 2hr.

Leave Crozon W by the D 308.

Windswept heathland follows after the pine groves.

Pointe de Dinan★★

Allow 1hr. Leave your car at the car park; continue on foot, by the path on the left for about 500m/545yds.

A fine **panorama** can be seen from the edge of the cliff; on the left are Cap de la Chèvre, the coast of Cornouaille and Pointe du Raz; on the right, Pointe du Penhir and the Tas de Pois. Skirting the cliff to the right you will see the enormous rocky mass of **Dinan Castle** (Château de), joined to the mainland by a natural arch.

Take the footpath over the natural arch to explore the rock which looks like a fortified castle in ruins *(30min on foot there and back, over rocky ground; wear non-slip soles)*.

③ FROM CROZON TO CAP DE LA CHEVRE★

11km/6.8mi – allow 2hr.

Crozon –

See ① above.

Leave Crozon by the D 887 SW.

Morgat⌂

Morgat is a well-sheltered seaside resort. The great sandy beach is enclosed to the south by a point covered with pine woods, Beg-ar-Gador. On the north side, a rocky spur separates Morgat Beach from that of Le Portzic. Fishing boats go out from the **harbour,** sheltering behind a jetty where 400 pleasure craft can also anchor.

⚹ Les Grandes Grottes★

Guided tour (40min) Apr–Sept, daily, depatures scheduled according to the tides, leaving from the port. 10€ (children 7€). Vedettes Rosmeur Croisières. 06 85 95 55 49.

The first group of big caves, situated beyond Beg-ar-Gador, includes Ste-Marine and the Devil's Chamber (Chambre du Diable). The second group is at the other end of the bay. The finest grotto is that of the Altar (l'Autel), 80m/260ft deep and 15m/50ft high.

Les Petites Grottes

These small caves at the foot of the spur between Morgat and Le Portzic beaches can be reached at low tide.

From Morgat to Cap de la Chèvre the road runs through an austere landscape of rocks and stunted heath, open to the ocean winds, with little hamlets of houses huddled together that seem to hide in the folds of the ground. To the left, the view gradually opens out over Douarnenez Bay, with the massive outline of the Ménez-Hom in the distance.

A short distance past **Brégoulou**, leave the car in the car park from which you can enjoy a good view of the Tas de Pois and Pointe du Raz.

The splendid beach of **Plage de la Palud** offers fine views of the rocky coastline. Bathing is forbidden owing to powerful waves breaking on the shore.

Cap de la Chèvre★

From the former German observation point there is a fine **view** over the Atlantic: (left to right) Pointe de Penhir ,Tas de Pois, the Île de Sein, Cap Sizun, Pointe du Van and Pointe du Raz to the south of Douarnenez Bay.

A **monument**, representing the wing of an aircraft, is dedicated to the aircrew personnel of Aéronautique Navale killed or missing in active service.

ADDRESSES

STAY

Hôtel de la Presqu'île – *pl. de l'Église. ℘02 98 27 29 29. Closed 8–31 Mar, 27 Sept–20 Oct Sun and Mon off season. 13 rooms. ⊇ 10€. Restaurant⊝⊝.* This former town-hall now houses soundproofed, stylish rooms.

Ferme Auberge du Seillou – *Seillou, 29590 Rosnoen. 20km/mi12.5 E of Crozon on the D 791. ℘02 98 81 92 21. www.fermeaubergeduseillou.com. Closed for three weeks Sept–Oct. 6 rooms. ⊇. Restaurant⊝⊝ (reservations necessary).* Old stones and quality farm products (meat, cider, *kig ha farz*), give a good name to this house which is hidden on a farm. Cute attic bedrooms and footpaths nearby.

Hôtel Vauban – *4 quai du Styvel, Camraet-Sur-Mer. ℘02 98 27 91 36. 16 rooms. ⊇ 6€.* Humble but pleasant hotel, well kept and reasonable prices. Great location and views.

Hôtel de France – *19 quai Gustave Toudouze, Camraet-Sur-Mer. ℘02 98 27 93 06. www.logis-de-france.fr. Closed Nov–Easter. 20 rooms. ⊇ 8€.* Simple rooms but well kept and soundproofed. Those at the back are smaller. As you'd expect from a Logis de France hotel, the food is good.

EAT

CAMARET-SUR-MER

Chez Philippe – *22 quai Gustave Toudouze. ℘02 98 27 90 41. Closed Mon and Thur eve in Winter.* A restaurant of regulars where you eat shoulder to shoulder and for almost nothing: daily special, *moules marinières*, tasty meat and fish dishes.

Les Frères de la Côte – *11 quai Gustave Toudouze. ℘02 98 27 95 42. Closed Nov–Apr and Mon–Wed.* Coming from the Caribbean island of Guadalupe, these brothers prepare Breton fish with exotic spices. Rum drinks are a speciality.

SHOPPING

Biscuiterie de Camaret – *route de Crozon. ℘02 98 27 88 08.* A huge range of regional products: preserves, sweets, hand-painted porcelain and faience. Free tasting of Breton cakes.

Landévennec★

Situated on the Presqu'île de Landévennec, which is part of the Parc Naturel Régional de l'Armorique, the village of Landévennec occupies a pretty site★ at the mouth of the River Aulne, which is best seen by taking the steep downhill road to the right from Gorréquer. A lookout point to the right offers a fine view★ of Landévennec. Below is the course of the River Aulne, with the Île de Térénez; beyond, the Presqu'île de Landévennec and the River Faou.

▶ **Population:** 349.
🖦 **Michelin Map:** Local map 308 F5 - Finistère (29).
🖹 **Info:** Rue St-Guénolé, 29560 Landévennec. ℰ02 98 27 78 46.
◗ **Location:** Take the D 60, which becomes the D 791 linking Le Faou to Crozon. Steep descent into the village.
🕙 **Timing:** A couple of hours should suffice.
🖎 **Don't Miss:** A tour of Le Faou to admire the site.

VISIT
Abbaye St-Guénolé
Halfway down the slope, bear right onto a tree-lined alley and follow the signposts.
http://abbaye-landevennec.cef.fr.
The very plain church contains a poly-chrome wood **statue** of St-Guénolé (15C), in sacerdotal vestments and a monolithic pink granite altar.

Ruines de l'Ancienne Abbaye
🕙*Open Jul–mid-Sept 10am–7pm; second half of Sept Sun–Fri 10am–6pm; Easter–Jun Sun–Fri 2pm–6pm; Oct–Mar, Sun and holidays only 2pm–6pm.* 🖦4€. ℰ02 98 27 35 90. *www.pnr-armorique.fr.*
The monastery founded by the Welsh St-Guénolé (Winwaloe) in the 5C and remodelled several times ceased to exist in the 18C and only the ruins of the Romanesque church remain. The layout can be deduced from the column bases, wall remains and doorway: a nave and aisles with six bays, transept, chancel

and ambulatory with three radiating chapels. At the entrance to the south transept, there is a monument thought to be the tomb of King Gradlon.
An **abbey museum** of a very modern design was inaugurated on this site. It houses objects unearthed during excavations, including a wooden sar-cophagus predating the 10C and models illustrating the different stages of con-struction of the abbey.

EXCURSIONS
Argol
◗*6km/3.7mi to the SW of Landévennec on the D 60.*
In Breton, Argol means "in danger of dying", and this is the place where Dahut, daughter of King Gradlon, is said to have died when the legendary city of Ys was engulfed by the sea.
The town's **Parish Close** (enclos par-oissial) church dates from 1576 with a calvary from 1593. The triumphal arch at

---

St-Guénolé (St-Winwaloe)
The son of a Prince from Britain, Guénolé was born about AD 460 and grew up in the area around St-Brieuc. Hearing of the death of St-Patrick he decided to go to Ireland to see his remains but before he set off the saint appeared to him in a dream telling him to found an abbey. He set up a small community on a desolate island at the mouth of the River Faou but soon gave this up to found the Abbey at Landévennec, the ruins of which can still be seen today. (*Abbey ruins open daily Jul–Aug 10am–7pm; Apr, daily exc Sat; Jun and Sept 10am–6pm; Oct–Mar Sun and public hols 10am–5pm; www.musee-abbaye-landevennec.fr*).

the entrance to the enclosure features an equestrian statue of Gradlon.

👥 Maison des vieux métiers vivants★

🕐Jul–Aug, 2pm–6pm; Apr–Jun and Sept, Tue, Thu and Sun 2pm–5.30pm, rest of the year, ask for details. ☞4€ (6-14yrs, 2€). ☎02 98 27 79 30. www.argol.fr.

Volunteers present rural and maritime occupations of yesteryear: basket making, saddlery, clog-making, pit sawing, spinning, lace making, toy making, etc. In summer, the museum also holds special events and demonstrations (fitting tyres onto cart wheels, harvest festival, threshing with a flail, sheep shearing, etc). Programme available on request.

👥 Parc de jeux bretons

200m/218yds from the Maison des vieux métiers vivants. 🕐 Jul–Aug 2pm–6pm, Apr–Jun and Sept, Tue, Thu and Sun 2pm–6pm. Free.

This annex to the museum offers the opportunity to try your hand at traditional Breton games, such as galoche or boulten, using skittles or pucks. Rules supplied on site.

Pont de Térénez

▷ 9.5 km/6mi away, heading S on the D 60 then left onto the D 791.

Spanning the River Aulne, this graceful bridge, whose central span 272m/890ft, offers a fine view of the valley.

Le Faou

▷ 20km/12.4mi E on the D 60 then left on the D 791.

The town, at the head of the Faou estuary, occupies a **site**★, which is full of character at high tide. The main street, rue Principale, is flanked on one side by old houses with overhanging upper storeys and slate-covered façades. The 16C **church** (🕐 open Mon–Fri 3pm–7pm; ☎02 98 81 90 55; ask for key in presbytery) stands on the river bank. It has an elegant 17C domed bell-tower, a double transept, a canted east end and an ornately sculpted south porch.

Argol triumphal arch
©Jakez/iStockphoto.com

ADDRESSES

🏠STAY / 🍴EAT

🛏🛏 **LOGIS Hôtel le Relais de la Place** – 7, place aux Foires, La Faou. ☎02 98 81 91 19. Pleasant hotel and restaurant located at the heart of the charming village of Le Faou. Good for seafood.

🛏🛏 **LOGIS la Vieille Renommée Hôtel de Beauvoir** – 11, place aux Foires, La Faou. ☎02 98 81 90 31. This fine building at the heart of le Faou is full of character and very welcoming. Its restaurant specialises in refined cuisine with a regional flavour.

🛒 SHOPPING

Écomusée de l'Abeille – Ferme Apicole de Térénez. 8km/5mi from Le Faou towards Crozon. ☎02 98 81 06 90. www.ferme-apicole-de-terenez.com. Open 10am–7pm. Beekeepers present their trade and products, such as royal jelly, wax and pollen. You can learn about apiculture, see the professional equipment and sample honey, gingerbread, mead and confectionery, which are all for sale in the on-site shop.

La Cornouaille★★

Historic Cornouaille, the kingdom and then the duchy of medieval Brittany, extended far to the north and east of its capital, Quimper, reaching Landerneau, the neighbourhood of Morlaix and Quimperlé. The area included in the tour is much smaller and is limited to the coastal districts of Cornouaille, west of Quimper. This very extensive coastline is marked by two rocky peninsulas, Cap Sizun, "Le Cap", and the Presqu'île de Penmarch, which are its main tourist attractions. Fishing plays an important part in daily life in this part of Brittany; the ports of Guilvinec, Audierne and Douarnenez specialise in the landing of sardines and spiny lobster. The interior is densely cultivated with potatoes and early vegetables, and the countryside, with its tranquil horizons, is covered with small hamlets of whitewashed houses.

🚗 DRIVING TOURS

1 CAP SIZUN★★

Quimper to Plozévet

128km/80mi – allow one day.

Quimper★★ – 🕪 *See QUIMPER.*

▷ *Leave Quimper NW by rue de Locronan and rue de la Providence.*

The road goes up the rural valley of the Steïr with its wooded slopes and then through undulating countryside.

Plogonnec

The 16C **church**, remodelled in the 18C, has a fine Renaissance bell-tower and 16C stained-glass windows. In the chancel to the left of the high altar the windows recount the Transfiguration, above the altar the Passion and to the right the Last Judgement.

Locronan★★ – 🕪 *See LOCRONAN.*

- 🕪 **Michelin Map:** Local map 308 F/H 5/7 - Finistère (29).
- 🛈 **Info:** 8 rue Victor Hugo, 29770 Audierne. ℘02 98 70 12 20. www.audierne-tourisme.com.
- 👥 **Kids:** Aquashow in Audierne and Haliotika in Guilvinec.
- 🕒 **Timing:** Allow a day for the beaches, little churches, walks and stunning views. Bring a picnic and sturdy shoes.
- 🕪 **Don't Miss:** The headlands.

▷ *The Douarnenez road with Forest of Nevet on its left, leads to the sea.*

Kerlaz

There is a good view of Douarnenez, which is reached after skirting the fine Ris Beach.
Note the 16C and 17C church with an openwork bell-tower.

Douarnenez★ – 🕪 *See DOUARNENEZ.*

▷ *Leave Douarnenez, go through Tréboul and make for Poullan-sur-Mer where you turn left and then right and right again.*

Chapelle Notre-Dame-de-Kérinec

The chapel, surrounded by trees, dates from the 13C and 15C; the elegant bell-tower was struck by lightning in 1958 but an exact replica, as it appeared in the 17C, has been rebuilt. Note the flat east end and to the left the rounded pulpit dominated by a calvary.

Église Notre-Dame-de-Confort

🕒*Open 9am–7pm.* The 16C church with its galleried bell-tower dating from 1736, has **stained-glass windows** in the chancel, one of which is a Tree of Jesse. Over the last arch in the nave, on the north side, hangs a carillon wheel with 12 little bells. The chimes are rung to beg the Virgin for the gift of speech for children who have difficulties in speaking.

Leave Confort in the direction of Pont-Croix and turn right, then left onto D 307 towards Beuzec-Cap-Sizun and again right after 2km/1.2mi.

Pointe du Millier★

A small lighthouse stands on this arid site. From the point *(15min on foot there and back)* there is a **view**★ of Douarnenez Bay and *Cap de la Chèvre.*

On leaving Beuzec-Cap-Sizun bear right.

Pointe de Beuzec★

From the car park there is a **view**★ of the approach to Douarnenez Bay, the Presqu'île de Crozon and in fine weather, of the Pointe de St-Mathieu.

Réserve du Cap Sizun★

Open 24 hrs. *Closed Oct–Mar.* *Guided tours.* 2€. 02 98 70 13 53.

The most interesting time for a visit is at nesting time in the spring. Starting in March, most birds finish nesting by mid July. The adults and chicks then leave the sanctuary progressively through the month of August. In the magnificent and wild setting of the Castel-ar-Roc'h, more than 70m above sea level, such seabirds as guillemots, cormorants, common herring gulls, lesser black-backed gulls, great black-backed gulls, which are the rarest of all, and black-legged kittiwakes can be seen, sitting on their nests and feeding their young.

Herring gull

M. Guillou/MICHELIN

Goulien

La Maison du vent (*Jul–Aug, 3pm–6pm; no charge;* 02 98 70 04 09) is at Le Bourg. The eight wind turbines at Goulien have intrigued visitors ever since they were installed in 2000. For those who want to find out more, this interpretation centre in the former local school provides both entertainment and scientific information.

The presentation takes an educational and artistic approach to various themes, such as the nature of winds and their effects, electricity, wind power and the impact of wind on plants, wildlife and the landscape.

Pointe de Brézellec★

Park the car by the lighthouse enclosure. Go to the rock platforms nearby.

There is a magnificent **view**★ along an exceptionally long stretch of coast of saw-tooth rocks and sheer cliffs: Presqu'île de Crozon, Pointe de St-Mathieu, Pointe du Van and Pointe de Tévennec can be seen.

Turn back and turn right towards Pointe du Van.

Pointe du Van★★

1hr on foot there and back.

The 15C **Chapelle St-They** stands on the left of the path. On the point itself follow the half-hidden path, bearing always to the left, which goes right round the headland. The Pointe du Van, which is too big to be seen all in one glance, is less spectacular than the Pointe du Raz, but it has the advantage of being off the tourists' beaten track.

There is a **view**★★ of the Pointe de Castelmeur, the Pointe de Brézellec, the Cap de la Chèvre, the Pointe de Penhir, the Pointe de St-Mathieu and the Tas de Pois rocks on the right; the Île de Sein, the Vieille Lighthouse and the Pointe du Raz on the left. The cliffs are dangerous and should not be climbed.

The landscape becomes ever harsher: no trees grow; stone walls and barren moss covers the final headland.

Turn round and take, immediately on the right, a small road that hugs the coast leading to the Baie des Trépassés and affording fine views of the jagged coastline from the Pointe du Raz to the Île de Sein.

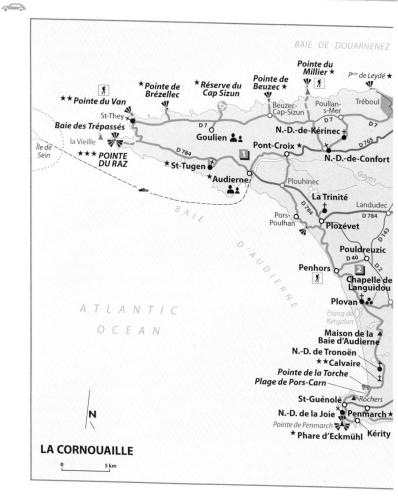

BAIE DE DOUARNENEZ

Pointe du Millier ★

P^{nte} de Leydé ★

★ Pointe de Brézellec

★ Réserve du Cap Sizun

Pointe de Beuzec ★

Tréboul

★★ Pointe du Van

Beuzec-Cap-Sizun

Poullan-s-Mer

St-They

D 7

D 7

Baie des Trépassés

Goulien

N.-D.-de-Kérinec

D 765

Île de Sein

la Vieille

D 784

Pont-Croix ★

N.-D.-de-Confort

★★★ POINTE DU RAZ

★ St-Tugen

Plouhinec

Goyen

★ Audierne

La Trinité

Landudec

D 784

D 784

Pors-Poulhan

Plozévet

D 143

BAIE

Pouldreuzic

D 40

D 2

D'AUDIERNE

Penhors

Chapelle de Languidou

ATLANTIC OCEAN

Plovan

Étang de Kergalan

Maison de la Baie d'Audierne

N.-D. de Tronoën

★★Calvaire

N

Pointe de la Torche

Plage de Pors-Carn

LA CORNOUAILLE

St-Guénolé

Rochers

N.-D. de la Joie

Penmarch ★

0   5 km

Pointe de Penmarch

Kérity

★ Phare d'Eckmühl

Baie des Trépassés

G. Targat/MICHELIN

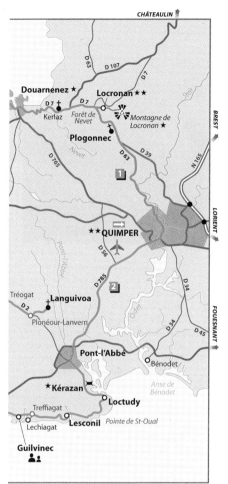

The swell runs unimpeded into the bay, where it breaks with an impressive display of force.

POINTE DU RAZ★★★

Maison du Site. ⏱*Open Apr– Jun, Sept and school holidays daily 10.30am–6pm; Jul–Aug, 9.30am–7.30pm.* 🚶*Guided walk (1hr 30)* ⧉*4€, minimum 4 persons.* ⊗*The walk is not advisable for those with vertigo.* ⧉*No charge for films and exhibitions.* ☎*02 98 70 67 18. www.pointeduraz.com.*

♲*Protective measures have been taken to preserve the site and its environment. To reach the end of the point, motorists must pay to leave their car in the parking area (*⧉*5€ for the day; 800m/0.5mi away from the point). It takes about 25min to follow the waymarked paths to the far end. A free shuttle provides transportation for those who have difficulty walking.*

Pointe du Raz is a rocky promontory at the tip of Cornouaille, jutting out into the treacherous Raz du Sein. This magnificent **site**★★★, which attracts numerous visitors in the summer, is heavily protected as part of France's national heritage. The best views are to be had on stormy days and at high tide.

🚶 Walk around the signal station in front of which stands a statue of Our Lady of the Shipwrecked (*Notre-Dame-des-Naufragés*) to enjoy a wide **panorama**★★ of the horizon: straight ahead is the Île de Sein and beyond, in clear weather, the Ar Men Lighthouse. Between the Île de Sein and the mainland is the fearful Raz de Sein or tide race which, so an old saying has it, 'no one passes without fear or sorrow'; to the northwest can be seen Tévennec Lighthouse (*Phare de Tévennec*) standing on an islet. The path runs along the edge of vertiginous chasms *(safety ropes)*.

The **Enfer de Plogoff** (Plogoff Hell) is a narrow jagged spur towering 70m above the sea and prolonged by a line

Baie des Trépassés

It was once thought that the drowned bodies of those who had been shipwrecked, and which the currents brought to the bay, gave the bay its name of Bay of the Dead. Another, less macabre explanation, based on the existence of a stream that flowed in the marshes, was that the original Breton name for the bay was *boe an aon* (bay of the stream), which became *boe anaon* (bay of the troubled souls). Now it is believed that the bay was the embarcation point from the mainland for Druids' remains, which were taken over to Île de Sein for burial. According to local legend, the town of Is once stood in the little valley, which is now covered in marshes.

Pointe du Raz

© pixpack/Bigstockphoto.com

of reefs; on the farthest of these stands La Vieille Lighthouse. This site is particuarlly impressive when storms are raging. The Raz de Sein is particularly dangerous and the Sémaphore is there to ensure safe navigation.

Take the road in the direction of Audierne and after 10km, turn right towards St-Tugen.

St-Tugen★
The nave and the tower of the **chapel** are in the 16C Flamboyant Gothic style, the transept and the east end in the 17C Renaissance style. There is a fine south porch surmounted by an elegant pierced tympanum, containing six statues of Apostles in Kersanton granite and three 16C statues of Christ, the Virgin and St Anne.
Inside are interesting 17C furnishings, including several altarpieces and a curious catafalque flanked at each end by statues of Adam and Eve.

Audierne★
This pleasure port and fishing village (lobster, sardines and crabs) lies on the estuary of the Goyen, at the foot of a wooded hill in a **pretty setting**★.

Aquashow★
Rte du Goyen, towards Douarnenez.
Open Apr–Nov: daily 10.30am–7pm; Oct–Mar school hols, 2pm–6pm.

Guided tours possible (3hr).
13.80€ (children 10.80€, free in the morning). 02 98 70 03 03.
www.aquarium.fr.
More than 180 species of fish and various sea creatures live here in this aquarium, which is well worth a two-hour visit. There are 'petting' areas where you can touch different fish and crustaceans. The sharks are favourites, and the the demonstration of diving and fishing birds is fascinating.

Pont-Croix★
Pont-Croix is a small town built up in terraces on the south bank of the Goyen, also known as the River Audierne. Its narrow streets, hemmed in between old houses, slope picturesquely down to the bridge. A great procession takes place here on 15 August. The church, **Notre-Dame-de-Roscudon**★ (*open Mon–Fri 10am–5.30pm*), is interesting. Its Romanesque nave dates from the early 13C. The chancel was enlarged in 1290 and the transept was built in 1450 and crowned by the very fine belfry with a steeple 67m high. The elegant south porch (late 14C) has three tall decorated gables.
Inside, the church contains fine furnishings: in the apsidal chapel is a **Last Supper** carved in high relief in wood (17C); on the right of the chancel, the Chapel of the Rosary (*Chapelle du Rosaire*) has fine **stained glass** (c. 1540).

▷ *Go to Plouhinec, the native town of the sculptor Quillivic, then on to Pors-Poulhan.*

Pors-Poulhan

This tiny port is sheltered by a pier. Before Plozévet, there are fine views of Audierne Bay and the Phare d'Eckmühl. The Gothic church at **Plozévet** has a 15C porch. A menhir, decorated by Quivillic, stands nearby as a WWI memorial.

▷ *Follow the route 1km further N.*

Chapelle de la Trinité

The chapel is T-shaped; the nave was built in the 14C and the remainder added in the 16C. Outside, note the charming Louis XII decoration (transitional style between Gothic and Renaissance with Italian influence) of two walls on the south transept side. Inside, the nave arches come down onto groups of columns with floral capitals.

▷ *Rejoin the coast, follow it to Penhors.*

Penhors

On the first Sunday in September the great *pardon* of Notre-Dame-de-Penhors, one of the largest of Cornouaille takes place. The night before there is a procession with torches. On Sunday afternoon the procession walks through the countryside until it comes to the shore line then back to the chapel *(accessed on a path to the beach)* where the benediction of the sea takes place.

Maison de l'Amiral

○*Open daily Jul–Aug 10am–8pm; Sept–Dec and 15 Feb–Jun, Tue–Fri 10am-noon, 2pm–6pm, Sat–Sun 2pm–6pm.* ✆*5.60€.* ♿ ℘*02 98 51 52 52. www.maison-de-l-amiral.com.*
This is an interesting place to take a break and admire the collection of thousands of seashells. Two rooms are devoted to displays of stuffed and mounted birds. There are five very short films on local sealife, and children are free to roam the park.

Pouldreuzic

Arriving in Pouldreuzic, you cannot miss the water tower decorated with the yellow and blue label featured on tins of Hénaff paté. The little town is Hénaff's stronghold and the company has even opened a museum.

La Maison du pâté Hénaff

℘ *02 98 51 53 76. www.henaff.fr. Museum: Jun–Sept. Possibility of a guided visit in low season by appointment or 10.15am, 2.15pm and 4.15pm in Jul–Aug.* ✆*5.20€ (12–16 years 2€). Tasting and sales. Shop: Jul–Aug: daily exc Sun 9.30am–1pm, 2pm–7pm; Sept–Jun. Tue–Fri 10am–12.30pm, 3.30pm–7pm. Closed Jan, Mar, Oct–Dec and public hols.*
The guided tour tells the story of Jean Hénaff and his descendents. In 1907, M. Hénaff first had the idea of canning the peas that he grew, before developing the pâté recipe that made his name. The canning process is also explained.

▷ *From Pouldreuzic, go back to Penhors and follow the signs along the "route du vent solaire", return to Plovan and la presqu'île de Penmarch.*

② PRESQU'ÎLE DE PENMARCH★

Plozévet to Quimper

70km/43mi – allow half a day.

The journey is made through Bigouden country, which has become known for the women's local costume, in particular their unique headdress in the shape of a little lace menhir.
The **Presqu'île de Penmarch** was one of the richest regions in Brittany up to the end of the 16C: cod-fishing (the 'lenten meat') brought wealth to the 15 500 inhabitants. But then the cod deserted the coastal waters, and a tidal wave brought devastation.
Final disaster came with the brigand **La Fontenelle** who took the locality by surprise in spite of its defences. He killed 5 000 peasants, burned down their houses and loaded 300 boats with booty which

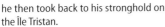

he then took back to his stronghold on the Île Tristan.

From Plozévet to the tip of Penmarch Peninsula the sea breaks against a great sweep of shingle, continually rolling and knocking the stones along this arc some 20km/12.5mi long.

The coastline is inhospitable and desolate, so inhabitants of the white-washed little villages with their white houses lying back from the coast, turn to the hinterland for their livelihood.

Plovan

A small 16C church adorned with beautifully coloured modern (1944) stained-glass windows and a fine turreted belfry. Nearby is a 16C calvary.

Chapelle de Languidou

The ruined 13–15C chapel still has some interesting elements, particularly the fine rose window.

▷ *From Plovan, you can make a return trip to go to la chapelle de Languivoa.*

Chapelle de Languivoa

1.5km/0.9mi E of Plonéour-Lanvern.
🕓*Open Jul–Aug, 2.30pm–6pm.*
𝓟*02 98 82 66 00.*
This 14C and 17C chapel (restored) forms an imposing ensemble adorned with rose windows and Gothic arcading. The dismantled belfry porch still dominates the devastated nave and Classical style entrance with its engaged Doric columns. The chapel contains the Virgin of Notre-Dame-de-Languivoa suckling her child. A *pardon* is held here on 15 August.

Maison de la baie d'Audierne

🕓*Open Jul– Aug 2pm–6pm; during the school hols Wed and Thur 2pm–6pm; rest of the year Wed 2pm–6pm.* 𝓟*02 98 87 65 07.*
The SIVU centre of the Bay of Audierne is an intercommunal organisation concerned with the protection of 209 hectares/516 acres of dunes and coastal marshes and preservation of the coast. In the summer you can visit the exhibitions or follow one of the leaders in a nature walk.

Calvaire and Chapelle Notre-Dame-de-Tronoën★★

The calvary and Chapelle of Notre-Dame-de-Tronoën stand beside Audierne Bay, in the bare and wild landscape of the dunes.

The **calvary**★★ (1450–60) is the oldest in Brittany. The childhood and Passion of Christ are recounted on two friezes. The intensity and originality of the 100 figures are remarkable and details of the sculpted figures are still visible despite wear from exposure. The scenes are depicted in the round or in high relief in a coarse granite from Scaer, which is friable and tends to attract lichen (the Last Supper and the Last Judgment on the south face are greatly damaged).

Three scenes on the north face are in Kersanton granite: the Visitation, an unusual Nativity with a sleeping Joseph and the Magi in 15C clothes. Christ and the thieves are also carved in hard granite.

The 15C **chapel** has a pierced belfry, flanked by turrets. Beneath the vaulted roof are old statues. The ornate south door opens on to the calvary. A *pardon* takes place annually.

▷ *Continue along the road bearing right and right again.*

Pointe de la Torche

The name is a corruption of the Breton Beg an Dorchenn: flat stone point. Note the tumulus with a large dolmen and the fine **view**★ of the St-Guénolé rocks and Audierne Bay. The two beaches, which are dangerous for swimming, attract surfing enthusiasts.

Plage de Pors-Carn

This great sandy beach along La Torche Bay is the terminal point of the telephone cable linking France and the USA.

St-Guénolé

Behind the fishing port (coastal fishing) are the famous **rocks** against which the sea breaks furiously.

Surf's up at Pointe de la Torche

G. Targat/MICHELIN

Musée Préhistorique Finistérien★

At the entrance to St-Guénolé. ◐*Open
Jun–Sept, Wed–Mon 10am–noon, 2pm
–6pm; Oct–May, Wed–Sun 10am–noon,
2pm–6pm.* ♿ ✆*02 98 58 60 35.*
A series of megaliths and Gallic steles
(obelisks) called *lec'hs* stand around the
museum. Start the visit from the left to
see the exhibits in chronological order,
from the Stone Age to the Gallo-Roman
period. On display are, in the first gallery,
a reconstruction of an Iron Age necropolis, Gallic pottery with Celtic decorations
and a Gallic stele with spiral carving; in
the south gallery are polished axes of
rare stone, flint arrowheads, bronze
weapons and chests with grooves.
The museum contains all the prehistori-
cal antiquities discovered in Finistère
except for the rich collection displayed
in the Musée des Antiquités Nationales
at St-Germain-en-Laye (●*see the Michelin Green Guide to Northern France and
the Paris Region).*

Chapelle Notre-Dame-de-la-Joie

This 15C chapel with its pierced bell-
tower is flanked by turrets. The 16C calvary is adorned with a *Pietà*. A *pardon* is
held on 15 August.

Phare d'Eckmühl★

◐*Open Apr–Sept, 10.30am–6pm.*
◦*2€.* ✆*06 07 21 37 34.*
Eckmühl Lighthouse stands at the very
end of the Pointe de Penmarch. The

lighthouse is 65m/213ft tall and its light
of 2 million candle-power has a range
of 54km/34mi. From the gallery at the
top of the tower (307 steps) there is a
view★★ of Audierne Bay, the Pointe du
Raz, the lighthouse on Île de Sein, the
coast of Concarneau and Beg-Meil and
the Îles de Glénan. Passing to the left
of the lighthouse, you will reach the
very tip of the point on which the old
lighthouse, a small fortified chapel and
a signal station stand. The sea is studded
with reefs covered in seaweed.

Kérity

This small fishing port leans more
towards pleasure boating each year.
The Église Ste-Thumette (1675) has an
elegant gabled front flanked by a turret.

Penmarch★

The parish includes several villages: St-
Guénolé, Kérity, Tréoultré and St-Pierre.
Église St-Nonna★ *(149 rue François Mer-
rien;* ◦◦ *guided tours Jul–Aug, Mon–Fri
10am–noon, 2pm–6pm;* ✆*02 98 58 60
16)* was built in the 16C in the Flamboyant Gothic style. At the east end and on
the buttresses on either side of the doorway, ships and caravels are carved into
high or low-relief sculptures, recalling
that the church was built with donations
from shipowners. A gabled bell-tower
crowns the roof. Inside there are several old statues: in the south chapel, St
Michael and St Anne carrying the Virgin

and Child; in the south aisle hangs the Vow of Louis XIII.

▷ *Proceed to Guilvinec by the coast road.*

Guilvinec

This active fishing port has an impressive fleet of some 130 boats. It forms a well-sheltered harbour with **Lechiagat**, a popular pleasure boat spot). Beaches unfold behind the dunes as far as Lesconil. The Haliotika Discovery Centre is a charming place to learn more about seafaring fishermen.

⚑ Haliotika

🕐 *Open 5 Jul–29 Aug, 9.30am–7pm, Sat–Sun and holidays 3pm–6.30pm; Mon–Fri, 6 Apr–4 Jul, 10am–12.30pm, 2.30pm– 6.30pm; rest of year times vary: see website.* ✆*6.30€ (children 3.70€).* ☐ ℘*02 98 58 28 38. www.haliotika.com.*

Follow your guide through the wholesalers fish market to see the daily fish auction. Audio guided tours in English are available at Haliotika's desk.

Learn how to recognise the fishing boats, the fishing techniques, the species of fish, the professional activities of the port.

A new exhibition called 'Grandfather, tell me about sea fishing' involves a retired

fisherman talking about the history of fishing in Brittany. From the panoramic terrace, witness the return of the colourful coastal trawlers bringing back the daily fish and crustaceans.

Lesconil

Lesconil is a small but bustling trawler fishing port. A picturesque scene occurs when the boats return around 5.30pm.

▷ *Make for Loctudy via Palue-du-Cosquer and Lodonnec.*

Loctudy – ☐ *See PONT-L'ABBÉ.*

Manoir de Kérazan★ – ☐ *See PONT-L'ABBÉ.*

Pont-l'Abbé – ☐ *See PONT-L'ABBÉ.*

▷ *Leave Pont-l'Abbé on the D 785 and return to Quimper.*

ÎLE DE SEIN

Regular service by boat from Audierne. There are daily crossings from Audierne (Ste-Evette) year-round aboard the Enez Sun III. Jul–Aug at 8.45am, 11.30am and 4.50pm, return journey at 10.20am, 3.30pm, 6.15pm; Sept–Jun at 9.30am, return journey at 4pm. ℘*02 98 70 70 70.*

Île de Sein with the lighthouse

©Daniel Sainthorant/Fotolia.com

Île de Sein – A Bit of History

For years, the island was the source of superstitious dread. In the 18C, its few inhabitants lived in almost total isolation, man y of whome were shipwreck looters. Now they are among the most active lifesavers. The women do all the manual labour, the men are sailors or fishermen. Fishing is the island's only means of livelihood.

Immediately after General de Gaulle's appeal of 18 June 1940, the men of the Île de Sein (130 sailors and fishermen) put to sea and joined the troops of Free French Forces in England. Nearly 3,000 French soldiers and sailors fled the occupying forces to reach the island and embark for England. When the Germans arrived on Sein they found only women, children, old men, the mayor and the priest. For several months fishing boats brought or embarked Allied officers. Of the sailors from the island who went to England 29 were killed on the battlefields. A commemorative monument stands to the right of the road to the lighthouse. General de Gaulle came in person in 1946 to award the Liberation Cross to the island.

Mid-Jul–mid-Sept, Sunday crossings from Brest at 9am and Camaret (aboard the André Colin, 196 passengers) at 9.30am, return journey at 5pm. ℘02 98 80 80 80 (Brest) or 02 98 27 88 22 (Camaret).
Sein Island makes a picturesque excursion. Lying just 8km/5mi off Pointe du Raz, it is less than 1.3sq km/0.5sq mi in area and is very low-lying; the sea sometimes covers it, as it did in 1868 and 1896.
The island is bare: there are no trees or even bushes; old fields are enclosed by low, drystone walls *(information ℘02 98 70 93 45; www.enezsun.com).*

Port and Village

The port provides a good shelter for pleasure craft. The village's small white houses with brightly painted shutters stand along alleys barely 90cm wide for protection from the wind. On a hillock near the church, two menhirs rise side by side, hence known as 'The Talkers'. Beyond the church, the Nifran Calvary is a simple granite cross resting on a tiered plinth. Behind it is the only dolmen on the island.
The **museum** *(quai de Pampolais; ⊙ open Jul–Aug, daily 10am–noon, 2pm–6pm; Jun and Sept, 10.30am–noon, 2pm–6pm; ⊚2.50€; ℘02 98 70 90 35)* commemo-rates the events of WW II by means of photographs, explanatory panels and diagrams: the departure of the men of the Île de Sein for England; the activities of the marine Free French Forces; the campaigns in which the activists of the Liberation took part; the losses of the Merchant Navy (45, 000 missing, 5, 150 ships sunk); and the anti-submarine struggle.
The **lighthouse**, on the island's western tip, is equipped with a 6kW light which has an average range of 50km/31mi. Left of the lighthouse stands the tiny Chapelle St-Corentin, an old hermitage. Beyond the point lies Sein Reef *(Chaussée de Sein)*, submerged or visible, it prolongs the island some 20km /12.5mi towards the open sea.
On one of these rocks, which is constantly pounded by the sea, the **Phare d'Ar Men** (Ar Men Lighthouse), which took 14 years of superhuman effort to build, was erected in 1881. Its light, with a range of 55km/34mi, warns sailors off the rocks.

Locronan★★

This little town once prospered from the manufacturing of sailcloth. Traces of its golden age are to be found in its fine **square**★★, with Renaissance granite houses, old well, large church and pretty chapel. The hill or mountain of Locronan, which overlooks the town, presents a unique sight on days devoted to *pardons*, which are known here as *Troménies*.

▶ **Population:** 800.

🦽 **Michelin Map:** Local map 308 F6 – Finistère (29).

🛈 **Info:** place de la Mairie, 29180 Locronan. ℘02 98 91 70 14. www.locronan.org.

◖ **Location:** East of Douarnenez and northeast of Quimper.

🕐 **Timing:** The Troménies take place in July.

🅿 **Parking:** Leave your car in the car park outside the village.

⊘ **Don't Miss:** The beautiful main square.

SIGHTS
Place Centrale
The main square of Locronan is emblematic of the city. It has been featured in films *(Tess d'Urberville,* for example*)* for the beauty and authenticity of the granite, Renaissance townhouses. Listed as a historic monument in 1936, it was formerly inhabited by merchants.

Église St-Ronan and Chapelle du Penity★★
🕐 *Open 8.30am–7pm in summer; 9am–6pm in winter.*

The adjacent and intercommunicating church and chapel form a harmonious ensemble. The 15C church is remarkable for its unity of style and stone vaulting. The decoration of the **pulpit**★ (1707) relates the life of St Ronan, and the 15C **stained-glass window**★ in the apse depicts scenes of the Passion.

Among the old statues note that of St Roch (1509). The 16C chapel houses the tomb of St Ronan (the recumbent figure dates from the early 16C and is one of the earliest works in Kersanton granite).

Note too a 16C Descent from the Cross in polychrome stone with six figures. The base is decorated with two beautiful **bas-relief sculptures**★, depicting the apparition of the resurrected Jesus to Mary Magdalene and the disciples of Emmaus, and two 15C statues (Christ in Fetters and St Michael weighing souls). From the cemetery behind the church there is a good view of the church's flat east end.

Place Centrale

G. Targat/MICHELIN

The *Troménies*

The **Petite *Troménie*** (👣 *see Calendar of Events*) consist of a procession that makes its way to the top of the hill, repeating the walk that St-Ronan, a 5C Irish saint, according to tradition, took every day fasting and barefooted.

The **Grande *Troménie*** ★★ takes place every sixth year on the second and third Sundays in July (*next in 2013*). Carrying banners, the pilgrims go around the hill (12km/7.5mi), stopping at 12 stations. At the different stations each parish exhibits its saints and reliquaries. The circuit follows the boundary of the former Benedictine priory – built on the site of the sacred forest or "Nemeton", which served as a natural shrine – founded in the 11C, which was a place of retreat. Hence the name of the *pardon Tro Minihy* or Tour of the Retreat, gallicized as *Troménie*.

Chapelle Notre-Dame-de-Bonne-Nouvelle

300m/328yds along rue Moal, which starts from the square and leads down the slope of the ridge. 🕐*Open 9am–6.30pm in season.* 📞*02 98 91 84 40.* This 14C chapel's calvary and fountain (1698) form a typically Breton scene.

Museum

On the Châteaulin road. 🕐*Open Jul–Aug, 10am–1pm, 2pm–7pm, Sun and holidays 2pm–6pm; rest of the year Mon–Fri 10am–noon, 2pm–6pm.* 🎫*2€.* 📞*02 98 91 70 14.*
The museum houses Quimper faience, sandstone objects, local costumes exhibits relating to the *Troménies* (👣*see above*) and to ancient crafts, pictures and engravings by contemporary artists of Locronan and the surrounding area.

EXCURSIONS

Montagne de Locronan★

▷ *2km/1.2mi E.* 🕐*Open only during the Troménies. The Petites Troménies are held every year on the 2nd Sun in July; the Grandes Troménies are held every six years from the 1st to the 2nd Sun in July.* 📞*02 98 91 70 14.*
From the top (289m), crowned by a **chapel** (note the stained-glass windows by Bazaine), you will see a fine **panorama**★ of Douarnenez Bay. On the left are Douarnenez and the Pointe du Leydé; on the right Cap de la Chèvre, the Presqu'île de Crozon, Ménez-Hom and the Monts d'Arrée.

Ste-Anne-la-Palud

▷ *8km/5mi NW. Leave Locronan by D 63 to Crozon. After Plonévez-Porzay, turn left.* 🕐*Open Easter to All Saints' Day daily 9am–8pm; rest of the year Sun only.* 📞*02 98 92 50 17.*
The 19C **chapel** contains a much-venerated painted granite statue of St Anne dating from 1548. The *pardon* on the last Sunday in August, one of the finest and most picturesque in Brittany, attracts thousands.
On the Saturday at 9pm the torchlit procession progresses along the dune above the chapel.

ADDRESSES

🛏🛏 **Hôtel Le Prieuré** – *11 r. du Prieuré.* 📞*02 98 91 70 89. www.hotel-le-prieure.com. Closed 11 Nov–15 Mar 15 rooms.* 🍽 *8€.* This discrete family run hotel-restaurant has renovated rooms in the front of the hotel and rustic rooms in the back. Traditional cooking and seafood served in the dining room furnished in Breton style.

🍴 **Crêperie Breizh Izel** – *place de l'Église.* 📞*02 98 91 82 23.* Don't hesitate to stop at this charming old house where you'll appreciate its fireplace, its attractive dining room and its fairly priced crêpes.

Douarnenez★

The four localities of Douarnenez, Ploaré, Pouldavid and Tréboul have merged to form the *commune* of Douarnenez, known today as a port city (with a museum-port, fishing port and sailing harbour), a European centre for fish canning, a seaside resort and a spa destination offering the seawater therapy of thalassotherapy. The town itself, nestled in a prettily curved bay, is full of colourful, picturesque façades that have seduced many an artist, including Auguste Renoir, Eugène Boudin and Emmanuel Lansyer. Although the so-called "era of the sardine" now belongs to the past, visitors will appreciate the old-fashioned atmosphere which permeates the maze of narrow streets encircling the port. According to local tradition, Douarnenez was the original site of the palace belonging to King Marc'h; the island located at the entrance to the estuary of Pouldavid bears the name of his nephew Tristan. Before being called Douarnenez in 1541 (*douar an enez* means the land of the island), the harbour was known as Hameau de St-Michel (St-Michael's Hamlet) and then, in 1520, Bourg de l'Île Tristan (Village of Tristan's Island).

▶ **Population:** 15,608.

◔ **Michelin Map:** Local map 308 F6 – Finistère (29).

▨ **Info:** 1 rue Docteur-Mével, 29100 Douarnenez. ℘02 98 92 13 35. www.douarnenez-tourisme.com.

◑ **Location:** A waterway divides the town: on one side the centre and Les Dames beach; on the other the marina and Tréboul beach.

▲ **Kids:** Port-Musée.

◷ **Timing:** A good place to explore the northern coast of Cornouaille, including the Sizun reserve and Pointe du Raz.

◻ **Parking:** Avoid the town centre and and try the car park near the marina.

A BIT OF HISTORY
La Fontenelle (16C)

In the 16C this island was the lair of Sire Guy Eder La Fontenelle, the most dangerous of the robber barons who devastated the country during the conflicts of the League.

La Fontenelle seized the Île Tristan. To obtain materials for fortifications he demolished those of Douarnenez. His cruelty was legendary. In 1598 he agreed

Douarnenez and the port

G. Couraud/MICHELIN

to lay down his arms on condition that he be allowed to keep the island; a request granted by Henri IV. But in 1602 the King took his revenge: involved in a plot, La Fontenelle was sentenced to be broken on the wheel in Paris.

WALKING TOUR
Chapelle St-Michel
⏱*Open Jul–Aug, 9am–noon, 2pm–6pm. ℰ02 98 92 13 35.*
Built in 1663, this chapel contains 52 panels from the 16C painted by Don Michel Le Noblets (1577–1652) who evangelised lower Brittany.
Halfway between Chapelle St-Michel and Chapelle Ste-Hélène, at the heart of the city, stands place Gabriel-Péri where a convivial, bustling open-air market takes place very morning.

Chapelle Ste-Hélène
This chapel, in the Flamboyant Gothic style, was remodelled in the 17C and 18C. Note the two 16C stained-glass windows at the end of the nave.
The west front is decorated with three low-relief sculptures representing a fishing boat, a gannet and a shoal – perhaps a hint at the fact that fishermen partly financed the church.

▷ *Take rue Hervé-Julien opposite the chapel.*

Port du Rosmeur★
Rue Hervé-Julien leads to a tiny square surrounded by fishermen's cottages. **Rue Anatole-France** runs down to the harbour that was once filled with sardine-fishing boats. When the sardine trade was at its peak, **rue du Rosmeur** was lined with canneries such as Capitaine Cook. You can see where the former canning plant, now a private residence, stood. It is easily identifiable by its bright façade and the old sign.

Port de Pêche
Built in 1951 on ground reclaimed from the sea, behind a 741m/2,400ft-long jetty, the fishing port boasts an important *criée* (fish auction) where the boats unload at about 11pm and bidding starts

at 6.30am. A walk along the jetty offers a good **view**★ of the bay beneath the towering Menez-Hom.

▷ *Walk along boulevard Jean-Richepin to Port-Rhû and admire the splendid view of Douarnenez Bay.*

The walk takes you past **Plage de Porscad**, then **Plage des Dames** and along boulevard Camille-Réaud, with picturesque views of Tristan Island.

▷ *A footbridge and a metal bridge for cars span the Port-Rhû estuary, linking Douarnenez to Tréboul.*

Tréboul
It is in this district with its cluster of narrow streets that the **marina** is located, which can accommodate up to 700 boats. Further away is **Plage St-Jean** followed by the vast **Plage des Sables-Blancs** near Pointe de Leydé and opposite Coulinec Island.

ADDITIONAL SIGHTS
Port-Musée★★
⏱*Open Jul–Aug, Tue–Sun daily 10am–7pm; rest of the year, 10am–12.30pm, 2pm–6pm; also open Mon during school holidays. ⏱Closed 1 Jan, 25 Dec. Combined ticket with visit to 'Musée à flot' ships on the water ☞7.50€ (children 4.50€). ℰ02 98 92 65 20. www.port-musee.org.*
This Port Museum is both a centre of conservation of boats and a permanent workshop where expertise in this field is passed on. It offers a good opportunity to rediscover the recent maritime past. The various elements of the Port Museum, established on the wonderful site of Port-Rhu, once the commercial harbour of Douarnenez, contain displays on all aspects of maritime and harbour life, from ships afloat, to construction sites and an onshore museum containing some 100 boats.

Musée du Bateau
This Boat Museum is located in an old canning factory and contains an **outstanding collection**★ of fishing, trans-

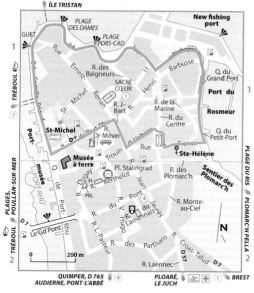

DOUARNENEZ

WHERE TO STAY

Kerveoc'h (Auberge de)....①

Manoir de Kervent
(Chambre d'hôte)..........④

Ty Mad (Hôtel).....................⑦

WHERE TO EAT

Clos de
Vallombreuse (Le)..........①

Tudal - Au Goûter
Breton (Crêperie)..........④

port and pleasure boats from France and abroad. The Irish curragh can be found beside the Welsh coracle or the Norwegian *oselvar*; clinker-built ships are next to carvel-built ships. Most of the exhibits are of wood; however, there are some boats made from the skins of horses, deer, seals or even whales. Many of the craft are displayed in full sailing rig. There are reconstructed scenes and short black-and-white files of famous rescues, as well as an exhibition of Douarnenez's canning tradition.

In summer, craftsmen are at work along the quayside, in an effort to keep alive traditional maritime crafts; various activities are scheduled (*programme of events available at the Port-Musée*).

Musée à flot

This comprises about 40 boats, 26 of which are open to visitors, moored in three harbour docks. In the first basin, fishing boats include: trawlers, lobster boats, shellfish boats, sardine boats and tuna boats. Visitors can go aboard one of the lobster boats, the *Notre-Dame-de-Rocamadour*. In another basin are larger coastal vessels such as the St-Denys, the *Anna Rosa* or the Northdown. The variety of boats displayed encompasses a British steam tug, a Norwegian coaster

and a Breton *sablier* (used for transporting sand). Pleasure craft include the Ariane, built in 1927, the Viviane, dating from 1859, as well as cruising vessels and modern racing boats moored on the premises.

EXCURSIONS
🏃 Sentier des Plomarc'h and Plage du Ris★

E of town: 2hr 30min on foot there and back. Access via rue des Plomarc'h, E of the town plan.

The path begins at Port du Rosmeur, runs along the side of a slope, affording some very picturesque **views**★ of Douarnenez, and leads to Plage du Ris. Return by the Locronan road.

Sentier des Roches-Blanches★

▶ *At Sables-Blancs Beach (Tréboul district), turn left on the road to Roches-Blanches and leave the car in the* 🅿 *parking area just after the Village de Vacances.*

A hiking trail forms a 6km/3.7mi-loop. The coast path is marked by orange blazes, and runs along the sea to **Pointe de Leydé**★ which affords a lovely **view**★ of the bay of Dournenez. For a longer hike, continue on to Poullan-sur-Mer instead of taking the road to Tréboul.

Église de Ploaré

▷ *Take the D 5 then rue Lannec.*
🕐 *Open Jul–Aug 10am–noon.* ✆ *02 98 92 03 17.*

The church dates from the 16C and 17C. It is crowned by a fine Flamboyant and Renaissance **tower**★, 55m/180ft high, with a crocketed steeple with four pinnacles at the corners (two Gothic, two Renaissance). The façade is flanked with Gothic buttresses surmounted by pinnacles, while those of the apse and transept are crowned with Renaissance lanterns.

Laënnec (1781–1826), the inventor of the stethoscope, is buried in the cemetery. Kerlouarnec, the country house where this eminent physician died, can be seen at the end of a fine avenue leading to the Chapelle de Ste-Croix (1701).

Le Juch

▷ *8km/5mi along the D 765. 6km/3.7mi further on, turn left for Le Juch.*

Fine **view** of Douarnenez Bay, the Presqu'île de Crozon and Ménez-Hom. Inside the 16C–17C **church** *(if closed, call* ✆ *02 98 74 71 38)*. The old 16C stained-glass window at the east end shows scenes from the Passion; to the left and right of the chancel are statues depicting the Annunciation, placed in niches with 16C painted shutters.

To the right of the sacristy door, in the north aisle is St-Michael overcoming a dragon known as the Devil of Le Juch. *Pardon* on 15 August.

ADDRESSES

🛏 STAY

🍽🛏 **Chambre d'hôte Manoir de Kervent** – *6 chemin Kervent. Rte d'Audierne by the D 765 then turn right after the traffic lights following the signs.* ✆ *02 98 92 04 90. www.gites-finistere.com. Closed Nov–Jan.* ⚘. *4 rooms.* ☺. This family-run countryside residence has four rooms. A hearty Breton style breakfast will be served to you by the mistress of the house before a visit (optional) to the nearby cooperage.

🍽🛏 **Auberge de Kerveoc'h** – *42 rue de Kerveoc'h.* ✆ *02 98 92 07 58. www.auberge-kerveoch.com. 13 rooms.* ☺ *8€. Restaurant*🍽🛏. This old farm with a pleasant garden also houses an equestrian centre. The bedcovers in the rooms are traditional to the region. The restaurant is housed in a former stable.

🍽🛏🛏 **Hôtel Ty Mad** – *22 Place Gambetta, 29100 Tréboul. 3km NE of Douarnenez.* ✆ *02 98 /4 00 53. www. hotelymad.com. 15 rooms.* ☺ *12.50€.* Just above St-Jean beach, this old presbytery overlooks the bay. Very pleasant and airy contemporary interior that favours natural materials such as plain wood or sea rush floors, and exposed stone walls.

🍴EAT

🍽 **Crêperie Tudal – Au Goûter Breton** – *36 rue Jean-Jaurès.* ✆ *02 98 92 02 74. www.augouterbreton.com. Closed last two weeks in Jun and Sun.* The clients are pressed shoulder to shoulder, attracted by the warm welcome and young, buzzing atmosphere. Inventive crêpes such as those filled with marinated sardines are popular.

🍽🛏 **Le Close de Vallombreuse** – *7 rue d'Estienne d'Orves.* ✆ *02 98 92 63 64. www.closvallombreuse.com. This maison de maître* was built by a canner in the early 20C. Pleasant shady garden and nicely decorated rooms. In the restaurant, elegant décor and seafood specials.

🏃ACTIVITIES

Thalasso Douarnenez – *Tréboul-Plage.* ✆ *08 25 00 42 30. www.thalasso.com. Open Mon–Sat 8.30am–12.30pm, 2pm–6pm.* Seawater spa treatments à la carte or with a half-day pass on reservation.

Rent a bike – La Bécane – *42 av. de la Gare (near the beach).* ✆ *02 98 74 20 07. Open daily (except Wed off season and Sun) 9am–noon, 2pm–7pm. Closed Oct.*

Pont-l'Abbé

This town, which stands at the head of an estuary, owes its name to the first bridge *(pont)* built by the monks *(abbés)* of Loctudy between the harbour and the lake. It is the capital of the Bigouden district which is bounded by the estuary of the Odet, the coast of Penmarc'h and Audierne Bay. The Bigouden costume is very distinctive and is still worn for special occasions.

SIGHTS

Église Notre-Dame-des-Carmes

Open 9am–noon, 2pm–7pm.
02 98 87 02 80.

Former 14C chapel of the Carmelite monastery. Entering, you will see on the right an 18C font whose canopy comes from the Église de Lambour. Above the high altar is a 15C stained-glass window with a rose 7.7m in diameter. To the left, the Chapelle Ste-Anne is a modern processional banner; in the nave are statues of the Virgin and St John, both from the 16C, flank Christ. As you come out, turn right to go round the church and look at the flat chevet crowned by an unusual domed belfry. A *pardon* is held on the Sunday after 15 July.

- **Population:** 8,132.
- **Michelin Map:** Local map 308 F7 – Finistère (29).
- **Info:** Square de l'Europe, 29120 Pont l'Abbé. *02 98 82 37 99. www.pont labbe-lesconil.com.*
- **Location:** There are two ways to get to Pont l'Abbé: from Quimper on the D 785 (19km/12mi NE) or from Bénodet on the D 44 (12km/7.5mi E).
- **Timing:** After a walk around the town, end your day on the banks of Île-Tudy.
- **Don't Miss:** The Manoir de Kerazan.

In the garden, on the north side of the church, note the **Bigouden monument** (1931) by Bazin, which stands among greenery on the river's edge.

Château

Open Jul–Aug, daily 10am–12.30pm, 2pm–7pm, Jun and Sept 10am–12.30pm, 2pm–6.30pm; Apr–May 2pm–6pm.
Closed Mon Apr–May, public holidays.
3.50€. 02 98 66 09 03.

©Djigibodgi.com/Fotolia.com

Bigouden Costume

This regional costume, worn by women, is usually only seen these days during traditional festivals such as the Embroidery Festival (second weekend of July) and the *pardon* (Sunday after 15 July). Local costumes became increasingly elaborate and colourful in the 19C, and the embroidered lace bonnet, the *bigou*, grew steadily with successive generations. From a tall sugarloaf shape around 1900, it reached 20cm/7.8in in the late 1920s and even taller just after WWII. Today, the cap hovers around the 30cm/12in-high mark, with a base as wide as 14cm/5.5in for stability. The full outfit consists of the *bigou* worn with a black dress that has been maginficently embroidered with geometric patterns of lace in red, yellow and orange tones.

This 14C–18C fortress has a large oval keep with a building attached. Go round the tower to see the turret overlooking *rue du Château*. Inside the keep you may visit the **Musée Bigouden** (audio commentary on each floor) housed on three floors *(79 steps)*, which has collections of Bigouden costumes, beautifully embroidered headdresses and 19C furniture (box beds, dressers, chests), models of boats, sailing equipment.

Ancienne Église de Lambour
The ruined church retains a fine 16C façade and some bays of the 13C nave. The bell-tower was razed during a peasant revolt (🐾 *see below*).

EXCURSIONS
Chapelle N.-D.-de-Tréminou
▶ *2km/1.2mi W on rue Jean-Moulin.*
🕒*Open Jul–mid-Sept and Heritage Days 2pm–6.30pm.* ♿ ☎*02 98 82 04 65.*
Standing in a shaded close, this 14C and 16C chapel (restored) has a belfry which is set above the nave.
Near this chapel, in 1675, the Cornouaille peasants in revolt adopted the "peasant code". Closely linked with the 'stamped paper' revolt, this mass uprising was severely crushed and many bell-towers in the vicinity were razed to the ground in reprisal. A *pardon* takes place on the fourth Sunday in September.

Manoir de Kérazan★
▶ *3km/1.8mi S along the Loctudy road.*
🕒*Open mid-Jun–mid-Sept, 10.30am– 7pm; Apr–mid-Jun and mid–end Sept, Tue–Sun 2pm–6pm.* ☞*6€.* ♿ ☎*02 98 87 40 40.*
The manor house is situated in a large park full of tall trees and consists of a main building with large windows, which was rebuilt in the 18C, and a wing set at right-angles, dating from the 16C. The estate was bequeathed to the Institut de France by Joseph Astor in 1928. The rooms, richly decorated and furnished, bear witness to the luxurious setting the Astors aimed to create.
Louis XV woodwork, both authentic and reconstructed, adorns the great hall, the billiards room, the corner room and the

Boat trips to Île-Tudy

The peninsula can be reached by CD 144 or by sea (♿no cars), with departures from Loctudy. There are several round trips a day (except weekends Sept–Jul). ☞*2€ return.*
From Loctudy, cyclists and pedestrians can sail to Île-Tudy, a fishing port which, despite its name, is not on an island, but a peninsula.

green hall. The dining room, decorated with painted panelling, contains a display of a number of works by **Alfred Beau** (1829–1907). This ceramic painter, who was associated with the Porquier de Quimper faience works, created many works of art from plates and trays, as well as by painting works on enamel which was then framed in either plain or carved wood, giving the impression that they were real paintings. The true masterpiece has to be the life-size cello made from polychrome faience, for which the manufacture process involved 15 different firings. The library is as it was arranged by Joseph Astor's father, mayor of Quimper and a great admirer of Beau; the furniture and the layout of the shelves have not been changed. The rooms contain a collection of paintings and drawings in which Brittany and the Breton way of life in days gone by play an important role. Various Schools are represented, from the 16C to the 20C (Frans Francken, Charles Cotter, Lucien Simon, Maurice Denis). The tour ends in the blue hall, once a chapel, which houses the Astor family's memorabilia and a collection of 19C weapons.

Loctudy
Loctudy is a quiet little seaport and resort at the mouth of the River Pont-l'Abbé.
The fishing **port** becomes animated on weekday evenings when the fishing fleet (prawns, burbot, sole, sea bass) is landed. A pretty view from the quays overlooks the Île Chevalier, in Pont-l'Abbé estuary and Île-Tudy and its beach.

The **church** (*1 rue de Poulpeye;* ⏱*open daily Jul–Aug Mon–Sat 9.30am–noon; 2.30pm–6.30pm, Sun 9.30am–noon, rest of the year 9.30–noon, 4.30pm–6pm;* ☞*guided tours Jul–Aug, Mon, Thu and Fri;* ☎*02 98 87 41 07)* dates from the beginning of the 12C and has been remodelled several times, the porch was added in the 15C and its façade and belfry were built in the 18C. In spite of the additions, the **interior**★ is elegant and well proportioned with its nave, chancel, ambulatory and radiating chapels in pure Romanesque style. Admire the capitals and column bases carved with small figures, animals, scrolls, foliage and crosses.

In the cemetery to the left of the church, near the road, is the 15C Chapel of Pors-Bihan. Left of the lane leading to the church is a **Gallic stele**, 2m high, surmounted by a cross.

ADDRESSES

STAY

🍴🍴 **Chambre d'hôte La Chaumière de Kéraluic** – *29120 Plomeur. 3km W of Pont l'Abbé on rte St-Jean-Trolimon.* ☎*02 98 82 10 22. www.keraluic.fr.* ☞*. 3 rooms and 3 studios.* This attractive stone cottage has three pleasant rooms on the first floor. On the ground floor there are three studios with their own terraces (rental: one week minumum). In winter, breakfast is served by the fireside.

🍴🍴 **La Tour d'Auvergne** – *22 Place Gambetta.* ☎*02 98 87 00 47. www.tour dauvergne.fr.* ☞ *7€. Restaurant* 🍴🍴*. 19 rooms.* Standard, slightly old-fashioned rooms and a pleasant wine bar. In the restaurant, menus are inspired by the land and the sea. There's a shady outside terrace and parking opposite.

🍴🍴 **Hôtel de Bretagne** – *24 Place de la République.* ☎*02 98 87 17 22. www.hotel debretagne29.com. Closed 28 Jan–10 Feb, 13–26 October and Sun eve off season.* ☞ *8€. Restaurant* 🍴🍴*. 18 rooms.* In this establishment located on the market place, it's not the little rooms with pastel tones that will seduce you most, but the welcoming family atmosphere, notably at lunch. Seafood takes pride of place in a rustic-style dining room or on the terrace in an inner courtyard.

🍴🍴🍴🍴 **Villa tri Men** – *16 rue du Phare, Combrit.* ☎*02 98 51 94 94. http://trimen.fr.* ☞ *14€.* Between Bénodet and Pont l'Abbe , this big family home dating from 1900 has been totally renovated. The result is elegant, with a beautiful terrace above the estuary of the River Odet.

EAT

🍴 **Crêperie Bigoudène** – *33 rue du Gén.-de-Gaulle.* ☎*02 98 87 20 41. Closed second fortnight of Jan, second fortnight of Nov, Sun and Mon except school holidays.* The country-style décor and traditional crêpes are just right after a visit to the Musée Bigouden.

🍴 **Le Bistrot Gourmand** – *Wine bar of the Tour d'Auvergne.* The décor features slate, wainscoting and dried grape vines. Have a drink and enjoy a quick snack: kidneys, fresh sea scallops, etc.

SHOPPING

Market – every Thursday on *place de la République* and *place Gambetta*. Local produce available from this traditional market right in the centre of town.

ACTIVITIES

Bicycle hire – Cycles MBK Le Loc'h – *28 pl. de la République.* ☎*02 98 87 12 41*

Water sports – Centre Nautique de Lesconil – *2 rue Victor Hugo, 29740 Lesconil.* ☎*02 98 87 89 43. www.centre nautiquelesconil.com.* Sailing, kayaking, other water sports and lessons.

Swimming – Parc Aquatique Aquasud – *17, route de Quimper. Open daily.* ☎*02 98 66 00 00.* ☞*7.50€.* Modern swimming pool complex with lessons and aquagym sessions available.

Bénodet☼☼

This charming seaside resort lies in a pretty, verdant setting at the mouth of the Odet estuary. Bénodet (Benoded in Breton) offers all the summer pleasures: a small harbour, fine beaches of pale sand, outdoor sports, sailing, a casino and a new film festival. **Éric Tabarly** (1931–98), the famous yachtsman who won many solo races including the transatlantic and transpacific and was lost at sea off the coast of Ireland, had a house on the banks of the Odet.

- **Population:** 3,159.
- **Michelin Map:** Local map 308 G7 - Finistère (29) .
- **Info:** 29 ave. de la Mer, 29950 Bénodet. ℘02 98 57 00 14. www.benodet.fr.
- **Location:** 16km/10mi S of Quimper, between Pont-l'Abbé and Concarneau.
- **Don't Miss:** A boat trip up the River Odet (allow and hour).

SIGHTS

Musée du Bord de mer

Espace J. Boissel - 29 av. de la Mer - ℘02 98 57 00 14. 15 Jun–15 Sept: 10am –1pm, 2pm–6.30pm ; rest of the year: daily exc Tue–Wed 10am–1pm, 2pm–6pm. Guided tours available. 4 € (5-12 yrs 2 €).

With its posters, paintings, photographs, films of regattas and models of boats, the museum transports visitors back to the era of classic yachting, which became popular at the same time as seawater bathing and the railways. Another side of life at the seaside is explored through bathing costumes, beach toys and holiday luggage. The collection also includes sailing artefacts that belonged to Éric Tabarly.

L'Odet

The resort takes its name from the River Odet: *ben* means "end" in Breton, so Bénodet means "the mouth of the River Odet". A **boat trip up the Odet** ★★ can be made (*duration 90mins departing from Bénodet;* *see Boat Trips down the Odet in Quimper, p279*).

Reached via the Avenue de Kercréven, the **vantage point for views of the Odet** gives fine view over the river and the marina.

Pont de Cornouaille

1km/0.6mi NW on the D 44.

This 610m/667yd bridge offers a fine **view**★ over the marina, Ste-Marine and the estuary, as well as upriver.

DRIVING TOUR

From Bénodet to Concarneau along the Coast

40km/25mi– allow 3hr.

Leave Bénodet E by D 44 towards Fouesnant and after 2km turn right.

Le Letty

A large lagoon separated from the ocean by a 4km/2.5mi sandbar and sheltered by a dune.

Retace the route to Fouesnant.

Le Perguet

On the right-hand side of the 12C chapel of Ste-Brigitte, a stone staircase on the roof gives access to the open-work bell-tower.

*At 2.5km/1.6mi fork right, leading to la pointe de Mousterlin (**see Fouesnant-les-Glénan, p312**). About turn. At 2 km/1.25mi, turn right and, at 4.5 km/2.8mi another right.*

Beg-Meil and Fouesnant☼

The road runs along Kerleven Beach, a long beach of fine sand, in the curve of La Forêt Bay, then after a steep descent (15% or 1:7), it skirts St-Laurent Cove and crosses St-Jean Bay to Concarneau. Beautiful **views**★, especially at high tide.

ADDRESSES

🛏️ STAY

🍴🛏️📶 **Hôtel du Bac** – *19 rue du Bac Ste-Marine, 29120 Combrit. 5km from L'O de Bénodet by Cornouaille bridge.* ☎️*02 98 56 34 79. www.hotelsaintemarine.com. 11 rooms.* ⌁ *9€.* Idyllic location, maritime décor and rooms with great views – not to mention delicious food.

🍴 EAT

🍴 **Crêperie La Misaine** – *Quai Jacques de Thézac, 29120 Combrit.* ☎️*02 98 51 90 45. Closed 15 Oct–27 Mar except Fri–Sun and school hols.* This little stone house half way between the chapel and the harbour of Ste Marine has great views over the bay – and the food is nice too!

🏃 ACTIVITIES

BOAT TRIPS

Vedettes de l'Odet – ☎️*0 825 800 801. www.vedettes-odet.com.* This company offers several cruises up the 'prettiest river in France'. From Apr–Sept you can go to Rosulien Manor (45min, 15€), Kérogan Bay (2hr, 25€) or Quimper (2hr15min, 25€). Or you can sail to the **Glénan Islands**, with a stopover on Île de St-Nicolas (30€); take a guided tour through the islands (39€) or board the Capitaine Némo, a catamaran equipped for underwater viewing (42€).

Fouesnant-les-Glénan★

This town is in the middle of one of the most fertile areas in Brittany; the villages stand among cherry and apple orchards. This is also where the best Breton cider is produced. The costumes and headdresses of Fouesnant can be seen at the Apple Trees Festival and at the *pardon* of St Anne (both in July). Its beaches and small ports make it a popular seaside resort. Built in the 12C, the church, remodelled in the 18C, was restored. Inside, the tall granite pillars are adorned with fine Romanesque capitals. An unusual stoup is built into an engaged pillar.

- ▶ **Population:** 9,716.
- 🧭 **Michelin Map:** Local map 308 G7 - Finistère (29).
- 📋 **Info:** Espace Kernévéleck, 49 rue de Kerourgue, 29170 Fouesnant. ☎️02 98 51 18 88. www.ot-fouesnant.fr.
- ▶ **Location:** On the D 44 between Bénodet and Concarneau.
- 👪 **Kids:** Les Balneides leisure centre; Capitaine Nemo boat trip.
- 👁️ **Don't Miss:** A dip in the clear waters of Glénan.

🚶 WALK

Cap-Coz⚓
This small resort is built on a sandy spit, between the cliffs of Beg-Meil and the channel to Port-la-Forêt.
Enjoy a pleasant excursion along the **coastal path** which runs from La Forêt Bay as far as La Roche-Percée, overlooking or crossing small coves and affording fine views of the coastline from Kerleven to the Pointe de Trévignon.

Beg-Meil⚓
5.5km/3.4mi S.
Beg-Meil (meaning the Point of the Mill) is located at the mouth of Baie de La Forêt and opposite Concarneau. This resort has beaches both on its bay and ocean front. On the bay side there are small, rocky, wooded coves: Oiseaux Beach and La Cale Beach. On the ocean side there are dunes and the well-equipped Sémaphore Beach. From the vast Dunes Beach (or *Grande Plage*), the Glénan archipelago is visible in the distance. From **Pointe de Beg-Meil**

Îles de Glénan

S. Sauvignier/MICHELIN

(Beg-Meil Point), there is a 7m-high menhir, which was laid on its side by the Germans during WW II.

Pointe de Mousterlin

6.5 km/4mi to the SW.
An extended view of the coast from the pointe de Lesconil to the right, the pointe de Trevignon to the left

Îles de Glénan★

Access by boat: Apr–Sept from Beg-Meil, Bénodet, Concarneau and Loctudy (1hr crossing). The Île St-Nicolas, where you disembark is a natural reserve with a fragile ecosystem. The local narcissus has been given special protection, but all of the flora should be observed only. Picking flowers is forbidden. Keep to the marked paths.

The archipelago consists of nine islets surrounded by reefs and lies off Concarneau. It is home to a unique plant species, the *narcisse des Glénan* (narcissus), discovered in 1803 by a chemist from Quimper, which flowers briefly in mid-April.

Boats go to the Île St-Nicolas which has a few houses, a diving school *(Centre International de Plongée)* and a breeding pool for crustaceans. A footpath goes round the island, affording good views of the coast from Penmarch to Le Pouldu.

To the north lies the **Île Brunec** and to the south the **Île du Loch**, which can easily be distinguished by its chimney as a former seaweed processing plant.

Both are privately owned.
Penfret with its lighthouse, **Cigogne** (The Stork), identified by its 18C fort and the annexe of the marine laboratory of Concarneau, **Bananec**, which is linked to St-Nicolas at low tide, and **Drénec** are islands from which the internationally famous sailing school, the Centre Nautique de Glénan, operates.

EXCURSION

La Forêt-Fouesnant

This village possesses a parish close and a 16C calvary with four corner pilasters. The church porch, dating from 1538, is adorned with two old, rough-hewn statues of St-Roch and St-Mélar. Inside, at the high altar are an altarpiece and, on either side, two 17C statues.

Port-la-Forêt

5.5 km/3.4mi E by the D 44.
The port lies between the beach and the town and can accommodate 800 boats. The launches take people to the Iles de Glene or to l'Odet.

⚓ Capitaine Nemo

Departing from Beg-Meil, this boat trip is equipped with underwater vision and travels around the Glénan archipelago. *8 Vieux Port, 29950 Bénodet. ℘02 98 57 00 58. www.vedettes-odet.com.*

ADDRESSES

⌂STAY

◖◗**Auberge du Bon Cidre** – *37 rue de Cornouaille, Fouesnant.* ✆*02 98 56 00 16. www.aubergeduboncidre.com. 28 rooms.* ⌘*7.50€. Restaurant*◖◗. This former pub is now a pleasant hotel and restaurant. Comfortable rooms overlook the flower garden. The restaurant offers both seafood and regional specialities.

◖◗**L'Orée du Bois** – *4 rue Kergoadic, Fouesnant.* ✆*02 98 56 00 06. www.hotel-oreedubois.com. 15 rooms.* ⌘*7.50€.*

Simple rooms and a friendly welcome near the church. Breakfast served in a room with nautical décor.

⚡ACTIVITIES

Centre Nautique de Fouesnant – *1 chemin de Kersentic.* ✆*02 98 56 01 05.*

Les Balneides – ✆*02 98 56 18 19. www.balneides.fr.* Leisure centre with the longest water slide in Brittany.

Concarneau★

Concarneau offers a fascinating picture of a bustling fishing port, the charm of a walled town enclosed in granite ramparts, and the facilities of a popular resort. France's premier fishing port, it is the leading market for tunny caught in African waters and in the Indian Ocean, has three fish canneries and holds a colourful fresh fish auction *(criée)*.
There is an attractive **panorama**★ of Concarneau, its fishing port and the bay from Moros Bridge (Pont du Moros).

WALLED TOWN★★
(Ville Close) *Allow 2hr.*
Narrow alleys cover the islet of irregular shape (350 x 100m) linked to the mainland by two small bridges between which stands a fortified building. Massive ramparts, built in the 14C and completed in the 17C, surround the town. Cross the two small bridges and pass under a gateway leading to a fortified inner courtyard. There is a fine well.

Musée de la Pêche★
⏱*Open Jul–Aug, daily 9.30am–8pm; Apr–Jun,& Sept–Oct 10am–6pm; Feb– Mar and school hols, 10am–noon, 2pm –6pm.* ⏱*Closed last three weeks Jan, 1 Jan and 25 Dec.* ⬤*6€.* ♿ ✆*02 98 97 10 20.*

▸ **Population:** 19,953.
⬤ **Michelin Map:** Local map 308 H7 - Finistère (29).
▤ **Info:** Quai d'Aiguillon, 29900 Concarneau. ✆*02 98 97 01 44. www.tourisme concarneau.fr.*
◉ **Location:** Southeast of Quimper on the D 783.
Kids: The fish auctions.
⏱ **Timing:** Allow a day for the ports and the old town.
▣ **Parking:** Use one of the public car parks at quai Carnot, Aiguillon or Pénéroff.
◉ **Don't Miss:** The old town and the views from Pointe du Cabellou.

This fishing museum is located in what used to be the arsenal, which also served as barracks and a fishing school.
In the courtyard, the *Commandant Garreau*, a lifeboat built in 1894, is exhibited. Accompanying notices, models, photographs, dioramas, and some 10 boats explain the history of Concarneau, its evolution as a port, traditional and modern fishing techniques (whale, cod, sardine, tuna, herring), boats, canning industry, shipbuilding, navigational equipment and rescue operations.

Concarneau

H. Le Gac/MICHELIN

Outside (via Major's Tower – Tour du Major) a fishing boat is moored; climb aboard *Hémérica*, a trawler put out of commission in 1981, and relive the hard life of the fishermen.

☆❧ WALKING TOUR
Ramparts

⏲ *Open Jun–Sept, daily 9.30am–7pm; Apr–May, 10am–12.30pm, 2pm–6pm; school hols 10am–5pm.* ⚠ *Access to the ramparts may be forbidden in adverse weather conditions or during the Blue Nets Festival.* ℘*02 98 50 39 17.*

▶ *Follow the signs. For the first part of the tour, go up a few steps on the left and follow the wall walk.*

Glimpses of the inner harbour and the fishing fleet can be caught through the loopholes. You also get an over-all impression of the New Tower (*Tour Neuve*).

▶ *For the second part of the tour, return by the same path to the starting-point and descend the steps.*

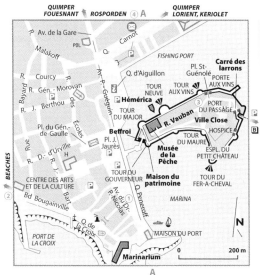

Concarneau harbour

©Daniel Sainthorant/Fotolia.com

After skirting Esplanade du Petit Château, giving onto the marina, you overlook the channel between the two harbours.

○ Return to the town by Porte du Passage. By the corner of the Hospice take rue St-Guénolé, which bears left towards place St-Guénolé.

From place St-Guénolé a short alley to the right leads to **Porte aux Vins** (Wine Gateway) through the ramparts. As you go through the gate *(porte)* you will get a typical view of the trawlers moored in the harbour.

○ Rue Vauban brings you back out of the walled town.

Harbours

By way of avenue Pierre-Guéguin and Quai Carnot, take a quick look at the **Port de Pêche** (fishing port), where the main fishing fleet (trawlers and cargo boats) is moored; you may see the day's catch being unloaded. Then, follow avenue du Dr-P.-Nicolas and walk round the **marina**. The embarcation point for excursions is at the end of this quay, on the left.

On the left of Quai de la Croix is the marine laboratory (Laboratoire Maritime) of the Collège de France. Inside

visit the **Marinarium** (○ *open Jul–Aug, daily 10am–7pm; Apr–Jun and Sept, 10am–noon, 2pm–6pm; Feb–Mar and Oct–Dec, 2pm–6pm;* ☞*5€;* ♿ ℘*02 98 98 50 81 64; www.mnhn.fr/mnhn/conc),* an exhibition devoted to the sea world: aquariums, dioramas and audio-visual displays.

After passing the picturesque old fish market, the 15C Chapelle Notre-Dame-de-Bon-Secours and a small lighthouse, you may skirt **Port de la Croix** (follow blvd Bougainville), which is sheltered by a jetty.

Looking back, there is a good view of the Pointe du Cabellou and, further on, of the Pointe de Beg-Meil. Out at sea are the Îles Glénan.

EXCURSIONS
Beuzec-Conq

○ 1.5km/0.9mi N. Follow rue Jules-Simon and cross D 783. Once in rue de Stang, go through the entrance gate on the left. ☞*Guided tour Jun–Sept (1hr) 10.30am–1pm, 2pm–6pm, Sat 10.30am –1pm.* ☞*5€.* ♿ ℘*02 98 97 36 50.*

The **Kériolet Mansion**, built in the 15C, was transformed in the 19C into a medieval-style fantasy dwelling by the wealthy Russian princess Zenaïde Narischkine-Youssoupoff. Prince Youssoupoff, one of the killers of Rasputin, also lived here.

Rosporden

◐ *13km/8mi NE along D 70.*
◐ *Open Jul–Aug, 10am–noon,
3pm–6pm. ☎02 98 59 21 65.*
The church **bell-tower**★ is reflected
in a pool formed by the River Aven.
There are many canning factories in the
town, which is also famous for its mead
(*chouchen* in Breton). The **church**, dating from the 14C–15C, was remodelled
in the 17C. The square **belltower**★ is
surmounted by an octagonal spire.

🚗 DRIVING TOUR

Concarneau to Pont-Aven by
the Coast Road

45km/28mi – about 2hr.

◐ *Leave Concarneau E on Quai Carnot
towards the D 783. Quimperlé and after
2.5km/1.5mi bear right.*

The road passes the Moros bridge, which
offers pretty views over Concarneau, its
port and the bay. Under the bridge is a
little island inhabited by ducks. At Pointe
du Cabellou, go round it starting from
the right.

Pointe du Cabellou★

The car park affords a fine **view**★ of the
site of Concarneau and the walled town.
The road skirts the rocky coastline amid
the villas and pine trees and offers pretty
views of Baie de la Forêt and the Îles
de Glénan.

◐ *Return to the main road and make
for Quimperlé. Turn right at Pont-
Minaouët and right again at Kermao.*

The road goes through **Pouldohan**
(which has a fine beach and large sailing school) and Pendruc.

Pointe de la Jument

◐ *15min on foot there and back.*

Enjoy the fine rocky site and view of
Cabellou, the bay and Beg-Meil, and the
coast of Loctudy in the distance.

◐ *Make for the Pointe de Trévignon
going via Lambell where you turn right,
Lanénos and Ruat.*

Pointe de Trévignon

An old fort stands at the tip of the headland; fishing boats and the lifeboat are
berthed in the tiny port to the west.
There is a fine **view**★ to the right of La
Forêt Bay and Beg-Meil, Bénodet Bay,
and on the left of the Îles de Glénan and
near the coast of Verte and Raguenès
Islands.

◐ *Follow the road along Kersidan
Beach and turn left to Kercanic.*

Kercanic

This picturesque hamlet has several
traditional thatched farmhouses.

◐ *Turn back and bear left.*

The road runs through the charming
village of **Kerascoët** (with many pretty
thatched cottages) towards Port-
Manech. In Trémorvezen, turn right
beyond the chapel.

◐ *The remainder of the excursion
is described in the opposite direction
under PONT-AVEN: Driving Tour.*

Thatched stone cottage in
Kerascoët village

A. Cassaigne/MICHELIN

ADDRESSES

🏠 STAY

Chambre d'hôte Le Manoir de Coat Canton – *Grand Bois, 29140 Rosporden. 13km N of Concarneua on the D 783 and D 70.* 📞*02 98 66 31 24. 4 rooms.* 🚭. 🚗. The manor, whose construction dates from 13 C to 17 C, only houses the reception area. The rooms, either medieval, Breton or English style, are in an old restored longhouse.

Hôtel Ker Moor – *plage des Sables Blancs.* 📞*02 98 97 02 96. www. hotel-kermor.com. 12 rooms.* 🛏 *12€.* The discreet façade of this 1900 villa hides a beautiful hotel. The atmosphere is reminiscent of a ship's cabin: onboard furniture, portholes, painted wainscots and model ships. All rooms have a view of the sea, and three have a terrace.

Océan – *plage des Sables-Blancs.* 📞*02 98 56 53 50. www.hotel-ocean.com. 53 rooms.* 🛏 *11.50€.* In a modern neighbourhood along the coast, this imposing new building shelters big rooms facing either the sea or the swimming pool. The comfortable dining room (closed Sun evening, Mon noon and Sat from Oct–Apr) has a nice view over the beach and the bay; seafood holds pride of place on the menu.

🍽/EAT

Le Cosy Bar – *8 av. du Dr Nicolas.* 📞*02 98 50 54 21. Open Tue–Sun 11am–1am.* Here's a lively spot that doesn't serve chips, mayonnaise or ketchup, but rather home made bread with good meat and fresh vegetables, tortillas, paninis and home made pizzas. Delicious!

Le Buccin – *1 rue Duguay-Trouin.* 📞*02 98 50 54 22. www.restaurantle buccin.fr. Closed Sun eve, Thu and Sat noon.* A dining room with a simple and fresh setting located on the ground floor of an old house; appetizing recipes that reflect the day's catch; warm and attentive service and welcome.

Grill l'Océania – *3 rue Alfred Le Ray.* 📞*02 98 50 81 58. Open Tue–Sun 7pm–midnight, Fri–Sat until 2am.* Delicious and copious dishes cooked over a wood fire; fish (swordfish, bluefin tuna) but also meat, and not only beef but African-style frogs' legs, ostrich and even kangaroo.

Chez Armande – *15 bis av. du Dr Nicolas.* 📞*02 98 97 00 76. Closed 10–25 Feb, 26 Aug–3 Sept, 16 Dec–7 Jan, Tue (except Jul and Aug) and Wed.* Enjoy your meal on the terrace in front of the marina: try lobster stew with mushroom sauce or a *cotriade Concarnoise*. If you like leg of lamb, try the *gigot de 7 heures'* or you may prefer fillet of fine "Salers" beef.

La Porte Au Vin – *9 pl St-Guénolé.* 📞*02 98 97 38 11. Open 20 Mar–mid-Nov and Christmas.* This restaurant is in the old town next to the gate where wine used to be delivered. Good value menus are served in traditional surroundings: stonework, vaulting, fireplaces, old photos and antiques.

🚶 ACTIVITIES

Tour of the Criée (fish auction) – From Easter–Nov, guided tours (1hr 30) are carried out daily by **Video-Mer** (📞*06 80 26 34 25, www.videomer.fr*) and by **À l'Assaut des Remparts** (📞*02 98 50 55 18, www.alassautdesremparts.fr*). Board fishing boats that have just returned from sea and assist with unloading the day's catch.

Town Tours – Concarneau is a Ville d'art et d'histoire and the Tourist Office runs several different themed tours (1hr 30): artists, military architecture etc.

Beaches – Boulevard Katherine Wylie offers beautiful views of the bay of Concarneau lined with the beaches of **Rodel**, **Les Dames** and **Miné**. Farther on, the beach of **Cornouaille** and the **Sables-Blancs** are reachable from the centre by urban bus BUSCO (n° 2).

🛒 SHOPPING

Conserverie Courtin – *3 quai de Moros.* 📞*02 98 97 01 80. www.conserverie-courtin.com. Open Mon–Sat 9am–12.30pm, 2pm–7pm.* This is one of the last canning factories, reputed for its confits of St-Jacques, soups, sauces and bisques. Free guided tours and tastings.

Pont-Aven★

The town lies in a very pleasant setting at the point where the River Aven opens out into a tidal estuary. The Aven used to drive numerous mills, hence the saying: "Pont-Aven, a famous town; 14 mills, 15 houses". Today, only one mill remains in operation. Pont-Aven is also famous for Galettes de Pont-Aven (butter cookies) and as a favourite resort of painters; the Pont-Aven School, headed by Gauguin, was formed here in about 1888.

▶ **Population:** 2,953.
- **Michelin Map:** Local map 308 I7 – Finistère (29).
- **Info:** 5 pl. de l'Hôtel-de-Ville, 29930 Pont Aven. ℘02 98 06 04 70. www.pontaven.com.
- **Location:** Pont-Aven is halfway between Lorient (39km/24mi E) and Quimper (34km/21mi W) on the N 165.
- **Timing:** The town gets very busy in summer.
- **Parking:** There's a large car park near the post office.
- **Don't Miss:** Pont-Aven museum.

A BIT OF HISTORY
Pont-Aven School
See INTRODUCTION: Art and Culture.
The *Caisse Nationale des Monuments Historiques* has set up *La Route des Peintres*, which includes five itineraries of one or two days each, described in a book of the same name (available in English). The tours start in an art gallery, concentrating on the works of local and visiting artists in Cornouaille, 1850–1950, then take the visitor off to discover the landscapes which inspired the art.

SIGHTS
The Banks of the Aven
Allow 30min on foot there and back. Walk to the right of the bridge towards the harbour.
Follow the river bank lined with rocks and ruined watermills. On the river's east bank there is an enormous rock called Gargantua's Shoe *(soulier de Gargantua)*. Near the square, beside the harbour, is a view of the fine stretch of water formed by the Aven.
The once prosperous port (oysters, wine, salt and grain) is now used by pleasure boats.

Promenade Xavier-Grall
Access via rue Émile-Bernard.
This promenade (named after the poet and reporter **Xavier Grall**, 1930–81), along the Aven, passes by the mill course and gates, which regulated the water to the mills, and old wash-houses scattered on either side of the river. Footbridges span the river, which winds between the Porche-Menu rocks.

Bois d'Amour★
Access via Promenade Xavier-Grall.
A footpath follows the meanders of the Aven and climbs the hillside (*about 1hr*). With the aid of maps produced by the Tourist Office, this pleasant walk shows visitors the places which inspired the painters of the Pont-Aven School.

Chapelle de Trémalo
Access via rue Émile-Bernard and right on D 24, the Quimper road (signposted).
This characteristic early 16C Breton country chapel is set amid fine trees. It has a lopsided roof, with one of the eaves nearly touching the ground. Inside is a 17C wooden Christ, which was the model for Gauguin's *Yellow Christ* where, painted in the background, is the village of Pont-Aven and Ste-Marguerite Hill.

Musée de Pont-Aven
Open Jul–Aug, daily 10am–7pm; May–June, Sept–Oct, 10am–12.30pm, 2pm–6.30pm; Nov–Mar 10am–12.30pm, 2pm–6pm. Guided tours available (1hr 30). Closed Jan and four days between temporary exhibitions. 6€.
℘02 98 06 14 43.

The modern wing is for temporary exhibits and the old wing recounts with photographs and documents the history of Pont-Aven: the town, port, Gorse-Bloom Festival, and the Pont-Aven painters and their lodgings (Pension Gloanec).

The first floor houses the permanent collection concentrating on the Pont-Aven School: Maurice Denis (Midsummer Bonfire at Loctudy), Émile Jourdan (Lanriot Chapel), Rouillet (The Port in Pont-Aven), Gustave Loiseau (View of Pont-Aven), and works by Paul Sérusier, Charles Filiger, Émile Schuffenecker. An audiovisual presentation illustrates the environment which favoured the development of the Pont-Aven School: the Golden Gorse Festival, the Gloanec boarding house where the painters lived.

Temporary exhibits present artists who worked in Brittany at the end of the 19C as well as contemporary artists, who are once more being welcomed in Pont-Aven.

🚗 DRIVING TOUR

Pont-Aven to Concarneau on the Coast Road

45km/28mi – allow 2hr.

▷ *Leave Pont-Aven by the D 783 W, then, after 2.5 km/1.6mi, turn left on to the D 77.*

Névez

This village has retained a number of 18C granite houses built of 2m-high standing stones. In the **Chapelle Ste-Barbe** there are some old wooden statues and a 17C high altar.

▷ *Retake the D 77 in the direction of Port-Manech then turn left onto the road to Kerdruc.*

Kerdruc

In a pretty **setting**★ overlooking the Aven, this small port still has some old thatched cottages.

🏃 Port-Manech

A charming resort with a well-situated beach on the Aven-Belon estuary.
A path cut in the hillside links the port to the beach and offers fine views of the coast and islands.

▷ *Go to Kerangall.*

Les jardins de Rospico

Névez-Port-Manech. ☎ 02 98 06 71 29. www.jardins-rospico.com. ♿. 14 Jun–6 Sept, 11am–7pm; 21 Mar–13 Jun and 6 Sept–7 Nov, 2pm–6pm. ☞6.50€ (6-16 yrs 2.50 €). ⊗Closed Sat. Shop and tea room.

This undulating floral park is a mix of gardens inspired by the English and Mediterranean styles, with plants for humid regions as well as perennial plants. Pools of water and waterfalls punctuate this perfumed walk.

EXCURSION
Nizon

The small **church** with its squat pillars dates from the 15C and 16C and contains many old statues. The colours of the stained-glass windows by the master glazier Guével are remarkable. The Romanesque calvary was used as a model by Gauguin for his *Green Christ*.

ADDRESSES

🛏 STAY

Chambre d'hôte Kermentec – *1km/0.6mi rte de Quimper then chapelle de Trémalo. ☎02 98 06 07 60. http://larour.veronique.free.fr. Closed Dec–Jan. 3 rooms.* Nestled in the heights of Pont-Aven, this little Breton house offers spacious and comfortable rooms.

Les Ajoncs d'Or – *1 pl. de l'Hôtel-de-Ville. ☎02 98 06 02 06. www.ajoncs dor-pontaven.com. 20 rooms. Closed Jan, 17–26 Oct, Sun eve and Mon off season. ⎕ 8€. Restaurant.* In the centre of Pont-Aven, a very pleasant place with elegant rooms (choose one in the main building) equipped with bright wood furniture and sea grass flooring. Cuisine inspired by the sea and a warm welcome await.

⊜⊜⊟ **Auberge Les Grandes Roches**
– 29910 Trégunc. 9km/6mi W of Pont
Aven on the D 783. ℘02 98 97 62 97.
www.hotel-lesgrandesroches.com. 17
rooms. ⊑ 14€. Closed 1 Dec–1 Feb.
A picture-postcard collection of farm
buildings in a park complete with
dolmen and menhir. Stylish, cosy rooms
and suites, and a charming restaurant,
which offers coastal cuisine.

⚑/EAT

⊜ **Le Talisman** – 4 rue Paul Sérusier.
℘02 98 06 02 58. Closed Sun lunch off
season and Mon. Owned and operated
by the same family since 1920, this
good *crêperie* bears the name of a small
painting by Sérusier (1888) depicting
the Bois d'Amour.

⊜⊜⊟ **Moulin de Rosmadec** – Near
the bridge in the town centre. ℘02 98
06 00 22. www.moulinderosmadec.com.
4 rooms. ⊑12€. Closed Feb holidays and
18–31 Oct. Reservations obligatory. An
unusual sight, this 15C former mill has
stylish rooms, but is best known for its
attractive dining room, summer terrace
and inventive food.

⚐ ACTIVITIES

River cruises – Vedettes Aven-Bélon –
℘02 98 71 14 59. www.vedettes-aven-
belon.com. From Apr–Sept, boat trips on
the Aven and the Bélon *(1h to 2h)*: small
ports, castles, beaches and sea birds.
10.50€–14.50€, depending on cruise
route (Bleu, Vert, Rouge).

Quimperlé★

This little town is prettily situated
at the confluence (*kemper*) of the
River Ellé and River Isole, which join
to form the Laïta. It consists of an
upper town, dominated by the Église
Notre-Dame-de-l'Assomption, and
a lower town grouped about the
former Abbaye of Ste-Croix and rue
Dom-Morice. Quimperlé was once a
fairly important harbour but today
it is chiefly used for small pleasure
craft that sail along the Laïta to
discover the Forêt de Carnoët and
the pretty seaside resort of
Le Pouldu.

SIGHTS

Église Ste-Croix★★

⏱ Open 8.30am–6pm.
The Église Ste-Croix is interesting
archaeologically, as it was based on
that of the Holy Sepulchre at Jerusalem. It includes a rotunda with three
small apsidal chapels opening into it
and a porch, the whole forming a Greek
cross. The church was built in the 12C,
but had to be rebuilt in 1862, except for
the apse and the crypt, when its bell-
tower collapsed. The new bell-tower
stands alone.

▶ **Population:** 10,725.
⛁ **Michelin Map:** Local map
308 J7– Finistère (29).
▤ **Info:** 45 pl St Michel 29300
Quimperlé. ℘02 98 96
04 32. www.quimperle
tourisme.com.
▷ **Location:** 20km/12.5mi NW
of Lorient on the N 165.
▲▲ **Kids:** Bat-watching in
St-Maurice Abbey.
🕐 **Timing:** There are not
many restaurants in
Quimperlé, so book ahead
when possible. Allow a
half a day for exploration.
▣ **Parking:** There are
plenty of car parks,
notably St-Michel near
the Tourist Office.
◈ **Don't Miss:** The medieval
houses in rue Dom-Morice.

The **apse**★★, with its blind arcades, columns, capitals and windows, is the finest
specimen of Romanesque art in Brittany.
A Renaissance stone **altarpiece**★ (part
of an old rood screen) stands against
the façade.

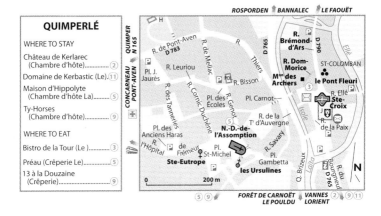

The **crypt**★★ has remarkable capitals and two 15C tombs with recumbent statues.

On leaving the church, take *rue Ellé* which skirts the north side and affords a good view of the east end and the bell-tower.

Rue Brémond-d'Ars

There are some half-timbered and old 17C houses at numbers 8, 10, 11 and 12. At number 15 note the staircase of the Présidial, a former Law Court. Also note the ruins of the Église St Colomban.

Rue Dom-Morice★

This narrow alley is lined with 16C half-timbered and corbelled houses; number 7, the **Maison des Archers** (1470) is noteworthy and stages interesting temporary exhibits (○*open daily Jul–Aug 10am–noon, 2.30pm–7pm; rest of year 2pm–7pm;* ○*closed Tue;* ℘*02 98 96 04 32; www.quimperletourisme.com*).

Église Notre-Dame-de-l'Assomption

○*Open Jul–Aug, 9am–6pm.*
℘*02 98 96 04 32.*
This 13C and 15C church, surmounted by a large square tower, is also known as St-Michel. Pass under the archway on the right, built into one of the buttresses, to get a glimpse of the fine carved porch (1450). Inside, look at the oak-panelled vault with a sculpted cornice.

Chapelle Ste-Eutrope (Hôpital Frémeur)

This old hospice dates back to 16C. The hospice used to be a 13C leper hospital. The *longère* retains the medieaval structure.

The gates opened and the ill were able to hear the mass celebrated in the adjoining chapel. Go back to place St-Michel and take the rue A-Briand.

Chapelle des Ursulines

A 17C convent built in Jesuit style with a tendency to baroque. It has a gold leaf ceiling. The town of Quimperlé organises contemporary art exhibitions.

🚘 DRIVING TOURS

1 DOMAINE DE CLOHARS-CARNOËT

Round trip of 43km/26.7mi – 2hr 30min.

▷ *Leave Quimperlé via Quai Brizeux.*

Forêt de Carnoët

Bordered by the River Laïta, the forest offers pretty sites and pleasant walks (◔*some paths are reserved for walking and riding*).

▷ *Some 500m/545yds beyond Toulfoën, turn left towards the Rocher Royal.*

The road winds through the forest to the banks of the Laïta where the **Rocher**

Royal can be seen, a rocky ridge towering above the river, and the ruins of the Château de Carnoët. This is the legendary dwelling of the Count of Commore, the Bluebeard of Cornouaille.

After hearing a prediction that he would die by the hand of his son, he put his first four wives to death as soon as they conceived. The fifth wife, Triphine, before she died, was able to save her son, who became **St-Trémeur**. Commore, on meeting the saint, was struck by his resemblance to his mother and immediately had him beheaded.

Then, according to the legend, Trémeur picked up his own head, walked towards his father's castle and threw a handful of earth against the building, which then collapsed, burying Commore alive.

Return to the Le Pouldu road, turn left and at a major junction, left again.

The **Pont de St-Maurice** over the Laïta gives a fine **view**★ of the river and its steep banks.

Turn round and after 700m/765yds, turn right.

St-Maurice
29360 Clohars-Carnoët. ⏱ *Open daily mid-Jun–mid-Sept 11am–7pm; Apr–mid Jun, Sun and public holidays 2pm–6pm; school holidays Sun–Fri 2pm–6pm.* *3€ (children 2€).* *02 98 71 65 51. www.clohars-carnoet.fr.*
This natural protected site, property of the *Conservatoire du Littoral* since 1991, is green and pleasant. Water is everywhere: on the left, the Laïta, on the right, a lake. The 13C chapter house is one of the oldest in Brittany.
Don't leave without taking a look at the bats in the attic. Thanks to an infrared camera, visitors can observe a colony of large bats which live in the eaves.

Maison Marie-Henry
10 rue des Grands-Sables. *Guided tours (45min) Jun–Nov, 10.30am–1pm and 2.30pm–7pm.* *4€.* *02 98 39 98 51.*
Reconstruction of the inn which Gauguin and members of the Pont-Aven

School decorated with paintings and drawings; the furniture dates from the 1880s. Temporary exhibitions devoted to these artists illustrate their influence on the Nabis movement.

Chapelle Notre-Dame-de-la-Paix
🔲 *To visit (min 10 people) contact Michelle* *02 98 96 91 51 or Pascal* *02 98 06 46 65.*
In a grassy close near Grands Sables Beach is an entrance flanked by a monument to Gauguin. The chapel escaped ruin by being transported 26km and rebuilt here. The bays have flame and lily shaped tracery with stained glass by Manessier and Le Moal. Below the timber roof, the rood beam carries a Christ with a red loincloth and a second group depicting a *Pietà*.

Drive along Grands Sables Beach then turn left towards Doëlan.

Doëlan
This small fishing port is a well-kept secret, commanding the entrance to a deep, sheltered estuary. Verdant river banks and Breton houses.

Return to Quimperlé via Clohars-Carnoët.

Port of Doëlan

G. Targat/MICHELIN

2 THE BÉLON REGION

Round trip of 37km/23mi – 1hr 30min.

Leave Quimperlé to the SW on D 16 and at Gare-de-la-Forêt, bear right.

Moëlan-sur-Mer

Several small harbours. In the **church** (*open Mon–Fri 9.30am–5pm*), note the four 18C confessional boxes in the Italian style.

Continue SW to Brigneau.

Brigneau

A tiny fishing port where pleasure craft also find shelter.

The road follows the coastline, with thatched houses along the way.

At Kergroès, bear left.

Kerfany-les-Pins

This small seaside resort has a pretty location and a sandy beach, set beside the River Bélon, with a fine view over Port-Manech and the Aven estuary.

Take the uphill road beyond the beach and at Lanriot, turn left.

Bélon

This locality, on the south bank of the Bélon, is famous as an oyster-farming centre. The oyster beds on the north bank can be seen at low tide.

Return to Quimperlé via Moëlan-sur-Mer.

EXCURSIONS
🏛🏛 Manoir de Kernault

At Mellac, 5 km/3.1m to the NW by the D 765. ℘02 98 71 90 60. Jul–Aug, 10am–12h30, 2–7pm ; Apr–Jun and Sept–Oct, daily exc Mon–Tue 2–6pm ; Feb–May and school hols : 2–6pm. 4 € (-18 yrs 2.50 €).

The beautiful 15C manor house surrounded by a 30 acre park is remarkable for its superb 16C timber-framed barn. This has become a cultural centre for temporary interesting exhibitions, events some for children.

Roches du Diable★

12km/7.5mi NE, plus 30min on foot there and back. Leave Quimperlé on D 790 towards Le Faouët and after 4.5km/2.8mi turn right and go through Locunolé.

There is a pretty run as the road descends towards the Ellé.

Cross the bridge and turn left towards Meslan; after 400m/438yds, leave the car in the car park to the left.

Paths leading up to the top of the Devil's Rocks drop vertically to the fast-flowing waters of the Ellé.

ADDRESSES

🛏 STAY

☕🍽 **Chambre d'hôte Ty Horses** –*Le Rouho, 56520 Guidel. 7km/4mi SE on the D 765 rte de Lorient and rte de Locmaria. ℘02 97 65 97 37. 🍴. 4 rooms.* Attractive rooms in this modern cottage each have their own colour scheme. Breakfast is served on the veranda, where you can watch the horses being exercised.

☕🍽 **Chambre d'hôte La Maison d'Hippolyte** – *2 quai Surcouf. ℘02 98 39 09 11. http://hote.hippolyte.free.fr/accueil.htm. 🍴. 4 rooms.* Located on the banks of the Laïta, this 19C house often hosts contemporary art exhibitions and poetry evenings. The bathrooms are tiny and the rooms simple, with parquet floors and wooden furniture. Hippolyte was a well-known local fisherman.

☕🍽🛏🍽 **Chambre d'hôte du Château de Kerlarec** – *℘02 98 71 75 37. www.chateau-de-kerlarec.com. 🅿 🍴 🍽. 5 rooms. Restaurant* ☕🍽. Splendid park setting for this opulent Second-Empire era château with modern amenities such as pool and tennis courts.

☕🍽🛏🍽 **Le Domaine de Kerbastic** – *Rte de Locmaria, 56520 Guidel. 7km/4mi*

SE on the D 765. *02 97 65 98 01. www.
domaine-de-kerbistic.com. Closed 30 Nov
– 14 Feb. 15 rooms. ⊑ 17€. Restaurant
⊖⊜🍽🍷. Luxurious mansion with
stylish rooms and charming gardens.

♀/EAT

⊜ **Crêperie Le Préau** – 3 rue des Plages,
29350 Moëlan-sur-Mer. *02 98 96 50 91.
Closed 23 Nov–14 Dec and Mon exc Jul–
Aug. Thur eve, Sun and Wed in Winter.
This old school near the church houses
a *crêperie*. Wonderful smelling crêpes
are made in front of you.

⊜ **Crêperie 13 à la Douzaine** – 22 rue
de Lannevain, 29360 Clohars-Carnoët.
*02 98 71 61 25. Closed Sun exc school
hols, Mon exc Jul–Aug. ⊿. Next to a
Celtic pub, you'll find this *crêperie* whose
produce is made with organic flour.
Gourmets will enjoy the St-Jacques
(scallops) with cream, curry, mushrooms
and a dash of cognac.

⊜⊜ **Le Bistro de La Tour** – 2 rue
Dom-Morice. *02 98 39 29 58. www.hotel
vintage.com. Closed Sun lunch in Jul– Aug,
Sun eve low season, Mon exc eve in Jul–
Aug and Sat. Located in a pleasant alley in
Quimperlé old town. More evocative of a
wine merchant than of a restaurant, the
façade here takes its cue from the owner,
chairman of the *Sommeliers de Bretagne*.
Oenophiles can purchase and taste their
favourite wines.

⚡ACTIVITIES

**Horse Riding – Ferme Équestre de
Kersperche** – Lieu-dit Kersperche, 29340
Riec-sur-Bélon. *02 98 06 50 22. Open
daily on reservation. Closed Sept. This
centre offers treks (10 people max) and
hosts paintball games.

🛒SHOPPING

Huîtrière du Château de Bélon – Port
de Bélon, 29340 Riec-sur-Bélon. *02 98 06
90 58. www.huitres-belon.com. Open daily
10.30am–2pm, 3pm–6.30pm. 45min-
oyster bed visits, tastings and sales.

Montagnes
Noires★★

Along with the Monts d'Arrée,
the Montagnes Noires form what
Bretons call the spine of the
peninsula. These two little mountain
ranges, mainly of hard sandstone
and quartzite, are not quite alike:
the Montagnes Noires are lower;
their crest is narrower; their slopes
are less steep and their heaths are
less extensive. The range's name
suggests that it was once covered
with forest (*noire* means black). As
in all inland Brittany, the ground
gradually became bare. After
several years of reforestation, the
fir woods once again justify their
name. Quarrying of Breton slate
was carried out on a large scale in
the past, and is now concentrated at
the eastern end of the range, in the
district of Motreff and Maël-Carhaix.

- 🗺 **Michelin Map:** Local
  map 308 I/J5 - Finistère
  (29 and Morbihan (56).
- 📄 **Info:** www.chateauneuf-
  du-faou.com
- 📍 **Location:** The Montagnes
  Noires extend for about
  60km/37mi from east to
  west, south of Carhaix-
  Plouguer. Quimper
  is about 40km/25mi
  SE on the D 15.
- 👪 **Kids:** Park and Château
  de Trévarez.
- 🕐 **Timing:** The driving tour
  takes about half a day.
- 👁 **Don't Miss:** The
  panorama from the Roc
  de Toullaëron or the
  exquisite stained-glass
  windows of the Chapelle
  Notre-Dame-du-Crann.

DRIVING TOUR

From Carhaix-Plouguer to Cléden-Poher

85km/53mi – allow half a day.

Carhaix-Plouguer –
♿ *See CARHAIX-PLOUGUER.*

▷ *Leave Carhaix-Plouguer W towards Pleyben (N 164) and then follow D 769 S.*

The road then enters the picturesque valley of the **Hyère**.

▷ *At Port-de-Carhaix, after crossing the Nantes-Brest Canal, bear right.*

About 1.5km/0.9mi further on, note the **Calvaire de Kerbreudeur** on the left, parts of which are thought to date from the 15C.

St-Hernin

In this place, where Ireland's St Hernin is said to have settled, is a 16C parish close. The church and charnel house were remodelled in the 17C. On the beautiful slender calvary note St-Michael slaying the dragon.

▷ *Take the road to Moulin-Neuf and bear right on the road Carhaix-Plouguer to Gourin. Old slate quarries can be seen to the right and left.*

Chapelle St-Hervé

Access via a road to the left.
This small 16C building with a pierced pinnacle is decorated in the Flamboyant Gothic style. A *pardon* is held on the last Sunday in September.

▷ *Head for Gourin via Minetoul.*

La Trinité-Langonnet

This village possesses a fine Flamboyant-style **church**. The **timbering**⋆ inside, dated 1568 and decorated with Renaissance designs, shows great craftsmanship and enhances the lofty, well-lit nave. In the richly ornamented chancel, note the carved recesses, corbels and purlins.

Gourin

Once a centre of slate production, Gourin also has white stone quarries and raises horses, cattle and poultry.

▷ *Follow D 301 N. The road climbs towards the crest of the Montagnes Noires.*

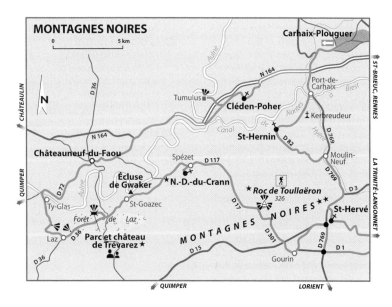

🚶 Roc de Toullaëron★

5km/3mi from Gourin – allow 30min on foot there and back. Leave your car and take a stony lane bordered with oak trees (private property, no picnicking) to the right. At the end of the lane, climb up the rocks.

From the top, which is the highest point in the Montagnes Noires (326m/1,070ft), a wide **panorama**★ may be enjoyed in clear weather: to the west is the densely wooded valley of Châteaulin; to the north, the Monts d'Arrée; to the south, in the distance, the Breton plateau slopes gently down to the Atlantic.

Make for Spézet; on leaving Spézet, take the Châteauneuf-du-Faou road and bear left.

Chapelle Notre-Dame-du-Crann★

Rte de Roudouallec. Guided tours mid May–mid Sept, daily 2pm–5.30pm; rest of the year, call Mme Arlaux at 02 98 93 92 92.

The chapel, built in 1532, stands on the side of the road in a verdant setting. It contains some remarkable 16C **stained-glass windows**★★.

In the south aisle you will see the window illustrating the legend of St-Eligius, who is the patron of farriers (specialists in equine hoof care). In the south transept are the Death and Coronation of the Virgin. Above the south aisle, is the stained-glass window of St-James the Greater, in three bays. The window in the chancel depicts scenes from the Passion in 12 bays.

Return to Spézet and before entering the village, bear left and after 2km/1.2mi, left again. At the entrance to St-Goazec, turn right.

Écluse de Gwaker

This is one of the many locks on the Nantes-Brest Canal. There is a pretty waterfall at the end of the large pool, which forms a pleasant setting.

After St-Goazec, bear right towards Laz. The road climbs into the lovely forest of Laz, which is mostly coniferous.

👥 Park and Château de Trévarez★

Open late Nov–early Jan, daily 1.30pm–6.30pm; Apr–Jun and Sept, 1pm–6pm; Jul–Aug, daily 11am–6.30pm; Oct–Mar, Wed, Sat, Sun 2pm–5.30pm. 5€ (12–25 years 3.50€; children under 11 free). 02 98 26 82 79. www.trevarez.com.

This 85ha/210-acre forest park is laid out around an imposing neo-Gothic château built in the Belle Epoque style. The sign-posted paths wind their way through the woods, making for a pleasant stroll whatever the season: admire the camellias (April), the azaleas and hydrangeas (July), fuchsias and rhododendrons.

A pond, a water garden and several fountains add a refreshing touch. The château terrace offers a **splendid view** of the Châteauneuf-du-Faou region. The former stables, whose original design was extremely modern for their time, have kept their stalls and loose-boxes; these have been converted into a small museum and are used for exhibitions and other educational activities organised throughout the year. This charming outing can be complemented by a train ride.

At Laz, turn right towards Kerohan.

The picturesque downhill road, hemmed in by rocky ridges, affords a fine view over the Aulne Valley.

After Ty-Glas, bear right towards Châteauneuf-du-Faou. The road crosses and then follows the Aulne.

Châteauneuf-du-Faou

This village is built in very pretty surroundings on the slope of a hill overlooking the Aulne. It is an angler's delight with salmon swimming up the Aulne from the sea, and also pike.

In the church, the baptismal chapel decorated in 1919 with scenes from the life of Christ by **Paul Sérusier** (1865–1927), a painter of the Nabis group, is of interest. A *pardon* is held on the third Sunday in August at the Chapelle Notre-Dame-des-Portes.

Lock at Bizernig, Châteauneuf-du-Faou

©Alain Hennequin/Bigstockphoto.com

The road from Châteauneuf to Carhaix-Plouguer is charming for the short distance that it follows the Aulne.

After 1.5km/0.9mi beyond the confluence with the Nantes-Brest Canal, bear left towards La Roche and then right after some 500m/545yds.

The road runs past farmyards to a hillock. From the top of the tumulus, there is a fine **view** of a loop of the Aulne.

Return to the road to Carhaix-Plouguer.

Cléden-Poher

The village has a fine **parish close**★ dating mainly from the 16C. The 15C–16C church contains interesting altarpieces: three Flemish-style 16C panels at the high altar; the altarpiece of the Rosary (1694) in the south aisle; the altarpiece of the Pentecost (17C) in the north aisle. Much of the vaulting has preserved its panelling painted in 1750. In the cemetery are an ossuary turned into a chapel with a fine timber roof, a calvary (1575) and two curious sacristies with keel vaulting.

Return to Carhaix-Plouguer.

ADDRESSES

STAY

Domaine de Koadig – *29270 St-Kernin. ℰ02 98 99 54 85. 2 gîtes (sleep 6 and 10). ⌕5€. Restaurant.* In the heart of the mountains, this vast estate offers a dream environment for nature lovers: animal park, Arab horses, sheep in the fields, trout fishing and numerous walks.

Hôtel du Relais de Cournouaille – *Rte de Carhaix, 29520 Châteauneuf-du-Faou. ℰ02 98 81 75 36. www.lerelais decornouaille.com. Closed Oct. 30 rooms. ⌕7€. Restaurant.* Installed in two adjoining village houses (one old, one new), this hotel has modernised rooms. The generous menu includes dishes for children.

EAT

Le Bienvenu – *84 rue Nicolas-le-Grand, 56110 Roudouallec. 9km/5.6mi W of Gourin rte de Quimper on the D 1. ℰ02 97 34 50 01. www.restaurant-hotels. com. Closed Feb holidays.* Hortensias and rhododendrons surround this village restaurant. In the simple dining room you can sample generous portions of traditional local cooking.

ACTIVITIES

Aulne Loisirs Plaisance – *Pen ar Pont, 29520 Châteauneuf-du-Faou. ℰ02 98 73 28 63. www.aulneloisirs.com. Closed mid Nov–mid Mar.* This water sports company offers trips on the Nantes-Brest canal, pleasure boat, kayak and bike rental.

Carhaix-Plouguer

In the Roman era, Carhaix was an important town commanding seven main roads; even today it is still the hub of a roadway network.

The town is a milk production centre in the centre of a cattle-rearing district. Threatened, like most rural areas, by a decline in its population, the town created the *Festival des Vieilles Charrues*, a popular traditional event which attracts 200, 000 visitors every year in July.

▶ **Population:** 7,648.

◔ **Michelin Map:** Local map 308 J5 finistère (29).

▣ **Info:** rue Brizeux, 29270 Carhaix-Plouguer. *℘*02 98 93 04 42. www.poher.com.

◑ **Location:** 60km/37mi NE of Quimper.

◔ **Timing:** After a walk around town, allow half a day to discover the plateau of Huelgoat.

◉ **Don't Miss**: The Vieilles Charrues music festival.

A BIT OF HISTORY
La Tour d'Auvergne
Carhaix's famous son is **Théophile-Malo Corret** (1743–1800), known as La Tour d'Auvergne. When still very young, he became keenly interested in the Breton language, but he was always a soldier at heart. During the Revolution his exploits were such that he, a junior captain at 46, was offered the most exalted rank; but he refused preferring to remain among his fellow troops. When there was a pause in his campaigns, he would bring his faithful Celtic grammar out. On retirement he devoted himself to the study of his favourite subject.

When the son of his Celtic master was called up for the army, La Tour, moved by the old teacher's grief, took the young man's place and enlisted, at 54 years of age, as a private soldier in the 46th half-brigade: new adventures followed. Bonaparte offered La Tour a seat on the Legislative Council, but failed to overcome his modesty. He was awarded a sword of honour and the title of 'First Grenadier of the Republic'. When he was killed in 1800, during the Rhine campaign he was mourned by the whole army. Every year, on the Saturday preceding 27 June, Carhaix celebrates the name-day of La Tour d'Auvergne.

SIGHTS
Église St-Trémeur
Rebuilt in the 19C, the church's porch opens onto the bell-tower (16C); the tympanum over the doorway is adorned with the statue of St Trémeur, whose legend dates from the 6C.

Maison du Sénéchal
6 rue Brizeux. ◔*Open daily Jul–Aug 9am–12.30pm, 1.30pm–7pm (Sun 10am –1pm). Jun and Sept Mon–Sat 9am– noon, 2pm–6pm; Oct–May Tue, Wed, Fri, Sat 10am–noon, 2pm–5.30pm.* *℘02 98 93 04 42. www.poher.com.*
This building has a 16C façade. The ground floor is of granite decorated with carvings and the corbelled upper storeys are faced with slate and adorned with statuettes. The Tourist Office *(syndicat d'initiative)* has its premises here (temporary exhibitions), and a small **museum** of local ethnography is open to the public on the first floor.

🚗 DRIVING TOUR

Plateau du Huelgoat
Round tour of 80km/50mi – 4hr.

▷ *Leave Carhaix by rue Oberhausen and rue des Abattoirs in the direction of Plounevézel. Turn right at Croissant Marie-Joffré. 3km further on, past the Lesquern hamlet on the left, take a bend on the right onto an unsurfaced road.*

Chapelle St-Gildas

The beacon of St-Gildas (238m/780ft) stands to the right of the chapel (view of Monts d'Arrée). The road leads through woodlands to the 16C chapel, which has a square bell-tower crowned by a stone spire and grotesques at the east end.

Return to the main road and turn right. Bear left towards Plourac'h.

Église de Plourac'h

This Renaissance church was designed in the form of a T and was built largely in the 15C and 16C. The south face is the most ornate. The porch, which is Gothic in character, contains statues of the Apostles surmounted by canopies. A beautiful Renaissance doorway with windows on either side is crowned by three gables adorned with coats of arms. Near the font is an 18C altarpiece depicting the mysteries of the rosary and statues of St-Adrian and St-Margaret. Among the many statues ornamenting the church should be noted those of St-Guénolé and St-Nicodemus (dressed as a doctor of law), and a Descent from the Cross in which the Virgin wears a Breton cloak of mourning.

Continue towards Callac.

Detail of the calvary, Pestivien

Callac

This town is dominated by the ruins of Botmel Church. In front of the stud farm stands a bronze statue of the stallion Naous, by Guyot. The town is also the home of the Breton spaniel, a pointer.

Take the road towards Guingamp and after 4km/2.5mi turn right.

Bulat-Pestivien

This former pilgrimage centre has retained a fine **church**★ built in the 15C and 16C with remarkable porches. The Renaissance tower, had a spire added in the 19C.

Inside is a monumental sacristy – adorned with a frieze of macabre design – with a loggia that projects into the church.

There is a curious lectern representing a peasant in the local Vannes costume and a massive table dating back to 1583. Offerings used to be placed at the table during the **pardon**, which still takes place every year on the Sunday following 8 September.

There is a fine calvary (1550) with a striking Entombment at Pestivien *(1km/0.6mi N of Bulat).*

Drive to Burthulet along the Rostrenen road.

Chapelle de Burthulet

A simple 16C chapel, with wall belfry, stands in melancholy surroundings. You would not question the local legend that: 'The devil died of cold here'.

Make for Ty-Bourg and bear right.

St-Servais

The writer Anatole Le Braz was born here. Note the 16C **church**.

Take the road opposite the church towards St-Nicodème. After 2km turn right.

Gorges du Corong★

1hr on foot there and back. From the roundabout at the end of the road follow the path leading to the gorges.

The path runs along the river and into the Duault Forest. The river disappears beneath a mass of rocks to reappear as a series of cascades.

◐ *Turn round and bear right, then right again in the direction of Locarn.*

Église de Locarn
☜ *Guided tours daily 10am–noon, 2pm–5pm.* ℘*02 96 36 66 11.*
The **church** contains 17C furnishings (altarpiece, pulpit and statues), a remarkable 16C stained-glass window, a carillon wheel and the panels of a Flemish altarpiece, also of that period. Displayed in the presbytery is the **treasury**★.

Note the following objects made of silver-gilt: 15C St Henrin's bust and reliquary (in the form of an arm), a processional cross (late 16C) and a 17C chalice.

◐ *Return to Carhaix-Plouguer via Trebrivan.*

ADDRESSES

🛏STAY

☕☕☕ **Chambre d'hôte Le Manoir de Kerladen**– *rte de Kerledan.* ℘*02 98 99 43 63. 3 rooms.* ☲. A restored 16C manor house set in 7 acres/0.4 hectares on the southern edge of town. Large comfortable rooms with luxurious en-suite facilities.

☕☕ **Noz-Vad** – *12 bd de la République.* ℘*02 98 99 12 12. www.nozvad.com. 44 rooms. Closed 21 Dec–11 Jan.* ☲ *8.50€.* Comfortable and quiet rooms; the fancy decoration has been made by regional artists: armchairs and sofas embroidered with flowery designs, warm colours and beautiful bedding to ensure you have a *noz vad* (a good night). Small garden.

🍴EAT

☕ **Crêperie Ty Gwechall** – *25 place des Halles.* ℘*02 98 93 17 00. Closed Sun evening and Mon.* Take care to lower your head as you enter this lovely stone house where the crêpes are prepared with the best products of the region: andouille of Guéméné, goat's cheese, etc.

☕☕ **La Ronde des Mets** – *5 Place de la Mairie.* ℘*02 98 93 01 50. Closed Mon and Thur eve.* Comfortably seated among the paintings made by regional artists, you will enjoy flavourful traditional cuisine.

🏃ACTIVITIES

Les Ânes sont dans le Pré – *Le Pellem.* ℘*02 98 99 44 21. www.lasdlp.com.* Walks accompanied by donkeys from.

EVENTS
Festival des Vieilles Charrues – ℘*0820 890 066. www.vieillescharrues. asso.fr, end of July.* One of the biggest festivals of French music (pop, rock, world). At this time of the year, the fields around the town are full of spectators.

🛒SHOPPING

Saveurs et Gourmandise – *19 rue du Gen. Lambert.* ℘*02 98 99 46 58. Open Tue–Sat 10–noon, 2pm–7pm.* This small grocery in the town centre abounds with products from the Brittany and other regions of France: sardines, cakes, caramels made with salted butter, foies gras, eaux-de-vie, flavoured teas, etc., but also tableware and a selection of amusing teapots.

Chatillon Chocolat – *46 Place Charles-de-Gaulle, Pleyben.* ℘*02 98 26 63 77. www.chatillon-chocolat.com. Open Apr–Sept, daily 9am–12.30pm, 2pm–7pm; off season, Mon–Sat 9am–12.30pm, 2pm–6.30pm.* Enjoy the florentin: a subtle biscuit made with honey, almonds, oranges and chocolate, that Michel Chatillon makes with perfection. Dozens of other typically Breton treats – chocolates, cakes and biscuits – are offered in this small shop.

Huelgoat★★

The forest, lake, trickling water and rocks make Huelgoat one of the finest sites★★ in inner Brittany. Situated within the Parc Natural Régional d'Armorique, Huelgoat is a favourite place for anglers (especially for carp and perch in the lake and trout in the river) and a good base for excursions.

WALKING TOUR

The town

The 16C **church** standing near the main square in the town centre has a modern belfry. Inside there are sculpted purlins and to the left of the chancel is a statue of St-Yves, the patron saint of the parish, set between a rich man and a pauper. Overlooking Huelgoat, this Renaissance **Chapelle Notre-Dame-des-Cieux** with its 18C bell tower, has curious painted low-relief sculptures depicting scenes from the life of the Virgin and the Passion around the chancel and the side altars. A *pardon* takes place on the first Sunday in August.

⚑ The Rocks

Allow 1hr 30min on foot.
From rue de Berrien past the lake, follow the signposted path.

Chaos du Moulin

The path cuts through the rocks dominating the course of the River Argent. This pile of rounded granite rocks, surrounded by greenery, is very picturesque.

Grotte du Diable

▷ To reach this, climb down an iron ladder. A brook babbles under the rocks.

Roche Tremblante

North bank. By leaning against this 100t block at a precise point, you can make it rock on its base.

▷ An uphill path, known as Lovers' Walk (Sentier des Amoureux), leads directly through the woods to Artus's

▶ **Population:** 1,622.

Michelin Map: Local map 308 I4 – Finistère (29).

Info: 18 pl Aristide Briand, 29690 Huelgoat. ℘02 98 99 72 32.

Location: East of the Monts d'Arée, in the heart of a wooded region.

Kids: Identify animal tracks at the Maison de la Faune Sauvage.

Timing: This is the perfect spot to walk and picnic.

Don't Miss: Walks along the river.

Cave and to Boars' Pool (℘ see The Forest, below).

Allée Violette

A pleasant path in the woods along the left bank of the River Argent ends this ramble through the rocks.

▷ To return to the centre of Huelgoat, at Pont-Rouge, turn right onto the road from Carhaix and then take rue du Docteur-Jacq.

The Forest

Extending over 1,000ha/2,471 acres, the Forest of Huelgoat lies at the foot of the southern slope of the Monts d'Arrée mountain range. Its tortured topography consists of a series of hills divided by deep valleys. The forest features a great many different landscapes and colours; it also contains strange, picturesque sites that have inspired many traditional tales and legends. (*information about these sites is available on signposts and in car parks; ℘ see below*).

⚑ Promenade du Fer à Cheval and Le Gouffre

Allow 30min on foot. After Pont-Rouge, take the Horseshoe Walk on the right.
A pleasant walk through the woods along the River Argent. A stairway (*39 steps*) leads down to the chasm. The River Argent flowing from the Lac

Rocks at Huelgoat

S. Sauvignier/MICHELIN

d'Huelgoat, falls into a deep cavity to reappear 150m further on. A path leads to a lookout point *(15min there and back – difficult and no safety ramp)* commanding a view of the chasm. You can continue this walk through the woods by the river passing near the *Mare aux Fées* (Fairies Pool) and combining it with the *Promenade du Canal*.

Follow the signposts to the mine (La Mine), turn right at the bridge into an unsurfaced road and at the former mine, continue along an uphill path to the right of the power station (usine électrique). A footbridge spans the canal and leads to the opposite bank.

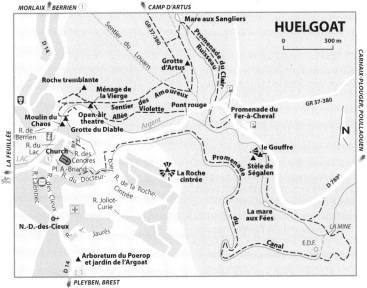

WHERE TO STAY	WHERE TO EAT
Ferme de Porz Kloz (Studios, gîtes La)....................①	Krampouez Breizh (Crêperie).....................①

Promenade du Canal

2hr on foot there and back on rue du Docteur-Jacq.

This walk follows the bank of the upper canal. A reservoir and two canals were dug in the 19C to work the silver-bearing lead mines, already known to the Romans. The waters were used to wash the ore and drive a crusher. From the far end of the canal walk you may continue on to the chasm (*This walk is described in the opposite direction* below.)

Promenade du Clair-Ruisseau

1hr 30min on foot there and back.
From the car park after Pont-Rouge, take Allée du Clair-Ruisseau.

This path half-way up the slope affords fine views of the rock-strewn stream bed. A stairway *(25 steps)* on the left leads down to the **Mare aux Sangliers** (Boars' Pool) in a pretty setting of rocks shaped rather like boars' heads, hence the name. Cross over the rustic bridge to Allée de la Mare on the left.

After the great stairway *(218 steps)*, which provides the quickest access to **Camp d'Artus** (Artus's Camp), you can see up above, on the right, the entrance to **Grotte d'Artus** (Artus's Cave).

Continue up the path which after 800m/0.5mi takes you to the camp. Boulders mark the entrance which was dominated by an artificial mound.

The cave is an important example of a Gallic fortified site, bordered by two enclosures. In spite of the encroaching vegetation, it is possible to go round the camp by a path *(1km)* following the remaining second elliptical enclosure which is fairly well preserved.
Northeast of Huelgoat *(13km/8mi)*, in the **Maison de la Faune Sauvage** (& *02 98 78 25 00*), you can learn more about the animals living free in the Armorique Regional Nature Park.
Set up in the former railway station at Scrignac, it houses exhibits on recognising animal tracks and contains about 70 stuffed and mounted specimens.

ADDRESSES

STAY

Auberge du Youdig – *Kerveguenet, 29690 Brennilis. & 02 98 99 62 36. www.youdig.fr. 4 rooms and 5 gîtes.* There is a passion for Breton heritage and legends here. Enjoy a night of tales, nature walks or themed weekends. Delicious regional cuisine.

Chambre d'hôte O'Brien's – *4 route de Berrien, 29690 Huelgoat. & 02 98 99 82 73. 4 rooms. Open all year.* Situated on the edge of Huelgoat with stunning views over the 'Rochers du Chaos' or over the lake from each room. Ideal for families.

La Ferme de Porz Kloz – *Trédudon-le-Moine, 29690 Berrien. 11km/ 6.8mi N of Huelgoat on the D 14 then take the D 42 left. & 02 98 99 61 65. Closed 15 Nov–Easter. Reservations obligatory. 4 rooms.* Time seems to have stood still in this collection of 17C farm buildings, formerly part of the Relecq abbey. Its rooms, furnished with family heirlooms, are particularly comfy.

EAT

Crêperie Krampouez Breizh – *pl. Aristide-Briand. & 02 98 99 80 10. www.creperie-krampouez-breizh.com. Closed 2 weeks in Mar and 2 weeks in Oct, Wed eve and Fri exc mid Jul – mid Aug.* Push the door of this *crêperie* and discover a warm room full of old furniture, beams and an imposing fireplace. Traditional *galettes* and specialities of the house such as the An Huelgoat (snails and garlic butter) and the Méli-Mélo (apples and sausages).

ACTIVITIES

Ti Ar Gouren – *Le Poullic. 4km from Huelgoat. & 02 98 99 03 80. www.tiar gouren.fr.* This centre for Breton sports, including traditional fighting, offers workshops, classes and traditional games. Enquire at the centre.

Monts d'Arrée★★

Solitary, barren, covered in heathland, often wet, these sharp crests of quartz have been incorporated into the Parc National Régional d'Armorique to better preserve their wild nature. In the midst of the park, the different sites which make up the Écomusée des Monts d'Arrée illustrate the rural way of life of times past. The mountain range is wooded in parts, especially towards the east, but the summits are usually quite desolate. There is not a tree on them; the heath is pierced by rocky scarps; here and there are clumps of gorse with golden flowers in spring and purple heather in September.

PARC NATUREL RÉGIONAL D'ARMORIQUE

Inaugurated in 1969, the Regional Park encompasses 39 communes on 172,000 ha/425,000 acres of land and ocean. There are four eco-zones on the site: the *Monts d'Arrée*, the Crozon Peninsula, the *Aulne Maritime* and the islands of the Iroise Sea.

- **Michelin Map:** Local map 308 G/I 3/4 – Finistère (29).
- **Info:** Parc Naturel Régional d'Armorique, 15 place aux Foires, BP 27, 29590 Le Faou. 02 98 81 90 08. www.pnr-armorique.fr.
- **Location:** Dividing the Cornouaille and the Léon, the Arrée Mountains are the highest in Brittany, yet their highest point is less than 390m/1,280ft.
- **Kids:** A nature walk in the Réserve Naturelle du Venec.
- **Don't Miss:** The view from Roc Trévezel.

The purpose of the park is the preservation of landscapes, flora and fauna; the creation of activities to foster local economic growth and the preservation of aspects of rural civilisation.

A network of 20 facilities ensures that different exhibit areas are open to the publi: Ferme des Artisans in Brasparts, open-air museums of the Monts dArrée in St-Rivoal and Commana, Museum of

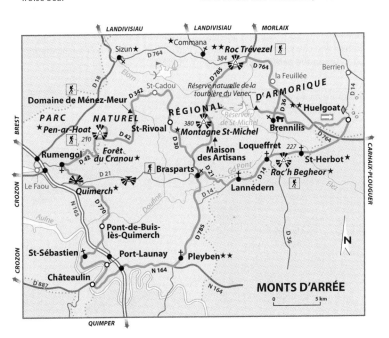

Lighthouses and Bouys and Niou Houses in Ouessant, Museum of Rural Schooling in Trégarvan, Mineral Museum in Crozon, River House in Sizun, Wolf Museum in Cloître-St-Thégonnec (ask at the park office for details).

🚗 DRIVING TOUR

Crossing La Montagne Pelée

122km/76mi – allow one day.

In nice weather, this route is a good way to appreciate the beauty of Brittany's interior.

▷ Leave Huelgoat S Towards Pleyben.

St-Herbot★

The **church**★ (🕐open Jul–Aug, 2pm–6pm), with its square tower, stands surrounded by trees. It is mainly in the Flamboyant Gothic style. A small Renaissance ossuary is located to the right of the porch. There is a fine crucifix-calvary in Kersanton granite (1571) in front of the building.

Inside, the **chancel** is surrounded by a remarkable **screen**★★ in carved oak topped by a Crucifixion. Against this screen, on the nave side, are two stone tables for the tufts of hair from the tails of oxen and cows, which the peasants offer during the pardon to obtain the

protection of St-Herbot, the patron saint of horned cattle. Note also the richly decorated stalls (lift the seats) against the screen.

Roc'h Begheor

🚶 15min on foot.
🅿 Car park to the right of the road.
A good **view**★ over the Monts d'Arrée and the Montagnes Noires.

Les Monts d'Arrée landscape

R. Mattes/MICHELIN

Lannédern

In the **parish close** is a Cross decorated with figures; note St-Edern riding a stag. Inside the **church** are six polychrome low-relief sculptures (17C) illustrating his life.

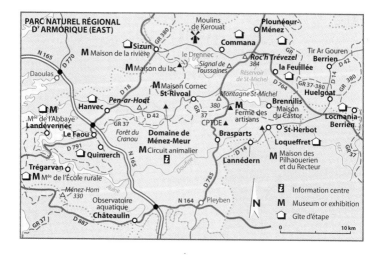

○ *Continue towards Pleyben and turn right after 1.5km/0.9mi.*

⚐ Brasparts

Perched atop a hill, this village has an interesting 16C **parish close**. Inside the church, by the nave (on the right), stands a splendid **Virgin of Pity**★ (16C).
For hikers: from the town, follow the hiking trails marked Du Méné *(11km)* and De Gorre *(16km)*.

○ *Head towards Pleyben*

Pleyben★★

The great feature of Pleyben is its magnificent parish close, built from the 15C to the 17C. There is a *pardon* on the first Sunday in August.

Parish Close★★

Constructed between the 15 and 17C in the local granite which is very difficult to work with.

Calvary★★

The most imposing calvary in Brittany. Built in 1555 near the church's side entrance, it was displaced in 1738 and given its present form in 1743. Since then new motifs and scenes have been added to the monument: the Last Supper and Washing of the Disciples' Feet date from 1650. The huge pedestal with triumphal arches enhances the figures on the platform.
To follow the life of Christ start at the corner with the Annunciation and move in an anticlockwise direction to discover the Nativity, the Adoration of the Shepherds and other scenes.

Church★

The church (○*open 9am–noon and 2pm–7pm*), dedicated to St-Germanus of Auxerre, is dominated by two belfries, of which that on the right is the more remarkable.
It has a Renaissance **tower**★★ crowned with a dome with small lantern turrets. The other tower has a Gothic spire linked to the corner turret at the balustrade level. Beyond the arm of the south transept is a curious quatrefoil

sacristy, dating from 1719, with cupolas and lantern turrets. Inside, the nave has 16C panelled **vaulting**★; the ribs and the remarkable purlin are carved and painted with mythological and religious scenes. At the high altar is an altarpiece with turrets and a two storey tabernacle (17C). At the centre of the east end is a 16C **stained-glass window**★ depicting the Passion. Note the pulpit, the organ case (1688), the Baptism of Christ over the font and the many coloured statues including St-Yves between the rich man and the pauper.

Chapelle Funéraire

🐾 *Guided tours* ○*Jul–Aug.*
Self-guided tours ○*9am–noon and 2pm–7pm the rest of the year.* ☏*02 98 26 60 11.*
A former 16C ossuary where exhibitions are held.

Châteaulin

Standing on a bend of the Aulne, in the green and deep valley through which the canalised river flows, this little town is a centre for freshwater fishermen. In fact, the tide does not reach Châteaulin but dies out a little way downstream at Port-Launay which harbours numerous pleasure boats.

Observatoire Aquatique

○*Open Mon–Fri 10am–5pm.* ☏*02 98 86 30 68. www.smatah.fr.*
This centre is dedicated to the observation of the main species living in the riv-

Salmon Fishing

Châteaulin is the salmon-fishing centre in the Aulne Valley; the salmon has always appeared on the town's coat of arms. Less often than in the past, the salmon come up the river to spawn, trying to leap the small waterfalls formed by the overflows from the locks. Angling (bait casting, spin casting) is done below the locks over a distance of some 100m/328ft, especially in March and April.

ers along the coast of the Finistère, such as Atlantic salmon. In summer, nature walks are organised in the Arrée hills.

Chapelle Notre-Dame
Access via rue Graveran and a road to the left, opposite the cemetery.
The castle's former chapel stands in an enclosure near some 17C houses. Pass through the triumphal arch, there is a 15C calvary cross presenting a rather unusual Last Judgement. Modified in the 17C and 18C, and extensively restored in 1991, the chapel retains some vestiges of the 13C (columns, capitals), and some 17C altarpieces.

Follow the south bank of the Aulne.

Port-Launay
This is the port of Châteaulin, on the Aulne. The long quay makes for pleasant walks.

Leave the Brest road on the right and continue along the Aulne, pass under the railway viaduct, bear right at the roundabout and 100m/110yds further on, turn left.

Chapelle St-Sébastien
Open Apr–Oct, 9am–6pm. ℘02 98 73 17 03.
In the 16C **parish close** stand a triumphal arch surmounted by St-Sebastian between two archers, and a fine calvary with figures including the saint pierced by arrows. The chapel contains splendid 17C **altarpieces**★ in the chancel and the transept; note, to the left, the panels depicting the story of Lorette, a small Italian town where, according to legend, the house of the Virgin Mary was brought from Nazareth by angels in the 13C.

Follow the small road over the railway line and the Quimper-Brest dual carriageway.

Pont-de-Buis-lès-Quimerch
On leaving the village, below the road, on the left a 300-year-old explosives factory can be seen.

Drive to Quimerch then Rumengol along D 770.

From the Quimerch viewing table, the view extends from Ménez-Hom to the *Forêt du Cranou* taking in the Brest roadstead and the Presqu'île de Plougastel.

Rumengol
Rumengol dates from the time of King Gradlon who built a chapel here in the 5C, just after the town of Ys disappeared. The **church** is 16C as shown by the south porch and the magnificent west front in Kersanton granite but significant alterations were made in the 17C and 18C.
The two **altarpieces**★ and altars date from 1686. In the centre of the village, near the church apse, is a sacred fountain (1792), an object of devotion on *pardon* days.

Forêt du Cranou★
The road, hilly and winding, runs through the state forest of Cranou, which covers over 600ha/1,483 acres and consists mostly of oaks and beeches. *Picnic areas.*

On leaving the Forêt du Cranou, bear right towards St-Rivoal; at the entrance to Kerancuru, turn left for Pen-ar-Hoat-ar-Gorré. In the hamlet (schist houses), turn left towards Hanvec and left again on to an uphill road.

Pen-ar-Hoat★
45min on foot there and back. Walk round the farm and bear left towards the line of heights; after passing between low walls, the climb ends among gorse bushes. Alt 217m/712ft.
The **panorama** extends over the heath-clad hills: to the north are the hills bordering the left bank of the Elorn; to the east the nearer heights of the *Arrée*; to the south Cranou Forest; and in the distance the *Montagnes Noires* and the Ménez-Hom; and lastly, to the west, the Brest roadstead.

Return to Kerancuru and bear left; 3.5km further on, left again.

Domaine de Ménez-Meur

⏱ *Open Jul–Aug, daily 10am–7pm; May, Jun and Sept, 2pm–6pm; Mar–Apr and Oct, Wed, Sun, public holidays and school holidays 1.30pm–5.30pm; Nov–Feb, 1pm–5pm.* 🚗3.30€. ☎02 98 68 81 71. www.pnr-armorique.fr

The estate sprawls over 400ha/988.4 acres in an undulating countryside. A nature trail *(about 1hr 30min)*, accompanied by panels giving information on the region's flora, winds through the large enclosures where ponies, sheep, deer and wild boar roam; you'll also find rare breeds like Ouessant sheep. La Maison du Cheval Breton looks at the horses' place in Breton life.

▷ *Take the D 342 then the D 130 to St-Cadou for St-Rivoal.*

St-Rivoal

After the village, below the Le Faou road, to the left, is the **Maison Cornec** *(⏱open Jul–Aug, daily 11am–7pm; Jun, daily 2pm–6pm; 1–15 Sept, Mon–Fri 2pm–6pm;* 🚗*1.50€;* ☎*02 98 81 40 99)*, a small farm dating from 1702. It is one of the many exhibits dispersed throughout the Parc d'Armorique, which make up the open-air museum devoted to the different styles of Breton architecture. The little house, built of schist and with a fine external covered stairway going up to the hayloft, comprises a large room with the living quarters for the farmer and his family around the great chimney and the domestic animals at the other end.

▷ *Take the D 30 in the direction of Brasparts.*

The road winds through a countryside of hills, and of green and wooded valleys whose freshness contrasts with the bare rocky summits.

▷ *After 5.5km/3.4mi, bear left onto D 785 towards Morlaix.*

Maison des Artisans

⏱*Open Jul–15 Sept, 10am–7.30pm; Apr–Jun, 16–30 Sept and school holidays Mon–Fri 2pm–6.30pm, Sat–Sun 10.30am–7pm; Oct–Mar, Sat–Sun 10.30am–7pm.* ☎*02 98 81 46 69. www.parc-naturel-armorique.fr.*

Part of the regional park and housed in St-Michel farmhouse, it displays the creations of over 200 Breton craftspeople.

▷ *Continue towards Morlaix; take the road which branches off to the left.*

Montagne St-Michel★

From the top of the rise (alt 380m/1,250) where there is a small chapel which reaches an altitude of 391m at its summit, there is a **panorama** of the *Monts d'Arrée* and the *Montagnes Noires*.

From the foot of the hill, a great peat bog called the Yeun Elez extends towards the east. In the winter mists, the place is so grim that Breton legend says it contains the **Youdig**, a gulf forming the entrance to Hell. Beyond it may be seen the St-Michel reservoir which supplies the *Monts d'Arrée* thermal power station at Brennilis.

Note the megalithic alignment on the rocky point to the right of the lake.

Fine views of the countryside, the mountains and Brennilis basin from the road passing by the Toussaines Signal Station *(Tuchenn Gador).*

🗺 Roc Trévezel★★

This rocky escarpment, which juts up into the skyline (384m/1,260ft), is in a remarkably picturesque spot.

Take the path (30min on foot there and back) near a signpost. Go towards the left, cross a small heath bearing to the right, and make for the most distant rocky point.

From here the **panorama**★★ is immense. To the north, the Léon Plateau appears, bristling with spires; in clear weather you can see the Kreisker spire at St-Pol-de-Léon and to the east Lannion Bay; to the west, the end of the Brest roadstead; to the south, the St-Michel Mountain and, beyond it, the dark line of trees on the *Montagnes Noires.*

▷ *By the Roc-Tredudon pylon turn right towards Huelgoat and after 6km/3.7mi, bear right to Brennilis.*

Roc Trévezel

S. Sauvignier/MICHELIN

Brennilis

This village has a 15C **church** topped by a delicate openwork belfry.

Return to the entrance to Brennilis and turn right. 90m/98yds further to the right, a signposted path leads to a covered alleyway partly hidden by a tumulus. Continue on the secondary road to Huelgoat.

Réserve Naturelle de la Tourbière du Venec

Nature walks (3hr) and other activities are organised Jul–Aug, Tue–Thu and Sat at 3pm. 4€ (children 2.50€). Ramblers: wear boots and appropriate attire. Information from Maison des Castors (see below).

Created in 1993, covering 47ha/175 acres, the park is mostly wetlands and peat fields covered with sphagnum moss.

The reserve is not accessible to the public (other than on an organised walk), but you can explore the **Maison des Castors et de la Réserve Naturelle du Venec** (*2 place du Calvaire, 29410 Le Cloître-St Thégonnec; 02 98 79 71 98*), which hosts an exhibition on the beaver population.

Return to the edge of Brennilis and turn right. About 91m on, to the right, there is a marked path leading to a **covered alley**, a megalithic monument partly covered by a tumulus.

Continue on the secondary road to return to Huelgoat.

ADDRESSES

STAY / EAT

Auberge du Poisson Blanc – *Pont Coblant, 4.5km/2.8mi S of Pleyben on the old rte de Quimper towards Briec. 02 98 73 34 76. Closed three weeks in Nov, Sun eve, Mon eve off season. 6 rooms. 6.50€. Restaurant.* The restaurant is more interesting than the accommodation. Regional cuisine such as warm sausage with lentils, and couscous on Thursdays.

SHOPPING

Chatillon Chocolat – *46 pl. Charles-de-Gaulle, Pleyben. 02 98 26 63 77. www.chatillon-chocolat.com. Open Mon–Sat 9am–12.30pm, 2pm–6.30pm.* Delicious honey, almond, chocolate and orange florentines are made here. Visit the workshop and enjoy a tasting.

Morbihan – "Little Sea" in Breton– is named after the glittering Gulf, the beautiful inland sea which is such a popular part of this *département* in the heart of southern Brittany. Driving itineraries from lively Vannes explore different sides of this enchanting body of water. Inland, the countryside is littered with mysterious prehistoric dolmens and menhirs, as well as sites linked to Arthurian legends involving Merlin, Vivian and Lancelot. Picturesque Belle- Île is idyllic, peninsulas are washed by the mighty Atlantic Ocean, and fascinating historic towns like Auray guarantee a varied trip, however long your stay.

A Bit of History

The territory covered in this section of the Guide corresponds with the modern *département* of the same name which lies in the south of Brittany between the *départements* of Finistère and Ille-et-Vilaine. The region is characterised by the inland sea of the Gulf of Morbihan with its tranquil waters broken only by many small islands, the Presqu'île de Quiberon and the appropriately named Belle-Île just to the south.

The relatively flat countryside to the north of the Gulf seldom rises above 200m/656ft and extends to the border with the Côtes-d'Armor *département* in the north, interrupted only by the massive plateau of the Landes de Lanvoux. Measuring 60km/37mi by 10km/6mi, the plateau runs east to west across the middle of Morbihan providing opportunities for walking and angling in a verdant and peaceful landscape interspersed with the occasional prehistoric standing stone. In the west, the waters of the Scorff and Blavet rivers discharge into the Atlantic at Lorient, while north of the Landes de Lanvoux the river Oust and its tributary the Claie flow towards a confluence with the Vilaine river at Redon.

Tourism, fishing and agriculture are the mainstays of the local economy. The Gulf of Morbihan is an ideal environment for producing a large volume of oysters. Shipyards at Lorient construct submarines, while at Vannes there is some light industry and canning plants can be found in harbour towns along the coast. There is much evidence of settlement in the area during prehistoric times, with the megalithic monuments at Carnac, in particular, and around the Gulf de Morbihan giving some idea of the importance of the region to the little-known

Highlights

1 Walking the meandering alleys and cobbled squares of **Vannes Old Town** (p345)

2 Cruising around the islands of the **Golfe du Morbihan** (p353)

3 Taking in Carnac's remarkable **megalithic monuments** (p364)

4 Driving along the deep valleys and past lush fields on **Belle-Île** (p373

5 Visiting **Josselin Château** (p395)

people who were here before the Celts. Later, in 56BC the Celtic Veneti tribe were defeated by the Romans under Julius Caesar at the Battle of the Morbihan Gulf in what is the first recorded naval engagement in the North Atlantic. Caesar's fleet, under the command of Brutus, completed destroyed the Celtic fleet and in doing so established Roman dominance in Brittany.

After the Romans left, a fresh wave of Celts from Britain came and by the 10C Vannes had been established as the capital of Brittany. Though no longer the capital of the region, it is the *préfecture* of Morbihan and today is a very pleasant small city to visit, with colourful timber-framed houses, 16C and 17C mansions and pleasant walks in the gardens below the ramparts.

Nearby Auray on the River Loch is also an excellent base for exploring the area as well as being an interesting town with a pretty harbour and connections to Benjamin Franklin, who disembarked here from the US on a trip to France to negotiate the first alliance between the two countries.

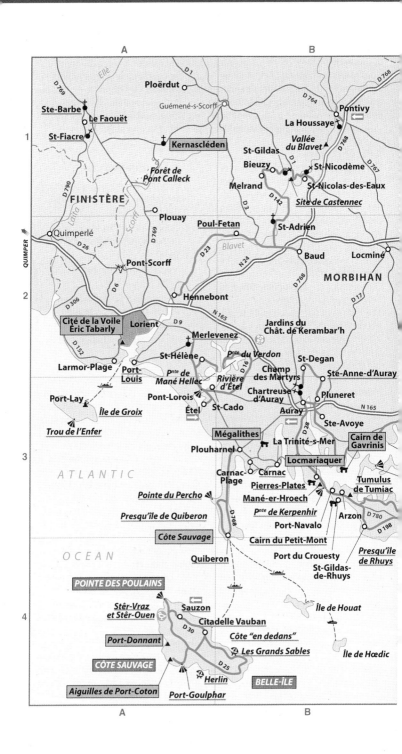

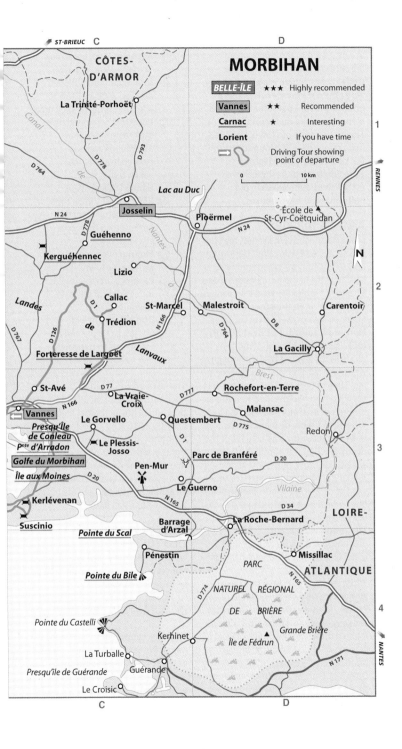

Vannes★★

Vannes, built in the shape of an amphitheatre at the head of the Golfe du Morbihan, is a pleasant city, very popular in season. It is also a good departure point for boat trips across the Golfe du Morbihan. The picturesque old town, enclosed in its ramparts and grouped around the cathedral, is a pedestrian zone where elegant shops have established themselves in old half-timbered town houses.

▶ **Population:** 5, 079.
◔ **Michelin Map:** Local map 308 O9 – Morbihan (56).
▯ **Info:** Quai Taberly, 56000 Vannes. ☎08 25 13 56 10. www.tourisme-vannes.com.
▸ **Location:** Separated from the sea by the Gulf of Morbihan, Vannes is crossed by the N 165 which comes from Nantes (112km/69mi).
▴▴ **Kids:** A boat trip on the Gulf; the aquarium; the butterflies in the Jardin aux Papillons.
◷ **Timing:** Allow a day to explore the town.
▱ **Parking:** Leave cars near the sea port or place de la République.
◎ **Don't Miss:** The old houses; La Cohue and the view from the ramparts.

A BIT OF HISTORY

During the period of the Veneti, the original settlement was called Darioritum and seems to have prospered well, at least until the Barbarian invasions of the 3C and 4C. In the 4C, Waroc'h, leading the Bretons from the other side of the Channel, took possession of the town.

Nominoë, founder of Breton unity (9C) – Nominoë, a Breton of modest origin, was discovered by Charlemagne, who made him Count of Vannes. Becoming Duke of Brittany (826) under Louis the Pious, he had decided to unite all the Bretons in an independent kingdom. When Louis died, he went into action. In ten years unity was achieved: the duchy reached the boundaries, which were to be those of the Province until January 1790. From the outset, Vannes was the capital of the new Breton kingdom, which later reverted to the status of a duchy.

The union with France (16C) – Anne of Brittany, who married Charles VIII and Louis XII successively, remained the sovereign of her duchy.

When she died in 1514 at the age of 37 without leaving a male heir, Claude of France, one of her daughters, inherited Brittany. A few months later, Claude married the heir to the throne of France, François of Angoulême, and after a few months, on 1 January 1515, became Queen of France. The King easily persuaded her to yield her duchy to their son, the Dauphin. Thus Brittany and France would be reunited in the person of the future king.

The last step was taken in August 1532. The States (councils), meeting at Vannes, proclaimed 'the perpetual union of the Country and Duchy of Brittany with the Kingdom and Crown of France'. The rights and privileges of the duchy were maintained: taxes had to be approved by the States; the Breton Parliament kept its judicial sovereignty and the province could maintain an army.

◢◣WALKING TOURS
OLD TOWN★★

Inside the ramparts and centred around the cathedral St-Pierre, the area has been pedestrianised.

▸ *Start from place Gambetta.*

This semicircular square, built in the 19C, frames **Porte Saint-Vincent** (St Vincent Gateway), which leads into the old town along a road of the same name, lined with beautiful 17C mansions. At the entrance to the road, the most remarkable of these, the Hôtel Dondel, was the headquarters of Général Hoche in 1795.

Wash-houses along the ramparts

J. Malburet/MICHELIN

Ramparts★

After crossing from the Promenade de la Garenne you will get a **view**★★ of the most picturesque corner of Vannes, with the stream (the Marle) that flows at the foot of the ramparts (built in the 13C on top of Gallo-Roman ruins and remodelled repeatedly until the 17C), the formal gardens and the cathedral in the background. A small bridge, leading to Porte Poterne, overlooks some old **wash-houses**★ with very unusual roofing.

La Cohue★

This term (literally, a bustling crowd) is commonly used in Brittany to designate the market place, the area where traders and the courts of law were found. In the 13C, the market was held in the lower part of the building; the upper floor was reserved for legal affairs. Beginning in 1675, the exiled Parliament of Brittany held its meetings there. During the Revolution, the building became a theatre, and remained so till the 1950s.

La Cohue Musée des Beaux-Arts

⏰*Open mid-Jun–Sept, daily 10am–6pm; rest of the year, daily 1.30pm–6pm.* ⏰*Closed public holidays off season.* €6€*(combined with Musée d'Histoire).* ☎*02 97 01 63 00.*
Now the beautifully restored building is a museum, and offers visitors a perma-

nent collection of 19C and contemporary paintings as well as religious sculpture. On the first floor, the courtroom (1550), with its fine oak timber ceiling, was the seat of the Presidial court of justice. It now houses, for the most part, 19C–20C works of art by local painters (Jules Noël, Henri Moret, Flavien Peslin, Félix Bouchor), who were inspired by Brittany and its folklore.

Cathédrale St-Pierre★

Men worked on this cathedral from the 13C to the 19C. The only trace of the 13C construction is the north tower of the façade (on place St-Pierre), which is surmounted by a modern steeple. In the garden next to the north side of the cathedral are the remains of some 16C cloisters. The rotunda chapel, which juts out, was built in 1537 in the Italian Renaissance style, rarely found in Brittany. Enter the church by the fine transept door (Flamboyant Gothic, with Renaissance niches).
In the entrance, on the left, a painting describes the death of **St Vincent Ferrier**, with the Duchess of Brittany present. This Spanish monk, who was a great preacher, died in Vannes in 1419 and was canonised in 1455. On the right is St Vincent preaching in Granada. In the second chapel of the north aisle, a rotunda chapel, is the saint's tomb.
In the apsidal chapel or Chapel of the Holy Sacrament and nave chapels, you

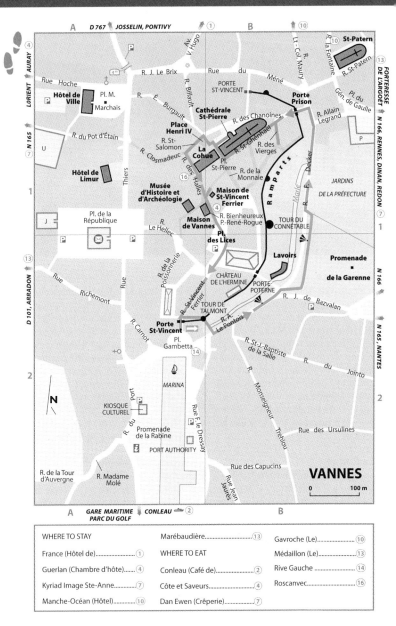

VANNES

0   100 m

A   **GARE MARITIME** 🚢 **CONLEAU** ⛴ ②
    PARC DU GOLF

B

will see altars, altarpieces, tombs and statues of the 17C and 18C.

Rue St-Guenhaël, lined with old houses, leads to the 15C **Porte Prison** (Prison Gate), flanked by a machicolated tower. Just before, on the right, rue des Vierges and a little passage lead to a section of the ramparts which gives a pretty view of the gardens.

Place Henri-IV★

Walk along rue des Halles then rue St-Salomon with its old town houses to this picturesque square, lined with 16C gabled houses. Glimpse down rue des Chanoines, too.

Musée d'Histoire et Archéologique de Morbihan★

🕐*Open mid-Jun–Sept, 10am–6pm; mid May–mid Jun, 1.30pm–6pm.* ⊛*6€ (combined with Musée des Beuax Arts).* ✆*02 97 01 63 00.*

This museum occupies three floors of Château Gaillard (15C), which once contained the Parlement de Bretagne (House of Parliament).

The museum is rich in prehistoric specimens, most of which come from the first megalithic excavations made in the Morbihan region: Carnac, Locmariaquer and the Presqu'île de Rhuys. Exhibited are a remarkable collection of **necklaces**, bracelets, **polished axes** and swords; another gallery contains a variety of objets d'art (13C–18C).

Maison de Saint Vincent-Ferrier

17 place Valencia.

In this house, remodelled in the 16C, Vincent Ferrier died in 1419. A fine example of a timber-framed house with a ground floor in stone.

Maison de Vannes

An old dwelling adorned with two carved wood busts of jovial peasants known as "Vannes and his wife."

Place des Lices

This square used to be the tilt-yard, where tilts and tournaments were held in 1532, the year France and Brittany were united under one crown. At one end of the square, set in the niche of a turreted house, is a statue of St Vincent-Ferrier. The saint preached here in 1418.

▷ *Return to Porte St-Vincent via rue A.-Le-Pontois and the Calmont Tower bridge.*

AROUND THE OLD TOWN
Quartier Saint-Patern

This area of the town, located outside its walls, is actually the oldest. Remnants from the gallo-roman settlement of Darioritum, dating from the first century

AD have been located here. It takes its name from the 5C Saint Patern, one of the seven founding saints of Brittany.

Promenade de la Garenne

The park of the former ducal castle of Vannes was arranged as a public promenade in the 17C.

The view of the ramparts, especially of the Constable's Tower, is attractive. In the upper part of the garden on a wall to the left of the War Memorial, a marble tablet recalls the shooting of the Royalists in 1795.

Hôtel de Limur

A late 17C town house with a fine stone staircase.

Hôtel de Ville

This building in the Renaissance style, erected at the end of the 19C, stands in place Maurice-Marchais, which is adorned with the equestrian **statue** of the Constable de Richemont, one of the great figures of the 15C – for it was he who created and commanded the French army which defeated the English at the end of the Hundred Years' War. He became Duke of Brittany, succeeding his brother in 1457, but died the following year.

Port de Plaisance and Conleau

This area has benefited from long term development. The Eric Tabarly Quai is dominated by contemporary buildings, which marry wood, steel and glass, and also houses an exhibition space.

On the other side of the water, the harbour master's office has a fine terrace on the first floor.

You can head south on the **promenade de la rabine**, which is a tree lined road which runs along the right bank of the Marle river. (Allow around 15 mins to reach the park on the bay).

Parc du Golfe

This park is located by the exit to the marina, and is the departure point for boat trips.

♨♨ Aquarium du Golfe★

⊙Open Jul–Aug, daily 9am–7.30pm; Apr–Jun, Sept and school hols, 10am–noon, 2pm–6pm; Oct–Mar, 2pm–6pm. ⊙Closed 1 Jan and 25 Dec. ∞10.80€ (children 4–11 yrs, 7.50€). ⅙ ℘08 10 40 69 01. www.aquarium-du-golfe.com.
More than 50 pools, in which the relevant natural environment has been reconstructed, house about 1 000 fish from all over the world (cold seas, warm seas, freshwater), which make up an incredible kaleidoscope of colour. In one 35 000l/7 700gal tank, a coral reef has been recreated and is home to numerous species of fish which habitually frequent this environment. A huge aquarium contains several varieties of shark and an exceptional sight: a huge 3m-long sawfish!

♨♨ Capitaine d'un Jour

⊙Open daily May–Sept, 9am–7pm; Oct–Apr, 9.30am–6pm. ⚓Guided tours (1hr 30min) available. ⊙Closed Jan and 25 Dec. ∞6€ (children 4.50€). ⅙ ℘02 97 40 40 39.
A museum-cruise that is fun and educational. See the Morbihan Gulf from another perspective. History, oyster beds, fishing, shipbuilding, coastal navigation are part of the tour.
There are many activities and games to interest children.

♨♨ Le Jardin aux Papillons

⊙Open Jul–Aug, daily 10am–7pm; Apr–Jun and Sept, 10am–noon, 2pm–6pm. ∞9€ (children 6.30€). ⅙ ℘02 97 46 01 02. www.jardinauxpapillons.com.
Visitors are free to stroll around at will among the many varieties of vibrantly coloured butterfly that are housed in this environment of tropical trees and floral shrubs. Glass hatching cases illustrate the various stages of development of the chrysalis.

🚗 DRIVING TOURS

1 PRESQU'ÎLE DE CONLEAU TO GRAND-CHAMP★

5km/3mi – plus 30min on foot there and back.

◯ Leave Vannes by Promenade de la Rabine. After 2km/1.2mi a good view of the Golfe du Morbihan unfolds before you. Cross the estuary of the Vincin on a causeway to reach Presqu'île de Conleau.

Presqu'île de Conleau
A small port well placed at the mouth of the Vincin; landing-stage for boat trip to the Île d'Arz. From the beach there is a good view over the Île de Boëdic between Pointe de Langle on the left, and Pointe de Kerguen on the right.

Presqu'île de Séné
10km/6mi S – about 45min.

◯ Leave Vannes by rue Ferdinand-le-Dressay which skirts the harbour's left shore, then bear left towards Séné.

Séné
Formerly known for its typical fishing boats, the **sinagots**, the village maintains its maritime tradition.

◯ On leaving Séné, bear right towards Bellevue and Port-Anna.

⚑ The old salt-marshes (almost 220ha/ 544 acres) have recently become a haven of peace for thousands of migratory or nesting birds of the region.
The **Reserve Naturelle de la Falguérec-en-Séné** (⊙open Jul–Aug, Mon–Sat 10am–1pm, 2pm–7pm; Feb–Mar, 2pm–6pm; Apr–Jun and Sept, 2pm–7pm; ∞5€; ℘02 97 66 92 76; www.reservedesene. com) is marked with nature trails for walkers and the seven observation posts are open to the public.
Bring your binoculars to observe birds such as the black-winged stilt, the elegant avocet or the redshank. The **Information Centre** houses exhibitions and a shop.

Port-Anna

This little port, frequented by fishing boats and pleasure craft, commands the narrow channel though which boats sail heading for Vannes.

▷ *Return to Bellevue and bear right towards the wharf.*

Embarcadère

This wharf is used for goods dispatched to the Île d'Arz.

From the car park, the **view**★ extends over the River Vannes with Presqu'île de Conleau to the left and Séné, at the end of a creek, to the right.

Château du Plessis-Josso

15km/9mi E. Leave Vannes on N 165 towards Nantes. 3km/1.8mi after Theix, turn left on D 183 towards Sulniac.

Guided tours (30min) Jul–1 Sept (and Patrimoine weekend in Sep), daily 2pm–7pm. 5€. 02 97 43 16 16. www.plessis-josso.com.

This charming castle, set in a verdant spot near a lake, is made up of three distinct parts added at three different periods: a 14C fortified manor house, a 15C main building with a polygonal staircase tower and a Louis XIII-style pavilion.

Temporary exhibitions are held in the outbuildings.

Grand-Champ

19km/12mi N. Leave Vannes on rue Hoche and take D 779.

In the nave of the **church** there are two carved wooden panels which come from Notre-Dame-de-Burgo, a ruined chapel in a pretty woodland setting, 2km/1.3mi east of the town.

2 LES LANDES DE LANVAUX

55km/34mi – 3hr.

▷ *Leave Vannes by rue du Maréchal-Leclerc and take N 166. After 14km, turn left to the castle.*

Forteresse de Largoët★

Walk 800m/0.5mi to reach the site.
Open Jun–Sept, 10.30am–12.10pm, 2.20pm–6.30pm; Mar–May and 23–31 Oct, weekends and holidays 2pm–6.30pm. 4.50€. Closed Tue exc Jul–Aug. 02 97 53 35 96. http://forteresselargoet.free.fr

These imposing feudal ruins, also known as **Tours d'Elven** (Elven Towers), stand in the middle of a park. The road (Vannes to Ploërmel road) to the towers branches off left between two pillars.

The Forteresse de Largoët belonged to Marshal de Rieux, who was first a councillor of Duke François II and then tutor to his daughter, Anne of Brittany. When the troops of the king of France,

Forteresse de Largoët

J. Malburet/MICHELIN

Charles VIII, invaded Brittany in 1488, all the Marshal's strongholds, including Largoët, were destroyed.

Pass through the 15C entrance fort built against the first entrance gate (13C). Of the castle there remains an impressive 14C keep, 44m high, with walls 6–9m thick (*stairs are not advisable for older persons or children*).

After Elven turn left on to the D 1.

Landes de Lanvaux

Contrary to what the name *landes* (moors) implies, this long crest of flaking, rocky land, which was not even cultivated until the 20C, is now a fertile region. Many megalithic monuments can be seen. The road passes the imposing Chateau de Trédion, surrounded by a landscaped 22ha/54.3 acre park.

Across from it, turn right and cross the built-up area, then go left, above the square.

The road drops into the rural valley of the Claie and its tributary, the Callac stream.

Trédion

If you are not able to stay in this imposing château, which was re-modelled and turned into a hotel in the 19C, you can enjoy its grounds.

Take the D 133 N towards Callac.

Callac

On the left of the road before a crossroads is a man-made grotto, a copy of the one at Lourdes.

To the left of the grotto a path climbs steeply; on either side are Stations of the Cross carved in granite. The path leads to a calvary from where there is a view of the Landes de Lanvaux.

Take the left-hand road. When it reaches the Plumelec road, turn left, and 600m/655yds later bear right. After 2km/1.2mi take the road on the left back to Vannes.

St-Avé

Open mid-Jul–Aug, Tue, Wed and Fri 2pm–7pm.

The **Chapelle Notre-Dame-du-Loc** rises by the old lie of the Vannes road. A calvary and a fountain stand before the 15C building. Inside, note the carvings on the purlins and tie-beams which depict angels, grotesques and animals; in the centre of the nave stands a calvary with figures, surmounted by a wooden canopy.

Return to Vannes along D 126.

ADDRESSES

STAY

Hôtel Le Marina – *4 Place Gambetta. 02 97 47 22 81. 14 rooms. 5.90€.* The rooms in this town-centre hotel, opposite the port, are soundproofed and well decorated, and most have views over the harbour. A good place from where to explore the town on foot.

Chambre d'Hôte Guerlan – *56400 Plougoumelen. 12km/7.5mi W of Vannes on the N 165, exit Ploeren towards Mériadec then first right after 3.5km/2.2mi 02 97 57 65 50. Closed 10 Nov–10 Mar. 5 rooms.* This imposing 18C building is ideally placed to explore the Gulf of Morbihan. Its rooms, a mix of ancient and modern, are spotless; one is for families. Visits to the farm on request.

Hôtel de France – *57 av. Victor Hugo. 02 97 47 27 57. www.hotelfrance -vannes.com. 30 rooms. Closed 21 Dec–5 Jan.* A small but pleasant terrace and comfortable rooms are just part of the cordial greeting visitors receive at this attractive establishment near the town centre.

Hôtel Manche Océan – *31 rue du Lt.-Col.-Mauray. 02 97 47 26 46. www. manche-ocean.com. Closed 22 Dec–6 Jan. 41 rooms. 8.50€.* In the heart of the town, this 1950s building is constantly evolving: most of its rooms have recently been renovated.

Kyriad Vannes Centre – *8 pl. de la Libération. 02 97 63 27 36. www.kyriad-vannes-centre.fr. 33 rooms. 8 €.* This central hotel offers comfortable rooms with air conditioning and sound insulation. The Breton-style restaurant provides a warm welcome and a traditional menu.

Marébaudière – *4 r. A.-Briand - 02 97 47 34 29. www.marebaudiere.com. 14 rooms. 10 €.* Five minutes on foot from the ramparts, this typical regional-style house has rooms decorated in blue, yellow and russet.

EAT

Café de Conleau – *10 allée des Frères-Cadoret. 02 97 63 47 47. www.le-roof.com.* An annexe of the hotel serving a brasserie menu. Low prices in a pleasant setting.

Crêperie Dan Ewen – *3 pl. du Gen.-de-Gaulle. 02 97 42 44 34. Closed one week in Feb and two weeks in Oct.* Breton culture is cultivated with passion in this restaurant near the *préfecture* – old-style crêpes, antique furniture, Celtic music.

Le Gavroche – *17 rue de laFontaine. 02 97 54 03 54. www.restaurant-le gavroche.com. Closed Sun. Reservations advised.* In a street filled with restaurants serving cuisine from around the world, here's one that stands out. Delicious traditional cuisine and an inner courtyard with a fountain.

Côte et Saveurs – *8 r. Bienheureux-Pierre-René-Rogues. 02 97 47 21 94. www.cote-et-saveurs.com. Closed Wed Sept–Mar.* The restaurant's name is well chosen as you can travel the world with the menu's exotic specialities such as pavé of ostrich (ostrich steak) with green pepper and red fruits. There are more dishes on a blackboard according to what is available in the market.

Rive Gauche – *5 pl. Gambetta - 02 97 47 02 40.* . Ground floor restaurant with small wooden tables and fabric tablecloths in a charming bourgeoise house located on the port. Menus and winelist on blackboard.

Le Médaillon – *10 rue Bouruet-Aubertot, 56610 Arradon. 02 97 44 77 28. http://lemedaillon.chez-alice.fr. Closed 21–27 Dec, Sun eve and Wed except 14 Jul–31 Aug.* Don't be put off by the plain exterior of this bar that has been converted into a restaurant; inside is a rustic dining room with beams and stonework and a terrace at the back.

Roscanvec – *17 rue des Halles. 02 97 47 15 96. www.roscanvec.com. Closed Sun and Mon (exc school hols). Reservations advised.* In a half-timbered house in the old town, the wonderful cuisine here is no-nonsense, with a menu that ranges from oysters with jelly of pork feet to caviar.

NIGHTLIFE

L'Océan – *4 pl. Gambetta. 02 97 47 22 81.* This bar is opposite the harbour in Vannes. The terrace is magnificent and overlooks place Gambetta, which is where the locals meet after work.

SHOPPING

Brasserie Mor Braz – *Zone St-Léonard Nord, 56450 Theix. 02 97 42 53 53. www.morbraz.com. Open Mon–Sat 9am–noon, 2pm–7pm.* A couple of Breton brewers make beer from seawater. Here you can taste and buy this beer "like no other'" – sweet and salty at the same time.

ACTIVITIES

Cruises – Navix – *Parc du Golfe. 0825 132 100. www.navix.fr. Closed Oct–Mar. Tour of the Gulf 29€; Belle-Île 30€–34€.*

EVENTS

Fêtes d'Arvor – *02 97 01 62 40. www.fetes-arvor.org. Mid-Aug.* Three days of Breton celebrations, animated by the Celtic groups and other *bagadou* including: concerts, fest-noz, shows and the election of a festival queen.

Jazz à Vannes – *02 97 01 62 44. www.mairie-vannes.fr/. Beginning of Aug.* The region's jazz festival.

TOURS

Vannes, a designated *Ville d'Art et d'Histoire*, offers guided tours during the holiday season, including evening walks. *02 97 01 64 00. www.mairie-vannes.fr.*

Golfe du Morbihan★★

The Morhiban Gulf, an inland sea dotted with islands, offers some of the most unusual scenery in Brittany. It has the most delicate light effects, and its sunsets are unforgettable. A visit, especially by boat, is essential.

A BIT OF HISTORY

In 1C BC the Veneti – after whom Vannes is named – lived around the Golfe du Morbihan. They were the most powerful tribe in Armor and when Caesar decided to conquer the peninsula he aimed his main effort at them. It was a stiff task, for the Veneti were fine sailors and had a fleet which made it useless to attack them by land. The decisive struggle, therefore, had to be waged afloat. The Roman leader had a large number of galleys, built and assembled at the mouth of the Loire which were under the command of his lieutenant, Brutus.

The encounter, which took place before Port-Navalo, is said to have been watched by Caesar from the top of the Tumulus de Tumiac. However, geologists believe that the gulf did not exist at the time of the Gallic War. In any event, it is certain that the battle took place somewhere off the southeast coast of Brittany.

The Gauls put to sea with 220 large sailing ships with high, strong hulls. The Romans opposed them with their large flat barges, propelled by oarsmen. The total and unexpected victory of Brutus was due to several causes: the sea was smooth and this favoured the galleys, which could not face bad weather; moreover, the wind dropped completely during the battle, becalming the Veneti in their sailing ships; and finally, the Romans had sickles tied to long poles, and when a galley drew alongside an enemy sailing ship, an agile sailor heaved the sickle into its rigging. The galley rowed on at full speed, the rope drew taut and the blade cut the rigging, thus mast and sails came tum-

- ◉ **Michelin Map:** Local map 308 N/O9 - Morbihan (56).
- ▣ **Info:** www.tourisme-vannes.com.
- ◐ **Location:** The Gulf of Morbihan starts south of Vannes and extends west to the river Auray. Its two ports, Port-Navalo and Locmariaquer, are accessible respectively by the D 780 and by the D 28 and D 781.
- ◐ **Timing:** Book boat trips the day before you want to travel.
- ◈ **Don't Miss:** A boat trip and an excursion to the Île de Gavrinis to admire the neolithic cairn.

bling down. Two or three galleys then attacked the ship and boarded it.

After this victory Caesar occupied the country of the Veneti and made them pay dearly for their resistance. All the members of their Senate were put to death, and the people were sold into slavery.

GEOGRAPHY

Mor-bihan means "little sea", while *Mor-braz* means "great sea" or ocean. This gulf, which is about 20km/12.5mi wide and 15km/9mi from the sea to the inner shore, was made by a comparatively recent settling of the land. The sea spread widely over land already despoiled by river erosion leaving inlets and estuaries which run far into the interior, and innumerable islands which give the Morbihan its special character. The River Vannes and River Auray form the two largest estuaries. The gulf is tidal; at high tide the sea sparkles everywhere around the low, flat and often wooded islands; at low tide, great mud-banks lie between the remaining channels. A narrow channel, before Port-Navalo permits passage both at high and low tide. Morbihan is thronged with boats fishing between the islands, as well as with

Abélard

A love story with a brilliant student, Héloïse, ended tragically when her outraged family had Abélard emasculated. The learned philosopher tried to find peace in this Breton solitude. His disillusion was quick and cruel: 'I live', he wrote to Héloïse, 'in a wild country whose language I find strange and horrible; I see only savages; I take my walks on the inaccessible shores of a rough sea; my monks have only one rule, which is to have none at all. I should like you to see my house; you would never take it for an abbey; the only decorations on the doors are the footprints of various animals – hinds, wolves, bears, wild boars – or the hideous remains of owls. Every day brings new dangers; I always seem to see a sword hanging over my head.' However, the monks used poison, not a sword, to get rid of their abbot. It was a wonder he survived and managed to escape through a secret passage in 1132.

pleasure boats and oyster barges using Auray and the port of Vannes. There are many oyster beds in the rivers and along the islands.

THE GULF BY BOAT★★★

The best way to see the gulf is by boat. About 40 islands are privately owned and inhabited; the largest are Île d'Arz and Île aux Moines, both *communes*.

Île d'Arz

🕒*Crossings year-round, 8.45am– 6.45pm. 15min crossing from Vannes-Conleau.* ✆*7.10–7.50€. Tour of the Gulf (Apr–Oct)* ✆*20€.* ✆*02 97 01 22 80. www.compagnie-du-golfe.fr*
The island, 3.5km/2mi long, has several megalithic monuments. A footpath runs along the coast, right round the island.

Île aux Moines★

Departures every 30min from Port-Blanc (5min) Jul–Aug, 7am–10pm; Sept–Jun, 7am–7.30pm. ✆*4.10€ return.* ✆*02 97 26 31 45. www.izenah-croisieres.com.*
This former monastic fief is the largest of the Morbihan Islands (7km/4.3mi long) and the most populous. It is a particularly quiet and restful seaside resort where mimosas and camellias grow among palm trees, lemon and orange trees. Its woods have poetic names: *Bois des Soupirs* (Wood of Sighs), *Bois d'Amour* (Wood of Love), *Bois des Regrets* (Wood of Regrets). The beauty of the island women, often sung about by Breton poets, is no doubt responsible for these gallantries.

There are several **sights** worth visiting: the town with its picturesque alleyways; from Pointe du Trech, north of the island, there is a good view of Pointe d'Arradon and the gulf – note the odd-looking calvary, its base composed of different levels and with stairs on its right side; southwards are the Boglieux and Penhap dolmens; and Pointe de Brouël, east of the island, affords a view of the Île d'Arz.

🚗 DRIVING TOURS

THE SHORES OF THE GULF★

1 FROM VANNES TO LOCMARIAQUER

49km/30.5mi – 3hr 30min.

Vannes★★ – *2hr 30min.*
👣*See VANNES.*

▷ *Leave Vannes on D 101. After 5km/3mi bear left towards Pointe d'Arradon. The road skirts Arradon.*

Pointe d'Arradon★

Turn left towards Cale de la Carrière. From here there is a very typical **view**★ of the Golfe du Morbihan in which you can distinguish, from left to right: the Îles de Logoden; in the distance, the Île d'Arz; then the Île d'Holavre, which is rocky, and the Île aux Moines. To reach the point take the path bordering the rocks behind the hotel.

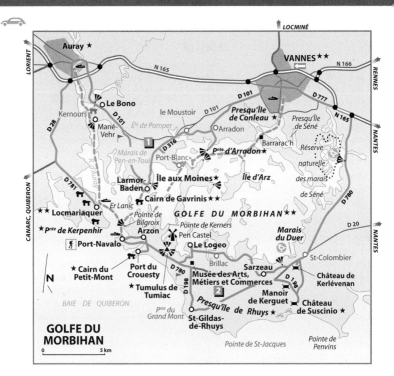

GOLFE DU MORBIHAN

0   5 km

▷ *Turn round and go to Le Moustoir and bear left.*

At the place called **Moulin de Pomper** note on the left the old tidal power mill (⌖ *see Vallée de la RANCE*).

Larmor-Baden

A little fishing port and large oyster-farming centre. From the port there is a fine view of the other islands and the entrance to the gulf.

Cairn de Gavrinis★★

During the visit, you will be able to glimpse lovely views of the River Auray.
⌖ *Guided tours (50min).* ⊙ *Jul–Aug, 9.30am–12.30pm, 1.30pm–7pm (reserve the day before); Apr, Jun and Sept, 9.30am–12.30pm, 1.30pm–6.30pm; May, 1.30pm–6.30pm, Sat–Sun and holidays 9.30am–12.30pm, 1.30pm–6.30pm; Oct–Nov and Mar, Thu–Tue 1.30pm–5pm.*
"Megaliths Circuit" Jul–Sept, departing at 5pm, Apr–Jun, departing 4.30pm.
⌖ *Boat and tour 12€, guided tour 15€.*
✆ *02 97 57 19 38. www.gavrinis.info.*

The **Gavrinis Tumulus** is the most interesting megalithic monument in Brittany. It is situated on the island of Gavrinis, at the mouth of the Golfe du Morbihan, south of Larmor-Baden, from which it can be reached. The tumulus – 6m/20ft high and 50m/165ft around, is made of stones piled on a hillock. It was discovered in 1832 and comprises a covered gallery 14m/46ft long with nine tables held up by 23 carved supports; the funeral chamber, probably a royal tomb (2.5m/8ft on one side), with a ceiling made of a single granite slab, resting on supports is also covered with carvings.

From the top of the tumulus there is a wide view of the Golfe du Morbihan.

Er Lanic

On the tiny island of **Er Lanic**, a little south of Gavrinis, are two tangent circles of menhirs (cromlechs) in the form of a figure of eight, half of which is submerged. This provides evidence of the subsidence of the soil which created the gulf in prehistoric times. At low tide, the menhirs reappear.

Le Bono

As you leave **Kernours**, on the right in a small pine forest is a right-angled dolmen. On this same road continue to **Mané-Verh**, which offers glimpses of the River Auray.

▷ Return to Le Bono.

From the new bridge is a picturesque **view★** of Bono, its river and harbour and the old suspension bridge. You will notice piles of whitewashed tiles used to collect oyster spat (*see CANCALE*).

Auray★ – *See AURAY.*

▷ Leave Auray by the D 28, then after 8km/5mi bear left on the D 781.

The road skirts megalithic monuments and leads to Locmariaquer★★(*see LOCMARIAQUER*).

2 PRESQU'ÎLE DE RHUYS

79km/49mi – about 4hr.

▷ Leave Vannes on the Nantes road on the town plan. After St-Léonard, turn right.

The road runs along the east bank of the bay; there are several viewpoints.

Presqu'île de Rhuys★

At St-Colombier you enter the peninsula, which encloses the Golfe du Morbihan to the south. Its flora is reminiscent of that of the south of France.

Château de Kerlévenan

Guided tour of the park (1hr). *Jul–mid-Sept, Sat–Thu 1.30pm–5.30pm. 2.30€. 02 97 26 46 79.* This 18C château built in the style of Louis XVI is reminiscent of the Petit Trianon in Versailles. Overlooking the gulf, the park has a chinese-style pavilion and a chapel.

Sarzeau

Birthplace of **Lesage** (1668–1747), satirical dramatist and author of *Turcaret* and *Gil Blas*. On the small square, to the right of the church, stand two lovely Renaissance houses.

▷ From Sarzeau go towards Brillac, the road follows the coast for some distance.

Le Logeo

A pretty little port sheltered by the Gouihan and Stibiden Islands.

▷ Go as far as Le Net and bear right.

Tumulus de Tumiac★

15min on foot. *Leave your car in the car park and take a dirt track to the right.* From the top of the tumulus there is an extensive **view★** of the gulf, Quiberon Bay and the islands. This was the observatory from which Caesar is supposed to have watched the naval battle agains the Veneti.

Arzon

In Arzon church, two stained-glass panels recount the vows made by sailors during the Dutch War in 1673. Since then, every Pentecost Monday, seamen take part in a procession from Ste-Anne d'Auray.

Port-Navalo⌂

A small port and seaside resort. The roadstead is enclosed to the south by a promontory on which stands a lighthouse (benches and telescope), and to

Port Navalo

J. Malburet/MICHELIN

the north by Bilgroix Point which offers a good **view**★ of the Golfe du Morbihan. The beach faces the open sea.

Port du Crouesty

Located on the bay of the same name and southeast of Port-Navalo lies this pleasure boat harbour. Alongside it is a large residential complex. The four docks are well sheltered and can hold over 1 100 boats. From the tourist car park there is a good view of the site. Fine walk along the quayside. The **Cairn du Petit-Mont**★ is located south of Port-Crouesty (*Jul–Aug daily 11am–6.30pm, Apr–Jun and Sept 2.30pm–6.30pm exc Wed; 6 €*). Situated on a spectacular promontory which overlooks the peninsula, this archaeological site dates back some 7,000 years. Among the impressive 10,000sq m/12,000sq yd of stones, lie several cairns. The first dates back to 4500 BC. It has no formal structure, unlike the second of the cairns, dating from 4000-3500 BC, which has a sepulchre centred around a stone block. The third cairn, which rings the two older sites was created between 2700–2500BC. During WWII the Germans destroyed one of the four dolmens to create a bunker.

Musée des Arts, Métiers et Commerces

Rd-pt du Net, Largueven on the D 780 near the junciton of the D 198. Apr–Sept 10am–noon, 2pm–7pm, Sun 2pm–7pm; Feb, Mar and Oct daily exc Mon 2pm–7pm. Closed 6 Nov–31 Dec, 1 Jan. 5.50 € (under 12 yrs, 3€). 02 97 53 68 25. www.musee-arts-metiers.com.
On a site of 900sq m/1,000sq yd, more than sixty professions are represented, either in shop or workshop reconstructions. There is a permanent exhibition of Breton costumes as well as themed exhibitions and a section devoted to the 1930s.

St-Gildas-de-Rhuys

Open daily 9am–7pm.
Guided tours available Jul–Aug, Mon–Fri 10.30am–noon, 4pm–6pm; rest of the year, call 06 61 85 44 06.

This village owes its origin to a monastery founded by St Gildas in the 6C. The most famous of the abbots who governed it was Abélard in the 12C.
The former abbey **church**★ was built at the beginning of the 11C and largely rebuilt in the 16C and 17C.
The Romanesque chevet has pure, harmonious lines; it is ornamented with modillions; note a small carving depicting a tournament. Inside, the Romanesque **chancel**★ is remarkable. Behind the Baroque high altar is the tomb of St Gildas (11C). In the north transept lies the 11C gravestone of St Goustan and in the ambulatory, lit by modern stained-glass windows, 13C and 14C gravestones of Breton children and gravestones of abbots and knights. At the end of the nave is a stoup made up from two carved capitals. Another capital is found in the south aisle.
The **treasury**★ (*guided tours Jul–Aug, Tue-Fri and Sun afternoon; 02 97 45 31 45*) contains valuable antique objects, well displayed: 14C and 18C shrines, reliquaries (15C) containing the arms and legs of St Gildas, and his embroidered mitre, a 17C silver-gilt cross bejewelled with emeralds etc.

Château de Suscinio★

3.5km/2mi from Sarzeau on the D 198. Open Apr–Sept, Thu-Tue 10am–7pm; Feb–Mar and Oct, 10am–noon, 2pm–6pm; Nov–Jan, 10am–noon, 2pm–5pm; also open Wed during school holidays, 25 and 26 Dec, 1 and 2 Jan. 7€. 02 97 41 91 91. www.suscinio.info.
The impressive ruins stand in a wild setting by the seashore, where they are buffeted by sea winds. It was the sea which used to fill the moat. The castle was built in the 13C and modified by the dukes of Brittany in the 15C, prior to becoming one of their favourite residences. It was confiscated by François I and fell into the hands of the French Crown which used it to house faithful servants and the then current Royal favourite. In ruins at the end of the Ancien Régime, the castle was sold to a private individual during the Revolution and was used as a stone quarry. Six of the towers have survived.

Château de Suscinio

G. Targat/MICHELIN

In 1955, the roofing of the New Tower *(Tour Neuve)* and the West Pavilion *(Logis Ouest)* were restored to its former glory. The rooms in the entrance pavilion, also restored, house a small **museum** devoted to the history of Brittany.

Having crossed the moat, enter the guard-room and the adjoining tower in which the history of the castle and its restoration are explained.

On the upper floors, the history of Brittany is described with the aid of literature, portraits, paintings and locally produced artefacts (*Scène de pardon* by Camille Chazal and a relief depicting Olivier de Clisson on horseback by Fremiet). Several rooms are devoted to

splendid 13C and 14C **floor coverings** in varnished ceramic, which came from a chapel outside the castle's curtain wall on the banks of the moat, since disappeared. The variety and quality of the decoration, which has been excellently preserved, make these an eloquent witness to medieval decorative art.

The Ceremonial Hall *(Salle des Cérémonies)*, which opens onto a small chapel, provides access to the north façade and to the terraces, offering a lovely **panorama** of the peninsula and ocean.

> From St-Colombier return to Vannes on the road on which you came.

ADDRESSES

STAY

Auberge du Parc Fétan – *17 rue de Berder, 56870 Larmor-Baden.* ℘02 97 57 04 38. www.hotel-parcfetan.com. *Closed 10 Nov–10 Feb. 25 rooms and 9 apartments.* ⌷8€. *Restaurant for guests.* A quiet road separates this hotel from a charming little creek with a small beach. Most rooms have a view of the Gulf, those on the second floor have air conditioning. Heated swimming pool from Apr–Sept.

Hôtel Glann Ar Mor – *27 rue des Fontaines, 56640 Port-Navalo.* ℘02 97 53 88 30. www.glannarmor.fr. *9 rooms.* ⌷8€. *Restaurant.* A nice establishment near the golf course with

simple, white rooms. The restaurant has an extensive French wine list. Full or half-board in-season.

Hôtel Le Gavrinis – *Toulbroch, 56870 Baden. 2km/1.2mi on the rte de Vannes.* ℘02 97 57 00 82. www.gavrinis.com. *Closed 8 Jan–12 Feb and 26 Nov–3 Dec. 18 rooms.* ⌷11.50€. *Restaurant.* This neo-Breton house surrounded by a beautiful garden has comfortable rooms. Pastel tones in the restaurant and a flower-filled terrace add to the charm.

EAT

La Rose des Vents – *5 rue St Vincent, 56370 Sarzeau.* ℘02 97 41 93 77. www.larosedesvents-sarzeau.com. *Closed Mon off season. Reservations advised.*

When you push the heavy door of this 1730 house, you wouldn't guess that there's a beautiful garden out the back where you can eat in summer. Attractive, rustic, antique-filled interior. Crêpes on the menu.

◒◒ **Les Embruns** – *rue du Commerce, 56780 Île-aux-Moines.* ℘*02 97 26 30 86. Closed Jan, Feb, 1–15 Oct and Wed.* A great stop for locals and tourists after fresh seafood prepared simply.

◒◒ **Le Boucanier** – *3 rue du Gén.-de-Gaulle, Port-Navalo.* ℘*02 97 53 89 22. Closed 15 Dec–15 Jan, Tue and Wed (except in season).* This established restaurant on the port has a new dining room with a marine theme. Large covered terrace with great views.

ACTIVITIES

Kayak – *Base nautique Varec'h, in Baden.* ℘*02 97 57 16 16. www.bretagne-kayak. com. Open 9am–6pm.* For beginners or those with experience.

Swimming – There are numerous small beaches on the gulf, notably on the Île aux Moines. The pretty beach at Suscinio is 3km/1.9mi long, and although the water may be cooler than in the gulf, it is much clearer.

Thalassotherapy – *Miramar Crouesty – Port Crouesty, 56640 Arzon.* ℘*02 97 53 49 00. www.miramarcrouesty.com. Open 9am–6pm. Closed Sun afternoon, 27 Nov –27 Dec.* All the usual treatments in a wonderful location. Pool, relaxation area and activities for children (6–12yrs).

MARKETS

Port du Crouesty, every Mon (am) in summer; Port-Navalo, Fri (am) Easter–Nov; Arzon, Tues (am); Sarzeau, Thur (am), as well as a market-fair on the third Wed of every month.

Auray★

This ancient town, built on the banks of the Loch or River Auray, is one of the eight Breton towns honoured with the title *Ville d'Art et d'Histoire*. Many visitors come to enjoy its attractive harbour, its old St-Goustan Quarter, and its proximity to the marvellous Golfe du Morbihan.

A BIT OF HISTORY

The Battle of Auray (14C) – The town is famous in Breton history for the battle that was fought under its walls in 1364 ending the Breton War of Succession (1341–1364). The troops of Charles of Blois, backed by Du Guesclin, held a bad position on a marshy plain north of Auray. Jean de Montfort, Charles's cousin, Olivier de Clisson, and the English, commanded by Chandos, were in a dominating position. Against Du Guesclin's advice, Charles attacked but was soundly defeated, before being slain by one of De Montfort's Breton soldiers.

▶ **Population:** 12,420.

Michelin Map: Local map 308 N9 - Morbihan (56).

Info: 20 rue de Lait, 56400 Auray. ℘02 97 24 09 75. www.auray-tourisme.com.

Location: Between Vannes (19km/12mi E) and Lorient (41km/25mi W).

Kids: Goélette St-Sauveur.

Timing: Spend a day discovering the river and beach and the evening wandering the old town.

Don't Miss: The St-Goustan neighbourhood.

Georges Cadoudal – A farmer's son from around Auray, he was 22 when the **Chouannerie**, a Breton Royalist revolt, broke out in 1793. He threw himself wholeheartedly into the cause. When the men of the Vendée were beaten, he carried on the struggle in Morbihan. He was captured, imprisoned at Brest, but

Quartier St-Goustan

G. Targat/MICHELIN

escaped and took part in the action at Quiberon. He came away unhurt, submitted to Hoche in 1796 and reopened the campaign in 1799. Bonaparte offered the rebel a pardon and the rank of general, without success. The struggle ended only in 1804; Cadoudal had gone to Paris to try to kidnap Napoleon; he was arrested, sentenced to death and executed.

SIGHTS
Promenade du Loch★
There is a good **view** over the port, St-Goustan Quarter and Auray River, crossed by an attractive old stone bridge with cutwaters.
Moored in the loch is a schooner, the **Goélette St-Sauveur** (*open Easter–Sept 10.30am–12.30pm, 2.30pm–7pm; 02 97 56 63 38; 5€*), which has been painstakingly reconstructed from an old hull. It contains information on the way of life in St-Goustan port during the last century, including slide shows with soundtracks. A display of tools belonging to maritime carpenters evokes the construction techniques which were once used.

Quartier St-Goustan★
This little port, particularly lively in the evening, still has some beautiful 15C houses and other pretty dwellings in place St-Sauveur and up some of the steep (in places even stepped) little lanes leading off the square.

The quay to the left of the square is named after **Benjamin Franklin**. In 1776, during the War of Independence, the famous American diplomat and statesman sailed from Philadelphia to negotiate a treaty with France and landed at Auray instead of Nantes due to the unfavourable weather conditions. The house (at number 8) where he stayed bears a plaque.

Mausolée de Cadoudal
Access by car from place du Loch along rue du Verger towards Le Reclus.
The mausoleum, a small domed circular building, stands opposite the general's family house.

🚗 DRIVING TOUR

Le Pays Alréen
23km/14mi – 3hr.

▷ *Leave Auray on avenue du Général-de-Gaulle.*

Chartreuse d'Auray
Open Apr–Aug, Wed–Mon 2.30pm–5pm, Wed 2.30pm–6pm. Closed Tue. No charge. 02 97 24 27 02.
On the battlefield where he defeated Charles of Blois, Jean de Montfort (who became Duke Jean IV) built a chapel and a collegiate church, which was later transformed into a Carthusian monastery (from 1482–1790).

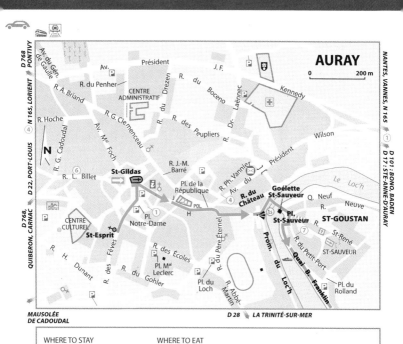

AURAY

0   200 m

NANTES, VANNES, N 165

D 101 : BONO, BADEN
D 17 : STE-ANNE-D'AURAY

D 768, PONTIVY
Av. du Gén. de Gaulle

N 165, LORIENT

D 22, PORT-LOUIS

D 768,
QUIBERON, CARNAC

MAUSOLÉE
DE CADOUDAL

D 28   LA TRINITÉ-SUR-MER

WHERE TO STAY		WHERE TO EAT			
Cadoudal (Hôtel Le)	①	Auberge (L')	①	Closerie de Kerdrain	⑥
Talvern (Chambre d'hôte)	④	Belle Bio (Crêperie La)	④	Frégate (Crêperie La)	⑦

The funeral chapel was built in the early 19C to hold the bones of exiles and Chouans who were shot on the Champ des Martyrs in 1795; in the centre, the black and white marble mausoleum bears 953 names.

Champ des Martyrs

The exiles and Chouans were shot in this enclosure during the Royalist insurrection (1793–1804). The Duchess of Angoulème had a chapel built in the style of a Greek temple on the site where they were executed and buried, before the remains were transferred to the Carthusian Monastery.

▷ *Follow the road to Ste-Anne-d'Auray.*

The road skirts the Kerzo Bog (on the right) where the Battle of Auray was fought on 29 September 1364.

▷ *After 500m/545yds bear left in the direction of St-Degan.*

St-Degan

Overlooking the deep valley of the Loch, the hamlet hosts the **Ecomusée** (🕐 *open daily Jul–Aug, 10am–7pm; Mar–Jun, Sept–Oct and school holidays Mon–Fri 2pm–5.30pm; ≈5€; ℘02 97 57 66 00*), which contains a collection of restored farm buildings from the 17C and 18C.

▷ *Go to Brech and turn right.*

Ste-Anne-d'Auray★

Ste-Anne is Brittany's premier place of pilgrimage. The first *pardon* takes place on 7 March; then, from Easter until Rosary (the first Sunday in October); there are parish pilgrimages (especially Wednesdays and Sundays from the end of April to the end of September). The *pardon* of St Anne on 26 July is the most attended, together with those on 15 August and on the first Sunday in October. In 1623 St Anne appeared to a ploughman, Yves Nicolazic, and asked him to rebuild a chapel which had been previously dedicated to her in one of his fields. On 7 March 1625, Yves unearthed, at the spot she had indicated, an old statue of St Anne. A church was built there the same year.

Basilique
Built in Renaissance style during the late 19C, the basilica took the place of the 17C chapel.

Trésor★
🕐Open Jun–Oct 2–6.30pm, Wed 2pm –6.30pm, 8.30pm–10.30pm. Rest of the year, daily exc Mon, 10.30am–noon, 3pm–6pm, Sun 3pm–6pm. ✆3€. 👓 ℘02 97 57 68 80.
Located in the cloister, it contains objects devoted to Ste-Anne, notably a relic of St-Anne presented by Anne of Austria in thanks for the birth of Louis XIV. A Breton art gallery contains 15C–19C statues.

Monument aux Morts
The war memorial was raised, thanks to public subscription all over Brittany, to the 250,000 Breton soldiers and sailors who died in World War I. It has become a memorial to all those who have died during wars since.
Not far away, on the other side of the road, a Franco-Belgian cemetery contains the graves of 1,338 soldiers.

Historial de Ste-Anne
🕐Open Mar–Oct, daily 10am–7pm. ✆4€. 👓 ℘02 97 57 64 05. www.musee-de-cire.com.
This waxwork exhibition presents the life of Yves Nicolazic and the origins of the annual pilgrimage.

Musée du Costume Breton
To the right of the war memorial.
🕐Mar–Oct, daily 10pm–noon, 2.30pm –6pm. Rest of year Sun 2.30pm–6pm. ✆1€. ℘02 97 57 68 80.
This museum displays a fine collection of old dolls in Breton costume and two small boats offered as ex-votos.

Maison de Nicolazic
🕐Open Apr–Oct, 10am–4pm. ✆No charge. ℘02 97 57 68 80.

The house where Sainte Anne appeared to the pious peasant. Inside is a chapel and some 17C furniture.

Monument du Comte de Chambord
Towards Brech, on the left about 500m/ 545yds from the town.
Each year, for St Michael's day, followers and friends made the pilgrimage to Ste-Anne. Representations of Bayard, Du Guesclin, St Geneviève and St Jeanne d'Arc frame the statue of Charles X's grandson.

▷ *Follow the D 17 heading S towards Pluneret.*

Pluneret
In the cemetery, alongside the central alley, on the right, are the tombs of Sophie Rostopchine, the Countess de Ségur, the well-known author of children's books and of her son, Mgr Louis-Gaston de Ségur.

▷ *Proceed along D 101 towards Bono and after 2km/1.2mi turn left for Ste-Avoye.*

Ste-Avoye
Among picturesque cottages, near a fountain, stands a pretty Renaissance chapel with a fine keel-shaped **roof**★. The polychrome decoration of the carved-wood **roodscreen**★ is remarkable: on the nave side, it depicts the Apostles; on the chancel side, the Virtues on the left by St Fiacre and St Lawrence; on the right by St Yves between the rich man and the poor man.

▷ *Turn back in the direction of Ste-Anne-d'Auray and bear left to Auray.*

ADDRESSES

🛏 STAY
🍽🍽**Hôtel Le Cadoudal** – *9 pl. Notre-Dame. ℘ 02 97 24 14 65. www.hotelle cadoudal-auray.com. Closed 2 weeks in Mar. 13 rooms. ⬜ 7 €.* You can expect a friendly warm welcome in this unpretentious hotel. Rooms are simply

equipped with double glazed windows. A very pleasant breakfast room and service *en terrasse* on fine days.

☺☺ **Chambre d'hôte Talvern** – *Talvern, 56 690 Landévant. ℘ 02 97 56 99 80. www.chambre-morbihan.com.* 🛏. *5 rooms.* 🍽. This 19C longère has comfortable, elegant rooms decorated with a spice theme. The table uses organic vegetables from the *potager* (kitchen garden).

⛨EAT

☺ **Crêperie La Belle Bio** – *4 rue Phllippe Vannier. ℘02 97 24 26 75. Closed Mon eve and Sun in winter.* Most of this restaurant's ingredients are organic. Rustic dining room and covered terrace.

☺ **Crêperie La Frégate** – *11 r. du Petit-Port (in port de St-Goustan). ℘ 02 97 50 71 95. Closed Jan, Tue and Wed exc school hols.* A half timbered house where you will be treated to delicious crêpes.

Tastings will be offered to bargain hunters who visit the nearby boutique.

☺☺ **Closerie de Kerdrain** – *20 r. L.-Billet. ℘ 02 97 56 61 27. www.lacloserie dekerdrain.com. Closed 5 Jan–1 Feb, Sun eve (exc Easter–Nov), Mon and Tue.* Charming Breton manor house in a garden. Classic rooms, elegant wood-work and a pleasant terrace where you can enjoy appetising cuisine.

☺☺ **L'Auberge** – *56 rte de Vannes. ℘02 97 57 61 55. Closed Wed lunch in Winter.* Behind its flowery façade, this little inn serves generous portions of local food in a pretty dining room filled with Breton furniture. Some rooms available.

⛒ SHOPPING

Au Régal Breton – *17 rue du Belzic. ℘02 97 24 22 75. Open 9am–12.30pm, 2pm–7pm. Closed Wed.* Plenty of regional goodies in this Breton pâtisserie.

Locmariaquer★★

The village, which commands the entrance to the Golfe du Morbihan, has retained several important megaliths.

SIGHTS
Ensemble Mégalithique de Locmariaquer★★

By the cemetery, take the signposted path to the car park. ◷*Open 1 Jul–4 Sept 10am–7pm; May–Jun 10am–6pm; 5 Sept–30 Apr 10am–12.30pm, 2pm–6pm.* ☛*Guided tours available (45min).* ◷*Closed 1 Jan, 1 May and 25 Dec.* ⛲*5€.* ♿*℘02 97 57 37 59. www.monum.fr.*
This group of three megaliths is an important part of a programme of con-servation and restoration of megalithic sites.

Grand Menhir Brisé

This menhir was probably broken on purpose as long ago as the Neolithic period, when it measured 20m/65ft and weighed almost 350t. It is made of

▸ **Population:** 1,598.
⛬ **Michelin Map:** Local map 308 N9 – Morbihan (56).
🛈 **Info:** 1 rue de la Victoire, 56740 Locmariaquer. ℘02 97 57 33 05. www.ot-locmariaquer.fr.
◖ **Location:** 13km/8mi S of Auray.
◷ **Timing:** Start with a visit to the megaliths followed by an afternoon on the beach.
☺ **Don't Miss:** The funerary chamber of the Table des Marchands.

a type of gneiss rock that can only be found 12km/7.5mi away. An axe carved on one of its sides is believed to be sym-bolic of the menhir's position within an important group of megaliths.

Table des Marchands

The origin of the name of this dolmen has provoked considerable dispute, and experts are not sure whether the

Entrance to the tumulus

G. Targat/MICHELIN

dolmen in fact bears the name of the family to which it belonged. It has been restored recently, and its tumulus has been rediscovered. A 7m/23ft corridor leads to a funerary chamber in which the base stele is decorated with crooks arranged symmetrically.

The slab that forms the ceiling is in fact part of a large menhir, the two other parts of which can be found at the Tumulus d'Er-Grah, not far from here, and in the *Cavin de Gavrinis*, 4km/2.5mi away. This slab features axe and crook motifs and part of a bovine figure.

Tumulus d'Er-Grah

This very elongated monument is situated north of the other megaliths. It is thought that its original length was more than 170m. The tumulus is currently the object of examination.

Dolmen de Mané-Lud★

This dolmen surrounded by houses on the right at the entrance to the village. The stones that remain standing inside the chamber are carved.

Dolmen de Mané-Rethual★

In the centre of the village and to the right of the former town hall, take a path that passes by a group of houses and gardens.

A long covered alleyway leads to a vast chamber, the supports of which are carved.

🚗 DRIVING TOUR

Megalithic Monuments
5km/3mi.

◐ *From place Évariste-Frick, follow rue Wilson.*

On leaving the village take the road on the right leading to **Kerlud** village, a remarkable group of small farms built in granite. Opposite the last house is the partly hidden **Dolmen de Kerlud.**

◐ *Return to the main road and bear right; beside the beach turn right again.*

Dolmen des Pierres-Plates★

A menhir indicates the entrance to this dolmen. Two chambers are linked by a long alleyway. Remarkable engravings decorate the supports. A terrace affords a fine view of the Pointe de Port-Navalo and the Pointe du Grand-Mont, the Île d'Houat with Belle-Île in the distance, and the Presqu'île de Quiberon.

◐ *Turn round and follow the shoreline as far as the Pointe de Kerpenhir.*

Pointe de Kerpenhir★

Continue past the blockhouse – the point where a granite statue of Our Lady of Kerdro stands protecting sailors (*kerdro* is Breton for safe return), affords a **view**★ onto the Morbihan channel.

The road to the left offers a fine glimpse of the bay.

Tumulus de Mané-er-Hroech★

At Kerpenhir take a path to the left of the road which climbs up to the tumulus. A stairway (23 steps) gives access to the funerary chamber and to the dry-stone structure forming the tumulus.

Return to Locmariaquer.

ADDRESSES

STAY

Hôtel Les Trois Fontaines – *rte d'Auray. ℰ02 97 57 42 70. www.hotel-troisfontaines.com. Closed 6 Nov–26 Dec and 6 Jan–7 Feb. 18 rooms. ⌑ 11€.*

At the entrance of Locmariaquer, this charming modern establishment has spacious rooms with a nautical theme. There's a pretty garden and a terrace.

EAT

Retour de la Marée – *Scarpoche. ℰ02 97 57 30 22.* Catch-of-the-day, pan-fried squid, locally sourced meat dishes cooked just right—a good address to share with your best friends. Friday is music night until 2am or later.

TOURS

The Tourist Office organises guided tours of the oyster beds, a local milk farm and the megaliths. Enquire within.

Carnac★

Carnac's megalithic monuments symbolise prehistory in France the same way as Stonehenge does in England. The museum of Prehistory is world-renowned for its collection of objects dating from that period. The town is also a seaside resort ideal for families.

MEGALITHIC MONUMENTS★★

A tour of the numerous mégalithes (alignments, dolmens, tumuli) to the north of Carnac makes a fascinating excursion.

Since the footsteps of innumerable visitors pose a serious threat to the soil (which is essential for the study of the mysterious origins of the megaliths) the public authorities have had to take action to protect the Ménec, Kermario and Kerlascan Alignments. If plant life is allowed to grow again, this will prevent any further erosion of the soil, which will in turn prevent the foundations of the menhirs from becoming exposed. At Kermario, if conditions are favourable, a temporary footbridge enables visitors

▶ **Population:** 4,444.

Michelin Map: Local map 308 M9 - Morbihan (56).

Info: 74 av. des Druides, 56340 Carnac. ℰ02 97 52 13 52. www.ot-carnac.fr.

Location: At the base of the Quiberon Peninsula.

Kids: A trip to the megaliths followed by a visit to the museum of prehistory to put them into perspective.

Don't Miss: The megaliths of Ménec and Kermario.

GETTING AROUND

BY BUS – The local shuttle **Tatoovu** operates from the 15 Jun–15 Sept between Carnac-Ville, Carnac-Plage and the alignments. Information at the Tourist Office.

BY BIKE OR SCOOTER – **Marie-France et Christian Besret** – 2 bis av. des Salines. ℰ02 97 52 88 92.

Alignements du Ménec

J. Malburet/MICHELIN

to observe the alignment in its entirety, as an example of Western Europe's first ever architecture.

👥 Alignements du Ménec★★

The Ménec Alignments (👥 *guided tours Jul–Aug (1hr);* 🎫 *4.50€ (under 18 yrs free);* ✆*02 97 52 29 81;* 🕐*closed 1 Jan, 1 May, 25 Dec)* over 1km/0.6mi long and 100m/325ft wide, include 1,170 menhirs arranged in 11 rows. The tallest is 4m /13ft high. They begin with a semicircle of 70 menhirs partly surrounding the hamlet of Ménec.

👥 Alignements de Kermario★

Some 990 menhirs in ten rows occupy an area similar to the Ménec Alignments.

Alignements de Kerlescan★

In this field (880 x 139m/960 x 152yds), 540 menhirs are arranged in 13 rows which are preceded by a semicircle of 39 menhirs.

▸ *From Kerlescan, take D 186 on the left, then turn right on the Chemin de la Métairie.*

👥 Alignements du Petit Ménec

Barely visible from the road, tucked in the woods, this enchanting place has not been developed for tourism.

Tumulus St-Michel★

The tumulus is 120m/394yds long and 12m/39ft high, a mound of earth and stones covering two burial chambers and some 20 stone chests.

Most of the artefacts found there are now in Carnac's Musée de Préhistoire and the Musée Archéologique du Morbihan in Vannes. The galleries were first explored in the early 20C, but for safety reasons visitors are no longer allowed inside.

Surmounting the tumulus are the Chapelle St-Michel, decorated with fine frescoes (1961) by Alic Pasquo, a small 16C calvary and a viewing table. The **view**★ extends over the megaliths, the coast and the islands.

Dolmens de Mané-Kerioned

A group of three dolmens; the first has eight uprights with stylised engravings of axes, spirals, coats of arms and more.

Tumulus de Kercado

Leave the car at the entrance to Kercado Castle. 🕐*Open 9am–7pm.*

This tumulus (3800 BC) is 30m/98ft across and 3.5m/11.5ft high and covers a fine dolmen. A menhir stands on the summit. Note the carvings on the table and four uprights.

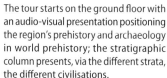

CARNAC-PLAGE⌂

Carnac-Plage, with its gently shelved beach, has been developed in the shelter of the Presqu'île de Quiberon. It boasts several beaches: Grande Plage to the south (2km/1.2mi long); Légenès, Ty Bihan and St-Colomban to the west; Beaumer and Men-du to the east. Windsurfers meet at St-Colomban Beach the whole year.

SIGHTS

♙♙ Musée de Préhistoire J.-Miln-Z.-Le-Rouzic★★

10 pl. de la Chapelle. ⏱*Open May–Jun and Sept, Wed–Mon 10am–12.30pm and 2pm–6pm; daily Jul–Aug 10am–6pm; Oct–Apr Wed–Mon 10am–12.30pm, 2pm–5pm.* ⏱*Jan, 1 May and 25 Dec.* ⏣*5€ (children 2.50€).* ♿ ☎*02 97 52 22 04.* *www.museedecarnac.com.*

This Museum of Prehistory was founded in 1881 by the Scotsman James Miln (1819–1881) (who had excavated in Carnac and Kermario) and then enriched by Zacharie Le Rouzic, native of Carnac. In its new surroundings, these exceptional, beautifully displayed collections, cover prehistory from the Lower Paleolithic (450 000 BC) to the early Middle Ages.

St-Cornély

A pope in 3C Rome, St-Cornély fled to Brittany after being persecuted by the Roman Emperor Gallus. Accompanied by two oxen carrying his luggage, he petrified the Roman soldiers who were pursuing him. Legend has it that these petrified forms are the Carnac alignments. St-Cornély later became the patron saint of horned animals and he is celebrated on the second Sunday of September in Carnac's churches. This tradition goes back to the Middle Ages when in order to turn the pagan cattle fair into a Christian festival, the beasts were blessed in St-Cornély's fountain, adjacent to Carnac's principal church.

The tour starts on the ground floor with an audio-visual presentation positioning the region's prehistory and archaeology in world prehistory; the stratigraphic column presents, via the different strata, the different civilisations.

Proceeding chronologically, the visitor is presented: Lower Palaeolithic (chipped stone, scrapers, points); Middle and Upper Paleolithic (panels and documents); Mesolithic (primitive tools in wood or bone, shell ornaments, a reconstructed burial chamber) and Neolithic. In the latter period, man lived in settled communities and turned to crop growing and stock raising, marked by the realisation of megalithic tombs: dolmens or collective burial tombs (placed with the dead were pottery, polished axes, jewellery); menhirs and alignments.

Also exhibited here are necklaces made of variscite (a green semiprecious stone), fine polished axes in jadeite or fibrolite, beads and pendants, pottery, engraved stones, dolmens and objects related to daily life.

The first floor covers the Bronze Age (socketed axes, gold jewellery), Iron Age (reconstructed burial tomb, salt oven, Celtic gold coins), to the Roman era (model of a villa, statuettes of Venus, coins, objects related to daily life).

Church★

This 17C church is dedicated to **St Cornely,** the patron saint of horned cattle; his statue stands on the façade between two oxen. A massive bell-tower topped by an octagonal spire dominates the building. The porch on the north side is surmounted by a canopy in the form of a crown.

Inside, the wooden vaults are covered with curious 18C **paintings** depicting the lives of the saint, Christ and St John the Baptist, and the Virgin. The communion table, pulpit and chancel screen are of the 18C and in wrought iron. In the chancel entrance, on the left, is a reliquary bust of St Cornely (18C gilt wood). The church's treasury is exhibited in the south aisle: chasuble, cross, chalices and monstrance.

EXCURSION

La Trinité-sur-Mer ☺

The village, built on a height, extends down the slope to the harbour and beaches on the River Crach estuary, which is lined with oyster beds. A small fishing port, a busy pleasure boat harbour and shipyards add to the activity of this resort, which has fine beaches along the Presqu'île de Kerbihan (*02 97 55 72 21; www.ot-trinite-sur-mer.fr*).

The **marina** can accommodate 1 200 yachts. La Trinité is a popular meeting place for sailing buffs, whether they prefer sleek competition models or lovingly restored old schooners. Regattas and races are held here all year long, including the *Spi Ouest-France*, where the competition is open to both amateurs and champions.

The **chemin des douaniers** is a path that leads from the marina to Pointe de Kerbihan, past numerous oyster beds along the estuary, then round to Kerbihan and Kervillen beaches. Beyond the latter, Île de Stuhan, a nature reserve, comes into sight.

Pont de Kérisper

From this great bridge over the River Crach there is a good **view**✶ of the estuary, the town and the port installations.

MEGALITH EXCURSION ★★

To the NW along the D 781 towards Lorient you can visit a number of sites of prehistoric interest.

To the left on leaving Plouharnel are the three underground chambers of **Dolmens de Rondossec**.

After the level crossing, the **Menhirs du Vieux-Moulin** stand in a field to the right of the road.

The **Alignements de Ste Barbe** are comprised of four menhirs on the edge of a field near the road in the direction of Kersilly campsite. Take a road to the right.

The **Dolmen de Crucuno** rises next to a farm in the centre of the hamlet of Crucuno. Only one chamber remains with the great table supported by 11 uprights. 500m /545yds beyond Crucono, on the left, Dolmen de Mané-Croch is a typical

dolmen with side chambers. To the right of the road at the entrance to Erdeven are 10 rows of some 1,130 menhirs at the **Alignements de Kerzerho**.

Strategically located on the Qiberon Bay, **Plouharnel** has some lovely old houses and a charming 16C chapel, Notre-Dame-des-Fleurs. Inside, there is a 15C Tree of Knowledge carved in alabaster. A path behind the chapel leads to a fountain. An old blockhouse houses the **Musée de la Chouannerie** (🕐 *open mid-Jun–Sept, daily 10am–noon, 2pm–6pm; Easter–mid-Jun, 2pm–6pm; ⊗5€; ⊛ *02 97 52 31 31*). The Chouannerie movement, a Breton Royalist revolt, is recounted with dioramas peopled with terracotta figures, depicting the movement's main antagonists and Chouan arms, costumes and guillotine.

Outside Plouharnel, on the road to Auray, you can see the abbey of **Ste-Anne-de-Kergonan**, founded in 1897. Benedictine monks live and work here. The ceramic shop is open to the public.

Abbaye St-Michel-de-Kergonan

3km/1.8mi by D 781 towards Plouharnel. This Benedictine abbey, founded in 1898, is part of the Abbaye St-Pierre in Solesmes. An imposing granite building includes a plain church with wooden vaulting held up by granite pillars.

Beyond the abbey shop (books, produce and objects made by the nuns), a gallery houses an exhibit on the Benedictine Order: its origin, Cistercian Law, expansion, the height of its power with Cluny, and information on Gregorian chants.

ADDRESSES

🛏 STAY

☜ **Chambre d'hôte Ty Me Mamm** – *Quelvezin. 5km/3mi N of Carnac by D 768 and C 202 rte de Quelvezin. *02 97 52 45 87. 4 rooms. ⊅. ⊑.* Hospitality and spontaneity are the key words on this farm dating from 1900. The bedrooms, which are named after Carnac's beaches, successfully blend rustic and modern décor. Large garden and lake.

⊜⊜ **Chambre d'hôte L'Alcyone** – *Imp. de Beaumer.* ☏*02 97 52 78 11. http:// lalcyone.blogspot.com. Closed last week of Nov and first week of Feb. 5 rooms.* ⌨. ⌨. This 1890 longhouse has been prettily restored: delightful terrace facing the fields and comfy sofas in the lounge. Pleasant rooms with white walls, parquet floors and quality textiles. Homemade jam and pastries for breakfast.

⊜⊜ **Hôtel La Marine** – *4 Place de la Chapelle.* ☏*02 97 52 07 33. www.lamarine carnac.com. 31 rooms.* ⌨ *7.50€. Restaurant* ⊜⊜. Located at the heart of the town. Rooms are well kept and the restaurant has a pretty terrace.

⊜⊜ **Hôtel Ostréa** – *34 cours des Quais, La Trinité-Sur-Mer.* ☏*02 97 55 73 23. www. hotel-ostrea.com. 13 rooms.* ⌨ *8€. Closed Dec–Jan, Mon off season and Sun eve. Restaurant* ⊜⊜. Bright and cheerful rooms; most open onto the port. Spacious terraces where you can take breakfast or seafood meals.

⚲/EAT

⊜ **Chez Céline** – *among the alignments of Kermario.* ☏*02 97 52 17 31. Open daily in summer 10am–9.30pm.* Enjoy a delicious buckwheat crêpe on the terrace, among the standing stones.

⊜⊜ **La Côte** – *at the Kermario stones.* ☏*02 97 52 02 80. www.restaurant-la-cote.com. Closed 6 Jan–12 Feb, 15–19 Mar, 4–8 Oct, Sat lunch, Sun eve, from Sept–Jun and Tue lunch in Jul–Aug and Mon.* Inventive cooking in this old farmhouse with a charming garden terrace

⊜⊜ **Kreiz An Avel** – *plage de St-Colomban, 1 av. de la Chapelle.* ☏*02 97 52 74 52. Open daily until midnight.* A restaurant and *crêperie* in a pleasant location with fish fresh from the bay.

⊜⊜⊜ **Auberge Le Râtelier** – ☏*02 97 52 05 04. www.le-ratelier.com. Closed 6 Jan–6 Feb, March and Wed out of season.* The original creeper-clad façade, hides a warm, rustic dining room. Regional cuisine here pays homage to the sea. Basic, cosy rooms available.

⊜ **Le Crêperie du Bourg** – *16 rue des Frères Kermorvant, La Trinité-Sur-Mer.* ☏*02 97 55 73 26. Closed Jan, Sun eve and Mon.* A small place in the old town, two steps from the marina. The kitchen is in the middle of two bright dining rooms. Warm welcome and a choice of crêpes, both sweet and savoury.

⊜⊜ **Le Quai** – *8 cours des Quais, La Trinité-Sur-Mer.* ☏*02 97 55 80 26. Open summer.* Gigantic meals, well prepared and nicely served. The "big meal" mixes seafood, Parma ham and salad. This is the place to find sailors, skippers and satisfied eaters.

♡ NIGHTLIFE

⊜⊜ **Le Baobab** – *3 allée du Parc, Carnac-Plage.* ☏*02 97 52 29 96. Open until 1am.* A pub, a café and an ice cream parlour rolled into one, set back from the shore. Savour some fish, oysters, a salad, or have an evening drink.

🏃ACTIVITIES

Carnac Thalassothérapie – *av. de l'Atlantique.* ☏*02 97 52 53 54. www.thalasso-carnac.com. Open 8.30am –6pm. Closed 2nd and 3rd week of Jan.* Relaxation is assured in this building, which is renovated every year. With four treatments per day, you'll discover watertherapy and seaweed-based therapies during a weekend stay. The swimming pool is open to the public.

Paragliding – *Hôtel Les Rochers, 6 bd de la Base Nautique.* ☏*02 97 52 10 09.* Tempted by the thought of gliding over the bay of Quiberon? Then get yourself to the Water Sports Café at the Hotel des Rochers. Solo or tandem flights from the pontoon 600m/655yds from the beach.

Presqu'île de Quiberon★

This former island is now attached to the mainland by a narrow isthmus. It offers a varied landscape of sand dunes fixed by maritime pines, a wild coast (Côte Sauvage) with an impressive jumble of cliffs, rocks, caves, reefs and wide sunny beaches.

A BIT OF HISTORY

Hoche repels the exiles (July 1795) – Quiberon saw the rout of the Royalists in 1795. The French exiles in England and Germany had made great plans; 100 000 men, led by the princes, were to land in Brittany, join hands with the Chouans and drive out the 'Blues'. In fact, the British fleet which anchored in the Quiberon roadstead carried only 10 000 men, commanded by Puisaye, Hervilly and Sombreuil. The princes did not come.

The landing began on the beach at Carnac on 27 June and continued for several days. Cadoudal's Chouans joined them. But the effect of surprise was lost; long preparations and talk among the exiles had warned the Convention; **General Hoche** was ready, and he drove the invaders back into the peninsula. Driven

- **Michelin Map:** Local map 308 M10 Morbihan (56).
- **Info:** 14 rue de Verdun, 56170 Quiberon. ✆0825 13 56 00. www.quiberon.com.
- **Location:** Opposite Belle-Île, only one road leads here: the D 768 which starts in Auray (28km/17mi NE). Traffic jams in summer.
- **Timing:** Come on Saturday morning for the market.
- **Parking:** Difficult to find parking spaces in summer.
- **Don't Miss:** The beaches and creeks.

to the beach at Port-Haliguen, the exiles tried to re-embark. Unfortunately, the British ships were prevented by a heavy swell from getting near enough to land and the Royalists were captured. The Convention refused to pardon them. Some were shot at Quiberon and others were taken to Auray and Vannes and shot there.

Quiberon ⌂

At the far end of the peninsula, Quiberon is a popular resort with its fine south-facing sandy beach and proximity to the Côte Sauvage.

Côte Sauvage

R. Mattes/MICHELIN

GETTING THERE

BY TRAIN – Presqu'île de Quiberon – avoid the traffic by taking the Tire-Bouchon train from Auray (28km/17mi, 9 stops). Eleven return journeys (5.10€) daily in Jul–Aug.

Île d'Houat and Île de Hœdic

From Quiberon – 6am–10pm. 30min trip (1 to 6 trips daily depending on the season). Contact SMN: ℘0820 056 000. www.smn-navigation.fr.

Port-Maria

This departure point for boat services to Belle-Île, Houat and Hœdic is a busy harbour and a fishing port.

EXCURSIONS

Île d'Houat and Île de Hoedic

These islands in the Ponant archipelago lie some 15km/9mi from the mainland. Their coastline is fringed by sandy beaches alternating with cliffs and rocky headlands. Tourism and fishing are the main activities. Peace and quiet is guaranteed. Leave your car on the mainland, as no motor vehicles are allowed on the islands.

Houat

The island of Houat (meaning "duck") is a granite ridge fringed by cliffs (5km/3mi long and 1.3km/0.8mi wide). Because of its location commanding access to Quiberon Bay, it was occupied three times by the English in the 17C and 18C. Pretty houses, whitewashed and flower-bedecked, line the winding streets and alleyways of the **town**, leading to a square in the centre in which stands the communal well, and on to another square next to the church.

The church, built in the 19C, commemorates St Gildas, an English monk and patron of the island, who visited Houat prior to founding the monastery of St-Gildas-de-Rhuys.

Go round the church and follow the path skirting the cemetery.

From the look-out point, there is a fine **view**★ of the harbour and of the Presqu'île de Rhuys.

Beaches – There are numerous beaches located in small creeks but the loveliest extends to the west, facing the Île de Hœdic, near the old harbour.

Hœdic

Separated from the Île d'Houat by the Sœurs Channel, Hoedic is the smaller of the two (2.5 x 1.5km/1.5 x 0.9mi); it has the same granite formation with beaches and rocky headlands. Two lagoons extend east of the town while the island is covered in sparse heathland where wild carnations, a few cypresses, fine fig trees and tamarisks grow. Fresh water is supplied by an underground water source.

The south-facing houses stand in groups of three or four in the **town**. Near the former beacon is the **Église St-Goustan** named after a Cornish hermit, who came to the island for a few years. It has fine 19C **furnishings**; note the two angels in white marble by the high altar.

The old **fort**, built in 1859 and partly hidden by the dunes, can be seen on the road to Port de la Croix. Footpaths by the sea take you round the island to discover the beaches and admire the lovely **view** of the mainland, Houat Island, Belle-Ile and of the reefs.

🚗 DRIVING TOURS

1 LA COTE SAUVAGE★★

18km/11mi round trip – allow 2hr.

Go to Port-Maria and bear right onto the coast road (signposted route côtière).

This wild coast is a succession of jagged cliffs where caves, crevasses and inlets alternate with little sandy beaches with crashing rolling waves (bathing prohibited; ground swell). Rocks of all shapes and sizes form passages and labyrinths in which the sea boils and roars.

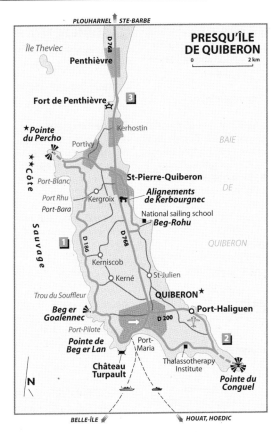

PRESQU'ÎLE DE QUIBERON

Beg er Goalennec
Go around the Café Le Vivier and over the rocks to reach the tip of the promontory from where there is a pretty view over the length of the Côte Sauvage.

> After Kroh-Kollé, bear left.

The road runs downhill towards **Port-Bara**, a cove prickling with rocks, before going inland. Surfaced roads lead to Port-Rhu and Port-Blanc; the latter has a nice white sandy beach.

Pointe du Percho★
Go on foot to the tip of the point.
A lovely **view**★ opens out, on the left, to the Côte Sauvage, on the right, to the Isthme de Penthièvre, its fort and beach, and beyond the islands of Belle-Île and Groix. The last stele indicates Beg en Aud, the furthest point on this coastline.

> Cross Portivy and drive to St-Pierre-Quiberon.

St-Pierre-Quiberon
This resort has two beaches on either side of the small port of Orange. Take rue des Menhirs to see the St-Pierre lines made up of 22 menhirs on the right.

② POINTE DU CONGUEL
6km/3.7mi round trip – allow 1hr 30min.

> Leave Quiberon to the E by boulevard Chanard.

Drive round the **Institut de Thalassothérapie**, which offers salt-water cures for arthritis, rheumatism, over-exertion and injury rehabilitation.

Pointe du Conguel
Viewing table. Allow 30min on foot there and back.

From the tip of the point there is a view of Belle-Île, Houat and Hœdic Islands, the Morbihan coast, Quiberon Bay and Teignouse Lighthouse.

Drive on to Port-Haliguen.

On the left there is an aerodrome with a runway for light aircraft. Beyond Fort-Neuf, note the bustle created on the beach by the various sailing clubs and schools. The view opens out over the bay and the Morbihan coastline. On your right you pass an obelisk commemorating the surrender of the exiles in 1795.

Port-Haliguen
A small fishing and pleasure boat harbour hosts summer regattas.

ADDRESSES

STAY

Hôtel Le Relais – *64 rte du Roch Priol, Quiberon.* ℘*02 97 50 10 56. www. hoteldurelais.fr.* *7.50€. Closed 19 Dec–5 Jan. 23 rooms. Restaurant.* Family-run hotel with functional rooms, some of which open onto the garden. Traditional seafood cuisine in the restaurant.

Hôtel Roch Priol – *rue des Sirènes, Quiberon.* ℘*02 97 50 04 86. www.hotel rochpriol.fr. Closed 16 Nov–14 Feb.* *7.50€. Restaurant. 45 rooms.* According to regulars, this place is the best one on the presqu'île. Its quiet, family atmosphere and value for money make it a great choice.

Hôtel de La Sirène – *rte du Port, Houat.* ℘*02 97 30 66 73. www. houat-la-sirene.com. Closed Nov–Mar. 20 rooms.* *12€. Restaurant.* Bright, standard rooms. Meals focus on seafood with a daily fish special.

EAT

Le Neptune – *4 quai de Houat, Port Maria.* ℘*02 97 50 09 62. Closed 6 Nov–31 Mar.* The restaurant focuses on fish and other types of seafood. Don't miss the *tournedos* of St Jacques (scallops).

3 ISTHME DE PENTHIÈVRE
This provides road and rail links between the former island and the mainland.

Leave Quiberon via D 768 towards St-Pierre-de-Quiberon.

Fort de Penthièvre
Rebuilt in the 19C, it commands the access to the peninsula. A monument and a crypt commemorate 59 members of the Resistance shot here in 1944.

Penthièvre
This small resort has two fine sandy beaches on either side of the isthmus.

La Chaumine – *36 Place du Manémeur, Quiberon.* ℘*02 97 50 17 67. Closed 10–31 Mar, 3 Nov–16 Dec, Sun eve low season and Mon.* Known for its inventive cuisine: try oysters au gratin with Muscatel and hazelnuts.

ACTIVITIES
Sofitel Thalasso Quiberon – *pointe de Goulvar.* ℘*02 97 50 20 00.* Sea-water swimming pools and all the spa treatments you could want.

SHOPPING
La Quiberonnaise – *30 rue du Port-de-Pêche, Port Maria.* ℘*02 97 50 12 54. www.laquiberonnaise.fr. Closed Sun.* This well-known cannery has a shop not far from the port: sardines, tuna, mackerel, anchovies.

BEACHES
ÎLE D'HOUAT AND ÎLE DE HŒDIC
Many beaches are hidden in the little creeks of Houat: in the west, there's Treac'h er Venigued and in the east, Treac'h er Goured.

Belle-Île★★★

The largest of the Breton islands is a schist plateau measuring about 84sq km/35sq mi. Its name alone is enticing, yet its beauty surpasses expectation. Valleys cut deeply into the high rocks forming beaches or harbours; wheat fields alternate with patches of gorse and whitewashed houses stand in lush fields.

A BIT OF HISTORY

Fouquet, Marquis of Belle-Île – Superintendent Fouquet bought Belle-Île in 1658, completed the fortifications and added 50 cannons. His immense wealth supported his own fleet and its flagship, the *Grand Écureuil*. But his daring behaviour, swindles and slights practised on Louis XIV were his undoing. The final act was played out at Nantes, where the Court was visiting in 1661. D'Artagnan and the Musketeers seized Fouquet as he came out of the castle and put him in a coach, which took him to Vincennes.

A fortified rock – Being the sole island between the Channel and the Mediterranean with fresh water in abundance, Belle-Île was attacked many times by British and Dutch fleets. The British captured the island twice – in 1572 and 1761 – and occupied it until the Treaty of Paris (1763) returned it to the French. The island has conserved its defensive system: in addition to Le Palais citadel, fortified by the military architect Vauban, there are several 18C and 19C isolated redoubts around the coast.

Acadians and Bretons – In 1766, 78 Acadian families came to live on the island; they brought with them the potato many years before Parmentier introduced it to France. These Acadians were descendants of the French who had lived in Canada since the beginning of the 17C and had refused to submit to the English, who had held Nova Scotia from the time of the Treaty of Utrecht (1713).
The Acadian families were moved to New England and then, after the Treaty of Paris, were moved by Louis XV to Belle-Île.

▶ **Population:** 4,489.
◔ **Michelin Map:** Local map 308 L10/11 – Morbihan (56).
▯ **Info:** Quai Bonnelle, 56360 Le Palais. ℘02 97 31 81 93. www.belle-ile.com.
◔ **Location:** The island is situated about 20km12.5/mi S of the Presqu'île de Quiberon and is reached by ferry.
◔ **Timing:** Walks – or sunbathing – on the beaches.
◔ **Don't Miss:** Citadelle Vauban, the charming port of Sauzon.

GETTING THERE

The Société Morbihannaise de Navigation (℘08 20 05 60 00 (0.12€/min), www.smn-navigation.fr) links **Quiberon** and **Le Palais** (passengers and vehicles), year-round. Departures from **Lorient** mid-Jun–end Aug.

GETTING AROUND

BY BUS – From *quai Bonnelle*, *℘02 97 31 32 32*. Four lines run between Sauzon, Bangor and Locmaria via beaches and main sights. About seven round trips a day in summer.
Locatourisle (*℘02 97 31 83 56, www.locatourisle.com*) is a car rental agency at the landing stand in Le Palais.
Roue Libre (*6 quai J. Le Blanc, Le Palais*, *℘02 97 31 49 81. www.belle-ile-evasion.com*) rents off-road bikes, tandems and child trailers. From ☞7€.

LE PALAIS
Allow 2hr.
The island's capital and main town is where most of the facilities are to be found. Inhabitants call it simply Palais.

Citadelle Vauban★
*Cross the mobile footbridge over the lock, go through Bourg gate and follow the path along the **huge moat**, cut from the rock itself, as far as Donjon*

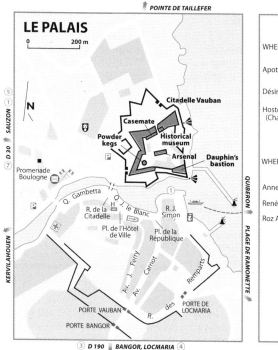

LE PALAIS

POINTE DE TAILLEFER

0   200 m

N

Citadelle Vauban

Casemate

Powder kegs

Historical museum

Arsenal

Dauphin's bastion

Promenade Boulogne

Q. Gambetta

Q. J. le Blanc

R. de la Citadelle

R. J. Simon

Pl. de l'Hôtel de Ville

Pl. de la République

Av. J. Ferry

Av. Carnot

R. des Remparts

PORTE VAUBAN

PORTE BANGOR

PORTE DE LOCMARIA

SAUZON

D 30

KERVILAHOUEN

QUIBERON

PLAGE DE RAMONETTE

D 190   BANGOR, LOCMARIA

WHERE TO STAY

Apothicairerie (Hôtel L')......①

Désirade (Hôtel La)..............③

Hostellerie La Touline (Chambre d'hôtes)............⑤

WHERE TO EAT

Annexe (L').................................①

Renée (Crêperie Chez)........④

Roz Avel.......................................⑦

gate. A signposted tour takes visitors past all the sights of the citadel. ⏱Open Jul–Aug, daily 9am–7pm; Apr–Jun and Sept–Oct, 9.30am–6pm; Nov–Mar, 9.30am–noon, 2pm–5pm. ⏱Guided tours (1hr) Jun–Sept. ☞6.50€. ☎02 97 31 84 17. www.citadellevauban.com.

Built in 1549, the citadel was enlarged by the Duke Gondi de Retz and Fouquet. Its double ramparts, powerful corner bastions and outward appearance show the influence of Vauban, who resided here in 1683, 1687 and 1689. Besieged at the end of the Seven Years' War, it fell into the hands of the English, who occupied it until the signing of the Treaty of Paris (1763). It was subsequently abandoned by the army and sold in 1960.

The most remarkable buildings include: the **historical museum**, set up in the Louis-Philippe blockhouses featuring "maple leaf" vaulting and displaying a host of documents on the history of Belle-Île and its illustrious visitors (Arletty, Claude Monet, Sarah Bernhardt); the **round powder magazine** and its strange acoustics; the large **arsenal** with superb oak timbering; the

Louis XIII **storerooms**; the **blockhouse** which contains the map room; finally the military prison and the cells.

The **Bastion de la Mer** and the **Bastion du Dauphin** afford remarkable **views**★ of Le Palais, the north coast and its harbour, the Île de Houat and the Île d'Hœdic.

🚗 DRIVING TOURS

1 LA CÔTE SAUVAGE DE BELLE-ÎLe★★★

Round tour of 49km/30.5mi – about 3hr 30min.

▷ *Leave Le Palais on Quai Gambetta and Promenade Boulogne and turn right towards the citadel. Near the coast, bear left and then right.*

Pointe de Taillefer

Near the signal station there is a fine **view** over Le Palais roadstead, the Pointe de Kerdonis, Hœdic and Houat Islands and the Presqu'île de Quiberon.

Turn round and make for Sauzon.

Nearby is **Port-Fouque** with a pretty, sheltered beach.

Sauzon★
This small port with its busy marina lies in a pretty **setting**★ on the east bank of the River Sauzon's estuary. A pleasant excursion *(1hr 30min on foot there and back)* starting from the port, takes you round the **Pointe du Cardinal** and affords views over the approach to the port, the Pointe de Taillefer, the Presqu'île de Quiberon and the Pointe des Poulains.

Pointe des Poulains★★★
30min on foot there and back.
From the car park, on the left is Fort Sarah Bernhardt, which is near the estate where the actress spent her summers. Make your way down the slip to the sandy isthmus which connects the island with the *Pointe des Poulains* on which stands a lighthouse and which is completely cut off at spring tide. From the point there is a vast **panorama**★.
The **Villa Lysiane**, which was named after the actress' granddaughter, is now the site reception centre, housing the reception, ticket office, shop and temporary exhibitions (open Jul–Aug, 10.30am–5.30pm; Apr–Jun and Sept, except Mon, 10.30am–5.30pm; free of charge; ℘ 02 97 31 61 29).
From here, a path leads you down to the Villa des Cinq Parties du Monde and the Fort Sarah-Bernhardt, which make up the Musée Sarah Bernardt.

Musée Sarah Bernhardt★★
Jul– Aug, 10.30am– 5.30pm; Apr–Jun and Sept, daily except Fri 10.30am–5.30pm. 4 € (14-17 yrs, 2 €). ℘ 02 97 31 61 29
The **Villa des Cinq Parties du Monde** was built for Sarah's son Maurice. Nowadays an entertaining exhibition with an audioguide narrated by Fanny Ardent introduces you to the great actress' extraordinary personality and tumultuous personal life, and above all, her relationship to the island and its inhabitants. In the **Fort de Sarah-Bernhardt**, which was where the actress lived when she was on the island, the décor has been recreated so successfully that you expect Sarah Bernhardt to walk through the door in person. The table is laid, and through the picture window you can see the lighthouse and the waves crashing on the rocks. A defensive system consisting of several of these little forts was built in the 1830s, and other examples can be seen on the island.

Musée Sarah Bernhardt

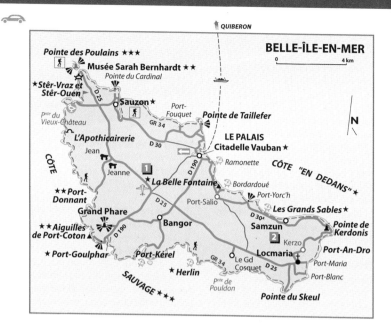

BELLE-ÎLE-EN-MER

From the fort, you carry on along the Chemin des Poulains to the lighthouse, across a little beach of white pebbles that can be submerged at high tide.
In the **lighthouse**, a warden will tell you about the rich natural environment of the headland.
🚶 From the Pointe des Poulains, you can follow the magnificent coastline on foot via the GR 34 hiking path, which initially skirts the edge of a golf course.

Port-Goulphar

©Bathilde Chaboche/Office de Tourisme de Belle Ile en Mer

Stêr-Vraz and Stêr-Ouen★

These *abers* cutting deeply into the coastline are at the foot of the **bird sanctuary** on the Pointe du Vieux-Château.
On Kerlédan Moor stand the menhirs **Jean and Jeanne**, said to be young fiancés punished because they wanted to meet before their wedding day.

Port-Donnant★★

30min on foot there and back. 🅿.
The setting is superb: a fine sandy beach and a rolling sea enclosed between high cliffs. ⚠*Bathing is dangerous.*

Grand Phare

🕐*Open 10 Jul–Aug, daily 10am–1pm, 3–5pm.* 🎟2€.
The lighthouse, opened near Goulphar in 1836, is 46m high and has a beam which carries 44.5km. From the balcony there is a fine **view**★★ of Belle-Île, the neighbouring islands and the coast as far as the Presqu'île de Rhuys.

🚶 Port-Goulphar★

This is one of the most charming sites on the island. After Goulphar manor house, take a steep road downhill *(15min on foot there and back)* to the port – a

Aiguilles de Port-Coton

©Bathilde Chaboche/Office de Tourisme de Belle Île en Mer

long, narrow channel at the foot of picturesque cliffs. A group of islets marks its entrance. The best view of this curious mass of rocks is from the cliff.

Aiguilles de Port-Coton★★
Port-Coton is called so because the sea there seems to boil and builds up a great mass of foam like cotton wool. At the end of the road loom the **Aiguilles** (Needles).

Bangor
The most primitive sites on the island are found in this village. It takes its name from Bangor Abbey (Northern Ireland), which was one of the most well known in Western Christianity, and from which came the first Celtic monks to settle on the island in the 6C.
In a rocky setting lies **Port-Kérel**, the most popular beach on the island.

▷ *Return to Le Palais.*

② POINTE DE KERDONIS★
Round trip of 33km/20.5mi – about 2hr.

▷ *Leave Le Palais by avenue Carnot and rue Villaumez on the left.*

The first part of this tour is devoted to seeing different beaches. Backing onto the point of the same name is the **Plage de Ramonette**.

▷ *At the entrance to Port-Salio, turn left, then 250m/273yds further, turn left again to reach La Belle Fontaine.*

This reservoir was created under Vauban's orders, to provide fresh water to high-ranking ships.

▷ *Turn back and bear left.*

The **Plage de Bordardoué** is a beautiful beach and perfect for families.

▷ *Turn round and bear left twice.*

The road descends towards **Port-Yorc'h** closed in by the Pointe du Bugul to the right and the Pointe du Gros Rocher to the left, which is extended by an islet on which an old fort stands. The road from Port-Yorck to the Pointe de Kerdonis commands superb **views**★★ over Houat and Le Palais roadstead.
The largest beach on Belle-Île is **les grands sables**, with traces of fortifications erected in 1747. In the 17C and 18C British and Dutch forces made several attempts to land on the island.

Pointe de Kerdonis
At the southern tip of the island stands a lighthouse which commands the sea lane between Hœdic and Belle-Île. Nearby is **Port-An-Dro**, a sandy beach off a small valley where the English forces landed in 1761.

Locmaria

The village is reputed among the island-ers as a place where sorcery occurs. A downhill road to the right of the church leads to **Port-Maria**, a deep cleft in the rocks which offers a fine sandy beach at low tide. Slightly further south, the cliffs of Arzic Point overlook the small cove of **Port-Blanc**.

ADDRESSES

STAY

 Hôtel L'Apothicairerie – *Sauzon 56360.* 02 97 31 62 62. *www.hotel apothicairerie.com. Open from Easter to Nov school hols. 38 rooms.* This modern hotel should be appreciated for its location on a rocky outcrop, rather than its intrinsic beauty. Its light and bright rooms enable guests to thoroughly enjoy the calm of this place.

 Chambre d'hôtes Hostellerie La Touline – *rue du Port-Vihan, 56360 Sauzon.* 02 97 31 69 69. *www.hostellerielatouline.com. Closed Nov–Mar. 5 rooms.* 13€. This fisherman's house hides charming antique-filled rooms with pretty names (Capitanine, Zanzibar etc.) behind its blue façade. The terrace overlooks the intimate garden. Solarium and jacuzzi.

 Hôtel La Désirade – *Rte de Port-Goulphar, 56360 Bangor.* 02 97 31 70 70. *www.hotel-la-desirade. com. Closed 4 Jan–30 Mar and 4 Nov–26 Dec. 24 rooms.* 16€. The rooms, set in three of the four pink houses with blue shutters that surround the pool, are spacious, comfortable and nicely decorated. The day's menu is served in the rustic dining room or on the terrace.

EAT

 Crêperie Chez Renée – *21 rue Sarah Bernhardt, 56360 Bangor.* 02 97 31 52 87. *Closed Mon–Thu off season.* This isolated former farmhouse, surrounded by fields, looks like a doll's house with its colourful rooms and shady terrace. Reservations are recommended.

Pointe du Skeul

Follow the unsurfaced road after Skeul hamlet.
This headland is a semicircle of jagged rocks in a wild setting.

 Return to the main road and Le Pailais, but make a slight detour to see the Acadian village, Grand-Cosquet.

 L'Annexe – *3 quai Yser, 56360 Le Palais.* 02 97 31 81 53. *Closed Mar, Mon and Tue from Nov–Feb and Wed.* The atmosphere is friendly, the service is quick and informal. People come here for the quality of the grilled seafood.

 Roz Avel – *56360 Sauzon.* 02 97 31 61 48. *Closed 1 Jan–15 Mar, 11 Nov–15 Dec and Wed. Reservations obligatory.* Behind the church, this traditional old house filled with Breton furniture is well loved by locals who like to catch rays on the terrace or enjoy seafood in the dining room.

SHOPPING

Biscuiterie La Bien Nommée – *ZA de Bordilla, 56360 Le Palais.* 02 97 31 34 99. *www.labiennommee.com.* Proudly carrying the name of the island on which it was founded, this family-run biscuit shop offers a range of old-fashioned products without colourings or additives. Free tours and tastings.

Le Grenier de Manon – *8 pl. de l'Hôtel de Ville, 56360 Le Palais.* 06 83 15 14 24. *Open Apr–Sept, 10am–1pm, 4pm–7.30pm.* Annick Lorec, an archaeologist mad about arts and crafts, has turned herself into a lace-maker with lightning-quick fingers. In front of your eyes, she makes napkins, tablecloths and bed linen, as well as offering courses.

Rivière d'Étel

This short river, which forms a bay west of the Quiberon Peninsula, follows a course that covers 15km/9mi from its source to the sea, yet the banks are so winding that they would measure 100km/62mi if stretched straight. These endless curves make the river banks a lovely place to enjoy nature.

Oysters have been farmed here since 1890. The oyster shells are a greenish-blue colour and have an interesting flavour often described as hazelnut-like.

SIGHTS
Étel
The river is known for its treacherous bank of quicksand *(barre)*, which offers a spectacular scene in bad weather. Navigation is difficult, even in good weather, and requires constant surveillance.

The view extends over Groix Island, Belle-Île and the Quiberon peninsula. The small fishing port of **Étel** lies on the river's south bank. It is home to a fleet of about ten fishing boats, which sail to the Azores, and a small fleet of trawlers, which fish along the coast.

Pont-Lorois
This short and pretty run gives a glimpse of the wide estuary, which on the left opens out into a bay and on the right narrows into a deep channel which winds down to the sea.

LEFT BANK
St-Cado
Located on an island linked to the mainland by a dyke, this hamlet with its little fishermen's houses make a charming Breton **scene**★, especially at high tide. Chapelle St-Cado is one of the few Romanesque buildings in the Morbihan with unornamented rounded arches, plainly decorated capitals and dim lighting.

It is in this chapel that the deaf sought help from St Cado, whose stone bed and pillow can still be seen. **Pointe du Verdon**.

- **Michelin Map:** Local map 308 K/L 8/9 - Morbihan (56).
- **Info:** place des Thoniers, 56410 Étel. 02 97 55 23 80.
- **Location:** The river separates Quiberon from Lorient. From Nostang, the D 158 follows the right bank while the D 16 gives access to the many little villages off the left bank.
- **Timing:** You can visit the area for a couple of hours but it's so pretty, you'll probably want to take your time.
- **Don't Miss:** St-Cado harbour for its charming fishermen's houses and the church at Merlevenez for its doorway.

As with all the points of the bay, the far end of the Pointe du Verdon is devoted to oyster farming; after crossing the isthmus and before taking the uphill road through the pines, bear right to reach a platform from which there is a fine view over the oyster beds. At low tide it is possible to walk round the point.

RIGHT BANK
Presqu'île de Nestadio
This village has some 16C houses. At the end of the peninsula, stands a small chapel dedicated to St-Guillaume.

Pointe de Mané-Hellec
By a small transformer station, turn left onto a surfaced road.
From here there is a lovely view of St-Cado and its chapel, Pont-Lorois, the River Étel and the Forêt de Locoal-Mendon.

Ste-Hélène
This village is known for its fountain where sailors used to come in pilgrimage before going to sea. If the bit of bread they threw in the fountain floated, it meant they would come back safe and sound from their fishing trip.

Merlevenez★

This little town's **church**★ is one of the few Romanesque churches in Brittany which has kept intact its elegant doorways with chevron and saw-tooth archivolts, its depressed arches in the nave, its historiated capitals and dome on squinches rising above the transept crossing. Modern stained-glass windows by Grüber illustrate scenes from the Life of the Virgin.

There is a fountain in Sainte-Hélène where local seamen used to come and pray before going to sea. Each one would throw a piece of soft bread into the fountain (&see above).

ADDRESSES

⌂STAY

⌂⌂**Hôtel Le Trianon** – *14 rue du Gen. de Gaulle. ℘02 97 55 32 41. Closed Jan, 5–20 Nov, Sun eve, Fri eve and Sat off season. 24 rooms. ⌂10€. Restaurant*⌂⌂. Pleasant rooms near the harbour – those in the adjoining villa are preferable. There's a lounge to relax in and a rustic dining room where traditional food is served in a welcoming atmosphere.

Port-Louis★

Port-Louis is a small fishing port and seaside resort popular with the inhabitants of Lorient. It still has its 16C citadel, 17C ramparts, as well as several interesting old houses. The town also has two fishing harbours: Locmalo in Gâvres cove and, opposite Lorient, La Pointe, a marina which has been equipped with 200 moorings for yachts.

A BIT OF HISTORY

Port-Louis was originally called Blavet. During the League, the Duke of Mercœur captured it with the help of the Spaniards. Forty young girls fled in a ship, but the Spaniards saw them and gave chase. Rather than be taken by the victorious enemy, all 40 girls joined hands and jumped into the sea.

It was under Louis XIII that Blavet took the name of Port-Louis in honour of the King. Richelieu made it a fortified port and the headquarters of the first India Company, which failed. When Colbert founded the second India Company, Lorient was built to receive it.

From that time on, Port-Louis declined. Under Louis-Philippe the town found new life in sardine fishing and canning in oil.

▷ **Population:** 2,980.
🜨 **Michelin Map:** Local map 308 8K – Morbihan (56).
▯ **Info:** 1, rue le Citadelle, 56290 Port-Louis. ℘02 97 84 78 00. www.lorient-tourisme.fr.
▷ **Location:** Opposite Lorient, the village is accessible by the D 781.
🕐 **Timing:** Allow a morning for exploration.
🜨 **Don't Miss:** The citadelle tower and the India Company Museum.

SIGHTS
Citadelle★

The citadel is at the entrance to the Lorient roadstead. Its construction occurred in different stages: in 1591, during the Spanish occupation by Juan del Aguila; continued in 1616–22, by Marshal Brissac and completed in 1636 under Richelieu. Built on a rectangular plan, the citadel is bastioned at the corners and sides; two bridges and a demilune protect the entrance. The citadel has always been a prison – among its 'occupants' was Louis Napoleon, the future Emperor Napoleon III.

A signposted path directs you to the parapet walk (note the cannons facing the Île de Groix) which looks onto two courtyards and the different parts of the edifice, some of which contain museums, the **Musées de la Citadelle** (🕐 open May–Aug, daily 10am–6.30pm; Feb–Apr and Sept–mid Dec, Wed–Mon 1.30pm–6pm; 🕐 closed mid Dec–mid Jan; ✆5.50€; ✆02 97 82 56 72. www.musee-marine.fr).

Citadelle

G. Targat/MICHELIN

Musée de la Compagnie des Indes★★

Housed in the new wing of the Lourmel barracks, this India Company Museum traces the history of this prestigious company from the founding of Lorient, its expansion in the 18C, its crews, cargoes, trading posts (in India, Africa, China), maps and engravings.

One gallery concentrates on the theme of the India Company's fleet: shipbuilding, cargoes, models of *Comte d'Artois* (with cargo and passengers) and *Comte de Provence* (both built in the Lorient shipyards).

Espace du Sauvetage en Mer

This museum traces the history of sea rescue in France from its origins in the middle of the 19C. Don't miss the lifeboat, *Commandant Philippes de Kerhallet,* manned by 12 oarsmen, built in Le Havre in 1857 and used between 1897 and 1939 at Roscoff.

Trésors d'Océans★

This museum focuses on the exciting finds that have been made by divers, notably Franck Goddio.

Pavillon de l'Arsenal – Musée de la Marine

Housed in the Arsenal, in a room which has fine woodwork, ship's models (corvettes, frigates, merchant ships, cruisers, etc.), portraits of seamen, paintings and documents pertaining to navigation on the Atlantic are on display. Reduced model of the Napoleon's (launched in Cherbourg in 1850) engine room.

Poudrière – Musée des Armes

The former Powder Factory contains 17C–20C arms and documents on naval artillery.

Ramparts

Built between 1649 and 1653 by Marshal Meilleraye, these ramparts envelop the town on two sides. On Promenade des Pâtis, a door in the wall leads to a fine sandy beach from where there is a view onto the Pointe de Gâvres, Île de Groix and Larmor-Plage.

It is well worth walking along rue de la Poste, rue des Dames, Petite Rue and rue du Driasker to see the interesting **old houses**.

EXCURSION
Riantec

This village on the shores of Gâvres lagoon is the popular with people looking for shellfish. The **Maison de l'île de Kerner** (🕐 open Jul–Aug, daily 10am–7pm; Apr–Jun and Sept, Tue–Fri 9am–12.30pm, 2pm–6pm, Sat, Sun 2pm–6pm; Easter and Nov school hols, 9am–12.30pm, 2pm–6pm, Mon 2pm–6pm; 🕐 closed 18 Dec–15 Jan; ✆4.10€; ✆02 97 84 51 49; www.maison-kerner.com) offers an insight into the local natural environment, including numerous migrating birds and oyster beds thrive. The botanical gardens contain a selection of salt-meadow and dune plants.

Lorient

The modern city of Lorient boasts proudly of being the site of five ports: the fishing port of Keroman; a military port, with dockyard and submarine base (capacity for 30 submarines); a passenger port, with ships crossing the roadstead and sailing to the Île de Groix; the Kergroise commercial port, which specialises in the importing of animal foodstuffs; and the Kernevel pleasure boat harbour, with a wet dock located in the centre of the city: it is the starting point for transatlantic competition. An annual Interceltic Festival (Festival Interceltique, *see Calendar of Events*) is held in Lorient.

A BIT OF HISTORY

The India Company – After the first India Company, founded by Richelieu at Port-Louis, failed, Colbert revived the project in 1664 at Le Havre. But as the Company's ships were too easily captured in the Channel by the British, it was decided to move its headquarters to the Atlantic coast. The choice fell on "vague and vain" plots of land located on the right bank of the Scorff. Soon afterwards, what was to be known as the 'Compound of the India Company' was born. Since all maritime activities

▶ **Population:** 116,174.

Michelin Map: Local map 308 KB - Morbihan (56).

Info: 6 quai de Rohan, 56100 Lorient. ☎02 97 84 78 00. www.lorient-tourisme.fr.

Location: The N 165 is to the north of the town.

Kids: *La Thalassa* fishing trawler and exhibition; Pont-Scorff Zoo.

Timing: Use the Batobus: very practical and pleasant "boat-buses" with six itineraries.

Parking: A modern town, there are plenty of car parks – the first half-hour is free in blue zones.

Don't Miss: The great parades and festivities during the Interceltic Festival in August.

were focused on India and China, the installations built on that site bore the name *l'Orient* (French for the East). In those days, the arrogant motto of the India Company – *Florebo quocumque ferar* (I shall prosper wherever I go) – was fully justified by the flourishing trade which it exercised. But a new naval war

Lorient harbour

© Photononstop/Tips Images

GETTING AROUND

BY BUS – The CTRL *(Compagnie des transports de la région lorientaise)* serves Lorient and 19 villages in its surroundings. ℘*02 97 21 28 29, www.ctrl.fr.*

BY BATOBUS – The CTRL also offers six boat links – very useful to go from one shore to the other of the harbour.

Every day of the year, except for line 5 (Sun only).

BY BIKE – There are 62km of cycle paths in Lorient and its surroundings. Rent bikes from the Tourist Office or at *Transports et Déplacements, gare d'échange, cours de Chazelles.* ℘*02 97 21 28 29.*

---

loomed ahead, so Seignelay turned the "Compound" into a royal dockyard patronised by the most famous privateers (Beauchêne, Duguay-Trouin).

In the 18C, under the stimulus of the well-known Scots financier Law, business grew rapidly; 60 years after its foundation, the town already had 18 000 inhabitants. The loss of India brought the Company to ruin, and in 1770 the State took over the port and its equipment. Napoleon turned it into a naval base.

During WW II, Lorient was occupied by the Germans on 25 June 1940. From 27 September 1940 the city was subject to bombardments, which intensified as the war raged on, culminating in a hugely destructive offensive in August 1944. The fighting between the entrenched German garrison and the Americans and locally based Free French Forces, which encircled the Lorient "pocket", devastated the surrounding area. When the townspeople returned on 8 May, 1945, all that greeted them was a scene of utter desolation.

VISIT
Ancien Arsenal

Until 2000, the naval dockyard was located in the former India Company's area; four docks were used for the repair of warships. Abandoned by the navy, the area is being modernised. The Breton television channel Breizh has located its headquarters along quai du Péristyle.

Église Notre-Dame-de-Victoire

Better known to the locals as the church of St-Louis, it stands in place Alsace-Lorraine, itself a successful example

of modern town planning. The church is built in reinforced concrete and has very plain lines. It is square with a flattened cupola roof and a square tower flanking the façade. The beauty of the church lies in its **interior**⋆. Little panes of yellow and clear glass reflect light into the building from the top of the rotunda, and the bays in the lower section consist of brightly coloured splintered glass.

Enclos du Port de Lorient

Enter through the 'Porte Gabriel'. Information on tours available from the Tourist Office: ℘*02 97 21 07 84. www.lorient-tourisme.fr.*

A tour of the dockyards recalls the heyday of the India Company: the Hôtel des Ventes, built by Gabriel in 1740, has been entirely restored in the original style. The **Tour de la Découverte** (1737), flanked by the Admirality mills (1677), once served as a watchtower. Climb the 225 steps to enjoy the superb **view**⋆ of the roadstead.

La Thalassa

Quai de Rohan. ⊙*Open Jul–Aug, 10am–7pm; Sept–Jun, daily Tue–Fri 9am–12.30pm, 2pm–6pm, Sat, Sun, Mon 2pm–6pm. Last entry 1hr 30min before closing.* ⊙*Closed 18 Dec–15 Jan.* ⊛*6.90€ (children 5.30€).* ℘*02 97 21 10 14. www.sellor.com.*

After sailing the seas of the world (nearly 38 times round the globe), this ship, launched in 1960 by Ifremer, is enjoying well-deserved retirement in Lorient. A tour of the three decks gives visitors a good idea of life on board, techniques of navigation, trawler fishing and oceanographic research. The tour continues on

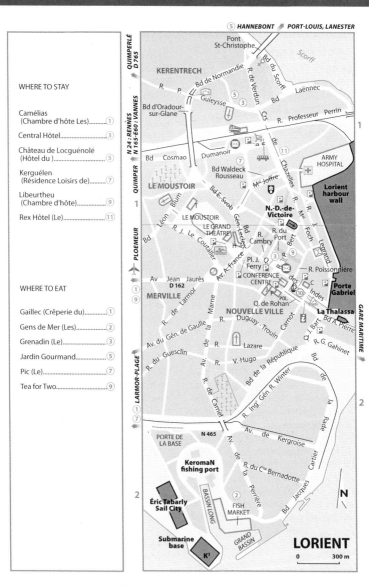

WHERE TO STAY

Camélias
(Chambre d'hôte Les)...........①
Central Hôtel..........................③
Château de Locguénolé
(Hôtel du)............................⑤
Kerguélen
(Résidence Loisirs de).........⑦
Libeurtheu
(Chambre d'hôte).................⑨
Rex Hôtel (Le).........................⑪

WHERE TO EAT

Gaillec (Crêperie du)..............①
Gens de Mer (Les)...................②
Grenadin (Le)...........................③
Jardin Gourmand.....................⑤
Pic (Le).....................................⑦
Tea for Two..............................⑨

LORIENT

0   300 m

land with an exhibition devoted to the fishing industry in Lorient.

Port de Pêche de Keroman

Best seen in the morning when the fishermen return with the day's catch (depending on the tide).

Partly reclaimed from the sea, the port of Keroman is the only French harbour designed and equipped for commercial fishing; it is the leading port in France for the value and variety of fish landed.

It has two basins set at right angles: the **Grand Bassin** and the **Bassin Long** (totalling 1,850m/1.1mi of docks). The Grand Bassin is sheltered by a jetty 250m/273yds long which is used by cargo steamers and trawlers. The basin has two other quays, one with a refrigerating and cold-storage plant for the trawlers and fish dealers; and the other, as well as the quay at the east end of the Bassin Long, where the trawlers unload their catch. In front of the quays is the

600m/655yds long **market hall** (criée) where auctions are held, and, close behind it, the fish dealers' warehouses which open onto the car park, where lorries destined for the rest of France are loaded. There is also a **slipway** with six bays where trawlers can be dry-docked or repaired.

The port of Keroman sends out ships for all kinds of fishing throughout the year. The largest vessels go to sea for a fortnight, and carry their own ice-making equipment (which can make up to 400t a day) to the fishing grounds.

Ancienne Base de Sous-marins Stosskopf★

Entrance by the Porte de Keroman.
Guided tours (1hr 15min) Jul–Aug and school holidays daily 12.30pm–5.30pm. Closed 1 May and 25 Dec.
7.50€. *02 97 84 78 00.*
www.lorient-tourisme.fr.

The submarine base is named in honour of a WW II maritime engineer who, by appearing to collaborate with the Germans, was able to keep abreast of activities on the base and inform Allies. When he was discovered, he was executed.

The three blocks were built in record time. The first two (1941) have slots for 13 submarines. The third (1943) has a reinforced concrete roof 7.5m/24.5ft thick. At the end of World War II, the French Navy took over the base for their Atlantic submarine operations, but have since abandoned it for this purpose. The last dry-dock operation took place in December 1996, and the *Sirène*, the last active submarine, left the base for the Toulon port in February 1997. The *Flore* is the only ship remaining; it has no military purpose but is kept up for display between blocks one and two. The Navy has progressively turned over the dockyards to the city of Lorient and various projects for the use of the area are underway or being considered.

EXCURSIONS
Larmor-Plage⌂

6km/3.7mi S of Lorient by the D 29.
Looking out over the ocean, across from Port-Louis, Larmor-Plage has lovely, fine, sandy beaches much appreciated by the people of Lorient.

The parish **church**, built in the 12C, was remodelled until the 17C. The 15C porch, uncommonly situated on the north façade because of the prevailing winds, contains statues of the Apostles and above the door a 16C painted wood Christ in Fetters.

The old road from Larmor follows the coast fairly closely, passing many small seaside resorts. After Kerpape the drive affords extensive views of the coast of Finistère, beyond the cove of Le Pouldu and over to the Île de Groix.

In the foreground are the coastal inlets in which lie the little ports of Lomener, Perello Kerroch and Le Courégant and the large beach of **Fort-Bloqué** dominated by a fort (privately owned). Go through **Guidel-Plages** on the Laïta estuary. From Guidel make for the Pont de St-Maurice (6km/3.7mi there and back) over the Laïta. The **view**★ up the enclosed valley is magnificent.

Hennebont

17km/10.5mi NE of Lorient.
Route passes through Lanester.
Hennebont is a former fortified town on the steep banks of the River Blavet *(good fishing)*.

The 16C basilica, **Basilique Notre-Dame-de-Paradis**, has a big **bell-tower**★ and is surmounted by a steeple 65m high. At the base of the tower is a fine flamboyant porch ornamented with niches leading into the nave, which is lit up by a stained-glass window by Max Ingrand.

Pont-Scorff Zoo★

15km/9.3mi N of Lorient. Open *Jun–Aug, 9am–7pm; Oct–Mar, 9.30am–5pm; Apr, May and Sept, 9.30am–6pm.*
15.50€ (children 10€). *02 97 32 60 86.*

In a woodland setting on the steep banks of the Scarve, the zoo specialises in breeding big cats and houses 450 types of animals from around the world including five Asian elephants – a record in France. There are animal shows, too.

Plouay

The start point for the Tour de France and a must for cycling enthusiasts, with a Véloparc and bike museum.

ADDRESSES

🛏STAY

🛏 **Chambre d'hôte Libertheu** – *23 rue de l'anse de Stole, Lomener, 56270 Ploemeur.* ℘02 97 82 86 22. http://lelostec. demaret.free.fr/. ⇥ *3 rooms.* Neo-Breton house with old furniture in the lounge and breakfast room. The rooms are smallish and cosy. Delicious breakfast: a choice of breads and homemade jam.

🛏🛏 **Central Hôtel** – *1 rue Cambry.* ℘02 97 21 16 52. www.centralhotellorient.com. *21 rooms.* ⊑ 8€. Built in the 1950s, this hotel sits just opposite Jules-Ferry park. The rooms are brightly coloured with attractive furniture and good sound-proofing.

🛏🛏 **Le Rex-Hôtel** – *28 cours de Chazelles.* ℘02 97 64 25 60. www.rex-hotel-lorient.com. Closed 26 Dec–3 Jan. *23 rooms.* ⊑8€. This hotel, situated on a long avenue lined with plane trees, is regularly updated. Most rooms have been renovated: new bed linen, furniture and Internet access.

OUTSKIRTS

🛏 **Résidence Loisirs de Kerguélen** – *Parc océanique, 56 260 Larmor-Plage.* ℘02 97 33 77 78. www.sellor-nautisme. com. *38 rooms.* ⊑ 5.40 €. This residence offers a young, sporty atmosphere. Simple, comfortable, low-priced rooms. Meals available. Activities for all ages can be found nearby on the beach.

🛏🛏 **Chambre d'hôte Les Camélias** – *9 r. des Roseaux, 56 260 Larmor-Plage.* ℘02 97 65 50 67. Closed late Sept–early Oct. ⇥. *4 rooms.* ⊑. A garden of trees surrounds this pretty house. The rooms are very well presented with bourgeoise style furniture and ornaments.

🛏🛏🛏 **Château de Locguénolé** – *56 700 Hennebont.* ℘ 02 97 76 76 76. www.chateau-de-locguenole.com. Closed 4 Jan–13 Feb. *18 rooms.* ⊑ 20 €. *Restaurant.* Two historic houses located in a park of 148 hectares/20 acres.

Spacious, elegant rooms. A pleasant dining room where dishes cmbine the tastes of the sea and the *potager* (kitchen garden).

🍽EAT

🍽 **Tea For Two** – *23 r. Paul-Bert.* ℘ 02 97 64 27 70 . Closed last week Jan, 1–15 May, 1–15 Aug and Sun. You will love the atmosphere and the hot colours of this delightful salon de thé. Patisseries maison, assiettes gourmands, brunches and the teas have already acquired the Salon a solid reputation.

🍽 **Les Gens de mer** – *14 bd Louis Nail.* ℘ 02 97 37 11 28. www.lesgensdemer.fr. Closed Sun eve. Opposite the port of Keroman and frequented by locals you can enjoy seafood at low prices.

🍽🍽 **Le Grenadin** – *7 rue Paul-Guieysse.* ℘02 97 64 30 01. http://legrenadin.free.fr. Closed first week of Jan, three weeks in Jul, Sun eve, Wed eve and Mon. This small traditional restaurant near the train station is renowned for the quality of its ingredients, mainly sourced from the sea. Contemporary décor and atmosphere.

🍽🍽🍽 **Le Jardin Gourmand** – *46 rue Jules Simon.* ℘02 97 64 17 24. www.jardingourmand.fr. Closed Feb school holidays, 22 Aug–15 Sept, Sun eve, Mon and Tue. A beautiful dining room with caramel-coloured furniture and a small terrace at one end; the cuisine is light and delicious. Good wine list.

🍽🍽🍽 **Le Pic** – *2 blvd. du Maréchal Franchet d'Esperey.* ℘02 97 21 18 29. www.restaurant-lepic.com. Closed Wed eve, Sat lunch and Sun. Behind an elegant façade, lies an old-fashioned setting and pub atmosphere for a traditional dishes based on the catch of the day.

OUTSKIRTS

🍽 **Crêperie du Gaillec** – *Hameau de Gaillec, 56 270 Ploemeur.* ℘ 02 97 83 00 26. creperie-gaillec@wanadoo.fr. Closed 1st week Jun and 1st 3 weeks Oct. Getting to this old farm may not be easy, but it is well worth the effort. Savour the crêpes made from organic flour and local artisan products. On fine days you can eat under the pergola.

Pipers at the Interceltic Festival

R. Mattès/MICHELIN

☺ NIGHTLIFE

Tavarn Ar Roue Morvan – *1 place Polig-Monjarret. ✆02 97 21 61 57. Open Mon–Sat 11am–1am.* A Breton tavern through and through. Enjoy regional cuisine with regular live music.

Café du Port – *52 rue du Port. ✆02 97 21 87 41. Open Mon–Sat 11am–1am.* Despite its name, this café is actually on a pedestrian street. Breton beers and rum drinks are the specialities.

🎋 ACTIVITIES

Boat trips – To discover the bay or the Blavet river. *Batobus – ✆02 97 21 07 84 or Beateau Taxi – ✆02 97 65 52 52.*

Ar Ganol, la Nin'Arion – *Quai de Pont Augan (leave Gare de Baud towards Quistinic), 56440 Languidic. ✆02 97 36 93 18. www.ninarion.fr. Closed 1 Oct–15 Apr.* This barge built in Nantes (1903) takes visitors up the Blavet *(2hr)*. Commentary on the history of Breton canals.

Centre Nautique de Kerguelen – *parc Océanique, Larmor-Plage. ✆02 97 33 77 78. www.sellor-nautisme.com.* Windsurfing, diving and sea kayaking, all year. Rentals and lessons available.

Centre Nautique de Port-Louis – *plage des Grands Sables. ✆02 97 82 18 60.* Sea garden (children from 4 years old) in summer, lessons and rental of catamarans, windsurfers, sea kayaks.

🎭 FESTIVALS

Festival Interceltique – *2 rue Paul Bert. ✆02 97 64 03 20. www.festival-interceltique.com. First fortnight of Aug.*

The big annual gathering of the Celtic cultures attracts hundreds of thousands of spectators and thousands of Celtic artists from around the world.

Fêtes Médievales de Hennebont – *Last weekend of July.* Jugglers, knights, old Breton games, medieval feasts, archery workshops and a craft fair in the centre of town over this weekend.

Grand Prix Ouest de France – *Late August. www.comitesdesfetes-plouay.com.* Three days of cycling heaven for all levels of experience in Plouay.

🛒 SHOPPING

Biscuiterie La Lorientaise – *Rond-Point de Kernours, 56700 Kervignanc. ✆02 97 76 02 09. Closed public hols.* This shop sells galettes, madeleines and Breton cakes.

La Cour des Métiers d'Art – *8 rue Prince de Polignac, 56620 Pont-Scorff. ✆02 97 32 55 74. www.pont-scorff.com.* The work of craftsmen and women from across France: glass, pottery, porcelain.

Ar Gwasked – *pl. de l'Église. ✆02 98 48 88 42.* This interesting shop sells knick-knacks made from wool, including mobiles, earrings, slippers, postcards.

Ferme d'Autruches de la Saudraye – *La Haye, Guidel. ✆02 97 65 04 54. www.autruches.fr. Visit May–Oct 10am–8pm. Shop open year-round 10am–1pm.* A 40ha wooded area is home to 1,500 ostriches and emus. From May to October, you can observe the hatching of ostrich chicks. In addition to feathers and leather goods from the birds, the shop sells meat, pâté and ready meals.

Île de Groix★

Groix Island is smaller than its neighbour, Belle-Île, but has the same geological form – a mass of schist rock. The coast on the north and west is wild and deeply indented, with cliffs, giant rocks, valleys and creeks. The east and south sides are flatter, with many sheltered sandy creeks along the coast. Small villages dot cultivated fields and the vast expanses on which gorse and heather grow.

EXCURSIONS
Port-Tudy

Sheltered by two piers, this port offers a direct link with Lorient on the mainland. Formerly a tunny fishing port, it is now a safe harbour for trawlers and pleasure boats.

Housed in an early 20C canning factory, the ♔♔**Ecomusée de l'Île de Groix** (♔ see Address Book) presents interesting exhibits (explanatory panels, photographs) on the island's geography, history and ethnography.

The *Kenavo*, the last coastal fishing cutter built on the Île de Groix, can be hired for a boat trip round the island; contact the Tourist Office for details.

St-Tudy (le Bourg)

This is the island's capital with its low slate-roofed houses grouped round the church. The bell-tower is crowned by a tunny fish weather vane, recalling the island's great tunny fishing days of the early 1900s.

From **Port-Mélite**, a rocky cove with a beach, the view extends from the Étel Bar to the Pointe du Talut. The island's largest beach, **Plage des Grands Sables** is situated southeast of Port-Mélite, along a convex section of coastline.

Locmaria

Facing the open sea, this village, with its winding streets, has a small harbour, where fishing and pleasure boats seek shelter behind a jetty.

▶ **Population:** 2,275.
⬡ **Michelin Map:** Local map 308 K - Morbihan (56).
▮ **Info:** Quai de Port Tudy, 56590 Groix. ☎02 97 86 53 08. www.groix.fr.
◉ **Location:** 3km/1.8mi from the mainland. It is 8km/5mi long and 2–4km/1.2–2.5mi wide and divided into two: Primiture to the east, with its beaches, and Piwisy to the west, which is wilder.
♔♔ **Kids:** The Ecomuseum.
◔ **Timing:** Allow a day to visit.

GETTING THERE
BY BOAT – The **SMN** (*Société Morbihannaise de Navigation*), serves Groix (Port-Tudy) all year, departing from Lorient (45min, about 28€ there and back). Best to avoid taking a car – take a bike instead. ☎08 20 05 60 00 (0.12€/ min). www.smn-navigation.fr.

GETTING AROUND
In minibus – In July-Aug, the **Taxico** shuttle serves the island four times a day. Departure points in town: Primiture (east of the island) and Piwisy (west). Single ticket 1.10€.
Bike/Scooter/Car Rental – **Coconut's Location** – *Port-Tudy*. ☎02 97 86 81 57. Rental of bikes, off-road bikes, scooters and cars (Jeep and off-road utility vehicles).
Bikini Bike – *Port Tudy*. ☎02 97 86 85 12. Conveniently situated at the port, this place rents out bikes as well as a child-friendly tandem.

Pointe des Chats

On this point, the lowest part of the island, stands a small lighthouse with a fine view of the south coast. There is a **mineralogy reserve** where visitors can see garnets, needles of blue glaucophane and green lepidolite, but of course the taking of samples is strictly forbidden.

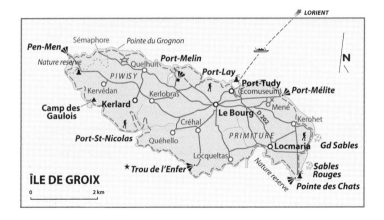

Trou de l'Enfer★

This deep opening (the Devil's Hole) in the cliff face, into which the sea surges with great force, is a wild barren site with a beautiful **view** of the Pointe St-Nicolas and the rocky coast.

Beyond Trou de l'Enfer, to the north-west, is **Port-St-Nicolas**, a large bay with deep, clear waters.

Pen-Men

The western tip of the island, to the right of Pen-Men Lighthouse, is a rocky headland, offering splendid views of the Morbihan coast extending from Talut Point to Port-Manech. This, the **Réserve Naturelle François Le Bail** (&see Address Book) is home to thousands of birds.

Plages des Grands Sables

This is the island's largest beach; garnets can sometimes be found in the sand.

Pointe de Biléric

Near the Beg-Melen signal station (⊶ closed to the public), many black-legged kittiwakes can be seen nesting in this bird sanctuary.

Port-Melin

The little creek can only be reached on foot down a steep slope.

ADDRESSES

STAY

⊖⊟ – ⊖⊟ **L'Escale** – 5 quai de Port-Tudy. ℘02 97 86 80 04. 7 rooms. ⊒ 7€. Located in front of the landing stage, this small establishment offers rooms with views over the harbour.

⊖⊟ **Chambre d'hôte La Grek** – 3 pl. du Leurhé, Le Bourg. ℘02 97 86 89 85. Closed Jan. ⊭. 4 rooms. This Art Deco style house gets its name from the nickname given to people from these parts. Its elegant, comfortable rooms have spacious bathrooms.

⊖⊟ **Hôtel de la Marine** – Le Bourg. ℘02 97 86 80 05. www.hoteldela marine.com. Closed Jan, Sun eve and Mon off season. 22 rooms. ⊒ 9.50€. Restaurant⊖⊟. Wood interior with a refined décor, rooms giving onto the terrace, the garden or the sea. The restaurant is popular and the welcome warm.

EAT

⊖ **L'Ocre Marine** – 22 rue de Tromor, Locmaria. ℘02 97 86 53 98. www.creperie -locremarine.com. A pleasant terrace where you can order a bottle of excellent cider to accompany crêpes made with organic flour.

⊖⊟ **Les Courreaux** – rue du Gén.-de-Gaulle, Port-Tudy. ℘02 97 86 82 66. 'Surf and Turf' specialities prepared with creative flair have made the reputation of this popular establishment.

Auberge du Pêcheur – *Port-Tudy.* ℰ*02 97 86 56 92. http://aubergedu pecheur.free.fr.* Tasty seafood cuisine served in an old house decorated with a collection of traditional coffee pots. Eight rooms are available (⊜⊜⊜).

ACTIVITIES

Walks – The coastal path, exclusively for pedestrians, goes all around the island (30km). To discover the rest of the island, nothing is better than a bike! Ask for the map *'Itinéraires de Découverte'* (for walkers and cyclists) at the Tourist Office.

Cycling – Cyclists and horse riders can enjoy 50km/31m of paths crossing the interior of the island, accessible to all, passing traces of prehistory, hamlets, lavoirs and fountains. There are several places to hire bikes with anti-theft devices, baby seats etc.

L'Écomusée de Groix – ℰ*02 97 86 84 60. http://ecomusee.groix.free.fr.* This museum offers different events all year long, devoted to discovering the island, the shipping trades and traditional fishing communities. You can learn about digging for shellfish, working on a sailing ship and rowing.

La Maison de la Réserve François Le Bail – *(behind Pen-Men; ℰ02 97 86 55 97; http://ile-de-groix.info/reserve)* offers various thematic trips and walks on the two sites of the game reserve: geology, ornithology, algae and fauna of the littoral.

La Roche-Bernard

This picturesque old town, on the spur of La Garenne, overlooks the River Vilaine. The port stands on a tributary of the river; the naval dockyards here were famous in the 17C. Formerly very prosperous due to its trade in wood, wheat, wine, salt and spices, the town is now a pleasure boat harbour (capacity for 300 boats).

A BIT OF HISTORY

A real Republican – The town of La Roche-Bernard welcomed the Revolution and opposed the Chouans. In 1793, 6,000 "Whites" (Royalists) easily defeated the 150 'Blues' (peasants) who were defending the town.
Mayor Sauveur refused to flee; he was imprisoned. He was ordered to shout, "Long live the King!" and he replied, "Long live the Republic!" He was shot down.
He became a hero of the Republic by decree; the town was named La Roche-Sauveur until 1802.

▶ **Population:** 761.
⬡ **Michelin Map:** Local map 308 R9 – Morbihan (56).
▯ **Info:** 14 rue du Dr-Cornudet, 56130 La Roche Bernard. ℰ02 99 90 67 98. www.cc-pays-la-roche-bernard.fr.
◖ **Location:** La Roche-Bernard is situated on the N 165, north of the Parc Régional de Brière, between Nantes and Vannes.
Kids: The animals and plants in Branféré.
◷ **Timing:** Allow half a day for the town and its environs.
◉ **Don't Miss:** Walks along the river Vilaine to Arzal dam and the view from pointe de Scal in Pénestin.

SIGHTS

Pont du Morbihan★

Located about 600m/655yds upriver from its predecessors, this bridge, inaugurated in 1996, is 376m/yds411 long and 21m/69ft wide. The roadway rests on an arch with a 200m/ft218yds span. Two footbridges enable visitors to stand more than 50m/164ft above the river and admire the breathtaking **view**⋆.

Viewpoint
At the hook of the road to La Baule, a rocky belvedere *(23 steps)* overlooks the Vilaine valley and its wooded slopes: on the right are the suspension bridges and on the left, the marina.

Old district
Across from the viewpoint and on the other side of the road begins **Promenade du Ruicard**, which overlooks the port. It goes into rue du Ruicard and leads through a maze of small streets, some of which are stepped. Houses of the 16C and 17C follow: numbers 6 and 8 are well restored, number 11 has an interesting doorway and number 12 has a turret.

Passage de la Quenelle, with its dormer windows surmounted by sculpted pediments, leads to **place Bouffay** where the guillotine stood in 1793. Situated on the square is the town hall, which is also known as the House of the Cannon (*Maison du Canon*) (1599) because of the cannon (from the *Inflexible* which sought refuge in the estuary after a sea battle) placed in the corner. On the left opens rue de la Saulnerie with a 15C house.

In rue Haute-Notre-Dame stands the small 11C Chapelle Notre-Dame, rebuilt in the 16C and 19C. The first church built in the city, it was converted into a Protestant church in 1561, and then used to store fodder during the Terror; it became Catholic once again in 1827.

Musée de la Vilaine Maritime
Open mid-Jun–mid-Sept, daily 10.30am–12.30pm, 2.30pm–6.30pm. 3€. 02 99 90 83 47.

The 16C and 17C Château des Basses-Fosses, on a spur on the west bank of the Vilaine, houses this museum of rural and maritime life on and along the river. The ground floor explains the intense maritime activity that the river once enjoyed, with a diorama recreating

the early 1900s. A reconstructed cabin shows life aboard a coastal fishing vessel. Upstairs, rural life is shown with exhibits of houses and different kinds of timber work, roofing, and dormers. The old carpentry, masonry and roofer trades are exhibited, as well as local costumes and headdresses.

Boat Trip on the River Vilaine
Boat trips (1hr 30) are available Jul–Aug, leaving from the Arzal dam or La Roche-Bernard at 2pm, 3pm, 4pm, 5pm, 6pm. 10€ (children 6€). Lunch/ dinner cruises Mar–Sept (4hr) departing from the Arzal dam daily at 12.30pm, Fri and Sat at 8pm.* 42€. 02 97 45 02 81. www.vedettesjaunes.com.
Boats go down the Vilaine to the Barrage d'Arzal (Arzal dam) or up to Redon.
A footpath (10km/6mi) leads from the old harbour to Arzal Dam.

EXCURSIONS

Missillac
13km/8mi SE by N 165 and the E 60.
Separated from the town by a small stretch of water beside the wood, the 15C **Château de la Bretesche**, with its low crenellated ramparts and water-filled moat, stands in an outstanding **site**⋆.

Foleux
18km/11mi N via D 774. At Péaule, take D 20 towards Redon; after 8km/5mi turn right.
The marina is located at the confluence of the Vilaine and Trévelo rivers.

After Foleux skirt the Vilaine from here there is a good view of the wide valley. Bear right then turn left three times before taking the road that leads to the château.

Château de Léhélec
Guided tours (30min). Jul–Aug, *Wed–Mon 2pm–7pm.* 5€. 02 99 91 84 33.
Surrounded by woodland, this manor house, built of ferruginous schist, offers on its south front an attractive perspective of the three courtyards bordered

by the 16C and 18C outbuildings. One of these buildings houses a small **rural museum** containing regional furniture and everyday objects.

Visitors are also admitted to two rooms lit by tall windows – the drawing room and dining room on the ground floor.

Barrage d'Arzal

◎ *12km/7.5mi W via D 34 then D 139.*
This dam on the Vilaine forms a fresh-water reservoir thus eliminating the effect of the tides and making the trip easier for the coasting vessels that ply upstream to Redon. The reservoir has an attractive stretch for pleasure craft. A road follows the crest of the dam over the river.

Le Guerno

◎ *18km/11mi NW along N 165 – E 60 towards Muzillac. Turn right after 8km/ 5mi and follow the new Route Bleue.*
The village, once a popular place of pil-grimage, has a 16C church built where a Templars' Chapel once stood. The church's exterior has on its south side a pulpit, stalls and bench (reserved for the clergy); the altar is backed against the calvary (on the square). The round tower, on the west side, is capped by an 18C lantern turret.

The inside is decorated with 16C stained-glass windows and choir stalls, and 22 16C carved panels in the loft. At the transept two cylindrical columns support the vaulting.

The trunk of the column on the left is hollow to collect offerings.

◎ *Once outside Le Guerno bear right then left onto the avenue that goes to Château de Branféré.*

On the way to Branféré, notice two 18C **fountains** (on the right side of the road), dedicated to St Anne and St Mary.

♠♠ Parc Zoologique de Branféré★

◎ *Open Jul–Aug 10am–6pm; Apr–Jun and Sept 10am–5pm; Sat–Sun, public holidays and school holidays (16 Apr– 8May) 10am–6pm; Feb–Mar and Oct– Nov 1.30pm–4pm.* ◎*12.50€ (children*

8.50€). ♿ ✆*02 97 42 94 66. www.branfere.com.*
The château stands in 50ha/124 acres of parkland, where over 2,000 animals and countless birds roam amid the trees and a series of lakes. The varied flora provide part of the animals' food.

Moulin de Pen-Mur

◎ *17km/10.5mi W on N 165 – E 60. Leave this road at Muzillac and follow the signs for Site de Pen-Mur.*
◎*Guided tours (45min).* ◎*Jul–Sept Tue–Sun 10am–noon, 2pm–7pm (last tour 1hr before closing); Apr–Jun 3pm– 6pm (tour at 3pm, 4pm, 5pm); Closed Oct–Mar and Mon exc Jul–Aug.* ◎*6€.* ✆*02 97 41 43 79.*
The mill, prettily located near a lake, con-tains an exhibition on the production of paper by hand using traditional 18C methods, showing all the stages from cutting up rags to the drying process.

Pénestin

17km/10.5mi W on the D 34.
For the Phoenicians it was a tin trad-ing post, these days it's a quiet seaside resort where mussel-growing is the main business.

The **pointe du Halguen** is covered with heath dotted with pines. On foot you can reach the rocky beaches, which are surrounded by low cliffs.

At the **pointe du Scal★** the Vilaine wid-ens between pointe du Halguen, on the left, and Pen-Lan. Here, you'll see many boats used for collecting mussels.

Opposite the pointe de Merquel, the **pointe du Bile★** offers views over two small islands and ochre cliffs.

ADDRESSES

⬤ STAY / ⑂ EAT

⬤ **Chambre d'hôte Le Moulin de Couedic** – *St-Cry, 56130 Nivillac.* ✆*02 99 90 62 47. www.moulin-du-couedic.com.* ⬤. *4 rooms.* A warm welcome awaits on this farm. Rooms are in the old stables and there's a gite for longer stays. The evening meal makes use of farm-fresh products.

Rochefort-en-Terre★

This charming, small town occupies a picturesque **site**★ on a promontory between deep dells. This landscape of rocks, woods, ravines, orchards and old houses bright with geraniums, attracts many painters.

▶ **Population:** 710.
🌄 **Michelin Map:** Local map 308 Q8 – Morbihan (56).
🏛 **Info:** pl. du Puits, 56220 Rochefort-en-Terre. ℘02 97 43 33 57. www.rochefort-en-terre.com.
◐ **Location:** The village is situated between the river Oust and the D 775, which links Redon (27km/17mi SE) with Vannes (40km/25mi W).
👪 **Kids:** The dinosaurs in Malansac.
🕐 **Timing:** Allow two hours for a visit.
👁 **Don't Miss:** The beautiful old houses in the village.

SIGHTS

Old Houses★
In the heart of the town stand 16C and 17C town houses which you can see as you stroll along rue du Porche, place des Halles and **place des Puits**. At place des Puits note the former law court, the entrance of which is surmounted by a set of scales.

Château
Guided tours (1hr). 🕐 *Jul–Aug, daily 10am–7pm; Jun and Sept, 2pm–6pm; Apr–May, Sat–Sun and public holidays 2pm–6pm.* 🎫 *2€.* ♿ *℘02 97 43 31 56.*
The only features that remain of the castle, destroyed in 1793, are the imposing entrance fort, sections of the walls, the underground passages and the outbuildings. The latter were restored at the turn of the century by the American Alfred Klots, with parts – most notably the dormer windows – from the 17C Kéralio manor house near Muzillac.
A small **museum of folk art** adjoining the old workshop of the owners evokes one or two aspects of the way of life in Rochefort in days gone by (lovely collection of headdresses). Another room contains the doors from the old dining room of a mansion, which were painted c.1880.

Église Notre-Dame-de-la-Tronchaye
🕐 *Open 9am–7pm.* ℘*02 97 43 31 50.*
The 12C, 15C and 16C church has a façade embellished with four gables pierced with Flamboyant bays. Inside, the chancel contains 16C stalls and, left of the high altar, a white stone Renaissance altarpiece. In the south arm of

Place des Puits
G. Targat/MICHELIN

the transept, a 17C altarpiece behind a fine 18C wrought-iron grille bears the venerated statue of Our Lady of La Tronchaye, which was found in the 12C in a hollow tree where it was hidden at the time of the Norsemen invasions. The statue is the object of a pilgrimage on the Sunday after 15 August. In the north arm of the transept is a wrought-iron font and white stone Renaissance altarpieces; one is decorated with three niches, each of which contains a painted wood statue.

EXCURSIONS
👤👤 Parc de Préhistoire

◗ *3km/1.8mi E on D 21 towards Malansac then D 134 to St-Gravé.*

🕐 *Open Apr–mid-Oct, daily 11am–7pm (last entry 2hr before closing); mid-Oct–mid-Nov, Sun, public holidays and school holidays 1.30pm–6pm.* 🚫 *Closed mid Nov–Apr.* 🎫 *10.50€ (children, 6.50€).* 🚶 🖉 *02 97 43 34 17. www.prehistoire.com.*

Gwenfol site, with its lakes and old slate quarries, is now an outdoor museum of prehistory. Different tableaux composed of people and animals (life-size models) accompanied by explanatory panels illustrate the Paleolithic to the Neolithic Ages, with such scenes as the discovery of fire, flint knapping, hunting, family life and the erection of a menhir.

Questembert

◗ *10km/6mi SW on the D 777 and D 7.*

A small, friendly town located in verdant countryside. The impressive **covered market** was built in 1552 and restored in 1675. The small 16C **Chapelle St-Michel** stands in the cemetery. On the north side is a calvary. This monument recalls the victory of Alain-le-Grand over the Norsemen in 888 at Coët-Bihan *(6.5km/4mi SE of Questembert).*

La Vraie-Croix

◗ *8km/5mi W by D 1.*

This charming village decked with flowers still has its chapel resting on ribbed vaulting. In the old days, the road used to run underneath the vaulting. The lower part of the building appears to date back to the 13C.

Josselin★★

This small town stands in a picturesque setting. Its river, the Oust, reflects the famous castle of the Rohan family. Old houses with slate roofs are scattered around the Basilique Notre-Dame-du-Roncier (Our Lady of the Brambles) behind the fortress-castle, on the sides and the summit of a steep ridge.

A BIT OF HISTORY

The Battle of the Thirty (14C) – By the mid-14C, Josselin Castle had already been razed and rebuilt. It belonged to the Royal House of France; Beaumanoir was its captain and the War of Succession was raging. The Blois party held Josselin, while the Montfort party held the city of Ploërmel, where an Englishman, Bemborough, was in command. The two garrisons had frequent encounters as they ravaged the countryside, before hand-to-handing fighting between 30 knights from each camp was arranged. After taking Communion and praying all night, Beaumanoir's men repaired, on 27 March 1351, to the rendezvous on the heath at Mi-Voie, between Josselin and Ploërmel (5km from Josselin at a

▸ **Population:** 2,582.

Michelin Map: Local map 308 P7 - MorbihaN (56).

Info: place de la Congrégation, 56120 Josselin. 🖉 02 97 22 36 43. www.josselin.com.

Location: Josselin is equidistant between Lorient (75km/46mi W) and Rennes (80km/49mi E) on the N 24.

👤👤 **Kids:** The Musée des Poupées and the insectarium at Lizio.

🕐 **Timing:** The town and surroundings will take about a day

Don't Miss: The view from the belfry in Notre-Dames-des-Ronciers basilica, the history of Breton resistance in the Musée St-Marcel.

place called Pyramide; a stone column marks the spot today). In the opposite camp were 20 Englishmen, six Germans and four Bretons. The day was spent in fierce fighting until the combatants were completely exhausted. Josselin won; the English captain was killed with eight of his men, and the rest were taken prisoner. During the struggle, which has remained famous as the Battle of the Thirty, the Breton leader, wounded, asked for a drink. 'Drink your blood, Beaumanoir, your thirst will pass!' replied one of his rough companions.

Constable de Clisson (14C) – Among the owners of Josselin the greatest figure was Olivier de Clisson, who married Marguerite de Rohan, Beaumanoir's widow, and acquired the castle in 1370. He had a tragic childhood; at seven his father was accused of betraying the French party in the War of Succession and beheaded in Paris. His widow, Jeanne de Belleville, who had been quiet and inconspicuous hitherto, became a fury. She hurried to Nantes with her children and, on the bloody head of their father nailed to the ramparts, made them swear to avenge him. Then she took the field with 400 men and put to the sword the garrisons of six castles who favoured the French cause. When the royal troops forced her to flee, she put to sea and sank every enemy ship that she met.

The Rohans at Josselin (15C and 17C) – In 1488, to punish Jean II de Rohan for having sided with the King of France, the Duke of Brittany, François II, seized Josselin and had it dismantled. When his daughter Anne became Queen of France she compensated Jean II, who was able in the rebuilding of the castle to create a masterpiece worthy of the proud motto of his family: "Roi ne puis, Prince ne daigne, Rohan suis" ("I cannot be king, I scorn to be a prince, I am a Rohan"). The owner of Josselin showed his gratitude to the Queen in the decoration of the palace; in many places, the letter 'A' is carved in the stone, crowned and surmounted by the girdle, which was Anne's emblem, and accompanied by the royal *fleur-de-lys*.

In 1629, Henri de Rohan, the leader of the Huguenots, Richelieu's sworn enemies, met the Cardinal in the King's antechamber where the cleric, who had just had the keep and five of the nine towers razed, announced with cruel irony: 'I have just thrown a fine ball among your skittles, Monsieur.'

CHÂTEAU★★

Pl. de la Congrégation. Guided *tours (45min) daily 14 Jul–Aug, 10am–6pm; 4 Apr–13 Jul 2pm–6pm; Sept 2pm –5.30pm; Oct, Sat–Sun, public holidays and during school holidays, 2pm–6pm.* 7.40€. 02 97 22 36 45.

To get a good **view**★ of the castle, stand on Ste-Croix Bridge, which spans the River Oust. From this point the building has the appearance of a fortress, with high towers, curtain walls and battlements. The windows and dormer windows appearing above the walls belong to the palace built by Jean II in the 16C. The castle is built on a terrace of irregular shape, surrounded by walls of which only the bases remain, except on the side which is seen from the bridge. The isolated 'prison tower' marked the northeast corner of the enclosure.

Chateâu de Josselin

G. Targat/MICHELIN

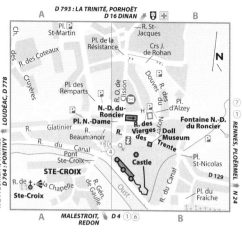

The delightful **façade**★★ of the main building that looks out onto the old courtyard, now the park, makes a striking contrast with the fortifications of the outer façade. Nowhere else in Brittany has the art of the sculptor in that hard material, granite, been pushed to such limits: brackets, florets, pinnacles, gables, crowns and curled leaves adorn the dormer windows and balustrades. Only the ground floor, restored in the 19C, is open to the public. In the panelled dining room stands an equestrian statue of Olivier de Clisson by Frémiet. After the antechamber, in which are hung portraits of the Rohan family, is the richly furnished drawing room with its delicately carved chimney, which bears the current Rohan motto: *'A plus'* (To more). There are over 3 000 books and some portraits in the library.

🚹🚺 Musée des Poupées

3 rue des Trentes. ⏱*Same hours as the castle.* ⬤*6.60€ (children 7–14, 4.60€).* ☎*02 97 22 36 45.*

In the castle's old stables, 500 dolls from the Rohan collection are exhibited. These come from many different countries (France, Netherlands, Austria, North America, etc.) and date from the 17C to the 20C.

The dolls (in wood, wax, celluloid, porcelain) are dressed in religious or traditional costumes. Miscellaneous doll accessories are also exhibited. There are temporary exhibitions here in summer.

Basilique Notre-Dame-du-Roncier★

⏱*Open 8.30am–7.30pm.* ✐✐*Guided tours available.* ☎*02 97 22 20 18.*

The name is based on a very old legend: around the year 800 a peasant, cutting brambles in his field discovered a statue of the Virgin and the site became one of pilgrimage and prayer. Founded in the 11C on the site of an oratory made of branches and several times remodelled (east end's spire built in 1949), the basilica is, generally speaking, Flamboyant in style; note the wonderful gargoyles that adorn its three sides and the stone statue of the Virgin at the entrance door. The basilica is famous for its great *pardon (*👉*see Calendar of Events).* Inside, in the south chapel, is the **mausoleum**★ of Olivier de Clisson and his wife Marguerite de Rohan (15C).

Tower

Access from place A.-de-Rohan. ⏱*Open mid Jun–mid Sept, 8.30am–7pm.* ℹ *Ask at the Town Hall.* ☎*02 97 22 24 17.*

The tower commands a view of the north-east façade, the castle's inner courtyard and the countryside beyond.

Old houses

There are many old houses around the basilica, especially on rue des Vierges and place Notre-Dame. Some of the most picturesque are in rue des Trente; note the former residence at number 7 (1624), now the Tourist Office, and beside it a house built in 1663.

Fontaine N.-D.-du-Roncier
Built in 1675, the fountain is still a place of pilgrimage.

Chapelle Ste-Croix
Built on the side of the hill is this chapel with its 11C nave. After a visit to the chapel, stroll in the picturesque Ste-Croix district with its narrow streets and old corbelled houses.

EXCURSIONS
Guéhenno
▶ *10km/6mi SW along D 24 then D778.*
The village has retained fine 16C and 17C stone houses. The **calvary**★ stands in the cemetery near the church. It dates from 1550, was destroyed in 1794 and restored in the last century. All its beauty lies in its perfect composition. Carved in the shaft of the central cross is Jesse, father of David. In front of it stands a column, with the instruments of the Passion, on which a cock is perched, in allusion to the denial of St Peter. Behind this monument is a small ossuary, whose entrance is protected by the figures of two guards on duty.

Lizio
▶ *10km/6mi S via D 4 then right onto D 147.*

Écomusée des Vieux Metiers
Bobhuet, 56460 Lizio. ◷ *Open Apr–Jun, 2pm–6pm; Jul–12 Sept 10am–noon, 2pm–7pm; 13 Sept–1 Nov, 2pm–6pm; rest of the year, by prior arrangement.* ◌ *Guided tours available (1hr 30min).* ◌ *5.80€.* ♿ ☎ *02 97 74 93 01.* *www.ecomuseelizio.com.*
More than 60 obsolete crafts and trades are illustrated in a large exhibition area. There are reconstructions of shops, farmhouse interiors, workshops and a wealth of tools and objects from bygone days.

♟ Insectarium
Rue du Stade. ◷ *Open Apr–Jun and Sept, 2pm–6pm; Jul–Aug 10am–7pm; Oct–Mar, during school holidays 2pm–6pm.* ◌ *7€ (children over 5€).* ♿ ☎ *02 97 74 99 12. www.insectariumdelizio.fr.*

Dozens of different species of insects are displayed here: centipedes, stick insects, moths, crickets, scorpions, trap-door spiders. Two films are shown and a microscope is available for observation of insects.

Univers du Poète Ferrailleur
▶ *On the road to Roc-St-André.*
◷ *Open daily Jul–Aug 10.30am–7pm; 5 Apr–Jun and 1–15 Sept, Sun and public holidays 2pm–6pm.* ◌ *6€.* ♿ ☎ *02 97 74 97 94. www.poeteferrailleur.com.*
Enter into the world of "the poet-junk-man", a fantastic artist whose unbridled imagination has breathed life into a collection of 60-odd strange and intriguing sculptures.

Ploërmel
▶ *13km/8mi E along D 24.*
This little town, in the centre of an agricultural area at the limit of Upper Brittany, was once the seat of the dukes of Brittany and it was from Ploërmel that the Englishman, Bemborough, set out for the Battle of the Thirty (1351).

Église St-Armel★
The church is dedicated to St-Arthmael, who founded the town in the 6C; he is shown taming a dragon whom he leads away with his stole.
The church dates from the 16C. The Flamboyant Gothic and Renaissance north **portal**★ presents two finely carved doors. The scenes depicted take both religious (Christ's Childhood, Virtue Trampling on Vice) and comic themes. The Apostles have been sculpted on the door panels.
The magnificent 16C and 17C **stained-glass windows**★ have been restored: Tree of Jesse (in the side aisle), life of St Arthmael (in the north transept); and modern windows by Jacques Bony.
In the chapel to the north of the chancel are white marble statues of Duke Jean II and Duke Jean III of Brittany (14C). In the south transept, behind the Kersanton granite tomb of Philippe of Montauban and his wife, is a fine 14C recumbent figure in white marble. Below the wood vaulting the purlins are worth noting.

Old Houses

Rue Beaumanoir, so-called in memory of the hero of the Battle of the Thirty, contains (at number 7) the 16C **Maison des Marmousets**★ adorned with woodcarvings, and opposite the 16C former house of the dukes of Brittany. Other old houses may be seen in rue des Francs-Bourgeois.

Horloge Astronomique (Astronomical Clock)

1 bd. Foch. ◓*Open 11.30am–1.30pm.* ♿ ✆*02 97 74 06 67.*

The clock, protected by a glass case, was created between 1850 and 1855 and was intended for the instruction of the future teachers of the schools situated along the coast.

Lac au Duc

2km/1.2mi N of Ploërmel via bd. du Mar.-Foch.

This lake (250ha/718 acres) has an artificial beach, a water sports centre and fishing facilities. A 3km/1.8mi footpath, starting from the parking area of the King Arthur Hotel, runs along the edge of the lake through an arboretum planted with 2,000 hydrangea of 220 different types. They flower from May to October.

La Trinité-Porhoët

▶ *15.5km/9.5mi N on D 793.*

This town owes its name to the intersection of three Roman roads and to the lords of Porhoët, powerful counts of Brittany. This massive **Église de la Ste-Trinité** was built to serve as a priory for the St-Jacut brothers. An unusual feature of the interior is the slanting floor, which rises towards the choir. A spectacular **Tree of Life**★ from the 17C embellishes the altar screen.

Malestroist

▶ *25km/15.5mi SE along D 4 and D 764.*

Near the Lanvaux Moors, this picturesque town, built along the Oust Canal, contains interesting Gothic and Renaissance houses. Malestroit was, during the Middle Ages, one of Brittany's nine baronies.

Half-timbered or in stone, **old houses** are located mostly in the St-Gilles precincts. On place du Bouffay one of the residences has humorous carvings on its façade, another has a pelican in wood. Stroll along rue au Froment, rue aux Anglais, rue des Ponts and the rue du Général-de-Gaulle.

Musée de la Résistance Bretonne

▶ *In St-Marcel, 3km/1.8mi W of Malestroit via D 321.* ◓*Open daily mid-Jun–mid-Sept 10am–7pm; mid-Sept–mid-Jun Wed–Mon 10am–noon, 2pm–6pm.* ◓*Closed 1 Jan, 24, 25 and 31 Dec.* ◔*8€.* ♿ ✆*02 97 75 16 90.*

A visit to the Musem of Breton Resistance starts with a film summarizing the significant events of WW II, including the German war effort, the invasion of Europe, the Allied landing, and the Liberation.

Audiovisual presentations, explanatory panels, models, arms, and uniforms show the war's effect on Brittany. To illustrate wartime rationing, a street has been reconstructed, with its local grocery store, petrol pump, and restaurant. In the park, part of the Atlantic Wall has been rebuilt, and farther on there is a garage from during the Occupation, with its gas-run cars, an American Army camp, and finally a collection of military vehicles and weapons belonging to both the German and Allied armies.

Nearby is a monument commemorating the battle that occurred between members of the *Maquis* (French Resistance Movement) Free French commandos and the Germans on 18 June, 1944, soon after D-day.

Locminé

▶ *25km/15.5mi W of Josselin along N 24.*

The name of this town (*lieu des moines* meaning a place where the monks are), derives from the abbey founded here in the 6C, which had two churches identical in layout: Église St-Sauveur (16C) and Chapel of St-Colomban. Only their façades remain; behind is a modern church (1975) built on the site of the naves.

Domaine de Kerguéhennec

▶ *10km/6.2mi E of Locminé.*

The Kerguéhennec **estate**, in a pleasant, verdant setting, includes a Classical-style château, wooded park and lake. It was acquired by the Morbihan *département* in the 1970s and transformed into a **Contemporary Art Centre** .

Park and Sculptures

◷ *Open Jul–Aug Tue–Sun 11am–7pm; rest of the year, Tue–Sun 11am–6pm.* ◷ *Closed public holidays.* ♿ *℘02 97 60 44 44. www.art-kerguehennec.com.*

An arboretum with fine trees is located in the 195ha/482 acre park. Dotted throughout the park are some 30 sculptures by artists including Giuseppe Penone, François Morellet, Tony Cragg, Michelangelo Pistoletto, Richard Long and Jean-Pierre Raynaud (*1,000 Cement Pots,* 1986)

To find your way in the maze of the park and to identify the sculptures that are scattered in it, ask for a map at the château or at the Café du Parc next door.

Château and outbuildings

The château, built in the early 18C by local architect Olivier Delourme, consists of a main building, with two projecting wings and symmetrically opposed outbuildings, the whole enclosing a vast court of honour, closed by a fine grille. It houses temporary exhibitions and conferences.

Chapelle Notre-Dame-du-Plasker

To the left of the east end of the modern church.

This 16C rectangular chapel is decorated in the Flamboyant style.

ADDRESSES

🛏STAY

🍴 **Camping Le Bas de la Lande** – *Le Bas de la Lande. ℘ 02 97 22 22 20. www.josselin.com ou www.guegon.fr. Apr–Oct. 60 pitches.* Near to the bank of the river Oust, this campsite has terraced pitches and chalets. Clean and functional toilets. Games room and free access to minigolf.

🍴🛢🛢🛢 **Hôtel du Roi Arthur** – *56 800 Ploërmel. At the Lac au Duc 1.5 km/ 0.9m by the D 8. ℘ 02 97 73 64 64. www. hotelroiarthur.com. Closed Feb school hols. 46 rooms. ⊠15 € .* In search of the Holy Grail? Perhaps it is hidden here between the lake and the golf course. Choose one of the recently renovated comfortable rooms. Think of the legend as you take your place around the round table to taste the modern cuisine.

🍴 EAT

🍴 **La Marine** – *8 r. du Canal, Josselin. ℘02 97 22 21 98. truchot.jacquet@ wanadoo.fr.* Bordering the river Oust with a lovely terrace in summer and near to the chateau. There is pretty sea side decoration in the two dining rooms. A good choice of crêpes with two specialities, la St Juoan and la Favorite.

OUTSKIRTS

🍴 **Crêperie Maël Trech** – *13 pl. du Bouffay, 56 140 Malestroit. ℘ 02 97 75 17 72. Closed Tue eve and Wed exc Jul– Aug.* An old house in the medieval centre. A menu of crêpes and house specialities such as *Mer Graal* (crayfish and asparagus flambéed in anis).

🍴🍴 **Le Cobh** – *10 rue des Forges, 56800 Ploërmel. 13km/8mi SE on the N 24 to Rennes. ℘02 97 74 00 49. www.hotel- lecobh.com. Closed 1–17 Jan, Mon, Tue and Wed lunch and Sun. 12 rooms. ⊠ 8.50€.* This old posthouse with a yellow façade is named after an Irish village. Warm welcome and contemporary interiors are inspired by Celtic legends and Breton culture. Traditional cuisine.

Pontivy

The old capital of the Rohan owes its name to the monastery founded in the 7C by St Ivy. The older part of the town has narrow, winding streets, in contrast to the geometrical town plan laid out by Napoleon.

SIGHTS

Old Houses★

Admire old half-timbered and corbelled houses of the 16C and 17C on **rue du Fil**, place du Martrat, the centre of Old Pontivy, rue du Pont, rue du Docteur-Guépin and on the corner of rue Lorois and rue du Général-de-Gaulle.

Château des Rohan

⏲*Open Feb–Mar and mid Sept–Nov, Wed–Sun 2pm–6pm; Apr–mid Jun, daily 10am–noon, 2pm–6pm.* ⊜*4.50€.* ☛*Guided tours* ⊜*6€.* ℘*02 97 25 12 93.*

The castle was built in the 15C by Jean II de Rohan. The façade is flanked by two large machicolated towers with

▶ **Population:** 13,518.
⚲ **Michelin Map:** Local map 308 N6 – Morbihan (56).
🛈 **Info:** Quai Nièmen, 56300 Pontivy. ℘02 97 25 04 10.
◖ **Location:** On the river Blavet and Nantes–Brest canal.
⊙ **Don't Miss:** The Château des Rohan.

pepper-pot roofs – all that remain of the four towers of the perimeter wall. The main building, remodelled in the 18C, is adorned with cusped pediments and a spiral staircase.

EXCURSIONS

Kernascléden★★

▷ *32km/20mi N of Lorent via D 769. Near the D 110, which goes around the forest of Pont-Calleck.*
This small village (population 355) possesses a beautiful church built by the Rohan family.

Church★★

⏲*Open 9am–8pm.* ℘*02 97 51 61 02. Key on request from Mr Lavolé-Bénoni.* ☛*Guided tours on request.*

Though the church at Kernascléden was consecrated in 1453, 30 years before the Chapelle de St-Fiacre (⚲ *see Le FAOUËT*), there is a legend that they were built at the same time and by the same workmen. Every day, angels carried the men and their tools from one site to the other. A characteristic feature of this church is the striving for perfection that appears in every detail. The very slender tower, the foliated pinnacles, rose carvings and delicate tracery help to adorn the church without overloading it. Two porches open on the south side. The left **porch**★, which is the larger, is ornamented with statues (restored) of the twelve Apostles. Inside, the church has pointed stone vaulting. The vaults and

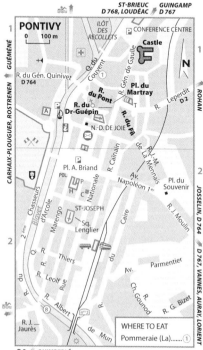

walls surmounting the main arches are decorated with 15C **frescoes**★★ representing episodes in the lives of the Virgin and Christ. The finest are the Virgin's Marriage, Annunciation (left of chancel) and Burial (right of chancel). In the north transept are eight angel-musicians; over the triumphal arch (on the chancel side), the Resurrection of Christ. On the walls of the south arm are fragments of a dance of death and a picture of Hell (facing the altar), which is remarkable for the variety of tortures it depicts.

There are many 15C statues in wood and stone: Our Lady of Kernascléden to the left of the high altar, St Sebastian and a Pietà in the nave.

Rood screen, Chapelle St-Fiacre

H. Le Gac/MICHELIN

Le Faouët★

▷ *On the D 769, which links Lorient (37km/23mi away) and Carhaix-Plouguer (34km/21mi away).*

This village (population 2,806) is the centre of a very picturesque district extending between the Stêr Laër and the Ellé, two rivers flowing from the Montagnes Noires. The 16C covered **market** with its great slate roof supported by a domed pinnacle houses a lively interior. In the shady square in front stands a monument to **Corentin Carré**, France's youngest soldier, who enlisted in 1915 aged just 15.

Chapelle St-Fiacre★

▷ *2.5km/1.5mi SE on D 790.* ◷*Open Jul–Aug, daily 9.30am–12.30pm, 2pm–7pm; Apr–Jun and Sept, daily 10am–noon, 2pm–6pm; Nov–Mar, Mon 1.30pm–4.15pm, Sat–Sun and public holidays 2pm–5pm.* ☎*02 97 23 23 23.*

The chapel is a fine 15C building. The façade has one of the best gable-belfries in Brittany. Inside, the **rood screen**★★ of lace-like woodcarving is a Flamboyant work of 1480. On the nave side, scenes of the Temptation of Adam and Eve, the Annunciation and the calvary are related.

The most curious figures are on the chancel side; they picture Theft (a man picking fruit from a tree), Drunkenness (a man vomiting a fox), Lust (a man and

a woman) and Laziness (a Breton peasant playing bagpipes and a bombard, a member of the oboe family). The decoration of the panels of the gallery and the corbels is quite varied. The stone altarpiece against the left pillar shows the martyrdom of St Sebastian.

There are fine 16C stained-glass windows in the chancel and transept: the Passion (chancel), the Life of St John the Baptist (south transept), the Tree of Jesse and the Life of St Fiacre (north transept).

Chapelle Ste-Barbe

▷ *3km/1.8mi NE of Le Faouët via D 790.* ◷*Open same as Chapelle St-Fiacre (⏷ see above).* ☎*02 97 23 23 23.*

This Flamboyant-style chapel is built in a rocky cleft on the side of a hill. The **site**★ is very pretty; from a height of some 100m, it overlooks the small Ellé Valley. The great stairway *(78 steps)*, built in 1700, leading up to the chapel, is linked by an arch to the St Michael Oratory (Oratoire St-Michel) crowning a rock spur. Nearby, in a small building, is the bell tolled by pilgrims to call down blessings from heaven. Paths lead down to the sacred fountain, below the chapel.

🚗 DRIVING TOUR

From Pontivy to Hennebont
90km/56mi – about 4hr.

▷ Leave Pontivy on rue Albert-de-Mun, driving towards Auray, and turn right at Talvern.

Chapelle St-Nicodème
This 16C chapel is preceded by a massive tower with a granite steeple. A Renaissance doorway leading to a 16C staircase opens at the base of the tower.
To the left of the chapel, a Gothic fountain empties into three pools in front of three niches surmounted by richly carved gables. There is a *pardon* on the first Sunday in August.

St-Nicolas-des-Eaux
The little town sits on the side of a hill. The chapel sits above the town and is surrounded by thatched-roof houses.

Site de Castennec★
This Celtic site became an oppidum and then a fortified Roman camp.

▷ Turn left after Castennec .

Bleuzy
To the left of the **church**, note the two Renaissance houses with a bread oven and a well. Inside the church, the stained-glass windows and the woodwork and beams are worth a look. A ringing stone located next to the pulpit, once used in guise of a bell, is believed to be a meteorite.

▷ Go to Melrand, passing through La Paule.

Le Village de l'An Mil
🕐*Open May–Aug, 10am-7pm; Sept–Apr, 11am–5pm, Sat–Sun 11am–6pm.* ⬤*3€.* ✆*02 97 39 57 89. www.melrand-village-an-mil.info.*
Deep in the countryside, excavations have brought to light the vestiges of the village of Lann Gouh ('old land'), which date back to around the year 1000. The village illustrates rural medieval architecture and the daily life of people and animals, who lived under one roof.

▷ Return to the centre of the town. Behind the church, take D 142 towards St-Barthélemy, where you will turn right towards St-Adrien.

Chapelle St-Adrien
The 15C chapel stands below the road, between two fountains: the one on the right is surmounted by a calvary. Inside, there is a simple rood screen, carved on the nave side and painted on the other.

▷ The road (D 237) follows the Blavet Valley through delightful countryside. Turn left towards Baud (D 3).

Baud
Some 30km/18.5mi from the the sea, the Baud region offers many pretty walks which show the more traditional side of Brittany. In the lower town, below the Locminé road, at the far end of the large car park, is the **Fontaine Notre-Dame-de-la-Clarté**.

Cartopole
🕐*Open mid-Jun–mid-Sept, 10am-12.30pm, 2pm-6pm (Jul–Aug until 7pm) mid-Sept–mid-Jun, Wed, Thu and Sat and Sun 2pm–6pm.* ⬤*5€ (children 2.50€).* ✆*02 97 51 15 14. www.cartolis.org.*
Here you will find a treasure chest of some 30,000 post cards that show the heritage of Brittany and the evolution of its society in the early 20C. There is a film, you can view 3,000 cards in the centre and all of them are available on a database.

▷ Leave Baud by the road to Hennebont. At Coët Vin bear left; 500m/545yds further on, leave your car in the car park on the right.

Vénus de Quinipily and Park

⏱Open May–Oct, 10am–7pm; Nov–Apr (except mid-Dec–end Jan), 11am–5pm. ◉3€. ☎02 97 39 04 94.

From the other side of a wooden gate, a steep path leads up to the Venus, placed above a fountain, set in the park of the restored Château de Quinipily. The origins of the statue are uncertain. It has been taken for a Roman idol or an Egyptian Isis. As it was the object of much reverent speculation, it was thrown into the River Blavet several times by zealous clergymen. The Count of Lannion installed it here in 1696.

◯ *Return to Baud and go towards Poule Fetan.*

Poul Fetan★

◯ *15km/9mi W along D 3. In Quistinic, turn onto the Hennebont road.* ⏱Open daily Jul–Aug, 10.45am–7pm; Jun and Sept, 11am–6.30pm; Apr–May, 2pm–6.30pm. ◉7€. ☎02 97 39 51 74. www.poul-fetan.com.

In a setting high above the Blavet Valley, a quaint little 16C hamlet has been painstakingly reconstructed from the ruins abandoned during the 1970s. Among the charming thatched cottages, note the Maison du Minour (The Chief's House), the inn *(auberge)* where you may enjoy a typical Breton meal, the former bakery and an *écomusée*. In the summer, craftspeople attired in regional costume demonstrate trades from typical peasant life of yesteryear: washerwomen rub steaming linens; a baker is busy at his oven; a farmer is making millet porridge while another is churning butter. A pottery workshop illustrates the traditional sculpting and firing techniques. Various farm animals include the "magpir", a small cow typical of the Breton region.

◯ *Retrace your steps tot take the D 159 and then the road to Hennebont.*

Hennebont –
◉*See LORIENT: Excursions*

ADDRESSES

⏱ EAT

◉◉ **La Pommeraie** – *17 quai Couvent.* ☎ 02 97 25 60 09. restaurant lapommeraie@wanadoo.fr. Closed 12–19 Apr, 16–31 Aug, 26 Dec–4 Jan, Sun and Mon. Yellow façade and a warm welcome in this colourful restaurant with a small courtyard alongside the river Blavet.

🛒 SHOPPING

Markets – On Mondays, a market in Pontivy is held in la place Aristide-Briand. There's also a local market on Sunday at Rohan, 17km/10.5mi to the east on tje D764.

🏃 ACTIVITIES

Bretagne Plaisance – ☎ 02 99 72 15 80 - www.locaboat.com. Pleasure boats for hire, end March to beginning November.

Base nautique de Toulboubou – *Toulboubou.* ☎ 02 97 25 09 51. Canoe-kayak practical courses. Equipment hire.

OUTSKIRTS

L'art dans les chapelles – *From 1st weekend of Jul –31 Aug: daily exc Tue, 2pm–7pm; 1st 3 weekends Sept: 2pm–7pm. Information at the Maison du chapelain, Chapelle St-Nicodème, 56930 Pluméliau.* ☎ 02 97 51 97 21. www.art chapelles.com. Every summer since 1992 (all year visits by prior arrangement) a number of chapels in the Blavet valley and country of Pontivy have welcomed exhibitions by established contemporary artists and also new artists.

Poul-Fetan – ☎ 02 97 39 51 74. Jul –Sept, afternoons. Local events breathe life back into Poul-Fetan. Local artisans distil lavender, bake their bread, grind their corn and shape their butter pats. A pottery workshop offers visitors the chance to try their hand at traditional methods of production and firing. Traditional local animals can also be seen, including a miniature cow – the "pie noire". Festivities take place during July and August.

NANTES AND AROUND

In the Breton language, Nantes is known as Naoned, which is also the name of the historic province that roughly corresponds to the modern Loire-Atlantique *département*. Prior to 1941, the city of Nantes was the official capital of Brittany. Loire-Atlantique, while no longer officially attached to the Brittany Region, retains numerous Breton traditions, and many inhabitants would like to see it restored to its previous status. The area is famous for its beaches, especially at the resort of La Baule, as well as the marshland of the Brière, a haven for wildlife and a bird-watcher's paradise.

Highlights

1 Stepping back in time at Nantes' imposing **Château des Ducs de Bretagne** (p414)

2 Cruising past green countryside and manor houses on a **river Erdre boat trip** (p418)

3 Discovering the salt marshes on the **Presqu'île de Guérande driving tour** (p431)

4 Swimming off Europe's most beautiful beach at **La Baule** (435)

5 Getting back to nature at the **Parc Naturel Régional de Brière** (p440)

A Bit of History

The territory covered in this section includes the city of Nantes itself and the Loire-Atlantique *département* north and south of the river Loire. It is surrounded by the Atlantic in the west, Morbihan in the northwest, Ille-et-Vilaine in the north, Maine-et-Loire in the east and the Vendée in the south. Generally, the landscape is quite flat, with the area to the north of St-Nazaire a mixture of marshland, canals and low-lying meadows which are frequently inundated with sea water. The National Regional Park of the Brière, for which a driving itinerary is given (see p441), is a vast wetland area that provides shelter to migrating birds and a habitat to beautiful flora, such as lilies and irises.

The southwestern-facing coast between Piriac-sur-Mer and St-Nazaire has been called the Breton Riviera thanks to its vegetation resembling that of the Mediterranean. This stretch of sandy beaches, rocky promontories and caves is more often known as the Côte d'Amour (the Love Coast) after readers of the local *La Mouette* newspaper coined the phrase at the turn of the 20C.

Nantes is a modern city of nearly 300,000 people at the confluence of five rivers, the mighty Loire, the Sèvre Nantaise, the Chézine, the Cen and the Erdre, whose combined waters all discharge into the Atlantic Ocean via the Loire at St-Nazaire. The centre and old town are situated on the right bank of the Loire. Its imposing Château of the Dukes of Brittany embodies the importance of the city back in the times of the last Duke, Francois II. Nantes was originally a Gallo-Roman city, but after the Romans left it suffered several invasions until in AD 936 its future was secured by Alan Barbe-Torte, or Crooked Beard. He returned from exile and chased the Vikings out of Brittany before becoming the first duke and establishing Nantes as the capital.

For centuries, the Prequ'île de Guérende northeast of Nantes has been one of France's main centres for the production of salt. Today, salt pans are still a familiar sight, along with the *paludiers* (salt marsh workers) gathering their "white gold". A driving itinerary is given for this unusual area (see p433).

Salt is very important to the local economy together with the shipbuilding, chemical and aerospace industries, and food processing. South of Nantes the Pays de Muscadet produces the world-famous white wine. You can discover the vineyards with our driving tour (see p419).

A driving itinerary is also given for the Pays de Retz (see p422). It takes in the western part of the medieval region located on the south bank of the Loire which the Bretons absorbed into their territory during the early middle ages.

Nantes★★★

Nantes is many cities combined: a city of the arts, of industry, and of education. Located at the confluence of the rivers Loire, Sèvre and Erdre, Nantes is the historic capital of the Dukes of Brittany and has become the capital of the modern-day Pays de la Loire region. The three ports of Donges, Nantes and St-Nazaire have merged and follow the estuary from Nantes out to the Atlantic Ocean. Among Nantes' more famous children are the writer Jules Verne (1828–1905) and sailor Éric Tabarly (1931–98).

A BIT OF HISTORY

Nantes, capital of Brittany – Nantes, first Gallic and then Roman, was involved in the bloody struggle between the Frankish kings and the Breton noblemen, but it was the Vikings who did the most damage.

In 843 pirates landed, rushed into the cathedral where the Bishop was saying Mass, and put the prelate, the clergy and the congregation to death. In 939, young **Alain Barbe-Torte** (Crookbeard), a descendant of the great Breton chiefs, who had taken refuge in England, returned to the country and drove the invaders out of Brittany. Having become duke, he chose Nantes as his capital and

▶ **Population:** 270,251.

♿ **Michelin Map:** Local map 318 G4 – Loire-Atlantique (44).

🛈 **Info:** 7 rue de Valmy, 44041 Nantes. ℘08 92 464 044. www.nantes-tourisme.com.

▶ **Location:** Capital city of the Loire-Atlantique region.

👥 **Kids:** Les Machines de l'Île, Natural History Museum, Planetarium, Hespérides gardens.

🕐 **Timing:** The Pass Nantes gives discounts on public transport and museum and attraction entrance fees.

🅿 **Parking:** Traffic in town is heavy. Leave your car in one of the many central car parks. Parking is limited to 2hr in the red zone and 3hr in the yellow zone.

◉ **Don't Miss:** The château of the Ducs de Bretagne, the Beaux-Arts museum and a boat trip up the Erdre valley.

rebuilt it. Nantes was the capital of the Duchy of Brittany several times during the Middle Ages, in rivalry with Rennes. The Dukes of the House of Montfort,

Fine mansions along the Loire

A. de Valroger/MICHELIN

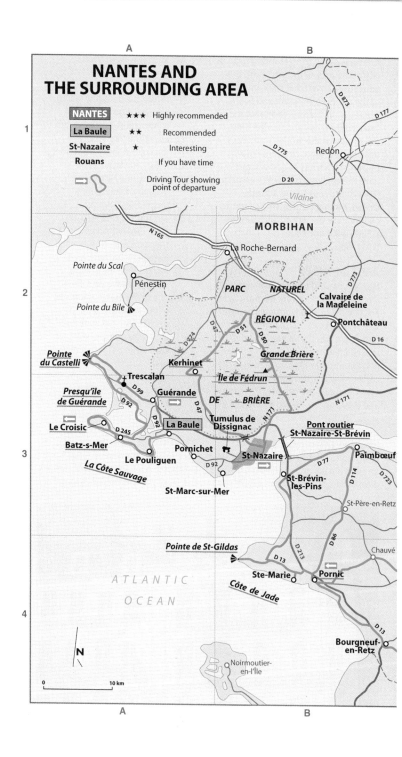

NANTES AND THE SURROUNDING AREA

NANTES ★★★ Highly recommended
La Baule ★★ Recommended
St-Nazaire ★ Interesting
Rouans If you have time

Driving Tour showing point of departure

MORBIHAN

D 873
D 177
Redon
D 775
D 20
Vilaine

La Roche-Bernard

Pointe du Scal
Pénestin
PARC NATUREL
Calvaire de la Madeleine
Pointe du Bile
RÉGIONAL
Pontchâteau
D 16
D 324
D 47
D 51
D 50
D 773
Pointe du Castelli
Kerhinet
Grande Brière
Trescalan
Île de Fédrun
Presqu'île de Guérande
D 99
Guérande
DE BRIÈRE
N 171
D 92
Le Croisic
D 245
La Baule
Tumulus de Dissignac
Pont routier St-Nazaire-St-Brévin
Batz-s-Mer
D 92
Pornichet
St-Nazaire
Paimbœuf
Le Pouliguen
St-Marc-sur-Mer
D 92
D 77
St-Brévin-les-Pins
D 114
D 723
La Côte Sauvage
St-Père-en-Retz
D 86
Chauvé
Pointe de St-Gildas
D 213
D 13
Ste-Marie
Pornic
ATLANTIC OCEAN
Côte de Jade
N
Bourgneuf-en-Retz
D 13
0   10 km
Noirmoutier-en-l'Île

A   B

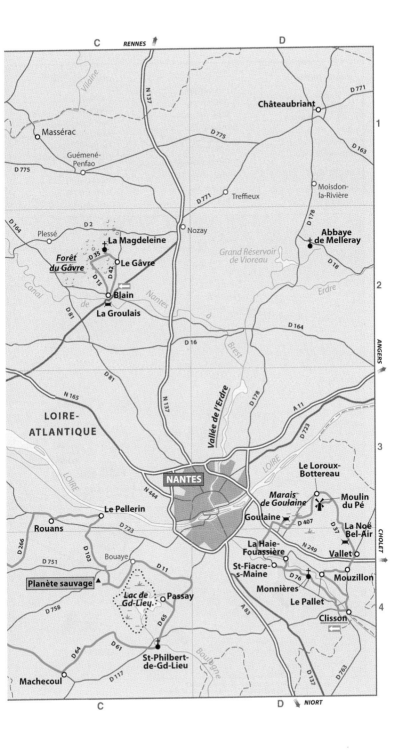

WHERE TO STAY

All Seasons Centre........................... (7)
Coin chez soi (Un)............................ (12)
Colonies (Hôtel des)........................ (1)
Graslin (Hôtel).................................. (4)
Petit-Port (Camping Le)................... (9)
Pommeraye (Hôtel)........................... (11)

WHERE TO EAT

Amour de Pomme de Terre..... (1)
Atlantide (L').................................. (4)

Café Cult' (Le)............................... (7)
Chez l'Huître................................ (11)
Cigale (La)..................................... (13)
Embellie (L')................................. (17)
Enfants Terribles
(Le Bistrot des)........................... (19)
Heb-Ken (Crêperie)...................... (21)
Montesquieu (Le)........................ (22)
Paludier (Le)................................. (3)
Tim Fish.. (2)

STREET INDEX

Bouffay (Pl. du)............................. 1
Flesselles (Allées)......................... 3
Fosse (R. de la).............................. 5
Kervégan (R.)................................. 7
Paix (R. de la)................................ 9
Petite-Hollande (Pl. de la)............ 11
Pré-Nian (R.).................................. 13
St-Léonard (R.)............................... 15
St-Vincent (Pl.).............................. 17
Ste-Croix (Pl.)................................ 19

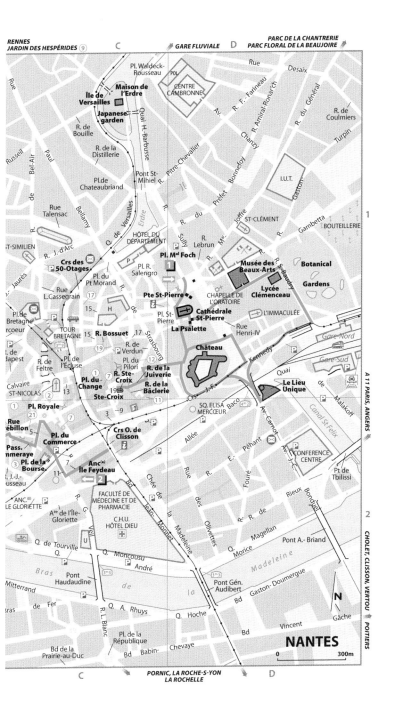

Childhood of a Visionary

The 20 years that Jules Verne spent in Nantes from his birth on Feydeau Island in 1828 until he set up house in Paris in 1848, undoubtedly helped to strengthen his vocation as a writer of fiction. His exceptional talent and boundless imagination successfully combined dream, scientific fact and adventure. The sight of the great port crowded with ships, or the equally fascinating scene of the steam-driven machines at the Indret factory; the tales of voyages he listened to from his uncle Prudent, once a privateer; lessons in reading and writing with Madame Sambin, the widow of the captain of an ocean-going vessel; or imaginary shipwrecks conjured up while playing among the little islands of the Loire, all played a part in inspiring the author's imaginative genius when he came to write *Voyages Extraordinaires*, which earned him the acclaim of more than 25 million teenagers even before he was universally acknowledged as a great writer.

especially **François II,** governed as undisputed sovereigns and restored the prestige of the town and its title of capital.

Edict of Nantes (13 August 1598) – In 1597, Brittany, tired of disorder and suffering caused by the League and also of the separatist ambitions of its Governor, Philip of Lorraine, sent a pressing appeal to Henri IV, asking him to come and restore order. Before the castle he whistled with admiration. "God's teeth!" he exclaimed, "the Dukes of Brittany were no small beer!" The royal visit was marked by a great historic event: on 13 August 1598, Henri IV signed the Edict of Nantes, which, in 92 articles, settled the religious question – or so he thought.

Sugar and ebony – From the 16C to the 18C, Nantes had two main sources of revenue: sugar and the slave trade, known discreetly as the ebony trade. In the Antilles, the slaver would sell the slaves bought on the Guinea coast and buy cane sugar, refined at Nantes and sent up the Loire. The ebony trade made an average profit of 200 percent.

Philosophers inveighed against this inhuman traffic, but Voltaire, whose business acumen is well known, had a 5,000-livres share in a slave ship from Nantes. At the end of the 18C the prosperity of Nantes was at its height: it had become the first port of France; its fleet included 2,500 ships and barques. The big shipowners and traders founded dynasties and built the fine mansions

on Quai de la Fosse and the former Feydeau Islet.

The Nantes Noyades – In 1793 some of the cruellest and most violent killings of the French Revolution took place in Nantes. Jean-Baptiste Carrier, the deputy for Cantal in the National Convention (Assembly) in Paris, was charged with setting up a Revolutionary Tribunal (to try political offenders) in Nantes. Carrier had already spent some time at Rennes. His mission was 'to purge the body politic of all the rotten matter it contained'. This being the Reign of Terror (12-month period when violent means were employed to dispose of enemies of the Revolution), Carrier soon disposed of the fair trials and invented torturous and inhumane ways of disposing of the prisoners.

As well as rounding up prisoners to be shot, he crammed clergy into boats, with trap doors for bottoms, on the River Loire. When the signal was given, the doors were opened. He also invented the so-called underwater marriages or republican baptisms, where naked priests and nuns were tied together before being drowned.

When informed, the Convention immediately recalled its delegate. He was put on trial and was sent before the Nantes Revolutionary court, sentenced to death and guillotined in December.

The Duchess's hiding place – In 1832 tragedy gave way to farce. The **Duchess of Berry**, a mortal enemy of Louis-

Philippe, was convinced that Brittany was still legitimist and scoured the Nantes countryside. Her failure was complete. She took refuge at Nantes but was betrayed. The police invaded the house and found it empty, but kept it under surveillance. Feeling cold, they lit a fire in one room. Their surprise was great when the chimney-shutter fell open and out on all fours came the Duchess and three of her followers, black as sweeps and half suffocated. They had spent 16hours in the darkness of the wall.

A new vitality – In the 1980s the shipyards closed down, threatening the town's economic prosperity but Nantes promptly turned to service industries (insurance, communications), which now represent the bulk of its economic activity. Nantes has also become an important university town with a large student population.

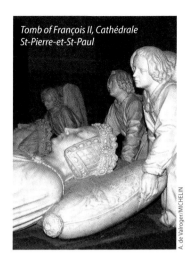

Tomb of François II, Cathédrale St-Pierre-et-St-Paul

A. de Valroger/MICHELIN

WALKING TOUR
1 AROUND THE CASTLE★★
Allow 3hr.

Place Maréchal-Foch
Two fine 18C hotels, built from the plans by Ceineray, flank the Louis XVI Column that was erected in 1790. From the square, commonly called place Louis XVI, which is met by Cours St-André and St-Pierre, you can readily appreciate the grand dimensions of the cathedral, in particular its soaring height.

Porte St-Pierre
This 15C gateway stands on the remains of a 3C Gallo-Roman wall. The gateway is built into an elegant turreted building.

Cathédrale St-Pierre-et-St-Paul★
◷*Open 9am–6.30pm.*
This imposing building is remarkable for its austere façade: two plain towers frame a Flamboyant window (note the 15C canopied niches that decorate the pillars supporting the towers). The cathedral was begun in 1434, completed in 1893, restored in 1930 and after fire damage in 1972. The three portals reveal finely sculpted recessed arches and on

the central portal stands a statue of St Peter.

Interior★★
Here, at Nantes, white stone replaces the granite used in purely Breton cathedrals. Being less heavy, this stone made it possible to build vaults 37.5m/123ft high (for comparison, the vaulting of Westminster Abbey is 30.5m/100ft high).

As you enter you will be struck by the nave's pure, soaring lines, a fine example of Flamboyant work. Stand under the organ loft to appreciate the effect; you will see a double row of vertical lines springing from the ground and shooting without a break up to the delicately carved keystones of the vaults where they cross.

The visual effect is of elevation. Seen from this angle, the slender ribs of the pillars mask not only the flat wall surfaces that separate them but all the lines, curved or horizontal, of the arcades, the triforium or the upper windows, which could break the harmony of the vista, which is composed entirely of parallel vertical lines.

▷ *Go around the building to the right.*

In the south transept is the decorative masterpiece of the cathedral and a great Renaissance work: the **tomb of François II**★★. It was carved between

1502 and 1507 by Michel Colombe, a sculptor who was born in Brittany but settled in the Touraine. It was commissioned by Anne of Brittany to receive the remains of her father, François II, and her mother, Marguerite of Foix, and it was placed in the Church of the Carmelites. The Revolutionary Tribunal ordered it to be demolished, but the courageous town architect of the time, instead of obeying the order, hid various pieces of the tomb in his friends' homes. It was reconstructed after the Revolution and transferred to the cathedral in 1817.

The Duke and Duchess recline on a black marble slab placed atop a rectangular slab in white marble. The statues grouped round them are symbolic: the angels supporting their heads represent their welcome to Heaven; the lion crouching at the feet of François stands for power, and Marguerite's greyhound stands for fidelity. The four large corner statues personify the four Cardinal Virtues: for the Duke, Justice (crowned and holding a sword) and Strength (helmeted and armed and expelling a dragon from a tower); Prudence and Temperance guard the Duchess. Prudence has two faces: in front, a young girl with a looking glass, symbolising the future, and behind, an old man representing the past. Temperance holds a bridle to signify control over passions, and a clock representing steadiness.

Below the recumbent figures are 16 niches containing the statues of saints interceding for the deceased, notably St-Francis of Assisi and St-Margaret, their patrons. Below the saints, 16 mourners, partly damaged, represent their people's sorrow.

This magnificent group is lit by a superb modern **stained-glass window** by Chapuis, 25m/82ft high and 5.3m/17ft wide, devoted to Breton and Nantes saints. The impression of height at the transept crossing is astonishing.

In the north arm of the transept is the **Cenotaph of Lamoricière**★, the work of the sculptor Paul Dubois (1879). The General is shown reclining under a shroud. Four bronze statues represent Meditation and Charity (at his head) and Military Courage and Faith (at his feet). Lamoricière (1806–65), a great African campaigner who came from Nantes, captured the Arabian Emir Abd-el-Kaderin 1847 during the wars in Algeria. He later fell into disgrace and when exiled by Napoleon III, he commanded Papal troops against the Italians. It is the Catholic paladin who is honoured here.

Skirt the cathedral façade; go through the portal to the left.

La Psalette

This 15C building with a polygonal turret formerly contained the chapter-house but is now part of the sacristy.

Take the vaulted passageway on the right.

From the small square you can see the other side of La Psalette.

Bear right on Impasse St-Laurent then left into rue Mathelin-Rodier (the name of the architect of the cathedral and part of the castle).

It was in the house at number 3 that the Duchess of Berry was arrested (see above).

Musée des Beaux Arts★★

10 rue George Clemenceau. Open Wed–Mon 10am–6pm, Thu until 8pm. Closed public holidays. 3.50€. 02 51 17 45 00.

The museum is housed in an imposing late-19C building, the main part of which is flanked by projecting wings. The collections, enriched by exhibits from the depository, cover the 13C to the present. A central patio is surrounded by large galleries with works exhibited in chronological order.

15C–18C

Note Perugino's (1448–1523) *St-Sebastian* portrayed as an elegant page holding an arrow; *St-Peter's Denial, The Angel Appearing to Joseph in His Dream* and *The Hurdy-Gurdy Player.* The 17C is represented by Georges de La Tour

(1593–1652), *The Guitarist* by Greuze (1725–1805) and *Harlequin, Emperor of the Moon* by Watteau (1684–1721).

19C
Classicism and Romanticism are represented by Ingres' fine portrait *Madame Senonnes,* Delacroix's *The Moroccan Chief* and Courbet's *The Winnowers.*

Modern and Contemporary Art
The 20C collections are displayed in seven large galleries. In the first, works illustrating the period from Impressionism to the Fauves include Monet's *Venitian Gondolas,* Émile Bernard's *Apple Tree Beating,* representing the Pont-Aven School, Sonia Delaunay's *Yellow Nude,* a Fauve work, and *Transatlantic Roll* by Nantes artist Émile Laboureur.

The second gallery contains a collection, which must be unique in a provincial museum, of paintings by Vasili Kandinsky executed during the years he taught at the Bauhaus (1922–33). The homogeneity of this collection, which features in particular *Black Frame* and the bright *Évènement Doux,* revolves around the idea of a 'microcosm'.

The third gallery exhibits different artistic movements from the period 1913–45, notably two works by the Constructivist Gorin, *Two Women Standing* by Magnelli, as well as two paintings by Chagall executed at a particularly testing time in his life, *Red Horse* and *Obsession.*

The fourth gallery plunges the viewer into the cultural context of the period 1940–60, with figurative works by Lapicque (*Sunset on the Salute*), Hélion (*Still Life with Pumpkin*) and abstract works by Poliakoff, Hartung, Bissière and the Nantes artist Camille Bryen.

The fifth gallery covers the period 1960–75. It focuses principally on the Nantes artist Martin Barré, but also exhibits the interesting work of François Morellet, representing Kinetic art.

The sixth gallery is largely given over to the 1970s and 80s. Note in particular *Promenade of the Blue Cavalier,* a charming abstract work by Thiéval, large "canvases" by Viallat and above all two Picassos, among the master's last works, *Couple*★ and *Man Seated with Walking Stick.* Finally, there are three works by Dubuffet, including *Setting with two Figures.*

The final gallery devotes a large area to contemporary European artistic expression. Rebecca Horn's *Hydrapiano,* with the bizarre behaviour of its long column of mercury, is particularly eye-catching.

Lycée Clemenceau
R. Georges-Clemenceau.

In 1886 this Lycée became the first French "sports academy". It was originally created by Bonaparte in 1803, and then rebuilt during the third Republic, by architects Antoine Demoget and Léon Lenoir.

Among its pupils is the writer Aristide Briand. It has been the only lycée in Nantes and indeed the *département* of the i-Atlantic for a long time, and has taken its place in the evolution of both the town's history and secondary education in France.

Le Lieu Unique
Open Mon 11am–8pm, Tue–Wed 11am–2am, Thur–Sat 11am–3am, Sun and public holidays 3pm–8pm. Access to the tower Wed–Sat 1pm–7pm, Sun 3pm–7pm. 2€. 02 40 12 14 34. www.lelieuunique.com.

Across from the Château, on the other side of the rail tracks, there stands a

Tower of Le Lieu Unique
H. Le Gac/MICHELIN

blue, white and red cupola. It is the last remaining trace of the biscuit factory founded by Jean Romain Lefèvre, husband of Pauline Isabelle Utile, in 1885. They joined their initials and created **Lu**, probably the best known of all bicuits in France, especially famous for the *Petit Beurre*. In 1986, the machinery moved to premises south of town. In 1999 the former factory was redesigned by architect Patrick Bouchain and renamed *Lieu Unique*. A cultural research centre was born in the stripped-down space with concrete and brick walls. You can see performances of dance, theatre or music, attend exhibitions, browse in the book shop, have a drink or visit the famous **tower** for a view over town and a look back at the former factory.

The moat surrounding the castle

A. de Valroger/MICHELIN

Château des Ducs de Bretagne

4 pl. Marc-Elder. ⏰*Open Jul–Aug, 9am –8pm, museum 10am–7pm; Jun and Sept, 10am–7pm, museum Wed–Mon 10am–6pm.* ⏰*Closed 1 Jan, 1 May, 1 Nov and 25 Dec.* ✆*5€; access to the courtyard, moat and ramparts is free.* ♿ ✆*02 51 17 49 00.*

The golden age of the castle was that of Duke François II, when court life was truly regal: five ministers, 17 chamberlains and a host of retainers attended

the Duke. Life was sumptuous and morals liberal.

The present building was begun by Duke François II in 1466 and continued by his daughter, Anne of Brittany. Defence works were added during the League by the Duke of Mercœur. From the 18C onwards the military took possession, destroyed some buildings and erected others lacking in style. The Spaniards' Tower (1), which had been used as a magazine, blew up in 1800 (the

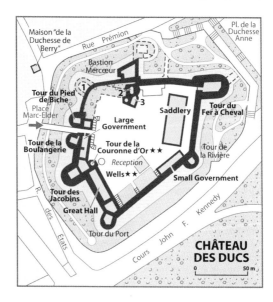

Maison "de la Duchesse de Berry"

Rue Prémion

Pl. de la Duchesse Anne

Bastion Mercœur

Tour du Pied de Biche

Place Marc-Elder

Large Government

Saddlery

Tour du Fer à Cheval

Tour de la Boulangerie

Tour de la Couronne d'Or ★★

Tour de la Rivière

Reception

Wells ★★

Small Government

R. des États

Tour des Jacobins

Great Hall

Tour du Port

Cours John F. Kennedy

CHÂTEAU DES DUCS

0   50 m

north part of the castle was destroyed – the sites of the destroyed buildings are indicated by a broken line on the plan). From the time of Charles VII to Louis XIV, nearly all the kings of France spent some time at the castle. Louis XII married Anne of Brittany in its chapel (1499); it was here that Henri IV signed the Edict of Nantes in 1598. Chalais, Cardinal de Retz, Gilles de Rais (Bluebeard) and the Duchess of Berry were imprisoned in its towers.

A tributary of the Loire washed up against the south, east and northeast walls until the building of a quay in the 19C and the filling of the branch in the 20C. The castle has recently reopened after a 15-year restoration programme and now houses the **Musée d'Histoire de Nantes**. The museum displays, chronologically and thematically, 800 objects in 32 rooms and highlights the history of the castle and Ducal Brittany, the Loire estuary, urban development, maritime and industrial heritage, WW II and the city's reconstruction, social movements, the city today and its future.

The fortress

The moat has now been re-established; the ditches that guarded the north and west sides have been turned into gardens and the old ditches have been restored on the other sides. An 18C bridge leads to the former drawbridge, which is flanked by two massive round towers dating from the time of Duke François.

Inside the courtyard

Behind the massive defensive walls, the court was used for jousting and tournaments, as well as the performance of mystery plays and farces.

The 15C **Bakery Tower**, also called Tower of Hell, was used as a prison, a theory confirmed by the graffiti visible on the walls.

The elegant **Golden Crown Tower**★ (Tour de la Couronne d'Or), whose name may be explained by the presence of a nearby well, presents fine Italian-style loggias and connects two pavilions pierced by rows of windows. The 15C **Jacobins Tower** (Tour des Jacobins) was also used as a prison (note the carved graffiti).

The main building, built by François II and extended two storeys by Anne of Brittany, was the ducal palace. It is decorated by five tall Gothic dormer windows with ornate pinnacles.

This part of the castle took the name **Governor's Major Palace** (Grand Gouvernement) after the 1670 fire, which destroyed a whole wing; later it became the home of the governor of Brittany. During the reign of the dukes, it had been their palace and had been used for meetings concerning the duchy.

Over the **well**★★, which probably dates back to the days of François II, there is a wrought-iron framework, which represents the ducal crown. The seven-sided curb of the well has seven pulleys and seven gargoyles for the overflow.

The Renaissance **Governor's Lesser Palace** (Petit Gouvernement) was built under François I; the military Saddlery, dating back to 1784 was the armory.

The **old keep (2)** is, in fact, one of the four polygonal towers that enclosed the original castle built in the 13C and enlarged in the 14C; it is part of an 18C mansion that houses the **porter's lodge (3)**.

The Horseshoe Tower is 16C. In the restored rooms, special lighting enhances the vaulting and its armorial-decorated keystones. Temporary exhibitions are held alternately, presenting the works formerly displayed in the Musée des Salorges.

Nantes derives its name from the Namnètes, a Gallic tribe who made the town their capital. The Romans developed it as a trading centre; the Vikings pillaged then occupied it. In the early 20C, a plan for urban renewal greatly altered the face of the town, as did the massive destruction of WW II. The cathedral, striking for its Gothic unity despite the long building period, was bombed during the war, and had been nearly completely restored in 1972 when fire largely destroyed the roof. The medieval castle is remarkable for its contrasts: outside, a fortress with its crenellated towers; inside, a typical Renaissance palace. These rare historic buildings are the architectural pride of Nantes.

Plateau Ste-Croix

This is an area where 15C and 16C half-timbered houses still stand: number 7 **rue de la Juiverie**, number 7 **rue Ste-Croix**, numbers 8 and 10 **rue de la Boucherie,** number 5 **rue Bossuet** and **place du Change.**

The 17C **Église Ste-Croix** is surmounted by the former town **belfry**★ crowned with trumpeting angels. The palm tree decoration of the chancel vaulting contrasts with the round vaulting of the nave. Large Flamboyant windows open onto the aisles. The furnishings are 18C. Bars and restaurants liven up the district in the evening and pavement cafés welcome visitors as soon as the weather turns mild.

▷ *To return to the historic city centre, follow cours Franklin-Roosevelt then cours Olivier-de-Clisson to rue Kervégan.*

② OLD NANTES

Allow 3hr.

Ancienne Île Feydeau★

Between 1926 and 1938 the islet was linked to the mainland and a second island, the Île Gloriette, by filling in several arms of the Loire. The islet has retained its 18C appearance, especially between place de la Petite Hollande and cours Olivier-de-Clisson (number 4 was the birthplace of Jules Verne).

It was here that rich shipowners used to build their vast mansions, which stretch from the central street, rue Kervégan, right back to one of the outer avenues, allées Turenne or Duguay-Trouin. Curved wrought-iron balconies and grotesque masks, probably the work of seafaring craftsmen, adorn the façades. The inner courtyards have staircases with remarkable vaulting.

Quartier Graslin★

It was the financier **Graslin**, Receiver General for farmlands at Nantes, who was responsible for the creation of this area in the late 18C. The Stock Exchange, built by Crucy in 1811–13, stands on **place du Commerce**. It now houses the Tourist Office. Further on, **place Royale**, designed by Crucy, is adorned by a fountain represetning Nantes (1865).

Opening onto rue Santeuil is a curious stepped shopping arcade on three levels. **Passage Pommeraye**★, built in 1843, leads to the Stock Exchange. Great fluted columns support galleries lined with elegant shops and rows of statues serve as pedestals for the lamps.

Place Graslin – narrow and busy, **Rue Crébillon** is very lively. It is the hub for taking a stroll in the town. It leads to a fine esplanade which houses the Corinthian theatre dating from 1783. La Cigale brasserie is classed as a national monument and has a fine 19C interior with mosaics. Just further on is **Cambronne** Square, created by Mathurin Crucy. Fine Napoleon I houses flank the square.

▷ *Having crossed the square, turn left and left again, then right, towards Quai de la Fosse.*

Musée de l'Imprimerie

24 quai de La Fosse. ◷*May–Jun daily exc Sun, 10am–noon, 2pm–5.30pm; Jan–Apr, 10am–noon, 2pm–5.30pm, Sun 2pm–5pm, possibility of a guided visit 2.30pm daily exc Sun.* ◷*Closed public hols.* ⊚*5 €.* ⏦ *℘ 02 40 73 26 55. www.musee.imprimerie.free.fr.*

This museum traces the history of the book. Techniques for preparation and printing are demonstrated using tools and machinery still in working order.

Quai de la Fosse

Several 18C mansions line this quay (numbers 17, 54, 70), including number 86, Hôtel Durbé, whose outbuildings served as a warehouse for the India Company.

Opposite quai de la Fosse, the île Beaulieu, renamed île de Nantes, is subject to a vast programme of urbanisation. The architect Jean Nouvel is responsible for the new glass and concrete law courts (palais de justice).

Église Notre-Dame-de-Bon-Port

🕓*Open 10am–7pm.*
Also known as Église St-Louis, this unusual building overlooks Place Sanitat. The great cubic mass (1846–58) is adorned with frescoes and a triangular pediment topped by a majestic dome. Massive hexagonal pillars support the dome decorated with panels of stained glass and frescoes.

Musée Archéologique★

⊶*Closed for major restoration from 2011.*
The first floor of this archaeological museum concentrates on Greek and Etruscan pottery and all that is Egyptian (sarcophagi, canopic vases – funerary urns, the covers of which are in the form of an animal or human head – bronze and painted statuettes).
The second floor concentrates on local civilisations covering prehistory to the invasion of the Norsemen, with displays of arms, tools, terracotta and bronze vases, jewellery, items from St-Nazaire dating from the neolithic to the Bronze Age, and Gallo-Roman objects excavated at Rezé (Loire-Atlantique).

Musée Dobrée★

⊶*Closed for major restoration from 2011.*
This Romanesque-style mansion was built in the 19C by the Nantes shipowner and collector **Thomas Dobrée** (1810–95).
The museum contains Romanesque and Gothic sculptures from Nantes and the Val de Loire medieval ivories and alabasters, champlevé enamels (12C–14C) from the Limousin, Rhine and Moselle regions, paintings and jewellery.
On the first floor are Chinese collections, Dobrée family memorabilia.
Opposite the museum is the **Manoir de la Touche** (🕓*open during temporary*

exhibitons). It was built at the start of the 15C by Bishop Jean de Malestroit. Jean V, duke of the house of Montfort, died here in 1442. The term *"tousche"* designates a small wood, which used to top the hill.

👥 Muséum d'Histoire Naturelle★★

12 rue Voltaire. 🕓*Open Wed–Mon 10am –6pm.* 🕓*Closed public holidays.*
3.50€ (under 18s, no charge), no charge on 3rd Sun of every month.
&.*02 40 41 55 00. www.museum. nantes.fr.*
Originally set up in the Cabinet Dubuisson in 1799, this Natural History Museum was later moved to the former Mint (Hôtel de la Monnaie) and inaugurated in 1875. It houses several important collections in such varied areas as zoology, regional fauna, osteology, palaeontology, prehistory, sciences of the earth, mineralogy and ethnography.
The section devoted to shells is remarkable on account of the sheer beauty and variety of the exhibits. A vivarium presents reptiles and batrachians from all over the world.

QUAI DE LA FOSSE TO BUTTE STE-ANNE

Escorteur d'Escadre Maillé-Brézé

Guided tours daily (1hr or 90min including machinery) 🕓*Jun–Sept 2pm– 6pm; Oct–May, Wed, Sat, Sun, school holidays and public holidays, 2pm–5pm;*
🕓 *Closed Mon, Tue, Thu and Fri 3pm.*
4.60€ (7€ including machinery).
09 79 18 33 51. www.maillebreze.com.
Docked on the Loire, this escort ship (132.65m/435ft long and 12.7m/41ft wide) was launched in 1957 and served until 1988. The visit includes antisubmarine and anti-aircraft weapons and detection systems, the command post and the officers' and sailors' living quarters.
In the officers' quarters, a small museum evokes the life of French Admiral Jean Armand de Maillé (1619–1646) through literature and various exhibits.

🔹 Planétarium

*Access by Quai E.-Renaud and rue
de l'Hermitage. 8 rue des Acadiens.*
🕐*Shows (1hr) daily (except Sat) at
10.30am, 11.30am, 2.15pm, 4.45pm; Sun
3pm, 4pm, 4.30pm, 5.30pm.* 🕐*Closed
public holidays.* ✎*5€ (children 3€).*
♿ ☎*02 40 73 99 23.*

In the planetarium, visitors discover
the mysteries of the universe: the sun,
moon, stars and planets are projected
onto the dome. Each show takes a different theme.

View from Ste-Anne Lookout point★

*Access via Quai E.-Renaud and rue
de l'Hermitage.*

From the terraced lookout point there is
a good view of the port installations with
cranes in the foreground and shipyards
and Île de Nantes in the distance.
A viewing table (table d'orientation)
helps the visitor pinpoint Nantes' main
sights and its new buildings.

Musée Jules-Verne★

3 rue de l'Hermitage. 🕐*Open daily Jul–
Aug 10am–6pm; Rest of year, Wed–Mon
10am–noon, 2pm–6pm, Sun 2pm–
6pm.* ☛*Guided tour Sun at 3.30pm.*
🕐*Closed public holidays.* ✎*3€
(children free), no charge 4th Sun of
the month.* ♿ ☎*02 40 69 72 52.
www.julesverne.nantes.fr.*

A 19C mansion houses the museum
devoted to Jules Verne (1828–1905), one
of the first to write science fiction novels
such as *Five Weeks in a Balloon, A Journey
to the Centre of the Earth* and *Around the
World in Eighty Days.*

L'ÎLE DE NANTES

Opposite the Quai de la Fosse, the **Île
Beaulieu** used to function as a shipyard. Re-named the **Île de Nantes** it has
benefitted from an urban development
programme.
The western section, surrounded by two
tributaries of the Loire, has nearly been
completed. On your left hand side, as
you cross the Anne-de-Bretagne bridge,
you can see architect Jean Nouvel's glass
and concrete building, which houses the
Palais de Justice.

🔹 Les Machines de l'Île

*Entrance on bd. L. Bureau behind the
law courts. Enquire at the Tourist Office
for details of tours and opening times.*
The old naval dockyards have been
transformed into workshops that produce fairytale machines. An elephant
(40t and 12m/39ft high) can take 35 passengers on its back or in its stomach! A
35-minute trip costs 6€.

THE ERDRE VALLEY
Boat Trip on the Erdre★

♿*See Addresses for details.*
This beautiful river isn't easy to explore.
The road doesn't follow the river and
the best thing to do is to hire a kayak
or take a boat trip. This is a favourite of
the Nantais, in pleasantly green countryside dotted with manor houses; the 16C
Château de la Gascherie with its ornate
windows is notable. The Erdre widens
beyond Sucé to form Lake Mazerolles.

Île de Versailles

*Entrance on quai de Versailles or quai
Henri-Barbusse.* 🕐*Open mid-Jan–mid-
Nov Wed–Mon 1.30am–6.15pm, Sat–
Sun and holidays 9.30am–12.15pm,
2.15pm–6.15pm; mid-Nov–mid-Jan,
Wed–Mon 1.30am–5.15pm, Sat–Sun
9.30am–12.15pm, 2.15pm–5.15pm.*
🕐*Closed Tue.* ♿ ☎*02 40 29 41 11.
www.jardins.nantes.fr.*

Once covered with marshland, the islet
was landfilled during the building of the
Nantes-Brest Canal. A charming Japanese garden has been landscaped with
rock gardens, waterfalls, and lanterns.

PARKS AND GARDENS

Nantes took an interest in botany as
early as the 17C and exotic plants such as
magnolias adorned the town's gardens,
which today cover an area of 800ha/
1,977 acres.

Jardin des Plantes★

Entrance on boulevard de Stalingrad (opposite the station) or place Sophie-Trébuchet. ◷*Open 15 Jan–19 Mar, 8.30am–6.30pm; 20 Mar–22 Oct 8.30am–8pm; 23 Oct–17 Nov 8.30am–6.30pm; 18 Nov–14 Jan 8.30am–5.30pm.* ♿ ☏*02 40 41 90 09. www.jardins.nantes.fr.*

This fine garden was created in 1807. It is beautifully landscaped and contains several fine ponds and wooden sculptures, in addition to the masses of white, pink, purple and yellow camellias, magnolias, rhododendrons and splendid trees. A statue of Jules Verne is a reminder that Nantes was the writer's native town. The greenhouses contain an extensive collection of cacti (👁*guided tours 3€*).

Parc de Procé

Entrance on boulevard des Anglais, rue des Dervallières or boulevard Clovis-Constant.

It is a pleasure to stroll through this undulating park (16ha/40 acres) landscaped with perspectives and rhododendrons, azaleas, oaks and more.

👥 Le Jardin des Hespérides

Ferme de la Hautière. 3km/1.8mi N via the ring road, exit: La Chapelle-sur-Erdre. ◷*Open May–mid-Oct.* 👁*Guided tour (1hr 30) at 4pm, Sun and holidays at 3pm, 5pm.* ✆*7.60€ (children 4.10€).* ♿ ☏*02 40 72 03 83. http://ferme.fruitiere.free.fr.*

This fruit-growing farm, run by the same family since 1810, has set aside a 1.5ha/4-acre theme-area which includes a strawberry garden, a Loire-Atlantique garden, a world garden (fruit from faraway countries), a new-fruit garden (hybrids), a wild-fruit garden, a Neolithic garden, a Mediterranean garden and a botanists' garden.

Visitors are invited to taste a cocktail of fruits and then buy some products, such as jams and sorbets, in the shop.

🚗 DRIVING TOURS

The following three driving tours allow you to explore the area south of the Loire Estuary: the wine country of Muscadet, the Pays de Retz and the Jade Coast.

☐1 LE PAYS DU MUSCADET DE SÈVRE-ET-MAINE

Tour of 65 km/40.5m – allow 4hr.

Clisson

Clisson is one of the gateways to the vineyards producing Muscadet de Sèvre-et-Maine, as well as those of the Gros-Plant du Pays Nantais. Stretching out on either side of the valley of the Sèvre Nantaise, along the river's sinuous course, you will find the winemakers' estates.

▷ *Head N out of Clisson for 8km, following the D 763 then the D 149 towards Nantes.*

Le Pallet

This village was the birthplace of the philosopher and theologian Pierre Abélard (1079-1142), a remarkable and enigmatic figure. He is most famous for falling in love with Héloïse, the niece of the cruel Canon Fulbert, whom he married in secret before she was placed in a convent.

In a huge modern building, this museum of the region's winemaking heritage, the **Musée du Vignoble nantais**, will introduce you to all the secrets of Muscadet wine (◷*early Apr–early Nov: afternoons;* ◷*closed Mon, 11 Nov–28 Feb, Easter Mon, Whit Mon, 1 and 11 Nov, 25 Dec;* ✆*5€ (18 yrs, 3 €); ☏02 40 80 90 13. www.vignoble-nantais.eu*).

Visitors can discover the different areas of production and the different tasks performed on the vineyard: grafting techniques, harvest, pressing, winemaking, cooperage and selling the wine.

The objects, machines and tools on display include secateurs, pruning knives, sprayers, ploughs, tractors and barrel scales, as well as a monumental 18C **long-beam press**.

In the **salle des cinq sens** (room of the five senses), you can learn about the different flavours of wine, before the final tasting. Outside, the museum presents the different grape varieties grown in the Pays Nantais.

Starting from the **Chapelle St-Michel**, a signposted route marks a pleasant walk through the vineyards.

Leave Le Pallet by the E and follow signs to Mouzillon.

Mouzillon

At the beginning of July, the village holds an evening of celebrations entitled "La Nuit du Muscadet". To the south of the church is a **Gallo-Roman bridge** over the Sanguèse.

From Mouzillon, head N on the D 763.

Vallet

This winemaking town is considered to be the capital of the Muscadet region.

Quittez Vallet par le nord-ouest en prenant la D 37.

Château de la Noë de Bel-Air

Free entrance to the park and grounds of the château all day. Free guided tours available on request.

This elegant château was destroyed during the French Revolution but rebuilt in 1836. Overlooking the park is a huge loggia with Tuscan columns. The use of brick in the construction of the outbuildings and the orangery is reminiscent of the Clisson style.

Follow the D 37.

Le Moulin du Pé

The top of this disused windmill offers a remarkable view over the vineyards and the marshland of the Marais de Goulaine.

Go back to the D 37 and continue in the same direction.

Le Loroux-Bottereau

The inhabitants of Le Loroux-Bottereau formed an élite corps during the 1793 uprising, earning the wrath of General Turreau, who had the town destroyed in 1794.

Église St-Jean-Baptiste – The church has two 12C frescoes illustrating the legend of St Giles. From the **bell tower**, you can enjoy a view over the vine-clad slopes.

From Le Loroux-Bottereau, head SE on the D 7.

Marais de Goulaine

This 1,500-hectare/3,700-acre expanse of lush vegetation is criss-crossed by numerous canals bordered by reeds. Heading up from the road, near the legendary Pont de l'Ouen, you can enjoy a fine **view** from the Butte de la Roche.

Promenade en barque – ℰ02 40 54 55 50. ○Apr–Sept: Boat hire, (○closed during the hunting season). Keys and oars from Tourist Office. ⊜10€ boat for 4 persons. (half day).

You can explore the heart of the Marais de Goulaine by boat or on foot on canalside walks.

Turn right onto the D 74.

Château de Goulaine

13km/8mi SE on N 149, then D 119 towards Haute-Goulaine. Guided tours (1hr 30) 3 Jul–5 Sept, daily 2pm–6pm; 28 Mar –2 Jul and 6 Sept–7 Nov, Sat–Sun and public holidays 2pm–6pm. ⊜8€. ℰ02 40 54 91 42. http://chateau. goulaine.online.fr.

The château, surrounded by vineyards, was built between 1480 and 1495 by Christophe de Goulaine, Groom of the Bedchamber to Louis XII and François I. He built it on the foundations of an old medieval fortress which, with those at Clisson and Nantes, had been used to defend the Duchy of Brittany against France.

Remains from this military past include a machicolated tower and a small castle in front of a bridge spanning a moat. This handsome residence consists of a

Gothic 15C main building of calcareous tufa from the Saumur region, and two wings added in the early 17C.

Inside, a spiral staircase leads to the first floor, which opens into the **Great Hall,** in which the most striking feature is the richly sculpted, monumental Renaissance chimney piece. A beautiful 16C Flemish tapestry depicting the Fall of Phaethon adorns the wall.

The **Blue Room** still has its early 17C décor intact: blue and gold coffered ceiling, chimney piece with Corinthian columns and caryatids, panelling decorated with pastel landscapes, and a large majestic Gobelins tapestry. The **Grey Room** has interesting panelling and mythological scenes on its piers.

Don't miss the permanent exhibition of the LU biscuit company from 1880 to today.

Volière à Papillons

An enormous greenhouse next to the castle's curtain wall contains tropical flowers and shrubs and houses many butterflies.

Return to the D 74 and continue in the same direction. At Haute-Goulaine, take the DF 105 southbound. As you come into Vertou, turn left, then take the D 59 towards Clisson. After 500m/545yds, take a left turn onto the D 539.

La Haie-Fouassière

This winemaking village takes its name from the fouasse, a delicious cake in the shape of a six-pointed star that can be found in local pâtisseries.

A wine centre, **Maison des vins de Nantes,** close to the water tower, is the headquarters of the Nantes wine trade association *(Pl. du Commerce; visit and (free) wine tasting by arrangement; ℘02 40 36 90 10. www.vinsdeloire.fr).*

It has extensive documentation on the region's wines and a selection of 104 different bottles.

The building also offers **good views** over the vineyards.

From La Haie-Fouassière, head S on the D74, crossing the Sèvre Nantaise.

St-Fiacre-sur-Maine

Sophie Trébuchet, the mother of Victor Hugo, used to spend her holidays in this little winemaking village tucked away in a verdant corner between the Sèvre and Maine rivers. The village also boasts the highest density of vines in the region and is home to a 19C Neo-Byzantine church and some very old farms. Other notable sights are the C15 Tour du Chasseloir, with its cellar decorated with imaginary creatures, and the Château de Coing, with its Italian-style outbuildings bearing a certain resemblance to the architecture of the town of Clisson.

Turn left onto the D 76, which runs alongside the river.

Monnières

As well as its 12C and 15C architecture, the church at Monnières has some interesting modern stained-glass windows inspired by the subject of wine and vines.

The D 76 will take you back to Clisson.

② LA CÔTE DE JADE★

70km/43mi tour – allow around half a day.

Pornic

From Pornic to St-Brevin-les-Pins, a string of popular resorts stretches along the coastline of the Pays de Retz, which is known as the Côte de Jade due to the vivid green colour of the waves. Between Pornic and St-Gildas, the cliff road skirting a coastline indented with sandy creeks is particularly attractive.

Ste-Marie

Near Mombeau beach, a cliff-top path offers a lovely **view** over the rocky coast with its beaches of fine sand. You will also notice lots of cabins on stilts built for fishing, known as *carrelets*.

Follow the signs for Le Porteau par la côte (Le Porteau via the coast).

From **Les Sablons** beach to Le Porteau beach, the road hugs the shore above the jagged coastline. Then from **Le Porteau to Préfailles**, the road moves inland, and only walkers can continue along the coast, via the Tour du Pays de Retz hiking path, which overlooks the ocean.

Pointe de St-Gildas★

🅿 *Leave your car at the car park by the marina (port de plaisance).*

The headland is covered in short moorland grass and dotted with remnants of the Atlantic Wall fortifications built by the Germans. Beyond are schist reefs pummelled by the waves. On 14 June 1931, a steamboat from Nantes, the *St-Philibert*, went down off the Pointe de St-Gildas, claiming the lives of 500 passengers returning from an excursion to Noirmoutier. The headland has a view of the Breton coast between St-Nazaire and Le Croisic, and down to Noirmoutier.

⬦ *Follow the Pornic road (D 313). After 1km/0.6mi, turn left onto the D 13, which follows the Côte de Jade for 20km/12.5mi.*

St-Brevin-les-Pins

In this charming resort, you will find villas dotted amongst the pines, an 8km beach of fine sand, a casino and a marina. It also encompasses **St-Brevin-l'Océan**, with its dunes stretching south from the rocky outcrop of Le Pointeau. A **tourist train** operates around the resort in the holiday season.

Of the many megaliths in the region, the **Dolmen de l'allée des Rossignols** in St-Brevin-l'Océan (5m/16.4ft in length) is one of the most accessible.

The **Musée de la Marine** (*Mindin, pl. Bougainville;* 🕐 *mid Jun–mid Sept. Daily exc Mon, 3pm–7pm;* 🅾*closed Oct–May and public hols;* ⊛*3 € (under 12yrs, free);* 𝄞*02 40 27 24 32; www.mairie-saint-brevin.fr*) is housed in a disused fort dating from 1861 and standing at the mouth of the Loire, on the Promontoire du Nez-de-Chien. Its exhibits chart the history of Mindin, in particular the 1759 Battle of Quiberon Bay, which was fought by the French and the English during the Seven Years' War, and led to

the sinking of the French ship the *Juste*. The ship's canons are on display at the entrance to the fort.

You can admire numerous models of ships from all eras, including three giants built in St-Nazaire: the Normandie, the France and the Batillus, a supertanker dating from 1976 that was one of the largest ever built. The grounds of the fort offer a **view** of St-Nazaire and its shipyards, and the elegant **St-Nazaire-St-Brevin road bridge★**.

⬦ *From Mindin head E for 11km/7mi on the D 277 then the D 77. At Paimbœuf there is a fine view over the Loire esuary. From Paimboeuf, head S on the D 114. When you reach St-Père-en-Retz, the D 86 will take you back to Pornic.*

③ PAYS DE RETZ

130km/80mi route – allow about a day.

⬦ *Begin by heading SE out of Pornic.*

The road follows the coast, passing through the resort of La Bernerie. South of Moutiers-en-Retz, you can enjoy fine views over the Bay of Bourgneuf and the Island of Noirmoutier.

Bourgneuf-en-Retz

An important crossroads giving access to the beaches of the Bay of Bourgneuf to the north and the Vendée oyster beds to the south.

The **Musée du Pays de Retz** occupies the 17C outbuildings of a former Franciscan friary (*6 r. des Moines;* 🕐*Jul–Aug, 10.30am–1pm, 2pm–6.30pm; Apr–Jun and Sept–Oct, daily exc Mon, 10am–noon, 2pm–6pm;* ⬦ guided visit on reservation; ⊛*4 € (-12 years2 €);* 𝄞*02 40 21 40 83; www.museepaysderetz.com*).

It offers collections covering mineralogy and archaeology, as well as local costumes and headdresses, a traditional late-19C rural cottage and several workshop reconstructions, bringing the traditional occupations of the Pays de Retz to life. As well as activities relating to the sea (oyster farming, work on the salt marshes, fishing and coastal wildlife), visitors can also learn about farming and the crafts of the clog-maker, cobbler, blacksmith, spinner, cooper, baker, innkeeper and brick-maker.

▷ *From Bourgneuf, head E for 12km/ 7.5m on the D 13.*

Machecou

During the holiday season, the historic capital of the Pays de Retz stages shows based on the region's history.

▷ *From Machecoul, head NE on the D 64. Around 2km/1.25m after St-Même-le-Tenu, turn right onto the D 71. At St-Lumine, take the D 61 for 7km/4.4m.*

St-Philbert-de-Grand-Lieu l'Abbatiale St-Philbert★

Access by the Tourist Office, ℘*02 40 78 73 88.* ◷*Jul –Aug, 10am–noon, 2pm– 6.30pm; Apr–Jun and Sept, 10am–noon, 2pm–6pm, Sat, Sun and Mon 2pm– 6pm; Oct–Mar: daily exc Mon, 10am– noon, 2pm–5.30pm, Sat–Sun, 2pm– 5.30pm.* ⟿ *Guided visit Jul–Aug, 3pm and 4pm. Closed 1 Jan., 1 May, 1 Nov, 25 Dec.* ⊜*2.50 € (under 6 yrs, 1.50 €).* ⟿*Guided visit 3 € (-6 yrs, 2 €), visit to gardens no charge.*

Construction of this amazing Carolingian church dates back to the 9C and was completed in two stages: the first from 815 and the second from 836 to 847. For a time, the church possessed the precious relic of St-Philbert (♨ see box below) and became an important destination for pilgrims. It underwent alterations during the Hundred Years' War and the Wars of Religion, then was used to store fodder for animals during the French Revolution. The structure suffered some ill-treatment in 1870, when people saw fit to lower the walls by more than 3m. It then became disused and was used as a chicken market until 1936. Since then, it has regained its role as a place of worship, and now stands as a moving example of a building that bears the scars of its long history, although the rehabilitation has subtly brought out the beauty of its architecture and given it back the solemnity it deserves.

Interior – The nave is both majestic and austere and stands out for its curious mixture of ancient tradition and Byzantine influence, which can be seen in the imposing, unadorned pillars and the alternation of bricks and Roman-style stonework. On the side walls, a white chalk line indicates the level of the ground before the building was cleared, and in the transept arches, you can see where materials from Roman buildings were reused in the construction, which was quite a common practice in the Middle Ages. In the choir, you will see the **crypt** of St-Philbert, which was designed with pilgrims in mind and contained openings allowing them to pray in front of the 7C **marble sarcophagus** containing the remains of the miracle-working saint. With the Viking threat looming large in 858, however, his remains were removed from the sarcophagus. Such was the veneration for the saint that the crypt was even walled up in order to protect his coffin.

📏**Maison du lac** – *Access by the Tourist Office.* ℘ *02 40 78 73 88. Apr–Sept, morning and afternoon, rest of the year, daily exc Mon and Sun afternoon. Closed 1 Jan and 25 Dec.* ⊜*2.50 € (6-12 yrs 1.50 €), combined ticket with the Abbatiale.*

This remarkable museum of birdlife is dedicated to the 225 species of nesting and visiting birds that can be found at the Lac de Grand-Lieu. It features an audiovisual presentation on the flora and fauna of the lake and a video on the nature reserve.

▷ *From St-Philbert, head N on the D 65 for 6km/3.75m then turn left onto the D 62 towards Passay.*

Lac de Grand-Lieu

This lake linked to the Loire estuary by the Acheneau channel, also known as the Étier de Buzay, has been a nature reserve since 1980. The rocky bottom, which lies 1m–2m/3.2ft–6.5ft under the surface according to the season, is covered in places by a thick layer of mud. The mud is said to have buried the town of Herbauge, which paid the price for its dissolute ways. According to the legend, you can still hear the bells peal in the middle of lake at midnight on Christmas Eve. The lake is an important nesting site for the grey heron and the rare spoonbill, and being situated on an Atlantic migration route, is visited by more than 200 species of bird, including snipe, ducks, teal, grebes, crakes and geese.

Boat trips – *During the feast day dedicated to fishermen, which takes place in Passy on 15 Aug and the following Sun.* Boat trips are only permitted on an exceptional basis, so the Maison du pêcheur in Passay is the only way to discover the lake's natural beauty.

Passay

This typical fishermen's hamlet is the only place from which you can approach the Lac de Grand-Lieu.

Maison du pêcheur – *Mid Jun–mid Sept: 10am –7pm; rest of the year, Wed and Sat, 2pm–5pm, Sun 2pm–6pm. Guided visit (1h30). Closed public hols.* 4 € (6-15 yrs, 2 €). 02 40 31 36 46. Standing at the foot of an **observatory tower** looking out over the lake and its surroundings, this little museum introduces you to the reserve's exceptionally rich natural habitat. It provides a clear presentation of the lake and its ecosystem (plants and wildlife), along with the activities that rely on them, particularly fishing and the specific techniques used by fishermen. Aquariums contain local species such as pike, zander, eels and carp.

From Passay, return to the D 65 and head NE. At Pont-St-Martin, take the D 11 heading W for 9km/5.6mi. At Bouaye, follow the signs for St-Mars-de-Coutais.

Planète sauvage★★

Apr– mid Nov, all day. Rest of the year; Sat Sun all day. Closed Dec–Mar. 17 € (4-13rs, 11 €). 02 40 04 82 82. www.planetesauvage.com.

Planète Sauvage is a haven for over 2,000 animals and one of Europe's leading reproduction centres for wild animals, accounting for some 250 births each year.

Safari tour – *about 2hrs. Possible rest break after 5km/3mi. Follow the safety advice: keep your windows closed and sound the horn if you have a problem, but do not get out of your vehicle.* Allow yourself to be transported to far-away lands as you observe some 150 species of wild animals close up, either from your own vehicle or on a guided 4x4 expedition (booking required).

Ten kilometres (6mi) of trails wind their way through 16 different wildlife areas recreating bushland and savannah habitats, where you can marvel at the hippos and elephants at play by the water or the amazing jumping skills of the impalas and springboks, see the American black bears taking a siesta on the rocks, watch the tigers and admire the lions, giraffes and the social behaviour of the African wild dogs.

Plenty of surprises are also in store at the **bushland village** (village de brousse), which can be explored on foot. At the **reptile arch** (arche des reptiles), you will come face to face with the amazing world of snakes, lizards, crocodiles and tortoises. At the **miniature farm** (ferme miniature), on the other hand, you will be charmed by the raccoons, porcupines, coatis, meerkats, parrots and other smaller animals. Another attraction is the **siamang and flamingo island** (île aux siamangs et aux flamants), where the gibbons mingle with the colonies of birds on the shore. Jungle track (parcours jungle) – daredevils will want to venture onto this suspension bridge hanging over the territory of 70 rhesus macaques!

Marine complex (cité marine) – for the well-being of the animals this area is equipped with innovative water treatment technology. The large pool hosts an amazing sea lion show (25min).

Go back to Port-St-Père and head 10km/6.25m to the N on the D 103 then the D 80.

Le Pellerin

At Le Pellerin, you can take a ferry across the Loire.

From Le Pellerin, head 10km/6.25mi W on the D 58 then the D 66.

Rouans
This village was the setting for Jean-Loup Hubert's film Le Grand Chemin, starring Anémone and Richard Bohringer, and their verbal sparring still seems to hang in the air!

▶ *Head W out of Rouans to rejoin the D 266, which takes you through the Forêt de Princé. At Chauvé, get back onto the D 6, which will take you back to Pornic.*

ADDRESSES

🛏STAY

NANTES
🛏 **Camping Le Petit Port** – *21 bd du Petit-Port, Bord du Cens.* ☎*02 40 74 47 94. www.nge-nantes.fr/camping. Reservation advised. 200 pitches.* The campsite has 200 pitches for tents, caravans and campervans just minutes from the town. 36 mobile homes are available. Free access to the swimming pool in Petit Port for campers.

🛏 **All Seasons Centre** – *3 r. Couëdic -* ☎*02 40 35 74 50. www.accorhotels.com. 65 rooms.* 🛏. Near the place Royale, this hotel has modern rooms (flat screen TV, internet), with a view of neighbouring rooftops from upper floors.

🛏 **Hôtel Pommeraye** – *2 r. Boileau.* ☎*02 40 48 78 79. www.hotel-pommeraye. com. 50 rooms.* 🛏 *9,50 €.* Close to the well known Passage Pommeraye and rue Crébillon's shops, lovers of contemporary design will delight in this hotel which is classified as a Clef Verte venue.

🛏 **Hôtel Graslin** – *1 r. Piron.* ☎*02 40 69 72 91. 47 rooms.* 🛏 *11 €.* This hotel offers two types of accommodation. Choose either the renovated Art Deco style rooms or the more traditional pine furnished rooms.

🛏 **Un coin chez soi** – *1 r. de Briord.* ☎ *06 64 20 31 09. www.uncoinchezsoi.net.* This hotel offers an alternative to a traditional hotel as it consists of private apartments situated in the town centre which can accommodate 2–4 persons. Immaculate decoration.

🛏 **Hôtel des Colonies** – *5 rue du Chapeau Rouge.* ☎*02 40 48 79 76. www.hoteldescolonies.fr. 38 rooms.*

🛏 *8€.* The pleasant breakfast room at this contemporary hotel serves as an exhibition space for local artists.

🍴EAT

NANTES
🍽 **Le Café Cult'** – *2 pl. du Change.* ☎*02 40 47 18 49. http://cafe-cult.com. Closed two weeks in Aug and Sun.* Take a trip back in time as you admire the façade of this 15C Nantes house, a listed building, then open the door to discover its medieval interior and bar where food is inspired by history.

🍽 **Crêperie Heb-Ken** – *5 r. de Guérande.* ☎*02 40 48 79 03. www.heb-ken.fr. Closed 20 Jul–19 Aug, Sun and public hols.* Reasonable prices for crêpes.

🍽 **Le Montesquieu** – *1 r. Montesquieu.* ☎*02 40 73 06 69. Mon–Fri noon–2pm and Wed–Sat 7pm–10.30pm.* Near to the Musée Dobrée, this restaurant serves authentic and tasty cooking.

🍽 **Amour de Pomme de Terre** – *4 rue des Halles.* ☎*02 40 47 66 37. www.amour depommedeterre.fr.* The potato reigns here in all its forms: as an accompaniment to grills or *raclettes*, in salads, au gratin...

🍽 **Tim Fish** – *4 r. de l'Arche Sèche.* ☎*02 40 47 11 46. www.timfish.fr. Closed Mon– Wed eve and Sun.* This small restaurant has developed a new way of tasting seafood. The assortment of fresh seasonal fish is served in a buckwheat cornet with vegetables.

🍽 **La Cigale** – *4 pl. Graslin.* ☎*02 51 84 94 94. www.lacigale.com.* With its listed tiles dating from 1900, which have appeared in several films, this atmospheric, animated brasserie is a favourite of the locals. A great place to come for market-fresh *plats du jour* and weekend brunches.

🍽 **Le Bistrot des Enfants Terribles** – *4 rue Fénelon.* ☎*02 40 47 00 38. Closed Sat lunch, Sun and Mon. Reservations advised.* Cosy restaurant where the dining room has fireplaces dating from the 16C and 17C, mirrors and benches. The caramelised pigs' cheeks, house terrines and St-Jacques (scallops) with mushroom sauce are delicious.

🍽 **Chez l'Huître** – *5 rue des Petites-Écuries.* ☎*02 51 82 02 02. www.chez lhuitre.fr. Closed 23 Dec–15 Jan and Sun* *except from 15 Jun–15 Sept.* Lovers of seafood are going to like this place, which has several varieties of oyster on offer. In summer, winkles and other crustaceans accompany your aperitif.

🍽 **L'Atlantide** – *Quai Ernest-Renaud. ☎02 40 73 23 23. www.restaurant-atlantide .net. Closed 20–23 May, 31 Jul–30 Aug, Sat lunch, Sun and holidays.* A contemporary dining room with Japanese influences on the fourth floor of this modern building. Well-regarded cuisine with views over the Loire and the city.

🍽 **Le Paludier** – *2 r. de Santeuil. ☎02 40 69 44 06. Closed Mon and Sat lunch, Sun.* Restaurant dedicated to seafood.

🍽 **L'Embellie** – *14 r. Armand Brossard. ☎02 40 48 20 02. www.restaurant lembellie.com. Closed Aug, Sun and Mon.* Close to the Anne de Bretagne tower. Dishes prepared with care.

NIGHTLIFE

The bars and restaurants in the *quartier du Bouffay* stay open until late. In the old town, the *rue de la Juiverie* is a good place to go and near the station, the post-industrial façade and white neon of the *Lieu Unique* hides a more intimate interior.

Bateaux Nantais – *Quai de la Motte-Rouge. Tram 2, stop Motte Rouge. ☎02 40 14 51 14. www.bateaux-nantais.fr. Daily 9am–11pm.* Discover the river l'Erdre, one of the most beautiful rivers of France, while having lunch or dinner. At night the boat trip is enchanting. **Pannonica** – *9 r. Basse-Porte. ☎02 51 72 10 10. www. pannonica.com. Ticket Office : Daily exc Sun and Mon, 1–6pm, Sat 9am–1pm. Closed mid Jun–mid Sept.* The concert hall at the Pannonica focuses on jazz, rock and new music. Some jazz greats have jammed in this Nantes hot spot. In June there is an international festival of improvised music –All'improvista.

ACTIVITIES

Boat trips – Bateaux Nantais – *as above.* François I claimed the Erdre one of France's most beautiful rivers. Panoramic trips (1hr 45min) pass many châteaux and cost 10€ for adults or 28€ for a family of four. Dinner or lunch cruises by reservation 59–80€.

Adventure Park – Les Naudières – *rte de Vannes, 44880 Sautron. 10km/6mi*

W of Nantes on the D 965 towards Vannes. ☎02 40 63 21 05. www.lesnaudieres.com. Open Jul–Aug, 10am–7pm; Apr–Sept see website. 9€. This adventure park has about 100 games spread over 7ha/17.3 acres. Toboggans, slides, bridges and tunnels will delight both small and big children.

Electric boats – *☎02 51 81 04 24. www.rubanvert.fr. Open May–Jun and Sept, 2pm–7pm, Sat–Sun and holidays 10am–7pm; Apr and Oct, Sat–Sun and holidays 10am–7pm; Jul–Aug, daily 10am–7pm.* Explore the **Erdre** or the **Sèvre Nantaise** on boats (no licence necessary). Departures from l'île de Versailles, Vertou or Sucé-sur-Erdre. Boat for 4 people from 25€/hr.

Kayak – *Kayak Nantais, rte de la Jonelière. ☎02 40 29 25 71. www.nack.fr. Open 10am–12.30pm, 2pm–6pm.* This club organises courses on the river.

Golf – Ligue de Golf des Pays de la Loire – *9 rue Couëdic. ☎02 40 08 05 06. www.ligue-golf-paysdelaloire.asso.fr.* Lessons and courses for all levels.

FESTIVALS AND EVENTS

See Calendar of Events. Also, be sure to find out about the performances of the **Royal de Luxe**, one of France's best-known street-theatre companies. Between its trips around the world, the company regularly comes back to Nantes, its home town, to invade the streets with articulate giants and legendary stories.

SHOPPING

Marché de Talensac – Undeniably part of Nantes' history, this markethall houses the city's most important market. There are more than 75 stalls, including some arts and crafts.

Passage Pommeraye – The films of Jacques Demy (*Lola*, 1961) and the prose of André Breton haunt this magnificent 19C arcade which now houses art galleries and boutiques.

Wine –Domaine des Herbauges – *44830 Bouaye. ☎02 40 65 44 92. www. domaine-des-herbauges.com. Open Mon–Sat 9am–noon, 2pm–6.30pm (Sat until 5.30pm).* The muscadet *Côtes de Grandlieu* is cultivated here by the fourth generation of winegrowers.

St-Nazaire ★

A visit to St-Nazaire, which is above all a great ship-building centre, is particularly interesting. Originally a small fishing port in the 15C, the town developed rapidly in 1856, when large ships, finding it difficult to sail up to Nantes, stopped at its deep-water port. Rebuilt in 1945 in the plainest fashion, St-Nazaire is nevertheless worth seeing for its port where everything is spectacular: the former submarine base, Escal'Atlantic, the museum show devoted to transatlantic sea journeys of bygone days and the docks where the world's largest liners are built.

▸ **Population:** 68,838.

Michelin Map: Local map 316 C4 – Loire-Atlantique (44).

Info: blvd. de la Légion d'Honneur, 44600 St-Nazaire. ℘02 40 22 40 65. www.saint-nazaire-tourisme.com.

Location: The city is served by the N 171 which comes from Nantes (65km/40mi E) and ends in Guérande (22km/13.5mi W).

Timing: Book in advance to visit the Airbus site.

Don't Miss: The view of the port from the submarine base.

A BIT OF HISTORY

From fishing village to major port – In 1850, St-Nazaire was no more than a village with 800 inhabitants. Six years later, the silting up of the Loire estuary led to the creation of a deep-water harbour for large ships unable to sail up to Nantes. At the same time, the *Compagnie Générale Transatlantique* established shipyards and set up the headquarters of its Central America shipping line in St-Nazaire.

At the turn of the 20C, the population of St-Nazaire had reached the 30,000 mark. However, the town was hard hit by the economic depression of 1929: the shipyards declined and the translatlantic shipping lines were transferred to Le Havre.

Opération Chariot – During WW II the town became a German submarine base. On 27–28 March 1942, a British commando unit caught the enemy by surprise, while the destroyer *Campbeltown* knocked down the Louis-Joubert entrance lock and the following day neutralised the lock by blowing itself up. A stele, reminding us of this heroic act, faces the sea on boulevard de Verdun. An obvious target for aerial bombardment between 1940 and 1945, the town got caught up in the fighting for the St-Nazaire Pocket and consequently was a desolate site when finally liberated.

St-Nazaire today – Since 1966, the Port Autonome de St-Nazaire has included several sites stretching some 60km along the Loire esturay: Donges specialises in crude oil; Montoire-de-Bretagne in natural gas, coal and foodstuffs; St-Nazaire handles traffic from local factories and continues to build ships.

HARBOUR INSTALLATIONS

Allow one day. Follow the signposts Ville-Port.

Leave the car in the parking area of the former submarine base. Combined tickets available for the different attractions on the site. Advisable to book tickets one week in advance.

Base de sous-marins

The submarine base, built during the German occupation from 1941 to 1943, was a very large reinforced concrete structure covering an area of 37 500sq m and measuring 300 x 125m/985 x 410ft. It had 14 bays, which together could take some 20 submarines. Machine shops were installed at the back of the bays. In spite of much bombing, the base came through the war undamaged and was used for the construction of warships until the late 1990s.

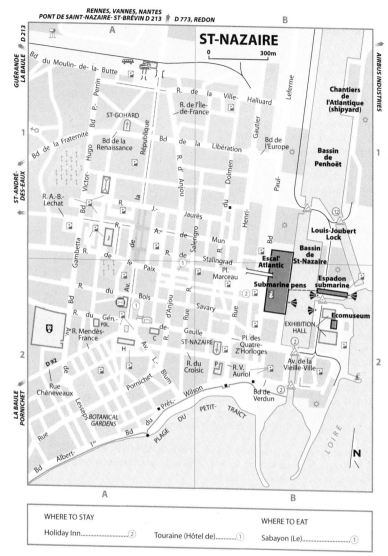

ST-NAZAIRE

0   300m

WHERE TO STAY	WHERE TO EAT
Holiday Inn...............② Touraine (Hôtel de)..........①	Sabayon (Le)............................①

But this huge bunker effectively cut the port off from the city. Later, it was used by the French Navy for building warships. Since the late 1990s, the installation of the Tourist Office has meant a reincarnation for the base, which is livelier and more integrated in the urban fabric.

👥 Escal'Atlantic★★

In the former submarine base. ◷*Open mid Jul–mid Aug , 10am–7pm; Apr–mid Jul and 27 Aug–30 Sept, 10am–12.30pm,* 2pm–6pm; Rest of the year by arrangement. Last entry 1hr 30min before closing. ◷Closed 1 Jan and 25 Dec. ➾12.50€ (children 8€) in summer, 9.90€ (children 6.90€) in winter. ♿ ℰ0 810 888 444. www.saint-nazaire-tourisme.com.

This vast area (3,500sq m/4,185sy yds has been given over to a recreation of the great ocean liners of the past from the *Liberté* to the *France*. The visit is like a cruise aboard one of these liners: uniformed staff welcome passengers who freely explore cabins, the music room, the bridge, the dining room, the piano-bar, dormitories reserved for immigrants and the holds.

Visitors can recline in deck chairs lined up along the promenade decks and admire a seascape created with special effects. Video clips bring famous passengers back to life: sail with Winston Churchill, Grace Kelly, Buster Keaton, Fred Astaire and others.

Terrasses panoramiques★★

In order to appreciate the full extent of the harbour installations, climb onto the roof of the submarine base (access via the ramp opposite rue Henri-Gautier or from inside the base by a lift located behind the Tourist Office).

The remarkable view of the harbour includes the Bassin de St-Nazaire and the Bassin de Penhoët, one of the largest in Europe with three types of dry dock. The Louis-Joubert lock was built between 1929–1932 to allow for the increase in tonnage of great Atlantic liners.

Écomusée de St-Nazaire

⏱Open mid Jul–mid Aug, 10am–7pm; Apr–mid Jul and 27 Aug–30 Sept, 10am–12.30pm, 2pm–6pm; rest of the year by arrangement. ⏱Closed Jan and 25 Dec. ⏱3€. ✆02 51 10 03 03. www.ecomusee-saint-nazaire.com.

On the banks of the Loire, at the heart of the port, a bright yellow building houses exhibits concerned with the St-Nazaire shipyards and the port's development: models of the shipyards, ocean liners (Normandie, Île de France, France), battleships (Jean Bart), dockers' old tools, portraits of people who contributed to the city's development and more.

Sous-marin Espadon

⏱Open mid Jul–mid Aug, 10am–7pm; Apr–mid Jul and 27 Aug–30 Sept, 10am–12.30pm, 2pm–6pm; rest of the year by arrangement. Last entry 1hr 30min before closing. ⏱Closed Jan and 25 Dec. ⏱8€ in summer, 6.90€ in winter. ✆0 810 888 444. www.saint-nazaire-tourisme.com.

Launched in 1957 from the Augustin Normand Shipyards in Le Havre, the Espadon was the first French submarine to cruise the polar ice caps. Seventy men lived on board; the torpedo room, engine room, sleeping area and control room can be visited.

Chantiers de l'Atlantique★

⏱Guided tours only (2hr), reservations required. The tour bus leaves from the submarine base. Wed and weekends, call ahead for times. ⏱Closed 31 Dec–6 Feb and 25 Dec. ⏱12€ in summer, 10.90€ in winter. ✆0 810 888 444.

Between the Bassin de Penhoët and the Loire lie the shipyards, made up of the former Loire workshops and dockyard and the Penhoët Dockyard; these were linked together in 1956 and since 1976 have been incorporated into Alsthom, now forming a subsidiary of the GEC Alsthom group. Among the ships which have come from the Atlantic Dockyard are the battleship Jean Bart, and the ocean liners Normandie and France. Cargo boats, container ships, ore carrying ships and tankers (capacity 550,000t) and passenger transport ships for French and foreign use are also built in the yards. Since 1987, the year in which Sovereign of the Seas (capacity 2, 600t) was delivered, the Chantiers de l'Atlantique have built a total of 11 cruise liners, including the largest in the world: Monarch of the Seas and Majesty of the Seas (capacity 2,770). Not for long, though, for in 2003 an even larger liner was launched: the Queen Mary II ordered by the Cunard Company. This ship, 345m/1132ft long and 41m/135ft wide, manned by a 1,310-strong crew, accommodates 2,800 passengers and crosses the Atlantic in six days at a speed of 30 knots.

The **exhibition** illustrates the evolution of the shipyards and the shipbuilding process from designing to launching.

A bus **tour of the yards** gives an insight into the extent of the complex. Three docks contain ships at different completion stages from the assembly of the hull to the finishing touches.

Built on a hill, surrounded by drystone walls, this tumulus, with two covered burial chambers, dates from 5C BC; two narrow passageways lead to these chambers.

Airbus St-Nazaire

Guided tours only (2hr) on reservation 48hr in advance (depart by coach from submarine base). Bring a passport for identification. Call about times of tours. Closed Jan–6 Feb. 12€ in summer, 10.90€ in winter. 0 810 888 444.

France's second Airbus site (after Toulouse) with 2,300 employees. Visitors will cross the huge hangars on foot and see new planes being assembled.

EXCURSIONS

Pont routier St-Nazaire–St-Brévin

Constructed in 1975, on the northeastern outskirts of St-Nazaire, this bridge spans the Loire and enables a link with Retz, La Vendée and the Charente.

St-Marc-sur-Mer

7 km/4.4mi W in the direction of La Baule.

St-Marc owes its notoriety to its most famous visitor – Jacques Tati's M. Hulot. Although the beach, surveyed by a bronze statue, doesn't seem to have changed much over the years, the hotel certainly seems to have profited from this media link.

La Grande Brière ★ (see p440)

North of St-Nazaire.

Tumulus de Dissignac

W by the D 492, then right towards Les Forges. 02 51 10 03 03 or 06 87 64 07 17. Visit with commentary (45mn) Jul–Aug: Tue–Sun. 10.30am–1pm, 2.30pm–7pm; Rest of the year: guided visit on request. 2 € (-15 yrs, no charge).

Located on a small mound, this tomb has two covered rooms and is surrounded by circular dry stone walls, which are terraced. It dates from 4000 BC. Two narrow corridors lead to the funeral chambers.

ADDRESSES

STAY

Hôtel de Touraine – 4 av. de la République. 02 40 22 47 56. www.hotel-de-touraine.com. 18 rooms. 6.20€. Closed 19 Dec–5 Jan. Very simple but well kept rooms (those at the back are quieter) in the town centre. Breakfast served in the garden in summer.

Holiday Inn – 1 r. de la Floride. 02 40 19 01 01. www.saint-nazaire. hiexpress.com. 75 rooms. Ideally situated in the new quarter of the town's port this hotel offers a totally contemporary setting. Comfortable rooms with excellent service.

EAT

Le Sabayon – 7 rue de la Paix-et-des-Arts. 02 40 01 88 21. Closed 3 weeks Aug, 2 weeks Apr, and Sun and Mon. Reservations advised. In this nautical restaurant, you'll find scallops sautéed in Guérande butter with a dash of wine, millefeuille of melon and locally caught fish.

EVENTS

At nightfall, the port is illuminated with red, blue and green hues: this is the 'Nuits des Docks', conceived by Yann Kersalé, a light sculptor.

BEACHES

Beaches, creeks and rocks stretch from the capitainerie to the Jaunais beach, an expanse of sand sheltered by a dune: no fewer than 20 beaches in total. Families should head to Villès-Martin or to Porcé. Surf fans should make for Courance and those who like tranquillity should seek out the creeks near Port Charlotte. The best way to explore the beaches is to follow the chemin des douaniers, preferably at low tide, from the base nautique (7km).

Presqu'île de Guérande★

This interesting district is home to a curious landscape of salt-marshes, several beaches (of which La Baule is the finest), the picturesque Côte Sauvage, busy fishing ports, Guérande and Batz.

A BIT OF HISTORY

The former gulf – In the Roman era, a great sea gulf stretched between the rocky Île de Batz and the Guérande ridge. A change of level of approximately 15m/50ft turned the gulf into marshland.

Sand brought down by the currents linked the Île de Batz with the mainland through the strip on which La Baule and Le Pouliguen stand. To the west the sandy Pen Bron Point has not quite reached the island; a channel remains open opposite Le Croisic through which the sea flows at high tide into the Grand and Petit Trait, vestiges of the former gulf. At low tide it retreats, exposing mud flats on which the coast dwellers raise oysters and mussels, clams and periwinkles. The rest of the marsh is used for salt pans.

Salt-marshes – The salt-marshes cover 1,800ha/4,448 acres divided into two basins: Mesquer and Guérande, forming a huge quadrilateral delimited by clay embankments.

◔ **Michelin Map:** Local map 316 B4 - Loire-Atlantique (44).

▤ **Info:** 1 pl. du Marché-au-Bois, 44350 Guérande. ☏02 40 24 96 71. www.ot-guerande.fr.

◉ **Location:** Guérande is 6km/3.7mi from La Baule.

⚐ **Kids:** Musée de la Poupée (Doll Museum).

▣ **Parking:** There are car parks around the ramparts.

◈ **Don't Miss:** The guided tours of the salt marshes, or the market on Wednesdays and Saturdays.

The sea, brought in by the tides through canals (*étiers*), irrigates the salt-marsh. Every 15 days, during the salt harvest, the salt pan worker allows the seawater to flow through a gate into a type of settling pond (*vasière*) used for removing the impurities (sand, clay etc). Then, with the drop in water level the water flows through a series of ponds where the wind and sun cause the water to evaporate, producing brine. In the 70sq m pools called *œillets*, the brine finally rests and crystallizes.

From June to September the salt-pan worker harvests two kinds of salt: table or white salt collected (3–5kg/6.5–11lb per day per *œillet*) with a flat spade

HERBIGNAC, LA ROCHE-BERNARD 🚢 D 774

D 99 🚢 LA TURBALLE, PIRIAC, PRADEL

Pte l'Abreuvoir Vannetaise
Bd
Bd Émile Pourieux
R. du Bouton d'Or
de
Rue Vannetaise
du Nord
Ramparts
R. des Capucins
St-Aubin
R. Ch. Muller
Av. de la Brière
ST-LYPHARD LA ROCHE-BERNARD
Pl. du Pilori
Pl. St-Aubin
N.-D. LA BLANCHE
R. de Bizienne
R. St. Michel
Pte St-Michel
R. Fg St-Michel
Doll Museum
R. du Saillé
R. du Tricot
Tour St-Jean
Pays de Guérande Museum
Bd
du
Midi
Bd de Dinkelsbühl
D 99 ST-NAZAIRE LA BAULE
Pl. du Marhallé
N
GUÉRANDE
Fg St-Armel
R. des Saulniers
H
0   200 m

D 774 🚢 LE POULIGUEN, LE CROISIC, SAILLÉ

(lousse) and coarse or grey salt collected (40–70kg/88–155lb per day per œillet) at the bottom of the pond with a large flat rake (lasse) onto a tray. The salt is put to dry on little platforms (trenets) built on the banks, then piled in large heaps (mulons) at the edge of the salt pans before being stored in sheds in September.

When not harvesting salt, the salt-pan worker looks after the salt-marsh: repairing the dykes, raking the settling pond (October-March), cleaning and preparing the salt pans (April-May) and removing the salt before the next harvest.

A hard struggle – The salt pans of Guérande were very prosperous until the Revolution, thanks to a relic of the former rights of the province. The salt could be sent all over Brittany without paying the *gabelle* or salt tax. Dealers or salt makers could exchange it in neighboring provinces for cereals. Trafficking by "false salt makers" or smugglers often occurred. Today about 7,000 œillets are harvested, producing an average of 10,000t of coarse salt a year. Guérande salt is rich in sodium chloride and weak in magnesium, potassium and other trace elements.

Cliffs and dunes – The cliffs and rocks of the Côte Sauvage, between the Pointe de Penchâteau and Le Croisic, offer a striking contrast to the immense sandy beach at La Baule. In 1527 a violent wind spread the sand accumulated in the Loire estuary over the village of **Escoublac**. After this gale, which lasted for several days, sand continued to accumulate, and in the 18C the last inhabitants finally left and the village was rebuilt several miles further back. The pines planted to fix the dunes from the Bois d'Amour of La Baule. The coast, which became very popular in the 19C, took the name of **Côte d'Amour.**

GUÉRANDE★

Standing on a plateau overlooking the salt-marshes and surrounded by ramparts, the town has retained its medieval appearance. Colourful markets are held on Wednesday and Saturday mornings inside the covered market and on place

Guérande salt

S. Sauvignier/MICHELIN

St-Aubin. Every year in August there is a three-day Inter-Celtic Festival at the foot of the fortifications.

Porte St-Michel – Chateau-Musée

🕐 Open Apr–Sept, daily (except Mon morning) 10am–12.30pm (noon in Oct) and 2.30pm–7pm. ∞4€. ℘02 28 55 05 55. www.ville-guerande.fr.

The gatehouse was once the governor's house (15C) and is now a local museum; a spiral staircase goes up to the different floors. Note the two reconstructed interiors: that of the Briéron inhabitant with its waxed furniture and that of the salt-marsh worker with its furniture painted a deep plum-red colour. The museum has porcelain from Le Croisic, pottery and other everyday objects typical of the area, part of the collegiate church's rood screen and old bourgeois, salt-marsh worker and farm tenant costumes. Particularly interesting is the relief map of a salt-marsh, which illustrates the salt-gathering process.

Ramparts★

The 14C/15C ramparts remain whole to this day. They are flanked by six towers and pierced by four fortified gateways. In the 18C the Duke of Aiguillon, Governor of Brittany, had the moats filled in (although the north and west sections still contain water) and arranged the present circular promenade, which you can follow by car or on foot. You can also walk along the **watch-path** from Porte St-Michel to beyond St-Jean Tower.

Collégiale St-Aubin★

This collegiate church, built between the 12C and 16C on the site of a baptistery, features a granite west façade decorated with bell turrets and crocketed pinnacles. To the right a 15C outside pulpit is embedded in a buttress.

The **interior** is imposing with large 15C pillars in the transept. The Romanesque columns of the nave support Gothic arches with **capitals** portraying grotesques and floral decoration. The 15C chancel, with aisles opening onto four 16C chapels, is lit by a magnificent 18C **stained-glass window** showing the Coronation of the Virgin and the Assumption. On the left, the small 14C lancet window shows the life of St Peter. The chapel to the right, oddly enough called the **crypt**, contains a Merovingian sarcophagus (6C) discovered under the chancel, a recumbent figure and a tombstone, both 16C. In the nave is a 16C carved wooden Christ.

♔♙ Musée de la Poupée

23 rue de Saillé. ◷*Open Apr–Sept 10am –1pm, 2.30pm–7pm; Nov–Mar Tue–Sun 2pm–6.30pm.* ◷*Closed Jan–5 Feb and 25 Dec.* ◠*4€; children 2.50€.* ♿ ✆*02 40 15 69 13.*

The museum houses hundreds of dolls made of porcelain or wood, displayed in an old-world setting scattered with miniature furniture and china.

🚗 DRIVING TOUR

Tour of 62 km/39mi departing from Guérande and takes a half day.

▷ *Take the D92, direction La Baule.*

Château de Careil

D 92 towards La Baule. 👁*Guided tours (45min).* ◷*Jun–Aug, daily 11am, noon, hourly 2pm–6pm. Tours by candlelight Jul–Aug Mon and Wed 9.30pm.* ◷*Closed Dec, Jan, May and Sept.* ◠*Guided tour 5.50€, by candlelight 8€.* ✆*02 40 60 22 99. www.careil.com.*

The first fortified castle to be built here was constructed in the 14C. It was renovated in the 15C–16C and is still inhabited today. Note the elegant Renaissance façade, as well as the guard-room and drawing room with their fine beams.

Le Pouligen and the Côte Sauvage – ♿ *See LA BAULE*

Batz-sur-Mer – ♿ *See LE CROISIC*

Saillé

Saillé is the salt capital of the region, set on an island amid the salt-marshes. A former chapel contains the **Maison des Paludiers** (◷*open daily Jun–Aug, 10am–12.30pm, 2.30pm–6pm; Nov–Jan, Sat, 2.30pm–5.30pm; Feb–Mar and Oct, daily 2.30pm–5.30pm; Apr, 10am–noon, 2.30pm–5.30pm; May and Sept, 10am– noon, 2pm–6pm* ◠*4.30€;* 👁*guided tours (1hr 30) of salt marsh Mon, Wed and Fri 4.30pm; May–Sept, 5pm;* ◠*6.30€;* ♿ ✆*02 40 62 21 96; www.maisondespaludiers.fr).* Engravings, tools, furnishings and costumes illustrate the life of the salt-marsh worker.

Pradel

The modern **Terre de Sel** exhibition centre (👁*guided visit Jul–Aug: 9.30am –7.30pm ; Apr–Jun and Sept–Oct: 10am– 6pm; rest of the year: 10am–12.30pm, 2pm–5pm;* ◷*closed 1 Jan, 25 Dec;* ◠*4 € (child 2.50 €) exhibition, 11 € (child 8 €);* ✆*02 40 62 08 80; www.terredesel.fr)* has been created to showcase the wellknown Guérande salt.

Visitors can appreciate how the salt is produced, as well as, gaining an understanding the importance of the salt pans to the environment. ◠Guided visits and bird watching trips are also available.

▷ *Continue NW on the D 92 for 6 km/3.75m.*

La Turballe

This lively artificial port is used by both pleasure boats and fishing vessels. The main catch is anchovy. It is also the departure point for Belle-Île, Houat and Hœdic in the Morbihan bay (♿*see p373 & p370).*

▷ *Go N along the coast for 5km/3.1mi.*

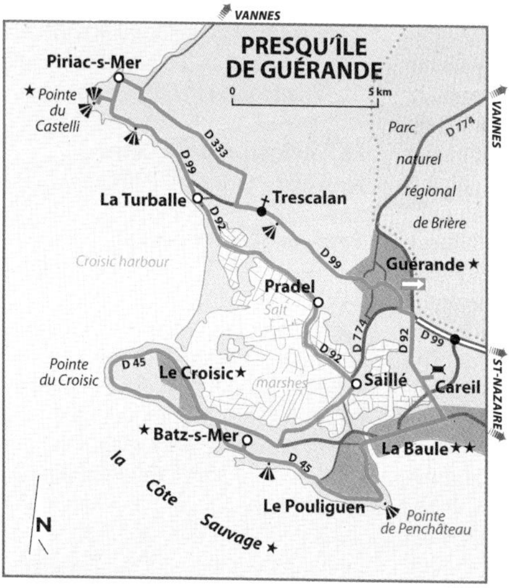

Piriac-sur-Mer

In front of the church in the square of this small resort and fishing village is a fine group of 17C houses. A path along the cliff ridge leads to **Pointe du Castelli**★, with a nice view of the rocky creeks. On the right Île Dumet and the low shore of Presqu'île de Rhuys are visible. On the left are the roadstead and peninsula of Le Croisic with the church towers of Batz and Le Croisic.

Around Piriac and at Lerat, there are several small beaches suitable for families and to the south of La Turballe there is a vast sandy beach facing west.

Trescalan

Buttresses and beautiful pillars with capitals are features of the **church** which contains a statue of St Bridget in silver cloth. Beautiful view of the coast on leaving **Lerat.**

ADDRESSES

STAY

GUÉRANDE

Camping L'Étang – *5 km/3.1mi from Guérande by the rte de St-Lyphard then 3 km/1.9mi by the D 48 on the right and turn left. 02 40 61 93 51 or 06 31 96 33 65. www.camping-etang.com. Open all year. Reservation advised. 119 pitches. Restaurant Jul–Aug.* As the name of the campsite suggests, it is near a lake but there is also a swimming pool. In addition to the normal pitches there are chalets and mobile homes to hire.

Hôtel Les Voyageurs – *Place du 8 Mai 1945. 02 40 24 90 13. Closed 23 Dec–21 Jan, Sun eve and Mon exc Jul–Aug. 12 rooms. 7€. Restaurant.* In front of the ramparts, old-fashioned but well-kept rooms and good regional cuisine is served in four dining rooms, one of which opens onto the terrace.

Chambre d'hôte La Guérandière – *porte Vannetaise. 02 40 62 17 15 or 06 86 77 84 43. www.guerandiere.com. Reservations necessary in winter. 6 rooms. 10€.* This spacious, distinguished house has comfortable rooms decorated in pastel tones, reached by a beautiful staircase. Breakfast is served in the garden on fine days.

LA TURBALLE

Chambre d'hôte du Manoir des Quatre Saisons – *744 bd de Lauvergnac, 44420 La Turballe. 1.5km/.09mi from La Turballe on the D 333. 02 40 11 76 16. www.manoir-des-quatre-saisons.com. 5 rooms.* This alluring Breton longhouse is set in a park. Whether you stay in the manor or the cottage, each room has its own colour scheme. Breakfast is served by the fireplace or next to the pool.

EAT

Roc Maria – *1 rue du Vieux-Marché-aux-Grains, Guérande. 02 40 24 90 51. www.hoelcreperierocmaria.com. Closed Mon Sep–Mar, 3 weeks from 11 Nov & last 2 weeks Jan).* A medieval building housing a *crêperie* and ten simple rooms.

Le Vieux Logis – *pl. de la Psalette, Guérande. 02 40 62 09 73. Closed 12 Nov–16 Dec, Tue eve and Wed (except Jul and Aug).* This beautiful old stone house has kept its 17C charm. The green, shady terrace is a pleasant spot. Grills are a speciality here.

😋🍽️🍺 **Les Remparts** – *14–15 bd du Nord, Guérande. ✆02 40 24 90 69. Closed 29 Nov–3 Jan. 13–19 Feb, Sun eve, Sat eve and Mon except public holidays.* Contemporary setting for regional cuisine and seafood seasoned with local salt.

😋🍽️🍺 **Le Terminus** – *18 quai St-Paul, 44 420 La Turballe. ✆ 02 40 23 30 29. http://laturballe.free.fr/restaurant-terminus. Closed 19–24 Oct, 2 weeks in Feb (school hols), Tue eve and Wed exc school hols.* Enjoy seafood dishes from a table near the windows or the veranda to watch the boats in the fishing port.

🏃 ACTIVITIES

Rent a bike – Bicycle Repair – *6 rue Gustave Flaubert, Guérande. ✆02 40 62 39 95.* Off-road and touring bikes.

Horse Riding – La Champagne – *On the D 744, 44350 St-Molf. ✆06 08 50 69 43. www.equitationlachampagne.com. Open 9am–12.30pm, 2pm–10pm.* Run by a friendly crowd, this large riding school offers outings on the beach, at night and on the banks of the river Vilaine. One hour or one day, one week or more.

🛒 SHOPPING

Markets – Guérande – Wed and Sat morning in the *halles* and on *place St-Aubin* in July and August.

Salt – Salines et Saveurs – *5 pl. de la Psalette, opposite the entrance to the church. ✆02 40 01 44 23.* A family of salt marsh harvesters offer all sorts of products made with salt from Guérande.

La Baule ☼☼☼

La Baule's long beach of fine sand, which boasts the title of 'Europe's most beautiful beach', stretches along southern Brittany. Water sports, tennis, a casino and golf make this one of the most popular seaside resorts on the Atlantic coast.

VISIT

Seafront★

Sheltered from the winds, this elegant promenade lined with modern buildings stretches for about 7km/4mi between Pornichet and Le Pouliguen. Unfortunately, the turn-of-the-century villas which were once the heart of the resort, have since fallen prey to developers.

La Baule-les-Pins ☼☼

La Baule is extended eastwards by this resort, which was built in 1930, in an area of pine forests.

The attractive Allée Cavalière leads to the Escoublac Forest.

▶ **Population:** 16,095.

🖐 **Michelin Map:** Local map 316 B4 – Loire Atlantique (44).

🏳 **Info:** 8 place de la Victoire, 44504 La Baule. ✆02 40 24 34 44. www.labaule.tm.fr.

🅿 **Location:** La Baule is 74km/46mi W of Nantes and 10km/6mi E of Le Croisic.

🕐 **Timing:** La Baule is a great day out.

👁 **Don't Miss:** Walks and dips in the sea on the Côte Sauvage.

Pornichet ☼

Originally a salt-marsh workers' village, Pornichet became a fashionable sea-side resort in 1860, popular with Parisian publishers. The town is composed of two distinct districts: Old Pornichet, to the southeast, which is busy all the year round, and Pornichet-les-Pins to the northwest, whose large villas sur-

Beach at la Baule

S. Sauvignier/MICHELIN

rounded by greenery are livelier in the summer. Also in the summer, horse races are held in the Côte-d'Amour's racecourse. And finally, the **boulevard des Océanides** runs along the beach and leads to the pleasure-boat harbour which can take over 1,000 boats.

Le Pouliguen ☖

Separated from La Baule by a channel *(étier)*, this village with its narrow streets became a fashionable resort in 1854, made popular by men of letters such as Louis Veuillot and Jules Sandeau. A sheltered beach and a pleasant 6ha/15-acre wood make Le Pouliguen a very pleasant place to stop.

Chapelle Ste-Anne-et-St-Julien

Place Mgr-Freppel. Guided tours Jul–Aug, Wed at 10.30am. ℘02 40 42 18 94.

Standing near a calvary, this Gothic chapel has a 16C **statue of St Anne** and a stained-glass window representing St Julian (in the chancel). At the west end, on either side of the porch are two interesting **bas-relief sculptures** depicting the Coronation of the Virgin and the Adoration of the Magi.

La Côte Sauvage★

This stretch of coast starts from the Pointe de Penchâteau. Skirted by a road and footpaths, the coastline alternates rocky parts with great sandy bays and

has numerous caves which are accessible only at low tide, in particular the cave of the Korrigans, where Breton legend has that little elves live.

Cycle Track

The road which runs along the coast is one-way only between Pouliguen and Batz-sur-Mer, allowing a track specifically for cyclists.

ADDRESSES

STAY

⊜ **Camping La Roseraie** – *20 av. Jean Sohier. NE of La Baule-Escoublac.* ℘02 40 60 46 66. www.laroseraie.com. 235 places. Open Closed Oct–Mar. This is the best campsite in the region. Two steps from the beach, you'll have access to large swimming pools, a gym, children's entertainment and lots more.

⊜ **Hotel Les Dunes** – *227 av. de Lattre de Tassigny, La Baule.* ℘02 51 75 07 10. www.hotel-des-dunes.com. 32 rooms. ⊆ 7€. Functional and well-kept rooms, quieter at the back. A warm family welcome and attractive prices make this a good choice.

⊜⊜ **Hôtel St-Pierre** – *124 av. de Lattre de Tassigny, La Baulle.* ℘02 40 24 05 41. www.hotel-saint-pierre.com. 19 rooms. ⊆ 9€. This hotel is nicely located between the beach and the casino. Modern rooms with blue décor.

Hôtel Le St-Christophe – *Place Notre-Dame, La Baule.* ℘*02 40 62 40 00. www.st-christophe.com. 45 rooms.* 🍽 *11€. Restaurant* ⬤⬤⬤. Comfortable rooms in four 1900-style villas. Elegant restaurant with terrace-garden for classic cuisine, including (but not limited to) seafood.

PORNICHET

Villa Flornoy – *7 av. Flornoy, 44380 Pornichet.* ℘*02 40 11 60 00. www.villa-flornoy.com. Closed Nov–Feb.* 🍽 *9€. 30 rooms. Restaurant* ⬤⬤. In a residential area, this 1920s house is done out in English cottage style: pastel tones, elegant individual rooms furnished with *toile de Jouy* and local porcelain. There's also a charming garden.

⅋ EAT

LA BAULE

La Croisette – *31 Place du Mar. Leclerc.* ℘*02 40 60 73 00.* Palm trees and a Medeterranean feel on the terrace, where you can enjoy pasta, pizza and grills.

La Villa – *18 av. du Gén.-de-Gaulle,* ℘*02 40 23 06 00.* The unusual décor is reminiscent of the East and exotic travel, and there are many cosy corners for diners. Simple dishes, oysters and a good wine list.

PORNICHET

La Cabane – *On the beach, facing the Régent hotel.* ℘*02 40 15 20 10. Open at noon all year, except Mon–Wed and Sun off season.* Mussels and crêpes, with your feet in the sand.

Le Danicheff – *45 av. du Gén.-de-Gaulle.* ℘*02 40 61 07 32. Closed Sun eve Nov and Feb school holidays.* Traditional setting and cuisine, very good value for money and good wines to enjoy in the restaurant or take away.

⅋ NIGHTLIFE

La Canne à Sucre – *136 av. du Gén.-de-Gaulle.* ℘*02 40 24 00 94.* Latino, zouk, salsa music and plenty of atmos.

Le Bax – *12 av. Pavie.* ℘*02 40 60 90 00.* An intimate atmosphere to start or end the evening. Popular with young professionals.

Casino – *24 espl. Lucien Barrière.* ℘*02 40 11 48 28. Open Sun–Thu 10am–3am. Fri–Sat 10am–4am.* Slot machines, games, restaurants and a disco.

THALASSOTHERAPY

Centre Thalgo – *av. Marie-Louise, La Baule.* ℘*02 40 11 99 99. www.lucien barriere.com. Open daily 8.30am–12.45pm, 2.30pm–8pm except Sun in Apr. Closed 1st two weeks Dec, 1 Jan, 25 Dec.* Inside the Hôtel Royal, a wide range of treatments and packages (energising, anti-stress, quit smoking). It is not necessary to be a guest at the hotel.

Relais Thalasso La Baule – *28 bd. de l'Océan.* ℘*02 40 11 33 11. www.thalasso-labaule.com. Closed 1st two weeks Dec.* Its three arcades include five levels of treatments. The space houses a pool, a hammam, a sauna and cabins, not forgetting the relaxation room. Various packages allow the discovery of hydromassage, beauty treatments and marine therapy.

⅋ ACTIVITIES

Golf Barrière-La Baule – *Domaine de St-Denac, 44500 St-André-des-Eaux.* ℘*02 40 60 46 18. www.lucienbarriere. com. Open Apr–Oct, Sat–Sun 8am–7pm (Sun 6.30pm), Mon–Fri 8.30am–6.30pm; Nov–Mar, Wed–Mon 9am–6pm.* This renowned golf course, near the ocean, has three courses in a 220ha/543.6-acre park.

⅋ SHOPPING

Markets – *La Baule*, covered market daily except Mon, Oct–Mar. *Le Pouliguen*, Tue, Fri and Sun. *Pornichet*, Wed and Sat morning. For a good choice of seafood, stop at the *Halle aux Poissons*: *Tue–Sun morning off season, mid-Jun–mid-Sept, daily*.

Le Croisic★

This pleasant fishing port is located on a peninsula overlooking the Grand Traict lagoon, which feeds the salt marshes of Guérande. It is only accessible by the N 171. Originally one of the first seaside resorts, today Le Croisic still attracts many summer visitors. Two companies offer **boat trips** to Belle-Île, Houat and Hoedic. A ferry service crosses the roadstead to La Turballe.

▶ **Population:** 4,121.
Michelin Map: Local map 316 A4 - Loire Atlantique (44).
Info: pl. du 18 Juin 1940, 44490 Le Croisic.
℘02 40 23 00 70.
www.ot-lecroisic.com.
Kids: Océarium aquarium, Musée des Marais Salants, Grand Blockhaus.
🕐 **Timing:** Allow a day.
Don't Miss: The Côte Sauvage landscape.

Le Croisic port

A. de Valroger/MICHELIN

SIGHTS

Port

The port extends between Mont-Esprit and Mont-Lénigo, two mounds formed by ballast unloaded by ships in former days (see below), and is well protected by the Tréhic jetty; 17C houses with wrought-iron balconies line the quayside over a distance of more than 1km. It is a picturesque and busy scene in winter with the arrival of prawn boats, and in summer is enlivened by tourists.

Hôtel d'Aiguillon

The pretty 17C building houses the town hall. Dumas' D'Artagnan stopped here.

Église Notre-Dame-de-Pitié

This unusual 15C and 16C church, with its 17C **lantern tower** (56m/184ft), overlooks the port. Inside it has a short nave, with a flat east end illuminated by a window with Flamboyant tracery and three side aisles. The doorway pier is adorned with a statue of Notre-Dame-des-Vents.

Old houses

To admire the beautiful corbelled and half-timbered houses, walk through the little streets near the church. Note numbers 25, 20 and 28 in rue de l'Église, number 4 place du Pilori and numbers 33 and 35 in rue St-Christophe.

Mont-Lénigo

Ships at one time unloaded their ballast here and in 1761 trees were planted. The **view**★ goes over the roadstead, the Tréhic jetty (850m/930yds long), and its lighthouse (1872) at the entrance to the port; the Pen Bron dyke (1724) is across the way as is its marine centre. A shaded walk goes down to the esplanade where there is the memorial (1919) by René Paris, erected to Hervé Rielle, the coxswain, who saved 22 ships of the French fleet from disaster in 1692, by directing them to St-Malo.

Océarium★

🕐Open daily Jun–Aug 10am–7pm; 5 Apr–30 Jun, 25 Oct–4 Nov, 10am–6pm; rest of year 10am–noon, 2pm–6pm. ⊕12€ (children 9€). ℘02 40 23 02 44. www.ocearium-croisic.fr. This star-shaped marine centre houses a collection of wonders of the deep from both temperate and tropical waters. Not to be missed is the amusing colony of penguins (watch them feed at 11am, 3pm and 5pm), the sharks, the nursery, the marvellous 11m-long tunnel that goes through an aquarium containing 300,000l/66,000gal of seawater, and the pool where visitors can look at and touch starfish, shellfish and crabs.

🚗 DRIVING TOUR

La Côte Sauvage from Le Croisic★

26km/16mi – 2hr.

▷ *Leave Le Croisic by D 45, the coast road.*

After St-Jean-de-Dieu, the road follows the coast passing St-Goustan and its salt-marsh where eels are raised. The Côte Sauvage (meaning wild coastline) with oddly shaped rocks (appropriately named the Bear, the Altar) ends at the **Pointe du Croisic**. Further on the view opens out over Pornichet, the Loire estuary and the coast as far as the Pointe St-Gildas.

Batz-sur-Mer ≜

Against a background of the ocean and the salt-marshes, Batz's tall church bell-tower acts as a landmark for the town. The rocky coastline is broken by the sandy beaches of Valentin, La Govelle (fun-board) and St-Michel, a small strand where locals gather to watch the waves crashing on the dyke.

Église St-Guénolé★

29 rue de la Plage.
☛*Closed for renovation. Information from the Tourist Office.*
The church was rebuilt in the 15C–16C. Its **bell-tower**, 60m high, surmounted by a pinnacled turret, dates from 1677. In the **interior**, you will notice at once the off-centre chancel, massive pillars supporting Gothic arches and the wooden roof shaped like the keel of a boat; note the remarkable **keystones** in the north aisle. The top of the **bell-tower** (182 steps) offers an extensive

panorama★★ along the coast from the Pointe St-Gildas to the shores of the Presqu'île de Rhuys and, at sea, to Belle-Île and Noirmoutier.

Chapelle Notre-Dame-du-Mûrier★

Legend has it that this fine Gothic chapel, now in ruins, was built in the 15C by Jean de Rieux de Ranrouët to keep a vow he made when in peril at sea. He was guided to safety by a burning mulberry bush (hence the name *mûrier*).

👥 Musée des Marais Salants

⏱*Open Jul–Sept, 10am–12.30pm, 2.30pm–7pm; Jan–May, Sat–Sun 10am–noon, 2pm–6pm; Jun, 10am–noon, 2.30pm–6.30pm; Oct–Nov, 10am–noon, 2pm–5pm.* ⏱*Closed 15 Nov–20 Dec, 1 Jan, 1 May, 1 and 11 Nov.* ⊜*4€ (children 6–12, ⊜2€).* ♿ ♪*02 40 23 82 79.*
This museum of popular arts and traditions contains a 19C Batz interior, salt workers' clothes, and other exhibits covering all aspects of working with salt. The tour ends with an audio-visual presentation on the salt-marsh and its fauna. **Guided tours**★ of the salt-marshes are available.

👥 Grand Blockhaus

Rte de la Côte Sauvage.
⏱*Open Apr–mid-Nov, 10am–7pm.* ⊜*6.50€ (children 5–12, ⊜5€).* ♪*02 40 23 88 29.* *www.grand-blockhaus.com.*
This is one of the largest bunkers of the Atlantic Wall defences. During WW II, it was camouflaged as a villa in order to avoid being bombed. It now houses the *Musée de la Poche de St-Nazaire* (St-Nazaire Pocket), the last European area to be liberated in 1945. The atmosphere of a bunker has been recreated: sleeping area, radio station, ammunition store, engine room, etc.

Le Pouliguen ≜≜ – 👁*See La BAULE.*

▷ *Take the D 45 back to Le Croisic.*

La Grande Brière★★

Also known as Grande Brière Mottière, this region covers 7,000ha/17,297 acres of the total 40,000ha/98,842 acres belonging to the Parc Naturel Régional de Brière. Lying to the north of St-Nazaire, the area is renowned for its wildfowl, fishing and interesting boat trips.

A BIT OF HISTORY

Brière in the past – In early geological times the area was a forested, undulating basin which reached the hills of Sillon de Bretagne. Neolithic man (7500 BC) was expelled from the area, when there was a momentary maritime incursion. Marshes formed behind the alluvial banks deposited by the Loire. The trees died and were submerged and vegetable matter decomposed to form **peat bogs**, often entrapping fossilised tree trunks, known as **mortas**, over 5,000 years old.

Brière from the 15C to the 20C – This swampy area was subdivided, water pumped and the drainage improved. In 1461, the Duke of Brittany, François II, decreed the area the common property of all Briérons, an act which was to be confirmed by several royal edicts. For centuries the Briérons (17 parishes divided into 21 communes) have cut the peat, gathered the reeds and rushes for thatching, woven baskets with the buckthorn, tended their gardens and kept poultry. They have trapped leeches, harpooned eels, placed eel-pots in the open stretches of water and wickerwork traps to catch pike, tench and roach; and hunted with their dogs in a boat hidden by a clump of willow trees. For ages the Briéron has propelled with a pole his **blin,** a flat-bottomed boat, loaded with cows or sheep going to pasture. In spite of these activities, the Briéron women also had to work to make ends meet. In the 19C and early 20C, two workshops in St-Joachim employed approximately 140 women to make wax orange blossoms. These flowers were used to make

- **Michelin Map:** Local map 316 C/D 3/4 - Loire-Atlantique (44).
- **Info:** 38 rue de la Brière, 44410 La Chapelle-des-Marais. ℘02 40 66 85 01. www.parc-naturel-briere.fr.
- **Location:** This strip of marshland is situated between the N 171, the D 774 and the the N 165.
- **Kids:** Go birdwatching in the Réserve Pierre Constant and Ker Anas; see the puppets in the Chaumière des Marionnettes.
- **Timing:** Go bird watching at dawn or dusk but don't forget to protect yourself from the mosquitoes!
- **Don't Miss:** The boggy prairies of the Île de Frédun and the thatched cottages in the hamlet of Kerhinet.

splendid brides' headdresses, exported throughout Europe.

The Briéron of the 21C has remained closely attached to the land but, by force of circumstance, he is turning more to local industries: metallurgy in Trignac and dockyards and aeronautics at St-Nazaire. Nevertheless, he continues to fish, shoot, graze animals or cut reeds and pay his annual fee. Change is inevitable: roads now link the islets, locks have been built, marsh has become pastureland, but despite it all, La Grande Brière has retained its charm and when the Briéron returns home he fishes and shoots for his own pleasure. Many of those who have boats will take visitors on trips along the canals and smaller channels, beautiful with yellow irises (mid-May to mid-June) and pearl-white water lilies (mid-June to late July).

PARC NATUREL RÉGIONAL DE BRIÈRE

Created in 1970, the **Brière Regional Nature Park** organises events celebrating regional traditions and folklore,

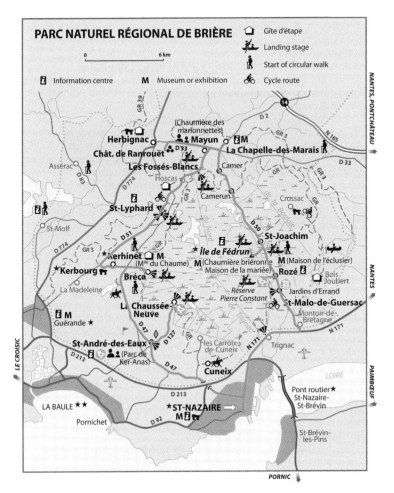

PARC NATUREL RÉGIONAL DE BRIÈRE

0   6 km

🏠 Gîte d'étape
🛶 Landing stage
🚶 Start of circular walk
🚲 Cycle route

ℹ Information centre   M Museum or exhibition

and offers opportunities for rambling, cycling and canoeing. It is a haven for bird watching.

🚗 DRIVING TOUR

From St-Nazaire

83km/51mi – half a day.

St-Nazaire

ⓘ *See ST-NAZAIRE.*

↪ *Leave St-Nazaire by N 171, the road to Nantes. Take the Montoir-de-Bretagne exit and turn onto D 50.*

St-Malo-de-Guersac

This, the largest of the islets (13m/43ft high), offers a **view** from Guérande in the west to the hilly region, Sillon de Bretagne, to the east.

Rozé

A boat-building centre, this small port was the former departure point for the boats plying upstream to Nantes and Vannes.

La Maison de l'Éclusier (*guided tours (1hr) Jul–Sept, 10am–1pm, 2.30pm –6.30pm, Apr–Jun, 2pm–6.30pm; ◉5€; 𝒫02 40 66 85 01; www.parc-naturel-briere.fr*). The house is located on Rosé Canal. The lock keeper operated the two locks which regulated the water level of the marsh. There is an exhibition devoted to the fauna (stuffed animals) and flora to be found in the marshland. An aquarium contains the main species of Brière fish. Slides and various documents illustrate the formation and evolution of the marsh.

Docked alongside the canal is a reconstruction of the Théotiste, which was used to transport peat.

👥 Réserve Pierre Constant

(behind the Maison, cross the bridge over the canal and take the path to the right to the reception building (pavillon d'accueil) 800m further on.

🕐*Jul–Sept, 10am (9am 1st week Sept)– 1pm, 2.30pm–6.30pm, Apr–Jun, 2pm– 6.30pm. ☞5€ (children 2.50€). ✆02 40 66 85 01. www.parc-naturel-briere.fr).*

A path *(about 2km/1.2mi)* cuts through this nature reserve (26ha/64 acres), with observation posts where silence and patience will be rewarded. There are descriptive panels to help you identify the flora and fauna. In a wood and reed building, Brière activities are displayed.

⬤ *Bear left before St-Joachim.*

Île de Fédrun★

Linked to the St-Joachim road by two bridges, this, the most attractive of the islets, is entirely surrounded by marshland. The islet has two roads: one which divides it in two and the other which runs around it. At number 130 of the circular road is the **Maison de la Mariée (Bride's House)** (🕐*open Jul–Sept, 10am–1pm, 2.30pm–6.30pm; Apr–Jun, 2pm–6.30pm; ☞5€; ✆02 40 66 85 01).* The interior of the house, arranged in typical Brière style, displays a collection of bridal headdresses decorated with wax orange blossoms and an explanation of how they are made.

St-Joachim

The village, once a wax orange blossom manufacturing centre, extends along the two islets of **Brécun** (alt 8m/26ft) and **Pendille**, dominated by the tall white spire of its 19C **church** *(place Julien Salnier; 🕐open 8am–6pm; ✆02 40 88 42 34).*

The road crosses the sparsely populated islets of **Camerun** and **Camer**.

La Chapelle-des-Marais

At the entrance to the village, on the right, is the **Maison du Sabotier** (clog-maker's house), where the last Briéron craftsman lived.

In the **church** the granite pillars stand out against the white stone; in the chapel to the right of the chancel there is a polychrome statue of St Corneille, protector of horned cattle.

⬤ *Take the road in the direction of Herbignac and after 4km/2.5mi turn left.*

👥 La Chaumière des Marionnettes

28 rue de la Herviais, Mayun.

🕐*Open year-round weekends and school hols, 2pm–7pm. Shows on Wed at 9pm. ☞5€. ✆02 40 53 22 40. Shop and workshops in puppet making.*

After travelling France putting on puppet shows for more than 30 years, this couple have finally settled in this charming thatched cottage. They take visitors on an imaginary journey to a mythical land of sorcerers.

⬤ *Go back to rte d'Herbignac and continue for 2km/1.2mi.*

Château de Ranrouët

🅿 *Leave the car in the car park (grassy) and go behind the old farm buildings.*

🕐*Open Jul–Aug, daily 10am–7pm; Apr–Jun & Sept, Tue–Sat 2.30pm– 6.30pm. ☞Guided tours (1hr) Jul– Aug ☞5€. 🕐Closed 1 May. ✆02 40 88 96 17. www.herbignac.com.*

This 12C–13C fortress, dismantled in 1618 by Louis XIII and burnt during the Revolution, is spectacular with its six round towers and moat (dried-up). Note in particular the 16C modifications designed to counter improved artillery (barbican, fortified curtain wall). Cannon-balls embedded in the right tower wall recall that the castle once belonged to the Rieux family, whose coat of arms included ten gold cannon balls.

Thatched cottage, Kerhinet

©Sylvaine Poitau/Apa Publications

 Make an about turn and retake the road to Herbignac.

Herbignac
This village has long been a centre of pottery tradition that dates back to the Gallo-Roman period.
For more information visit the **Maison du tourisme et du patrimoine** (*open Jul–Aug; 02 40 19 90 01*).

 From Herbignac retake the road until Mayun, where the craft of basket making has been revived, and turn right.

Les Fossés-Blancs
From a landing-stage on the canal to the north, there is a fine view of the Brière. A tour of the marsh provides an opportunity to study the flora and, occasionally, the fauna.

St-Lyphard
In the **church's belfry** (135 steps; *guided tours (30min) Jul–Aug, daily 11am–6.30pm (Sun 6pm); Apr–Jun and Sept, 11am–5.30pm; rest of the year (Tue–Sat) 11am–5.30pm. closed 1 Jan, 1 and 11 Nov and 25 Dec; 3€; 02 40 91 41 34; www.saint-lyphard.com*) a lookout point has been set up.
A **panorama** ★★ extends onto the Brière and from the Loire estuary to the mouth of the Vilaine encompassing Guérande and its salt-marshes.

 Follow the road towards Guérande and turn left.

Dolmen de Kerbourg★
This covered alleyway stands on a mound near a windmill.

 Continue in the direction of Le Brunet.

Kerhinet
One of the thatched cottages of this charming hamlet presents a modest **Brière interior** (dirt floor, meagre furnishings and kitchen utensils) and houses the **Musée du Chaume** (*guided tours (1hr) Jul–Sept, 10am–1pm, 2.30pm–6.30pm; Apr–Jun, 2pm–6pm; no charge; 02 40 66 85 01*). In the shed are tools used for peat harvesting, farming and fishing.

 Go on to Le Brunet and from there continue to Bréca offering a good view over the Brière and Bréca Canal. Return to Le Brunet and follow D 47.

St-André-des-Eaux – Parc Ornithologique de Ker Anas
Open Jul–Aug, 10am–8pm. Guided tours (2hr) Tue and Thu at 10am; Apr–Jun and Sept, 2.30pm–6.30pm. 6.50€ (children 3.20€). 02 40 01 27 48. www.keranas.fr.
The nature trail of this park extends over a kilometre (about half-a-mile). Along the way visitors can see a great variety of birds from different continents: geese, teals, swans and ducks from all over the world. At the entry you can buy a bag of food to feed them yourself.

▶ *Follow D 127 to La Chaussée-Neuve.*

La Chaussée-Neuve

It was from this former port that the boats loaded with peat used to leave. From here there is a wide **view**★ over the Brière.

▶ *Return to St-André-des-Eaux, and bear left to return to St-Nazaire.*

EXCURSIONS
Pontchâteau

▶ *12km/7.5mi NE of St-Joachim along the D 16.*

The church of Pontchâteau, which is perched on a hill in a region of unused, overlooks the little town with its houses built in terraces on the banks of the River Brivet.

Calvaire de la Madeleine

▶ *4km/2.5mi W. Leave Pontchâteau on D 33 towards Herbignac.*

🅿 *Leave the car in the car park on the left side of the road.*

St Louis-Marie Grignion de Montfort (1673–1716), a famous preacher, had the calvary built in 1709 on the heath of the same name. Destroyed under Louis XIV, it was rebuilt in 1821.

From the Temple of Jerusalem – a fortress-type oriental palace – an alley crosses the park and leads to Pilate's Court or Scala Sancta, the five high-relief sculptures of which represent the Passion. It is the first station in the Stations of the Cross which, further on (on the left) are continued by large white statues derived from the local folklore. From above the calvary the view extends to the Brière, St-Nazaire and Donges.

ADDRESSES

🏠 STAY

🛏 **Hôtel Le Bretagne** – *Pont d'Armes, 44410 Assérac (10.5km/6.5mi NW of Brière) ℘02 40 01 71 03. Closed two weeks in Feb and two weeks in Nov. 12 rooms. ☐ 6.50€.* The marshland is at arm's length, and the Atlantic 5km away. The rooms are simply furnished but attractive. Breakfast is served on a veranda overlooking the garden.

🛏🛏 **Chambre d'hôte Ty Gwen** – *25 Île d'Errand, 44550 St-Malo-de-Guersac. 3km/1.8mi from St-Malo, after the church, towards Errand. ℘02 40 91 15 04. Closed Oct–Mar. ☐. 3 rooms.* Incredibly romantic, this pretty thatched cottage welcomes its guests with cosy comfort. Ceiling beams, fireplace and well-chosen fabrics create a refined atmosphere. Its charming garden and swimming pool add to the pleasure.

🍴 EAT

🍽 **Les Calèches Briéronnes** – *À Bréca, 44410 St-Lyphard. ℘02 40 91 33 24. www.creperie-de-breca.com. Closed Nov–Easter.* Old oak trees and marshes surround this house where you can munch on a galette, a salad, a grill or an ice cream. Simple dining room with bay windows and a pleasant terrace in summer.

🍽🍽🍽 **Auberge de Bréca** – *Road to Bréca (follow the signs to the restaurant). 02 40 91 41 42. www.auberge-breca.com. Closed 19 Dec–3 Jan, Tue eve from Nov–Mar, Sun eve and Thu except Jul–Aug.* This restaurant and ice cream salon, located in an old hunting lodge, offers a quick bite or a little refreshment to those who have enjoyed a long boat trip.

BARGE TOUR

Barge outings★★ are available all year; refer to the map of the park to find embarkation points. The Brière is delightful in every season: abloom in the spring, lush green in the summer, orange and red in the autumn, and silver in the winter. **Anthony Mahé** *(port de la Chaussée-Neuve, 44117 St-André-des-Eaux, ℘02 40 91 59 36)* offers guided tours *(2hr)* from 10am–6pm for 8€.

Blain

An old Roman crossroads, Blain plays an important commercial role between Nantes, Redon and the Anjou. The Nantes-Brest Canal separates the town from its castle (whose first construction dates from 1104). Nearby Gâvre forest, the largest wooded area in Brittany, is criss-crossed with footpaths.

VISIT

Le Musée de Blain

2 place Jean Guihard. ◯*Open Tue–Fri 2pm–6pm, Sat 2pm–5.30pm, Sun 2.30pm–5.30pm.* ◯*Closed public holidays.* ⊚*3€ (children 1.50€).* ✆*02 40 79 98 51. www.musee-de-blain.fr.* Located in the old presidial of the Dukes of Rohan, this museum revives the past of the Blain area. Two rooms are devoted to popular Christmas traditions: one room displays thousands of bean kings (lucky trinkets hidden in Twelfth Night cakes), the other about 100 Nativity cribs from all over the world.

Château

This fortress originally belonged to Olivier de Clisson, and later became Rohan family property. Despite the fact that in 1628 Richelieu razed the ramparts, impressive ruins still stand, including the 14C **Tour du Pont-Levis** topped by a pepper-pot roof, which houses the museum (◯*open mid-May–mid-Oct, Tue–Sun 10am–noon, 2.30pm–6.30pm;* ⊚*3€;* ✆*02 40 79 07 81)* and the 15C **Logis du Roi** with its pinnacled Renaissance dormer-windows. Receptions are held here. There is a fresco centre and an ancient print shop.

🚗 DRIVING TOUR

The Forêt du Gâvre★

Round tour of 13km/8mi NW on D 15, the road to Guéméné-Penfao.
The road crosses the stands of oak interspersed with beeches and pines, which cover 4,400ha/10,872 acres, to reach the Belle Étoile crossroads.

▶ **Population:** 8,799.
⚐ **Michelin Map:** Local map 316 F3 – Loire-Atlantique (44).
🏳 **Info:** 2 place Jean Guihard, 44130 Blain. ✆02 40 87 15 11.
◐ **Location:** Between the forest of Gâvre and the little forest of Groulais, to the north-west of Nantes.
👥 **Kids:** Musée de la Fève et de la Crèche.
◯ **Timing:** Consider a walk along the canal in the morning and a stroll in the forest in the afternoon.

◐ *Turn right towards Le Gâvre and at La Maillardais turn left.*

Chapelle de la Magdeleine

This modest 12C chapel has a 15C polychrome Virgin, Notre-Dame-de-Grâce.

◐ *Return to La Maillardais and continue straight on to Le Gâvre.*

Le Gâvre

The **Musée Benoist** (◯*open Mar–Nov, Tue–Sun 2.30pm–6.30pm;* ⊚*3€* ✄; ✆*02 40 51 25 14; http://maisondelaforet 44.free.fr)* is housed in a 17C residence flanked by a corner turret. The ground floor exhibition is concerned with the Forêt du Gâvre; the upper floor with traditional crafts. A lively programme of activities is held throughout the year (in French) to bring the forest environment to life.

Not far from the school *(école),* the **wooden shoemaker's home** shows the life of the shoemaker.

🚗 *Leave from the car park of Gâvre campsite.*

Use a booklet from Blain Tourist Office to follow Guenael, the monk's path through the forest (4km/2.5mi).

◐ *Return to Blain.*

ADDRESSES

🏠STAY

BLAIN

🛏 **Camping municipal le Château –**
*Rte de St-Nazaire. Exit SWby the N 171,
rte de St-Nazaire and turn left, at 200m/
219yds from the Nantes–Brest canal.
𝄞 02 40 79 11 00. www.ville-blain.fr.
Open May–Sept. ⇌ Reservation advised.
45 pitches.* This pleasant campsite near
the castle and the Nantes–Brest Canal
is very well maintained. A lively site in
a green environment with many trees
and a library with tourist information.

♈EAT

LE GÂVRE

🍲🍲🍲 **Auberge de la Forêt –**
*La Maillardais - 44 130 Le Gâvre. At
8 km/5mi N of Blain by the D 42 and
D 35. 𝄞 02 40 51 20 26. www.auberge-
delaforet.fr. 8 rooms.* This restaurant
offers a good compromise between
gastronomy and traditional cuisine.
Good service in a large and elegant if
somewhat impersonal dining room.
The rooms are simple and well kept
making this inn a friendly place on the
edge of the forest.

Châteaubriant

This old fortified town with its
imposing château stands on the
border of Brittany and Anjou,
surrounded by woods dotted with
lakes. By preserving and enchancing
its historic and cultural heritage,
Châteaubriant has become a lively
tourist destination.

SIGHTS

Château★

🕐*Open May–Sept, Wed–Mon, 11am–
6.30pm; rest of year 2pm–5.30pm.
Guided tour May–Sept. 🕐Closed 25
Dec, 1 Jan, 1 May, 1 Nov. ⊛3€.
𝄞02 40 28 20 20.*
Part of the castle, which has been
remodelled several times, is feudal while
another part, dating from the Renaissance, was built by Jean de Laval. You
can stroll round the castle along the

From the Hoof to the Plate

Châteaubriant has the second-
largest livestock market in France
and is one of the country's biggest
beef-producing areas. To cook the
perfect 300g/10oz fillet, it must
be seared on the outside and just
warm and bloody on the inside. It is
traditionally served with dauphinois
potatoes and Béarnaise sauce.

▶ **Population:** 12,065.
🜚 **Michelin Map:** local
map 316 H1 - Loire-
Atlantique (44).
🛈 **Info:** 22 rue de Couëré,
BP 193 Châteaubriant.
𝄞02 40 28 20 90. www.
tourisme-chateaubriant.fr.
◑ **Location:** 70km/44mi
north of Nantes on the D 31.
🕐 **Timing:** Allow an hour
to visit the château.
◉ **Don't Miss:** The château.

esplanade and the gardens which go
right down to the Chère. All that remains
of the feudal castle is a large keep, connected with the entrance fort and the
chapel by walls against which the two
wings of the main building stand. The
three wings of the Seigneurial Palace
(Palais Seigneurial), opposite, are connected by elegant Renaissance pavilions. The roof is ornamented with dormer windows, which are emblazoned
with the coats of arms of Châteaubriant,
Laval and Montmorency.
The tour takes you up the central staircase (**1**) to a balcony from where there
is a lovely view onto the Main Courtyard, embellished with gardens and
a huge chestnut tree, the keep, and
the city's rooftops. Continue on to the
room (**2**) of Françoise de Foix with its

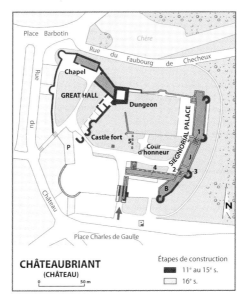

Place Barbotin
Chère
Rue du Faubourg de Checheux
Rue
Chapel
GREAT HALL
Dungeon
Rue du
Castle fort 5
Cour d'honneur
SEIGNIORIAL PALACE
P
1
J
4 2 3
B
N
Place Charles de Gaulle

CHÂTEAUBRIANT
(CHÂTEAU)
0   50 m

Étapes de construction
■ 11ᵉ au 15ᵉ s.
□ 16ᵉ s.

coffered ceiling and monumental early 17C carved wood chimney. Next to it is the oratory (**3**) with the tombstone of Françoise de Foix with an epitaph by Clément Marot (French Renaissance poet). The Magistrate's Court (Tribunal d'Instance – **J**) occupies a part of the palace while the public library (**B**) is housed in the south wing.

There are only two sections left of the colonnade that surrounded the Main Courtyard: the covered gallery (**4**), which ends at a charming staircase-pavilion, and the other section (**5**) enclosing the Main Courtyard.

Église de St-Jean-de-Béré

The church's oldest parts (comprising the chancel and the transept crossing), are built of fine red sandstone and date from the late 11C; the nave is 12C.

Outside, near the picturesque south porch (16C), is a rustic altar from which services were held at the time of the plague. Inside you will find the ornately decorated altarpiece (1665).

La Sablière

At the town gates on the road to Pouancé, the Carrière des Fusillés is a memorial to the 27 hostages executed by the Nazis on 22 October 1941. The recesses at the base contain soil from the areas where the Resitance movement was particularly active.

EXCURSION
Abbaye de Melleray

▶ *21km/13mi S via D 178; turn left on D 18 at La Meilleraye-de-Bretagne (towards Riallé).* ℘ *02 40 55 26 00.*
Founded in 1142 near a lovely lake, the buildings of this Cistercian abbey date from the 18C. The **Église Notre-Dame-de-Melleray,** completed in 1183, has been restored to its Cistercian severity, including a series of grisaille windows. Note the pointed white-stone arches resting on square pink-granite pillars. In the flat chevet, admire the 17C wood polychrome **statue of the Virgin**.

ADDRESSES

STAY

Hôtel La Ferrière – *Rte de Moisdon-La-Rivière . ℘ 02 40 28 00 28. www.hotel laferriere.fr. 19 rooms. ☲ 10.50 €.*
A comfortable hotel with outlying buildings in its own grounds. Rooms are decorated with style and have modern bathrooms. The dining room has a veranda overlooking the grounds.

INDEX

INDEX

INDEX

INDEX

INDEX

♀/EAT

INDEX

MAPS AND PLANS

MAP LEGEND

	Sight	Seaside resort	Winter sports resort	Spa
Highly recommended ★★★		≜≜≜	❄❄❄	♯♯♯
Recommended	★★	≜≜	❄❄	♯♯
Interesting	★	≜	❄	♯

Additional symbols

🛈		Tourist information
═	═	Motorway or other primary route
❶	❶	Junction: complete, limited
⊨	═	Pedestrian street
⊨ ═ ═ ═ ⊨		Unsuitable for traffic, street subject to restrictions
⊥⊥⊥	- - - -	Steps – Footpath
🚂	🚃	Train station – Auto-train station
🚌	S.N.C.F	Coach (bus) station
—		Tram
Ⓜ		Metro, underground
🅿		Park-and-Ride
♿		Access for the disabled
✉		Post office
☎		Telephone
✉		Covered market
⦁╳⦁		Barracks
△		Drawbridge
⋃		Quarry
✕		Mine
Ⓑ	Ⓕ	Car ferry (river or lake)
⛴		Ferry service: cars and passengers
⛴		Foot passengers only
③		Access route number common to Michelin maps and town plans
Bert (R.)...		Main shopping street
AZ B		Map co-ordinates

Sports and recreation

🏇		Racecourse
⛸		Skating rink
🏊	🏊	Outdoor, indoor swimming pool
🎥		Multiplex Cinema
⛵		Marina, sailing centre
⛺		Trail refuge hut
▭■▭■▭		Cable cars, gondolas
▭+++++▭		Funicular, rack railway
🚂		Tourist train
◊		Recreation area, park
🎢		Theme, amusement park
🦌		Wildlife park, zoo
✿		Gardens, park, arboretum
🐦		Bird sanctuary, aviary
🚶		Walking tour, footpath
😊		Of special interest to children
		Restaurant: non-smoking section
♿		Rooms accessible to persons of reduced mobility

The prices correspond to the higher rates of the tourist season

Map Legend continued overleaf

Abbreviations

A	Agricultural office (Chambre d'agriculture)
C	Chamber of Commerce (Chambre de commerce)
H	Town hall (Hôtel de ville)
J	Law courts (Palais de justice)
M	Museum (Musée)
P	Local authority offices (Préfecture, sous-préfecture)
POL.	Police station (Police)
🛡	Police station (Gendarmerie)
T	Theatre (Théâtre)
U	University (Université)

Selected monuments and sights

	Tour - Departure point
	Catholic church
	Protestant church, other temple
	Synagogue - Mosque
	Building
	Statue, small building
	Calvary, wayside cross
	Fountain
	Rampart - Tower - Gate
	Château, castle, historic house
	Ruins
	Dam
	Factory, power plant
	Fort
	Cave
	Troglodyte dwelling
	Prehistoric site
	Viewing table
	Viewpoint
	Other place of interest

COMPANION PUBLICATIONS

ROAD MAPS FOR THIS REGION

Motorists who plan ahead will always have the appropriate maps at hand. Michelin products are complementary: for each of the sites listed in *The Green Guide*, map references are indicated which help you find your location on our range of maps. The image below shows the maps to use for each geographic area covered in this guide.

To travel the roads in this region, you may use any of the following:

♦ the regional map at a scale of 1:200 000 **no 512**, which covers the main roads and secondary roads, and includes useful indications for finding tourist attractions.

This is a good map to choose for travelling in a wide area. At a quick glance, you can locate and identify the main sights to see. In addition to identifying the nature of the road ways, the maps show castles, churches and other religious edifices, scenic view points, megalithic monuments, swimming beaches on lakes and rivers, swimming pools, golf courses, race tracks, air fields, and more.

And remember to travel with the latest edition of the **map of France no 721**, which gives an overall view of the region of Brittany, and the main access roads which connect it to the rest of France. The entire country is mapped at a 1:1 000 000 scale and clearly shows the main road network.

INTERNET

Michelin is pleased to offer a route-planning service on the Internet: **www.ViaMichelin.com**.

Choose the shortest route, a route without tolls, or the Michelin recommended route to your destination; you can also access information about hotels and restaurants from *The Michelin Guide*, and tourist sites from *The Green Guide*.

You know the Green Guide

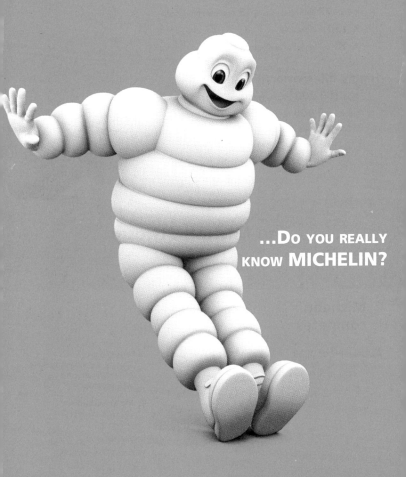

...Do you really know **MICHELIN**?

• Data 31/12/2009

The world No.1 in tires
with 16.3% of the market

A business presence in over **170 countries**

A manufacturing footprint
at the heart of markets

In 2009 **72** industrial sites in **19** countries produced:

- **150** million tires
- **10** million maps and guides

Highly international **teams**

Over **109 200** employees* from all cultures on all continents

including **6 000** people employed in R&D centers

in Europe, the US and Asia.

*102 692 full-time equivalent staff

The Michelin Group
at a glance

Michelin competes

At the end of 2009

Le Mans 24-hour race
12 consecutive years of victories

Endurance 2009
- 6 victories on 6 stages in Le Mans Series
- 12 victories on 12 stages in American Le Mans Series

Paris-Dakar
Since the beginning of the event, the Michelin group has won in all categories

Moto endurance
2009 World Champion

Trial
Every World Champion title since 1981 (except 1992)

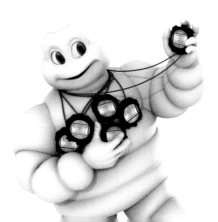

Michelin, established close to its customers

○ **72 plants in 19 countries**

- Algeria
- Brazil
- Canada
- China
- Colombia
- France
- Germany

- Hungary
- Italy
- Japan
- Mexico
- Poland
- Romania
- Russia

- Serbia
- Spain
- Thailand
- UK
- USA

● **A Technology Center spread over 3 continents**

- Asia
- Europe
- North America

○ **Natural rubber plantations**

- Brazil

Our mission

To make a sustainable contribution to progress in the mobility of goods and people by enhancing freedom of movement, safety, efficiency and the pleasure of travelling.

Michelin committed to environmental-friendliness

Michelin, world leader in low rolling resistance tires, actively reduces fuel consumption and vehicle gas emission.

For its products, Michelin develops state-of-the-art technologies in order to:
- Reduce fuel consumption, while improving overall tire performance.
- Increase life cycle to reduce the number of tires to be processed at the end of their useful lives;
- Use raw materials which have a low impact on the environment.

Furthermore, at the end of 2008, 99.5% of tire production in volume was carried out in ISO 14001* certified plants.

Michelin is committed to implementing recycling channels for end-of-life tires.

*environmental certification

**Passenger Car
Light Truck**

Truck

Michelin
a key mobility enabler

Earthmover

Aircraft

Agricultural

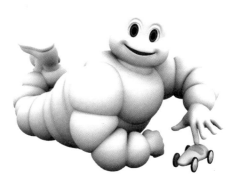

Two-wheel   **Distribution**

Partnered with vehicle manufacturers, in tune with users,
active in competition and in all the distribution channels,
Michelinis continually innovating to promote mobility today
and to invent that of tomorrow.

Maps and   **ViaMichelin,**   **Michelin**
Guides   travel   **Lifestyle,**
                    assistance   for your travel
                    services   accessories

MICHELIN
plays on balanced performance

- **Long tire life**
- **Fuel savings**
- **Safety on the road**

... MICHELIN tires provide you with the best performance, without making a single sacrifice.

The MICHELIN tire pure technology

1 Tread
A thick layer of rubber
provides contact with the ground.
It has to channel water away
and last as long as possible.

2 Crown plies
This double or triple reinforced belt
has both vertical flexibility
and high lateral rigidity.
It provides the steering capacity.

3 Sidewalls
These cover and protect the textile casing
whose role is to attach the tire tread
to the wheel rim.

4 Bead area for attachment to the rim
Its internal bead wire
clamps the tire firmly
against the wheel rim.

5 Inner liner
This makes the tire
almost totally impermeable
and maintains the correct inflation pressure.

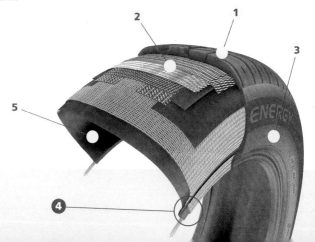

Heed
the MICHELIN Man's advice

To improve safety: I drive with the correct tire pressure

I check the tire pressure every month

I have my car regularly serviced

I regularly check the appearance

of my tires (wear, deformation)

I am responsive behind the wheel

I change my tires according to the season

Michelin Apa Publications Ltd

A joint venture between Michelin and Langenscheidt

58 Borough High Street, London SE1 1XF, United Kingdom

No part of this publication may be reproduced in any form
without the prior permission of the publisher.

© 2011 Michelin Apa Publications Ltd
ISBN 978-1-907099-07-6
Printed: November 2010
Printed and bound in Germany

Although the information in this guide was believed by the authors and publisher to be accurate
and current at the time of publication, they cannot accept responsibility for any inconvenience,
loss, or injury sustained by any person relying on information or advice contained in this guide.
Things change over time and travellers should take steps to verify and confirm information,
especially time-sensitive information related to prices, hours of operation, and availability.